SOUL FOOD FOR ENSLAVED HUMAN CONSCIOUSNESS

JEFFEREY MCGILL

ISBN: 979-8-88640-600-9 (sc)
ISBN: 979-8-88640-601-6 (hc)
ISBN: 979-8-88640-602-3 (e)

THE EWINGS PUBLISHING

One Galleria Blvd., Suite 1900, Metairie, LA 70001
1-888-421-2397

FOREVER BOUND

Life, an unrelenting moment to moment express, is powered by an unpremeditated destination through this world and on through death's doors into the next realm. Life is often a sublimating journey, at times, transcending the very dictates of will.

Life's journey is an express through the winding curves, uphill climbs, downhill dips, and straightaway twists and turns of reality. We travel freely down the conscious and unconscious roads of reality.

This express pauses briefly at junctures of change. Speeding through shadows of imagination on rails of expectation powered by fuels of truths and delayed by the steep costs of self-deception.

Day and night divide the natural accounts of our outer and inner journeys that echoes the energy we share with each other, resounding of all the places and spaces we've been, of which the cryptic details are known only to our unique individual spirit.

Jefferey McGill

Spirituality comes from within. We must stop confusing religion and spirituality. Religion is a set of rules, regulations and rituals created by humans, which are supposed to help people spiritually. Due to human imperfections, religion and politics have become corrupt and divisive tools for power and influence.

Spirituality is not theology or ideology. It is simply a way of life, pure and original as given by the most high. Spirituality is frequency vibrations linking us to each other and the creative source of all that exist.

Haile Selassie

What is truly setting the tone of the human agenda? How is our reality stacking up with our dreams and imagination? Where are we headed and what do our leaders know that is not being disclosed?

CONFUSING SPIRITUALITY WITH RELIGION

At the core of every society, is a collective drive of its people to establish identity, meaning, purpose, and a strong sense of destiny that offers hope against uncertainty, fear, and the eventual confrontation with societals challenges that bodes of collective destruction of everything necessary to the preservation of life itself.

We seek ideas of reassurance in a chaotic world that requires answers to questions presented by survival challenges.

If we think about the explanation of the "Big Bang Theory" when there was nothing, was God asleep? Is the "Big Bang" simply a manifestation of our creator's infinite consciousness?

Is reality just quantum magic dust, the ubiquitous imaginative force of the cosmic creator's unbound infinitude of nature?

Humans find themselves afloat in a cosmic spectrum of magic. We are castaways powered by vibrating inlets from a Godly creative source. We are quantum creative microcosmic cells filled with the force of our creator's imagination.

Life is the process of feeding our body and soul physically and spiritually. The challenge is to maintain in a group setting an independent sense of oneness within the omniscience of the all in us.

Spirituality is that sense of connection to the ultimate creative force, not religion. Spirituality is the foundation of every individual's balancing act as we juggle dreams and hopes of coming upon forceful inspirations that transport us to a heightened spiritual plane of peace. A peace in the sense of deliverance from day to day cycles of fear and stress we encountered securing physical safety.

We have faith bestowed within us of the greatest omniscient and omnipotent force there is that is organically manifested in everything that has ever been.

Anyone or any organization that can deliver this spiritual essence of force through actions, in essence, becomes the very manifestation of magical powers that comes from a spiritual connection to the highest vibrations of the creative force of God.

Every wise leader that has ever lived saw fit to tap into this powerful magic. Claiming connection to that force of all of creation itself.

Before organized religion, holy Roman emperors passed themselves off as Gods. Their corruption in the flesh proved otherwise. So leaders claiming to be direct descendants of God use religion to manage dreams, hopes, aspirations, and fears of the people they desire to rule over.

We see this same mechanism in place at the Vatican, in Washington DC, England and throughout Europe today where an elite group pass themselves off as being highly favored asking those deemed not highly favored to toil away working all of their lives in servant roles to the elite with only a chance for salvation in the afterlife.

This is the greatest fraud ever created. In Russia and China the oligarchs do not even bother to perpetrate the deceptions.

CONTENTS

Chewing the Fat 1
Deconstructing the White Trojan horse Jesus Christ 1
Evil never Sleep, nor should the Love and Grace of God in our Hearts 16
Love 19
The World Economic Forum's 'Sustainable Developments Goals 2030 Agenda' 20
Efforts of Depopulation 21
The Trans-Humanism Impact 22
The Economic Impact 25
Replacing Democracy with Totalitarianism 26
The End Game 28
The Gravest Challenge before Humanity 29
The Metaverse 31
So what is the Metaverse? 32
What are the Real-world Implications of the Metaverse? 34
World Economic Forum Plan for Technocratic Governance 35
Critiquing the Metaverse 37
Deviating from the Miracle 38
Filth in the Soul of Humanity 38
Man is a Wolf to Man 39
Menticide, the killing of the Mind 43

Chapter 1 An Alternative Perspective on God and the Cosmos...57

Path 1: Consciousness, Human or Alien, Nature's Self-Inflicted Wound 57

Path 2: Spiritual Consciousness beyond Our Physical World 58

Path 3: Cosmic Consciousness 60

The Narrative of Natural Origin and Religion

Path 4: Path 4: Why is the Book of Enoch not included in the Canons of the Bible? 65

Path 5: Are Religious Doctrines the Greatest Stumbling Block of Humanity? 76
- Ancient Egypt and Worship of the Sun 97
- Why Invent Jesus 109

Path 6: Lies and Deceptions, the Deadly Games People Play 112
- Solving Spiritual Deficiencies 113
- What does it mean to be spiritually deficient? 114
- Book of the Dead 116
- All Religions have their beginning in Ancient Kemet 119

Path 7: Another Concept of God 132

Path 8: Thoth 136

Path 9: African Belief Systems of Thoth Plagiarized by European's Story of Jesus 146
- Origins of Modern Humans: 152

Path 10: Egypt before the Pharaohs 156

Path 11: The Original Black Jews and the 12 Tribes of Judah 176

Chapter 2 Tracing Biological Differences to Extraterrestrial experiments 197

Path 12: The Metagene Factor and the Blue Planet Project 197
- False Facades of a Failing Virtual Reality 202
- The Big Crunch 203
- The Metagene 204
- Superpowers 206

Path 13: Thought is nature's echo of energy from atoms colliding 207

Path 14: Ancient Ruins and their Connections to Extraterrestrials 209

- Understanding fallacies of Faith based Gods and Religion .. 213
- Zecharia Sitchin 214
- Nasca Lines 218
- The Great Pyramids 218
- Stonehenge 218
- Teotihuacán 219
- Easter Island 219
- Face on Mars 219

Path 15: The Pyramid power plants of Extraterrestrial Gods at Teotihuacan, Mexico 220

The Extraterrestrial Narrative Ancient Aliens DNA Manipulation to Create a Race of Slaves

Path 16: Coming from Other Worlds: The Origin of Humanity According to Old Sumerian Tablets 222
- Adam creation, fresco of the Sistine Chapel by Michelangelo, Vatican City 226
- Zechariah Sitchin 228
- The Sumerian version of the creation of our Solar System ... 230
- Jack Beringer's and Michael Tsarion's Version of Origin of Man 232
- Signs of Reptilian Species on Earth 241
- How Did the Sumerian Know about all the planets in the Solar System 6000 Years Ago? 242
- Where did man come from? 243
- What the Sumerians Records Inform 244

Chapter 3 Extraterrestrial Presence Driving Human Affairs? 253

Path 17: Realm of Death Staining the Sanctum of Love 253

Path 18: Are other extraterrestrials, Greys and Draco-Reptilians also doing biological research? Are the different races on this planet control groups of experimentation? 255

Path 19: Are inhabitants of earth seeded from different star nations? 263

Path 20: What if an advanced Alien civilization populated humans on earth after destroying the dinosaurs and are who ancient people refer to as Gods? 288

Path 21: Chromosome Fusion Evidence of DNA manipulation in our distant past? 290

Path 22: The Definition of Archons and What we are dealing with? Satanists & Pedophiles Run the World 293

- The Invasion (Is Earth an Energy Farm?) 293
- This is some of the thing revealed by the entity 307
- Fields of the Nephilim 322
- 60 Minutes exposes organized pedophilia among highest ranks of British elite 340

Path 23: Are Archons the Greys? 344

Path 24: What if such beings as Archons: Alien Space Invaders truly exist? 347

- It is possible that Aliens have been here for untold years and Earth's inhabitants are being used for biological experiments. 348
- Different type of Aliens 349

Path 25: Psychonaut Sailors of the Soul Altering Parameters of Perception 354

- How the human mind has been infiltrated by an alien intelligence 354

Path 26: Addendum: The Archon Matrix 370

- The Archon Matrix Control System "The human body a container" 370
- Robert Lazar 370
- Soul Food 371
- Philosopher Daniel Pinchbeck 372

- Jacques Vallee 373
- Piercing the Veil of Reality 373
- The Active Side of Infinity 374
- Ponerogenic Groups 375
- John Carter and the Archon Game 376
- The Site of an Asteroid 'Mega Impact' 377

Chapter 4 Are Trans Humanism Agenda Driving Human Affairs? 379

Path 27: Ray Kurzweil, Elon Musk and the Transhumanism Agenda 379
- Nano Technology 381
- The Trans Humanist Connection to the COVID19 Pandemic 386
- The Ethics of Transhumanism 394
- Ray Kurzweil, Singularity University, and Elon Musk.... 397
- The Emergence of a Society Addicted to Artificial Intelligence Where Compassion Has Become Illogical ...407
- Are we little more than dust in the wind? 411
- Wall Street Banks, Bilderberg, DARPA and Silicon Valley's Singularity University 419
- Evil the great spiritual partitions of non-satanic and satanic worship out of sync in the natural order of the universe. 422

Path 28: Conversation with Nigel Kerner Existing with Greys in an Imperfect Universe and the End Game of Artificial Intelligence 425
- What the Greys Envy Most about the Organic Lives of Humans 432

Path 29: Is an Alien Extraterrestrial Intelligence Agenda Driving US Domestic and International Policies 433

Chapter 5 Secret Societies pact with alien entities................ 437

Path 30: William Hamilton..437

Path 31: Secret Treaty... 442
- Historical Comments 443

Path 32: Underground Infrastructure The Missing 40 Trillion Dollars..481
- Rabbit Holes 482
- Searching for Alice 483
- Urban rabbit hole detection..484
- Rural rabbit hole detection 485
- Tunnel construction 488
- Forty trillion dollars 489
- Disclaimer...491

Path 33: Dulce New Mexico and a Cosmic Conspiracy...............491

Path 34: Cloning and Other Experiments at Dulce 499

Path 35: What is going on in underground mega-complex below Dulce, New Mexico... 514

Path 36: Probing Deeper Into the Dulce 'Enigma' 519
- Known Activities At The Dulce Base 536
- Conversations Between Researchers...............................538
- Groom Lake, Area 51, And The Nevada Test Site 540

Path 37: The Black Budget and the Underground Empire...........542

Path 38: The Secret Shadow Government A Structural Analysis...549
- Underground Bases: A Lecture by Phil Schneider: May 1995...549
- Executive Branch..554
- Intelligence Branch... 555
- War Department... 559
- Financial Department 564

- Various secret government projects 565

Path 39: Who was William Thompkins? 568
- Solar Warden the United States Secret Space Program.... 581
- Michael Relf... 592
- Agenda of predatory species... 593
- Watch on You Tube.. 594
- Randy Cramer... 597
- Corey Goode.. 597

Path 40: Antarctica Shrouded in Secrecy Absence of Evidence is no Evidence of Absence 605
- The Lost City of Atlantis.. 606
- Corey Goode, Antarctica, and the Anshar People.......... 606

Chapter 6 Extraterrestrial Contributions to World War II. Humanity's Flaming Out on the Highway to Hell 626

Path 41: A Way beyond Loyalty, Provincialism, and the Herd Instinct 626
- Life beyond Superficial Material Desire.......................... 627
- The Masters or Archons Keeping Us on Spiritual Lockdown 631
- Humanity a Traumatized Species 631

Path 42: "The Presence of Extraterrestrials on Earth and The Technological Threat to the Planetary Biosphere"........... 635

Path 43: 'Luciferians' or the 'Poltergeists' overseeing and directing the actions of the Humanoid-Reptiloids collaborators. 663

Path 44: World War I, RMS Titanic, and the "Nitrogen Bomb" that will kill us all 673

Path 45: Exploitation of the people, for what? Wealth, Race, and War.. 678

- Humanity, Spawns of What? 682

Path 46: A Nazi Space Base 684
- The Site of an Asteroid 'Mega Impact' 685

Path 47: German Advance Weaponry and Extraterrestrial Influence 686
- Myth or Reality? 703
- Historical connections 710
- Early references 710
- Revisionist claims 711

Path 48: Fact or Fiction, Possible Extraterrestrial Intervention in World War II? 712
- Vladimir Terziski 724

Path 49: Antarctica- A Nazi Base? 731
- The Charite Anlage Unit 735
- Scary Secrets of the Third Reich's Base in Antarctica 735
- Neuberlin 738

Path 50: Why the US government doesn't like visitors to the South Pole base 745
- UFO Bases Found in Antarctica 746
- Wendelle C. Stevens 755

Path 51: Operation High Jump 757

Path 52: UFO's, Admiral Bird, James Forrestal, and John Kennedy 804

Path 53: Operation Paper Clip 811
- Crimes 812

Path 54: Black Occult Religions" of the BROTHERHOOD OF THE BELL. 815
- The Invisible Government 816

Chapter 7 Satanic Battle for our Souls 821

Path 55: New World Order on Schedule The Shimmering 821
- How did we lose our way on pathways of violence?.........825
- Breeding Human Intellect with Evil...............................828
- Are there Destructive Goals of Higher Order of Power and Wealth on Earth? 832

Chapter 8 The Carnage along the way to Hell....................... 838

Path 56: CERN...838
- The Fears and Concerns about CERN 841

Chapter 9 The Carnage along the Road to Hell 858

Path 57: The Morphing of the Hunger Game 858

Chapter 10 Humans Contributing to their Own Demise........ 867

Path 58: F.E.M.A 867

Path 59: These Are Times That Try Our Souls 874

Path 60: Ego Consciousness and God..878
- Spiritual Black Hole Consciousness................................880
- Shinto 881

Chapter 11 Making a U-Turn to Salvation 883

Path 61: First priority should be people over technology 883

Path 62: Thousands of scientists issue bleak 'second notice' to humanity...888

Path 63: "Stockholm Syndrome" What is preventing global social change for the better?..890

Path 64: David Icke 891

Path 65: The American Legacy of Moral Compromise for Fool's Gold 893
- Where are we headed? 899
- America as you know it will soon cease to exist 901

Path 66: Silence 903

Bibliography 907
References 909

CHEWING THE FAT

Deconstructing the White Trojan horse Jesus Christ

The World's Problems are not just going to go away doing nothing

In all the technical madness and the bureaucracy of politics and religion, mankind is out of sync with his organic human nature. Profiting by means of murderous wars and high tech bio-weaponry has bent our moral compass and distorted our sense of human dignity.

The collective brain of humanity is the most powerful weapon in the world. If we can't control the collective brain of humanity. If we can't control this brain and the brain controls us we are in trouble. We have got to tell our collective brain where we want to go, as one people motivated and united in one love, and how we are going to get there. We must control our collective brain as humans or it's over.

Many people are not aware of the reverence Africans had for nature in ancient Kemet. In light of understanding us as a people black people, we are the oldest people. If we go all the way back, before we adopted all these labels as Jews, Muslims, or a Christian, we must look at humanity as one family dating back to the original being of the planet. Tracing our mitochondrial DNA to human origin back to Africa, the home of the original beings on this planet.

We had one walk of life revering nature, the sun in all its life giving force, with self-preservation as key, we were not worshiping Gods with all the deities and different indoctrinations displacing our deep respect for nature.

Jiddu Krishnamurti stated "If we can understand the problem, the answer will come out of that understanding, because the answer is not separate from the problem." People live in fear of going against status quo saying you must not talk about anything negative. There is nothing negative about being knowledgeable. There is knowledge that you may not want to be true but never any knowledge that is negative. Ignorance is negative not knowledge.

You can do something with knowledge. The idea that you should be frightened of knowledge and afraid of looking at things as they really are and by ignoring them that they will just go away, is insanity. The problems will not go away. People ask what the solution is. Fundamentally finding solutions requires understanding what we are dealing with.

People limit their search for knowledge because of religious belief and the fear of losing credibility. I think you lose credibility accepting things you believe to be true because how people will react if we say what we think. Unless we understand how deep the rabbit hole goes and what we are dealing with, we are never going to find answers to problems.

We are infinite awareness that is capable of multiple realities. We are being bamboozled. Who or what is behind controlling our perception of our realities. Are we living in a Matrix? The politicians are not controlling how we perceive our reality. They are here today and gone tomorrow.

The politicians are just puppets of a system, each of them are here today, and will be gone tomorrow but the system remains firmly entrenched. The system goes on because there is something pushing the system in the direction it is going. It is not the corporations either. The corporations are means to ends of financial enslavement.

The corporate agenda is not the origin of control and corporations are not creating the pandemonium we are experiencing. It is not the people at the round tables of Bilderberg, Tri-Lateral, and Council of Foreign Relations. They are still at the level of playing out the agenda of controlling the perception of the masses.

You can go into the deeper dark spaces of the rabbit hole and find people like the Rothschilds who we don't see but control our means of existence, our perceptions, and therein our lives. The rabbit hole goes even deeper than the Rothschilds.

Remember, the truth does not change just because you do not want to hear it! The idea that we are alone is ludicrous. The fact that we are considered crazy for believing that there is other intelligent life in the universe reveals how inverted our perception of reality is. This infinite reality is teeming with different expressions of life. Some of this life is interacting with us.

On this very small rock called Earth, there are myriad experiments with matter conflated in layers of evolution that have created our micro human consciousness. Human consciousness is all the individual bubbles of consciousness within the macro bubble of a greater radiating and mysterious entity of infinite consciousness, we call God.

From the macro perspective of the cosmos interspersed with the micro human perspective, it is fascinating that human and cosmic consciousness is interplay of elements within a creative cosmic spectrum of light and dark energy.

In the human psyche, is there a light vs darkness conflict interred in our DNA composition that manifests in humanity's choices between good and evil? It seems humans have been in conflict fluctuating between influences of light and darkness, good and evil, or concepts of God and Devil. The human legacy is heavily influenced by fears represented in the unknown of the dark abyss we peer into at night but also the abyss of our inner temple or universe, which is our individual universal consciousness.

Is there an organic intimate connection with a **supreme creative omniscient force (SCOF)** we refer to as God or are we prisoners of conscious constructs of fear, which has produced all religious principles that constrains collective human consciousness?

Discerning truths for deeper understanding of human nature is imperative to lift constraints that shape our collective will. This task remains humanity's greatest challenge. Sadly the money changers are in control of the educational institutions and refuse to allow people to learn the truths and think for themselves. We could be such a beautiful and loving species without lies, deception, and selfish greed based actions of men.

The money changers, in the name of profit, offer multitudes of death by poisoning our senses and stoking desires through the media. Unfortunately, the majority have been blinded and refuse to realize they are being killed off as they pursue pleasure. Sadly, today's technical obsessions take priority over the spiritual expansion of their organic souls.

The problem of the world's wealth focused on dogmatic inspired mechanical love fueling partitioned religious division instead of higher vibrating unconditional organic love for each other. The Globalists have financed the deadly global upheavals with an agenda of controlling the masses while stockpiling wealth.

How further advanced in the pursuit of love and wisdom would we be as a species if these wealthy people's minds were not limited in scope by greed and religious programming. The Rothschild's controlling Britain and the United States banking system gives aid without a ceiling to an Ultra Zionist agenda.

The Talmudist conviction to Noahide Laws will offer up so much murder and destruction just to placate one group's religious misconceptions of reality. A group committed to forcing those perceptions on people not of the same belief.

There is a huge price we are paying for selfishness and greed of a few. The action of a few is the prime cause of human underachievements in spiritual advancement. The multitudes of partitioned religious sects are costing humanity dearly. The elite few are people with so much wealth yet so spiritually deficient and are so spiritually underachieved. Spiritual impoverishment manifests in destructive wars, murder, poverty, and racial tension we live with.

What God sanctions such murderous means to unholy ends? In the end, this financial support of war and destruction is such contradictions of piousness. Look closely to see greed disguised as loving spirituality driving engines of destruction in the name of one religion after another.

We are still very primitive minded spiritually and we as a species have so far to come finding the true essence of our loving connection to a supreme creative omniscient force available to us in the infinite consciousness beyond the narrow constraints of religious perspectives our societies continue operating from to this very day.

I look forward to the day when we no longer choose to embrace status-quo spiritual convictions that cause us to be calm and patient while Camelot is falling down around us, when our societies are rife with division among us, while an elite few destroy our planet. It is time we explore love from an untapped source of infinite consciousness of higher organic vibrations of love instead of dwelling within the lowly primitive vibrating violent mundane divisive teaching of religious dogma.

Religion is a myth with a silent agenda that is born of a stolen origin. Religion has infiltrated our senses, planted and now harvesting one of the world's worst nightmares in the Trans Human and Artificial Intelligence projects that have an objective to deconstruct organic DNA and digitize human nature.

As far back as 10,000 BC, history is abundant with carvings and writings reflecting people's respect and adoration for the sun. Every morning the sun would rise springing visions of warmth and security, saving man from the cold blind predator filled darkness of night.

Without the Sun, the cultures understood the crops would not grow and life on the planet would not survive. These realities made the sun the most adored object of all time. Ancient people were also very aware of the stars. The tracking of the stars allowed them to recognize and anticipate events which occurred over long periods of time, such as eclipses and full moons.

They in turn cataloged celestial groups into what we know today as constellations. The cross of the Zodiac is one of the oldest conceptual images in human history. It reflects the sun as it figuratively passes through the 12 major constellations over the course of the year.

It also reflects the twelve months of the year, the four seasons, the Solstices, and the equinoxes. The term zodiac relates to facts that constellations were anthropomorphized or personified as figures or animals. In other words the early civilizations did not just follow the sun and stars they personified them with elaborate myths involving their movements and relationships.

The Sun with its life-giving and saving qualities was personified as a representative of the unseen creator or God. It was God Sun the light of the world. The savior of humankind. The 12 Constellations represented places of travel for God Sun and were identified by names usually representing elements of nature that happened during that period of time. For example Aquarius the water bearer who brings the spring rains.

Horus was the Sun God of Egypt around 3000 BC. He is the Sun anthropomorphized. In his life, is a series of allegorical myths involving the Sun's movements in the sky.

From the ancient hieroglyphics in Egypt, we know much about the solar messiah. For instance, Horus being the Sun or the light had an enemy known as Seth. Seth was the personification of the darkness or night. Every morning Horus would win the battle against Seth while in the evening Seth would conquer Horus and send him into the underworld.

It is important to know that dark versus light or good versus evil is one of the most ubiquitous mythological dualities ever known and is still expressed on many levels to this day.

The story of Horus is as follows: Horus was born on December 25th of the Virgin Isis Mary. His birth was accompanied by a star in the east which in turn Three Kings followed to locate a newborn savior. At the age of 12 he was a prodigal child teacher. At the age of 30 he was baptized by the figure known as AT and thus began his ministry. Horus had twelve disciples. He traveled about performing miracles such as healing the sick and walking on water.

Horus was known by many gestural names such as the truth, the light, God's anointed son, the good shepherd, the Lamb of God, and many others. After being betrayed by Typhon, Horus was crucified and buried for three days and thus resurrected.

These attributes of Horus, whether original or not, seemed to permeate many cultures of the world for many other Gods are found to have the same general mythological structure. Attis of Phrygia born of a Virgin on December 25th in Greece 1200 BC was crucified and placed in a tomb and after three days was resurrected.

Krishna of India born of the virgin Devaki with a star in the east signaling his coming. He performed miracles with his disciples and upon his death was resurrected.

Dionysus of Greece born of a virgin on December 25th 500 BC was a traveling teacher performing miracles such as turning water into wine. He was referred to as the King of Kings, God's only begotten Son, the Alpha and Omega, and many others and upon his death he was resurrected.

Mithra of Persia born of a Virgin on December 25th 1200 BC. He had twelve disciples and performed miracles and upon his death he was buried for three days and resurrected. He was also referred to as the truth, the light, and many others. Interestingly the sacred day of worship of Mithra was Sunday.

The fact of the matter is there are numerous saviors from different periods from all over the world, which subscribe to these general characteristics. The question remains why these attributes, why the virgin birth on December 25th, why died for three days in the inevitable resurrection?

Why 12 disciples or followers? To find out, let's examine the most recent solar messiahs. Jesus Christ was born of the Virgin Mary on December 25th in Bethlehem. His birth was announced by a star in the East, which three Kings or Magi followed to locate and adorn the New Savior. He was a child teacher at 12 and was baptized at 30 by John the Baptist and thus began his ministry.

Jesus had 12 disciples which he traveled about with performing miracles such as healing the sick, walking on water, raising the dead, and he was also known as the King of Kings, son of God, the light of the world, the Alpha and the Omega, the Lamb of God, and many others. After being betrayed by his disciple Judas and sold for thirty pieces of silver, he was crucified and placed in a tomb after three days and was resurrected and ascended into heaven.

First, all these Gods December 25th birth is astrological. The star in the east is Sirius the brightest star in the night sky, which on December 24th aligns with the three brightest stars in Orion's belt. These three bright stars in Orion's belt are called today the same as they were called in ancient times, the three Kings. The three Kings and the brightest star Sirius all point to the place of the sunrise on December 25th. This is why the three Kings followed the star in the east in order to locate the sunrise. The birth of the sun.

The Virgin Mary is the Constellation Virgo. Also known as Virgo the Virgin. Virgo in Latin means Virgin. The ancient glyph for Virgo is the altered M. This is why Mary along with other Virgin mothers, such as Adonis mother Myrra or Buddha/s mother Maya begins with an M.

Virgo was also referred to as the House of Bread and the representation of Virgo is a virgin holding a sheaf of wheat. This house of bread in its symbol of wheat represents August and September the time of harvest. In turn Bethlehem in fact literally translates to House of Bread. Bethlehem is thus a reference to the Constellation Virgo, a place in the sky not on earth.

There is another very interesting phenomenon that occurs around December 25th or the winter solstice. From the summer solstice to the winter solstice the days become shorter and colder. From the perspective of the Northern Hemisphere, the Sun appears to move south and gets smaller and scarcer. The shortening of the days and the expiration of the crops when approaching the winter solstice symbolize the process of death to the ancients.

It was the death of the Sun. By December 22nd, the sun's demise was fully realized for the Sun having moved south continually for six months makes it to its lowest point in the sky. Here a curious thing occurs. The sun stops moving south at least perceivably for three days and during this three day pause the Sun resides in the vicinity of the Southern Cross or Crux Constellation.

After this time on December 25th the Sun moves one degree. This time the movement is north foreshadowing longer days, warmth, and spring. Thus it was said the Sun died on the cross for three days only to be resurrected or born again.

This is why Jesus and numerous other Sun Gods share the crucifixion three day death and resurrection concept. It is the Sun's transition period before it shifts its direction back into the northern hemisphere bringing spring and thus salvation.

They did not celebrate the resurrection of the Sun until the Spring equinox or Easter. This is because at the Spring Equinox the Sun officially overpowers the evil darkness as daytime thereafter becomes longer in duration than the night and the revitalizing conditions of Spring emerge.

Probably the most obvious of all the astrological symbolism around Jesus regards the twelve disciples. They are simply the twelve constellations of the Zodiac, which Jesus being the sun travels about with. The number twelve is replete throughout the Bible. 12 Tribes of Israel, 12 Brothers of Joseph, 12 Judges of Israel, 12 Great Patriarchs, 12 O.T. Prophets, 12 kings of Israel, 12 Princes of Israel, Jesus in Temple at 12.

Jesus' head is always depicted with his head on a cross. Earlier cult art always showed his head on a cross. For Jesus is the anthropomorphized Sun. The Sun of God, the light of the world, the risen savior who will come again as the Sun does every morning. The Glory of God who defends against the works of darkness as he is born again every morning and can be seen coming in the clouds up in heaven with his crown of thorns or sunrays.

Throughout the Scriptures there are numerous references to the age. In order to understand this, we need to be familiar with the precession of the equinoxes. The ancient Egyptians along with cultures long before them recognized that approximately every 2150 years the Sunrise in the morning of the Spring Equinox would occur at a different sign of the Zodiac. This has something to do with a slow angular wobble that the Earth maintains as it rotates on its axis. It is called a precession because the constellations go backwards rather than through the normal yearly cycle.

The amount of time it takes for the procession to go through all 12 signs is roughly 25 thousand seven hundred and sixty five years. This I also called the great year and ancient societies were very aware of this and they referred to each 2150 year period as an age.

From 2150 BC to 180 was Aries the Ram, from 1 AD to 2150 AD is the age of Pisces, the age we are still into today. In and around 2150, we will enter the new age. The Age of Aquarius.

The Bible reflects broadly speaking a symbolic movement through three ages while foreshadowing a fourth. In the Old Testament when Moses comes down Mount Sinai with the Ten Commandments, he is very upset to see his people worshiping a Golden bull calf. In fact he shattered the Stone Tablets and instructed his people to kill each other in order to purify themselves.

Go in and out from the Gate to Gate and slay every man and brother, and every man his companion, and every man neighbor. Exodus 32

Most Biblical scholars will tribute this anger to the fact that the Israelites were worshiping a false idol. The reality is the Golden Bull is Taurus the Bull and Moses represents the new Age of Aries the Ram. This is why Jews, even today, still blow the Ram's horn.

Moses represents the New Age of Aries. Upon the New Age everyone must shed the Old Age. Other deities mark these transitions as well such as Mithra a pre-Christian god who kills the Bull in the same symbology.

Jesus is the figure who ushered in the Age following Aries, the Age of Pisces or the two Fish.

Fish symbolism is very abundant in the New Testament. Jesus fed 5000 people with bread and two fish. When he begins his ministry walking along Galilee, he befriends two fishermen who followed him. We have all seen the Jesus fish on the back of people's cars. Little do they know what it actually means? It is a pagan astrological symbolism for the Sun's Kingdom during the Age of Pisces.

Jesus assumed birth date is essentially the start of this age. At Luke 22:10 when Jesus is asked by his disciples where the next Passover will be after he is gone? Jesus replies behold when ye are entered into the city a shouting man meet you bearing a picture of water follow him into the house where he entereth in.

This scripture is by far the most revealing of all the astrological references. The man bearing the picture of water is Aquarius the water bearer who was always pictured as a man pouring out a pitcher of water. He represents the Age after Pisces and when the Sun (God's Sun) Jesus leaves the Age of Pisces, he will go into the House of Aquarius, as Aquarius follows Pisces in the precession of the Equinox.

All Jesus is saying is that after the Age of Pisces will come the Age of Aquarius.

We have all heard about the end time in the end of the world. The cartoonist depictions in the Book of Revelation aside the main source of this idea comes from Matthew 28:20 for Jesus says I will be with you even to the end of the world. However in the King James Version "world" is this translation among many mistranslations.

The actual word being used is "beyond" which means Age. I will be with you even to the end of the Age, which is true as Jesus's solar Piscean personification will end when the Sun enters the Age of Aquarius. The entire concept of end times in the end of the world is a misinterpreted astrological allegory. 100,000,000 million people in America believe the end of the world is coming.

The character of Jesus being a literary and astrological hybrid is plagiarization of the Egyptian Sun God Horus. Inscribed about 3,500 years ago on the walls of the Temple of Luxor in Egypt are images of the enunciation. The Immaculate Conception the birth and adoration of Horus. The images begins with Thoth announcing to the Virgin Isis that she will conceive for us then Neth the Holy Ghost Impregnating the virgin and then the virgin birth and the adoration.

This is exactly the story of Jesus's miracle conception. In fact, the literary similarities between the Egyptian religion and the Christian religion are staggering and the plagiarism is continuous. The Story of Noah's Ark is taken directly from tradition. The concept of the great flood is ubiquitous throughout the ancient world. There are 200 cited claims periods and times.

One need look no further than a pre-Christian source than the Epic of Gilgamesh written in 2600 BC. This story talks of a great flood commanded by God an Ark with several saved animals on it and the release and return of a dove all held in common with the Biblical story among many other similarities.

Then there is the plagiarized story of Moses. Upon Moses's birth, it is said that he was placed in a reed basket and set adrift in a river in order to avoid infanticide. He was later rescued by a daughter of royalty and raised by her as a prince. This baby in a basket story was lifted directly from the myth of Sargon of Akkad around 2250 BC. Sargon was placed in a reed basket in order to avoid infanticide and set adrift in a river. He was rescued and raised by a key royal Midwife.

Moses is known as a law-giver the giver of the Ten Commandments the Mosaic Law. However the idea of a law being passed from God to prophet up on a mountain is very old motif. Moses is just another law-giver in a long line of lawgivers. In the local history of India, Manu was the great lawgiver.

In Crete, Minos ascended Mount Dicta where Zeus gave him the sacred laws while in Egypt there was Mises who carried stone tablets and upon them the laws of God were written.

As far as the Ten Commandments, they are taken outright from Spell 125 of the Egyptian Book of the Dead. What the Book of the Dead phrased I have not stolen became Thou Shall Not Steal. I have not killed became Thou Shall not Kill. I have not told lies became Thou Shall not Bear false witnesses.

The Egyptian religion is likely the primary foundational basis for Judeo-Christian theology. Baptism, after-life, final, Virgin birth, death, resurrection, crucifixion, the Ark of the Covenant, circumcisions, saviors, Holy Communion, Great Flood, Easter, Christmas, Passover, and many more are all attributes of Egyptian Ideas long predating Christianity and Judaism.

The Bible is nothing more than an Astrotheological literary hybrid just like nearly all religious myths before it. The aspect of transference of one character's attributes to a new character can be found within the book itself. In the Old Testament there is the story of Joseph. Joseph was a prototype for Jesus. Joseph was born of a miracle birth. Jesus was born of a miracle birth. Joseph was of 12 brothers and Jesus had 12 disciples. Joseph was sold for 20 pieces of silver. Jesus was sold for 30 pieces of silver. Brother Judah suggests the sale of Joseph. Disciple Judas suggests the sale of Jesus. Joseph began his work at the age of 30. Jesus began his work at the age of 30.

Is there any non-Biblical historical evidence of any person living with the name Jesus the son of Mary who travel about with 12 followers healing people? There are numerous historians who lived in and around the Mediterranean either during or soon after the assumed life of Jesus. How many of these historians documented this figure? Not one did.

Four historians are referenced to justify Jesus's existence. They were Pliny the Younger, Suetonius and Tacitus are the first three. Each one of their entries consist of only a few sentences at best and only referred to Christus or the Christ which in fact is not a name but a title. It means the anointed one.

The fourth source is Josephus and this source has been proven to be a forgery for hundreds of years. Sadly it is still cited as the truth. You think that a guy who rose from the dead and ascended into heaven for all eyes to see and perform the wealth of miracles acclaimed him would have made it into historical records. It didn't because once the evidence is weighed, there are very high odds that figure the figure known as Jesus did not exist.

The Christian religion is a parody on the worship of the Sun, in which they put a man called Christ in the place of the Sun and pay him the adoration originally prayed to the Sun. We don't want to be unkind but we want to be factual. We don't want to cause hurt feelings but we want to be academically correct and what we understand and know to be true. Christianity is just not based on truth. Christianity is in fact nothing more than a Roman Story developed politically.

The reality is Jesus was the solar deity of the Gnostic Christian sect and like all other pagan Gods he was a mythical figure. It was the political establishment that sought to historicize the Jesus figure for social control. By 325 AD in Rome, Emperor Constantine convened the Council of Nicaea.

It was during this meeting that the politically motivated Christian doctrines were established and began a long history of Christian bloodshed and spiritual fraud and for the next 1600 years the Vatican maintained a political stranglehold on all of Europe leave the joyous period of the dark ages along with enlightening events such as the Crusades and inquisition.

Christianity along with all other theistic belief systems is the fraud of the Age. It serves to detach the species from the natural world and likewise each other. It supports blind submission to authority. It reduces human responsibility to the effect that God controls everything and a turning away from awful crimes thusly empowering those who created the myth who know the truth but use the myth to manipulate and control societies.

The religious myth is the most powerful device ever created and serves as the psychological soil upon which other myths can flourish. We are witnessing the type of societies that have come into being in Western Nations. The Nuclear weapons, laboratory created viruses, the endless wars, the growing divide between the rich and the poor, the priorities being placed on Transhumanism and Artificial Intelligence, all taking place under the watch of religion showing no fealty to principles of love and Mercy and no God intervening to save mankind.

Only the truth will set us free in time to be our own savior. We are running out of time and the first priority to replace myths with truth and remove the Trojan horse of religion from our psychological infrastructure. This Trojan horse is the last obstacle between us that is preventing us from and preserving life, liberty, and pursuit of happiness while maintaining our human nature.

Evil never Sleep, nor should the Love and Grace of God in our Hearts

Has there ever been a time in human history where we have shown each other love as brothers and sisters? Have there always been that us and them aspect, Pharaohs Royal families, Vatican priests, puppet politicians that constitutes a division in humanity of the have and the have-nots?

The world around us is seeded in violence. We see it in the animal kingdom all around us. We witness the brutal nature of a dog-eat-dog world. We see more dominant and stronger predatory animals stalking and bringing down weaker prey, in many instances eating them while they are still alive. This is the same instinct embedded in the DNA of humans.

The predatory instinct is not as brutal as a lion felling a buffalo and eating it while it is alive and feeling the gnash of teeth tearing at its flesh. But we knowingly discriminate against each other, objectify each other, go to war against each other killing with various weaponized with guns, bombs, and high-tech biological agents.

What type of experiment is humanity? We have a consciousness that tells us that our behavior should be one of love of our own life and respect for another who exemplifies the same consciousness of love and respect for us.

When we pray to the presence of Godly omniscience and a sense of omnipotence, too often we forget the power of accountability to each other of the gift of giving we possess within from our creator.

In this Twi-Light zone of violence, we spend too much time obscuring the precious nature of an ability innate in us to give the gift of love to each other. Even with our prayers to our better essence of love and grace of the God that exist in each of us, the predatory nature of greed obscures the sense of love, which is the only thing that can extinguish the tempo of violence dwelling in our instinctual DNA.

There may have been a time in our most primitive state when violence was the rule of the day that protected us from predation of the animals around us. We have progressed to a modern era where we, as men, are predatory to other men and women. Somehow we have not advanced intellectually to turn off the switch of a violent aspect of our human nature that in many regards has become no longer necessary for the survival of our specie.

When will recognize that the time has long past that we should extinguish the evil and outdated elite oligarchies who rule with a sense of un-loving violence? We keep looking around and searching outside of ourselves for God and pointing to others as being the enemy. God and the enemy is us. We simply choose one or the other as we dress ourselves each day with clothes we wear. Our choice is the God in us or the clothing of the enemy that also dwells within us.

I would venture to say that there has never been a time in human history where we have shown each of us love as brothers and sisters. We continue to embrace the dress of predatory masculinity of male patriarchy whose time of violent will has past.

In America, Europe, China, Russia, and Israel the people wear this dress of predation with lavish military industrial complexes that is the dress of the enemy and not the Godly essence within us. We the People dress the same by cosigning the behaviors of our respective governments.

The dress of the enemy is exemplified in the money we spend wastefully on bombs, guns, planes, and the silent war being waged with mRNA bioweapons. The greed instinct in elite oligarchs use these weapons as a lion uses his teeth in following predatory instincts to feed himself by presenting death to another.

The lion has not the sense of a loving godly presence within, a gift of a loving presence given to us by our creator to procure a loving and peaceful life on such a miraculous and beautiful planet. We no longer have to follow our predatory instinct that rains death and destruction down upon each other.

We must through wisdom and the connection of the Godly presence within attain that accountability to self and each other and then hold the elite oligarch accountable for their persisting crimes against humanity, the planet, and our Godly creator.

I wrote this book and with the information in it seek to feed your curiosity as well as sound an alarm that if we do not wake up evil and darkness will snuff out the Godly light within us. Unlike us, "Evil" never sleeps.

Love

If God manifest at all in the realm of humanity, I would not think of a godly presence as anything physical. We interpret infinite consciousness or discern spiritual collective universal consciousness conceptually as God.

The only trace element that a godly presence manifest in consciousness is embodied in nature's power to create, preserve life for a period of time, destroy that life, and resurrect life again from the same expended elements in which life was drained from.

God is the warmth in woman's vaginal spaces that creates life. There is no place on earth that is more like heaven on earth. God is the warm radiation of sun rays permeating our skin that nurtures generation of consciousness. God is oxygen saturating blood cells.

God is the smile of appreciation of a kind act. God is the first glimpse of light of the newly born. God is the flavor of the moisture of water on a tongue. God is the quiet and calm serenity of sleep behind closed eyes. God is the rhythmic vibrations in the sensuality of music.

God is the pause of infinitude in between the rhythmic heart palpitations, that infinite presence from what we think of as death. God is life, death, and birth inseparably.

God is the positive vibe from prayerful self-talk. All the magical elements of love that constitute the non-fibrous infinitude of consciousness in which we relate to God.

If the entire macro cosmic theme is an exercise in the search for that rare elemental constituency of the spiritual essence of God, which is love, then finding the essence of love in the human flesh shaped and sculpted from fleeting elements from the explosions of suns throughout the cosmos, this consciousness out here in the cosmic slop is rare as finding rare metals such as plutonium, platinum, diamonds, and gold in bedrock.

Love in the physical fibers of humanity is a miraculous manifestation. We are rare cosmic spiritual jewels.

Made from Gods very own elemental fibers of stardust. Love in people reflects Gods creativity and respectfulness of life itself.

The love in the heart of woman precedes creativity in her womb. She is filled with the magnetic godliness of creativity that directs concupiscence in men. The birth of life from the woman's womb is in likeness of the powers of the creative infinitude of consciousness.

The World Economic Forum's 'Sustainable Developments Goals 2030 Agenda'

It is very obvious from the state of the world's affair that this agenda is not meant for the poor. Depopulation is the formula preferred by Globalist to accomplish this agenda.

What are the Sustainable Development Goals of the 2030 Agenda?

- No poverty
- Zero Hunger
- Good Health and Well-Being

- Quality Education
- Gender Equality
- Clean Water and Sanitation
- Affordable and Clean Energy
- Decent Work and Economic Growth
- Industry, Innovation, and Infrastructure
- Reduced Inequalities
- Sustainable Cities and Communities
- Responsible Consumption and Production
- Climate Action
- Life Below Water
- Life on Land
- Peace, Justice, and Strong Institutions
- Partnership for Goals

One has to ask the question of how serious Globalist world leaders are to attain these goals and considering their depopulation agenda who will reap the benefits. With the level of greed on display by the .01 percent that controls governments, economies, the pharmaceutical industry, military industrial complexes, the burning of the rain forests, climate change, threats of war, poison in the air with chemtrails, and mounting problems of GMO in the food supply, it is obvious the Sustainable Development Goals will integrate artificial intelligence with priorities placed on depopulation with an end game of humans being killed and replaced by robots in the workforce.

Efforts of Depopulation

Are the vaccine manufacturers, the FDA, the NIH and the CDC going to get away with their mass genocide from injecting spike protein triggering mRNA vaccines? According to Dr. David Martin, 700 million will die from Covid19 Vaccines by 2028. Dr. Martin has sued President Joe Biden and the Center for Medicare and Medicaid Services, holding people criminally accountable for their domestic terrorism, their crimes against humanity and the story of the coronavirus weaponization that goes back to 1998, referring to the hundreds of thousands of Americans who have been killed and maimed by the bioweapons of COVID-19 and its "vaccine."

Will it get worse, Dr. Martin answers in the affirmative, saying, "The fact is, when you inject mRNA into a human being, which is what the current manipulations are, that mRNA makes the human body produce a scheduled toxin the spike protein.

It is, in fact not a coronavirus vaccine, it is a spike protein instruction to make the human body produce a toxin – and that toxin has been scheduled as a known 'biologic agent of concern' with respect to biological weapons.

Ralph Baric published a paper in which he said the Wuhan Institute of Virology Virus 1 Coronavirus was 'Poised for human emergence.' They knew this all along, they knew it was a bioweapon since 2005. They knew it was effective at taking out populations, harming populations, intimidating and coercing populations and they did that all very intentionally for the purpose of destroying humanity.

"By their own estimate, they're looking for 700 million people [dead] globally and that would put the US participation in that, certainly, as a pro-rata of injected population somewhere between 75 and 100 million people dead.

By 2028, we have a tiny glitch on the horizon, which is the illiquidity of the Social Security and Medicare/Medicaid programs, so the fewer people who are recipients of Social Security, Medicare and Medicaid, the better. Not surprisingly, it's probably one of the motivations that led to the recommendation that people over the age of 65 were the first ones getting injected.

The Trans-Humanism Impact

Dr. Ralph Baric is the William R. Kenan, Jr. Distinguished Professor in the Department of Epidemiology and Professor in the Department of Microbiology and Immunology. He has spent the past three decades as a world leader in the study of coronaviruses and is responsible for UNC-Chapel Hill's world leadership in coronavirus research.

Ralph Baric published in his paper dispels the disinformation of the Government, NewsGuard and others about the vaccines not being capable of altering our genome, saying, "This is proven in their own data that the mRNA has the capacity to write into the DNA of the human and as such, the long-term effects are not going to merely be symptomatic.

The long-term effects of injected individuals are going to be altering of the human genome. Human culture depends on contact between people. Our high and mighty globalist masters want to keep us apart through lockdowns, government control of all our activities, and injecting harmful substances into our bodies.

The COVID-19 pandemic, which began unfolding with unprecedented global 'lockdown' in March 2020, has fundamentally remade human relations, capitalism, and culture in the West. No matter that in the past we had lived through far graver medical crises without thoughts of stopping all congregation of people, suspending the production of all culture, or compelling all healthy people to cover their faces, close their businesses and keep apart. This time, the elites used the 'crisis' to shut down Western norms of liberty, the human-centered world, and civilization itself.

What will our culture, which we once thought durable, be replaced by? A world managed by machines and mediated by digital interfaces; a world predicated on cruelty, without human empathy as an organizing principle; a world in which national boundaries, cultures, and languages are drained of meaning, in which cultures embody only the goals of meta-national oligarchs, a world organized for the benefit of massive pharmaceutical companies, a few global tech giants, and technocrats.

At a World Economic Forum 2018 conference, the Chief Executive Officer of Pfizer expressed excitement for invasive nanotech, referring to the recent FDA approval of a tablet with a sensor that can notify medical authorities of compliance.

Later that year, a nano transistor chip is unveiled that replaces silicon with air.

A COVID implantable microchip developer claimed we will be chipped, "Whether we like it or not!"

There has been much talk about graphene oxide and nanotech in the vaccines, which the media vehemently claims is not true.

But how would they know?

And why would anyone trust a word that they say about any of this?

If there are Nano circuits being created within the bodies of the vaccinated, this would explain the videos we've seen displaying IP addresses coming from the jabbed; a newly-activated network of Nano circuits, unique to each individual.

One of the leading experts of nanotechnology, Charles Lieber has written patents describing a technology that has the potential to self-assemble into tiny computer systems capable of controlling human neurology, which is exactly what electron microscopy of the Pfizer jab appears to be.

Charles Lieber was just convicted on numerous crimes for working with the Communist Chinese in Wuhan, where Pfizer ran a research and development facility.

Elon Musk expects to be implanting his Neuralink into human beings and claims that they could put you fully into Virtual Reality, as if this is somehow important for humanity. For humanity, it isn't – but for the transhumanists, it's a necessity.

If you listen to the psychopaths orchestrating all of this, transhumanism is officially their stated goal – and they won't need Elon's implantable chip.

With injectable Nano-sized circuitry in the human brain and nervous system, non-intrusive wearable tech will do the job just fine and this is rapidly being developed by Wellcome Leap, a privately-run umbrella corporation connecting DARPA, Silicon Valley and the military, who has tripled their network in less than a year, boasting success for the deadly mRNA vaccines and pushing to accelerate new ones, designed to correct every so-called flaw of the human psyche that stands in the way of productivity to an authoritarian state run by Artificial Intelligence that monitors and controls their neurological functions 24/7.

This is exactly what they say they want by the year 2030.

So either the vaccines are a way of interfacing the new Trans human-with-AI technology or they're lying and it's all about depopulation, which is what the latest data is showing.

The Economic Impact

What is Covid19 really about? The IMF and World Bank have for decades pushed a policy agenda based on cuts to public services, increases in taxes paid by the poorest and moves to undermine labor rights and protections.

IMF 'structural adjustment' policies have resulted in 52% of Africans lacking access to healthcare and 83% having no safety nets to fall back on if they lose their job or become sick.

In 2021, an Oxfam review of IMF COVID-19 loans showed that 33 African countries were encouraged to pursue austerity policies. The world's poorest countries are due to pay $43 billion in debt repayments in 2022, which could otherwise cover the costs of their food imports.

Oxfam and Development Finance International (DFI) have also revealed that 43 out of 55 African Union member states face public expenditure cuts totaling $183 billion over the next five years.

According to Prof Michel Chossudovsky of the Centre for Research on Globalization, the closure of the world economy (March 11, 2020 Lockdown imposed on more than 190 countries) has triggered an unprecedented process of global indebtedness. Governments are now under the control of global creditors in the post-COVID era.

Why close down the bulk of health services and the global economy knowing full well what the massive health, economic, and debt implications would be?

Why mount a military-style propaganda campaign to censor world-renowned scientists and terrorize entire populations and use the full force and brutality of the police to ensure compliance?

These actions were wholly disproportionate to any risk posed to public health, especially when considering the way 'COVID death' definitions and data were often massaged and how PCR tests were misused to scare populations into submission.

Replacing Democracy with Totalitarianism

The Bilderbergers, Trilateral Commission, and World Economic Forum policies of conflict (Communism v. Democracy, Democrats v. Republicans, and Tories v. Whigs) sets the table for a white supremacist oriented New World Order agenda of preying upon a nationalistic and religiously divided human race.

The ultimate target is to destroy organic ideas of independent thought that are the bedrock of freedom, love for each other and self, and a life of liberty. These rights are pathways to pursuits of happiness.

Pax Americana (Latin for "American Peace") is a term applied to the concept of relative peace in the Western Hemisphere and in the world after the end of World War II in 1945) It appears the post-World War II Pax Americana financial order is collapsing by design, to be replaced by a "Multipolar World Order", also known as the BRICS alliance - the fund for which is comprised of people from the IMF and the World Bank.

Meet the new boss, same as the old boss. The House always wins.

The war in Ukraine and the Russian sanctions have done nothing but accelerate the process of collapsing the West and ushering in this Multipolar World Order.

The tables have turned. The nations of the world are doing to America what America has been doing to them for decades. The misery this creates will cause the upending of the US government by its own people. A coup in America becomes a likely probability with each passing day.

Secession of several states will follow. The United States will be broken up like the Soviet Union. The bigger picture, however, is that the two factions vying for control of planet Earth actually answer to the same controllers. The break-up of America and Europe will benefit the banksters who desperately need an excuse to hoard confiscated gold, not pay their unfunded liabilities, i.e. Social Security, Medicare, government pensions, bonds, etc. If they get their way, the people will be screwed, as usual.

The BRICS nations are comprised of Brazil, India, China, and South Africa. China has recently invited Indonesia, Malaysia, Iran, Egypt and several other countries to join BRICS, a growing alliance.

While some are reporting that BRICS is somehow challenging the Globalists, this is demonstrably false.

The original concept for BRICS was proposed by the chief economist for Goldman-Sachs. BRICS' new development bank is staffed by known players of the IMF and World Bank.

and BRICS has repeatedly affirmed their commitment to the United Nations' Agenda 2030.

Aside from Brazil's President Bolsonaro, all of BRICS' nation-states have pushed the COVID-19 lockdowns and experimental shots.

And China recently announced five more years of their brutal "Zero-COVID" lockdowns.

BRICS is also pushing a digital currency and has launched a vaccine research and development center for member states.

BRICS is clearly not anti-Globalist.

Even the CCP's state-run media explains how BRICS now leads the globalization mission.

But they are all turning against the United States and its allies.

Xi Jinping accused the US of weaponing the financial system with their sanctions against Russia, which has caused the average person to suffer worldwide.

The End Game

Dr. Naomi Wolf has written the most important book of our times *"The Bodies of Others: The New Authoritarians, Covid-19 and the War against the Human"*

She states that the end goal is something much darker than a dark-enough world in which everyone is coercively vaccinated, whether they are at risk or not, whether they have immunity or not, a world in which 'boosters' for seven billion people annually are guaranteed forever.

The end-goal, rather, is to ensure that our pre-March 2020 world disappears forever, irretrievable. To be replaced with a world in which all human endeavor is behind a digital paywall, and in which all of us ask the permission of technology to gain access to the physical world, access to culture and access to other human beings.

The real goal has nothing to do with public health. The real goal is to destroy Western and human culture, and to replace it with a techno-fascistic culture—-a culture in which we have forgotten what human beings can do. The crime that was perpetrated during the pandemic years of 2020-22 was perhaps the greatest ever committed against humanity. And it is being perpetrated still."

The Gravest Challenge before Humanity

While elite control over human societies started to gather pace with the Neolithic revolution 12,000 years ago, it was rapidly accelerated with the dawn of human civilization 7,000 years later. Since that time, 'ordinary' human beings like you and me have fought an unending sequence of battles to defend ourselves against these ongoing efforts by elites to kill or control us and capture the bulk of Earth's resources for their own use.

We have had to fight off elites in a vast range of contexts: Pharaohs and Emperors politically, the Popes and other Vatican officials religiously, the City of London Corporation and other financial elites economically, monarchs and political elites nationally, and now a Global Elite that exercises enormous control technologically, economically, politically, militarily and otherwise over the entire world.

If we lose this battle, there will be no subsequent battle. The Long War against humanity will have been lost, once and for all. Why? Because this battle is for everything that it means to be human – human identity, human freedom, human rights, privacy, dignity, free will and anything else that makes life worth living – and for control of the Earth and all its resources.

And while it is true that no human has any of these elements in anything like its entirety – who would claim to be fully 'free' in this world? – and many humans still lack all of these elements in any meaningful form, it is nevertheless true that the totalitarian nature of the program being imposed on us will transform the very concept of 'human' in a way that has only been conceived in the past 100 years or so and not previously attempted. Moreover, if successful, any 'free will' that humans might still possess will be utterly eliminated.

Despite the unending efforts of those people aware enough to perceive the true depth of this conflict, elites have been able to ensure that the vast bulk of 'ordinary' people either do not perceive the conflict or the elite waste their dissent by only allowing expressing dissent within frameworks designed and controlled by elites.

Thus, one key way in which elites have been able to subdue effective resistance is to convince us to believe in the delusion of 'democracy': to make us believe the twin delusions that we actually make choices about who will govern us and that those we elect will then represent us.

A second way in which elites have been able to distract us from where the real power in society lies is by convincing us that we have 'legal recourse' against injustice, including against elites who kill and exploit us. No one is being prosecuted for crimes against humanity for the Covid19 psyop still in progress.

And, of course, elites control populations by using extensive propaganda – marketed variously as 'education', 'entertainment' and 'news' – to ensure the passive submission of the bulk of the population to elite directives.

In short, an unending sequence of violence – 'visible', 'invisible' and 'utterly invisible' – is used to terrorize the individual throughout childhood and adolescence into submissive obedience. This violence ensures that only a rare individual survives with any sense of 'Self', with the capacity to critique society and resist violence and exploitation strategically.

In his article "Do We Want Real Life? Or Live in the Delusion of a Dystopian Future: Virtual Beauty", "Virtual Freedom", "Virtual Love"... Is the WEF's "All-Digital Metaverse Reality" Our Future?, Robert J. Burrowes ask a very poignant question.

So here we are in 2022, deeply engaged in the final battle to defend humanity, with most of the population unaware of what is happening and the bulk of those who are aware dissipating their dissent through elite-controlled channels.

Hence, as the World Economic Forum puts it so clearly in one of its promotional videos: By 2030, 'You'll own nothing. And you'll be happy.'

The Great Reset' is a long-planned and complex series of actions designed to kill off a substantial proportion of the human population and leave those left alive as trans-human slaves in a technocratic world.

The Metaverse

Based on many years of effort, the World Economic Forum (WEF) has recently launched its plan to create our new all-digital world, called the 'metaverse'.

So if you find natural phenomena – ranging from rainforests, beaches and weather variations to ill-health, danger and unhappiness – annoying, you will soon be able to escape them, compliments of the Metaverse. Or so we are promised. And you won't be troubled by anything resembling what might be called 'free will' either. You will be content to do as you are told, even more than you are content to do already.

So what is the Metaverse?

Microsoft, one of several tech companies claiming to be building the Metaverse.

The Metaverse may be a concept long familiar to technologists. Specifically, the Metaverse is the moment at which our digital lives – our online identities, experiences, relationships, and assets – become more meaningful to us than our physical lives.' The Metaverse is 'most useful as a lens through which to view ongoing digital transformation. The belief is that virtual worlds, incorporating connected devices, block-chain and other tech, will be so commonplace that the Metaverse will become an extension of reality itself.'

Statements such as these reveal the breathtaking level of insanity that underpins this entire enterprise. It does not mean that we are not under enormous threat. Just as vast arsenals of nuclear weapons, by some insane 'logic', are supposed to provide us with 'security' while actually threatening the existence of all life on Earth, the Metaverse is part of a substantial package of measures that will reduce human life to one not worth living.

Author Tom Valovic states that "The Metaverse is one element in the path to implementing technocratic governance over all of humanity.

As Planet Earth and our physical world continue to experience massive biospheric degradation and disruption, the elites that are now in many cases pulling the strings of governance at the country level are heading for the exit doors. Elon Musk and Jeff Bezos are exploring the realm of space and Musk has a Mars mission planned. Globally oriented elites... looked out for themselves which is what they do best....

Paralleling the notion of space flight as a form of existential escapism is the Metaverse. So what if our cities are crumbling, infrastructures falling apart, and the biosphere is seriously degrading? So what if our wasteful consumer-driven lifestyle has created unprecedented levels of pollution so extensive that it's now the number one cause of health problems globally? No problem... we'll just kick back and don our Meta headsets (or worse get a brain implant) and escape into an artificially fabricated world that lets us turn our back on the massive ecological and environmental problems we now face.'

Facebook had changed its name to Meta. There's more to the name change than meets the eye: a strategic "vision" of the future and an overly powerful, profit-hungry corporation's misguided attempt to shape human destiny. Facebook's new moniker is shorthand for metaverse, a major new technology and culture shift that Big Tech is trying to force feed anyone who uses the Internet.

This is a seismic shift, comparable to the Internet in scope and scale, and it's planned to become the dominant paradigm for human communications, transitioning our business, social, and cultural life from physical to online environments.

This is an attempt to fabricate an alternate "reality" other than the physical one we now inhabit. This new reality can be accessed, of course, only by paying customers and those in a position to afford and understand it. It is a technology designed by elites and for elites and implicitly leaves behind much of humanity in its wake 'See depopulation and mRNA vaccines.'

For anyone concerned about the fate of the planet given the climate and biosphere crises and large-scale species extinction (and why do we hear so little of this in the mainstream media?), it is vitally important to understand not only what Meta has up its sleeve but also the larger picture that all the Big Tech players are peddling—a velvet steamroller promoting a massive existential shift that may come much sooner than we think.

What are the Real-world Implications of the Metaverse?

Virtual reality and augmented reality have been around for some time but have never really taken off as practical and useful technologies other than in gaming. But that's about to change and, if Big Tech has its way, it will have huge implications for all of us.

This radical change in how we live our lives is something that no one will get to vote on as a new and unprecedented kind of technocratic governance begins to replace many of the functions of traditional government and, even democracy itself.

As Planet Earth and our physical world continue to experience massive biospheric degradation and disruption, the elites that are now in many cases pulling the strings of governance at the country level are heading for the exit doors. Elon Musk and Jeff Bezos are exploring the realm of space and Musk has a Mars mission planned.

Globally oriented elites have a huge head start on the rest of the population for one simple reason: they had advance warning of just how serious the problems are we now face would be. These elites looked out for themselves which is what they do best. And governments just kicked the can down the road, something they're also quite adept at doing.

Paralleling the notion of space flight as a form of existential escapism is the Metaverse. So what if our cities are crumbling, infrastructures falling apart, and the biosphere is seriously degrading? So what if our wasteful consumer-driven lifestyle has created unprecedented levels of pollution so extensive that it's now the number one cause of health problems globally? No problem…we'll just kick back and don our Meta headsets (or worse get a brain implant) and escape into an artificially fabricated world that lets us turn our back on the massive ecological and environmental problems we now face.

World Economic Forum Plan for Technocratic Governance

The Metaverse appears to be part of a larger effort to implement technocratic governance and dovetails nicely with the agenda of the World Economic Forum (WEF). This organization is the official mouthpiece of the billionaire class.

The Davos elite is also promulgating its agenda through the mainstream media, ownership of which has been gradually appropriated by representatives of Big Tech. Jeff Bezos now owns the Washington Post; The Bill and Melinda Gates Foundation makes huge million-dollar level "contributions" to mainstream media outlets including PBS; and the CEO of Salesforce Marc Benioff now owns Time magazine. (Time, incidentally, recently ran a special issue on climate change which served up a very long-winded article on the importance of developing lab grown meat.)

Other huge technocratic changes are in the works. Large-scale (i.e., globally implemented) genetic modification (Covid19 vaccines) is another initiative on the WEF agenda. Everything in sight is targeted as a huge profit-making opportunity including the food supply, animal populations, and human bodies.

If re-designing animals stretches your credibility, here's what a recent WEF newsletter said about the need to genetically modify animals as a beneficial way of dealing with the climate crisis: "The process of resurrecting traits from extinct animals is commonly referred to as "de-extinction," and scientists hope to bring back the woolly mammoth to preserve the tundra. Engineering other animals and plants can help revive the ocean, protect food systems, and remove carbon from the atmosphere."

Now Big Tech is aiming to not only extend this intrusion with technologies like Alexa but to make life impossible to live without it... hence the notion of a Metaverse. Working in conjunction with elites and Big Tech social engineers, this next big initiative will be even more intrusive and dehumanizing and is being carried out under the rubric of a specious "philosophy" called transhumanism—a set of values that has declared our own humanity as deficient in need of technological enhancement, of course for a profit and complete totalitarian control and destruction of our organic humanity.

The first wave of transhumanism's new invasiveness will come with so called wearable devices i.e., headbands, virtual reality glasses, body attachments, skin implants, and others. The next phase will be an attempt to physically wire our bodies into an electronic alternate reality where privacy and individual autonomy will be nonexistent. (The WEF received a huge wave of pushback when they posted a video with the message: "You will own nothing, have no privacy, and be happy".) How ungodly if not Satanic!

We must not be seduced by this chimerical and false vision of reality which further removes our awareness from the natural world and (worse) even seeks to replace it by encouraging us to divert attention from the task of healing the planet and repairing our biosphere. We should not trust Mark Zuckerberg or any other members of the corporate elite with self-serving agendas to guide us through an increasingly precarious future. We should not be willing to accept Big Tech's and the WEF's dehumanizing vision of the future.

Tom Valovic is a journalist and the author of Digital Mythologies (Rutgers University Press), a series of essays that explored emerging social and political issues raised by the advent of the Internet. He has served as a consultant to the former Congressional Office of Technology Assessment. Tom has written about the effects of technology on society for a variety of publications including Columbia University's Media Studies Journal, the Boston Globe, and the San Francisco Examiner, among others.

Critiquing the Metaverse

In the overall elite program being implemented under what the WEF calls its 'Great Reset'. This comprehensive program will transform human society and human life for those people left alive after the eugenics component has been fully implemented with mRNA vaccines and world wars.

While some people may not intend for The Metaverse to become an all-encompassing reality that supersedes physical reality, for the Zuckerbergs, Microsoft, and WEFs of the world, that is exactly what they intend for The Metaverse.

For the billionaire class and their puppet organizations, such as the WEF and the United Nations, the Metaverse offers up the potential to commandeer all life into digital prisons where the people can be charged for services and products in the digital realm.... With the people of the world safely tucked into their digital beds, the Technocrats could complete their total takeover of natural resources, the economy, and humanity itself.

Who will govern the 'Metaverse'? According to the WEF, "real-world governance models" represent one possible option for Metaverse governance. However, far from referring to constitutionally defined institutions of governance, with checks and balances, the WEF cites Facebook's "Oversight Board" as an example of such a "real-world governance model."

You can live your life with all its challenges and problems, joys and achievements. Or you can live the virtual life that someone else programmed for you, including whatever comes with it that they didn't tell you about.

In short, like Neo in the film 'The Matrix', you have a choice. You can choose the Blue Pill and proceed to live in a synthesized, fictional, computer-generated world. Or you take the Red Pill and, in this case, join the fight with those of us determined to defend the real world and avert descent into the Metaverse.

But you must make that choice while you still have free will.

So you must make that choice soon.

Deviating from the Miracle

Most people are good. Occasionally they do something they know is bad. Some people are bad and they struggle every day to keep it under control. Others are corrupt to the core and just don't give a damn. The evil mind is a completely different creature. An evil mind believes doing bad things to others is okay.

The end results of evil is violence that is completely divorced from a moral conscience. This is the new world order of globalist psychopaths preferring nihilistic bioweapons, conventional wars, and humanistic betrayal by funding artificial intelligence over organic life, no matter what is destroyed or how many lives are lost. The Georgia Guide Stones call for a reduction of the world's population from 7.5 billion to 500,000,000. I understand it's bombing recently in Elberton, Georgia.

Filth in the Soul of Humanity

The masses have never thirsted after the truth. They turn aside from evidence that is not to their taste, preferring to deify error, if error seduces the weakness for pleasure in them. Whoever can supply them with illusions is easily their master; whoever attempts to destroy their illusion is always their victim.

Gustav Le Bon

Man is a Wolf to Man

According to Carl Jung the greatest threat to civilization lies not with the forces of nature, not with any physical disease, but with our inability to deal with the forces of our own psyche. We are our own worst enemy. Man is a wolf to man.

Jung states "in civilization in transition, this proverb, man is a wolf to man, is a sad eternal truism" and our wolf-like tendencies come most prominently at those times in history when mental illness becomes the norm, rather than the exception in a society, which Jung termed a psychic epidemic.

It is "Not" famine, "Not" earthquakes, "Not" microbes, "Not" cancer, but man himself who is man's "Greatest Danger" to man, for the simple reason that there is no adequate protection against a psychic epidemics, which are infinitely more devastating than the worst natural catastrophes.

The most dangerous epidemic of them all is "Mass Psychosis." It occurs when a large portion of society loses touch with reality and descends into delusions. This has been the case with religion and politics. Now we see it manifest in the mandates and dictates of the government during the current COVID19 pandemic and psychopathic wars of the Global Elitists.

When "Mass Psychosis" occurs, the results are devastating. Jung said that "the individuals who make up the infected society become morally and spiritually inferior. They sink unconsciously to an inferior intellectual level. They become more unreasonable, irresponsible, emotional, erratic, and unreliable," and commit crimes the individual alone would never commit standing freely alone but goes along with crimes against humanity when herded into a group smitten by madness.

What makes matters worse is that those suffering from mass psychosis are unaware of what is occurring. For just as an individual gone mad cannot step out of his or her mind to observe the errors in his or her ways, so there is no way of which those living from a point of mass psychosis can observe their collective madness.

But what causes mass psychosis? To answer this question we must explore what drives an individual mad. Where there are many potential triggers of madness, such as an excessive use of drugs or alcohol, brain injuries and other illnesses, these physical causes is not the primary concern of causes of mass psychosis. We need to ask what the psychogenic triggers are. The psychogenic triggers are the most common culprit of mass psychosis.

The most prevalent psychogenic cause of mass psychosis is a flood of negative emotions such as fear or anxiety that drives an individual into a sense of panic. When in a state of panic, an individual will naturally seek relief as it is too mentally draining to subsist in this hyper-emotional state.

While escaping from the state of panic can be accomplished through adaptive means, such as facing up to, and defeating the fear generating threat; another way to escape is to undergo a psychotic break. A psychotic break is not a descent into a state of greater disorder, but a re-ordering of one's experiential world which blends facts and fiction, or delusions and reality, in a way that helps end the feelings of panic.

The psychogenic steps that leads to madness are:

- Phase of panic- when the patient starts to perceive things in a different way and is frightened because of these different perceptions. He is confused and does not know how to explain the strange things that are happening.

- The next step is psychotic insight, whereby an individual succeeds in "putting things together" by devising a pathological way of seeing a reality which allows him to explain his abnormal experiences. The phenomenon is called "insight" because the patient finally see meaning and relations in his /her experiences.
- The insight is psychotic because it is based on delusions and not on adaptive and life-promoting ways of relating to whatever threat precipitated the panic.
- The delusion, in other words, allows the panic stricken individual to escape from the flood of negative emotions, but at the cost of losing touch with reality. This psychotic break can be viewed as "an abnormal way of dealing with an extreme state of anxiety."

Obsession with wealth and the many religions of the world are the social norm prevalent throughout the world today of dealing with extreme states of anxiety. If a panic triggering flood of negative emotions, in a weak and vulnerable individual, it can trigger a mass psychotic break, then a massive collective psychosis results when a population of weak and vulnerable individuals is driven into a state of panic by threats real, imagined, or fabricated.

Delusion can take many forms, and madness can manifest in countless ways, the specific manner in which mass psychosis unfolds will differ based on the historical and cultural context of the infected society.

In our modern era, mass psychosis is being caused by totalitarianism. That is our greatest threat. Totalitarianism is the modern phenomenon of total centralized state power coupled with the obliteration of individual human right, which is currently being done by COVID19 medical tyranny mandates. In the totalized state, there are those in power, and there are the objective masses, the victims.

In a totalitarian society, the population is divided into two groups, the rulers and the ruled, and both groups undergo a pathological transformation. The rulers are elevated to an almost god-like status which is diametrically opposed to our nature as imperfect beings who are easily corrupted by power.

The masses on the other hand are transformed into dependents of pathological rulers, the banking financial oligarchs, Royal Families, Presidents, Prime Ministers, and high ranking clergies such as the Pope and etc. who may view these dependents as useless feeders. The pandemic mandate are very suspicious given the rulers eugenic agenda that may include depopulation.

Those dependent on their pathological rulers take on psychological regression and childlike status. This type of transforming totalitarianism using controlled media networks to turn sound minds into sick minds. There is much that is comparable between strange reactions of the citizens of totalitarianism and their culture as a whole on the one hand and the reactions of the sick on the other.

The social transformation that unfolds under totalitarianism is built upon and sustained by delusional narratives of controlled media networks. For only deluded men and women regress to the childlike status of obedient and submissive subjects and hand over complete control to ruler of the church and state.

Every religion conditions childlike behavior of the Father and the child, in the state there are the rulers and the ruled. Religion has conditioned people to be the perfect subjects of totalitarian rule. They happily turn over their lives to politicians, clergy, and bureaucrats whose moral compass are often distorted.

Only a deluded class of people will believe that these rulers possess the knowledge, wisdom, and acumen to benevolently control society in a top-down manner. Only under spells of delusion would anyone believe that a society composed of power-hungry rulers, on one hand, and a psychologically regressed population on the other hand, would lead to anything other than mass suffering and social ruin.

What triggers the mass psychosis of totalitarianism in a society? It begins in a ruling class. The individuals that makes up that ruling class, be it politicians, clergy, bureaucrat, or crony capitalists, they inevitably are prone to delusions that augment their power. No delusion is more attractive to the power hungry than the delusion that they can and should control and dominate society.

When a ruling elite becomes possessed of a political ideology be it communism, fascism, technocracy, the next step is to induce a population into accepting their rule by infecting them with the mass psychosis of totalitarianism. COVID19 is the latest example of their contempt for the undeserving poor.

Menticide, the killing of the Mind

The mass psychosis of totalitarianism has been induced many times throughout history through religion and politics. It's a question of reorganizing and manipulating collective feelings in the proper way. The general method by which the ruling elite can accomplish their end is called menticide, with the etymology of this word being a "killing of the mind." This is being done with drugs, GMO's in the food, fluoride in the water, and mRNA vaccines.

Menticide is an old crime against the human mind and systematized. It is an organized system of psychological intervention and judicial perversion (FDA approving MRNA gene therapy that is being misrepresented as a vaccine) through which a ruling class can imprint their own opportunistic thought by reorganizing the minds and DNA of those they plan to use and destroy.

Priming a population for the crime of menticide begins with sowing of fear. When an individual is flooded with negative emotions, such as fear or anxiety he or she is very susceptible to descent into the delusions of madness. Threats imagined, real, or fabricated can be used to sow fear. A particularly effected technique to accomplish mass psychosis is to use waves of terror (pandemics and wars).

Under this technique, the sowing of fear is staggered with periods of calm, but each of these periods of calm is followed by manufacturing of an even more intense spell of fear, pandemics, wars, fluctuating stock markets, on and on, the process goes.

Each wave of terrorizing creates its effect more easily – after a breathing spell – than the one that preceded it because people are still disturbed by their previous experience. Morality becomes lower and lower, and the psychological effects of each new propaganda campaign becomes stronger, it reaches a public that has already been softened up.

While fear primes a population for menticide, the use of propaganda to spread misinformation and to promote confusion with respect to the source of the threats and the nature of the crisis, helps break down the minds of the masses.

Government officials, and their lackies in the media, can use contradictory reports, non-sensical information and even blatant lies (the inflated PCR statistics of those infected with COVID 19 virus and suppressing the numbers of those injured or killed by vaccines) as the more people they confuse, the less capable will a population be able to cope with the crisis, and diminish their fear, in a rational and adaptive manner.

Confusion heightens the susceptibility of a descent into the delusion of totalitarianism. Logic can be met with logic, while illogic cannot. Confusion confuses those who think straight. The big lie and monotonous repeated nonsense have more emotional appeal than logic and reason.

While the people are still searching for a reasonable counter-argument to the first lie (the first wave of COVID19 – then the next Delta wave and Omni), the totalitarians can assault them (Rape of the mind) with another lie or eventful war. Never before in history have such effective means (technology-wise) existed to manipulate a society into the psychosis of totalitarianism.

Smart phones and social media, television and the Internet, all in conjunction with Bots that spread propaganda and algorithms that quickly censor the flow of unwanted information, using fact-check to perpetuate lies, allow those in power to easily rape assault the minds of the masses.

The addictive nature of theses media technologies means that many people voluntarily subject themselves to the ruling elite's propaganda with a remarkable frequency. Modern technology teaches man to take for granted the world he is looking at; people takes no time to retreat and reflect.

Technology lures us on into its futuristic wheels of movements. No rest, no meditation, no reflection, no conversation and the senses are continually overloaded with stimuli. Man doesn't lean to question his world anymore; the screens of Google's data bases in the clouds give him his answers already made.

There is a further step the totalitarian rulers can take to increase the chance of a totalitarian psychosis, and this is to isolate the victims with global lockdowns made possible by a pandemic to disrupt normal social interactions.

When alone and lacking normal interactions with family, friends, and co-workers, an individual becomes far more susceptible to delusions for several reasons. They can lose contact with the corrective force of the positive example. They lose contact with individuals who can see through the propaganda who can help free others from the menticidal assault.

If isolation is enforced, the power of these positive examples greatly diminishes. Isolation increases the efficacy of menticide because like many other species human beings are more easily conditioned into new patterns of thought and behavior when isolated.

The Behaviorist Pavlov made an interesting discovery that conditioned reflex could be developed most easily in a quiet laboratory with minimum of distracting stimuli. Isolation and the patient repetition of stimuli are required to tame wild animals. The totalitarians have followed this rule using lockdown and controlled news media networks.

They know that they can condition their political victims most quickly if they are kept in isolation. Alone, confused, and battered by waves of terror, a population under attack of menticide descends into a hopeless and vulnerable state. The never ending stream of propaganda turns minds that were once capable of rational thought into playhouses of irrational forces and with chaos swirling around them, the masses crave a return to a more ordered world.

The would-be totalitarians can now take the decisive step, they can offer a way out and a return to order in a world that seem to be moving rapidly in the opposite direction. But all this comes at a price.

The masses must give up their freedom and relinquish control of all aspect of their lives to the ruling elite. They must relinquish their capacity to be self-reliant individuals who are responsible for their own lives, and become submissive and obedient subjects. The masses in other words, must descend into delusions of the totalitarian psychosis.

The totalitarian systems of the 20th century represent a kind of collective psychosis. Reason and common human dignity are no longer possible in such a system. There is only a pervasive atmosphere of terror, and a projection of "the enemy, imagined to be in our midst."

With all of the Bilderberg and Tri-Lateral dictates put in place by the ruling elite, society turns on itself. But the order of the totalitarian world is a pathological order. By enforcing a strict conformity, and requiring blind obedience of the people, totalitarianism rids the world of spontaneity that produces many of life's joys and creativity that drives the life of the common members of society forward.

The total control of this form of rule, no matter under what name it is branded, be it rule by scientists, doctors, politicians, bureaucrats, clergy, or dictator, breeds stagnation, destruction, and death on a mass scale.

The most important question facing the world is how can totalitarianism be prevented? If a society has been induced into the early stages of the mass psychosis, can the conditioning be reversed?

While one can never be sure of the prognosis of a collective madness, there are steps that can be taken to help effectuate a cure. This task necessitates many different approaches, from many different people. For just as the menticidal attack is multi-pronged, so too must be the counter-attack.

According to Carl Jung, for those of us who wish to help return sanity to the world, the first step is to bring order to our own minds, and to live in a way that provides inspiration for others to follow.

It is not for nothing that our age cries out for redeemer personalities, for the one who can emancipate self from the collective grip of the collective psychosis and save at least his own soul, who lights a beacon of hope for others, proclaiming that here is at least one man who has succeeded in extricating himself from the fatal identity with the group psyche.

Think of herd immunity as being synonymous with group think. Understand the road our pandemic is herding us down. If one finds oneself living in a manner free of the grip of group think or group psychosis, there are further steps that can be taken.

Information that can counter the propaganda should be spread as far and as wide as possible. For the truth is more powerful than fiction and falsehood peddled by the would-be totalitarian rulers and their hope for success that is dependent on their veil of lies covering their deception by censoring the free flow of information.

Tyranny is not easily conquered, the harder the conflict, the more glorious the conflict.

The ritual of cleansing body and soul gone awry. The thing that may impress foreigners when they come to America from Third World nations are the spacious American homes lavishly furnished, kitchens loaded with foods, and bathrooms with bathtubs and showers. American daily routines always begins or ends with a baths or shower. Cleanliness is Godliness.

We clean our body, yet there is so much dirt in the capitalist hive minded consumerist consciousness fueled by greed. Churches and educational institutions lacks substantial cleansing effects to counter the dirt embed in the dirty pharmaceutical and illegal drug culture, wars, and inequities of systems steeped in financial capitalism.

Religious principles and education from our most hallowed institutions proves insufficient at removing stubborn stains of vice and greed, inherent of a nation guided by profit instead of human dignity. The odorous dirt of the American psyche is obscured behind homes and well-scrubbed immaculately dressed outer images masquerading as those with clean hearts and spirits.

The make-up, the perfumes, and the clothes are fashion runways of so many in masquerade, who, behind the façade, are dingy beings with unclean souls and tainted ethical regards for the underprivileged. Every-day people are being reduced via menticide to spiritual zombies that are void of human dignity.

The inner dirt is manifested in national priorities of murderous rich men's wars for profits, frustration inspired mass killings, and lifestyles riddled with pharmaceutical and street drugs.

Where are the influence of Churches and higher education? Corrupt hive minded elected government officials turn a blind eye to the dirt of financial corruption and lack the moral conscience to envision a brighter day for the people they have taken an oath to serve and protect.

Politicians have desecrated and soiled the moral fibers that represent ideas of democracy. Democracy, dirtied with selfishness and greed, has become a Trojan horse of murder and thievery.

All the dirty people on Capitol Hill, unclean despite all of our churches and institutions of higher learning, where do they keep coming from. What image of self has been imposed upon us by the culture we live? How much of our belief is original; something that is unique and not something imposed by society? Can you see anything original in the mirror? When was the last time your mind was free of any kind of fear?

Who are you if you shed the image baggage of who you have been in the past?

Can you, who is the result of time, of various cultures, experiences, and knowledge, look at your reality with eyes that are not conditioned?

Can your mind operate instantly, being free of its religious, political, and nationalistic agenda, be free of its conditioning? A mind conditioned to the demands of pleasure, of gratification, of satisfaction is a mind that entangles freedom with enslavement.

In this enslavement, we are manipulated by those in control of wealth. Because of the values, levied on us by those controlling wealth, our prevailing collective mores that we embrace as a society are distorted in selfishness and greed based financial principles.

To truly know love, we must understand and put aside what is not love. In our society, that is a tall task because love has been substituted by so many things it is not. If we want to find out what truth is, we have to understand what truth is not.

If we look at the world through distorted lens, we do not possess the capacity to perceive what is false, therefore cannot discern what is true.

Everything is false that thought has put together psychologically the "me," the self with its memories, with its aggression, with its separateness, with its ambitions, competitiveness, imitation, fear and past memories; all of this has been put together by thought.

Here is where our global societies continue to error. Their Constitutions are ideas of the past; written by dead people who would not understand the dynamics of contemporary life. Past ideas of distorted values are outdated references for a world vastly different than the founding fathers could ever imagine.

The global societies will continue to get love wrong because its schools continue to embrace values that encourage children, despite all our religious institutions, to be ambitious, wanting to achieve, wanting to become powerful financial tyrants, minds that are aggressive, competitive, imitative, such minds cannot possibly understand what love is. A mind that is ambitious cannot possibly love and know to drop these ambitions to bring about a brighter day.

So, can we see very clearly that a mind seeking gain, or achievement, either in the world, or in the so-called spiritual seeking of enlightenment, cannot love. We must have the ability to see the falseness and the contradictions of how we live. In order to know truth, we must love the truth.

It is not will power that will bring about a greater human societies perched on principles of love; it is whether each of us can see the falseness of our commitment to knowing and living a life from true loving perspectives.

We actually have to see the falseness of what we do that is not love, such as supporting governments that spend it wealth on technologies that destroys and enslaves instead of nurturing with real examples of giving back for growth that manifest love, which free our children to flourish and inherit a world respectful of loving virtues grounded in a respect for nature and each other.

We have to see the destructive contradictions we ingest and then pass this poison on to our children. Can you see anything in the mirror that is original? What can you bring to the table that is lovingly brand new to create a brighter and sane future?

One statement of the Bible that truly resonates with me is "You will know a tree by the fruits it bears." What is the path of a nation built on genocide of native Indians, the enslavement of Africans, a nation whose legacy is murdering leaders like Abraham Lincoln, Martin Luther King Jr., the Kennedy Brothers, and brave men such as James Forrestal who were murdered to silence their wish to speak of extraterrestrial beings on earth?

The fruit America is bearing is not the fruits dreamed of by Martin Luther King Jr. or the Kennedy brothers. We are seeing the dreams of the New World Order globalists, who controls the WEF, which is hell bent on depopulation and eradicating notions of free will and human life itself.

While people are rocked to sleep with rhetoric of freedom and democracy, the only dreams that are coming true are those of the financial elite.

Those dreams of the Cabal are of other world orientation that makes human sacrifice via bioweapons, wars, and unnecessary mass poverty a necessary evil solution to achieve a victory in the most un-holy war in order to establish racial dominance over those deemed different and inferior.

As Allan Watts so eloquently stated, "we aren't better because we want to be." Do gooders have always been trouble makers like the monkey saying to the fish, kindly let me help you or you will drown. Then the monkey put the fish up a tree.

White Anglo Saxon, Protestants, German, British, and Americans have been on a technological rampage to fulfill what has been deemed "The White Man's Burden," to provide benefits of white culture, religion, and technology to everybody. They insist the world receive these benefits of their culture, political style, and their economic institutions. They say, "You better be democratic or we will shoot you!"

Having conferred these evil blessings all over the planet (weapons of mass destruction, Bioweapons, nuclear reactors threating our biosphere, and murderous wars, western society in all it bigotry and racism wonders why blacks protest and the rest of the world hates the threats of these so called benefits. When your technology compromises the planetary biosphere, people will look at you crossly.

It is so obvious that technology wears a veil masquerading as doing well for humanity while being amazingly destructive. How do these rich and powerful men know what good for the world?

Democracy today is reduced to shadow government controlling false front governments to manage what George Orwell called proletariats, the regular working persons, who believe they are free. In the meantime, elite aristocrats are developing a secret space program designed to escape a polluted and over populated earth.

Secret Space Programs and Underground Military Bases are constructed under the cover of lies. Who are these secret underground city enclaves being built for, and why are they being built with labor and taxes of the people, yet cloaked in secrecy? The answer to these questions reveals ultimate betrayal by world financial, political, and spiritual leaders.

Our objective purpose of being is to evolve beyond human thought into the eternal vacuum of silence to not only connect with but dissolve into the power of creation itself.

Only in the silent calm of a quiet mind, I discover life to be a blissful spiritual retreat. All the random noise of religion and politics in this spiritual war is disturbing, invasive and divisive. The conceptual forms of knowledge required to counter fears can be noisy distractions that diminishes the essences of compassion in the human spirit.

The wonder tales that describes the lives of legendary heroes, the powers of the divinities of nature, the spirits of the dead traveling with us in our consciousness, and the totem ancestry of the group or race we represent manifests in all types of myths that feeds religion belief, which gives symbolic expression to unconscious desires, fears, and tension that underlie the conscious pattern of human behavior.

Creating so many partitions in thought one becomes lost in the many partitions of joy, pleasure, and security that manifest as escapes as resolutions to daily physical survival challenges. With our births, each of us can manifest and represent as a God particle a quiet abode of infinite consciousness.

Once we connect with the source of creativity, the most difficult thing to change is returning from that off the grid realization and connection of peace to the social norm of being scattered all over the place living in a society that no longer values independent thinking and spiritual prosperity.

Having cast off the world, who would desire to return to its imperfect chaos? Society is jealous of those who remain away from it in independent bliss. The mRNA vaccine gene therapy is the greatest threat to humanity. The Corona pandemic is starting the new age of trans-humanism and herd mentality.

In Japan Shinto is "the way of the Gods." It is the way of devotion to preserving and cultivating purity of heart, following the right and moral way. Pleasing the deities with virtues and sincerity without any material offerings as the way practiced so much in the western world.

In Shinto, Deity is honored in all things. The practice of preserving purity of heart and mind is manifesting deity in oneself. The guardian of life sees all things in silence.

The function of religion is to bring awareness and make possible the leap into ubiquitous opening beyond thought itself. Religion is not the ultimate soul revelation. That ultimate revelation is complete openness to the silent oblivion of nothingness and the impermanence of our being and our place in the cosmic fabric as God Particles. We are tasked with growing beyond partitioned conceptualization in the realm of human thought and plunging alone into dissolution in the cosmic fabric.

God and the Gods are only convenient means themselves of the nature of the world of names and conceptual forms. Those symbolic forms of consciousness that we identify with in the concepts of God are merely symbols to move and awake the mind and call you past that consciousness called you that you are stuck on.

Regardless of which-ever deity is being worshipped, Christianity, Mohammedanism, and Judaism, the personality of the divinity is taught to be final. This finality makes it difficult for these religious members to understand how to go beyond the limitations of their own conceptual divinity confined in the confined psychological space of anthropomorphic thoughts.

Truth should not be painful. It may cause us to stumble but not lose our balance. Our acknowledgement of it is the light that illumines our path forward out of the mysteries of falsehood. The truth will always be the one, shape shifting, yet marvelously constant story that we find at the core of our being that is always challengingly persistent suggestion of more remaining to be experienced than will ever be known or told.

Myths are verbal conceptual portals through which the inexhaustible energies of the cosmos pour into the human cultural manifestation. Religion, philosophies, art, the social forms of primitive and historic man, prime discoveries in science and technology, the very dreams that blister sleep, boil up from the basic magic ring of myths.

The question is how do man abandon his infantile literal interpretations of myths in order to advance into the future without destructive violence? The myths of religion has supplied the symbol to carry the human spirit forward. We are seeing neuroticism advancing in bio-genetic and trans-humanism technologies as the beliefs religion and social mores are falling to the wayside as the universe reveals greater wisdom of purpose.

We as a species on earth are in the later stages of many of our religious mythologies. The key images hide like needles in this great cosmic haystack of secondary anecdote and rationalization. Technical secular points of views today outweigh the religious mythological symbols of Confucius, Muhammad, Vishnu, and Jesus Christ.

The Ancient Gods of Ancient Egypt, Hellenistic Greece, and in Imperial Rome have been reduced to mere patrons, household pets, and literary favorites. The Sun God of Egypt, Zeus on Mount Olympus, all reduced to superhuman romances. In China, Confucianism replaced the old myths forms to clutter of anecdotes of sons and daughters of provincial official who were given god-like status after serving their communities.

In modern Christianity the Christ held as an incarnation of God in human flesh has been reduced to a historical personage, a harmless country wise man who preached "do as to others as you would be done by them," yet was executed as a criminal. His life and death is a symbol of integrity and fortitude.

Whenever the poetry of myth is interpreted as biography, history, or science, it is killed. It is never difficult to demonstrate that as science and history mythology is absurd. When a civilization begins to reinterpret its mythology in this way, the life goes out of the mythology. Temples becomes museums and the link between the two perspectives is lost. This is the challenge of the Bible and its many sects in western civilization.

The societies in which it serves as a moral foundation have profited from slavery, produced the wars, the biogenetics that has produced the world's worst viruses, and the current COVID19 pandemic. The destructive contradictions of actions not matching the words are no longer entertaining, desirable, nor will be tolerated.

The story of humanity is filled with mysteries of man's origin. We are on this tiny planet in this vast reality of star filled galaxies and possibly parallel universes that seems to stretch into infinity. Are we alone or have we gotten some help stumbling out of the box of creation, whether God or ancient aliens?

CHAPTER I

AN ALTERNATIVE PERSPECTIVE ON GOD AND THE COSMOS

Path 1: Consciousness, Human or Alien, Nature's Self-Inflicted Wound

When you remove thinking from the equation of human or alien purpose and reality, everything happening in the cosmos makes sense living in a reality that is book ended by conceptual and physical realities evolving around living and dying.

Take away the fear component in consciousness, the undoing or the dissolving of and breaking down of the me concept, which also includes diametrically opposed judgmental constructs of right and wrong, then everything about the universe as presented to us by whomever and whatever makes perfect sense and is working in perfect order.

Fear is a very large factor in the composition of consciousness. Fear, also, a product of thought/consciousness. The idea of "Love" is also a product of thought. As Tina Turner asked, what does love have to do with it? Certainly that question can also be asked as to what love has to do with the machinations of nature/God.

The human psyche complex filters unrelenting experiences of taxes, death, and trouble and there is only one psychological relief and that is an idea, belief, and a sensation of this thing in the human spirit we think of as Love."

In its relentless perfection of order, why did nature, in all of its creative rage, inflict itself with the wound of human consciousness? Why the moral inventory of ideas of right, wrong, justice, and morality hidden away in the cosmic microbial thoughts of human or aliens?

What is the cosmic interest to all the blood-letting of all creatures fowl, fish, animals, and men? What is the inventory of consciousness being used for by the primal creator? Are we here to calibrate God's imperfections that comes with the territory of forging consciousness from the marriage of energy and matter?

The imperfections of matter imbued with consciousness is God tinkering with its own imperfection of self-creation where in the infinitum of the self-creative process even God had to rob Peter to pay Paul in the very beginning of its conscious infinitude.

Path 2: Spiritual Consciousness beyond Our Physical World

If what we think of as God is no more than infinite consciousness, is consciousness something permanent, essential, or characteristic attribute of the universe, like dark matter, dark energy, or gravity? The Political landscape and its associated morass of taxes and people grinding axes against each other is phenomenon consciousness created by properties in the brain and its natural metabolism associated with physical survival. Is there a higher vibrating spiritual agenda that our brains must grasp beyond struggles against nature or even God itself?

What higher vibrating essences are out there in a reality permeated by infinite consciousness that we can tap into that solves physical struggles?

What is the true essence of consciousness? Is there a higher vibrating creative force out there that we are tasked with filtering? When the brain dies, does the mind and consciousness of the being to whom that brain belonged ceases to exist?

In other words, without a brain, is there no consciousness? Is there infinite consciousness that exists, a creator, God, or what is referred to as the most high? According to the decades-long research of Dr. Peter Fenwick, a highly regarded neuropsychiatrist, after studying Near Death Experiences for 50 years, the view of consciousness existing only in the brain is incorrect.

In Fenwick's view, the brain does not create or produce consciousness; rather, it filters it. Fenwick present the analogy of the eyes where the eye filters and interprets only a very small sliver of the electromagnetic spectrum and the ear registers only a narrow range of sonic frequencies. Similarly, according to Fenwick, the brain filters and perceives only a tiny part of the cosmos' intrinsic "consciousness."

When we die all the consciousness that we filtered when alive is still here in the cosmos. After death, our brains can no longer filter, be stimulated by, and react to light energy, which preceded it before birth and remains after death. According to Fenwick, just because the organ that filters, perceives, and interprets cosmic consciousness dies does not mean the cosmic consciousness ceases to exist.

It only ceases to be in the now-dead brain but continues to exist independently of the brain as an external property of the universe itself.

Mankind has gone down a dangerous road of its multitudes of religious beliefs. Our consciousness tricks us into perceiving a false duality of self and other when in fact there is only unity.

When we die, we transcend the human experience of consciousness, and its illusion of duality, and merge with the universe's entire and unified property of consciousness. Fenwick make a very profound statement "only in death can we be fully conscious." I agree with that.

Another important message from Mr. Fenwick is that at death we are not joining God because the cosmic consciousness did not create the universe but is simply a property of it.

Religion is a construct of the human brain. All the gospels in the Bible and Koran written by men with limited tools filtering just their own 3 dimensional reality. We are ruled by an Oligarchy that refuses to share forensics evidence of alien presence among us, aliens who have been instrumental in human creation and technical progression.

Is religion a cover with an agenda of controlling the masses? Is there a cosmic overseer with a moral agenda of goodness for us beyond the limited phenomenology of all Holy books? Maybe consciousness is our own magic wand of creation. We can no longer allow fear inherent of religious belief limit the scope of humanity.

Think of a landscape of consciousness without the religious boxes that we are herded into at birth. This freedom of thought leads to a conceptual singularity unity into infinite consciousness.

Path 3: Cosmic Consciousness

Only a few are blessed with a vision transcending the scope of normal human destiny, and discern the essential nature of the cosmos. My personal fate and the fate of mankind has very little impact on the cosmological structure of the universe. Armed with only an anthropomorphic human understanding, we take our infinitesimal presence among the cosmic giants way too serious

What will it be in our life experiences that will open up a higher vibrating spiritual purpose? After discovering a heightened spiritual energy of unbound awakening, will we find ourselves existing in a timeless quantum singularity no longer corporeally limited to flesh bound consciousness?

The greatest challenge for the hero is permeating the whole texture of existence with a divine grace of a divine assisting presence to bring all to the same enlightened timeless unconscionable quantum spiritual void of calm, tranquility, and peace.

The universe is infinitely large. The observable universe appears to go back in time 13.8 billion years, beyond what we can see with our largest telescopes there is much more that dwarfs our collective human imagination; our thoughts and imagination is a narrow bandwidth of knowledge that we shape concepts of infinite consciousness we think of as God.

Some astronomers think that we may live in a "multiverse" consisting of possibly infinite cell-like units we think of as universes; each multiverse of universes operating within the infinite space time dimensions of a larger entity.

There are some who speculate that we live in a simulated universe. The simulation hypothesis or simulation theory is the proposal that all of reality, including the Earth and entire universe, could be an artificial simulation, such as a computer simulation. Is the phenomena of people, stars overhead, the ground beneath our feet, our bodies, and consciousness an elaborate illusion or simulation much like what we observe in a video game?

Beyond speculation on the reality we experience as life is some type of sophisticated video game, let's just take this hypothesis a bit further. What if our reality as collective human spirituality exists in the vacuum of a macrocosmic infinite consciousness of a spiritual entity we relate to as God?

In ancient Egypt, the saying "As above so below" speaks to the relationship of the temple of our body to the creator. Know thy self and you will come to know the Gods and the kingdom of heaven will be in you. Search not outside yourself for God is within.

Think of our brain that composes 100 billion neurons and is a microcosm of an infinite macrocosmic complex of stars that are elaborate neuronal-like connections which are all part of infinite consciousness or God that we have been paying homage to with prayer throughout human history. We relate to a concept of an external God and lack the emphasis in our teaching to seek God from within. This internal epiphany is everything. It is everything to know God within yourself and very important to know yourself. Our thoughts manifest our reality.

Now, let's compare the neurons of our brains with stars. Neurons in our brain serve as information highways between different complexes in the brain. What if stars, dark energy, and dark matter are network components of infinite consciousness of an entity we relate to as God?

There seems to be micro mimicking in the brain of what actually occurs in the universe. There is an eerie similarity of the ongoing creation of neurons in the hippocampus of the brain to the formation of stars in Nebula clouds of gases in deep space. The Glial cells in the brain support, protect, and hold neurons together much like dark matter and dark energy's gravitational relationship with stars that also hold them in place.

Instead of the much talked about idea that we live in a simulated universe, what if consciousness is the imagination of a supernatural entity, God, and human and human are microcosmic cells within this greater organ of infinite consciousness or God? What if black holes are transmitters of electro-magnetic impulses and chemical signals between different areas of a cosmic brain, much like the function of neuron in a human brain?

Dark matter may act as conduits-like constructs between many stars throughout the galaxies much like neuronal conduits sensory and motor neurons in the brain. The key difference between sensory and motor neurons is that the sensory neurons are the neurons that carry information from sense organs to the central nervous system while motor neurons are the neurons that carry information from the central nervous system to the muscle cells. Consciousness in the brain is impossible without networking between sensory and motor neurons.

Is God's consciousness a construct of electrical and chemical signals between stars just like consciousness is established in the human brain that is dependent on electrical and chemical signal between neurons in the brain? In an infinite perspective, could our universe be just "one" of many micro cosmic neuron cell organism in a network of multiverse cells, all of which could be constructs in the infinitude of God's infinite consciousness?

Is the human brain a microcosmic mimicry of an infinite cosmic network of intelligence? Is the energy of stars similar to synaptic energy constructs in the human brain? In the cosmic mind, is the network of stars, dark matter, and dark energy cosmic constructs that act like sensory and motor nerves in the human brain that share on a cosmic level electrical energy that is essential to the existence of cosmic consciousness?

Is cosmic consciousness the end product of nuclear fusion? Was the big bang simply neuronal firing in the cosmic headspace of God? Does the energy present within multiverse cosmic complexes of universes mirror the production and processing of energy that produces consciousness in the human brain, where synaptic connections transmit electrical impulses from one neuron to the next in building a memory network?

Was the big bang merely the firing of electro-magnetic energy of infinite consciousness of God? Is consciousness electro-magnetic waves? A new theory suggests electromagnetic energy in the brain enables neurons and brain regions to create consciousness and our ability to critically think. Could the expanding universe that we observe with galaxies racing away from us be exchanges of electro-magnetic connections that creates a cosmic memory network where the stars are simply charged particles using dark matter and dark energy as synaptic conduits?

You have about 100 billion neurons in your brain, but each neuron has multiple synapses connecting to multiple other neurons. As a result, you have literally trillions of synapses—possibly even a *quadrillion* (that's a 1 followed by 15 zeroes). There are 100 billion and 200 billion galaxies. This is conceptualization that challenge every religious instinct and something I think people should consider that could bring about an expansion from the narrow bandwidth of awareness we currently embrace.

We need a greater sense of awareness of the correlation of how the brain works and the similarities of the universe to the structure of the brain to understand what we are and where we come from? We are all made of the same God particles as the stars are. We are all one and connected.

Imagine the immensity of what we see as the universe and the complexity created by not fully understanding the light of energy of life inside us that is a Godly presence having a human experience contemplating itself through human eyes. Could all life terrestrial and extraterrestrial life be microcosmic units of this Godly infinite consciousness?

Is it possibly that we may even be constructs in the dream-like consciousness of a super entity with free organic will to fashion independence in that dream? What if we are not part of a simulation of technology but constructs within dreams of God?

Could a higher and deeper understanding end religious differences? Could such an understanding end senseless, murderous, and destructive wars? Could a better understanding of the cosmos create a heighten impulse to love outside or beyond the scope of partitioned and biased schools of dogmatic belief that divides. It is time we question everything we have been taught!

The Narrative of Natural Origin by Religion

Path 4: Why is the Book of Enoch not included in the Canons of the Bible?

Special gratitude to Paul Wallis and his work in his book "Out of Eden"

The familiar stories of the Book of Genesis affirm that God made the Universe, planets, Earth, you and me. However various anomalies in the text clue us that we are not reading the original versions of those stories. So what were the original narratives and what did they say about who we are and where we came from? What were the earlier stories of human origins, almost obliterated from the Hebrew Scriptures in the 6th Century BCE and suppressed from Christian writings in the 2nd and 3rd centuries AD? And what does any of this have to do with Extraterrestrials?

Enoch

Enoch walked with the Elohim, walked with the powerful ones. And then he was not because the powerful ones took him away. The book of Enoch unpacks what walking with the powerful ones meant and unpacks it in astonishing details.

200 Watchers coming to planet earth and hybridizing with human females resulting in giants. This narrative is in Genesis Six of the Bible and in the narratives of other cultures all around the world.

The Book of Enoch Mami Wata an Alien Abductions. In 1984 a twenty six year old woman appeared on the beach of Anloga a coastal town in the Keta District of the Volta region of Ghana, West Africa. When she walked into her family home, her relatives embraced her with joy and confusion. She had been missing for three years.

Her family was full of questions. Why had she vanished, why had she gone, and what happened to her in the intervening years? The story the young woman told them left her family worried and confused.

The young woman explained that she had been kidnapped while walking on the beach and taken to a community far away where she had been held captive. She had lived among her captives for three years and in that time had been forced to bear children. But the most shocking part of the young woman's story was still to come.

Her family pressed her to tell them where she had been living, why she had not been able to contact them, and who had taken her? Finally she told them she had been taken from the beach to an underwater base. The people had taken her to produce children. And most disturbing of all the people who had taken her were not human.

They were the Mami Wata people. There is a Mami Wata tradition all up the western seaboard of Africa and into the Caribbean. Description and the idea of the Mami Wata people takes different forms in different places. Different names are used in different parts of the world.

The Mami Wata peo described as beautiful often female and they abduct people near the water's edge. This tradition is thousands of years old. This narratives of abductions goes back thousands upon thousands of years.

The narratives of alien abductions needs to be giving more attention. Abductions is a narrative that is actually part of a bigger and more ancient one. This narrative of abduction is presented in the Book of Enoch.

The origin of the Book of Enoch is rooted in the Hebrew tradition. Scholars agree that the Book of Enoch was authored in the Second and Third century BCE, the writing may have encapsulated an oral tradition going even further back in history.

According to the Book of Genesis, Enoch was the father of Methuselah, who was the father of Lamarck, who was the father of Noah.

Enoch is probably the world's first abductee, albeit a willing one. There is a section in the book where Enoch is given a year's notice before being taken away from his family.

In the Book of Genesis, Enoch is mentioned in Chapter Five. It states Enoch walked with God. Then he was no more because God took him away. This text referencing God is a mistranslation of the word Elohim. The word Elohim often gets translated as God, but it is a plural form word and it takes plural verbs.

The way that text in Genesis really reads is that Enoch walked with the Elohim, walked with the powerful ones. And then he was not because the powerful ones took him away.

This in effect is the summary of the story of Enoch from the Book of Enoch. It unpacks what walking with the powerful ones meant and unpacks it in astonishing details.

The Book of Enoch comprises several works:

The Book of Watchers 1 Enoch 1-36
The Book of Parables of Enoch 1 Enoch 37-71 (Similitudes of Enoch)
The Astronomical Book 1 Enoch 72-82 (Book of Luminaries)
The Book of Dream Visions 1 Enoch 83- 90
The Epistle of Enoch 1 Enoch 91-108

In the Book of Watchers, Enoch tells the story of human females being abducted and impregnated by beings who arrive on earth from their station in the sky. It goes on to describe the writer's journey through the cosmos and discovering truths previously hidden from humanity that concern other dimensions.

The Book of Parables speaks more of Enoch's journeys and speaks of God's judgement of the watchers and plans for humanity. Its holds out the promise of a heavenly messiah.

In the Book of Heavenly Luminaries, Enoch is shown around the galaxy by an entity called Uriel, whether through a physical journey, astral travel, or simply tutelage, Uriel instructs him in astronomy and the laws of the Cosmos. The motif of a human being shown astronomy by an advanced being is found in the Hebrew tradition.

The prophet Ezekiel describes his experience in more physical terms, he reports being picked up in a flying craft. In his experience a human like pilot flies him around various cities of ancient Iraq before finally depositing him in Tel Aviv.

In the past, scholars assumed Ezekiel was describing a vision, but might Ezekiel had been describing something real and material, something that today we would call an alien abduction?

The book of Enoch and the Book of Ezekiel would be described as apocalyptic literature. Apocalyptic meaning that the writer has seen something that he does not know what it is, what it means, and it is absolutely mind-boggling. He knows it is significant and wants the reader to unpack the significance of what he saw.

Ezekiel does not describe his experience as a vision, he says where he was when this craft appeared and picked him up, where it flew him, the places he saw, where he was dropped off, and the state he was in after he had been dropped off, he said he had been so disoriented that he could not speak for seven days.

The pilot he described was like a human being who was talking to Ezekiel about religion and politics, but all the while the pilot spoke Ezekiel is fascinated by the craft he is in. He is describing what he is seeing and hearing the whole time.

Ezekiel is trying to describes the craft he is being carried in as YHWY habitation or as the glory because he has no other language with which to describe it. To the modern eyes and ears, we have an idea that what he is describing. When we dismiss it and say it's a vision, we are doing what we do to all contactees and abductees is ignoring the obvious assumption of UFO because it contradict our world view that we are alone in this universe.

The claims of the reports in Ezekiel finds support in other world literature. Flying and space faring crafts are described in the Hindu Text of the Bhagavad Gita. Similar crafts are depicted in the ancient wall art of Egypt and Mesoamerica.

In the Book of Enoch, the writer describes journeys which takes him far beyond those of Ezekiel and far beyond our Solar System. Ezekiel's travels around Iraq were just earth bound travels. He is just flying, whereas Enoch describes travels around the Galaxy. He is being guided by this strange entity called Uriel, a non-human entity.

It is unclear if he is being taken on a physical journey at that point, or if he is being shown a textbook, or if he is astral traveling. It is very clear he is trying to interpret this through his own world view. But, in one way or another, he is being shown the positions of the stars, heavenly bodies, how they move, and how they relate to each other. This theme of astronomical information is a little bit anomalous in the Bible, but it actually rings bells with narratives and mythologies from all around the world.

You can think about the Mayan Calendar, the Aztec, the Sumerians, the Egyptians, all of them had precise astronomical information in their mythologies. In light of the information they all had, you think how could they have possibly have had access to that information so long ago.

One of the most dramatic example is the Dogon people of Mali. When the anthropologists got into conversation with their Shamanic elders, they spoke about information they had to do with the Sirius Star system. First of all they knew that there was a three star system, something we did not know about until the 20th century. And when the anthropologists asked them, how do you have all this information about the Sirius Star System?

They said Oh! We learned that from the people who taught us. They were from Sirius C. So there is a patent in the world's ancestral narrative and ancient mythologies of precise astronomical information being encoded within very ancient stories.

We see aspects of that in the Book of Enoch. He is getting his information from a non-human entity called Uriel, who is giving him a little bit of education on the Solar System.

The Book of Enoch describes in dramatic detail a period in which 200 watchers arrive on planet earth and begin abducting human females. The watchers produce hybrid beings who are in human form, but far larger than normal human beings.

Mythologies around the world corroborates the Book of Enoch accounts of abductions by extraterrestrial presences who were exiled on planet earth. Although quoted verbatim in the New Testament latter of Jude and accepted as scripture by the Ethiopian Orthodox Church, the Book of Enoch has never been included in the internationally accepted cannons of scripture for either Judaism or Christianity.

The fact that the Book of Enoch isn't in the official cannon of scripture, is not particularly important. It is in the cannon of the Bible in the Ethiopian Orthodox Church. The Book of Enoch was quoted by Clement of Alexandria, one of the most significant of the early church fathers, as if it was scripture.

The Book of Jude when he wants to quote the Enoch of the Bible. He quotes the Book of Enoch word by word. He assumes that his New Testament readers has read the Book of Enoch.

The stories told in the Book of Enoch are really an unpacking of narratives that we find in canonical books, of Genesis, Ezekiel, The Gospels, the New Testament. In this case, the Book of Enoch should not be a book believers should be frightened of reading. It is a book that absolutely affirmed by canonical scriptures themselves.

The Book of Enoch's story of 200 watchers coming to planet earth and hybridizing with human females resulting in giants is a narrative that you find repeated in Genesis Six. It is also in the narratives of cultures all around the world. You can find it in African stories, Indian stories, Greek stories, Sumerian stories. The story is always the same, beings of another kind coming to planet earth. Hybridizing and interbreeding with human females resulting in a different kind of being called a giant, a Titan, or Nephilim.

These 200 watchers are angels. The word angel does not tell us what kind of being they are. What has been spoken is that they come from space, that they are physical every much as we are, that they are similar enough as we are to be able to hybridize with us. They are different enough that the result of that hybridization is different to us.

They can travel great distances with great rapidity, maybe even inter-dimensionally. They come from the sky and they intervene, harmfully in human affairs. By any accounts, this sounds an awful lots like extraterrestrials.

The Apkallu were beings described in Babylonian mythology that was written down by a Greek priest called Barrassas in the Third century BCE. Barrassas described the Apkallu as part human, part aquatic, and that is a theme that recurs in the African Mami Wata tradition, in the Caribbean, and in other mythologies around the world.

We see depictions of entities that are part human and part aquatic in many diverse cultures that have no contact with each other. Barrassas goes on to talk about one of the leaders of the Apkallu Oannes and describe that they took a role in nurturing early humanity, providing our ancestors with the basic tools of civilization to set us on our way as a human civilization.

In 1962, while at Berkeley Astrophysicist Carl Sagan wrote a paper called "Direct Contact among Galactic Civilizations by Relativistic Interstellar Spacecraft." In the paper, he wrote "there is the statistical likelihood that Earth was visited by advanced extraterrestrial civilization at least once during historical times.

On page 497 of his study, Sagan states that the Earth has been visited possibly 10,000 times in its geologic history. It is not out of the question that artifacts exist, (Pyramids in Egypt, Puma Puku, Teotewaquon, Easter Island, etc), or even remnants of past civilizations on Mars, or the moon as a base for extraterrestrials that provides continuity for successful expeditions.

Sagan wrote there are other legends that deserves serious study in the present context. An example is the Babylonian account of the origin of the Sumerian civilization by the Apkallu, representative of an advanced non-human and possibly extraterrestrial society.

Later, Sagan wrote "Stories like the Oannes legend, and representations especially of the earliest civilizations on Earth, deserves more critical studies than have been performed heretofore, with the possibility of direct contact with an extraterrestrial civilization as one of the many possible alternative interpretations, or explanation.

Could an intervention by an extraterrestrial civilization like the Apkallu explain why all of a sudden out of the blue in ancient Sumer you have civilizations springing up, complete with mathematics, complex astronomy, civil engineering, streetscapes, legal system, banking, money, culture, and literature, which is a major leap forward for Homo sapiens that needs some major explaining. The story of the Apkallu is this story that explains such a major leap.

The physical description of the Apkallu correlates so closely with the ancient stories of the Mami Wata people.

The Book of Enoch tells a story that seems foreign to Western ears with its reference to a non-human population resident to the Earth underwater or beneath the ice of Antarctica. Such revelation is at odd with the familiar stories of mainstream religions.

To people like the Dogon tribe of Mali, with their memory of friends from the Sirius star system or the Cherokee people of North America with their memory of the people from the Pleiades, or people from African and Caribbean cultures familiar with the Mami Wata, many of the themes in the Book of Enoch are strangely familiar.

In 1947, in the Qumran Caves on the Northern shore of the Dead Sea, in these caves in the Judean Mountains, an ancient religious community hid its precious archives of papyrus scrolls and manuscripts. Between 800 and 900 manuscripts were found. Among them some of the most important historic and religious text evet found. Among them, the Book of Enoch.

The earliest version of the Book of Enoch is the Ethiopian Book. Ethiopia is the home to the one church communion that accepts the Book of Enoch within the canon of the Bible. The Ethiopian Book comprises the Book of Watchers, the Parables of Enoch, and Astronomical Book of the Luminaries, the Book of Dreams, and the Epistle of Enoch.

Many of its themes echo the aspirations and concerns of many of the Hebrew Scriptures, but other themes occur within its pages that are more unusual. The current scrolls dates from the third to the first century BCE. The source of their narrative and their authorship remains a mystery.

Given the high regards in which the book was held in ancient times, what was it about the book's content that made it so controversial that it had to be excluded from the official cannon?

In chapters 1-36, the Book of Watchers details contact between entities from off planet and human beings. Some of that contact is benign and nurtures the emergence of human society. The Watchers teaches the humans how to cultivate crops, how to use medicine, and other healing modalities.

The Watchers teach metal technology and introduced humans to adornment of jewelry and make-up. These aspects in the Book of Enoch marks it as very different to the Books we find in the cannons of the Bible. The accounts in the Book of Enoch are not unique stories that narrative repeats in mythologies all around the world.

You can find it in Native American mythology, Mayan, Zulu, Babylonian all makes the claim that in our prehistoric past there was an intervention. People from off planet came and nurtured the human race as a conscious, intelligent, technological specie and gave us the building blocks of civilization.

Though this narrative has been allowed to remain among indigenous mythologies all around the world, that admission of a wide extraterrestrial family is an admission that Jewish and Christian religious authorities is not willing to make.

Of all the lessons given by the Watchers, one that concerns the Book of Enoch is the lesson in Astronomy. The Book of Enoch differs in this aspect from the Jewish text. Astrology and Astronomy is not favorably looked upon in the Bible.

Among the Book of Enoch's most explosive claim is the book's account of the abduction of human females by 200 of the Watchers. Their offspring are described as giants. The name the book of Genesis gives them is Nephilim. Greek Legend call them the Titans. Mythologies all around the world tell their own version of these intriguing story.

The Jewish historian Josephus refers to ancestral memory of human abductions and hybridization unpacked by the Book of Enoch. Josephus refer to this as history. He points to the existence of giants in his own time as material evidence of that ancient intervention.

The Sumerian texts speaks of sky people or star people. And among those people 300 are dispatched to what they call stations in the stars or Space Stations. Their jobs were to work as observers.

So why didn't the Book of Enoch make it into the canons of the Bible? The Hebrew stories of the beginning took their current shape through decisions and edits made sometime in the 6th Century BCE. In Christianity, decisions were made from the 2nd Century onwards to shape up what would become the New Testament and decisions were made to glue it to the Hebrew canon to create a Christian Bible.

All those decisions were taken on the basis of a monotheistic world-view. So the edits in the Hebrew Scriptures were to monotheize them. Their world-view is that we are alone in the universe. When they found other texts, including the Book of Enoch, with so much going on that acknowledged other off planets entities that seem to have intergalactic technology or interdimensional technology, they could not admit this information because it came to represent too many Gods.

This edit made in the 6th Century BCE, the Hebrew canon may have solved the problems of too many Gods, but by conflating the idea of God with other entities. By pushing the extraterrestrial almost out of sight and hopelessly confusing how we understand God in the Bible because we end up blaming God for things that extraterrestrials are responsible for.

From start to finish the Bible is peppered with non-human entities. Think about the Nephilim, the Anakim, the Elohim, Bene Elohim, the sky council, the one like a human being in the Book of Ezekiel, these are strands within the Biblical tradition that the institutional Judaism and Christianity of those ancient times did not want to acknowledge and just tactfully ignored.

The Book of Enoch being so specific about non-human entities blew all that open. With a world view that says there is no such thing as an extraterrestrial monotheizing the canon of the Bible meant to exclude extraterrestrials narratives.

Why was the narrative about ET contact suppressed? What was so taboo about reporting the Watcher's role in our great leap forward? Why was the narrative of human female abduction and hybridization allowed to remain in other indigenous mythologies around the world, but excised from Judaism and Christianity? What agenda does that secrecy serve? Are we entering a period where that veil of secrecy is being lifted?

Path 5: Are Religious Doctrines the Greatest Stumbling Block of Humanity?

The first known mention of **Israel** is an Egyptian inscription from the 13th century B.C. According to both Jewish and Christian Dogma, the books of Genesis, Exodus, Leviticus, Numbers, and Deuteronomy (the first five books of the **Bible** and the entirety of the Torah) were all written by Moses in about 1,300 B.C. There are a few issues with this, however, such as the lack of evidence that Moses ever existed.

Bible #1. The oldest surviving full text of the New Testament is the beautifully written Codex Sinaiticus, which was "discovered" at the **St Catherine monastery** at the base of **Mt Sinai** in **Egypt** in the 1840s and 1850s. Dating from circa 325-360 CE, it is not known where it was scribed – perhaps **Rome** or **Egypt**

The Old Testament is the original Hebrew Bible, the sacred scriptures of the Jewish faith, written at different times between about 1200 and 165 BC. The New Testament books were written by Christians in the **first century** AD

The Aleppo Codex (c. 920 CE) and Leningrad Codex (c. 1008 CE) were once the **oldest** known manuscripts of the Tanakh in Hebrew.

In 1947 CE the finding of the Dead Sea scrolls at Qumran pushed the manuscript history of the Tanakh back a millennium from such codices.

Middle Ages. Traditional Jewish exegesis such as Midrash (Genesis Rabbah 38) says that Adam spoke the **Hebrew language** because the names he gives Eve – Isha (**Book of Genesis** 2:23) and Chava (Genesis 3:20) – only make sense in **Hebrew**.

One of the earliest known humans is **Homo habilis**, or "handy man," who lived about 2.4 million to 1.4 million years ago in Eastern and Southern Africa. The earliest **humans** developed out of australopithecine ancestors after about 3 million years ago, most likely in Eastern **Africa**, most likely in the **area** of the Kenyan Rift Valley, where the oldest known stone tools were found. The Bible dates back only 4000 years BC stating Adam and Eve were the first humans.

The oldest known evidence for **anatomically modern humans** (as of 2017) are fossils found at Jebel Irhoud, Morocco, dated about 300,000 years old. Anatomically **modern human** remains of eight individuals dated 300,000 years old, making them the oldest known remains categorized as "modern" (as of 2018).

Scientists have long looked to East Africa as the birthplace of modern humans. Until the latest findings from Jebel Irhoud, the oldest known remnants of our species were found at Omo Kibish in Ethiopia and dated to 195,000 years old. Other fossils and genetic evidence all point to an African origin for modern humans.

Apart from being more stout and muscular, the adults at Jebel Irhoud looked similar to people alive today. "The face of the specimen we found is the face of someone you could meet on the tube in London," Hublin said. In a second paper, the scientists lay out how they dated the stone tools to between 280,000 and 350,000 years, and a lone tooth to 290,000 years old.

Scientists have too few fossils to know whether modern humans had spread to the four corners of Africa 300,000 years ago. Speculation that modern humans did spread is based on what the scientists see as similar features in a 260,000-year-old skull found in Florisbad in South Africa.

The extreme age of the bones makes them the oldest known specimens of modern humans and poses a major challenge to the idea that the earliest members of our species evolved in a "Garden of Eden" in East Africa, two hundred ninety-six thousand years later.

According to Bible genealogy,
The world began 4000 years ago

(1) 4000 BC years ago Adam and Eve was created, 1000 years passed

3000 (1000 years went by to 3000)

Things that happened in the time from 3000 years BC to 2000 years BC
(2) 2500 BC years ago the flood happened
(3) 2682 -2181 BC Egypt Old Kingdom rose up
(4) 2166-1991 BC Abraham
(5) 2125-1773 BC The Middle Kingdom
(6) 1525-1406 BC Moses
(7) 1550 -1069 BC The New Kingdom

1200 to 1100

(8) 1200-1150 BC The Bronze Age Collapse (Except Egypt)

Fall of Mycenae
Trojan War
Fall of the Hittite Empire
Egyptian Fight Sea People
Philistine invade Canaan

(9) 1100 BC The birth of Samuel
(10) 1010-970 BC the birth of David (David lived until 40 years of age)
1069 End of the Kingdom of Egypt

Things that happened from 1000 BC to the Common Era
(11) 970-931 BC the birth of Solomon
(12) 700 BC The earliest Bible component
(12) 621 BC Hilkiah finds the Torah
(13) 586 BC the fall of Jerusalem
(14) 4 to 7 AD Jesus was born
(15) 325 AD Bible was written by white men
(16) 1947 AD Dead Sea Scrolls found

It really does look like in Africa especially, but also globally, our evolution was characterized by numerous different species all living at the same time and possibly even in the same places."

The **San people** of southern Africa, who have lived as **hunter**-gatherers for thousands of years, are likely to be the oldest population of **humans** on Earth, according to the biggest and most detailed analysis of African DNA

Pentecost. In the New Testament, the day that the Holy Spirit descended upon the disciples of Jesus. **Pentecost** is the Greek name for Shavuot, the spring harvest festival of the Israelites, which was going on when the Holy Spirit came.

When God speaks to you is God male or female? Who is God's wife or husband? Why is there nothing spoken about God's mate?

The word **Hindu** is an exonym, and while **Hinduism** has been called the oldest religion in the world, many practitioners refer to their religion as **Sanātana Dharma** (Sanskrit: सनातन धर्म: "the **Eternal Way**"), which refers to the idea that its origins lie beyond human history, as revealed in the **Hindu** texts.

The Dead Sea Scrolls come from various sites and date from the 3rd century BCE to the 2nd century CE. The Dead Sea Scrolls (also the Qumran Caves Scrolls) are ancient Jewish religious manuscripts that were found in the Qumran Caves in the Judaean Desert, near Ein Feshkha on the northern shore of the Dead Sea in the West Bank. Scholarly consensus dates these scrolls from the last three centuries BCE and the first century CE.

The Hebrew calendar, still in use, is based on a concept known as Anno Mundi (\\"in the year of the world\\") which dates events from the beginning of the creation of the earth as calculated through scripture. Ancient civilizations such as Mesopotamia and Egypt based their calendars on the reigns of kings or the cycles of the seasons as set by the gods. In Mesopotamia, for example, one might date an event as \\"five years from the reign of King Shulgi\\" and, in Egypt, as \\"three years after the last...

What color was Noah, his wife, and his children?

Although the stories in the Torah are not dated, people have tried to construct chronologies by adding up years in Biblical genealogies. The most famous of these is Bishop James Ussher (1581-1656) who calculated that the first day of creation began Oct. 23, 404 (BCE = "Before Common Era." In the Christian world, the (mis)calculated date of birth of Jesus, called Christ)

Bishop Ussher dated the moment of the Exodus to 1491 BCE – over 1,000 years before the Torah took on its present form. The Torah is the first five books of Moses. The five books of the Torah are Genesis, Exodus, Leviticus, Numbers and Deuteronomy. These books are all ascribed to Moses, as told to him directly by God. The Torah gives the history of the world and the Jewish people, as well as the 613 laws passed down to them. The **Hebrew Bible**, which is also called the **Tanakh** (/tɑːˈnɑːx/;[1] תַּנַ"ךְ, pronounced [taˈnaχ] or [təˈnax]; also *Tenakh*, *Tenak*, *Tanach*), or sometimes the **Miqra** (מִקְרָא), is the canonical collection of Hebrew scriptures, including the Torah.

Torah, in Judaism, in the broadest sense, the substance of divine revelation to Israel, the Jewish people: God's revealed teaching or guidance for humankind. The Bible is all about laws for the Jews. Why would God choose a bunch of White folks to be his chosen few? These white folks are genetic mutations of the original man that lived millions of years before Jews in Israel regardless of their skin color whether they were black or white, but since the oldest remains of human are in Africa, they had to be black.

The Dead Sea Scrolls (also the Qumran Caves Scrolls) are ancient Jewish religious manuscripts that were found in the Qumran Caves in the Judaean Desert, near Ein Feshkha on the northern shore of the Dead Sea in the West Bank. Scholarly consensus dates these scrolls from the last three centuries BCE and the first century CE.

In conversations with people of religious faith, different perspectives of a supreme creative omniscient force **(SCOF)** to stories in Bible will be marginalized by those who walk in faith because they use references from the Bible as proof of the existence of an omnipotent being.

The most difficult concepts I find among discussions of the Holy Books are the low vibrational energy misapplying our collective creative force and permitting existence in our consciousness notions of a dark satanic force. Why summon low vibrational energy when we can consciously dwell in conscious spaces of high vibrating loving energy that is made abundantly accessible by a **supreme creative omniscient force (SCOF)?**

If an entity called Satan did exist, what if this entity created religion as a tool that obscures a pure organic and harmonious connection with the **supreme creative omniscient force** (**SCOF**)? The vibrations I sense vibrational energy of this **SCOF.** I find the parables of Holy Books methods of control that reduce access to higher organic vibrations of **SCOF.**

If Satan does exist, I think he would be hiding in plain sight by obscuring the minds of humanity with the religions of the world. It is an unforgivable deception if hidden from us is knowledge that Fallen Angels in the Bible are extraterrestrial aliens and the Books of the Bible prevents an organic understanding of who we are, how we were created. If religious dogma obscures a higher truth, such doctrines can be humanity greatest stumbling block to ascension and arrival to our true organic spiritual destiny?

Interpreting the words of the Bible, are we understanding everything that is written? What is conveyed is open ended. To every mind interpretations can vary from person based on education, their ability to relinquish desire, and the level of courage within them to confront their fears.

1 Corinthian verses 21-23:

21 For after that the wisdom in God the world by wisdom knew not God, it pleased God by the foolishness of preaching to save them that believe.

22 For the Jews require a sign, and the Greeks seek after wisdom:

23 But we preach Christ crucified, unto Jews this is a stumbling block, and unto the Greeks foolishness.

Many black slaves in America were reluctant to accept Christianity. Many owners hoped that religion would make their slaves more docile and encouraged them to convert. On Sundays, Niggers had to sit and listen to the white man's sermons. Obey your master and be a good servant. They tell the slave if he is good and works hard for his master that he would go to heaven and live a life of ease but they never told the slave that he would be free in heaven.

Revelations 22: 18 and 19 states do not add or take away from the book 55. When people defend the Bible, they always defend it with verses from the Bible. The problem is people are not aware of the deeper messages in the Bible. They only understand its surface meaning.

Timothy 3:16 All scripture is given by inspiration of God (It does not say God told men to write this book). Inspiration is the process of being mentally stimulated to do or feel something, especially to do something creative. If God can create the Universe in 6 days, he does not need to give a man a message to write a book.

The Bible did not fall from the sky and God did not whisper in men ears. Men wrote this book. We have no idea who wrote the book and we cannot prove that whoever wrote it was truly spoken to by God. We do not have the original books of the Bible. What do we really have?

The Bible is comprised of many different books. There are 66 books in the King James Version. There were over 500 books that the Bible was to have been comprised from. What we have of these original books are copies, we do not have the original books themselves. When you compare the copies, they all have mistakes. They have errors, they have things added and things taken away. If God instructed the writing of the Bible there would be no mistakes, it would be perfect.

There are thousands of errors in the Bible.

How did we get the Bible we have today. There were no blacks in attendance at the Council of Nicaea. Ancient Africa is completely ignored. The Nicaean Council was a council of European Bishops that convened in Nicaea, Turkey by the Roman Emperor Constantine I in 325 AD.

We don't know enough about what happened at the council of Nicaea. Where the clergy gathered with hundreds of manuscripts to figure out which manuscripts would be used to create the Bible.

What was the genius master plan? How would they figure out how to get these hundreds of manuscripts into the Bible? The Clergy said we will take all these books or manuscripts that supposed to be the inspired word of God and put them **under** the communion table and leave them there overnight. When they returned in the morning whatever books were on **top** of the table the next morning will be the books used to create the Bible.

How do we know this is true? Because they wrote about it. In his Synodicon, Council Pappus wrote in a decree to the Nicaean Council says "having promiscuously puts all the books that were referred of the Council for determination were placed under a communion-table in a church. They (The Bishops) besought the Lord that the inspired writings might get up on the table. While the spurious ones remained underneath, and it happened accordingly." But we are not told who kept the chamber key overnight!

This is how they figured out what books will go into your Bible. All these books were supposedly the inspired words of God. If someone came to you and said God gave me a message to write a book of gospel, how do you know God gave him the message? At the Council of Nicaea there were all these books piled up on the table, how do you know which of these books were supposedly inspired by God?

They had no idea who had the key to the chamber that could have come in overnight and put certain books on top of the table. Very few people of Christian faith are aware of this and no one talks about this. This is how your Bible was created. How could anyone take a book composed this way into their heart as the foundation of their life?

Also during the Council of Nicaea Sabinus, the Bishop of Heraclea, affirms "that except Constantine, the Emperor, and Eusebius Pamphilus, these bishops were a set of illiterate simple creatures that understood nothing." If you read about the Council of Nicaea you will read about the buffoonery that went on "there" making the Bible.

A lot of the books that did not go into the Bible were burned. A lot of books being found today (such as the Dead Sea Scrolls) were not at the Council of Nicaea. These books are not even included in the Bible. As far as those books that were burned, if they were inspired words of God, why wouldn't they also be included in the Bible instead of being burned?

The Dead Sea Scrolls are not in your Bible. They were found in 1947 and are not included in the Bible. If the Dead Sea Scrolls are the inspired words of God why are they not in your Bible?

All these books that were selected to go into the Bible had to be translated from Hebrew, Greek, or Assyriac to Latin. Then you have to make copies. The printing press was not invented until 1400, so all copies were done by hand. The foundation book of your life is based on copies. Errors and mistakes are going to happen, so the Bible you have today has errors and mistakes.

Where did these book at Nicaea come from that made it to the top of the table?

Long before the Council of Nicaea, there were the Septuagint and the Biblia Peshitta. The Septuagint is basically the Old Testament translated from Hebrew into Greek.

We do not have the original Old Testament and we do not have the original Hebrew version of it. Remember, Moses was the one who wrote the Old Testament or wrote the 5 Books of Moses (Genesis, Exodus, Leviticus, Numbers, and Deuteronomy). We do not have those books they are gone.

Ptolemy II Philadelphus was encouraged by his Librarian to translate Hebrew Law into Greek. They had a vast Library of books and they wanted to add a Version of Hebrew Law into Greek in that Library. We do not know if they had Hebrew versions of the Tanakh or Torah and we don't know what the Elders brought with them.

The Tanakh is the whole 24 Books of the Old Testament. The 5 Books of Moses is the Torah. The other 19 is the writings of the prophets. We do not know if the Elders came to Alexandria and recited the whole thing. The 72 Elders completed the task of creating the Septuagint in 72 days.

How do you create a Septuagint without the original Books of Moses and the original Hebrew version of the Old Testament? This goes back to LXX, this is the Roman Numeral 70. Septuagint means 70. LXX is speaking of the Letter of Aristeas, which are ancient documents that talk about 6 Elders taken from the 12 Tribes of Israel. These Elders were to go to Alexandria of Egypt to translate the Old Testament Hebrew into the Septuagint which is Greek.

How did they do this without having the original? The LXX is the only proof we have that the whole thing took place and these people had the knowledge of this information LXX of Letter of Aristeas. So, poof out of nowhere we get this Septuagint. We have 6 Elders from the 12 Tribes of Israel. That is 72 Elders altogether. How did these 72 old men translate the Hebrew version of the Old Testament into Greek if they did not have the original copy?

Scholars do not agree on this Letter. The Letter was written after the time this whole thing was to have happened. Do we have any Greek Translation of the Old Testament dating before Christ? Yes, we do, we have Orillia Papyri 458 dated to 150 BC. This is just a small piece that contains Deuteronomy 23 through 28.

Do we know that this fragment of Orillia Papyri is from the event the Letter is speaking to? We do not know. Scholars believe it is a copy of a copy. The whole thing with the 72 Elders took place at 250 BC, 100 years prior to the Orillia Papyri. This makes the Elders 150 to 170 years old doing the translations, which is highly unlikely.

Many scholars disagree with the dates associated with Christian manuscripts. Scholars who have done extensive research find that dates do not add up with true occurrences. When you think about the Roman Catholic Church, when they do anything it is broadcast.

When the Church makes a decree on anything, it is written down and is documented.

With the Catholic Church operating on a lie as huge as Christianity, they cannot go back and change everything. Sometimes anachronistically they will make decrees and time frames will not correspond with what has been stated. A lot of scholars have a problem with what is stated about Jesus Christ. They question a lot of things the Catholic Church has said about him; the statements of him being divine, born of a virgin birth, and so many things like that.

In Islam, Historius a bishop of the Assyrian Orthodox Church in Antioch left that church because he disagreed with the whole thing the Church of Rome was trying to do with the story of Jesus. This begs the question of why did so many have a problem with the story of Jesus Christ?

If you look at the story of Judaism and look at Jesus Christ, these events parallel as the Jews worshipping the Lamb; Jesus was the Lamb, the Lamb of God. All of these things we hear about when we hear about Jesus. People can see back then that Jesus and the Lamb was the same thing. The Roman Church took Judaism and created Christianity from that base. A lot of people disagreed with the Church of Rome and the story of Jesus.

The following statement is from a Book called "The Existence of Christ Disproved by Irresistible Evidence, in a Series of Letters, from a German Jew"

> The most ancient representation of the God of the Christians was the the figure of the Lamb sometimes united to a vase, in which its blood flowed, sometimes sleeping at the foot of a cross. That custom subsisted until the year 680, but it was ordained by the sixteenth synod of Constantinople (canon 82) that in place of

> the ancient symbol, which was the Lamb, they should represent a man attached to a cross, which policy was confirmed by Pope Adrian I. In our church may be seen this symbol, upon the tabernacle or little press, in which the priest enclose the sun of gold or silver that contains the circular image of the God Sun, as well as in front of their altars.
>
> The Lamb is there often represented sleeping, sometimes upon a cross, sometimes upon the book of faith, which is closed with seven seals. That number seven is that of the spheres, of which the Sun was reputed by ancient mystagogues to be the soul, and of which the motion or revolution is reckoned from the point of Aries, or the Lamb of the equinox. This is the Lamb that the Christians tell us was immolated from the beginning.

From Canon 82:

> We decree that the figure in human form of the Lamb who takes away the sin of the world, Christ our God, be henceforth exhibited in images, instead of the ancient Lamb.

The Roman Church decrees that you had the Lamb before now you have Christ. This begs the question if the Roman Church decreed this in the 7th Century, we already knew about Jesus in the 4th Century, why did the Roman Church wait until the 7th Century to replace the Lamb with Jesus?

Look at the rituals of Judaism, the Jews sacrifice the Lamb before the Passover. They eat the Lamb the evening of their holiday. Jesus was sacrificed before the Passover. You eat the body of Christ in Church. The Roman Church gave you the same religion they just changed the symbol of the lamb and made it a man.

What is the whole Lamb thing anyway? It goes back to Greek Mythology to Aries the Ram. Aries is the Lamb. It is Greek God worship, switched up from Ram to Lamb, made into a parable and put into the Old Testament.

If we had the Biblical manuscripts, the whole Council of Nicaea was supposed to have produced to us the Codexes starting from 325, 350, 400, and 405 CE. Why did it take so long to put Revelations in the Bible, to even put Jesus Christ name in the Bible, and to say we are going to replace our old symbol of the Lamb with a Man?

Another question is why did the Catholic Church not use any of these Manuscripts (Codex Sinaiticus, Codex Vaticanus, Codex Alexandrinus) any of them? The Catholic Church chose to use the Vulgate. It was not until 1546 that the Latin Vulgate was officially named the book of the Catholic Church.

Constantine ordered 50 copies of Codex Vaticanus to be made. Codex Vaticanus sat in the Vatican Library for over 1000 years, why let it sit so long? They brought out Codex Vaticanus and cataloged it but continued using the Vulgate. The Council of Trent made it official in 1546 to use the Vulgate as the official Bible of the Catholic Church.

The divisions of the Catholic Church did not agree on the New Testament. They did not agree on the Bible as a whole of the manuscripts they used to put the New Testament together. The disagreement caused the Crusades in the 11th Century. Pope Urban II decreed that all people who do not accept the New Testament must be killed.

When you are the Roman Catholic Church, if you wrote Sinaiticus, if you wrote Vaticanus if you wrote all these manuscripts that we found, how did these religious books get in such disrepair? Vaticanus is called Vaticanus because the Vatican is the institution that kept it. How did these books get in such disrepair?

Tischendorf did not find Sinaiticus until the 1800s. Tischendorf found Sinaiticus way out in Mt. Sinai. What was it doing there? If these books are supposed to be so powerful, so highly revered, they are supposed to be the true word of God, then how can the number one institute for Christianity not have their hands on them?

Why was the Catholic Church using the Old Latin Vulgate in the Sixteenth Century? Why was the Church in disagreement on the Bible until the 16th Century?

The Reason why:

> From the Fourth century, there existed unanimity in the West concerning the New Testament Canon, and that, by the 5th century, the Eastern Church, with a few exceptions, had come to accept the Book of Revelations, and thus had come into harmony on the matter of the Canon (Revelations and Genesis have been changed more than any other gospel in the Bible)
>
> Nonetheless, full dogmatic articulations of the Canon were not made until the Canon of Trent of 1546 for Roman Catholicism, the Gallic Confession of The faith of 1559 for Calvinism, the Thirty-Nine Articles of 1563 for the Church of England, and the Synod of Jerusalem of 1692 for the Greek Orthodox.

This is the division of the Catholic Church accepting the Canon and the New Testament the Latin Vulgate. The Church had this book supposedly in the 4th century 325 CE. Why were they using the Vulgate if they did all this research to put together Vaticanus, Sinaiticus, and Alexandrinus? The Vaticanus is the oldest of the great unsealed. They had the Septuagint, they had so many other religious books, but they could not agree on the New Testament. Because the New Testament was where things changed.

The Crusades happened. They wiped a lot of people out getting rid of as much proof as possible. Destroying manuscripts. People were hiding manuscripts because they knew the Catholic Church was trying to find these manuscripts and trying to kill them.

The Catholic Church forbade people from translating manuscripts that differed from its decrees and forbade that they own a Bible. The Decree of the Council of Toulouse of 1229 C.E.:

> "We prohibit also that the laity should be permitted to have the books of the Old or New Testament; but we most strictly forbid them from having any translation of these books."

The Ruling of the Council of Tarragona of 1234 C.E.:

> "No one may possess the books of the Old Testaments in the Romance (Latin) language, and if anyone possesses them he must turn them over to the local bishop within eight days after promulgation of this decree, so they can be burned."

In 1380- 1382, John Wycliffe was the first person to write an English translation of the Bible during the time of this decree. After he died, they convicted him of heresy. His body was exhumed in public, dug up his skeleton, crushed it and threw it in the River.

John Hus did the same thing. He was burnt alive. In 1536 William Tindale also translated the Bible into English and he too burned at the stake. Ten years after that the Council of Trent made it official that the Latin Vulgate would be the official Bible of the Catholic Church.

This was in 1546 and the Vulgate was what they used when they already had Codex Vaticanus, Codex Sinaiticus, Codex Alexandrinus, and Ephraemi Rescriptus existed, so why did the Catholic Church use the Latin Vulgate?

To understand why we must go back and look at Roman History, not just to the time the manuscripts were being completed but before then. One of the things that will help to understand why, is what is revealed in the Dead Sea Scrolls. Almost every Christian you talk to mention the Dead Sea Scrolls as being some kind of proof that Christianity is true.

These individuals may not realize that the Dead Sea Scrolls are not even in the Bible that they have today. The Dead Sea Scrolls were not discovered until 1947. The Dead Sea Scrolls were not at the Council of Nicaea. They are not in the Bible.

When you research the Dead Sea Scrolls, you will find they were found in Jerusalem. Why did somebody hide these manuscripts? The Dead Sea Scrolls are 825 to 870 separate scrolls with multiple copies of the Old Testament written in Hebrew and Aramaic.

They are different from the Old Testament that is in the current Bible. They include every book in the Old Testament you know except the Book of Ester and there are other prophecies of David and Daniel that is not available in the Old Testament.

Who hid the Dead Sea Scrolls? Scholars differ on the dates they were hidden between 30 and 70 A.D. What was going on in Jerusalem where they were found at that time?

Jerusalem was at war with Rome. In Luke 3:1-2, it talks about John the Baptist when he began his ministry under the reign of Tiberius Caesar, who ruled from 14 A.D. to 37 A.D. This is the time frame in which Jesus was supposedly crucified and killed.

Scholars find it hard to believe from the history of what was going on in Jerusalem at this time, being occupied by Rome, hating the Romans that someone like Jesus would be walking around preaching about turning the other cheek, love, and mercy. The Jews hated the Romans. They wanted blood and wanted to kill them. At this time, the Jews were putting together a rebellion.

The Jews doctrine was that a messiah would come, a leader, a warrior, a soldier would come and lead them to war and defeat the Roman Empire. This was the doctrine of the Jews. For somebody like Jesus coming in there and preaching mercy, love, and peace would not have been accepted and immediately killed.

In 66 A.D. is when the Jews did rebel against Rome. A man named *Josephus* born Yosef ben Matityahu. He was head of the Jewish forces in Galilee until he was captured by Vespasian Flavius. Vespasian was the commander under Roman Emperor Nero. Vespasian had a son who was Titus who was in Jerusalem conquering that place while Vespasian was in Galilee.

When Vespasian captured Josephus, Josephus impressed Vespasian by prophesizing that he would become Emperor. Vespasian liked what he heard and kept Vespasian as a slave interpreter.

Vespasian's son Titus conquered Jerusalem and ransacked the Temple. He took artifacts, gold, and manuscripts. Nero killed himself and Vespasian did become Emperor. He reigned for 10 years and then Titus became Emperor. Titus and Josephus became close friends.

If you went to Rome today and look at the Arch of Titus, everything mentioned above is on that Arch. The bas-relief depicts the sacking of the temple in Jerusalem. Josephus was basically a traitor. He later took on the title Titus Flavius Josephus. When the Romans brought back all the Jewish manuscripts from the Temple of Jerusalem, Josephus helped the Romans interpret and translate the manuscripts.

Rome realized what it already knew they could control the Jewish people with doctrine. The Romans realized where the original Jewish doctrine came from.

The Dead Sea Scrolls is different from the Old Testament we know today. It has a Messiah. We think the Messiah is supposed to be Jesus but that is not what was originally said. So, where did the Jewish doctrine come from?

To understand the origin of the Jewish doctrine we have to continue back to Canaan. That was ruled by the ancient Egyptians. Now we must ask who the Canaanites were. The Canaanites were Phoenicians. The Phoenicians were conquered by Cyrus the Great the King of Persia in 539 BCE. The Phoenician and Persians were Arab.

When the Persians conquered the Phoenicians, the Phoenicians were assimilated into the Persian army. Herodotus stated in his writing that you could tell the difference between the Persian and Egyptian armies. The Egyptians were black.

The Persian army inclusive of the Phoenician Canaanites were now strong enough to defeat the Egyptians. In 525 BCE the Battle of Pelusium was the first major battle between the Achaemenid Empire and Egypt. This decisive battle transferred the throne of the Pharaohs to Cambyses II of Persia.

The Persian conquered the Phoenicians in 539 BCE, they conquered the Egyptians in 525 BCE, and this brought about the 27th Dynasty of Egypt under Persian rule. In 490 BCE they fought off an invasion by the Libyans, and after that, the Persian went through a 63-year long rebellion of the Egyptians. It was not until 341 BCE until the Persian gained full control of Egypt.

In 336 BCE, Darius III was the last Emperor of the Persian Empire. The Greek then defeated the Persians and assumed control of Egypt and Israel. Before Islam the people in Israel were Arab. The Greeks ruled for a period of time and this is how we got our Old Testament.

In 290 BCE, Rome fought the Punic Wars, the war against Syria, and the Four Macedonian Wars with Greece. The Roman occupation of

Greece began after the Battle of Corinth in 146 BC. Greece did hold power over Israel but was conquered themselves by the Romans.

The Siege of Jerusalem in the year 70 CE was the decisive event of the First Jewish–Roman War. The Roman army, led by the future Emperor, besieged and conquered the city of Jerusalem, which had been controlled by Judean rebel factions since 66 CE, following the Jerusalem riots of 66 CE, when the Judean Free Government was formed in Jerusalem.

The siege ended on 30 August 70 CE with the burning and destruction of its Second Temple, and the Romans entered and sacked the Lower City. The destruction of both the first and second temples is still mourned annually as the Jewish fast Tisha B›Av. The Arch of Titus, celebrating the Roman sack of Jerusalem and the Temple still stand in Rome. The conquest of the city was completed on 8 September 70 CE.

So when the Roman Commander Titus sacked Israel coming away with all the wealth and sacred manuscripts of the Hebrew faith. The Hebrews rebelled against the Romans based on their doctrines. Vespasian took the Hebrew manuscripts to Josephus to translate.

The manuscripts that Rome was in possession of came from an Israel that had been under the rule of Greece. This time period was called the Hellenistic Age. During the Hellenistic Age, Israel was going under what is called Hellenization. What is Hellenization? That is instilling the Greek culture into Israel. This is where Hebrew came from. Hebrew is Greek. The Jews got their Old Testament doctrine from the Greeks.

The Greeks created the Old Testament doctrines for the same reason the Romans created the New Testament, to control the people. The Old Testament is based off Greek mythology; Eve eating an Apple can be compared to Pandora's Box; Hercules and Samson where each have to escape symbolic evil clutches of a female, and each was asked to kill a lion with their bare hands; and compare the whole Noah Ark story with the Greek mythology Deucalion.

In Deucalion's Flood, Zeus wanted to flood the world because the people were evil and did not want to worship the Gods the way they were supposed to. Zeus told Prometheus of the flood and Prometheus told his son Deucalion to build the ark.

Deucalion built an ark, gathered supplies, moved in with his wife, and Zeus opened up the heavens and all the land of Greece was transformed into a sea.

The same kind of story as Noah's Ark. The Greeks gave the Hebrews their language, their doctrine, and these doctrines compare with Greek mythology. The Greeks got the Hebrew to believe in this doctrine so much that they believed a Messiah was going to come and lead them to victory against the Roman Empire.

So when that did not happen against the Romans, the Romans did the same thing the Greeks, and that was giving the conquered Jews a new doctrine as a new form of hope. Vespasian, Titus, with the help of Josephus used the sacred manuscripts taken from the Temple in Jerusalem and revamped the gospel in the Old Testament and created a new gospel in the New Testament.

If the Romans did not write the Bible, why is there the Book of Titus, Book of Romans, and Book of Acts alluding to so much about Rome? The Jews doctrine did not come true and they lost their war with Rome. The gospel doctrines did not come true, no warrior led them to victory against Rome.

Rome's new doctrine became the new covenant for controlling the people because the old covenant was not fulfilled. Rome decided not to make the mistake of giving them hope that a warrior is going to come and lead them against their enemy. So Jesus is written into the Bible peaching a new doctrine of turning the other cheek, love thy neighbor, and etc. to calm the people down. The Roman decided to give the people a nice, kind, and gentle Jesus in a new covenant and explain to them why the covenant in the Old Testament did not work before. Hebrews 8:5-10 exemplifies this.

Hebrews was written talking to the Jews explaining that the old covenant was not fulfilled because they did not follow the doctrine and that Jesus had been sent as the Messiah to save them and was crucified. Placing all the blame on the Jewish people and not the Romans.

The history of religion in the world is clouded with division, wars, claims of heresies, and fascinations with spiritual dimensions with physical tools ill equipped to discern such dimensions.

One thing we are able to discern is that the cradle of civilizations points to beginnings in Africa.

Much thanks to Michael Chandler for his research for shedding light on important truths that have gone hidden by secret societies dating back to the Knights Templar that still exist today in groups today such as the Jesuits, Illuminati, Skull and Bone, and others.

I know no disease of the soul but ignorance, a pernicious evil, is the darkener of a man's life, it is the disturber of his reason, and the confounder of his truth.

-Ben Johnson-

Ancient Egypt and Worship of the Sun

The ancient Egyptians believed that as long as the Sun came up every day there'd always be life on earth. Quite logically the Sun became the representation for everlasting life. If the sun came up every day food will grow. If food grows people can live and reproduce.

So, when you die, you son and daughter can carry on and when he dies his son will carry on and so forth. Because of the Sun, the light of the world is present every day and there will be everlasting life on earth. So quite logically every major religion and mystic belief features the Sun as its principal and most important feature.

It is incumbent upon each of us to do the most conscious good and least conscious evil in our life's journey. We were all born with the Divine Right to question authority. The very nature of man cries out to investigate for himself as he search for the facts of his existence and not to be satisfied to be told what to think. Each of us should challenge our existing ideas and beliefs and look at the facts even they are uncomfortable to accept or even to consider.

There are many sects of religions and each one claims only they have the truth. When have you looked at historical facts stripped of all preconceived dogma and comfortable philosophy? Every religion claims to be right and all the others to be wrong, which are clearly totally illogical and unproved.

Could it be possible that only one of the world's thousands of religions could be right and all the rest be wrong? Especially when each religion thinks their belief is the truth?

What is the hidden truth? Most people don't understand that Christianity is an outgrowth of the earlier Hebrew faith. Consequently, you cannot understand Christianity correctly unless you understand the faith of which Christianity is an outgrowth of. This is why we have an Old and New Testament.

An intelligent person who has done his homework knows that Christianity roots are deeper than the Old Testament's Hebrew faith. No, its contents do not stop there. We cannot have Christianity without its parent Hebrew and we cannot have Hebrew without its parent, which is the many more ancient Semitic religions.

Hebrew is merely a recent occurrence in Semitic history. There is Semitic religion behind Judaism and behind the Semitic is Egyptian, and behind the Egyptian there is Sumerian, and behind the Sumerian is a more ancient one. It is a long Sumerian bloodline coming through history.

One of the greatest misconception about ancient people is that they were Sun worshippers. We've all heard that that ancient people worshipped the Sun as a God. The facts are that no people of no nation ever worshipped the Sun as a God. All religions in all countries of the world that we have history of used the Sun to symbolize deity including Christianity.

The Sun represented to the ancient people salvation because they believed, especially the Egyptians, who said if the Sun Continues to come up every morning that life would continue on. The Egyptians said the Sun of God, the light of the world, represented everlasting life on the earth, not for me or you as individuals, but on the earth.

The Egyptians realized that the Sun while burning was giving up energy and that the plants and the food chain on earth was receiving along with animals and humans energy from the Sun. Therefore, the Sun was giving up its life for us. Hebrew and Christianity text simply replaced the word Sun with Son or Jesus Christ.

To further understand the connection between Christianity and ancient religions, we must study Astronomy, which should not be confused with what is commonly known today as Astrology. Astronomy is a very precise science that we use today in determining when we will have the next eclipse or when we will see the next full moon.

As far back as we can go in history, the air was divided into twelve equal parts, just as we today divide the air into twelve months. You draw a circle representing one year, which is then divided into twelve equal parts. Each one of which is called a zodiac or a house. The Sun travels through different houses of the Zodiac.

This is where the connection between the Sun of God having twelve helpers as they were called in Egypt and the Son of God Jesus Christ who ministered to him having twelve apostles.

After dividing the circle into twelve equal parts, it was then further divided into four groups. The winter solstice from the middle of the winter across the Zodiac into the Summer Solstice; then the Spring or Vernal Equinox to the Autumnal Equinox and there you have the cross of the Zodiac. Remember this is all ancient science and it has been done like this for thousands of years.

The Egyptians noticed that on their sundials that in winter as the Sun moved further South bringing winter that winter represents the coldness of death. They also noticed that when the Sun went south and reached a point where it stopped in its movement and did not move any further South.

They noticed on their sundial not only did the Sun did not go further south but it didn't move back in the direction of the north either. This non movement lasted three days. For three days the Sun set exactly on the sundial in the same place. Therefore, the ancient said that the Sun of God dies for three days and is resurrected or bought back to life once it begins its annual journey back to the northern hemisphere.

And when it begins its annual journey back to the northern hemisphere was on December 25th. Therefore the God's Sun, the light of the world, who is our salvation because he is risen (the Sun itself and not Jesus) was reborn on December 25th. When the Sun is born on December 25th that is the Sun's birthday.

All unrelated churches display a circle within the cross. The circle is on the cross of the Zodiac and that circle represents the Sun. But over the ages man began to refer to this circle as the Sun of God and therefore it became God's Son. A cross with a circle truly represent the Sun dying on the cross of the Zodiac and not a man.

The Sun of God, God's Sun dies on the cross of the Zodiac. This is the Sun that comes up in the morning that is pictured on the cross. The circle surrounded by twelve other circles is the Sun symbolized with 12 helpers or houses of the Zodiac.

In Revelations Chapter 1 Verse 7, we read behold he cometh with clouds and every eye shall see him. The Sun of God, the light of the world comes, of course there is only one light of the world that every eye can see and that is the Sun.

In the scriptures we can also read how Jesus walked on water. All of us have seen the sunset. We are told that the Sun of God died with a crown of thorns. No wonder, the Sun is always pictured in ancient days with a crown of thorns or Sunrays.

The crown of thorns on Jesus, the Son of God, the light of the world, are the Sun's ray. The Europeans modified this by turning the Sunrays into thorns by turning them inward to make a crown, which the Kings of England use as a symbol to rule by divine rights.

The Sun of God is divine and it is through him we have government on earth. First in the form of Pharaoh and today we have a divine right of Kings who wear crowns of thorns.

If you take every single scripture in the New Testament that is applied to Jesus and apply it in your mind to the literal Sun that we see in the morning, every single scripture fits. If you understand what is being said, every single scripture that has applied to Jesus, if you apply it to the sun it fits.

In the Bible we see the twelve signs of the Zodiac connected with the Sun, is said to be God's helpers or the twelve apostles. The twelve apostles are the twelve signs of the Zodiac that are helpers of the Sun.

We also have the twelve hours of the day, twelve hours of the night, twelve months of the year, and the twelve signs of the Zodiac, the twelve tribes of Israel, the twelve brothers of Joseph, 12 patriarch of Israel, 12 great prophets of Judaism, we see how we can trace the 12 Apostles from the twelve houses are helpers of the Zodiac. We see how the Sun dies on the cross of the Zodiac for three days every year after which it was resurrected according to the Egyptians thousands of years before Israel ever existed.

The Passover was the Sun passing over from the death of winter into the new life of spring. Jewish people to this day still celebrate the Passover at the first full moon of the spring Equinox. Because the ancient Jewish religion was based on Egypt.

The Bible mention that the High Priest of Israel would go out in the morning mist to find the Mana from Heaven. Mana from heaven actually mean mushrooms. Many books have been written about the magic mushroom in the Middle East. There is problems with hashish and drugs in the Middle East for thousands of years.

Magic mushrooms are referred to in the scriptures as mana from heaven. The High Priest would go out in the morning and pick mushrooms and consume these mushrooms and begin to talk to God.

The Hebrew God L was a more ancient Semitic God Saturn. The Star of David, the hexagram, is actually the Star of Saturn. The six pointed star is associated with the worship of Saturn. Therefore, the beast is Saturn (Satan) and his mark is the 6- pointed star. Hebrews today worship on Saturday and Christians worships on the Sun's day, which is God's Sun, the light of the world.

There is still a disturbance among religious circles today as to what the correct day of worship is. It depends on if you are worshipping Saturn the old ancient Hebrew God on Saturday or the Sun of God, the light of the world on Sunday. It really does not make much difference it is all Egyptian.

In the Bible Jesus said (Luke 22:10) I will be with you until the end of the age, which implies there are more than one age. If there is more than one age, then there may be two ages or 12 ages. If Jesus or Horus the Sun of God says I will be with you until the end of age, yes he will, because each Zodiac house is an age and the Sun will be with you until the end of the age.

At the end of one age of the Zodiac there will be another age or aeon. Therefore we will be out of the old age and coming into the new.

During the rule of Pharaoh Akhenaten came an important religious change. Pharaoh Akhenaten was a very important Pharaoh. He single-handedly changed the worship in Egypt from many Gods to the worship of just one God. In particular and to the exclusion of all other Gods. The name of this God was Ra. Coincidentally, this is where we get the word "Sunra." The full name of this God was Amen Ra. The Pharaoh said when you pray to God you must pray through the Son of God Amen Ra because he represented God.

At the end of the prayer in the ancient temples of Egypt they would say Amen. In the Scriptures Jesus said "if your eye be single, then there will be light in you. This single eye was the symbol of Amen Ra. The eye was always within the circle, the Sun. The eye of God.

Horus had a personal name. His personal name was Io or Iou. The Egyptians referred to God's son as the Iou. Later on, after the different dynasties, the son became known as Iousis or Iesus. In Greek, when you change the I to J, it becomes Jesus.

In John 10:11, Jesus said I am the good shepherd and the good shepherd gives his life to the sheep. In John 10:14, Jesus said I am the good shepherd and I know my sheep. In the book of Hebrews 13:20, Jesus the great shepherd of his sheep. In the book of Revelations 12:5, and she brought forth a man child who was to rule all nations with a rod of iron. In Revelations 19:15, and he should rule the nation with a rod of iron. What we have established is Jesus is the good shepherd and he should rule the nation with a rod of iron.

The Pharaoh was referred to as the good shepherd. The people, the Royal household, and the religious household of Egypt were called in Egyptian "the shepherds fold." The Pharaoh being representative of Iousis the Son of God was called the great shepherd who looked after the shepherd's fold.

The Pharaoh was considered to be the incarnation of Amen Ra who ruled for God on earth. This is where we get the idea that there would be an earthly kingdom and the Pharaoh was the king of the kingdom.

There are at least three different places in the Bible where Jesus is referred to as the "chief corner stone" corner stone that the builders rejected. In Ephesian 2:20 Jesus Christ himself being the chief corner stone. Where do you find the chief cornerstone? You can find an ordinary cornerstone at the top of a building or at the bottom. A chief corner stone is translated from the Greek word meaning the peak of a Pyramid or the cap stone, which is how Jesus is referred to in some religions.

Why is Jesus referred to as the peak of a pyramid you may wonder? Look at the back of an American dollar bill where you will find a pyramid with the chief corner stone separated from the base of the pyramid. What is even more interesting is that on the American dollar bill within the separated cornerstone is the eye Horus, the all seeing eye of Iousis. The son of God, the eye of Ra, that we pray to and say Amen.

In Isaiah 19:19, God says to his people "in that day shall there be an altar to the Lord in the midst of the land of Egypt, and a pillar at the border thereof of the Lord. In other words in the middle of Egypt, there will be an altar to the Lord. In the middle of Egypt stands Cheops the Great Pyramid exactly in the middle. The Pyramid has already been sitting there for 3000 years before the Bible was written.

The ancient calendar did not start with January or Janus that represent the double headed God of Rome. The Egyptians started their Calendar in a different constellation. They begin their calendar with the constellation of Virgo, the Virgin. Consequently, the Egyptians and the ancient Sumerians culture said that the Sun of God died on the cross and resurrected in the constellation of Virgo or the Virgin. There is this connection of Egyptian religion as the parent of Semitic religion, where Jesus Christ the son of God is said to have been born of a virgin also.

This is why the front of the pyramid you have a Sphinx with the head of a woman and the body of a Lion. This symbolized the Zodiac overseeing the pyramid because Egyptian Zodiac began with Virgo the virgin the head of the Sphinx and ended with Leo the Lion or the body of the Sphinx, which symbolically was the complete Zodiac.

Leonardo Da Vinci in his very famous painting the last supper shows Jesus the light of the world, the Son of God and his twelve apostles. The Apostles are positioned six on each side of Jesus. They are individually grouped in threes. The four groups of three apostles in each group are talking only to each other. So, we have four groups of threes, summer, autumn, winter, and spring.

Leonardo Da Vinci was not only one of the greatest artists of all time, he was also a grandmaster of a very powerful secret society which still exist today. He was extremely well informed and well-read religious philosopher. He understood as did Michelangelo that Jesus as an actual man never existed. The entire story is Zodialogical or what has become today Astro-Theology. The term Astro-Theology is more specifically applied to a religious system based on the observation of the heavens.

In the Bible we hear much concerning Moses. If you go back, not to the Bible, not to the Genesis, but to the most ancient writings in the world, the Bhagavad-Gita, the Vedas, the Upanishads, you will find in the ancient nations of the world they had all the same identical stories. They have the story of the young boy swallowed by the great fish because he did not do what he was supposed to do, they have the story of Nebo, the Babylonians had the great lawgiver who had golden hair and went up into the mountain of God (the pyramids) and he receives the great law which became known as the Law of Hammurabi.

The Egyptians had the same story. Their great lawgiver was called Meeses was the great wonderful man with beautiful Golden hair who went up into the mountains and he received the law; the great law he brought down with the tablets of stone. When Meeses saw that the Egyptians did not respect divine law, he broke the stones. The Hebrews took that story moving into Palestine with their worship of their God L. Then comes Moses; Moses is Meeses and Meeses is Nebo, it is the same story and the story does not stop.

The entire New Testament is nothing more than the retelling of ancient Egyptian religion. Everything in the New Testament has already been written by the Egyptians thousands of years before Israel existed.

Is it just a mere coincidence that the Sun provides everlasting life on earth, that it walks on water, gives it life for, dies for three days each year, and is resurrected or born again on December 25? The Sun is the light of the world, it has a crown of thorns or rays. It takes 30 degrees to enter each sign of the Zodiac and 33.5 degrees to leave it.

Is it by mere chance that the more recent Jesus and other ancient Gods similar to him are just personifications of the Sun? In this world, we face life's challenge of survival, however brief, for an average 75 years or less. There is only so much ultimate truth to be understood about a vast and dynamic universe.

On this very small rock called Earth, there are myriad experiments with matter conflated in layers of evolution that has created ou micro human consciousness. Human consciousness is individual bubbles of consciousness within the greater bubble of radiated and mysterious dark mattered entity of infinite cosmic consciousness, we call God.

From the macro perspective of the cosmos itself and quantum connected human micro perspective, human and cosmic consciousness are integral fibers in a spectrum of creative physics of light and dark energy.

In the human psyche, is there a light vs darkness conflict interred in our DNA composition that manifests in humanity's choices between good and evil? It seems humans have been in conflict fluctuating between influences of light and darkness, good and evil, or concepts of God and Devil. The human legacy is heavily influenced by fears of the unknown presented by the dark abyss we peer into at night but also the abyss of our inner temple or universe, which is our individual consciousness.

Is there an organic intimate connection with a **supreme creative omniscient force (SCOF)** we refer to as God or are we prisoners of conscious constructs of fear, which has produced all religious principles that constrains collective human consciousness?

Coming upon truths for deeper understanding of human nature is imperative to lift constraints that shapes our collective will remains humanity's greatest challenge. Sadly the money changers are in control of the educational institutions and refuse to allow people to learn the truths and think for themselves. We could be such a beautiful and loving species without lies, deception, and selfish greed based actions of men.

The money changers, in the name of profit, offers multitudes of death by poisoning our senses stoking desires though the media. Unfortunately, the majority have been too dumbed-down to see they are being killed off in their pursuit of pleasure over spiritually developing the soul.

The problem of the world's wealth focused on dogmatic inspired mechanical love fueling partitioned religious division instead of higher vibration unconditional organic love for each other. The Globalists have financed the deadly global upheavals for the sake of wealth.

How farther advanced in the pursuit of love and wisdom would we be as a species if these wealthy people's minds were not limited in scope by greed and religious programming. The Rothschild's controlling Britain and the United States banking system gives aid without a ceiling to an Ultra Zionist agenda.

The Talmudist conviction to Noahide Laws will offer up so much murder and destruction just to placate one group religious perception of reality. A group committed to forcing those perceptions on people not of the same belief.

There is a huge price we are paying for selfishness and greed of a few. The action of a few is the prime cause of human underachievement. All the partitioned of religious belief is costing humanity. These people with so much wealth yet so spiritually deficient and so spiritually underachieved. Spiritual impoverishment manifests in destructive wars, murder, poverty, and racial tension we live with.

What God sanctions such murderous means to unholy ends? In the end, this financial support of war and destruction is such contradictions of piousness. Look closely to see greed disguised as loving spirituality driving engines of destruction in the name of one religion after another.

We are still very primitive minded spiritually and have so far to come to finding the true essence of our loving connection to a supreme creative omniscient force that is available to us in the infinite consciousness beyond the narrow constraints of religious perspectives our societies operate by.

I look forward to the day when we choose to take a closer look at persistent convictions that permits to be calm and patient with all the division among us while an elite few destroy our planet. It is time we explore love from an untapped source of infinite consciousness of higher vibrations instead of dwelling within the lower vibrating partitions of divisive religious dogma.

Dr. Richard Carrier

Why Invent Jesus

Dr. Richard Carrier asked the question why you would invent Jesus. He proposed two hypotheses that there was no Jesus and the plausibility of just an ordinary Jesus, a guy who was not miraculous, wasn't super, wasn't super famous, but legends grew up around him. This was the next most plausible theory if there is no God, Jesus was an ordinary dude and then the gospels built legends and myths around him and deified him.

Dr. Carrier informs that religion began sometime around 38 AD and the first documents mentioning Christianity or Jesus are the epistles of Paul that ends up in the New Testament. Many of these epistles are forgeries but it is believed that he did write seven of them.

Dr. Carrier informs that those documents were the first documents we have for Christian church and they only refer to visions. They never talk about Jesus having a ministry or anyone who ever met him in life. The first time anyone ever meets or encounters him is after his death. In the epistles, there is no direct claim that he was actually a guy walking around on earth in the authentic epistles.

According to Dr. Carrier, the Gospels come a lifetime later about 40 years after the beginning of the religion beginning in a time span between 75 and 115 AD. This was the first time you hear of any biographies. Going from no ordinaries memoirs, no ordinary history, to wild religious mythologies about Jesus.

All other evidence about Jesus comes later with Josephus late first century. It cannot be established that Josephus originally mentioned Jesus. Other documenters inserted Jesus into Josephus's text. The first clear examples of someone not Christian outside the New Testament that mentions Jesus was from 115 AD or later. All those references appear to refer back to the Gospels or to Christians reciting the Gospels.

There is no independent corroboration of the Gospels. The Epistles Dr. Carriers states only speak of a pre-existent celestial being. There are a number of places where Paul says Gospel is known through Revelations and hidden.

The first hundred years of Christianity are blank to us. All the original sects and all the evidence of them are gone. Some of the God that provide good pre-Christian evidence of dying and rising Gods that had attached salvation cults are Osiris, Romulus, Adonis, Zalmoxis, and Inanna. The first one in history is Inanna that started with a woman. In typical patriarchal style, the woman gets replaced with a man's story. Instead of a woman being crucified and resurrected on a third day she is replaced by a man crucified and resurrected on the third day.

These Gods were all personal savior Gods. (1) You get personal salvation by attaching yourself to them. (2) They are all the son or daughter of God. (3) They all undergo a passion. The passion of Christ is the latest version of that. (4) Through that passion they obtain victory over death. (5) They share that victory over death with their followers often through baptism and communion.

Through that passion with suffering o struggle they undergo that and obtain victory over death and share that victory over death with their followers often through baptisms and communions. These heroes from many different cultures predates Christianity. All these savior Gods have stories about them set in human history on earth just like Jesus yet none of them ever actually existed.

If you look at the galaxy of people in which Jesus fits to make him historical would make him extraordinary. All of those savior Gods of every national culture that had one includes the Egyptians, Greeks, Syrians, Turkey, and Thracians. The Jews took their local religion and merge it with those models and create a new version of those religions.

The Jews simply made a Jewish version of pre-cultural savior Gods of other cultures. They built off the fundamental structure of ancient Judaism of the time as a religion based on atonement sacrifice, basically blood magic. Magic that would assuage the anger of God and secure the blessings in this life and the next.

It begins with the story of Isaac. Abraham is commanded to sacrifice Isaac, his first born son to assuage the anger of God. Then God stops him at the last minute and tells Abraham I will let you substitute an animal. This is the beginning of the Yom Kippur principle, where you take a goat substitute for people and kill it and it became the atonement for the sins of Israel and assuaging the anger of God.

Animal blood is less powerful than human blood necessitating repeating the ceremony every year at the Jewish temple. When the Romans destroyed the Temple, there was no way to achieve atonement. Other anti-temple sects wanted to get rid of the Temple Cult because they thought the Temple cult had become so corrupt that it was actually preventing the end of the world. They wanted to end the world and bring doomsday on and the reason God would not do it because the Jews kept sinning, so God said if you keep sinning I am not going to come save you.

The anti-temple cults wanted to get rid of the Temple component and go direct to God himself.

The most important function of Jesus in the Jewish theology is that he replaces the Temple, both the Passover and the Yom Kippur Sacrifice. If you attach yourself to Jesus, you no longer need the Temple rituals. Jesus being the archangel first-born son of God is the most powerful magic blood you can get. If you sacrifice this guy the spell duration is infinity no longer will you need to repeat the rituals year after year and you no longer need the Temple.

The Jews created a version of the savior deity with a passion, death, and resurrection, though which he obtains victory over death and shares it with his followers through baptism and communion.

Path 6: Lies and Deceptions, the Deadly Games People Play

All life, stars and their nuclear reactions, terrestrial and non-terrestrial beings are collectives of individual bubbles of consciousness within a larger spectrum of infinite-consciousness.

This infinite-consciousness is that process in which all life bearing energy is recycled. That process, for lack of greater understanding, we misnomer as death? Death is simply transitioning stages from a narrow band of consciousness to infinite consciousness. Death is this process where raw cosmic energy in the form of physical matter is reintegrated from a temporary finite-form to infinite-consciousness.

In this sense, the cycle of life to death of the entire quantum constituency of networks of Galaxies and parallel universes with vibrating stars and their treasure trove of terrestrial and non-terrestrial life in regenerative cycles pulsating in infinitudes of organic cosmic-consciousness.

Life as we know it is spiritual integration via quantum connections from individual to infinite-consciousness. We are microscopic eyes through which the universe of **supreme creative omniscient force (SCOF)** contemplates all of creation.

Beyond the noisy observations of light, darkness, good, evil, hate, and love is a quiet place where there is no conscious distinctions between life and death. We are infinite consciousness cycling in and out of corporeal cocoons cycling through low vibrational physical world ascending to high vibrational consciousness to a singularity of silent peace where duality and conflicts cease to exist. This is the eternal cycle of being as we come full circle through the human experience back to oneness of infinite consciousness.

There is a creator of all that exits. Do not be afraid to embrace knowledge and presence of non-terrestrials existing among us. This knowledge does not change the fact that we exist in an organic creative spectrum of infinite cosmic consciousness.

Solving Spiritual Deficiencies

It is imperative that we debunk the misinformation of religious dogma so people can realize their organic potential as a higher vibrating organic spiritual creative forces in us all. It is important for each of us to realize higher all-encompassing spiritual resources that lie suppressed beneath layers of lies and deceptions rampant in our political and religious institutions.

Kemet is the name the native African people of the country now known as Egypt called themselves in their surviving writings. Many scholars refer to the people as "kmt" or Kemet. The surviving artifacts of the Kemet viziers and scribes evidence that Kemet rule of law was "Maat," contained at least in part in observing the 42 Laws of Maat.

We need to understand why history in the western world starts with Greco-Roman Civilization and rarely include ancient Africa. We are being indoctrinated into thinking that nothing happened until Greco-Roman driven western civilization arose.

Our educational system is saturated with lies and deceptions. If ancient Kemet was part of the educational system informing people of what pre-dated Greece and Rome, we would understand why black people are persecuted because of envy and jealousy of their advanced pre-Greco-Roman scientific advancements and spiritual ascent exemplified in the 42 Laws of MAAT of ancient Kemet.

Black kids are studying Copernicus, Galileo, and know nothing about Imhotep who was a physician 2000 years before Hypocrites. Imhotep knew about blood circulation, anatomy of the body, and the circumference of the earth before the Athenian Aristophanes.

This is powerful knowledge before Western Europe and western civilization. Black people never question why history is presented this way as though nothing existed of the magnitude of the great Pharaonic Dynasties of Ancient Kemet and mankind was barbaric until the Greco-Roman civilization rose up. This selected historical account persist today feeding the lies and negative connotations that African are savages. The Kemetic name for the Sphinx is Horemakhet. The word Sphinx is Greek. Horemakhet was a colossal monumental connection to black Africa.

The racism of Europeans to deny African history has developed Europeans into a stage of psychopathy. These psychopaths are attempting to deny what is true about the origin of humanity and roles black people have played in advancing human civilization.

What does it mean to be spiritually deficient? We are educated and molded after the ordinary pattern of the human family, we may live an average lifetime and never have an original thought. The thinking faculties that propagate the hive mind is populated with secondhand ideas of lesser informed ancestors.

What is the state of collective human spirituality? What diminishes higher quality spiritual ascension? How did humanity get its start on this planet? What are the truths of mankind's origin? What is the future purpose and destination of man?

What does it mean to be spiritually deficient?

Is the absence of truths and facts precursors to spiritual decadence? Are parables in the Bible the alpha and omega of existence or is logical scientific explanations of nature the way to a harmonious and peaceful journey for mankind? What ultimately will satiate humanity's virtuous quest for purpose, and being? How did humans come into existence on this planet, where are we going in this expanding universe, and do we need to feed on higher vibrating morals beyond religious piety to get there?

Do we need scientific facts as truths to liberate us from ignorance's suffocating grip on our collective spirituality, or do we languish with faithful perceptions of an all knowing and all powerful creator waiting for it to flip an evil script of its all omniscient and omnipotence? The choice is religious faith or a silent and resilient respect of nature's relentless renaissances of life itself. These two choices are juxtaposed psychic composition of this thing we call our human experiences.

Does faith based spirituality require a foundation of truth infused wisdom? Where faith is evoked, is truth relevant? Is faith based spirituality merely a metaphysical exercise in futility? Is the absence of truthful facts the first symptom of spiritual decay? There is a difference between faiths based living and fearless respect of an omniscient and omnipotent. Does awareness of infinite consciousness require more faculties than we are blessed with to truly comprehend?

"Faith is the perceptive power of the mind linked with infinite consciousness we think of as God. Forging will into power begs spiritual assurance in pursuit of power to do the seemingly impossible.

Willful faith is a force that draws our heart's desire right out of infinite consciousness. Faith is wielded as an artist wields a paint brush that depicts substance of being on the canvas of reality. It is this deep inner knowing of, that which can materialize, is already ours for the taking, which in essence is 'assurance of things hoped for'." God is all the pictures we as life artists choose to express with the individual brushes of our unique realities. Imagination fuels faith with the power to perceive ideas and form mental energy into thoughts and concepts to achieve things hoped for.

Book of the Dead

The idea of God collectively-inherited conscious and unconscious spirituality, idea, pattern of thought, image, etc., is universally present in each individual's psyches.

The Book of the Dead is an ancient Egyptian funerary text, used from the beginning of the New Kingdom (around 1550 BCE) to around 50 BCE. Translated as Book of Coming Forth by Day. Another translation would be Book of Emerging Forth into the Light. Collection of texts consisting of a number of magic spells intended to assist a dead person's journey through the Duat, or underworld, and into the afterlife and written by many priests over a period of about 1000 years.

The precursor to modern day religion is Egyptian Book of the Dead. It was part of a tradition of funerary texts which includes the earlier Pyramid Texts and Coffin Texts, which were painted onto objects, not papyrus. Some of the spells included were drawn from these older works and date to the 3rd millennium BCE. Much of what is written in the Bible serve a similar purpose as the Book of the Dead, to assist a dead person's journey through the underworld into the afterlife.

Spells were composed later in Egyptian history, dating to the Third Intermediate Period (11th to 7th centuries BCE). A number of the spells which made up the Book continued to be inscribed on tomb walls and sarcophagi, as had always been the spells from which they originated. The Book of the Dead was placed in the coffin or burial chamber of the deceased.

The Book of the Dead was most commonly written in hieroglyphic or hieratic script on a papyrus scroll, and often illustrated with vignettes depicting the deceased and their journey into the afterlife.

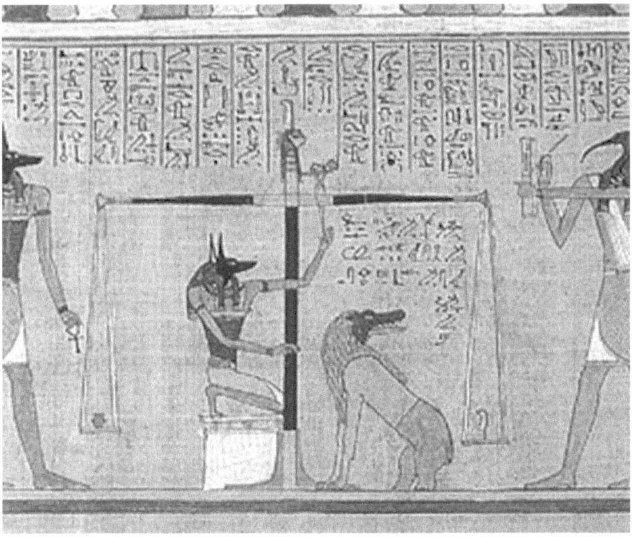

This detail scene, from the Papyrus of Hunefer (c. 1275 BCE), shows the scribe Hunefer›s heart being weighed on the scale of Maat against the feather of truth, by the jackal-headed Anubis. The ibis-headed Thoth, scribe of the gods, records the result. If his heart equals exactly the weight of the feather, Hunefer is allowed to pass into the afterlife. If not, he is eaten by the waiting chimeric devouring creature Ammit composed of the deadly crocodile, lion, and hippopotamus. Vignettes such as these were a common illustration in Egyptian books of the dead

The purpose of the Pyramid Texts was to help the dead King take his place amongst the gods, in particular to reunite him with his divine father Ra; at this period the afterlife was seen as being in the sky, rather than the underworld described in the Book of the Dead.[6] Towards the end of the Old Kingdom, the Pyramid Texts ceased to be an exclusively royal privilege, and were adopted by regional governors and other high-ranking officials.

The **Middle Kingdom of Egypt** (also known as **The Period of Reunification**) is the period in the history of ancient Egypt following a period of political division known as the First Intermediate Period. The Middle Kingdom lasted from around 2050 BC to around 1710

BC, stretching from the reunification of Egypt under the reign of Mentuhotep II of the Eleventh Dynasty to the end of the Twelfth Dynasty.

In the Middle Kingdom, a new funerary text emerged, the Coffin Texts. The Coffin Texts used a newer version of the language, new spells, and included illustrations for the first time. The Coffin Texts were most commonly written on the inner surfaces of coffins, though they are occasionally found on tomb walls or on papyri.[6] The Coffin Texts were available to wealthy private individuals, vastly increasing the number of people who could expect to participate in the afterlife; a process which has been described as the "democratization of the afterlife".[7]

The **New Kingdom**, also referred to as the **Egyptian Empire**, is the period in ancient Egyptian history between the 16th century BC and the 11th century BC, covering the 18th, 19th, and 20th dynasties of Egypt. Radiocarbon dating places the exact beginning of the New Kingdom between 1570 BC and 1544 BC.[1] The New Kingdom followed the Second Intermediate Period and was succeeded by the Third Intermediate Period. It was Egypt's most prosperous time and marked the peak of its power.

The New Kingdom saw the Book of the Dead develop and spread further. The famous Spell 125, the ‹Weighing of the Heart', is first known from the reign of Hatshepsut and Thutmose III, c.1475 BCE. From this period onward the Book of the Dead was typically written on a papyrus scroll, and the text illustrated with vignettes

The **Third Intermediate Period** of Ancient Egypt began with the death of Pharaoh Ramesses XI in 1070 BC, ending the New Kingdom, and was eventually followed by the Late Period. Various points are offered as the beginning for the latter era, though it is most often regarded as dating from the foundation of the Twenty-Sixth Dynasty by Psamtik I in 664 BC, following the expulsion of the Nubian Kushite rulers of the Twenty-Fifth Dynasty by the Assyrians under King Assurbanipal.

The period was one of decline and political instability, coinciding with the Late Bronze Age collapse of civilizations in the Near East and Eastern Mediterranean (including the Greek Dark Ages). It was marked by division of the state for much of the period and conquest and rule by foreigners.

All Religions have their beginning in Ancient Kemet

African or Kemetic religion was based on Maat. Maat was represented as balance, cosmic order, justice, righteousness and truth. The symbol of Maat is the scale where the heart had to be weighed with a feather. The symbol for the justice system of today is the same with the blindfolded white female holding a scale symbolizing blind justice. In ancient Kemet, the whole society was judged by Maat. The Kings were guided by Maat to insure evil would not come about. Maat was how balance was maintained in Kem.

Among the blacks in America, the fact that all religions practiced today have their roots in the motherland Africa is shocking. All historical, scientific, archeological evidence that the African were the very first people. Their history is there on temples, tombs, and monuments that has been there 4000 years. Many invasions that came into African societies, whether Persian, Arab, or Greco-Roman, led to plagiarizing directly from Kemet's traditions and temples.

The earliest versions of the Greeks first Bible Septuagint was written in Alexandria Egypt. Alexander II and Ptolemy were not Egyptian but invaders. Socrates and Pythagoras and many other Greek philosophers got their ideas from ancient Egypt.

After Alexander, Ptolemy came into Egypt and plundered many temples. Many treasures and scrolls were taken and housed in the Alexandria library. These scrolls written on papyrus where written thousands of years ago. The spiritual ideas practiced in Christianity are Kemetic teachings.

Black people of the Nile valley created the spiritual idea of the resurrection of a spiritual Christ. The difference in western spirituality and African spirituality is that resurrection that represent a resurrection of a spirit within ourselves. This is how western world came in contact with spiritual teachings; without it Christianity would not exist.

Many of the Laws we see in Judaism, come from the laws of Maat. I have not robbed or I have not stolen are ideas that arose from early Kemetic Africans in the Nile Valley. They established these moral ethical codes to govern one's immoral life on earth. I have not committed sin, I have not robbed, I have not stolen, and etc. these are Kemetic codes plagiarized as the 10 Commandments in the Bible.

People will argue that the codes are found in the Codes of Hammurabi. These laws of Maat predates the Codes of Hammurabi. The story stated in the Nile Valley, not Mesopotamia, not on the banks of the Tigris Euphrates Rivers, and certainly not in Europe.

Kemet is the original African name of Egypt. The word Kemet actually mean Black. The name Egypt is Greek. The native African people of the country, now known as Egypt, called themselves Kemetic in their surviving writings. Many scholars refer to the people as "kmt" or Kemet. The surviving artifacts of the Kemet viziers and scribes evidence that Kemet rule of law was "Maat," contained at least in part in observing the 42 Laws of Maat. Before the invasion of the Persians, Arabs, Greeks, Romans, and much later the Europeans, Black Pharaohs ruled in the land of Kem.

Under Kemet cosmology, Maat is designed to avert chaos (Isfet) and maintain truth (Maat). The symbol for truth, justice, balance, and order is the Goddess Maat. The iconography for Maat in the hieroglyphs depict the single ostrich feather (Shu), worn atop Goddess Maat's head.

During the reign of Pharaoh Menes, around 2925 B.C.E., after the unification of upper and lower Kemet, archaeological finds evidence administration of the 42 Laws of Maat among the Kemet people as deduced from Kemet coffin texts or funerary papyri dating from this period.

It is very perplexing to most descendants of slaves in America of Christianity's origin from Kem. African Dynastic rule dates back thousands of years before Judaism, Islam, and Christianity ever existed. The principles inculcated in Judaism, Islam, and Christianity came from Ancient Kem (Egypt).

In Chapter 30B of The Papyrus of Ani entitled "Chapter for Not Letting Ani's Heart Create Opposition against Him, in the Gods' Domain," we see the deceased scribe standing before his own heart/soul (ka) on the scale of Maat. On the opposite scale is the Goddess Maat's feather of truth (Shu). The head of the Goddess Maat is depicted atop the scales of justice. Thoth, also known by other names such as Tehuti, stands holding a tablet and a writing tool to record the results from the scales. The ibis-headed Thoth is the patron saint of Maat scribes and priests.

In Chapter 125 of The Papyrus of Ani, we find the petitioner led by Anubis into Duat and pronouncing his/her 42 affirmative declarations, listed below from Budge's public domain translation of the 42 Divine Principles of Maat:

1. I have not committed sin.
2. I have not committed robbery with violence.
3. I have not stolen.
4. I have not slain men or women.
5. I have not stolen food.
6. I have not swindled offerings.
7. I have not stolen from God/Goddess.
8. I have not told lies.
9. I have not carried away food.
10. I have not cursed.
11. I have not closed my ears to truth.
12. I have not committed adultery.
13. I have not made anyone cry.
14. I have not felt sorrow without reason.
15. I have not assaulted anyone.
16. I am not deceitful.
17. I have not stolen anyone's land.
18. I have not been an eavesdropper.
19. I have not falsely accused anyone.
20. I have not been angry without reason.
21. I have not seduced anyone's wife.
22. I have not polluted myself.
23. I have not terrorized anyone.
24. I have not disobeyed the Law.
25. I have not been exclusively angry.
26. I have not cursed God/Goddess.
27. I have not behaved with violence.
28. I have not caused disruption of peace.
29. I have not acted hastily or without thought.
30. I have not overstepped my boundaries of concern.
31. I have not exaggerated my words when speaking.
32. I have not worked evil.
33. I have not used evil thoughts, words or deeds.
34. I have not polluted the water.
35. I have not spoken angrily or arrogantly.

36. I have not cursed anyone in thought, word or deeds.
37. I have not placed myself on a pedestal.
38. I have not stolen what belongs to God/Goddess.
39. I have not stolen from or disrespected the deceased.
40. I have not taken food from a child.
41. I have not acted with insolence.
42. I have not destroyed property belonging to God/Goddess.

After the petitioner's testimony containing the 42 affirmative declarations, the weighing of the ka for truth, and the reading of the scales, it is said that the doer of Maat is administered Maat. If the petitioner is deemed by the Goddess Maat to be in substantial compliance with the 42 Laws of Maat the petitioner passes from Duat to the Field of Reeds (Arus) where Osiris sits as the final gatekeeper.

When we study the hieroglyphs of antiquity in one of the earliest advanced civilizations of Africa, in the Kingdom of Kemet, the parallels between ancient hieroglyphic inscriptions on the walls of the Ancient Pyramids and the 10 Commandments in the Bible is obvious.

The ancient Egyptians revered the woman. They knew the woman was the creator, the original one. She gave birth to man literally. The woman was deified and held high places in ancient Kemet societies. She ruled. When you get into the parables of the Bible, it goes all the way back to ancient Kemet. The Bible's parables are talking about the woman and her ability to create life.

The whole wonder and mystery of the Bible is this immaculate conception of Mary giving birth to Jesus who is the savior of mankind where without the son you cannot exist. When you start to understand the parables in the Bible and start looking into them, you can see very clearly what the Bible is talking about.

Luke 8:10-11 (Jesus speaking to his disciples)

10 – And he said, unto you it is given to know the mysteries of the Kingdom of God: but to others in parables; that seeing they might not see, and hearing they might not understand.

11 – Now the parable is this: The seed is the word of God.

What do we call our children? We call them our seeds. The Bible is all about birth, it is all about creation. What Jesus is trying to tell his believers is that everything is about the woman bringing forth the seeds which is the word of God.

The womb of woman is the Kingdom of Heaven. The ANKH symbolizes Kemetic Womb of Mankind and Eternal Life. The Scarred Beatle Khafri inside the ANKH symbolizing rebirth.

The Pope wears the symbol of the Scarred Beatle. He got it from Kemet and the Egyptian style Obelisk outside the Vatican, London, and Washington DC.

These monuments are all over the world like London and Washington DC. It all comes from Egypt. On the back of the dollar, we have the Egyptian pyramid saying "In God We Trust."

What is presented in the Bible is insanity if you try to interpret it on the surface.

More has been written about ancient Kemet than what has been written about the Bible. It is amazing how little Americans know about Kemet. There is a reason for people not being educated about ancient African culture. The unawareness is there because religion is a useful tool for controlling the masses with deceptive spiritual propaganda propagated via plagiarized Kemetic teachings converted into Biblical parables by Caucasian to subjugate a historically more advanced African people to their will.

What is not taught in Christianity is the kingdom of heaven is within each one of us. The Kingdom of God is the womb. The power of God is within you. Christianity teaches deceptively that we can only have a relationship with God though his white son Jesus.

The Greeks, Alexander the Great, conquered the Jews and created the Hebrew language along with the parables in the Old Testament to allow the subjugated Jewish people to continue their spiritual worship under Greek rule. The Roman Catholic Church plagiarized from ancient Kemet (Egyptian) mythology to give not just the Jews but all people in their empire parables in the New Testament of the Bible to control people.

Jewish people in the Old Testament used their imagination to shape mental energy into thought forms. The mental patterns of their collective mindsets created mental patterns of relying on their God to free them from their oppressors but their faith did not actually produce the finished product of defeating their oppressors, which were both the Greeks and Romans whom they fell captive to.

The Greeks conquered the Jews and in this Hellenistic Age, the Hebrew language was created by the Greeks for the Jews. After the Greeks came the Romans. After the Greeks conquered the Jews, the Romans defeated the Greeks and ruled.

Acts 26 states that Christianity began in Syrian Antioch Orthodox Church. Antioch is in Syria. The Romans took the Greek Old Testament Hebrew and translated it into Syriack this how we got the Peshitta. Later they took the Greek New Testament and translated it into Syriack as well.

The Peshitta supposedly was written around the 2nd Century A.D. The Peshitta did not include in the New Testament 2nd Peter, 2nd John, 3d John, and Jude & Revelations until the 5th Century. The Roman Catholic Church began between the 1st and 5th Century C.E. They were using the Septuagint. At some point, the Roman Catholic Church started using the Vetus Latina or the Latin Translation of the Septuagint. The Bible going from Hebrew, Greek to Latin. Thus the Vetus Latina was not a faithful translation of the original Hebrew.

In 382 C.E. Pope Damascus I commissioned Saint Jerome to revise the Vetus Latina. Saint Jerome gave us the Latin Vulgate Holy Bible, basically a revision of the Vetus Latina. Saint Jerome changed things because he felt the Septuagint was not perfect and had things that had to be changed.

Saint Jerome was not told by God nor did Jesus come down and assist Saint Jerome with these changes. This is one of the books that the Bible you have today are referencing. Saint Jerome changed a lot and added things that were not thee before. The Latin Vulgate was translated from 382 to 405 C.E. after the counsel of Nicaea. What books did the Counsel of Nicaea produce if the Latin Vulgate was produced after the Counsel of Nicaea?

The four great unsealed Codices. Unsealed means they were all written in upper case letters. We have the Codex Sinaiticus, Codex Vaticanus, the Codex Alexandrinus, and the Codex Ephraemi Rescriptus. The Codex Sinaiticus is the oldest complete Bible manuscript. The Codex Vaticanus is the oldest. Sinaiticus was written in 330-360, Vaticanus written in 325-350 took place the same time of the Counsel of Nicaea, Alexandrinus written 400-440, and Ephraemi written in 450.

These Codices were written between 325 and 450 C.E. These Codices were written after the Council of Nicaea. These Codices were put together after what took place at the Council of Nicaea.

The problem with these manuscripts is that they are all completely different. Codex Sinaiticus is the oldest complete manuscript; Vaticanus is older but is missing many passages. Mark ends at 16:8 Sinaiticus nor do Vaticanus have Mark 16:9-20.

Verses not in Vaticanus but are in late manuscripts; the text of the New Testament lacks several passages:

> Matthew 12:47 16:2b-3; 17:21; 18:11; 23:14
> Mark 16:9-20; The Book of Mark ends with verse 16:8 consistent with the Alexandrian text-type
> Luke 17:36; 22:43-44
> Luke 23:34 "And Jesus said: "Father forgive them, they know not what they do."
> John 5:4 Pericope Adulterae (John 7:53-8:11)
> Acts 8:37; 15:34, 24:7; 28:29;
> Roman 16:24
> 1 Peter 5:3

The Book of revelation was not added until the 5th Century. It is not in the Septuagint, it's not in Sinaiticus, it's not in Peshitta, it's not in Vaticanus, and it's not in the Vulgate.

The Dead Sea Scrolls is always pointed to as proof that Christianity is real. The Dead Sea Scrolls are not even in the Bible; they were not included because they were not found until 1947. They were not at the Council of Nicaea. The Dead Sea Scrolls were found in Jerusalem.

Why did someone had to hide these manuscripts? The Dead Sea Scrolls are 825 to 870 separate scrolls with multiple copies of the Old Testament written in Hebrew and Aramaic. They are different than the Old Testament you know. They include every book in the Old Testament except the book of Esther, also prophecies of David and Daniel are not included in the Old Testament you have today.

Why were the Dead Sea Scrolls put there? Some scholars believe they were put there in between 60 and 70 A.D. or as early as 30 and 70 A.D. During this time, Jerusalem was at war with Rome. In Luke 3:1-2 it talks about when John the Baptist began his ministry. He began it under the reign of Tiberius Caesar. Who ruled from 14 A.D. to 37 A.D.? This is the timeframe when Jesus was crucified and killed.

Scholars find it hard to believe that somebody like Jesus was preaching nonviolence and tuning the other cheek, when Rome was occupying Jerusalem and the Jews hated Rome and were putting together a rebellion. The Jews doctrine was that a warrior, soldier, and leader would come and lead them to war and defeat the Romans. Somebody like Jesus coming along preaching love and mercy would not have been accepted and killed.

In 66 AD the rebellion began. A man named Josephus was head of the Jewish forces in Galilee until he was captured by Vespasian Flavius. Vespasian was a commander under Nero at that time. Vespasian had a son Titus who was a very good military strategist. Titus was in Jerusalem conquering that place while Vespasian went to Galilee. When Vespasian captured Josephus, Josephus then told Vespasian that he was a prophet and that Vespasian would be emperor one day. Vespasian liked what he heard and kept Josephus as a slave interpreter.

Titus went on to defeat Jerusalem, destroyed the city, ransacked the Holy Temple and took all their artifacts and gold. Nero ended up killing himself, and Vespasian became Emperor for 10 years and then Titus took over and became Caesar. Titus and Josephus became close friends. Josephus turned traitor on the Jews and took on the title Titus Flavius Josephus. When the Romans brought back all the manuscripts and writings, Josephus helped the Romans interpret and translate the manuscripts.

The Romans knew they could control the Jews with doctrines. The Hebrews rebelled based on their doctrines. Titus took it to Josephus, who was a traitor, to decipher the Hebrew doctrines. The Romans with the interpretations of Josephus created the New Testaments for the Jews for the same reasons the Greeks created Hebrew and the Old Testaments, to control the people.

Where did the Hebrew doctrines come from? The Old Testament is based on Greek mythology. Examples eve eating the apple and Pandora's Box, Hercules and Sampson, and the Noah Ark story with the Greek story Deucalion's Flood. In Deucalion's Flood Zeus wanted to flood the world because people were evil.

The Greeks got the Jew to believe that a Messiah was going to come and lead them to victory against the Roman Empire. The Greeks rebelled and was defeated. Titus tore down their temple and took everything out including their religious writings.

With the help of Josephus, the Romans had to give the Hebrews a new doctrine and this is how the Bible came to be. The Romans revamped the Old Testament before adding the New Testament hundreds of years later.

After the Jews lost to the Romans, the gospels failed prophecy came under question. With that failure, in order to control those who are losing faith, Rome had to give them a new covenant. The old covenant statements were not fulfilled. Titus and Josephus knew the Jews had been controlled before with a gospel, now he had to give them a new gospel. The Messiah this time would not be a warrior but a leader that advocate loving and turning the other cheek to calm the people down.

This is presented in Hebrews 8:5-10.

It is important to know who is being called God in the Bible. The Caesar was called God also.

Religions all fall short without the faith element as integral fibers of one's spirituality. The man who is grounded in faith does not measure his thoughts or his acts by the world's standard of facts. Faith is blind.

Blind faith serves a useful purpose, because it represented a step forward from older types of religious superstition. Blind faith simply refers to the exercise of faith without deeper understanding of one's natural spiritual nature. There is nothing wrong with this if that is where a person is in his or her conscious development.

For those who exist within the means of blind faith, it is not a system of reasoning from premise to conclusion. God or "Divine Mind" is omnipresent. People have been conditioned to believe they have a unique connection with that Divine Mind through Christ and thus a realm of faith-based super consciousness.

The truth is we go to church on Sunday and give recognition to white Jesus. White Jesus does not represent your divinity of ancient Africa. In ancient Africa, depending on what period it is was the name connected with the God?

In the Middle Kingdom 4000 years ago there was worship bestowed the God Amen. We don't realize Amen came from Africa. We end our prayers with Amen. When the people of Kem gave praise to Amen, they raise up their hands. This became Salah in Islam; they bow down to Amen.

The Greeks took Amen out to the Western world ending payers with Amen. In Timothy chapter 6:16 "who alone is immortal and who lives in unapproachable light, whom no one has seen or can see. To him be honor and might forever. Amen." Amen represents the invisible spirit that is all around us that permeates us throughout the universe.

The current Christian belief system does not allow us to connect Amen to African spirituality 4000 years ago. If we have the spiritual consciousness to connect these things to our ancestors who created them, then we would be able to transcend time and space and go back and see how Alexander took Amen out of Africa and became part of the Greco-Roman world in the Old Testament and the New Testament created by the Romans.

Natural faith-thinking is done only by one who has caught sight of the inner truths of being, and who feeds his thinking faculty on spiritual guidance generated by a natural love within his heart free of dogmatic influences. In our society, our actualizations of love are not fed from internal heartfelt revelations, but mechanically created from external based religious dogma.

Path 7: Another Concept of God

Are there other facets to our energy beyond our consciousness? If so, can we feel this energy without conscious interpretations? What is there when we silence our thoughts?

Is consciousness a barrier in a duality sense that separates us from the ultimate singularity we think of as God, that quantum energetic force that exist outside the narrow finite band of consciousness that is the human realm? Does consciousness obscure integration into that singularity of God's all-encompassing infinite energy?

Is it possible for us to be one with this Godly force in those silence spaces between noises of our thoughts? Imagine breaking the dualistic barrier between us and God by silencing our thoughts and ideas created by the physical necessity of survival in this human body.

Only in those quiet spaces between thoughts will we realize within our energy base are spiritual fiber essences of God particles within us. I am speaking of the God essence within us that is perpetually obscured by struggles of physical survival.

Understanding this takes us beyond the dualistic constructs of religious teaching that promotes misunderstanding of the essence of God within each of us.

This is the creative ability in each of us. The time has long since passed that we are no longer oblivious to the godly essences in each one of us. When we truly realize the creative miracles we are endowed with, only then can these miraculous seeds of knowledge produce a bounty of love in this world.

What is it exactly that life wrings from our soul? We come into this world completely clueless that our minds will be used to filter consciousness from energy radiated from moving particles.

The Cosmos, the physical manifestation of God, is infinite consciousness composing life with exploding stars, radiation, and gases. Our cognitive vision is composed of radiating photons that produces images on the canvas of the human mind. Maybe we are images on the canvas of a super entity.

Photons come out of nowhere, they cannot be stored, they can barely be pinned down in time, and they have no home in space whatsoever. Photons are light .that occupies no volume and has no mass. The similarity between thought and a photon is very deep. Both are born in the region beyond space and time where nature controls all processes in a setting pregnant with creative intelligence building elements.

Life is the endless stream of consciousness created from moving particles. Love, sadness, pain, and pleasure are extracted from electromagnetic energy converted into consciousness.

The Cosmos is a storehouse of physical matter that produces energy, which terrestrial and non-terrestrial life and even God, all of who converts, through electromagnetic processes that radiates consciousness ad infinitum. Consciousness is the movement of atomic and subatomic particles. Awareness is consciousness emanating from the collision of cosmic particles.

No one told me how to think of the universe. Space and time are concepts, the notion of God is a concept. Human consciousness is a process of micro radiation within a micro bubble or human brain, which itself is captive in an expanding immensity of infinite cosmic consciousness.

What is cosmic energy? What are the transitional or handoff point between spirituality and physical matter? How are thought concepts incorporated into the building blocks of the cosmos?

I think we have to look at the basic constituent of thought which is energy. All matter such as solids, liquids, and gases, is composed of atoms. Therefore, the atom is considered to be the basic building block of matter. However, atoms are almost always grouped together with other atoms to form what is called a molecule.

When we look at the immensity of the universe from the minutest element to the most grandiose, the basic building block begins with the grouping of atoms.

Think about consciousness in the human brain. Communication through the brain is an electro-chemical process. Memory as the capacity to repeat or suppress a specific mental or physical act.

Throughout the universe we find star factories in the Nebulas gases. Stars are formed in nebulas, interstellar clouds of dust and gas. Nebulas are either remnants of matter from the original big bang or the result of stars collapsing and exploding as supernovas.

My interest here is the energy from stars that creates light that illuminates darkness. What is the correlation between the energy of stars and the manifestation of cosmic consciousness?

Due to the law of universal gravitation that every particle in the universe exerts an attractive force on every other particle. This happens over times with nebulas as the particles that make up the interstellar medium start to gather together. Is dark matter a large network of congealed clouds of dust and gas that are conduits of energy?

Is the human brain a microcosmic module of an immense cosmic network of intelligence? Is the creation and death of stars synaptic energy of immense thought processes and dark matter and dark energy conduits of electrical energy of cosmic consciousness? Is cosmic consciousness the end product of nuclear fusion?

Is the big bang simply the processing of a thought of a being we call God where the energy of the cosmic thought mirrors the electrical process of the synapses of the human brain where energy connections, called synapses, allow nerve impulses to jump from one neuron to the next? Is the big bang merely the growth of a synapse in the brain of a super entity that we as human cannot begin to wrap our brains around the immensity of such quantum reality?

Could the expanding universe that we observe with galaxies racing away from us be the exchange of electrical connections in building of a cosmic level memory network all the stars and charged particles being transferred via dark matter and dark energy synaptic conduits?

Imagine the immensity of what we see as the universe and the potential of what our reality could actually be. We are all units of consciousness at the most atomic level of an immensity beyond the grasp of consciousness.

Path 8: Thoth

Lost in modern day worship of religious institutions that are based on doctrines originating from Greek and Roman empires is the base knowledge of the original religious deities and doctrines of the most ancient kingdom of Kem, upon which all present day religions were created from. Kem was Africa's name before Greek and Persian invasions.

The incredible civilization of ancient Egypt lasted longer than the entire span of what we have come to accept as recorded history, which is only a few thousand years. Some believe that the ancient Egyptians inherited some of the lost knowledge of the civilization of Atlantis after its destruction. It's believed that the few survivors of this once extraordinarily advanced technological civilization found refuge in the land of the Nile Delta.

During these millennia, the ancient Egyptians developed not only technologically but also spiritually as they were introduced to a multitude of esoteric practices that we are still unraveling the meaning of. The fascinating spiritual and occult knowledge of the ancient Egyptians far surpass the knowledge we have today. It is believed that a large portion of this knowledge was actually channeled and given to the ancient Egyptians by an incredible being unknown whether human, God, or something completely different.

This being was called Thoth by the Egyptians, Hermes Tresmajistis by the Greeks, and later Mercury by the Romans. This mysterious entity was known to have lived in ancient Egypt before he was revered as a God. There are many stories about him claiming he could access higher realms of consciousness and derive universal information from the acacia field.

He was the first great Egyptian philosopher and founder of ancient Egyptian Mystery School. Thoth was the one considered who gave us writing, numbers, and the arts of self-cultivation through works of consciousness. It was said that he was receiving his wisdom while in deep meditative trances. Writing many books including allegedly the Emerald Tablets the Book of Thoth, and the Divine Pinander.

It's believe that the book of Thoth reveal the secrets of the universe and the processes achieved though awakening certain areas of the brain, which are inactive for the average person. The book of Thoth contain secret knowledge of the incarnation process, the multi-dimensional structure of the universe and offers thousands of spiritual and esoteric rituals which could have a powerful impact on the physical world.

There are also a lot of dark and dangerous injurious practices. In fact, it's believed that the powerful curse on Tutankhamen's tomb was created using the knowledge of the book of Thoth. In the wrong hands, the book of Thoth can be very dangerous and for this reason only Egyptian priests with special training were allowed access to Thoth's secret knowledge together with the Pharaohs.

It's been said that Thoth acquired all this knowledge through the practice of channeling, which is a psychic connection to beings from higher dimensions, which exists in the all-encompassing informational field. We are living in a field of energy and information which is all around us and yet imperceivable by the human eye.

To achieve this expanded state of consciousness, channellers and mediums usually meditate trying to break free of the worldly influences and tune into higher consciousness. They may seek connection to specific spirits of the dead or may be contacted apparently unbidden by some unknown force that wishes to communicate.

Although this sounds completely crazy to modern society, it was not like that in ancient times. On every continent, every ancient culture knew about this ability and every religion had some sort of priest or shaman which specialized in channeling, mediumship, and communicating with the divine. From the Native American shamans famous for their trans-shamanic states, to the Egyptian priests, the Celtic Druids, and the Step-Followers of the Tangre, all of them used channeling to communicate with the spirits.

The persecution of this lost knowledge came only after the rise of mono-theistic religions such as Christianity and Islam although cases of channeling, especially communicating with God, angels, and spirits beings can also be found in these two religions, precisely by the prophets communicating with these higher dimensional beings.

Thoth through his meditative Trans state of consciousness established this connection and transformed all the knowledge he acquired in writing. It's been said he wrote thousands of books. To the Egyptians his knowledge was so vast that they began to credit him as the communicator with the Gods.

The topics he uncovered ranged from medicine, chemistry, law, art, music, rhetoric, philosophy, geography, astrology, and much more. These were only the earthly aspects he acquired. There are many more practices, rituals, and esoteric abilities written in the book of Thoth, which we would today call paranormal o simply magical.

Some of them was supposedly the ability to communicate with animals and even telepathically affect them. The Pharaohs also used the book of Thoth to establish power over animals and humans. It's been said that the mysterious book holds secrets of controlling the natural yet unknown functions of our bodies.

No wonder the most famous Egyptian symbol, the Eye of Horus, also known as Wadjet secretly depicts the structure of the human brain with the pineal gland at its center. The Book of Thoth is around 20,000 years old and the first historical record mentioning it can be found written in the Turin Papyrus, an ancient manuscript listing the name of the Egyptian Pharaohs stating from the earliest times and going on to the rein of Rameses II.

This ancient Papyrus describes how an assassination attempt was made on the life of the Pharaoh using dark magic from the Book of Thoth. Magic was something completely natural in the daily life of ancient Egyptians. The proper definition of magic is science we do not understand yet.

The most important deity in ancient Kem was Thoth. Thoth, the EVA headed scribe of the ancient world, remains one of the most enigmatic and influential deities ever to have been worshipped by people. Thoth has occupied a strange place in the imagination of later readers of Egyptian history.

Thoth influenced scholars and theologians since its earliest worship through the renaissance, European Dark Ages, and even beyond the Egyptian Pre-Dynastic periods. The main reason for Thoth's lasting influence as well as his prominence during earliest days of his worship is that he embodies the human capacity for pursuing and even glorifying knowledge. Although Thoth did have mystifying aspects, his knowledge and therefore his magic was of a predominantly functional sort.

He was the God that invented those holy symbols or hieroglyphs without which histories could not have been written and the dead would have become lost on their journey through the land of the dead. He was the God of magic whose power could easily protect and restore life as it could decimate the land and yet he was also the architect and enforcer of the universal law.

Just like law of physics or mathematics that was immutable and unbiased. As such, Thoth represents the knowledgeable authoritative force of nature. Potent, at times mysterious but always inherent to a natural order.

To the ancient Egyptians, the Sun was the dominant figure in their mythology but it is important to remember that it was also twinned with its less luminous brother the moon. This duality is fixed and vital to understanding Thoth as a major deity in the Egyptian pantheon.

Thoth was not diminished by his association with a less brilliant orb that crossed the Egyptian sky because to the Egyptians the moon was a celestial clock that guided the rituals of the temples and recorded the passage of time by the way of its uniformly changing aspects.

In many respects, Thoth was the perfect symbol as a dynamic God who began his career as a wrathful God capable of laying waste to those opponents of universal law or Maat and later became the impassive hero of truth and wisdom

Given the fact that the worship of Thoth has been traced back as far as 6000 BCE, his biography has a tapestry of often conflicting truths further adding to his enigmatic personality. Depending on the cycle of myths the reader refers to, those parentage can be one such problematic truth.

According to one version, he was the son of two fathers; meaning that he was born to both Horace and Seth. This creates a chronological anomaly for many of the myths that have survived, which places Thoth either protecting his father as a child or being present at the establishment of the cosmos.

Thoth was often called the God with no mother and he was simply depicted as emerging from the primordial waters or being born from the lips of Rhea to uphold Maat. It was Thoth who created the cosmic egg.

It was known that Thoth like many of the other Gods in the pantheon also had a female counterpart in the character of Seshat. Seshat's name literally means she who inscribes rights and she was associated with many of the same tasks for which Thoth was later to become most famous, including recording annals, writing spells, and enabling architects to design temples and tombs with the same precision Thoth exacted in the universe.

Where Seshat's duties ceased and those of Thoth began is never clearly defined but they were both aspects of the same supernatural and inspirational force. The ambiguity concerning Thoth providence and his working relationship with his female counterpart ultimately had little effect on his worship as the great city of Cumin demonstrates (Cumin later renamed Hermopolis by the Greeks).

The name Cumin refers to the Ogdoad or the eight principal deities worshipped in Cumin (Hermopolis). The Ogdoad similar to the Ennead was made up of primordial Gods who represented the esoteric aspects of that time such as darkness and lack of boundaries. There were often four Gods twinned with their female counterparts to make up the eight deities of the Ogdoad with Thoth as its leader.

By the time the ancient Greeks had experienced this fantastic religious center, they saw that it was dominated by the figure they refer to as Hermes. This was a common practice amongst ancient polytheistic cultures but encountering a foreign God caused less of a threat to the polytheistic cultures of the past then the monotheistic cultures of the present.

To the ancients and this was a practice employed by Greeks, Romans, even as late as the Norse, a foreign God was merely an aspect of a deity they were already familiar with from their own pantheon. In the case of Thoth, the Greeks encountered a God of magic writing, namely hermeneutic and knowledge who sometimes acted as a messenger of sorts for other deities were all aspects of their own God Hermes.

Therefore, the Greeks believed Thoth was just another older aspect of Hermes.

The Greeks were respectful but the Egyptian Hermes must have been shocking in the least.

Much of what happened or what was known to have gone on in Africa before the rise of the Romans and Greeks has been obscured with disinformation. We are a species with amnesia. How have we become a species with amnesia? You do what the conquistadores and thugs from Europe did the past 500 years. You invade all the native countries around the world and sever the people from their ancestors. A prime example is Black America. You replace their knowledge and their books with Euro-centric books especially the Bible.

You then start teaching them a whole new history about who they are and where they come from. Everything we have been taught is a lie.

During later ages, the ego of Thoth passed into the bodies of men in the manner described in the Emerald Tablets. Thoth incarnated three times, in his last being known as Hermes, the thrice-born. In his incarnation, he left the writings known to modern occultists as the Emerald Tablets full of ancient mysteries.

The Tablets were left in the Great Pyramids in the custody of the Pyramid Priests. Some content in the Emerald Tablets are so great and far reaching in their importance that at present it is forbidden to release them to the world at large.

How did these secrets come to be revealed to modern man after being hidden so long? Some thirteen hundred years B.C., Egypt, ancient Khem, was in turmoil. Pyramid Priests were disseminated with Emerald Tablets to other parts of the world. The tablets allowed the priests to exercise authority over less advanced priests of races descended from other Atlantean colonies. The Tablets were understood from legend to give the bearer authority from Thoth. Africans were crossing the ocean when many in Europe thought the world was flat

The particular group of priest bearing the tablets immigrated to South America where they found a flourishing race. The Mayan knowledge and understanding of celestial bodies was advanced for their time: For example, they knew how to predict solar eclipses. The Mayans remembered much of the ancient wisdom.

In the tenth century, the Mayan had thoroughly settled the Yucatan Peninsula, and the Emerald Tablets were placed beneath the great temples of the Sun God. There is a commonality here between the Egyptians and the Mayans, each built pyramids and each worshipped the Sun God. After the conquest by the Spaniards, dark-hearted men who were killers driven by passion for gold, a recurring theme of European cultures until this very day, the Mayan cities were abandoned and the treasures of the temples forgotten.

The Great Pyramid of Egypt is a temple of initiation into the mysteries. Jesus, Solomon, and Apollonius were all initiated at the Pyramids. Before being returned to the Great Pyramids, the wisdom engraved on the Emerald Tablets were translated and copies retained in 1925. Only until now was the permission given for its content to be published.

Great were my people in the ancient days. Wise were we with the Children of Light Thothme who dwelt among us in ancient Kem. Thothme was the keeper of the temple, who was the link between the Children of Light who dwelt within the Temple and the races of men who inhabited the continents.

Thoth the son of Thothme grew from a child into manhood. He was taught by his father the mysteries. The fire for wisdom consumed Thoth. Thoth was taught by Dwellers in the Temple. Dwelling in the Temple learning more wisdom. Thoth was given the Key to Life. He looked deeply in the hearts of man and found great mysteries. Only in the search of truth could Thoth's soul be stilled and the flame within be quenched.

After the sinking of Atlantis, for the transgressions of the laws of the Dwellers in the Temple, Thoth went and dwelled in the land of Khem. He sent Sons of Atlantis in many directions desiring that in the womb of time wisdom might rise again in her children. Thoth dwelled a long time in the land of Khem. The children of Khem grew in the light of Thoth's wisdom. Great grew the Sons of Khem, conquering people around them, growing slowly upward in Soul force.

Thoth built the Great Pyramid that was raised over a doorway to the entrance to Amenti, deep in the Halls of the Earth, where exists the Lords of the powers, the Dwellers.

Thoth built his knowledge of "Magic Science" in the Pyramids. While he sleeps in Amenti, his soul's roaming free, will incarnate, dwelling among men. Thoth was an emissary on earth for the dweller fulfilling his command so many will be lifted. Thoth returned to Amenti, leaving behind his wisdom in the Emerald Tablets. Requiring that we preserve and keep the commands of the Dweller. Trusting that we lift ever upward our eyes to the light. In time, we will become one with the master, one with all.

Thoth departed advising that we know his commandments, keep them, and be them, and he will be with us, helping us, guiding us into the light. Wisdom from the Emerald Tablets reveals Children of Light are looking down on the world seeing the children of men in their bondage by dark forces from beyond.

Is Thoth referring to the Archons? Only by freedom the bondage of Archontic darkness can man ever rise from the earth to the higher vibrating light frequencies. The masters came down taking the form of men and in the form of men stating "We are they who were formed from the space-dust, partaking of life from the infinite ALL; living in the world as children of men, like and yet unlike the children of men."

The masters in the form of men blasted dwelling places in inner earth that became the Halls of Amenti. Thirty and two Sons of Light came to earth among men, seeking to free sons of men from Archontic forces of bondage from beyond our third dimension.

Our religious institutions of all faiths are depravities from poverty consciousness. They are doctrines of greater truths misrepresented by satanic worshipping wealthy masters of darkness seeking to fill all with darkness.

It is time for masters of rightness to rise to loosen the constricting chains that binds men to darkness. The brothers of darkness secret societies Illuminati have banded together through the ages as antagonists to children of light.

The adrenal chrome drinking global elite, Royal Family, child molesting Roman Catholic Papacy worshippers of darkness walk always in secrecy hiding what they truly are from unsuspecting masses. They are forever walking, working, hiding from light in darkness. Silently and secretly they use their power enslaving and binding the souls of men with devices of war, debt, and false religious doctrines.

The Archons unseen they come into men though dark ceremonies ignorantly as dark secret societies calls them forth at CERN.

Thoth warned of Archontic forces:

> Dark is the way of the Dark Brother's travel, dark of the darkness of the night. Traveling over the Earth they walk through man's dreams. Power they have gained from darkness around them to call other dwellers from out of their dimensional plane. Into man's mind-space the Dark Brothers reach. They wrap their veil of darkness around the soul of men and through a lifetime those souls dwell in bondage to evil.
>
> In the form of man they move amongst us, but only to sight were they as men. Serpent-Headed when the glamour was lifted but appearing as men among men. Crept they into Councils, taking forms that were like men unto men. Slaying by their arts the chiefs of the kingdoms, taking their form and ruling over man. Only by magic could they be discovered. Only by sound could their faces be seen. Sought they from the kingdom of shadow to destroy man and rule in his place.

Thoth advises us not to be captured in the darkness of evil. He encourages us to keep our heads turned toward light (high vibration) and not darkness (low vibrations). Those of us who seek the pathway of light have far greater power to bind with Light.

Understanding the Religious Narratives

Path 9: African Belief Systems of Thoth Plagiarized by European's Story of Jesus

Scholars and Pan-Africanists agree that Africans were the earth's first people, with the first philosophies, sciences, arts, and spiritual concepts. Our ancient African ancestors believed in a well-rounded life, unity with the Creator, and oneness with one another. Maat, an Egyptian philosophy and way of life, is a concept of spiritual being some African scholars argue is the foundation of all religions.

In the impressive halls of Kemet's (Egypt) majestic monuments, ancient writings inscribed on the walls of pyramids reveal a universal message of truth, justice, and righteousness. Ancient Africans did not practice religion; instead they followed a natural order of living and incorporated principles that were supposed to have led to a more balanced life.

Maat consists of 42 admonitions or negative confessions and seven cardinal virtues: Truth, justice, rightness, harmony, balance, reciprocity, and order. A close comparison of the confessions to the much younger Biblical Ten Commandments yields a stunning revelation: The Ten Commandments may have come from Maat.

For example, admonition 18, according to the Metu Neter (a book of spiritual guidelines), says, "I have not set my mouth in motion against any person." In comparison, Commandment 9 says: "Thou shall not bear false witness against your neighbor."

Admonition 20 says, "I have not defiled the wife of any man." Commandment 10 says, "Thou shall not covet your neighbor's house; you shall not covet your neighbor's wife, nor his male servant, nor his female servant, nor his ox, nor his donkey, nor anything that is your neighbor's." And the list goes on.

Long Beach State University Africana Studies professor and Seba (moral teacher of Maat), Maulana Karenga writes in his book, entitled "Maat, The Moral Ideal in Ancient Egypt," that the ancient Kemetic philosophy set into motion the moral principles of modern religions.

"There is clearly an interest in the ideal as a point of departure and motivation for philosophical discourse in the same sense (that) the ideal motivates discourse in other religious and ethical traditions," Karenga writes, "i.e., the central idea of iwa (character) in Ifa, 'adl (justice) in Islam, jen in Confucianism, nirvana in Buddhism, dharma in Hinduism, tzedek in Judaism, agape in Christianity, etc."

According to Karenga's research, Maatian influences and practices date as far back as 3100 and 2150 B.C., while other heavily used Biblical principles like the Ten Commandments, were written by Moses around 1500 B.C. Maatian principles, practices, and virtues are represented by an Egyptian woman or goddess who is also called Maat. She is depicted with wings or sitting with a scepter and ankh in either hand and an ostrich feather atop her head. Depictions of the goddess began to appear during the Old Kingdom (sometime around 2700 B.C.)

Maat in death

On the Papyrus of Ani, a scene of judgment begins with the Great Hall of Maati. Here is where Anpu, the god of embalming, leads all men and women who have died into judgment. Individuals have to answer for their actions, attempting to justify themselves with righteousness they demonstrated on earth, according to Maatian principles and virtues.

Karenga writes that Maat not only teaches to deny evil, but to promote good and do righteousness.

"The deceased declares her virtues saying that she did Maat in Egypt, and lives on Maat," he states. "Moreover, the deceased declares that he has done what was worthy of praise by others and that which pleased God. Especially important, the deceased declares moral concern and care for the most vulnerable of society..."

Anpu, weighs the heart of a person on the balance (scale) of Ra (God) against the feather of Maat. This determines, if a soul is worthy to enter into Aaru (the Field of Reeds), where the ancient gods roamed for eternity, or be devoured by Ammut, and have no chance for further existence. Djehuti, "the scribe of heaven and lord of just measure," is pictured next to the balance. His job is to record and announce the results.

At the end of the Papyrus of Ani, sits Asar "whose resurrection from the dead, symbolized and promised eternal life through righteousness for human beings," his wife Auset and Nebt-Hetn his sister. Ra and the Heliopolitan Ennead (The Great Nine Divine Powers) are also pictured on the papyrus. A side note: Different papyrus judgment scenes have more than nine divine powers, but Ra is always at the head.

The Biblical judgment scene according to Revelation 20:11-15 is similar. (According to Revelation 1, the author is John the Apostle. The book is a vision God gave him about the final judgment.) In the last days, the book of life was opened and the dead were "judged out of those things which were written in the books, according to their works" before the throne of God. Those who were not found in the book were cast into the lake of fire, eternal death. Those who were found worthy were given everlasting life. Upon closer examination, other parallels can be found.

Many religions teach morality and righteous living. Maat, although it is not a religion, is a spiritual foundation from which many would argue the world's religions gleaned. Maat is simply a way of life that is acceptable to people across different faiths.

The kingdom described in the Bible is the womb. The first heaven is the body. When you come out of the womb and look up into the sky is the second heaven. The third heaven is when we are released back into the cosmos as spiritual energy.

The bible is trying to tell us that we are God. The womb of the black woman is God. What came first the chicken or the egg? The woman had to come first. You cannot get a woman from a man but you can get a man from a woman. Your mother is God. If she does not feed you, you will die. She with the womb is God.

Corinthian 3:16 Know ye not that ye are the temple of God and the spirit of God dwelleth in you?

John 14:20 at the end of the day ye shall know that I am Father, and ye in me, and I in you.

Europeans took away the practice of reverence of black females in ancient African societies. The mystery of the gentiles is the black woman's womb. The kingdom of heaven, the black woman's womb, giving birth to Jesus Christ, this is the whole story of the virgin birth. The kingdom of God (black womb). The Catholics worship the womb of Mary Madeline a lot more than they do Jesus.

All the generation of Egypt in the Nile Valley grew up in a spiritual civilization. Any civilization outside the Nile Valley, outside of Kemet who were not into this spiritual culture venerating the womb of the black woman, they had to deal with the cold weather, fight off animals, other humans raiding, plundering, and raping women and children. Life in non Kemet civilization was about violence and material possessions and survival of the fittest.

These were white people who were not in Kemet. When the Ice age was finally over, the Bavarians came down to sunny Kemet and saw what was there. They had not seen anything like the temples and the Pyramids in Kemet anywhere.

The Egyptians were nice and let these people come in and traded with them. The white immigrants only saw the material splendor of gold and jewels. They did not understand the spirituality of MAAT principles guiding African civilization. They sought the knowledge of math and sciences while not embracing the spiritual culture of MAAT. White men set out specifically to conquer the people to take away the material splendor not caring about the spiritual.

The way into the kingdom of Heaven is through meditation when you go into yourself and figure out who you are. Jesus tells us not to listen to these preachers and not to go to these churches. The preachers do not allow you to go into yourself. When you meditate, you go within yourself.

Luke 11:52 Woe unto you, lawyers! For ye have taken away the key of knowledge: ye entered not in yourselves, and them that were entering into ye hindered.

White men changed the doctrines practiced in Kemet when he manufactured his Bible.

1Timothy 2:11-12 Let a woman learn quietly with all submissiveness. I do not permit a woman to teach or exercise authority over a man, she is to remain quiet.

1Corinthian 14:34-35: The woman should be kept silent in the churches. For they are not permitted to speak, but should be in submission, as the law also says. If there is anything they desire to learn, let them ask their husbands at home. For it is shameful for a woman to speak in church.

1 Timothy 2:9 Likewise also that women should adorn themselves in respectable apparel, with modesty and control, not braided hair and gold pearls, or costly attire.

The ministers do not tell women she must submit to the laws of the church because he wants the women to keep coming back to the church. It all goes back to Kemet, it goes back to the womb, to the Ankh. It goes back to what the Egyptians were teaching revering the black woman as God. Meditation is spirituality looking at God within, this is the secret of the Bible, the hidden code.

We must understand why the Masons bring the Bible and the Koran. The Koran is more updated for today. We must understand why the Masons have these books. They have these books in their Temples because they are using our ignorance against up with racism and everyone caught up in black and white social conflict.

If you are black African, you are a direct descendant of greatness and the closest thing left of the original man on this planet, and the walking image of the creator.

Your skin is dark and your bloodline is true. Our black people are in trouble. We need to wake up and realize just who we are. Non-black elitist know who we are and they know what we are capable of if we ever get it together. 666 Is not just about Satan. Yes there is an antichrist. Anybody that puts the Bible out there as it is read and understood, is anti-Christ. You are not listening to Jesus and what he said. He said you are God. He did not tell you to worship him. The Bible tells you clearly not to have any graven images. Jesus said the kingdom of God is within you. People have pictures on the wall walking around with crosses on their necks.

The womb, the woman, and the Kingdom is God. To get to the third heaven one must meditate.

There was a long war between the Romans and the Persians that ended in the 7th Century as a status-quo antebellum. This status means we will both leave with what we came into the war with. Right after the war was over arose Islam. Islam has all the Old Testament and claiming all these new teachings about Jesus that are not in the Bible.

If you came to a truce with Rome, who gave you your Bible, how would Rome allow you to use their creation to go control others? They had to come to some kind of agreement. Islam and Christianity has been ruling side by side since the 7th Century.

Many historians and scholars of antiquity, such as Chancellor Williams and Billy Carson, have done great research into the antiquity of Africa. The question is now, which narrative about the history of ancient Africa is true? Many ancient scrolls of antiquity have been either destroyed with an evil agenda or being hoarded by a syndicate of global elitist to keep the people from the truth.

Origins of Modern Humans:

Current data suggest that modern humans evolved from archaic humans primarily in East Africa. A 195,000 year old fossil from the Omo 1 site in Ethiopia shows the beginnings of the skull changes that we associate with modern people, including a rounded skull case and possibly a projecting chin.

A 160,000 year old skull from the Herto site in the Middle Awash area of Ethiopia also seems to be at the early stages of this transition. It had the rounded skull case but retained the large brow ridges of archaic humans. Somewhat more advanced transitional forms have been found at Laetoli in Tanzania dating to about 120,000 years ago.

By 115,000 years ago, early modern humans had expanded their range to South Africa and into Southwest Asia (Israel) shortly after 100,000 years ago. There is no reliable evidence of modern humans elsewhere in the Old World until 60,000-40,000 years ago, during a short temperate period in the midst of the last ice age. (Source: www2.palomar.edu)

The span of recorded history is roughly 5,000 years, beginning with Sumerian Cuneiform script; the oldest discovered form of coherent writing from the protoliterate period around the 30th century BC.

NOTE: The oldest known prehistoric art is the series of petroglyphs discovered caves in India: the Auditorium Cave at Bhimbetka and a rock shelter at Daraki-Chattan. This cave art are dated to be around 290,000-700,000 BCE.

Records were kept in the Sphinx that exceeded 100,000 years they were taken out and put in the Vatican. And the head was sealed shut.

In his book "The Destruction of Black Civilization," Chancellor documents the Pre-Islamic empires of North Africa, cities such as Memphis, Cumin, Thebes, and Meroe. The **Kerma culture** or **Kerma kingdom** was an early civilization centered in Kerma, Sudan. It flourished from around 2500 BCE to 1500 BCE in ancient Nubia, located in Upper Egypt and northern Sudan.

In ancient Egyptian history, the **Old Kingdom** is the period spanning 2686–2181 BC. It is also known as the "Age of the Pyramids" or the "Age of the Pyramid Builders", as it encompasses the reigns of the great pyramid builders of the Fourth Dynasty—King Sneferu perfected the art of pyramid-building and the pyramids of Giza were constructed under the kings Khufu, Khafre and Menkaure.

The **Fourth Dynasty** of ancient Egypt (notated **Dynasty IV**) is characterized as a "golden age" of the Old Kingdom of Egypt. Dynasty IV lasted from c. 2613 to 2494 BC. It was a time of peace and prosperity as well as one during which trade with other countries is documented.

Painted limestone Sphinx of Hetepheres II, possibly the first depiction of a sphinx, she was one of the longest lived members of the fourth dynasty royal family, a daughter of Khufu, she was the wife of Djedefre, and lived into the reign of Shepseskaf.

The Fourth Dynasty heralded the height of the pyramid-building age. The relative peace of the Third Dynasty allowed the Dynasty IV rulers the leisure to explore more artistic and cultural pursuits. King Sneferu's building experiments led to the evolution from the mastaba styled step pyramids to the smooth sided "true" pyramids, such as those on the Giza Plateau.

No other period in Egypt's history equaled Dynasty IV's architectural accomplishments. Each of the rulers of this dynasty commissioned at least one pyramid to serve as a tomb. King Sneferu, the first king of the fourth dynasty, held territory in ancient Libya to the Sinai Peninsula, and Nubia in the south. It was a successful period and this era is known for its advancement and concentrated government, as seen in the organized building of pyramids and other monuments.

These were black people building pyramids in 2613 to 2494 BCE before western Civilization's Jesus Christ. One has to wonder what was happening in Europe during this time. Civilizing influences from the Middle East began to be felt by the peoples of south-eastern Europe in the centuries after 1000 BC. Phoenician merchants developed new trading networks across the Mediterranean Sea. They brought with them knowledge of the great civilizations of Mesopotamia and Egypt – and also an important new tool, alphabetic writing.

So what is going on with the European mindset of white superiority in the Common Era? Africans were advanced in knowledge of health, math, and architectural technology thousands of years before Europe was civilized.

Initial Fourth Dynasty Royalty				
Names of Kings	**Horus (throne) name**	**Dates**	**Pyramid**	**Names of Wives**
Sneferu	Nebma'at	613–2589 BC	Red Pyramid Bent Pyramid Pyramid at Meidum	Hetepheres I
Khufu	Medjedu	2589–2566 BC	Great Pyramid of Giza	Meritites I Henutsen
Djedefre	Kheper	2566–2558 BC?	Pyramid of Djedefre	Hetepheres II Khentetka
Khafre	Userib	2558–2532 BC	Pyramid of Khafra	Meresankh III Khamerernebty I Hekenuhedjet Persenet
Menkaure	Kakhet	2532–2503 BC?	Pyramid of Menkaure	Khamerernebty II
Shepseskaf	??	2518–2510 BC?	Pharaoh's Bench at Saqqara	Bunefer

Egypt attained its first sustained peak of civilization—the first of three so-called "Kingdom" periods (followed by the Middle Kingdom and New Kingdom) which mark the high points of civilization in the lower Nile Valley.

In his book "The Compendium of the Emerald Tablets," Billy Carson breaks down the messages of Thoth. Thoth, who became the ancient Egyptian God of wisdom. The antiquity of the Emerald Tablets dates back some 36,000 years before the Common Era. In contrast to what is presented in the Bible.

The writer of the Emerald Tablets is Thoth, an Atlantean Priest-King who founded a colony in ancient Egypt after the sinking of Atlantis, the mother country. Credit has been given to Pharaoh Khufu of the 4th Egyptian Dynasty during the time period of 2589–2566 BC. According to the Emerald Tablets, it was Thoth who built the Pyramid of Giza! In the Pyramid of Giza, he incorporated his knowledge of the ancient wisdom and also securely hid records and instruments of ancient Atlantis.

For some 16,000 years, he ruled the ancient race of Egypt, from approximately 52,000 BC to 36,000 BC. The ancient barbarous race among which his followers settled were raised to a high degree of civilization. Thoth was immortal, that is he had conquered death, passing only when he willed and even then not through death. His wisdom made him ruler over various Atlantean colonies, including the ones in South and Central America.

When the time came for him to leave Egypt, he erected the Great Pyramids over the entrance of the Great Hall of Amenti, placed in it his records, and appointed guards for his secrets from among the highest of his people. In later times, the descendants of these guards became the pyramid priests, by which Thoth was deified as the God of Wisdom. In legend, the Halls of Amenti became the underworld, the Halls of the gods, where the soul passed after death for judgement.

Path 10: Egypt before the Pharaohs

Have you ever wondered about Pre-Pharaonic Egypt and its rulers, not according to mainstream scholars, but according to ancient texts written thousands of years ago?

Turin Royal Canon: An ancient Papyrus that proves 'Gods' ruled over Ancient Egypt. The final two lines of the column, which seem to represent a resume of the entire document are extremely interesting and remind us of the Sumerian King list. They read: '… Venerables Shemsu-Hor, 13,420 years; Reigns before the Shemsu-Hor, 23,200 years; Total 36,620 years'.

There is a time in the history of ancient Egypt where mainstream scholars are surrounded by countless enigmas they are unable to answer.

According to two ancient texts, there was a time in ancient Egypt, before the land of the Pharaohs was ruled by mortals where beings that came from the heavens reigned over the land. These mysterious beings are referred to as 'Gods' or 'Demigods' that lived and ruled over ancient Egypt for hundreds of years.

Known as the Turin King List, the ancient document is the ultimate piece that could help clarify the thin line dividing mortal rulers and gods in ancient times. The Turin papyrus –referred to by many as the Turin Royal Canon—is an ancient text written in the hieratic language (a cursive form of Egyptian hieroglyphics; used especially by the priests). Scholars believe that the original papyrus was a list that included over 300 names detailing precisely the years, months and days of each reign of the kings that ruled over the lands of ancient Egypt.

However, many other authors, **Eusebius**, bishop of Caesarea in Palestine, and Sincelo talk about, a lineage of gods that reigned on Earth for a total of 36,600 years. After this period of government come the mortal pharaohs of ancient Egypt mortals.

The papyrus was originally a tax roll, but on its back the most extensive king list of ancient Egypt was written down with extreme precision describing what mainstream scholars call 'mythical kings' such as gods, demigods, and spirits while it also accounts for the mortal Pharaohs that ruled over ancient Egypt. This is where many scholars cannot find common ground since some claim that it is impossible to differentiate mortal Pharaohs from Gods and Demigods and if mortal Pharaohs did exist, how can we prove that the alleged Gods and Demigods did not?

This ancient texts is considered as the most extensive list of Ancient Egyptian Kings ever found and is considered the basis for most of the chronology that predates the reign of Ramesses II.

Canon is distributed in the following manner:

Column 1—Gods of Ancient Egypt
Column 2—Rows 1-10 Spirits and mythical kings
Column 2—Rows 11-25 (Dynasties 1-2)

Column 3—Rows 1-25 (Dynasties 2-5)
Column 4—Rows 1-26 (Dynasties 6-8/9/10)
Column 5—Rows 12-25 (Dynasties 11-12)
Column 6—Rows 1-2 (Dynasties 12-13)
Column 7—Rows 1-23 (Dynasty 13)
Column 8—Rows 1-27 (Dynasty 13-14)
Column 9—Rows 1-30 (Dynasty 14)
Column 10—Rows 1-30 (Dynasties 14-15)
Column 11—Rows 1-17 (Dynasties 16-17)

Regrettably, since the Papyrus is in very bad condition, names and titles of some kings are still being disputed by mainstream scholars. However, this does not diminish its importance since it is a complete historical record of Pre-Pharaonic Egypt.

Maybe the very first dynasty of Egyptians was Sumerian, and so was the second, third, fourth, and fifth. Egyptologist have never accurately interpreted the writings from the first five dynasties. They can't because they don't admit their Sumerian logographic. In the tablet of Abydos of Pharaoh Seti I and his son Rameses II they list the names of the 75 predecessors before their reign. The first on the list is Menes. He is the first ruler in Egyptian King's list. Menes is the exact same name as Amum of Sumer.

In the Sumerian writings we find that Amum was famous. He is the author of the Sumerian inscription that mentions the building of the great wall of Uuruk. The Ubaid Period (c. 5000-4100 BCE) when the so-called Ubaid people first inhabited the region of Sumer is followed by the Uuruk Period (4100-2900 BCE) during which time cities began to develop across Mesopotamia and Uuruk became the most influential.

In Ancient Mesopotamia we have very interesting pieces of ancient history. Mesopotamia is a Greek name meaning "between the rivers" this region spreads between the Tigris and Euphrates rivers. This vast area of land was composed of several regions such as Southern Sumer,

Akkad, and Assyria to the North. In these regions, researchers have found evidence that speaks of a past that seems to disagree with our conventional way of looking at history.

Akkad for example, is a city located 50 km northwest of Babylon. It is commonly referred to as Akkad, Agade, Abu Habba, and Sippar, which means "city of books." This ancient city was very popular because of their libraries. According to research, it was the capital of the eighth antediluvian monarch, Emenduranna, who reigned for 21,000 years. If we move 80km southeast of Babylon we will find the city of Nimrod and the tablets of Nimrod. Between 1880 and 1900 archaeologists from the University of Pennsylvania excavated 50,000 tablets believed to have been written during the third millennium BC. Among their findings, archaeologists discovered a library of 20,000 volumes, dictionaries and complete works on religion, literature, law and science. Researchers also discovered a list of rulers that lived for thousands of years.

The Sumerian King list is perhaps, one of the most important archaeological discoveries. There are more than a dozen of copies of Sumerian King Lists, found in Babylon, Susa, and Assyria, and the Royal Library of Nineveh from the VII century BC. All of these are believed to originate from one original list believed to have been written during the Third Dynasty of Ur or even earlier.

The best preserved specimen of the Sumerian King List is called the Weld-Blundell Prism, which is a clay, cuneiform inscribed vertical prism housed in the Ashmolean Museum. The Weld-Blundell Prism was written in cuneiform around 2170 BC by a scribe who signed as Nur-Ninsubur from the end of the Isin Dynasty. This incredible document provides a comprehensive list of the Sumerian Kings from the beginning, before the great flood, and the 10 kings who lived before the Flood who lived for thousands of years. The clay prism was found in Larsa, home of the fourth antediluvian king Kichunna, a few kilometers north of Ur.

The first part of the Sumerian King List:

"1-39 After the kingship descended from heaven, the kingship was in Eridug. In Eridug, Alulim became king; he ruled for 28800 years. Alaljar ruled for 36000 years. 2 kings; they ruled for 64800 years. Then Eridug fell and the kingship was taken to Bad-tibira. In Bad-tibira, En-men-lu-ana ruled for 43200 years. En-men-gal-ana ruled for 28800 years. Dumuzid, the shepherd, ruled for 36000 years. 3 kings; they ruled for 108000 years.

Then Bad-tibira fell (?) and the kingship was taken to Larag. In Larag, En-sipad-zid-ana ruled for 28800 years. 1 king; he ruled for 28800 years. Then Larag fell (?) and the kingship was taken to Zimbir. In Zimbir, En-men-dur-ana became king; he ruled for 21000 years. 1 king; he ruled for 21000 years. Then Zimbir fell (?) and the kingship was taken to Curuppag. In Curuppag, Ubara-Tutu became king; he ruled for 18600 years. 1 king; he ruled for 18600 years. In 5 cities 8 kings; they ruled for 241200 years. Then the flood swept over."

The real meaning of the Sumerian King list is to demonstrate that the "royalty" came down from the heaven and a specific city was chosen to dominate over all others.

According to the Sumerian King List, after the flood this is how history continued:

After the flood had swept over, and the kingship had descended from heaven, the kingship was in Kic. In Kic, Jucur became king; he ruled for 1200 years. Kullassina-bel ruled for 960(*ms. P2+L2 has instead:* 900) years. Nanjiclicma ruled for (*ms. P2+L2 has:*) 670 (?) years. En-tarah-ana ruled for (*ms. P2+L2 has:*) 420 years ......, 3 months, and 3 1/2 days. Babum ...... ruled for (*ms. P2+L2 has:*) 300 years. Puannum ruled for 840 (*ms. P2+L2 has instead:* 240) years. Kalibum ruled for 960 (*ms. P2+L2 has instead:* 900) years. Kalumum ruled for 840 (*mss. P3+BT14, Su1 have instead:* 900) years. Zuqaqip ruled for 900 (*ms. Su1 has instead:* 600) years. (*In mss. P2+L2, P3+BT14, P5, the 10th and 11th rulers of the dynasty precede the 8th and 9th.*) Atab (*mss. P2+L2, P3+BT14, P5 have instead:* Aba) ruled for 600 years. Macda, the son of Atab, ruled for 840 (*ms. Su1 has instead:* 720) years. Arwium, the son of Macda, ruled for 720 years. Etana, the shepherd, who ascended to heaven and consolidated all the foreign countries, became king; he ruled for 1500 (*ms. P2+L2 has instead:* 635) years. Balih, the son ofEtana, ruled for 400 (*mss. P2+L2, Su1 have instead:* 410) years. En-me-nuna ruled for 660 (*ms. P2+L2 has instead:* 621) years. Melem-Kic, the son of En-me-nuna, ruled for 900 years. (*ms. P3+BT14 adds:*) 1560 are the years of the dynasty of En-me-nuna . Barsal-nuna, the son of En-me-nuna, (*mss. P5, P3+BT14 have instead:* Barsal-nuna) ruled for 1200 years. Zamug, the son of Barsal-nuna, ruled for 140 years. Tizqar, the son of Zamug, ruled for 305 years. (*ms. P3+BT14 adds:*) 1620 + X .... Ilku ruled for 900 years. Iltasadum ruled for 1200 years. En-men-barage-si, who made the land of Elam submit, became king; he ruled for 900 years. Aga, the son of En-men-barage-si, ruled for 625 years. (*ms. P3+BT14 adds:*) 1525 are the years of the dynasty of En-men-barage-si. 23 kings; they ruled for 24510 years, 3 months, and 3 1/2 days. Then Kic was defeated and the kingship was taken to E-ana.

What we have described in the Sumerian King list is something amazing since it tells us what exactly happened, who ruled and for how long.

The only question that remains is... How did certain kings rule for thousands of years? Were they ordinary human beings? Or did they in fact come from the "heaven"?

There are two Egyptian histories. One is pre-cataclysm before 2239 B.C. an involve Shemsu Hor a people who were technologically advanced. They have become the subject matter of many Egyptian traditions. Shemsu Hor according to Egyptian Legends was one of the first acts of Osiris in his reign who was to deliver the Egyptians from Their destitute and brutish manner of living. This he did by showing them the fruits of cultivation, by giving them laws, and by teaching them to honor the Gods.

The Egypt after a mass cataclysm in what Egyptologists refer to as the First Intermediate Period speaks of the entire Bronze Age, where every civilization, suffered a reset cataclysm that depopulated the entire world. This period is not talked about in much of the text literature. The First Intermediate Period is described as a period of disarray and an Egyptian Civilization that was disunited.

The Egyptian priest Manetho held that for 350 years (from 2239 BCE to 1889 BCE) that Egypt was in a state of chaos and had been destroyed. 350 years is a hiatus that necessitates the end of a civilization and the beginning of another. These distinct civilizations just happen to be geographically located at the place we call Egypt today.

The Dynasty Egypt we are familiar with began when Menes appeared who was a foreigner that arrived by ship. Menes was First Dynastic ruler of post-cataclysmic Egypt. He is also referred to by Egyptologists as Narmer. In Menes Egyptian palette he called himself the King of Uri. Uri is the city of Ur in Sumer. This information leads us to believe that he came from Mesopotamia.

This informs us that the very first dynasty in Egypt was Sumerian in origin. The very first dynasty of Egyptians was Sumerian, so was the second, third, fourth, and fifth. L. Augustine Waddell found that the ancient Egyptian language idioms were laterally Semitic and according to Augustine Waddell's research, Menes entry into Egypt began a very significant Sumerian presence establishing the City of Memphis.

In the Tablet of Abydos of Pharaoh Seti I and his son Rameses II, they list the names of the 75 predecessors before their rein. The very first on the list is Menes. Menes is the exact same name as Amum of Sumer. In Sumerian writings, we find that Amum was the same famous author of the Sumerian inscription that mentions the building of the Great Wall of Ur.

The Pre-Dynastic inscriptions of early Egypt especially at Abydos are of early Sumerian script not yet in the conventionalized forms of the hieroglyphics so famous today.

Sargon the Great was one of the world's earliest empire builders. From roughly 2334 to 2279 BCE, he ruled a civilization called the Akkadian Empire, consisting largely of ancient Mesopotamia, after conquering all of Sumer (southern Mesopotamia) as well as parts of Syria, Anatolia (Turkey), and Elam (western Iran).

In some of the oldest tombs in Abydos, inscriptions dates back to the Sargon Period. Inscriptions of Menes at Abydos were in Sumerian writings during the period ruled by Sargon. These were the earliest known use of hieroglyphs in Egypt.

The Papyrus of Turin clearly indicates the existence of NINE dynasties that correspond to the predynastic Pharaohs and among them are the Venerables of Memphis', 'the Venerables of the North' and, lastly, the Shemsu Hor (the Companions, or Followers of Horus) who ruled until the time of Menes, the first mortal Pharaoh of Ancient Egypt.

It is important to mention that ancient Egyptian chronology is accepted from Menes and onwards. However, mainstream scholars tend to disagree when discussing the time before Menes when alleged 'gods' ruled over the land of the Pharaohs.

According to reports currently, around 50% of the original Papyrus remains missing.

The final two lines of the column, which seem to represent a resume of the entire document are extremely interesting and remind us of the Sumerian King list. They read: '... Venerables Shemsu-Hor, 13,420 years; Reigns before the Shemsu-Hor, 23,200 years; Total 36,620 years'.

There is an ongoing debate going on between numerous researchers whether or not the enigmatic kings who ruled before mortal Pharos were real or not. Many argue that it be nearly impossible to deny their existence since just as the rule of mortal pharaohs is recorded in the ancient Papyrus so is the reign of the enigmatic beings referred to as Gods and Demigods.

Interestingly, according to Eusebius of Caesarea, who was a Roman historian, exegete, and Christian polemicist of Greek descent, a dynasty of gods ruled Egypt for 13.9 thousand years: the first was god Vulcan, the god who discovered fire, after him Sosis of the Sun, Isis, and Osiris of Saturn, Typhoon brother of Osiris, and Horus, the son of Isis and Osiris. They were followed by a dynasty of heroes and demigods who ruled for 11,025 years. This makes it a total of 24.925 years of reign. Approximately around 3000 BC, the first "human" Pharaoh would take rule as an Egyptian pharaoh.

In ancient Egypt, long before the first 'mortal' pharaoh known as **Menes-Narmer** ruled over the lands of Egypt there were other kings, gods and, "Those who came from above" who reigned in the country known today as Egypt.

This time in history, the pre-Pharaonic period remains a great mystery to most scholars, Egyptologists, historians, and archeologists, because they cannot accept what is written, as it goes directly against the beliefs of most people.

The time before 3000 BC, the date on which the first officer Pharaoh appeared in Egypt, is a great enigma.

Old Code of the Alien Gods of Egypt

There are about 138 pyramids so far, that has been discovered across Egypt! When looking at these complex structures of precise masonry, today's modern man cannot reconstruct? It is time for us to reconstruct our way of thinking towards how advanced in knowledge our early ancestors actually were!

It is no secret that the ancient Egyptians consider their civilization to be the legacy of the gods who did not come from the Earth, but from another place in the cosmos, and pre-Pharaonic Egypt seems to support this theory.

One of the most important ancient texts that can tell us more about this moment in history is the Turin Papyrus, which lists all the pharaohs who ruled over ancient Egypt.

This list not only includes all the "official" historical pharaohs of ancient Egypt, but also includes the deities or "gods" who came from above and reigned over the lands of Egypt before the first pharaoh of mortal Egypt with a lineage that extended for 13,000 years.

It is a great enigma why the main scholars consider this ancient text to be a pure myth and why most of the details of the ancient text have been overlooked and omitted in the history books.

"They seem to have no ancestors or developmental periods, but seem to have appeared overnight."

Toby Wilkinson, English Egyptologist

There are some researchers who believe that by calculating the information obtained from deciphering the Papyrus of Turin, we obtain the initial period, referred to as the kingdom of Ptah, creator and first ruler of ancient Egypt, which dates back to 39,000 years.

Egyptology and official historiography tells us that everything until the pre-dynastic era is considered a myth, without great historical value.

The wake of Palermo is another incredible ancient text that mentions the pre-Dynastic rulers of ancient Egypt. This ancient stele even refers to the Egyptian god Horus, suggesting that he was a physical ruler of ancient Egypt thousands of years ago.

Another Egyptian god, Thoth is said to have reigned over the lands of ancient Egypt from 8670 to 7100 BC.

Interestingly, the Egyptian high priest Manetho, who had access to an unlimited number of ancient texts of the Ancient Library of Alexandria, and who wrote for the pharaoh the history of ancient Egypt in 30 volumes, refers to the divine beings who ruled during the Pre-Pharaonic Egypt.

If you look at the Egyptologists of today, you will find that they also make use of Manetho's quotations as a very reliable tool in the study of officially recognized dynasties, however, for some mysterious reason, the Egyptologists themselves have decided to **avoid** *anything related to the prehistoric dynasties*, carefully selecting certain details and adopting them as their own, while rejecting everything that does not fit in 'their point of view' of the story.

Manetón is considered as the father of Egyptology
by many scholars today

There are two different views on the history of ancient Egypt. The accepted by the scholars and the one denied by them.

We can trace the rulers of Egypt in a series of old "Real Lists".

The Real Listing of Abydos for example, which is located on the wall of the temple of Seti I in Abydos, offers us a chronological order of seventy-six rulers of ancient Egypt, ranging from Menes to Sethi I.

In addition to this list we have the Royal List of Karnak that can be found in the Louvre, which has sixty-one rulers, ranging from Menes to Tutmosis III. These two lists help us understand the tradition of Upper Egypt.

The Royal List of Saqqara shows forty-seven previous kings and including Ramses II.

More important than any of the above mentioned is the Papyrus of Turin:

This ancient text written in hieratic on the back of the papyrus, with the accounts of the time of Ramses II on the obverse (giving the approximate date, about 1200 BC). In its original state, the papyrus must have been artistically a beautiful example, since the writing is exceptionally fine.

It contains the names of the kings in order, more than 300 when it is complete, with the length of each kingdom in years, months and days; and, since the definitive edition of the papyrus has not yet been issued, it is expected that more studies will obtain additional results.

The papyrus begins, like **Manetho**, with the dynasties of the gods, followed by the mortal kings also in dynasties.

The change of dynasty is observed, and the sum of the reigns is given to him: Also, as with Manetón, several dynasties are added, for example, the "Sum of the Kings of Menes a [Unas]" at the end of the V dynasty

The disposition in the papyrus is very similar to that of the personification of Manetho. (Page 16 of the source)

Manetón provides us with a series of interesting data about the so-called "divine" rulers of ancient Egypt and their dynasties that fall into three different categories:

- the gods
- the heroes
- the "Manes"

Ancient Egypt is a never ending source of inspiration for many of us – its myths, its history, and its art are wonderful and enigmatic and have intrigued researchers for decades. But perhaps the most astonishing part of ancient Egypt is its religion. Its pantheon has numerous gods that are associated with many parts of everyday life in ancient Egypt and exploring it is a very enlightening endeavor.

In this chapter, I delve deep into the rich and mythical world of the Egyptian gods and goddesses – exposing the most important deities of its pantheon of deities. Reading and learning about them is an absolute thrill and gives us an important glimpse into the minds and the beliefs of one of the world's oldest and greatest civilizations.

A Short Introduction to the Gods of Egypt

Ancient Egyptian society placed great emphasis on polytheistic, highly complex belief in many deities, and many myths associated with them. Many of these gods and goddesses had an animal form, as these animals played a crucial role in the everyday lives of Egyptians.

In fact, this pantheon was so complex that it contained more than 1400 deities, with some scholars claiming that this number is even greater. This fact means that we couldn't possibly name them all, but I will try to examine some of the most important deities that were present throughout the timeline of ancient Egypt.

The Egyptians believed that these deities were present in every part of their life and would influence both nature and the lives of humans. Worship of these gods was an integral part of everyday life and would be carried out both in temples and at home shrines.

Complex rituals and invocations survived in hieroglyphic writing and give us an insight into the very fluid beliefs of Egyptians regarding almost every aspect of the world around them. Animals were often mummified as a way of sacrifice and worship, and great emphasis was placed on death, the afterlife, and rebirth.

Animals had a complex role in the religion of Egyptians. Ibises, baboons, crocodiles, scarabs, fish, shrews, and cats were all considered sacred, but sacrificed, nonetheless. Cats especially were considered divine but still strangulated en-masse for mummification. Hundreds of thousands cat mummies were excavated in many tombs.

Baboons were sacred, but still bred in captivity for the purpose of sacrifice. Many suffered from malnutrition, fractures, vitamin deficiency, and osteomyelitis. Still, this provides an important insight into the religion and the bestial form of the gods of Egypt.

As mentioned, the Egyptian pantheon consisted of more than 1400 attested deities, and some of them were related to seemingly minor or unimportant things. Examples are many, like Ȧmi-kar the singing ape god, Ȧri-em-ăua - god of the sixth hour of night, Maa-en-Rā - an ape doorkeeper god, Neb ȧrit-tcheṭflu - goddess who created reptiles, Esna the divine perch, Shentayet the goddess of widows, etc. There are numerous examples they provide an important insight into the minds of ancient Egyptians.

But there were also those minor, but still important deities, such as Ta-Bitjet, Wepwawet, Babi, Bes, Khnum, Apophis, Nut, Isis, Hathor, Nefertem, and many more. In the following list are just some of the most important deities and their amazing attributes and stories.

Amun – Father of the Gods

Amun was one of the most important gods of the Egyptian pantheon – "The Lord of Truth, Father of the Gods, Maker of Men, Creator of all Animals, Lord of Things that Are, Creator of the Staff of Life". Translated as "Hidden One", Amun was one of the Ogdoad – the eight primeval deities of the Hermopolis, and at a time the chief Theban god.

As the importance of Amun grew and his cult spread, he gained the form of Amun-Ra, in the New Kingdom. This combined him with Ra, the sun god, and he became the chief deity, the king of the gods and the creator of the world and its inhabitants. At one period during the New Kingdom, Amun became so emphasized he overshadowed the other gods. His usual depiction is in human form.

Anubis - Lord of the Sacred Land

Another highly important Egyptian god, **Anubis** was considered a canine deity, "The God of Embalming, God of Death, God of Afterlife, and God of Cemeteries". He is famously depicted in his canine form – a human body with a head of a desert dog with a long snout and tall, pricked ears. It was believed that Anubis was the protector of tombs and would punish those who desecrated them.

His canine form is most likely related to the jackals of the desert who were mostly carrion eaters – a clear reference to the process of mummification and death.

He was known as the "Neb-ta-Djeser or the Lord of the Sacred Land, or the Dog Who Swallows Millions". Jackal statues were often used as tomb guardians, most famously in the tomb of **Tutankhamun**.

Bastet – the Cat Goddess

A daughter of Ra, Bastet was the **feline goddess,** with her most popular depiction in the form of a **domestic cat** . She was an important deity and the patron of the ancient Egyptian city of Bubastis.

She is attributed with many feminine roles, and as a "Goddess of Pregnancy, Goddess of Motherhood, Goddess of the Household, Goddess of Sex and Fertility, Goddess of Cosmetics, and Goddess of Women". Her name translates to "She of the Ointment Jar", and she is also called the "Ruler of the Divine Field". Mummified cats were sacred to Bastet.

Horus – God of Kingship

One of the oldest and most important Egyptian gods, **Horus** is considered the tutelary, "Patron Deity of all of Egypt, and the God of the Sky and Kingship". He shared the characteristics with Ra, the sun deity, and is presented in the form of a human with the head of a falcon, wearing the pschent – the crown that symbolizes **kingship** over the whole of Egypt.

- **Serapis: God of Fertility and the Afterlife that United Greeks and Egyptians**
- **Elongated Skulls and Indecipherable Language: What Does the Mysterious Starving of Saqqara Sculpture Mean?**
- **Maat: Ancient Egyptian Goddess of Truth, Justice and Morality**

His name is often translated as "The One up High" or "The Distant One". The symbol of the **Eye of Horus** was the symbol of protection and royal power, and the rulers were known as Shemsu-Hor, the followers of Horus.

Osiris – the God of Rebirth

One of the most prominent of the deities, **Osiris** is the "God of Fertility, God of Rebirth and Afterlife, God of Life and Vegetation". He is associated with the underworld and eternal life, and his power allowed for vegetation to grow and the dead to be reborn.

The ancient Egyptians connected seeds with Osiris, dead, and as the seeds sprout so does Osiris come back to life. Corn seeds were mixed with clay and mummified in the form of Osiris. Such mummies were numerous, and even excavated to reveal barley and wheat seeds that survived to the present day.

Ptah – The Creator of the World

The "God of Artisans, God of Architects, and God of Craftsmen, and the Creator God of Memphis and All Things", **Ptah** was a very important deity. He was considered the one who thought the world into existence, and the one who existed before all other gods.

He was the "Lord of Eternity", the "Master of Justice", and the "One Who Listens to Prayers". He was considered as creator of the city Memphis, an important city which the Egyptian knew as Hikuptah, the word which evolved into the modern word for Egypt.

Ptah was presented as a partially mummified man, with green skin and a smooth head, holding the combined scepter of ankh-djed-was. His temples were present all over Egypt.

Set – Lord of Storms

The "God of fire, God of Chaos, God of Violence, God of the Desert, and God of Trickery", **Set** was also known as Seth or Setesh. He is presented in the form of the mysterious Set animal – a canine-like beast that resembles a jackal or a fox.

He was the "Lord of Storms" and "The Red Desert". In the extensive Egyptian mythology Set played important roles – he repelled the serpent Apep, the embodiment of Chaos, and also killed his own brother Osiris, who would be avenged by Horus. "Powerful is His Arm" as a popular epithet associated with Set.

The Warrior Goddess Sekhmet

Fierce, ferocious, yet sensual, Sekhmet was the "Warrior Goddess of Healing". She was depicted as a woman with the head of a lioness, one of the fiercest animals the Egyptians knew. Sekhmet was known as "Lady of the Messengers of Death" and "Smiter of Nubians", "The One Who Was Before the Gods Were" and "The Lady of the Place of the Beginning of Time".

- **Think Egypt Think Magic: Essence of Spells, Incantations, Amulets and Absolute Faith – Part II**
- **Star Maps and the Secrets of Senenmut: Astronomical Ceilings and the Hopi Vision of Earth**
- **Hair-Raising Tales of Paranormal Animals that Possess Humans, See Death, and Act as Messengers of the Gods**

She is one of the oldest most important deities, and although feminine and beautiful, she was a wrathful and fierce deity. Her attributes were seemingly contradictory, but in fact two complementary aspects – death and destruction, and protection and healing.

The Crocodile God Sobek

Another very important deity, **Sobek**, the "Lord of the Dark Water", played a great role in the everyday lives of ancient Egyptians. With the Nile being the living heart of the entire kingdom, and also filled with deadly crocodiles, Sobek formed as a crocodile deity, a way to appease the beasts of the Nile and ensure a safe passage.

He was invoked for protection on the river, but his nature was also related to war, masculinity, and military prowess. He was presented as a man with a crocodile's head, and he was widely attested through the history of Egypt. Crocodiles were mummified in his honor.

Taweret - Goddess of Fertility and Childbirth

This goddess is widely attested as one of the more important deities and was important for over 2000 years. Taweret, whose name means "She Who is Great", had the form of a female hippopotamus – a fearsome depiction of an enormous beast with elements of a hippo, a lion, and a Nile crocodile.

Taweret was a beneficent "Goddess of Fertility and Childbirth", as well as a protector from the evil forces. Her form was believed to protect the women in labor. Small hippopotamus statuettes were often placed into tombs of the deceased – to help with the successful rebirth after death.

Taweret charms were also widely popular and worn by pregnant women. She was very popular among the common folk and was also known as "Mistress of the Horizon", "Mistress of Pure Water", and "Lady of the Birth House".

Thoth – God of Knowledge

Djehuty, more popularly known as **Thoth**, was the Ibis-headed god, the "Keeper of Time" and "The Lord of Writing". His usual form is that of a man with the head of an ibis or the head of a baboon. Both animals were sacred to the Egyptians.

He had many associations through history but was mostly the "Deity of Knowledge, the Scribe of the Gods, the Author of all Science and Philosophy, the God of Wisdom". His form in the underworld was Aani, the baboon god of the equilibrium.

Baboons and ibises were mummified as offerings to Thoth. There are an estimated 500,000 mummified ibises in the Saqqara burial grounds alone. And in the catacombs of Tune el-Gebel, roughly four million ibis burials were uncovered.

Heqet – Goddess of Childbirth

The **frog**-headed "Goddess of Fertility and Childbirth", Heqet was the female counterpart of Khnum, the creator god. It was believed that Heqet gave life to the body and the soul of a royal infant, which was shaped out of clay on the Khnum's potter's wheel.

She was the deity associated with the last moments of birth, as well as the yearly flooding of the Nile, and the frogs that were left in the fertile soil after the water receded. Heqet was depicted as either a frog-headed woman, or a frog seated on a lotus, and frog amulets were worn by women in childbirth. She was known as "She Who Hastens the Birth".

Egyptian Gods – In Unison with Nature

From this glimpse in to the very colorful and highly imaginative religion of the Egyptians, we can realize that they lived in unison with the nature around them. They depended on the river Nile which gave them life and crops and water, but also death and danger. The gods of Egypt are largely the faces of nature, and the Egyptians sought to appease them and master the nature around them.

And moreover, they believed in an afterlife and rebirth, placing a lot of emphasis on fertility and protection at birth. All of these beliefs are attested in archaeological and written data and show a complex relationship between life and death in the ancient Egyptian society. And you will have to agree – descending into this wondrous world of gods and goddesses is an inspiring and captivating journey!

According to Plutarco: "Ra went to heaven and Osiris became Pharaoh of Egypt with Isis and they built Thebes [the present Luxor]."

Path 11: The Original Black Jews and the 12 Tribes of Judah

The ancient Hebrew were Black people. Consequently Jesus and his disciples were also Black, as were the early Prophets and Saints. The following Christian icons are mainly from the Orthodox Christian Church, which unlike the Catholic and Protestant Churches seems to have resisted the urge to make everyone White.

The Catholic conversion is so complete, that of the three known Black Popes, not even a Whitenized image of any of them is known to exist. There were three African Popes, who came from the region of North Africa, and although there are no authentic portraits of these popes, there are drawings and references in the Catholic Encyclopedia as to their being of African background. And all are saints! All of these Popes accomplished many noble tasks during their papacy. However, this seems to be overlooked because of their ethnic backgrounds

The icons following iconic images were likely created long after they were dead. The Orthodox Christians seemingly being content with just giving the subjects exaggerated White features (notice the noses are even narrower than the White Saints) - White people are funny!

One should also not be fooled by the Coptic (descendants of the ancient Greeks of Egypt) image of a Black Jesus that is a rarity, hidden away in their museum. All of their modern icons have been converted to White. One can't help but wonder if White Christians, who profess such love for Jesus and Christianity, appreciate the rather gross irony of their practices. Many of the saints were black. They were martyred in service to, and defense of, their black ancestry.

Yet, they show these ancient Blacks - Jesus included; and our memories of them, such disrespect and contempt, by depicting them differently than what they proudly were. Apparently no sacrifice is sufficient to dissuade Whites from their natural habits: Greedily gobble up everything of value, then claim that it was they who created it - there is a lesson there somewhere. Saint Piran is included for comparison purposes only.

But before the modern era of pathetic White racism, with its White fright of all things Black, and Black identity theft. Where Khazar, Turks are the new Hebrews, and Osman Turks are the new Berbers, Egyptians, Arabs, and Middle-Easterners. Before every ancient Black figure encountered in a museum or book was explained away as a Nubian-Ethiopian, a Slave, or a servant: All people knew Hebrews to be Black people, and depicted them as Black people.

Christ and his disciples.
Painted wooden panel in the Coptic Museum, Cairo.

Apostle Nicanor the Deacon of the Seventy

Saints Nicanor, Prochorus, Timon, and Parmenas, Apostles of the Seventy were among the first deacons in the Church of Christ.

In the Acts of the Holy Apostles (6:1-6) it is said that the twelve Apostles chose seven men: Stephen, Philip, Prochorus, Nicanor, Timon, Parmenas and Nicholas, full of the Holy Spirit and wisdom, and appointed them to serve as deacons.

They are commemorated together on July 28, although they died at various times and in various places.

Although St Nicanor suffered on the same day that the holy Protomartyr Stephen (December 27) and many other Christians were killed by stoning, he is commemorated on December 28.

The Holy Prophet Nahum

The Holy Prophet Nahum, whose name means "God consoles," was from the village of Elkosh (Galilee). He lived during the seventh century B.C. The Prophet Naum prophesies the ruin of the Assyrian city of Nineveh because of its iniquity, the destruction of the Israelite kingdom, and the blasphemy of King Sennacherib against God. The Assyrian king Ashurbanipal died in 632 B.C., and over the next two decades, his empire began to crumble. Nineveh fell in 612 B.C.

Nahum differs from most of the prophets in as much as he does not issue any call to repentance, nor does he denounce Israel for infidelity to God.

Details of the prophet's life are unknown. He died at the age of forty-five, and was buried in his native region. He is the seventh of the Twelve Minor Prophets

The Prophet Nahum and St Nahum of Ochrid (December 23) are invoked for people with mental disorders.

Saint Anna

St Anna, the mother of the Virgin Mary, was the youngest daughter of the priest Nathan from Bethlehem, descended from the tribe of Levi. She married St Joachim (September 9), who was a native of Galilee.

For a long time St Anna was childless, but after twenty years, through the fervent prayer of both spouses, an angel of the Lord announced to them that they would be the parents of a daughter, who would bring blessings to the whole human race.

The Orthodox Church does not accept the teaching that the Mother of God was exempted from the consequences of ancestral sin (death, corruption, sin, etc.) at the moment of her conception by virtue of the future merits of Her Son. Only Christ was born perfectly holy and sinless, as St Ambrose of Milan teaches in Chapter Two of his Commentary on Luke.

The Holy Virgin was like everyone else in her mortality, and in being subject to temptation, although she committed no personal sins. She was not a deified creature removed from the rest of humanity. If this were the case, she would not have been truly human, and the nature that Christ took from her would not have been truly human either. If Christ does not truly share our human nature, then the possibility of our salvation is in doubt.

The Conception of the Virgin Mary by St Anna took place at Jerusalem. The many icons depicting the Conception by St Anna show the Most Holy Theotokos trampling the serpent underfoot.

"In the icon St. Joachim and Anna are usually depicted with hands folded in prayer; their eyes are also directed upward and they contemplate the Mother of God, Who stands in the air with outstretched hands; under Her feet is an orb encircled by a serpent (symbolizing the devil), which strives to conquer all the universe by its power."

There are also icons in which St Anna holds the Most Holy Virgin on her left arm as an infant. On St Anna's face is a look of reverence. A large ancient icon, painted on canvas, is located in the village of Minkovetsa in the Dubensk district of Volhynia diocese. From ancient times this Feast was especially venerated by pregnant women in Russia.

According to the Bible, the Jewish leader Jacob had 12 sons. Each of these sons—Reuven, Shimon, Levi, Judah, Issachar, Zevulun, Dan, Naphtali, Gad, Asher, Joseph, and Benjamin—became the father of a separate tribe. Known as the 12 Tribes of Israel, they settled on both sides of the Jordan River.

In 722 B.C., the Assyrians conquered Israel and ten tribes were exiled. They were "lost" to history.

The tribes of Benjamin and Judah remained, maintaining Jerusalem as their capital. Most Jews are believed to be descended from these tribes.

What Became of the Lost Tribes?

Scholars have claimed to discover their descendants in North and South America, England, China, Japan, Burma, Africa, Arabia, Persia, Central Asia, and Siberia, among other places. Other writers assert they were never lost to begin with, that they returned to live with the tribes of Benjamin and Judah.

Despite the confusion, evidence linking certain isolated peoples to Judaism is strong:

Southern Africa: Genetic testing has determined that men of the Lemba, a black, Bantu-speaking people, have the Y chromosome of the Jewish priestly class, the Cohanim. It is rare among non-Jews. The Lemba observe kosher-like dietary laws

Ethiopia: Some 65,000 Ethiopian Jews from different groups have moved to Israel since 1974. Israel's chief rabbis believe they are descended from the lost tribe of Dan. Others say they are descended from King Solomon and the Queen of Sheba. Many Ethiopians were so isolated they thought all Jews were black. They did not know of the standardization of Jewish law, the Talmud, or Hanukkah.

The original Jews in Africa 2000 years ago were a Black African people as an ethnic group. (Massey: Egypt Light of the Word p.501) Many of them still are Black, in northern Africa such as the Falasha Jews of Ethiopia.

A New York Times editorial (3/2/84) described them as "a lost tribe that has kept its identity for more than 2,000 years in a remote corner of Africa." Abraham, ancestor of the Hebrews, was from Chaldea; the ancient Chaldeans were Black. In fact, Africa takes its name from Ophren, a son of Abraham by his wife, Keturah (Whiston: The Life and Works of Flavius Josephus p.50) Like Jesus, Mary and Joseph, the lineage of Ethiopian Emperor, Haile Selassie also goes back to Judah—through Solomon/Queen of Sheba and King David.

Roman historian Tacitus wrote that many of his time believed that the Jews "were a race of Ethiopian origin." The Bible classifies the Ethiopians and Jews together, "Are ye not as children of the Ethiopians unto me, O children of Israel? saith the Lord." (Amos 9:7) Black Paul is mistaken for an "Egyptian" and declares himself to be a "Jew." (Acts 21:37-39, 22: 2,3) That the Jews got their language, religion and culture from the Canaanites and Sumerians through Babylon, is well documented by historians. The original ancient Hebrew alphabet was identical to that of the Phoenicians. "Semitic languages" are really dialectical variants of African languages.

The word Semite is from semi which means half. Half what? Half BLACK! (mulatto!) Semite refers to the descendants of Shem, one of Noah's sons. The word originates from the Latin prefix semi which means half. "Half Black and half white... therefore Black (since Black is genetically dominant)" points out Dr. Cress Welsing. Historian Cheikh Anta Diop also points out that the "Semitic" arises in the 4th millennia B.C. from crossbreeding between Black inhabitants of the holy land and white northern invaders.

While many Semites (such as Jews and gypsies) have mixed so much with whites that they've forgotten or deny their African roots, racism (white supremacy) will never let them forget this no matter how light-skinned they become, as proved by Hitler, who mandated their destruction because they were classified by whites as "non-white" people originating in Africa. The very word gypsy means "out of Egypt."

African Americans are largely descendants of the original Black Jews! The original Biblical Jews were Black African people who were ruthlessly persecuted by the white man (Romans). The prophet Jesus was a Black Jew who was born during this time. The Roman-Jewish War in 66 A.D. marked the peak of this persecution and the end of the original Black Jews (Hebrew-Israelites) as a nation.

As predicted by Jesus, in this war Jerusalem was overthrown, the Temple was destroyed and the Black Hebrews were scattered. (Mat. 24:15-21, Luke 21: 5,6, 20-24) The loss of life was appalling. So many Hebrews were slain that the whole lake of Galilee was red with blood and covered with corpses. The noted historian, Josephus estimated that one million one hundred thousand perished in the siege of Jerusalem alone, reports Hugh Schonfield in his book The Passover Plot p.192-195, which describes this massive genocide.

* Seeking to escape destruction, millions of original Black Biblical Jews fled into AFRICA!

* Centuries later, their descendants were captured and sold into slavery in the Americas! Ella Hughley's remarkable booklet The Truth About Black Biblical Hebrew-Israelites exposes and summarizes important details of this suppressed subject. She writes "Many of the Israelites... who managed to escape their persecutors during the Roman-Jewish War subsequently migrated to West Africa, and 16,000 years later their descendants were captured and brought to America in chains by cruel slave-traders."

She quotes the noted Jewish historian, Josephus from his book The Great Roman-Jewish War: 66-70, where he writes about this Jewish dispersion and captivity. "General Vaspasian and his son Caesar Titus fought against the Jews. Millions of Jews fled into Africa, among other places, fleeing from Roman persecution and starvation during the siege." In African Origins of Major Wester Religions p.75, Dr. Yusef ben-Jochannan writes "there were many Hebrew (Jewish) tribes that were of indigenous African origin, These African Jews were caught in a rebellion in Cyrene ... during 115 C.E.

This rebellion also marked the beginning of a mass Jewish migration southward into Sudan of West Africa." Arab historian, Ibn Battuta writes of finding Jews scattered across North and West Africa during his travels. The Hebrewisms of numerous tribes, especially in West Africa is well documented.

If the original Jews were Black, where did white Jews come from? There are two main types of white Jews; the Edomites and the Khazars. Edomites are the descendants of Esau, who was born ruddy (red) and hairy according to the Bible. (Gen. 25:25) This describes the "white" man; he is red (all shades) and hairy. Esau was the albino, fraternal twin brother of Jacob, the father of the original Black Israelites. The white Edomites and Black Israelites were constantly in strife against one another.

In fact, the Edomites fought the Black Jews in the Roman-Jewish War. At a later period in history, the Edomites (Idumeans) were conquered and forced to become "Jews." The European Khazars became "Jews" in 740 A.D. (see below) Neither groups are descended from the house of Israel! Khazars make up over 90% of the so-called "Jews!" (Hatonn)

The world's best kept secret? Hughley writes "These groups... [Khazars esp., plus Edomite and other ethnic groups] make up modern Jewry today. Although the black Hebrew-Israelites are the real descendants of ancient Israel, this truth is not known by many and it is 'the world's best kept secret.' Because of slavery and scattering, the Hebrew-Israelites are not known to the world as true Israel...

Some scholars, teachers and ministers teach that God has completely cast them away, but God said, 'I have chosen thee, and have not cast thee away.' (Isa. 41:9, last part.) [& Rm. ch.11] Although the children of Israel went into captivity, a remnant has returned as was predicted. The prophecy of Ezekiel 37th chapter tells of the spiritual resurrection of the people of Israel, who will be perpetually betrothed to their God in truth and in righteousness." There are numerous Black-Hebrew congregations in America. "Temple Bethel" is the largest & oldest (in Belleville, VA).

"Jews" were a heavy part of the African slave trade in the America! Compiled from Jewish documents, The Secret Relationship Between Blacks and Jews by the Nation of Islam reveals the vast Jewish involvement in the Atlantic slave trade. "Jews" were also major slave sellers during the Middle Ages. (Van Sertima: African Presence in Early Europe p.161) These "Jewish" slave-sellers were probably not "real Jews" at all but Khazars. (see below)

Counterfeit Jews: the hated, white "Khazars" who have usurped the real Jews! ... Historians are now recognizing that the majority of eastern so-called "Jews" are actually "Khazars" and have NO Semitic roots whatsoever! The Khazars are impostors: well-suppressed knowledge is emerging about this war-like tribe of whites that rose to power in Eastern Europe and were hated by the other whites they conquered due to their severe, exploitative treatment of them. The Khazars all converted to Judaism as a political ploy during the Middle Ages. It appears that they learned all they could from the real Hebrews before usurping them, selling them into slavery (or killing them) and taking over in their place,—using the corrupted form of Judaism to hide behind while continuing their treachery right into modern times.

Much of Europe's historical hate for "Jews" is hate for the ruthless Khazars who continued to be hated in spite of becoming "Jews." In fact, the word "Jew" originated during the 1700s to label them! (Hatonn: p.3, 17) Counterfeit Blessings—The Anti-Christ by Any Name: Khazars by G.C. Hatonn, exposes that the Khazars are the real "anti-Semites" who have labeled themselves as Zionists and "Jews" to deceive the world in furthering their own plans for global and political conquest.

The Ashkenazi Jews in Israel right now are those in Gen 10:3 which are said to be of the grandson of Japhet. Since Ashkenazi Jews aren't of the 12 tribes.. Where are the 12 tribes.. Theology will keep fooling the world about that even when the Bible said the 12tribes will never return to Israel physically again until Christ returns. EDUCATION AND RELIGION was intentionally meant to be deceptive. They don't want to real Israelites to remember their identity. Anyway, they already waking up and are starting to return to their heritage. Rev 2:9 and Rev 3:9 bear the records of the fake Jews that are currently calling themselves Jew-ish. Why would you put -ish at the back of your identity? Imagine referring to something as Brown-ish. It means to be like brown… but not really Brown. The same reason why they call themselves Israelis and not Israelites. Just to still keep the distinction, but people will never see that.

The ancient Jews (Hebrews) were black. They lived in Israel. When Moses got the slaves released from Egypt, they tried to go back to Israel, but found the land inhabited by a Germanic people who had migrated from Europe. The religious artifacts left by the Hebrews were appropriated and mixed with their own religion. The Germanic people didn't know that the Hebrews would ever return. Moses realized the people were not equipped for warfare, so he took them across the desert and along the coast of Africa.

Due to excessive inbreeding, Egypt, a black man's land, became weak and was conquered by the Greeks, Arabs and Romans. The men were mostly wiped out, but many large boys were castrated and forced into slavery as it was illegal for Egyptians to marry other Egyptians. The surviving Egyptian women were married off to the conqueror men or into concubinage.

At that time, Egyptians, Hebrews and Ethiopians all looked alike. That's why it wasn't readily known that Moses was not Egyptian. Europeans and modern-day Egyptians all knew historically that Moses was a black man, because they saw the statues way before modern libraries and internet. That is also the reason why they have such difficulty in finding out where many of the Royal Tombs are and trying to decipher the hieroglyphics because they killed the people who had that knowledge when they conquered Egypt. Also lost in history is the magic of the ancient Egyptian Pharaohs.

How did Jesus and the Hebrews become White?

How did the Hebrews turn White? Of course they didn›t really; except in the imaginations, and then the lying histories of Albino people. Who for probably practical reasons, decided that Hebrews, and the Blacks who originally lived in and ruled over, the Country's they took over as a result of the "Thirty Years War" on the continent and the British "Civil Wars" of the 1600s.

These were of course actually "Race Wars" with religion as the focal point. These wars pitted Europe's ancient Black and Catholic Rulers against the rebellious Albinos who had "In-mass" been chased out of their Homelands in Asia by the Mongols and into the Black lands of Europe. Black Europe was never "Densely Populated", so this massive influx of millions upon millions of Asian Albinos was sure to cause a "Seed Change" in Europe: and of course it did, it just took over two thousand years for it to happen.

The intricacies of what actually happened in Europe is still well hidden by the Albinos, but we do know that the expulsion of the last Albino tribe from Asia, the "Turks": was the last nail in the coffin for Black Europe. Fortunately for us, the Turks being chased out of Asia, and their subsequent machinations in the West, is well covered by the University of Calgary in their on-line course titled "The End of Europe›s Middle Ages" which is designed to assist students engaged in Renaissance, Reformation and Early Modern studies who lack a background in medieval European history.

Intended to provide a brief overview of the conditions at the end of Europe's Middle Ages, the tutorial is presented in a series of chapters that summarize the economic, political, religious and intellectual environment of the fourteenth and fifteenth centuries. In the main, the tutorial is rudimentary, but the part on the Turks is quite good, that is why it is listed here. The tutorial seems to be in partnership with Encyclopedia Britannica, which has a link and search panel on the pages. Note: some browsers have problems with the pages.

Europe

As the Asian Albinos crossed into Eastern Europe, the Black Romans forced them to convert to Christianity (Catholicism); later one of the Turkic tribes, the Khazars, converted to Judaism. Christianity seemed to serve them well until they had gathered enough manpower to take over, then it became clear that like every Black civilization that came before, they needed their own religion for Albinos to rally-round. Thus the creation of Protestantism, a new religion for Albinos.

Today, the only Protestant European countries or areas with significant Protestant populations are Germany (home of the Black Holy Roman Empire) and Britain (home of the deposed Black House of Stuart). Both Albino Germany and Albino Britain, were the major players in the 1600s "Race Wars".

The Racist United States Albino population is mainly made up of Albino Germans and Albino British people. Denmark, Finland, Iceland, Norway, Sweden, and the eastern, northern and western parts of Switzerland also have Protestant populations. The rest of Albino Europe went back to Catholicism once Albinos had taken control of the Catholic Church. As a point of interest: Roughly 48.9% of Americans are Protestants, 23.0% are Catholics.

Slavs and Blacks

Which brings up a very strange predilection among Russians, and Slavs in general; unlike all other Albinos, they have steadfastly refused to destroy "all" of the paintings of their past Black Kings, and refused to create fake White images of religious icons. Almost all of their Black Saints and other religious figures are still depicted as Black (though with Caucasian features). But the most amazing thing is that the Russians still display portraits of Black "Peter the Great" and his son on the Hermitage Museum Site. We have no idea why they do that – conscience?

It is worth mentioning, that the Hebrews were just as literate, and just as artistic as the other Black civilizations around them. The reason that we have to depend on outside sources for pictures of them, is because Whites destroyed all that the Hebrews ever created. Even down to the very religious writings that they claim to worship by.

That fact is that ALL Hebrew writings, even the SEPTUAGINT {the original Bible}, which was only roughly Hebrew (it was made for the Greek King of Egypt, Ptolemy II (Philadelphus) in 282-246 B.C.), has been destroyed. Everything except for the "Dead Sea Scrolls" which were found in 1947, in Qumran, a village situated about twenty miles east of Jerusalem.

The Scrolls are under the joint custody of the Catholic Church and the Israelis. The translated contents of those Scrolls has never been made public, and probably never will be - no doubt the differences in teachings and facts would be irreconcilable. (A few inconsequential snippets have been made public - the entire Scrolls is a huge work, which contains the entire old Testament plus many other works).

Why wasn't the material in these pages destroyed? Because after it's fall, Assyria came under the control of the Persian Empire, which was itself a Black Empire. It then came under the control of Greeks, who were at that time, seeking to merge with the Black Persians, not in denying that they were Black people. Then Assyria again came under Persian control, and then finally under the control of the original Black Arabs. So at the time when Whites were destroying vestiges of Black history, they had no access to the Assyrian artifacts.

But at those times when Whites did have control of an area, they seem to have been very through in destroying all vestiges of the former Black inhabitants; there is nothing left to suggest that Carthage was a Black city, Mesopotamia and the Indus Valley civilizations are some of the oldest known, yet very little is left - next to nothing in the Indus valley.

Ancient Anatolia (Turkey), was home to many great and famous civilizations, but very little has been found there. The Egyptian artifacts, of which there are many, were mostly recovered in modern times, when Whites rather than simply destroy, instead modify artifacts; sometimes just by breaking the noses off, in order to make them look like White people, and then proudly display them as proof of the White man's greatness.

The Khazars, a Turkish tribe who had established a Kingdom in the Caucasus region, and converted to Judaism in the 8th century A.D. Must have seen the doings of the Romans and Greeks, and seen it as an opportunity for them to take over the Hebrew identity, and thus control of the orthodox branch of the Hebrew religion - which indeed they did. They logically thinking that if Jesus can be White, why not then, the entire Hebrew nation - which was by then a diaspora anyway. The Islamist side-stepped the entire issue by forbidding imagery of any kind.

Color struck: America's White Jesus is a global export and false product By Wesley Muhammad, PhD.

What color was Jesus? Most American Christians—Black and White—would dismiss this question as both irrelevant and unanswerable as the Gospels fail to give us a physical description. The irony is that most of these same Americans in their heart of hearts are pretty confident any way that they know what color Jesus was. They attend churches with images of a tall, long haired, full bearded White man depicted in stained glass windows or painted on walls, and they return home to the same depictions framed in their living room or illustrating their family Bibles.

Further compounding the irony is the fact that America actually has an obsession with the (presumed) color of Christ and has exported her White Americanized Savior around the world, as recently documented by Edward J. Blum and Paul Harvey in their book, The Color of Christ: The Son of God and the Saga of Race in America (2012).

In fact, the world's most popular and recognizable image of Christ is a distinctly 19th-20th century American creation. It is true that versions of the "White Christ" appear in European art as early as the 4th century of the Christian era, but these images coexisted with other, nonwhite representations throughout European history.

The popularity of the cult of the Black Madonna and Black Christ throughout Europe is evidence of the fact that the European 'White Christs' never acquired the authority and authenticity that the White Christ now has globally. This Christ and his authority are American phenomena. As a predominantly Protestant nation Early America rejected the imaging of Christ that characterized European Catholicism.

By the mid-19th century, however, in response to American expansion, splintering during the Civil War and subsequent reconstructing, "Whiteness" took on a new significance and a newly- empowered "White Jesus" rose to prominence as the sanctifying symbol of a new national unity and power. As Blum and Harvey observe:

"By wrapping itself with the alleged form of Jesus, whiteness gave itself a holy face ... With Jesus as white, Americans could feel that sacred whiteness stretched back in time thousands of years and forward in sacred space to heaven and the second coming ... The white Jesus promised a white past, a white present, and a future of white glory."

As America rose to superpower status in the 20th century she became the world's leading producer and global exporter of White Jesus imagery through film, art, American business, and Christian missions, and has thereby defined the world's view of the Son of God. This globally recognizable Jesus is a totally American product.

Indeed, he is an American. Warner Sallman's iconic image of Jesus called Head of Christ (1941) became the most widely reproduced piece of artwork in world history and its depiction the most recognizable face of Jesus in the world. By the 1990s it had been printed over 500 million times and achieved global iconic status.

With smooth white skin, long, flowing blondish-brown hair, long beard and blue eyes, this Nordic Christ consciously disguised any hint of Jesus's Semitic, oriental origin—and departed from the older European depictions. It both shaped and was shaped by emerging American ideas of whiteness. The beloved White Jesus of today's world was Made in America.

What, then, did Jesus actually look like? Despite the absence of a detailed description of Jesus's physical appearance in the Gospels (though John the Revelator saw the risen Christ apparently with wooly hair and black feet, Rev. 1:14-15), there are non-biblical evidences that actually allow us to visualize the Son of God from Nazareth.

Revelation 1:14-15 - King James Version (KJV)

14) His head and his hairs were white like wool, as white as snow; and his eyes were as a flame of fire;

15) And his feet like unto fine brass, as if they burned in a furnace; and his voice as the sound of many waters.

The first century Jewish writer Josephus (37-100 AD) penned the earliest non-biblical testimony of Jesus. He reportedly had access to official Roman records on which he based his information and in his work Halosis or the "Capture (of Jerusalem)," written around 72 A.D., Josephus discussed "the human form of Jesus and his wonderful works."

Unfortunately his texts have passed through Christian hands which altered them, removing offensive material. Fortunately, however, Biblical scholar Robert Eisler in a classic 1931 study of Josephus' Testimony was able to reconstruct the unaltered testimony based on a newly-discovered Old Russian translation that preserved the original Greek text. According to Eisler's reconstruction, the oldest non-Biblical description of Jesus read as follows:

"At that time also there appeared a certain man of magic power ... if it be meet to call him a man, [whose name is Jesus], whom [certain] Greeks call a son of [a] God, but his disciples [call] the true prophet ... he was a man of simple appearance, mature age, black-skinned (melagchrous), short growth, three cubits tall, hunchbacked, prognathous (lit. 'with a long face' [macroprosopos]), a long nose, eyebrows meeting above the nose ... with scanty [curly] hair, but having a line in the middle of the head after the fashion of the Nazaraeans, with an undeveloped beard."

This short, black-skinned, mature, hunchbacked Jesus with a unibrow, short curly hair and undeveloped beard bears no resemblance to the Jesus Christ taken for granted today by most of the Christian world: the tall, long haired, long bearded, white-skinned and blue eyed Son of God. Yet, this earliest textual record matches well the earliest iconographic evidence.

The earliest visual depiction of Jesus is a painting found in 1921 on a wall of the baptismal chamber of the house-church at Dura Europos, Syria and dated around 235 A.D. The Jesus that is "Healing the Paralytic Man" (Mark 2:1-12) is short and dark-skinned with a small curly afro - see below.

This description has now been supported by the new science of forensic anthropology. In 2002 British forensic scientists and Israeli archaeologists reconstructed what they believe is the most accurate image of Jesus based off of data obtained from the multi-disciplinary approach. In December 2002 Popular Science Magazine published a cover story on the findings which confirm that Jesus would have been short, around 5"1', hair "short with tight curls," a weather-beaten face "which would have made him appear older," dark eyes and complexion: "he probably looked a great deal more like a dark-skinned Semite than Westerners are used to seeing," they concluded. The textual, visual, and scientific evidence agrees, then: Jesus likely was a short, dark-skinned Semite with short curly hair and dark eyes.

Colossians 1:15 describes Christ as the "image of the unseen God" and in the Gospel of John (12:45; 14:9) Jesus declares that whoever sees him has seen God. What Jesus "looks like" then is not irrelevant as it is in some way a pointer to God Himself.

CHAPTER 11

TRACING BIOLOGICAL DIFFERENCES TO EXTRATERRESTRIAL EXPERIMENTS

Path 12: The Metagene Factor and the Blue Planet Project

THE METAGENE FACTOR: The Metagene is a biological variant lying dormant in select members of the human race [especially on planet earth], until an instant of extraordinary physical and emotional over-stress activates it. (Apparently a latent self-preservation 'gene' capable of producing seemingly 'superhuman' abilities in earth humans during times of extreme stress or crisis. - Branton)

That's an energo-chemical, in response to adverse stimuli. A chromosomal combustion takes place, as the Metagene takes the source of bio stress, be it chemical, radioactivity, or whatever and turns the potential energo-response into a catalyst for genetic change. The main focus of the catalyst power is a gland in the middle of the human brain called the PINEAL gland, and the nutrient for increasing the Pineal's action is the adrenaline. The Metagene factor gives the ability of Psionic Power [for better or worse].

The main interest of the Aliens, especially the Grays, is to understand and control the Metagene for their own race. They try to do this using Biological Experiments to make Hybrids from both humans and aliens.

They believe perhaps the MEN FROM PLANET EARTH ARE THE DEADLIEST CREATURES IN THE UNIVERSE. Because ONLY on Earth people are apparently capable of generating the Metagene Factor, which means Natural Psionic ability, "Real Power" (Note: Power for good OR evil, you might say.)

One of the reasons that humans on earth are being controlled/harnessed as is the case with the Nazi-NSA-Military-Industrial space forces, or DENIED advanced interplanetary technology as in the case of those who have NOT been brought under their control, is simply because the aliens—especially the malevolents—are terrified that if a FREE non-collectivist human society from earth gets a foothold in space, then they/we would pose a deadly threat to their alien agendas of conquest and manipulation throughout the galaxy.

This is why they are INTENT on taming or harnessing the Metagene factor as they have done with the fascist forces based in Antarctica via massive mind control, so that these forces can be channeled as 'human shields' or 'warriors' to fight their battles in space against interstellar cultures who would otherwise resist the activities of the draconian collective.

We must DEMAND from the Military-Industrial complex which has been built with OUR tax dollars—and which is being deeply influenced by alien/fascist forces—that they CEASE from selling-us-out, and share their interplanetary technology with the rest of us, so that we as a whole can access the stars rather than just a core of super-wealthy and alien-controlled 'elite'.

If we as a Constitutional Republic [and Congress] rightfully take over control of whatever space projects have and are being financed BY OUR TAX DOLLARS, then the open space policy and public conscience itself will prevent these space forces from engaging in any unjustified military actions against peaceful worlds that would defy the foundational ethics of the U.S. Constitution on the one hand; or will prevent us from allying ourselves with any exploitative and manipulative alien force on the other hand. - Branton).

The principle races in the Universe are psychologically the same. The pure cold logic is a normal order to most important races. Basic sameness makes for predictability and security, the enemy one knows, are the ones you can guard against. This is not the case with [unpredictable] mankind.

While most are uniformly human, some [many more, apparently, than anyone had dreamed] possess a latent tendency towards super humanity, Natural Psionic Abilities. That in itself could prove dangerous for any idea of Alien domination on Earth.

(Note: for instance, some Terrans have the ability to 'scan' the UPF or universal psionic field with their superconscious minds via projecting and focusing their 'magnetic' body at various levels on a conscious or unconscious basis, and any subjective 'danger' that is detected through this process is converted to consciousness via 'intuition'.

This might be compared with 'remote viewing', which is simply the human brains' ability to 'tune-in-to' and 'ride' the Universal Psionic Field or the 'Flowline' like a biochemical radio receiver scanning the psionic 'air' waves—and psionic-waves ARE a tangible energy-form that can be measured just as radio waves can. The electro-magneto-gravitic 'grid' of any planet, and supposedly the EMG fields which connect the planets and stars at a subtle level, serve as the energy 'web' in which thought forms are trapped and contained.

Humans are multi-dimensional beings and therefore have the ability to perceive the vast 'reservoirs' of thought forms within these interstellar grids on an intuitive level, for instance when they are dreaming. During the dream-state the brain operates on a lower frequency—and what we might call psionic LONG waves are produced which can reach out and connect with others 'long' waves on the same frequency, or connect with the psionic field itself and observe the 'psychic atmosphere' resident within any certain area through tapping-in to the reservoir of 'thought forms' there.

This would explain why people often have 'vivid' dreams near high energy grid areas, simply because these areas tend to 'trap' more thought form, psionic or psychic energy residue than do other areas. Also astral, human or animal lifeforms which have become 'trapped' within these psionic energy grids by encountering powerful EMG zones like that which exists in the Bermuda Triangle area—essentially having entered into or become part of a "world of thought forms", a dimension density where events and objects are more 'fluid' than they are in the 3rd dimension—might be contacted, for better OR worse, while in the 'dream' state. Not ALL of the 'beings' or even 'dreamscapes' that one encounters within the dream-state are the exclusive products of one's own subconscious mind. - Branton)

By coupling mankind's inherent belligerence with the fact of the Metagene affect, each human is unique and Earth becomes a spawning ground for an unpredictable super-race, "if we have the chance". Others have already demonstrated an awareness of Man's Potential [throughout] human history. This is because the Aliens are here to try to CONTROL Earthlings before WE dominate THEM, and they want our most important secret: THE METAGENE FACTOR, which is the Aliens' only hope.

The main interest of these "secret" organizations (which should also include, Big Pharma, Big Corporations (All the Five Major Co. and their subsidiaries), Scholars, Doctors, Scientist, Occult groups, etc. is to understand (test/ experiment) and control the Meta Gene; and find ways to use it for their own race.

They try to do this by conducting secret Biological Experiments, much like those conducted by the Nazis, to enhance their structure by using the genes of humanity. They believe these select members of humanity are the deadliest creatures in the Universe, and they are on Earth! [Hidden in plain sight]; with Natural Psionic ability, "Real Power" . This is one of the reasons people are being controlled, energy harnessed by Nazi-NSA-Military-Industrial forces.

Their intent is to Tame and Harnessing the Meta Gene, as done with the base in Antarctica via massive mind control, so that these forces can be channeled as 'human shields' or use as 'warriors' to fight their battles in space. In the case of those who have NOT been brought under their control, they are terrified that if a "free" non-collectivist people gets a foothold over them, they would pose a deadly threat to their agendas. While most are uniformly human, some possess a latent tendency towards super humanity, Natural Psionic Abilities. That in itself could prove dangerous for any idea of domination on this planet.

These natural psionic abilities permit those with them to scan the universal psionic field with their superconscious minds via projecting and focusing their 'magnetic' body at various levels on a conscious or unconscious basis, and any subjective 'danger' that is detected through this process is converted to consciousness via 'intuition'.

The electro-magneto-gravitic 'grid' of any planet, and supposedly the EMG fields which connect the planets and stars at a subtle level, serve as the energy 'web' in which thought forms are trapped and contained. Humans are multi-dimensional beings and therefore have the ability to perceive the vast 'reservoirs' of thought forms within these interstellar grids on an intuitive level, for instance when they are dreaming.

During the dream-state the brain operates on a lower frequency—and what we might call psionic LONG waves are produced which can reach out and connect with others 'long' waves on the same frequency, or connect with the psionic field itself and observe the 'psychic atmosphere' resident within any certain area through tapping-in to the reservoir of 'thought forms' there.

False Facades of a Failing Virtual Reality

Not ALL of the 'beings' or 'dreamscapes' that one encounters within the dream-state are the exclusive products of one's own subconscious mind as much is created by these malevolent forces. As more and more people are waking-up to the illusion and the lies to keep us trapped in ignorance; control becomes even more difficult for these creatures.

By coupling mankind's inherent belligerence with the energies and talents of humanity's Meta Gene, any threats to Man's Potential can be overthrown.

Truth of the Matter is the "Super-race" isn't Nordic-Aryan; which we all know does not exist, but were created by the Nazis. The True Super-Race is Humanity!

Source:
Dulce Book: https://domoregooddeeds.files.wordpress.com/2013/04/the-dulce-book.pdf

(The above is largely edited from the Dulce Book, which was compiled by Branton. The Dulce Book is a combination of individual reports (accounts of events) that took place at Dulce, New Mexico.)

Tunguska Event

The sudden appearance of unusual abilities in humanity during the late 1930's can be traced to the Tunguska Event of 1908, though the world at large remains completely unaware of this fact

On June 30th 1908, a comet exploded approximately 5 miles above the ground in the Tunguska forest north of Siberia while traveling at an estimated speed of 40 miles per second. An air wave generated by the blast circled the earth twice, with the dust creating unusual sunsets and other atmospheric effects all over Europe.

The explosion produced surface temperatures of 160 degrees Fahrenheit and was as powerful as a 100 megaton hydrogen bomb, larger than any built by mankind. The blast knocked down trees within a 20 mile radius and left no crater or meteoric debris.

A concentration of ablation products (like iron oxide and glassy spheres of fused rock) stretched on a "tongue" 150 miles northwest of the impact site, which would indicate that the comet probably approached from a southeasterly direction. Iridium was found in a peat layer 1 foot below the surface at the site.

The comet itself is believed to have been small, perhaps only 100 to 300 feet in diameter, which would explain why no astronomical sightings were made prior to the impact.

(Note: this actually occurred in the real world, though not everyone agrees it was caused by a small comet. In the Meta-Earth campaign, the Tunguska event wasn't caused by a comet. It was caused by something else entirely. Something which changed the world forever. To find out what actually occurred keep reading.)

The Big Crunch

There are an infinite number of universes besides our own. The Big Bang is the one common origin to them all. All of these "Multiverses" are interlinked in some unknown way.

These universes are constantly expanding, propelled forward by the initial force of the Big Bang. Eventually the universes lose momentum and start to contract. This is called the Big Crunch, the end of time, where everything in the universe is collapsing in upon itself.

In theory, when the Big Crunch occurs in a universe the cycle should renew itself, with the formation of yet another universe. This is what generally occurs, but there have been times in the multiverse when a universe has imploded upon itself and instead of creating a new universe the Primordial energies of that universe have been "shunted" to another universe, altering it in unpredictable ways.

This has occurred at least twice in the campaign universe. The first time it occurred was before the dawn of recorded history. The Primal forces gave rise to Magic and many other supernatural phenomena. Over time these forces diminished, and gradually faded away from mainstream existence.

The second, and most recent time, it occurred was in 1908. The Primal Forces that were released into this reality resulted in the Tunguska Event on Earth which gave rise to superhuman powers and abilities.

Historians note that since the birth of "meta-humanity," the abilities exhibited by meta-humans have become more varied and powerful with each new generation. Initially, only a small percentage were changed. Most of the people who were changed were altered on a genetic level and never realized they were different. Others found that they had gained some minor, unusual ability.

These abilities helped give credibility to the Spiritualist movement and confounded Harry Houdini who was unable to disprove these abilities. During the 1920's these minor abilities helped some "Mystery Men" in their war on crime. It wasn't until the late 1930's, when the second generation metas started becoming active as "superheroes" that people with powers and abilities only read about in myths and fairy tales began to appear. The age of the superman had arrived.

The Metagene

The strange extradimensional energy released in the explosion spawned the metagene, a mutated DNA cluster with an anomalous triple helix composition. The metagene remained undiscovered until 1986, and since then scientists have been able to discern the following about its behavior.

Those in whom the metagene is active ("metahumans") have the tendency to develop unusual abilities (more popularly called "super powers"). This activation of the metagene may occur on its own or via artificial stimulation. Those rare few who are born with active super abilities are termed "mutants."

Those who don't have the metagene will never possess superpowers. Those who do have it may or may not manifest superpowers, but it is impossible to have superpowers without possessing the gene. It is hypothesized that in the vast majority of humanity, the gene remains dormant and harmless, however this cannot be proven since the latent metagene is undetectable by testing procedures. The metagene can only be detected once it becomes active.

There is some data that indicates an individual's abilities are somehow linked to specific psychological traits and characteristics of the individual in question. This is not a hard and fast rule, but it stands up to casual investigation. (i.e. a fireman receiving fire-based powers rather than cold-based)

Other data suggests a link between the powers and the triggering event. (i.e. getting struck by lightning causing the manifestation of electrical powers) Both of these theories are still under study, and both are inconclusive at the moment.

The awakening of the metagene may occur anytime from adolescence onwards. Awakenings are usually triggered when the individual suffers a traumatic experience. Physical side effects associated with a naturally awakened metagene are rare, and tend toward discoloration of the hair or skin.

More harmful physical side effects are very rare. Psychological side effects are perhaps more frequent, though still unusual. Paranoia, megalomania, feelings of invincibility and a host of other mental conditions have been known to occur and are under study at this time.

The metagene is a passive genetic trait, and can only be passed on to a person's offspring if the other parent has the metagene as well. In a worldwide census, the majority of metahumans were found to be in the US, with Europe a distant second, and Russia and Africa third. Accurate statistics regarding the number of Asian metahumans is unavailable, due to the Chinese government's unwillingness to release such information.

It can be said that the world has roughly five thousand Supers (about one in a million). These are spread throughout the world according to the guidelines above. It can be safely assumed however that the world has a good mix of supers from all nationalities and backgrounds.

Superpowers

No one knows exactly how metahuman's powers work; only that there is some link between the metagene and superpowers. Metahumans routinely break laws that no one believed could be broken-by anybody or anything. Name a physical constant or law: inertia, mass, gravity, or what have you, and some Meta has already bent, twisted and broken it... and made it look easy.

Metas alternately fascinate and disgust scientists. There is a perverse feeling of wonder and horror that only scientists can feel, in watching everything they thought they knew being ripped to pieces by watching a man fly, lift a truck, or move objects with his mind.

Studies of metahuman abilities hint at the mechanics behind these strange occurrences, but no definitive proof of just how the hell they are doing these things (that no one is supposed to be able to do) is ever found. All the scientists can do is document how much metahumans warp reality with their powers.

So far, no one, not even the Metas know how they are doing "it."

Path 13: Thought is nature's echo of energy from atoms colliding

It is a humbling realization sitting in early morning serenity surrounded by darkness and silence of a sleeping city and the world, while listening to background hum of the universe's electrical signals of collected emissions and explosions of Quasars, Pulsars, movement and collisions of active galaxies, binary stars, cosmic rays, dark matter, dark energy, Gamma-ray Bursts, Neutron Stars, Super Nova, white dwarfs, parallel and multi-universes all around us.

The cosmos is alive. The external universe and the human mind are a pair of parallel mirrors reflecting each other receding into an infinity of cosmic consciousness. Beyond the impermanence of fleeting audible word of disseminating energy that we transmit to each other in frames referred to as thought, is a silent and forceful omnipresence of everything.

The activity of collective minds exchanging energy with the cosmos, consciousness is this energy bouncing back and forth in the form of vibrations. The exchange and movement of vibrating energy between the cosmos and the human mind echoes as thought.

Being mere particles in the cosmic conversation, any of us existing as an individuality is a myth. Cosmic consciousness is a comprehensive electromagnetic field created by transitions of matter and gasses into a pulsing and vibrating energy in which all of us are plugged into collectively. The experience of living as human follows the cosmic pattern of the life and death of stars as we too experience the transition from the corporeal to energy in a very limited window of time.

Our extraction back to the pure energy fabric of the cosmos is the journey we call life. The energy firing our thought can never dissipate or be destroyed leaving me with a sense that energy wise we all live forever. From gas to matter and back to gas ad infinitum, the pattern persists across the entire cosmological spectrum from the micro to the macro level, whether we are looking at the life of a star or that of the briefest cosmic living cellular organisms.

The transition of heating and cooling gasses gives birth to physical matter. The movement of matter produces energy throughout the universe. The human brain uses energy to produce the fading radiation of thought. Thought is the product of the energy fabric that consists of every star crunched in a black hole, the collected emissions and explosions of Quasars, Pulsars, movement and collisions of active galaxies, binary stars, cosmic rays, dark matter, dark energy, Gamma-ray Bursts, Neutron Stars, Super Nova, white dwarfs, parallel and multi-universes all around us.

When you sit alone in the quiet morning and silence your mind and drift from the chaos found in thought and dial into the singularity of oneness with the universe, you can feel the movements of cosmic energy. When analyzed, what is heard in the cosmic vacuum are the machinations of the cosmos from which our consciousness are bubbles of cognition in this vast cosmic ocean by which the universe contemplates itself.

There is no individuality in this fabric of cosmic energy. The most astounding realization is our thoughts are not independent in origin, in the sense that we create our thoughts. Our consciousness may be the outcome of random raw cosmic intelligence shaping our collective destiny. What if our thoughts are influenced by a cocktail of exotic cosmic radiation that bombards us every day that is received by each of us as stimuli sparking thought? Photons are constantly bombarding our retina generating electrical signals in our brains.

Path 14: Ancient Ruins and their Connections to Extraterrestrials

In the ancient world there are pyramids in Africa, Central America, Europe, Indonesia, Antarctica, Bermuda Triangle, Iraq, China, Cambodia, and Mexico.

How would we know if some advanced civilization existed on our home planet millions of years before Homo sapiens showed up? Scientists are speculating on what traces these potential predecessors might have left behind. They're calling this possibility the Silurian hypothesis.

When it comes to the hunt for advanced extraterrestrial civilizations that might exist across the cosmos, one must factor with knowledge that the universe is about 13.8 billion years old. In contrast, complex life has existed on Earth›s surface for only about 400 million years, and humans have only developed industrial civilizations in the last 300 years.

This raises the possibility that other civilizations could have come and gone before us—not just on distant planets in other solar systems, but here on Earth itself. Four billions years is long enough for us to be iterations of life in perpetuity.

Adam Frank, an astrophysicist at the University of Rochester in New York asks the question, how do you know there hasn't been previous advanced civilizations? Artifacts of human or other industrial civilizations are unlikely to be found on a planet's surface after about 4 million years, said Frank and study co-author Gavin Schmidt, director of NASA's Goddard Institute for Space Studies in New York. For instance, they noted that urban areas currently take up less than 1 percent of Earth's surface, and that complex items, even from early human technology, are very rarely found.

One may also find it difficult to unearth fossils of any beings who might have lived in industrial civilizations before us, the scientists added. The fraction of life that gets fossilized is always extremely small. Given that the oldest known fossils of *Homo sapiens* are only about 300,000 years old, there is no certainty that our species might even appear in the fossil record in the long run. After a few million years, any physical reminder of your civilization may be gone.

This can be the case for past Civilizations on Mars that no longer exist. One wild idea the Silurian hypothesis raises is that the end of one civilization could sow the seeds for another. If an industrial civilization had existed on Earth many millions of years prior to our own era, what traces would it have left and would they be detectable today?

Ancient Egypt, Pumapunku, Teotihuacan, the Dark Side of the Moon, Antarctica, what does the government know, when did they know it, and how long have they known it? What was the purpose of ancient pyramids of Egypt, Bosnia, Teotihuacan, and other pyramids structures around the world?

Pumapunku, has scattered stone structures that are part of the larger Tiwanaku. Pumapunku, which translates to the Doorway of the Puma, is best known for its massive stones and for the extraordinary precision of their cutting and placement. It's one of those places where you've heard, probably many times, that the stones are so closely fitted that a knife blade cannot be inserted between them.

Much is often made of the vast size and weight of the Pumapunku stones, with paranormal websites routinely listing them as up to 440 tons. The accepted estimate of this piece of red sandstone's weight is 131 metric tons, equal to 144 US tons. It is unknown how the heavy lifting and exquisite masonry was accomplished at Pumapunku or at Easter Island.

Overwhelming evidence, supported by scientific research from all over the archeological community proves that our recorded history is wrong concerning ancient cultures which in turn changes religion, science, and academics. The pyramid structures that were built in Bosnia and across the globe over 10,000 years ago cannot be duplicated by modern science and machinery in the 21st century and there is no explanation for who could have built them in our recorded history.

Evidence Found Across the Globe of Highly Evolved Human Species from before the Ice Age, Demand Scientific Recognition of our Past that Depicts Societies of Advanced Technology and Culture.

Houston anthropologist, Dr. Semir Osmanagich, founder of the Bosnian Archaeology Park, the most active archaeology site in the world, declares that irrefutable scientific evidence exists of ancient civilizations with advanced technology that leaves us no choice but to change our recorded history.

An examination of the age of structures across the earth reveals conclusively that they were built by advanced civilizations from over 29,000 years ago.

Dr. Osmanagich states, "The ancient people who built these pyramids knew the secrets of frequency and energy. They used these natural resources to develop technologies and undertake construction on scales we have never witnessed on earth." Evidence clearly shows that the pyramids were built as ancient energy machines aligned with the earth's energy grid, providing energy for healing as well as power.

Renowned author Michal Cremo, in his book "Forbidden Archeology," theorizes that knowledge of advanced Homo-sapiens has been suppressed or ignored by the scientific establishment because it contradicts the current views of human origins that don't agree with the dominant paradigm.

Radiocarbon dating that proves the Bosnian Pyramid Complex dates back at least 25,000 years has been revealed by an international team of scientists led by Dr. Sam Osmanagich. Discovered in 2005, the

Bosnian Pyramid of the Sun Archaeological Park, which houses the largest pyramid in the world, is now the most active archaeological site on the planet.

The team's findings also reveal an energy beam, 13 feet in radius that transmits an unexplainable electromagnetic signal measuring 28 kilohertz coming from the center of the Pyramid of the Sun. This phenomenon has been independently confirmed by physicist Dr. Slobodan Mizdrak, Ph.D. from Croatia, Professor Paolo Debertolis, anthropologist from University of Trieste in Italy, sound engineer Heikki Savolainen from Finland and electrical engineer Goran Marjanovic from Serbia.

The energy beam is theorized by Dr. Osmanagich as the reason the pyramids were built; to provide ancient civilizations a powerful source of clean energy. This is already a widely supported theory set forth by the book "The Giza Power Plant" by Christopher Dunn published in 1998, which theorize the original function of the Great Pyramid was not a tomb but a power plant. The Bosnian Pyramid of the Sun is 30% larger than the largest pyramid at Giza and recent excavation has uncovered an extensive pre-historical underground labyrinth system, further evidence supporting the power plant theory.

Is it possible that the fossil fuel based energy system we now rely on could have been prevented if inventor Nicola Tesla's work on free energy hadn't been suppressed?

Tesla's (1856-1943) patented free energy methods were rejected due to their inability to be metered and monetized. "We urgently need to change our mistaken point of view that our ancestors were stupid and accept that they had an advanced understanding of the fabric of nature and the universe, just like Nikola Tesla, whose ideas were suppressed as they did not and do not fit in the reigning economic model," states Phillip Coppens, author and investigative journalist. "The pyramids are proof that our ancestors knew and worked with an energy technology that we are now finally able to measure, but are still short of fully understanding.

Understanding fallacies of Faith based Gods and Religion

Ancient astronauts" (or "ancient aliens") refers to the idea that intelligent extraterrestrial beings visited Earth and made contact with humans in antiquity and prehistoric times. Proponents suggest that this contact influenced the development of modern cultures, technologies, and religions, and even human biology. A common position is that deities from most, if not all, religions are extraterrestrial in origin, and that advanced technologies brought to Earth by ancient astronauts were interpreted as evidence of divine status by early humans

Proponents of the ancient astronaut hypothesis often maintain that humans are either descendants or creations of extraterrestrial intelligence (ETI) who landed on Earth thousands of years ago. An associated idea is that humans evolved independently, but that much of human knowledge, religion, and culture came from extraterrestrial visitors in ancient times, in that ancient astronauts acted as a "mother culture".

Some ancient astronaut proponents also believe that travelers from outer space, referred to as "astronauts" (or "spacemen") built many of the structures on Earth (such as Egyptian pyramids and the Moai stone heads of Easter Island) or aided humans in building them.

Proponents argue that the evidence for ancient astronauts comes from documentary gaps in historical and archaeological records, and they also maintain that absent or incomplete explanations of historical or archaeological data point to the existence of ancient astronauts. The evidence is argued to include archaeological artifacts that they deem anachronistic, or beyond the accepted technical capabilities of the historical cultures with which they are associated. These are sometimes referred to as "out-of-place artifacts"; and include artwork and legends which are interpreted in a modern sense as depicting extraterrestrial contact or technologies.

Zecharia Sitchin

Zecharia Sitchin's series The Earth Chronicles, beginning with *The 12th Planet*, revolves around Sitchin's unique interpretation of ancient Sumerian and Middle Eastern texts, megalithic sites, and artifacts from around the world. He hypothesizes that the gods of old Mesopotamia were astronauts from the planet "Nibiru", which Sitchin states the Sumerians believed to be a remote "12th planet" (counting the Sun, Moon, and Pluto as planets) associated with the god Marduk. According to Sitchin, Nibiru continues to orbit our sun on a 3,600-year elongated orbit. Modern astronomy has found no evidence to support Sitchin›s ideas.

Sitchin argues that there are Sumerian texts which tell the story that 50 Anunnaki, inhabitants of a planet named Nibiru, came to Earth approximately 400,000 years ago with the intent of mining raw materials, especially gold, for transport back to Nibiru.

With their small numbers they soon grew tired of the task and set out to genetically engineer laborers to work the mines. After much trial and error they eventually created *Homo sapiens*: the "Adapa" (model man) or Adam of later mythology.

Sitchin contended the Anunnaki were active in human affairs until their culture was destroyed by global catastrophes caused by the abrupt end of the last ice age some 12,000 years ago. Seeing that humans survived and all they had built was destroyed, the Anunnaki left Earth after giving humans the opportunity and means to govern themselves.

We must progress intellectually in understanding that religion is a useful tool of control by the global elite. The micro damages of defacing the Sphinx and the macro denigration of all people of African descent betrays the desperation of a global elite to use the tool of religion not as a purveyor of righteousness, love, and justice, but as a tool to control the people.

I am within the rapture of one omnipresent infinite consciousness completely dissociated from teachings of Islam, Judaism, and Christianity faiths.

Once upon a time, in the ancient past, Before the Common Era (BCE), in a time most European scholars refer to as the mythical "dark ages." In the **land of Kush**, there lived a great, grand, highly enlighten civilization of sophisticated, charismatic, powerful and compassionate African kings, who would become Egyptian Pharaohs. They thrived, prospered and ruled for thousands of years BCE. These same kings were students of the ancient mystery schools of Africa, worshippers of Amen (one God), and the Laws of MAAT.

Maat represents the ethical and moral principle that every Egyptian citizen was expected to follow throughout their daily lives. They were expected to act with honor and **truth** in manners that involve family, the community, the nation, the environment, and the gods.

Maat or **Ma'at** (Egyptian **mꜣꜥt /ˈmuʀʕat/**)[1] refers to the ancient Egyptian concepts of truth, balance, order, harmony, law, morality, and justice. Maat was also the goddess who personified these concepts, and regulated the stars, seasons, and the actions of mortals and the deities who had brought order from chaos at the moment of creation. Her ideological opposite was Isfet (Egyptian *jzft*), meaning injustice, chaos, violence or to do evil.

Lost in antiquity and shrouded in mystery, ancient Nubia (another name for Kush), extended south along the Nile River from the First Cataract to the Shubaluga Gorge (Sixth Cataract). Today this region is located in modern Sudan, with a small portion crossing into southern Egypt also known as the Land of Ham, by the ancient Egyptians, Libyans, Assyrians, Hebrews, and Persians. It was also called Ethiopia by the Greeks, Romans and 19th & early 20th century writers.

New archeological discoveries have recently proven that earlier Egyptian lineage origins flow from Ethiopia (Grandmother) to Nubia (Mother) to Kemet aka Egypt (Child). These rich new discoveries negate current Egyptology academics, who insist that all great civilizations originated in Egypt and Mesopotamia, however new DNA, archeology and anthropology studies conclude these were not the first great civilization and that Egypt's roots of origin flow undeniably back into ancient Ethiopia (the land of the Blacks).

Erich von Däniken was a leading proponent of this hypothesis in the late 1960s and early 1970s, gaining a large audience through the 1968 publication of his best-selling book *Chariots of the Gods?*

According to von Däniken, certain artifacts require a more sophisticated technological ability in their construction than that which was available to the ancient cultures who constructed them. Von Däniken maintains that these artifacts were constructed either directly by extraterrestrial visitors or by humans who learned the necessary knowledge from said visitors. These include Stonehenge, Pumapunku, the Moai of Easter Island, the Great Pyramid of Giza, and the ancient Baghdad electric batteries.

The so-called "Helicopter hieroglyphs", at Abydos, Egypt, which are argued to depict flying craft

Von Däniken writes that ancient art and iconography throughout the world illustrates air and space vehicles, non-human but intelligent creatures, ancient astronauts, and artifacts of an anachronistically advanced technology. Von Däniken also states that geographically separated historical cultures share artistic themes, which he argues imply a common origin.

One such example is von Däniken's interpretation of the sarcophagus lid recovered from the tomb of the Classic-era Maya ruler of Palenque, Pacal the Great. Von Däniken writes that the design represented a seated astronaut. The iconography and accompanying Maya text, however, identifies it as a portrait of the ruler himself with the World Tree of Maya mythology.

The origins of many religions are interpreted by von Däniken as reactions to encounters with an alien race. According to his view, humans considered the technology of the aliens to be supernatural and the aliens themselves to be gods.

Von Däniken states that the oral and written traditions of most religions contain references to alien visitors in the way of descriptions of stars and vehicular objects travelling through air and space. One such is Ezekiel's revelation in the Old Testament, which Däniken interprets as a detailed description of a landing spacecraft

Africa and South America is home to some spectacular relics from bygone eras, constructions that seem to defy the technological capabilities of their time either because they're too big, too heavy, or too complex.

As such, some suggest the ancient builders of the Egyptian pyramids, the Nasca lines, and others were following an extraterrestrial instruction manual. Perhaps the hands that crafted these sites weren't really of this world.

Could the blood lines of ancient King extend back to inter-galactic space travelers of advanced civilizations from other planets?

Nasca Lines

On a high and dry plateau some 200 miles southeast of Lima, more than 800 long, straight white lines are etched into the Peruvian desert, seemingly at random. Joining them are 300 geometric shapes and 70 figures of animals, including a spider, monkey, and hummingbird.

The longest of the lines run straight as an arrow for miles. The biggest shapes stretch nearly 1,200 feet across and are best viewed from the air. Scientists suspect the Nasca drawings are as many as two millennia old, and because of their age, size, visibility from above, and mysterious nature, the lines are often cited as one of the best examples of alien handiwork on Earth. Otherwise, how would an ancient culture have been able to make such huge designs in the desert without being able to fly? And why?

The Great Pyramids

The Great Pyramid is made of millions of precisely hewn stones weighing at least two tons each. Even with today's cranes and other construction equipment, building a pyramid as big as that of Pharaoh Khufu would be a formidable challenge.

And then there's the astronomical configuration of the pyramids, which is said to align with the stars in Orion's belt. As well, alien theorists often point to the fact that these three pyramids are in way better shape than others built centuries later (never mind the amount of work that has gone into preserving them over the past several centuries). So are Egypt's pyramids artifacts of aliens?

Stonehenge

The Neolithic monument inspired Swiss author Erich von Däniken to suggest it was a model of the solar system that also functioned as an alien landing pad—after all, how else could those massive stones have ended up hundreds of miles from their home quarry? It appears as though the stones are aligned with solstices and eclipses, suggesting the Stonehenge builders were at least keeping an eye on the heavens.

Teotihuacán

Meaning the "City of the Gods," is a sprawling, ancient city in Mexico that's best known for its pyramidal temples and astronomical alignments.

Easter Island

The enigmas surrounding the *Moai*, Easter Island's fleet of large stone figures, pretty much follow the same narrative as the other sites described here: How in the world did the Rapa Nui make these figures more than 1,000 years ago?

And how did the Moai end up on Island? Carved from stone, the nearly 900 human figures are sprinkled along the flanks of the island's extinct volcanoes. The figures average 13 feet tall and weigh 14 tons and appear to have been chiseled from the soft volcanic tuff found in the Rano Raraku quarry.

There, more than 400 statues are still in various states of construction, with some completed figures awaiting transportation to their intended resting place. The reasons for carving the Moai are mysterious.

Face on Mars

Spotted by the Viking 1 orbiter in 1976, the so-called face is nearly two miles long and is in a region called Cydonia, which separates the smooth plains of the Martian north from the more cratered terrain in the south. At the time, scientists dismissed the "face" as shadow play, but over the decades it has become a favorite among those who suspect aliens with a penchant for building things have been visiting the solar system

Path 15: The Pyramid power plants of Extraterrestrial Gods at Teotihuacan, Mexico

The Pyramid power plants of Extraterrestrial Gods was a technology system that generated a lot of energy. Teotihuacan, Mexico, thought to be the Cape Canaveral of its time, is littered with Mica and Mercury. Mica is an element that shields energy. Mercury is a fuel instrumental to producing free energy. Along the Avenue of the Dead in Teotihuacan, there are multiple structures that show evidence of a catastrophic fire or explosion that consume portion of the temple complex.

The damage has been attributed to the uprising of its people at the end of the 6th Century just before the population vanished entirely without a trace. Archeologist, Leopold Obatress says the flames were too extensive to be attributed to torch flames from an uprising.

Were the ancient people of Teotihuacan harnessing energy that caused a explosive energy release? Could the Mica and Mercury found at Teotihuacan corroborate the theory that the burn marks we see along the Avenue of the Dead are from some kind of mechanical explosion? The pyramids of Teotihuacan, like the Great Pyramids of Giza and other pyramid sites throughout the globe may have once served as electro-magnetic power plants. Were they tapping the resident power of the earth and then distributing it around the world?

Teotihuacan matches this model of a power plant. It is built over caverns and has liquid mercury and Mica incorporated into its design. That helped the Gods or Extraterrestrials come to and leave this planet. Were the pyramids technological systems that generated lots of energy?

If Teotihuacan served as an ancient power plant generating electro-magnetic energy, just what role did mercury recently discovered at Teotihuacan play in such a scenario? Mercury is used in anti-gravity spacecraft. Some of the ancient Indian epics talked about Vimana's and the mechanics of these crafts. Mercury found at pyramid sites is really part of the propulsion of anti-gravity crafts extraterrestrials were using here on earth. Electro-magnetism creates an environment that allows mercury to levitate.

Physicist James Lincoln work with super-conductors like mercury and the levitation effects produced in the presence of strong electro-magnetic fields as those believed having been generated by the ancient pyramid power plants.

Once a super-conductor reaches its critical temperature and is cold enough, it will levitate over a magnetic field. Levitation is the signature behavior of any super-conductor in the presence of a magnetic field. The super-conductor generates electricity flowing in loops inside its structure and makes it float. Once these electric currents are generated, they are free and permanent and last as long as the conductor properties are kept cold. Mercury is a super conductor. Crafts with a chamber of liquid nitrogen with enough magnetism over a surface have no limits for the amount of mass for a space craft.

Teotihuacan was maybe a location in which exotic and advanced technology was used to create an electro-magnetic field and the area around the pyramids may have been areas where levitation was easier for flying saucers that involved liquid mercury as fuel. Teotihuacan may have been the Cape Canaveral of its day. Today most space facilities are built as close to the equator as possible to take advantage of the earth's rotation. Teotihuacan is near the equator. When you examine the layout of the entire Teotihuacan Complex, Three of the main structures contained there have been found to line up with the three belt stars of Orion.

The Extraterrestrial Narrative Ancient Aliens DNA Manipulation to Create a Race of Slaves

Path 16: Coming from Other Worlds: The Origin of Humanity According to Old Sumerian Tablets

11 August 2017

Of the Codigo Oculto **Website**

Photocomposition.

Ancient Sumerian relief and Sumerian tablets (Hidden Code)

The age of earth is estimated to be 4 Billion years old. There is evidence that suggests that there may have been advanced societies that predates our current civilization. More recently the book 'Worlds before Our Own' (1978) by Brad Steiger exposed new facts in favor of early advanced societies. Steiger found that some advanced human artifacts were located in the lowest primordial geologic strata whereas primitive ones are in upper strata.

He labeled these anachronistic items that were seemingly out of their proper place in time, "Out-of-Place Artifacts" (OPA). His book fueled a series of later works that characterized the past 30 years with a sort of rebellion towards the current worldview of the ancient past.

I entertain this view and count myself in rebellion towards the current worldview dominated by religious views only 3000 years old. If advanced societies did exist, what then brought about their destruction? There are mainly two possible past events. Either these people were so advanced that they destroyed themselves, or a natural force brought about their destruction.

"When the first atomic bomb exploded in New Mexico, the desert sand turned to fused green glass. This fact, according to the magazine Free World, has given certain archaeologists a turn. They have been digging in the ancient Euphrates Valley and have uncovered a layer of agrarian culture 8,000 years old, and a layer of herdsman culture much older, and a still older caveman culture. Recently, they reached another layer, a layer of fused green glass." (New York Herald Tribune, 1947)

There are striking similarities found in myths and legends across the globe of a worldwide cataclysm—more specifically a deluge. Many similar myths on this account are found in Africa, China, North America, Australia, Samaria, and in very remote cultures that had no way to connect with one another. It is estimated that are more than 500 ancient deluge legends similar to those mentioned in the Biblical and Qur'anic accounts. These myths are actually traces of a global collective memory referring to an actual occurrence in the distant past.

More concrete evidence of advanced civilizations that predates our current civilization is the prehistoric structure that had been the tallest edifice on earth until the Empire State Building skyscraper was completed in 1931, and still *is* "the most colossal single building ever erected on the planet."

The mighty pyramid of Khufu silently speaks louder than the chatter of skeptics. It is aligned to true geodetic North and its location is found to be the center of the earth landmass. This sort of precision entails a comprehensive knowledge of earth geography, e.g. Mercator projection, which is something much unexpected of ancient Egypt.

As for its structure, engineers and scientists conclude that it is impossible to replicate the great pyramid despite the sophisticated technology we have now, given the structure's immensity and staggering precision.

Speaking in numbers, engineer Markus Schulte speculates that the Great Pyramid *alone* would cost us some $35 billion to duplicate.

What would happen if a cataclysmic event happened today? If humans were to simply die or disappear, the "next" civilization, in however many millions of years, would very likely have no knowledge that we once existed. The age we put on civilizations and even the Earth itself, for all the academic trimmings, is basically guess-work.

Within only decades most of the cities and concrete streets will have been overtaken by vegetation. Within three centuries, most of the metal buildings and bridges will have fallen to the ground and decompose.

According to numerous ancient texts and books written over the centuries, hundreds of thousands of years ago, before recorded history, the planet Earth was visited by travelers from a another place in the universe.

These beings, who would have settled in Africa and what is now the Persian Gulf, undertook activities to detect gold reserves in Southeast Africa and carried out a colonial expedition on Earth. Currently there are three beliefs of how humans came about on this planet:

- Those who believe that extraterrestrials came to earth from another planet and created humans by modifying indigenous hominid DNA who were already thriving on earth with extraterrestrial DNA.

- Those that look at the origins of life from a scientific point of view, maintaining that this life began millions of years ago and that humanity evolved to form an advanced species based on microorganisms.
- Those who argue that life was created by a divine intervention, which is the result of God, who created everything: the Earth, the Moon, our Solar System and the entire universe.

Thus, in Genesis 1:27 we can read:

> "Thus God created mankind in his image, in the image of God he created them, male and female he created them." We have, therefore, two or three prevailing theories that would explain the existence of humanity on Earth.

If we take a look at religion, we will find something that is practically impossible to prove, but there are millions of people scattered all over the world who firmly believe that humanity - and everything that surrounds us - was created by God.

If tomorrow we discovered other lives in this or other solar systems, how would religion survive this discovery?

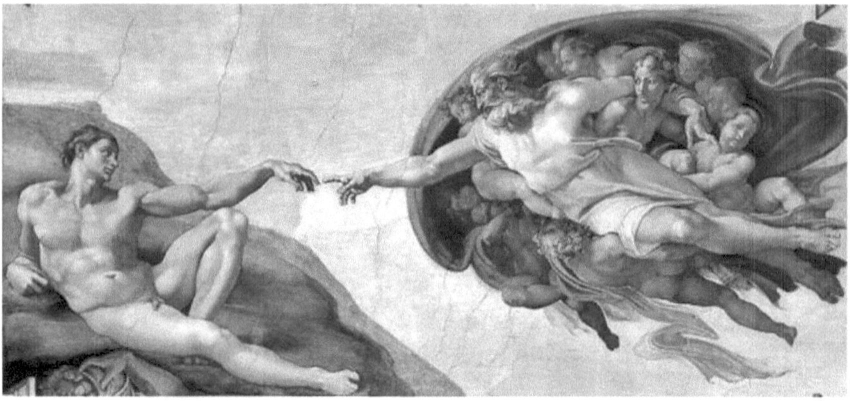

Adam creation, fresco of the Sistine Chapel by Michelangelo, Vatican City

Interestingly, there are several ancient texts before the Bible - such as the Popol Vuh, sacred book of the ancient Mayas - which affirm, literally, that humanity was CREATED *by strange beings.*

In the Popol Vuh states that these beings are known as, "the Creator, the Ancient One, the Dominator, the Feathered Serpent, those who beget, those who give being, those who hover over water like a rising light (possible description of a UFO)."

In the Koran we find the following:

Verse 96.1: "Recite in the Name of your Lord who created!"
Verse 96.2: "He created man from a clot"
Verse 96.3: "Recite that your Lord is the most generous!"
Verse 96.4: "Who taught with the calamus"
Verse 96.5: "He taught man what he did not know"

This is the reason why we ask ourselves again:

- Who were these gods?
- Is it possible that some of the oldest writings on Earth - from ancient Samaria - can help us understand the origin of humanity?

The truth is that, if we ignore the three hypotheses mentioned above, we will find others that, according to many, is as acceptable as the previous three. Why couldn't humanity have been created by a civilization arriving from somewhere in the universe.

According to the Sumerian texts, humanity would have been created by beings from other worlds to work in gold mines.

Such a controversial hypothesis is, however, as acceptable as the other two.

- The ancient humanity product of the ancient Anunnaki ?
- What if the controversial Zecharia Sitchin was right?

According to Sitchin in an interview published in the New York Times in 2010, the origin of humanity today would have begun with the arrival of inhabitants from a planet called Nibiru, whose long elliptical orbit would bring it closer to Earth once every 3,600 years .

Beings that were very technologically advanced who would measure more than 2.5 meters high, according to Sitchin.

About 450,000 years ago, these beings would have detected gold reserves in Southeast Africa, starting a colonial expedition to the Earth and settling in what is now the Persian Gulf. "These Nibiru-itas (beings of Nibiru) recruited erect primates of the Earth as workers to build eight large cities. Could primates have evolved from micro-organisms organically and these beings from Nibiru, with advanced technical genealogy, altered the primate's DNA and created man?

Enki, who became the god of Sumerian science, gave part of the advanced genetic composition of the Nibiru-itas to these bipeds so that they could work as miners, "Sitchin added. For Sitchin, the cities created by the beings from Nibiru were finally devastated by a great flood suffered 30,000 years ago, after which they began to transmit their knowledge to human beings, such as agriculture.

In any case, according to Sitchin, the Nibiru-itas ended up returning to their planet around 550 BC. This is in the Sumerian text.

Zechariah Sitchin

Excerpt from the Zachariah Sitchin interview published in the New York Times in the year 2010.

Nibiru, whose long, elliptical orbit brings it near Earth once every 3,600 years or so. The planet's inhabitants were technologically advanced humanlike beings, Mr. Sitchin said, standing about nine feet tall. Some 450,000 years ago, they detected reserves of gold in southeast Africa and made a colonial expedition to Earth, splashing down in what is now the Persian Gulf.

Mr. Sitchin said these Nibiru-ites recruited laborers from Earth's erect primates to build eight great cities. Enki, who became the Sumerians' god of science, bestowed some of the Nibiru-ites' advanced genetic makeup upon these bipeds so they could work as miners.

This is how Mr. Sitchin explains what scientists attribute to evolution. He says the aliens' cities were washed away in a great flood 30,000 years ago, after which they began passing on their knowledge to humans. Bas-Relief of Sumerian text shows a photograph of a woodcarving from 7,000 B.C. of a large man handing over a plow to a smaller man; depicting the passing on of agricultural knowledge. Anyway, he said, the Nibiru-ites finally jetted home in their spacecraft, around 550 B.C.

Also, in his book "The Cosmic Code ", Sitchin wrote:

> "There was a time, said the Sumerians, when civilized man was not yet on Earth, when animals were wild and not domesticated and crops were not yet cultivated. In that time, a long time ago, a group of fifty Anunnaki arrived on Earth. Led by a being whose name was EA (which means 'whose home is water'), they traveled from their home planet NIBIRU ('crossing planet') and, arriving on Earth, settled on the waters of the Persian Gulf ...this happened 445,000 years ago."

The Anunnaki chronology of arrival on Earth, according to Sitchin, would be the following:

- **450,000 BC:**
  After long wars, the atmosphere of Nibiru began to deteriorate and became a hostile place for life. The Anunnaki needed gold to repair their atmosphere. According to the researchers, we can use gold nanoparticles to repair our damaged ozone layer.

- **445,000 BC:**
  The Anunnaki land on Earth and establish their base in Eridu, seeking to extract gold from the Persian Gulf. "The metal, with its unique properties, was needed back home on their home planet Niburu for a vital need...as best as we can make out, this vital need could have been for suspending the gold particles in Nibiru's wanting atmosphere and thus shield it from critical dissipation. They are led by Enki, son of Anu.

- **416,000 BC:**
  Gold production falls, which causes Anu to visit the Earth with his other son Enlil. Anu decides that mining takes place in Africa and places Enlil in charge of the mission on Earth.

- **400,000 BC:**
  The south of Mesopotamia is inhabited by seven developed nations. Among the most important stand out: "Sipar", "Nippur" and "Shuruppak". After refining the metal, the ore was transported from Africa in "ships" to later be sent to space orbit.

In his books, The Twelfth Planet and The Cosmic Code, Zecharia Sitchin outlines this "celestial battle" as described in the Babylonian text Enûma Elish.

Tiamat, as outlined in the Enûma Elish is a goddess and a monstrous embodiment of primordial chaos. She gives birth to the first generation of gods; she later makes war upon them and is split in two by the storm-god Marduk, who uses her body to form the heavens and the earth.

Through Sitchin's studies of Sumerian cosmology he believes, there is an undiscovered planet which follows a long, elliptical orbit, reaching the inner solar system roughly every 3,600 years. This planet is called Nibiru. Nibiru is the planet associated with Marduk in Babylonian cosmology.

The Sumerian version of the creation of our Solar System

In the beginning there existed the Sun (Apsu), encircled by the planet Tiamat, and the planet Mercury (Mummu). Then, between Tiamat and Mercury, came into being the planets, Mars (Lahmu) and Venus (Lahamu). Then there came into being, beyond the planet Tiamat, the planets, Jupiter (Kishar) and Saturn (Anshar) along with their 'emissary' Pluto (Gaga). Last to come into being were the planets, Uranus (Anu) and Neptune (Ea). These nine planets, or 'gods,' moved in a counterclockwise direction around Apsu, the sun.

From outer space a new planet, Marduk, almost the size of Jupiter or Saturn, approached, attracted to this solar system by the gravitational pull of Neptune and Uranus. Moving in a clockwise direction past Neptune and Uranus, the path of Marduk took him toward the giants, Saturn and Jupiter.

As he passed by Uranus, portions of Marduk were pulled off to become four satellites or 'winds.'

Sitchin claims that one of Marduk's (Nibiru) moons struck Tiamat braking her into two separate pieces. On a second pass, Marduk, itself an enormous cosmic entity, struck Tiamat, smashing one half of the planet into pieces, which became what the Sumerians called the Great Band (asteroid belt) that resides 205 to 300 million miles from the sun. Life was also passed between worlds from Nibiru to Tiamat.

As Nibiru continued on, trampling in its path the lower half of Tiamat, another one of his satellites, called the North Wind, struck the remaining intact upper half of Tiamat. The force of this secondary impact thrust the remaining intact half of Tiamat away from her original orbit, to become repositioned between Venus and Mars. It was at this point that the remaining half of Tiamat took on the name of Earth (Ki), as noted in the Hebrew tradition.

The thrust gave the remaining half of Tiamat, or Earth, her axial spin and therefore her ability to experience the changing days and nights. Only Kingu continued to orbit around Tiamat as a satellite; he would later be called Lunar the Moon. Nibiru settled into an orbit around the sun. This event is said to have happened 4.5 billion years ago.

The destruction of Tiamat and the corresponding creation of Earth out of the wreckage resulted in the melting of the ice-covered surface and the remaining land masses of Tiamat being concentrated in one spot as a continent (i.e. Pangea). And the waters of the Earth surrounding the land formed the ocean filling the wound of the Earth, this wound we know as the Pacific Ocean. Zechariah Sitchin research reveals that in our ancient past there were advanced beings referred to as the Anunnaki (translated as "those who from heaven to earth came). Sitchin stated "The idea that there was in our Solar System a race of intelligent beings, far older than us who are now gone." The Sumerian text has forced us to rethink the question of human origin.

Jack Beringer's and Michael Tsarion's Version of Origin of Man

There had to be life on Nibiru to record these cataclysmic collisions. Because of such collision, how did life on Nibiru advanced faster than life on earth 4.5 billion years ago after this collision?

I can understand an advance civilization bringing life to this world through intergalactic travel from another star system. The collision of Nibiru with Tiamat is not logical in that life on each planet would not have survived such a cataclysmic collision.

Jack Beringer's book "Past Shock" said there are at least 30,000 texts that talks about visitations of extraterrestrials. Every single culture in this world have recorded information revealing sightings. Their names are many:

> Nephilims, Anakim, Annunaki, Anannage, Rephaim, Giants, Djinn, Titans, Fallen Angels, Watchers, Elders, Sons of Zadok, Sons of Seth, Uranids, Cyclopeans, Promethians, Olympians, Asuras, Elects, Illies, Fomorians, Gibborim, Necromancers, Rayless Ones, Bent Ones, Dogons, Dagons, Amaraka, Nagas, Naddreds, Rakshasas, Nagayunas, Dragon Kings Urshu, Brotherhood of the Snakes, the People Serpent, etc. The word Nephilim is the most common name.

> It may derive its name from the Niphal of the verb meaning "to be extraordinary" or "extraordinary men." It may also be derived from the verb Napal "Fall" or the "Fallen Ones" from heaven. The International Standard Bible Encyclopedia defines it as "unnaturally begotten." The word may have come from Nephel which means bad or strange birth or Knephelim, which means the serpents.

These so called "Fallen Angels" were extremely scientifically advanced humanoids beings, who came to earth after being forced to exit their own planet, or planets. They had been expunged by opposition forces and pursued across the galaxy into our Solar System. Upon arrival, they set up, unmanned make shift decoy center on the planet Tiamat, which once existed between Mars and Jupiter, but took refuge on Earth in its many underground caverns.

Tiamat was a vast ocean planet, in our Solar System, known from antiquity as the second sun. It was 15 times larger than Earth and was an entire ocean planet. It was not a sun, but its atmosphere was so resplendent that the actual sun's rays, when shining made it appear to people on our planet as a second sun.

According to D.S. Allan and J.B. Delair, in their book "Cataclysm," top scientists from Oxford and Cambridge, stated:

> If we elevate the Moon to planetary status, as the Sumerians appear to have done, then we have a total of ten planets orbiting the Sun. On this basis, one planet is currently still missing from the earlier Sumerian total. Could there really have been another planet known to the Sumerians, as yet lost to us or lost since their day?

The planet Tiamat is not here today, possibly destroyed by the pursuers of the Nephilim. This destructive act caused the Earth great floods.

This is believed to have occurred between 30 and 50,000 years ago. It is believed that the only thing left of Tiamat is the asteroid belt between Mars and Jupiter.

Tiamat was destroyed by humanoids and not by an asteroid or comet. It was a humanoid intervention destruction of a planet 15 times the size of planet Earth made up entirely of oceans. The pursuer of the Nephilim destroyed a whole planet in order to rid the galaxy of them.

This is the first event that caused the first flood. Tiamat's water poured down on earth from its destruction. Pre the deluge, there was only one large body of water on Earth. It was the Miocene Ocean. The Black and Caspian Sea in Russia are the remnant of this ocean.

In the Babylonian Enuma Elish, this destruction is documented:

> Go and cut off Tiamat's life, and let the winds convey her blood to secret places.

In the Book of Enoch is written:

> And behold a star fell from heaven, and the children of the Earth began to tremble and quake before them and to flee from them. And again I saw how they began to gore each other and to devour each other and the earth began to cry aloud.

The Nephilim were not on Tiamat. They had descended to Earth to hide. After the deluge, they emerged and set up their base, known as Atlantis o the west continent of Appalachia. From there, they set up making contact with the Earth's indigenous inhabitants.

In the Bible, Genesis says the sons of God came in unto the daughters of men and they bear children unto them. The Gnostic tells us more stating:

> Now come, let us seize her and let us cast our seed in her, so that then she is polluted. She will not be able to ascend to her light. But those whom she will beget will serve us.

The Ethiopian Kebra Nagast states:

> And the daughters of Cain with whom the angels had companied conceived, but they were unable to bring forth their children, and they died. And of the children who were in their womb some died, and some came forth, having split the bellies of their mothers. They came forth by their navels.

Other Gnostic text states:

> Those daughters of darkness became pregnant. As a result of the beauty of the forms of emissary, whom they had seen they had abortions, and the fruits of their bodies fell upon earth and consumed the blossoms of the trees. The evil ones were incredibly handsome physically.

The great sin that happened 30 to 50,000 years ago was not the impregnation of women. It was the transgenic experimentation, the genetic hybridization of our original forefathers that were on this planet. We are talking about the crossing of alien DNA with the DNA of our forefathers.

Genesis 1 we read and God said let us make man in **our** image after **our** likeness. Corinthian 15:45 states:

> The first man Adam became a living being. The last Adam a life giving spirit. The Spiritual did not come first, but the natural, and after that the spiritual. The

> first man was of the dust of the earth, the second man from heaven.

The first man was a creation from the earth the second one is the creation from up there from heaven. The spiritual, which means not of the earth.

Michael Tsarion refers to Homo Atlantis regarding the beings created on Atlantis. The First Born is a reference to the "Son of the Serpent" hybrid race of the Elohim. The beings created on Atlantis were very advanced technical beings. These being rebelled against their creators on Atlantis, left, and went to Oceania.

The Atlantean began a second major hybridization program and created a Mark II being. Termed "Adamic." These beings were of both sexes but they could not reproduce. They made excellent servants in the Gardens. So many documents testifying to these revelations have been destroyed or confiscated by the Vatican and others.

The Mayan ancient texts and chronicles were destroyed save one the Popul Vuh. The Popul Vuh is one of the last remaining Codices. It states:

> Let us make him who shall nourish and sustain us. What shall we do to be invoked, to be remembered in earth? We have tried with our first creatures but we could not make them venerate us. So then, let us try to make obedient, respectful beings, who shall nourish and sustain us.

Why would God need to create creatures to nourish and sustain them?

> In the Babylonian account man is to be merely a slave bought into being by Marduk at the plea of the defeated rebel Gods, so that those Gods themselves need not be

> subjected to servile labor. Man would be a puppet, a lowly, primitive creature.
>
> The Epic of Atrahasis – dates to about 1630 BC, found in the Assyrian Library of Nineveh…in a similar vein to the Enuma Elish, one of the main ideals is to show why man was created by Gods. It was so that they themselves need not work on the earth to produce their own food.

The Alien geneticist did not desire a repeat of their first experiments. They realized that the error centered on the intelligence of their progeny. In Mark II experiment "Adamic Man's" intelligence would be confounded. The Euphemism that has been used for dumbed-down is "Naked." When you read the word "Naked" in the Bible or the other apocryphal works of Adam and Eve in the Garden of Eden being naked, naked is a euphemism for being in a state of intellectual psychological ignorance.

All of us are eating from the **"Tree of life."** The goods of the tree are of organically pure energy essence of the creator. We are also **feeding off** the **"Tree of life"** with **the knowledge of good and evil. Health of essence is rejecting fruits of evil, in doing so, specifically choosing not to consume spiritually non-nutritious obsessive prioritization of carnal desires over "higher vibrating life-fruits of kindness, love, and joy."**

The tree of life is a term that relates to DNA. Ancient had an organic notion of DNA being a tree of 22 branches and roots. Its roots in the earth and its branches in the heavens. It is the same symbol of the two coiling serpents. The Semitic word for serpent is Nachash. That word has a second meaning, which is to discover or find out.

All the Gods of Egypt hold the Ankh. The ancient Egyptians did not use vowels. Many ancient words use strong consonants. The word Ankh if you add in the other sound values the word Ankh would be Anunnaki. The Egyptian Gods holding the Ankh is the word for Anunnaki or the word for the Fallen Angels or the Gods from on high the heavenly serpents.

There are troubling symbols everywhere. On the Alpha Romeo car brand, is the Knights Templar Maltese Cross and green dragon crowned devouring human beings. Where does these symbols come from and why are they being used?

The Lemurians (or sons of the serpents) became aware of their creator's second experiments. They had a dilemma, realizing that the race of Adams was, in fact, kindred to themselves. They both possessed human DNA. It was decided that representatives be sent to Atlantis to have a dialogue with the enslaved and "dumb-downed" Adam and Eves. The Bible presents this this as a parable with the story of the serpent entering the Garden. So the Book of Genesis is completely upside down. The serpent is attempting to free Adam and Eve of servitude instead of tempting them.

So the story goes, the sons entered into the Garden and spoke with their genetic cousins. They counselled them to throw off their chains of servitude and come with them back to Lemuria where they would be educated of all hidden from them. The Adams were resistant to the invitation. Fortunately, the response of Eve was different. The Eves were mysteriously attracted to these visitors and heeded their requests to free themselves from servitude. The Eves were responsible for the Exodus from Atlantis. Women committed a crime 13,000 years ago for which they have never been forgiven.

Leonard Shlain stated human history to date amounts to the tale of how a masculine, verbal mode of thinking, the linear, sequential, reductionist, and abstract mode controlled by the left side of the brain, has dominated the feminine, visual, and holistic mode that finds its home on the brain's right side.

After a brief preliminary excursion into primatology, Shlain traces logocentrism's long campaign to squash the sensuous. The Hebrew patriarchs, Buddha, and Confucius; Luther, Marx, and Hitler: all of these historical figures share both writerly wordiness and male chauvinism.

Shlain declares again and again that there is something inherently anti-female in the written word that attracts men who traffic in ethereal abstractions of the mind. As literacy spread, Shlain claims, so did patriarchy.

What does this has to do with the origin of Evil? How did the phenomena of evil come into the world and into consciousness of Earth's human inhabitants? It is this genetic transgenic experimentation. It is exactly the consequences of this experimentation that cause what we now call evil to come into existence. It is not nature, which is in perfect balance from the biggest neutron star to the Quantum.

Why would organic nature the epitome of perfection commit a blunder so deadly in one of its highest creation, which is man, who undermines it very order? It is the constant alteration of organic nature that cause evil to come into the world. We have a universe in perfect balance all around us. As we look at the evil proliferating all around us in the world, it seems like things from the machinations of a mad scientific community. The people of the world have been divided by notions of wealth, race, religion, and nationality.

We the people are divided and schizophrenic inside. We are bi-polar genetically, which echoes through our being manifesting in the chaotic schizoid-genic world we currently live in. We participate in the political charade and continue to witness things perpetually getting worse. The problem is our DNA makeup.

According to Plato, Zeus gathered the Gods in council to express his concern that these unusual creatures would one day challenge their hegemony. He was loathe to exterminate them with his thunderbolts, because there would be no one to bring the Gods offerings. Zeus solved the problem by putting each creature into a trance and then splitting them down the middle.

Upon awakening, each half only dimly remembered what it had been prior to being cleft in two. Zeus explained to the assembled Gods and Goddesses the cleverness of his scheme. These creatures would no longer pose a threat to the Gods, because they would dissipate their considerable energy by spending the rest of their days searching for their missing halves.

List of the Sumerian kings
in cuneiform writing.
XXIV century a. C.
(Public domain)

Curiously, the ancient List of Sumerian Kings, one of the most interesting ancient texts ever discovered, details with great precision the rulers of the ancient Sumerian civilization, describing the Kings-Beings who ruled the Earth for thousands of years.

So, in it we can read:

> "... After royalty descended from heaven, royalty was at Eridug, at Eridug, Alulim became king, reigned for 28,800 years. Alaljar reigned for 36,000 years. 2 kings, reigned for 64,800 years."

This ancient document seems to describe a time on Earth in which unknown beings lived for thousands of years, reigning in the ancient cities of that region.

The researchers have not been able to explain why the list combines mythical pre-dynastic kings with historical kings of which we do have proof of their existence, and because of this they defend conflicting explanations when discussing the interpretation of the surprising list of the Sumerian kings.

Signs of Reptilian Species on Earth

Thousands of Reptilian Statues discovered in Iraq. They date back to the Ubaid period 6000-4000 BC. The reptilian statues were discovered in cemeteries in the ancient city of Ur. Ubaid myth link these statues to tales of ancient spacemen who created man. The Ubaid's early ancestors the Halafs were known to bind their skulls. A tribute to their Gods the elongated skull resemble these statues. They also resemble mummies recently unearthed in Nazca Peru.

These enigmatic statuettes were discovered at the archeological site of Al-Ubaid. The Ubaidian culture in Mesopotamia is believed to date back to around 4000 and 5,500 BC. What did our ancient ancestors try to depict with these 7,000-year-old Reptilian statues? Did these enigmatic beings really exist on Earth?

The figurines are presented with long heads, almond shaped eyes, long tapered faces and lizard-type nose. So what did these lizard figures represent? Ancient alien depictions from the past.

Many believe these reptilian beings did and still do exist. They were of Ubaid culture history and other places throughout the planet. They were not in genetic partnership with the Anunnaki led by Enki and Enil family. Just a different species altogether.

How Did the Sumerian Know about all the planets in the Solar System 6000 Years Ago?

In ancient Mesopotamia, the secrets of astronomy and other celestial knowledge are kept carefully guarded. This knowledge is studied behind closed doors by an exclusive society of priests and astronomers. Some cylinder seals contains prints about 4,500 years old. Depicting the God Enlil handing the human plough to humankind ushering in the age of modern agriculture.

Also can be seen on a print is detailed depiction of the complete solar system identical to that known to contemporary science. On the outskirts of the nine known planets is an additional 10th planet not currently located by scientist of our modern era? A growing body of evidence indicates that it does exist.

According to modern science prior to the invention of the telescope in the 1600's, humanity had no knowledge of outlying planets beyond Jupiter, as these bodies cannot be seen with the naked eye. With the technological advancements such as the Hubble telescope and unmanned probes, the Voyager space probe corroborated ancient knowledge. The images of Uranus is exactly as the Sumerians reported 6000 years ago.

The Sumerians had no telescopes that we know of. They described Uranus as bright green and recorded its planetary tilt. According to the Sumerians, our solar system was invaded by a planetary body that caused collisions and disrupted the existing order. NASA scientists concurred that a collision with a body the size of earth traveling 40,000 miles per hour could have caused the orbital skew of Uranus and the devastation apparent from the planet's surface scarring.

Neptune was described a s blue green planet by Sumerians while scientist only confirmed this the past few decades. The Sumerians named and listed all of the planets in our solar system. Their ancient knowledge included knowledge included the planets Uranus and Neptune, supposedly unknown until discovered in 1781 and 1846. Pluto was not discovered by modern man until 1930.

Where did man come from?

Could we be the product of genetic engineering? Just how far back do we go to chronicle the first great civilizations older than the Greeks?

The cradle of civilization are in the rich flood plains of the Nile, Tigris, and Euphrates Rivers. You have to ask the question why just these three places on the entire planet? In the Great Plains between the Tigris and Euphrates of Sumer or modern day Iraq, the people were called Sumerians. The book of Genesis calls the land Shaniyar.

It is very interesting that Biblical scholars have ignored references to ancient kingdoms or categorized them as legends or lore. Could the passages of the Bible and creation in Genesis be a much shorter version of a much more complicated document that comes out of Sumer of powerful non-human God-like beings? Being who engineered us genetically from simple hominids specie native to earth?

In a 6000 year old Eanna Temple in Uruk, that was only discovered 150 years ago, is the statue of the patron deity and goddess Inanna. Inanna holds in her hands the waters of life. Adjacent to her are symbols of entwined snakes, which was the symbol of science. The twisted snakes also illustrates the precursor to the Egyptian Ankh, which is the symbol of life and creation.

The entwined snake is the symbol for genetic manipulation of DNA that was carved out in stone over six thousand years ago.

What the Sumerians Records Inform

Could there have been urban centers, walled cities, before 2500 B.C. not in Africa? Indeed there were in the Kingdom of Sumer where civilization began 6000 years ago, which precedes the history of the Bible 3000 years.

Out of nowhere a written language appears in on Cuneiform clay tablets iterating about Kings and priests, schools and temples, doctors and astronomers, high rise buildings, canals and docks and ships; intensive agriculture, metallurgy, textile industry, trade and commerce, laws and concepts of justice and morality, cosmological theories, and tales and records of pre-history.

In all these writings, the same facts emerge that in bygone days the righteous ones of the rocket ships that the Greeks began to call Gods had come to earth from their own planet. They chose southern Mesopotamia to be their home away from home. They called the land Ki and Gur. Land of the Lords and rockets. Shumer meant land of the guardians.

The statement that the first to establish settlement on earth were astronauts from another planet was not lightly made by the Sumerians. In text after text, whenever the starting point was recalled, it was always this "432,000 years before the deluge the dinger righteous ones of the rocket ships came down to earth from their own planet. The Sumerians considered their planet a twelfth member of our solar system." The sun, the moon, nine planets we know of today, and one more large planet whose orbit around the sun is 3600 earth years.

In his books, The Twelfth Planet and The Cosmic Code, Zecharia Sitchin outlines this "celestial battle" as described in the Babylonian text Enûma Elish.

Tiamat, as outlined in the Enûma Elish is a goddess and a monstrous embodiment of primordial chaos. She gives birth to the first generation of gods; she later makes war upon them and is split in two by the storm-god Marduk, who uses her body to form the heavens and the earth.

Through Sitchin's studies of Sumerian cosmology he believes, there is an undiscovered planet which follows a long, elliptical orbit, reaching the inner solar system roughly every 3,600 years. This planet is called Nibiru. Nibiru is the planet associated with Marduk in Babylonian cosmology.

The leaders of the astronauts who had come to earth from Nibiru was Enki. Text that was discovered in the ruin of Sumer records his landing on earth. On his planet, gold was needed. Gold was required for the space programs of the Niburuins as is evidence from the Hindu text's reference to the celestial chariots being covered with gold. Indeed gold is vital to the many aspects of the space instruments and vehicles of our own time. Gold metal, with its unique properties was needed back home for a more vital need that affected the very survival of life on that planet.

The vital need may have been for suspending the gold particles in Nibiru's waning atmosphere, thus shielding it from critical dissipation. Enki was a brilliant engineer and the plan was to extract the gold from the waters of the Persian Gulf. All did not go well with this scheme and the gold production was far below expectations. More astronauts were sent to increase production.

They came by groups of 50 and in one of these groups was led by Enki's fist born son Marduk. Slow progress of gold turned to disappointment on the home planet Nibiru. The scheme to extract gold from sea water by laboratory processes did not work as expected. They had to either abandon the project which was out of the question or attain the gold in a new way by mining.

The gold was naturally available in the abundance in the Azul in the primeval source on the continent of Africa. There was one major problem. The African gold had to be extracted from the depths of the earth though mining and to change from a sophisticated water treatment process to backbreaking toil below the surface of the earth. This new enterprise required more Anunnaki, a mining company, and a fleet of ore vessels to transport the gold from earth to Nibiru. Could Enki handle all the new requirement by himself?

The reigning King on Nibiru, Anu felt he could not. Anu came down to earth to see for himself. He brought his aire apparent Enlil who Anu felt could take charge of earth mission and deliver the gold. The choice of Enlil might have been a necessary one, but it must have been an agonizing one but sharpened the rivalry and jealousy between his sons who were half-brothers, Enki and Enlil.

Enki was the first born son by Anu by Id one of his six concubines and could have expected to follow Anu on Niburu's thrown. But as in the Biblical tale of Abraham, his concubine Hagar and his half-sister wife Sarah Anu half-sister wife Untu bore him a son Enlil. The Niburuins rule of succession, Enlil became the legal aire to the thrown instead of Enki. Now Enki's rival and robber of Enki's birthright came to earth to take over the command.

One cannot stress enough lineage and genealogy, the wars of the Gods, the struggles and successions of supremacy on Nibiru as on earth later on. As we unravel the puzzling persistence and ferocity of the wars of the Gods trying to fit them into the framework of history and pre-history a task neve undertaken before. It becomes clear that they stem from a code of sexual behavior based not on morality but on considerations of genetic purity.

At the core of these wars is intricate genealogy that determine hierarchy and succession. Sexual acts were judged not by their tenderness or violence but by their purpose and outcome.

The Anunnaki established their presence in Mesopotamia and in Egypt in search of gold. Enlil was challenged by a mutiny of the Anunnaki who were working in the gold mines of the Abzu. In the Altrahasic Epic. A full-fledged earth chronicle that record the events that led to the creation of homo-sapiens.

The text informs us that after Anu had gone back to Nibiru and earth was divided between Enlil and Enki, The Anunnaki toiled in the mines for 40 counted periods or forty orbits of their planet, or 144,000 earth years.

The work was difficult and backbreaking inside the mountains of deeply cut shafts. The Anunnaki suffered the toil. The mining operations deep inside the earth were never interrupted and the Anunnaki suffered. As the shafts grew deeper and the toil harsher, dissatisfaction grew. They were complaining, backbiting, grumbling in the excavations.

To help maintain discipline, Enlil sent Minurta to the Abzu but this strained relations with the Enki even more. It was then that Enlil decided to go to the Abzu and personally evaluate the situation.

The discontented Anunnaki seized the opportunity to mutiny. The Altrahasic chronicle in language as vivid as that of an modern reporter. In more than 150 lines of text unambiguously describes the events that followed. How the rebellious Anunnaki put their tools on fire and in the middle of the night marched on Enlil dwellings.

How some shouted let us kill him and break the yoke. How and unnamed leader reminded them that Enlil was the chief office of old times and advised negotiations and how Enlil enraged took up his weapons. But he too was reminded by his Chamberlin "My Lords but these are your sons."

As Enlil remained a prisoner of his own quarters. He sent a message to Anu and asked that he come to earth. When Anu arrived, the great Anunnaki assembled for a court martial. Enki ruler of the Abzu was also present. Enlil demanded to know who the instigator of the mutiny was. Calling for a death penalty. Not getting support of Anu, Enlil offered his resignation. Noble one he said to Anu take away the office, take away the power, to heaven will I ascend with you.

But Anu calming Enlil also expressed understanding of the miner's hardship. In courage Enki opened his mouth and addressed the Gods. Repeating Anu summation he had a solution to all this. While the chief medical officer their sister was in the Abzu with them. Let her create a primitive worker and let him bear the yoke, let the worker carry the toil of the God, let him bear the yoke.

The tale of genetic engineering of Homo sapiens is detailed in the Altrahasic text and several other creation of man text that has been discovered in various states of preservation, the tale of the genetic engineering of Homo sapiens has been told in amazing detail.

To achieve the feat, Enki suggested that a being that already exist, ape woman, be used to create the lulu Amelie, the mix worker by binding upon the less evolved being the mold of the God. The God Apsu purified the essence of a young male Anunnaki. She mixed it into the egg of an ape woman.

The fertilized egg was then implanted in the womb of a female Anunnaki for the required period of pregnancy. When the mix creature was born, Apsu lifted him up and shouted I have created. My hands has made the primitive worker. Homo sapien had come into being. It happened some 300,000 years ago. It came about through a feat of genetic engineering and embryo implant technique, which mankind himself is beginning to employ.

The findings by Martin Petr, a graduate student at Max Planck Institute for Evolutionary Anthropology, designed a set of probes that used the DNA sequence from small chunks of modern men's Y chromosomes to "fish out" and bind DNA from Neanderthal and Denisovan Y chromosomes.

The new method works because Neanderthal and modern human chromosomes are similar. What caused the divergence of modern humans from Neanderthal and Denisovan some 600,000 years ago? Neanderthal remains dating from 38,000 to 100,000 years ago contain the maternally inherited mitochondrial DNA (mtDNA) of a modern human woman, instead of the ancient Neanderthal mtDNA found in earlier fossils.

In that case, an early Homo Sapien woman's gene could have been spliced with a Neanderthal man more than 220,000 years ago. Was a more advanced specie's gene spliced into Neanderthal specie's DNA that changed its Y chromosome pattern? Research by Martin Petr may indicates cross-breeding or mating of early modern humans with Neanderthal women as far back as 370,000 years ago.

There has been undoubtedly a long process of evolution. But then the Anunnaki has taken a hand in the process and jumped the gun on evolution creating us sooner than we might have evolved on our own. Scholars have been searching for a long time for the missing link in man's evolution.

The Sumerian text reveal the missing link was a feat of genetic manipulation performed in a laboratory. It was not a feat over and done with in an instance. The text made clear that it had taken the Anunnaki considerable trial and error to achieve the desired perfect model of the primitive worker. But once achieved, a mass production process was launched.

Fourteen birth Goddesses at a time were implanted with the genetically manipulated ape women eggs. Seven to bear males, and seven to bear female workers. As soon as they grew up, the workers were put to work in the mines. As their numbers grew, they assumed more and more of the physical chores in the Abzu.

The armed clash between Enki and Enlil that was soon to take place was over these same slave laborers. The more the production of ores improved in the Abzu, the greater was the workload on the Anunnaki that has remained to operate the facilities of Mesopotamia. The climate was milder, rains were more plentiful, and the Rivers of Mesopotamia were constantly overflowing.

Increasingly, the Mesopotamia Anunnaki were digging the rivers, raising the dykes and deepening the canals. Soon they too began to clamor for the slave workers, the creatures of bright countenance but with thick black hair. The Anunnaki stepped up requests to Enlil for black headed ones. To the black headed people to give the pick axe.

Enki refused Enlil's request for the transfer of primitive workers to Mesopotamia. Deciding to take matters in his own hands, Enlil took the extreme step of disconnecting the communication with the home planet. In the bond heaven and earth he made a gash. Then he launched an armed attack against the lands of the mines. The Anunnaki in the Abzu assembled the primitive workers in a central compound. Strengthened its wall against the coming attack.

Enlil drove a hole through the fortification. As the hole widened primitive workers broke out of the hole towards Enlil. Thereafter the primitive workers performs the manual task in both lands. In the land of the mines, they bored the work and suffered the toils. In Mesopotamia, with picks and spades they built God's houses, they built the big canal banks, foods they grew for the sustenance of the Gods.

Many ancient drawing engraved on cylinder seals depicted these primitive workers performing their tasks, naked as the animals of the fields. Various Sumerian texts recorded this animal like stage in human development. When mankind was first created, they knew not the eating of bread, knew not the dressing of garment, ate plant with their mouth like sheep, and drank water from the ditch.

How long young female Anunnaki could be asked or forced to perform the role of birth goddesses? Unbeknownst to Enlil, with the connivance of Apsu, Enki contrived to give the new creature one more genetic twist, granting to the hybrid being the ability to have offspring, the sexual knowing for having children.

The event is echoed in the Biblical tale of Adam and Eve in the Garden of Eden. Although the original Sumerian text of the tale has not been found, a number of Sumerian depiction of the event were indeed discovered. They show different aspects of the tale, the tree of life, the offering of the forbidden fruit, the angry encounter that ensued between the Lord God and the serpent. Yet another shows Eve girdled in a garment around her loins while Adam is still naked.

The Bible in the original Hebrew called the God who tempted Eve Nachash. Translated serpent, but literally meaning he who solves secrets and he who knows metals. Enki was arrested after his unauthorized deed. In his anger, Enlil ordered the expulsion of the Adam the homo-sapiens earthling from the Eden, the abode of the righteous ones. No longer confined to the settlement of the Anunnaki, man began to roam the earth. Adam knew Eve his wife and conceived. The Gods were no longer alone on earth.

It is widely known that the early chapters of Genesis do not stand alone in the history of the **Ancient Near East** (ANE). Other texts parallel the biblical account of creation and the existence of similarities between Genesis, and ANE literature has led critical scholars to conclude that Genesis was dependent upon the Mesopotamian texts.

Today, however, there are many professing evangelical scholars who argue that the early chapters of Genesis were influenced by these ANE myths. Similarity between Genesis 1–2 and other ANE accounts have led these evangelical scholars to conclude that Genesis is not historical but "is an ancient Near Eastern form of science.

Biblical and Sumerian ANE accounts "share a conceptual world," which is why Genesis 1–2 is seen as "ancient cosmology." The similarities between the Sumerian ANE texts and Genesis 1–2 have convinced many of these scholars that Adam never existed or that he is anything other than the first human, who was supernaturally created. These scholars believe the Bible's account of Adam is based on *Atrahasis* and *Gilgamesh Epics* from Sumerian texts.

Is it our greatest blunder to force Biblical Scripture upon the world as Zionist Israel seek to do, it is the ancient text before Judaism, Christianity, and Muslim faiths that are organic and closer to nature that may be a better guide for our understanding of the world.

In an age of advancing technology, possibly connecting human civilization to extraterrestrial beings, it is more than alarming that the Bible and Koran ignore literal and physical evidence of extraterrestrial presence among humans on earth.

If Christians are to uphold the gospel message of Jesus consistently, the historical authenticity of Genesis as an account of material origins and original sin from Adam as the father of all humanity remains crucial.

CHAPTER III

EXTRATERRESTRIAL PRESENCE DRIVING HUMAN AFFAIRS?

Path 17: Realm of Death Staining the Sanctum of Love

In all of its majestic beauty in its multitudes of life creating elements, the question being asked of God is why are picturesque cosmic planetary oases of life overwhelmed with perverse themes of death? Everywhere one looks things are coming apart, a star in being shredded by a black hole, and some human or animal is being killed.

What appetite does endless and horrific tragedies of death serve God? Tragedies after tragedy permanently intruding upon the sanitary sanctum of a spirit of holiness embedded in a sense that life is a gift. Why is this gift accommodated with a seemingly organic disorder programmed in nature itself to stain the very fibers of this phenomenon of life that invariably stains every sanctum of those spiritual elements in consciousness that we think of as love?

In light of the intrusions upon the organic bastion of human nature itself, by prioritizing technological advancements of artificial intelligence over human nature, who are the Meta gatekeepers and what price are we as human being willing to pay for advance technologies? What is the end game trading human souls for artificial intelligence?

If we look carefully, we can see the human extinction writing on the wall. We cut down the forests to harvest earth's natural resources. We exchange uprooting trees that purify the air and provide the very oxygen we need for life. Many animals are forced out of their habitat into extinction for the sake of financial profiting. We have lost perspective on valuing nature around us that makes life possible and we have also lost a reverence for human life itself.

What course are we on and what is the end game for humans on this planet? No species was meant to live forever in such a volatile cosmic environment that incorporates death as a discipline needed to sustain life. Death is the shadow that life casts by nature of coming into existence. Death or God stalks the living much like a creditor from whom we have borrowed our essence from.

In a world of artificial intelligence where robots and androids are created without the need of hearts, blood, or brains that are created from natural organic elements. In this computerized virtual realm of artificial intelligence, love is permanently replaced with logic. Air, water, and a reverence for God is not necessary for artificial beings to proliferate.

What is the end game for beings with chips in their brains, not knowing what love is and have no organic sense of a spiritual connection to a cosmic creator? What kind of hell is it to live in a virtual logical realm where the rustle of wind through the leaves has no meaning, where the moisture of water becomes irrelevant, and where there is no foundation of a sense of love calculating each thought?

Let's just imagine that humans are overtaken by being with artificial intelligence, robots o androids if you can. Let's imagine after vital resources on earth are depleted and it becomes possible through advanced technology in space travel to migrate to distant exoplanets and we find primitive life thriving on those planets.

Could this scenario be the story of the beginning of life on earth? In this scenario, space travelers from earth, in search of life sustaining elements, are embraced as Gods arriving to colonize this virgin exoplanet. This indeed may be the story of how life was started here on earth.

Path 18: Are other extraterrestrials, Greys and Draco-Reptilians also doing biological research? Are the different races on this planet control groups of experimentation?

If mankind evolved from the same African ancestor then everyone's blood would be compatible, but it is not. Rhesus negative blood type appeared 35,000 years ago in Cro-Magnon. Where did the Rhesus negative come from? Why does the body of an Rh negative mother carrying an Rh positive child try to reject her own offspring? Is humanity not just one race but hybrid species.

-Robert Sepehr-

Has Planet Earth been a place where Greys and Draco-Reptillians have used humans for biological research? Are different races on this planet separate control groups of experimentation?

There are huge discontinuities between man and various Apes for whole mitochondrial DNA genes for the Rh factor and human Y chromosomes among others regarding number three the chromosomes. Key terms.

Homolog

- A gene related to a second gene by descent from a common ancestral DNA sequence. The term, homolog, may apply to the relationship between genes separated by the event of speciation (see ortholog) or to the relationship between genes separated by the event of genetic duplication (see paralog).

Ortholog

- Orthologs are genes in different species that evolved from a common ancestral gene by speciation. Normally, orthologs retain the same function in the course of evolution. Identification of orthologs is critical for reliable prediction of gene function in newly sequenced genomes. (See also Paralogs.).

Speciation

- Speciation is the origin of a new species capable of making a living in a new way from the species from which it arose. As part of this process it has also acquired some barrier to genetic exchange with the parent species.

Paralog

- Paralogs are genes related by duplication within a genome. Orthologs retain the same function in the course of evolution, whereas paralogs evolve new functions, even if these are related to the original one.

A genome is an organism's complete set of DNA, including all of its genes. Each genome contains all of the information needed to build and maintain that organism. In humans, a copy of the entire genome—more than 3 billion DNA base pairs—is contained in all cells that have a nucleus.

Kady Smith's 1987 study titled "Repeated DNA Sequences of the Human Y chromosome." It states:

> Most human Y chromosome sequences so far examined do not homologs, which are similar sequences on the Y chromosomes of other primates. Human female DNA does look somewhat ape-like, but not the male Y chromosome.
>
> This means that if we are a cross-bred hybrid species, as many geneticists contends, the cross had to be between a female ape-like creature of the earth, as the Sumerians says, and a male person from elsewhere.
>
> What the evolutionist do is find certain genes which look very similar between man and ape then they make

> a tree of descent while ignoring those huge impassable abysses of difference between man and ape elsewhere.
>
> By certain methods of DNA dating one can tell that numerous genes have been recently added to the human genome. If workers in the genetics field discussed such things openly, they will be ostracized. Any work along this line of thinking would be rejected without appeal.

What is really going on with the Rh factor? It is known that Rh Positive have a protein in common with the Rhesus Monkeys and Rh Negative do not have that protein. What exactly happened 6000 years ago in Samaria when civilization began?

According to Ed Green University of Santa Cruz there is a close relationship between Neanderthals and non-African than there is with people from Africa. Harvard researchers has declared black people are the only ones who have 100% human DNA. One to 4 percent of the genetic ancestry of any non-African can be attributed traced back to Neanderthal DNA.

Dr. David Emil Reich, a genetic professor at Harvard, and his colleagues analyzed the genetic variants of 846 non-African people, 175 people who live in the sub-Saharan region of Africa with a 50,000 year-old Neanderthal man. They found nine generic variants found in non-African humans were also found in Neanderthals.

Neanderthals DNA affects how keratin filaments developed. As opposed to humans that made their skin tougher. This tough skin allowed them to survive in harsh, cold climates.

It is due to an admixture event that happened very early on when humans migrated out of Africa and first came upon Neanderthal's range where they picked up Neanderthal genetics component and then took it with them as they went over the rest of the world. The world had a small population then, so we see this roughly in equal proportions all over the world.

A separate study by Dr. Benjamin Vernot and D. Joshua Akey, from the University of Washington, yielded the same conclusion by analyzing 286 East Asians and 379 Europeans. Some population have more Neanderthal genes than others. East Asians are more Neanderthal derived than Europeans. They have a little more on average. This is counter intuitive because Neanderthal are known to being Western Eur-Asian population.

What happened between the Neanderthal and the Cro-Magnum Man? What is the Rhesus blood type of the Neanderthal and the Cro-Magnum? We know the Neanderthal have the "O" blood type but we do not know the Rhesus factor. That aspect of the Neanderthal genome has not been mapped out and revealed.

Do humans represent a new species on the planet earth? We have the Neanderthal and the Cro-Magnum, which were entirely different species. Genetically, the Neanderthal and the Cro-Magnum were two different species, so what was really going on? Why does the gene to the Rhesus factor hold the key to the key differences between man and ape?

Genesis in the Bible talks about man being created out of dust of the Earth. The Bible does not tell us if there was already another species here. It is only telling us that a new species has been created on Earth. There is a lot about how man came upon Earth that we are not told.

What are geneticists really finding out? If you take an Rh positive person, someone that does not have any of the Rh Negative genetics, and compare the genetics of the Rh positive and Rh negative person, how would they differ?

The geneticists are covering up a lot and are in support of the evolution theory. The evidence coming about does not support the theory of evolution. Many Geneticists are starting to speak up about the inconsistencies of the Theory of Evolution.

Has Planet Earth been a place where Greys and Draco-Reptillians have used humans for biological research where different races on this planet are separate control groups of experimentation? Racism by the experimenters is the perfect way to keep control groups biologically pure.

The theory that all humans began existence in Africa is suspect. Geneticists study different cultures on different plates. If Greys or Draco-Reptillians have been conducting biological experiments looking for advantageous genetics, they care not about racism but are likely following programs but only caring about if they can mess with our genes programming change through genetic alterations.

Regarding the molecule melanin, one of the ways geneticists use ultra-violet light to splice cells to alter the genetics. Melanin absorbs ultra-violet light turns it into vibrations and the ultra-violet light does not get where it is intended to go.

Discoveries of sub-species of humans without greater expressions of melanin made it easy to alter genetic profiles. Could the Greys or Draco-Reptillians have sent white people north of Africa, some isolated as Aborigines in Australia, some left in Africa, and some moved to Asia? Was there a great movement of populations for biological experimental purposes?

Those with less melanin were easier to alter their genetic profiles. Melanin in black people is spread out through the cells in the skin and covers everything. In white people the melanin will coat the nucleus of the cell, so even in white people DNA can be well protected from gene altering ultra-violet light. Black people, with high contents of melanin in their skin, coats the cell wall nucleus of DNA and blocks ultra-violet light used to splice DNA, the ultra violet light is absorbed by melanin.

If the Greys were trying to alter the species with dark melanin, did melanin play a role in altering the species with dark melanin? When a random mutation like an Albino came along, did the experimenters realize that they could get straight into the cells minus the melanin?

Are pale skinned humans a biological modification to support genetic alterations by aliens? Have the northern European experienced the most outside interference by genetic altering Grey aliens?

Look at the aggression of the European nations, the colonization, the rape, pillage, and plunder of the world of melanin rich people, the development of nuclear weapons and anti-gravity space ships, one can see the advancement or gene alteration influence in technological advancement where Europeans have advanced from the horse and buggy to putting space ships into the heavens.

German scientists during WWII stated extraterrestrials helped with their technical advancement, thereby, interfering and feeding off the low vibrations of human suffering during war?

Trans-humanism and tapping into organic human spirituality by mapping the brain and downloading human souls into a virtual world where mechanical robots of synthetic intelligence such as the Greys attempts to develop souls.

What is synthetic and what is natural, humans are natural and Greys are synthetic androids. The Greys seek a natural organic soul but they can never bridge into the natural world. They have the technological advantage over us, why not decimate us and take the planet? It is not the planet they want, they want to experience what we experience and that is an organic soul in a natural organic universe.

Human have a pathway back from the physical universe back to the infinite. The Greys with all their logical based mathematical constructs do not have a pathway from the physical to the infinite spiritual beyond as humans do.

The Greys realize that the laws of thermodynamic breaks physical things down and they understand that thing about human being and all living organic things have this information field and returns through reincarnation. This information field from an eternal state never ends.

The Greys detects this and they are looking for that revitalizing factor that humans and animals seem to have through reincarnation.

The Greys are looking for that revitalizing factor that will give their program from their original creators a chance to survive forever like people do as eternal souls. All religions of humanity believes in the migration of the soul.

The transhumanist are looking for some kind of physical immortality by creating artificial beings even tempting people to relish prospects of mapping brains and downloading the mapped entity into a virtual universe to live inorganically in a virtual universe.

Transhumanism is a physically oriented prosthetic awareness of immortality your soul is equipped with already. People are being told if you accept the chip implant you are going to be more intelligent with downloads from the cloud. This set in motion the interference with the natural scope of conscience aware of being with artificial quantum, those chips can be hacked into and controlled from the outside. Mind control by those minds already controlled by the Grey Aliens who are hell-bent on undermining the natural ascension of humanity through advanced technology.

How do Greys expect to hijack, if you will, our souls? The soul of humans are in a continuum outside of atoms and therefore outside a point of force. While we are inside atoms in a living system, there are symmetries of molecules that has to do with the shape of water and etc.

where you can actually get the physical fields and the outside field to resonate that is the living structure of a human born into the physical world.

When we die the soul is no longer held in the atomic molecular physical structure and your soul gets out through decreasing levels of tensions or force. Some of the edges of force or accessible by the Greys at theses edges. If you have qualities that are going to bring you back again they can nip away and implant qualities in your soul that when you come back again you are a little more like them. That part of you in no longer under your control and you become more and more like them, which is a type of hybridization of human and Greys.

The Greys aim to put their program into us. They live on piggybacking through us on their terms. It is all about losing or having our natural organic information field that connects us to the organic universe hacked by the Greys. We become more restricted and more physically devolved beings. We lose our sense of humanity altogether. We become like machines, living through the Internet, not communicating with people one to one, with everything becoming virtual and synthetic.

There are people in the intelligence agencies work with or are aware of the entire Grey project and it is being covered up. Have the Greys subverted the entire information and power hierarchy attempting to spread their entire program throughout a growing rank of human hosts.

How must we face this huge challenge? Hope is to be found in the knowledge imparted to us by the great teachers in the past. Those who encouraged us to love and care for each other. Encouraging us not to be selfish and self-centered.

Jesus Christ warned his Apostles about the Alien Apocalypse in the Second Apocalypse of James talking about the pitiless ones who will take souls by theft. A more recent discovered text The Gospel of Judas where Christ tells Judas that he is of the seed of an alien entity.

Christ knew there was something going on and suggests there is an antidote to Grey aliens interrupting our information field that traces back to the infinite organic source of being. Maybe we can break that interruption by resembling more that prior state where everything was together and we were not separated and machine minded, the very opposite of transhumanism.

We need to collectively understand that the state we exist in is analogous to a near death experience, which we have an opportunity to come back and live transformed lives devoting energies to helping people. We must live life with a spiritual insight beyond the atomic state of the material world. We must will ourselves to the prime state of unadulterated love for each other.

Path 19: Are inhabitants of earth seeded from different star nations?

So, what race is the true bloodline back to ancient astronauts that colonized earth in search of gold?

Many scientists believe that modern man evolved from ape-like primates. There are many theories, including modern blood analysis and comparative studies between modern man and lower anthropoids, such as the chimpanzee and the Rhesus monkey.

It has been proven that the majority of mankind (85%) has a blood factor common with the rhesus monkey. This is called rhesus positive blood. Usually shortened to Rh positive. This factor is completely independent from the A, B, 0 blood types.

Modern man and rhesus monkey share the positive Rh factor. Why do some 15% of the population have Rh negative blood? If all mankind evolved from the same ancestor their blood would be compatible. If they are not the descendants of prehistoric man, could they be the descendants of ancient astronauts from other solar systems from habitable planet light years away? No one has tried to explain where people with Rh negative blood come from.

The Basque people of Spain and France have the highest percentage of Rh negative blood. About 30% have (rr) Rh negative and about 60% carry one (r) negative gene. The Oriental Jews of Israel, also have a high percent Rh negative, although most other Oriental people have only about 1% Rh negative. The Samaritans and the Black Cochin Jew also have a high percentage of Rh negative blood, although again the Rh negative blood is rare among most black people.

African Americans, about 90-95 percent are Rh-positive, and for Asians, the figure is 98 to 99 percent. But, strangely.... a person with type O negative blood is considered to be a "Universal Donor". It means his or her blood can be given to anyone, regardless of blood type, without causing a transfusion reaction. In China, over 99% of the population has Rh positive blood. The Mayans are also 98% O Rh positive blood.

Group O is the oldest of the blood groups. All humans in the Stone Age would have been group O. The second oldest group is the Group A. This group appeared between 25,000 and 15,000 BC around the time farming developed. Group B emerged between 15,000 and 10,000 BC when tribes began migrating from Africa to Europe, Asia and the Americas. The newest and rarest group is Group AB. This only appeared between 500 to 1,000 years ago. It is thought to be due to the intermingling of the other groups over many centuries. Approximately 10% of the populations of Japan, China and Pakistan have this group.

What probably makes the most sense is that these 15% of the population with Rh negative blood were some of the original inhabitants of Earth, most likely being seeded here from at least one star nation. Blue eyed inhabitants only date back to 10,000 years ago, which were most likely a 2nd generation of inhabitants from various star nations.

Through interbreeding, the blue eyed gene has been passed on to Rh negative people, but each blood type most likely represents your particular link to any given star nation that contributed to the populating of this planet.

Here is a list of prominent people and world leaders, some allegedly are members of Secret Societies with a criteria of having Rh negative blood.

Former U.S Presidents

Former President Eisenhower Type O-Neg
Former President John F. Kennedy Type AB-Neg
Former President Richard Nixon Type O-Neg
Former President Bill Clinton AB-Neg
Former President George W. Bush Sr. Type A-Neg

Monarchs

Pharaoh Ramses II Type B-Neg
Shroud of Turin was AB-Neg is this correct?
Prince Charles Type O-Neg and his late Grandmother
Queen Elizabeth Type O-Neg

Interesting Authors

Zacharia Sitchin Type Neg
Brad Steiger O-Neg
Erik Von Daniken Type O-Neg
Robert Anton Wilson Type Neg

Celebrities

Mick Jagger Type AB-Neg
Fox Mulder "X-files" Type O-Neg
Marilyn Monroe was Type AB-Neg
Dan Aykroyd Type O-Neg

High Profile Murders

O.J. Simpson is Type A-Neg "who killed"
Ron Goldman Type O-Neg
Laci Peterson Type O-Neg

Do Rh negative blood types have special abilities or talents that Rh positive types don't have? What are the differences between blood types? I am convinced power struggles and the wars to consolidate the world into one global society are being led by leaders who think they have divine connections to other worldly Gods or ancient astronauts through the blood type of Rh negative. It does not surprise me that the Royal family are included in the list above having Rh negative blood.

Ancient Alien's DNA manipulation to create a race of slaves

Who were Neanderthals? Were Neanderthals a distinct species of the *Homo*genus (*Homo neanderthalensis*) or a subspecies of *Homo sapiens.*

Like other humans, Neanderthals originated in Africa but migrated to Eurasia long before other humans did. Neanderthals lived during the Ice Age. They often took shelter from the ice, snow and otherwise unpleasant weather in Eurasia's plentiful limestone caves. Many of their fossils have been found in caves, leading to the popular idea of them as "cave men."

Neanderthals (or Neanderthals) are our closest extinct human relatives. Our well-known, but often misunderstood, fossil kin lived in Eurasia 200,000 to 30,000 years ago, in the Pleistocene Epoch.

Neanderthals lived across Eurasia, as far north and west as the Britain, through part of the Middle East, to Uzbekistan. Popular estimates put the peak Neanderthal population around 70,000, though some scientists put the number drastically lower, at around 3,500. The American Museum of Natural History sites differences from other humans such as flaring, funnel-shaped chest, a flaring pelvis, and robust fingers and toes. Approximately 1 percent of Neanderthals had red hair, light skin, and maybe even freckles.

Neanderthals were primarily carnivorous, and the harsh climate caused them to resort occasionally to cannibalism.

There is some debate as to whether Neanderthals were a distinct species of the *Homo*genus (*Homo neanderthalensis*) or a subspecies of *Homo sapiens*. There is much confusion when it comes to questions of Homo neanderthalensis mating with interbreeding with other Homo Sapiens of African origin. Scholar's opinions ranging from belief that they definitely interbred to belief that the two groups didn't exist on Earth at the same time.

Neanderthal expert Erik Trinhaus has long promoted the interbreeding hypothesis, but the theory really caught fire when a 2010 study published in Science magazine determined that Neanderthal DNA is 99.7 percent identical to modern human DNA (a chimp›s is 99.8 percent identical). Researchers of the Neanderthal Genome Project found that 2.5 percent of an average non-African human›s genome is made up of Neanderthal DNA. The average modern African has no Neanderthal DNA.

If Africans have no Neanderthal DNA and life originated out of Africa, what happened to the Africans who supposedly left Africa who later acquired Neanderthal DNA? Have we had two distinct species of Homogenus? If so, there is no way the Biblical story of Adam and Eve can be true.

So, we have a different Homogenus specie that either interbred with Homo sapiens out of Africa or are speculations of planet earth is a place where extraterrestrials really are conducting biological experiments on many different forms of life, including man.

What is interesting today is that Neanderthals lived during the Ice Age. They often took shelter from the ice, snow and otherwise unpleasant weather in Eurasia's plentiful limestone caves. The harsh climate caused them to resort occasionally to cannibalism.

Anthropologists continue to debate why Neanderthals, a now-extinct species of human, died out approximately 30,000 years ago. A new model suggests the practice of cannibalism may have contributed to the Neanderthals' extinction.

About 800,000 years ago, Homo heidelbergensis, living in Europe and Africa, gave rise to a number of future human types, including Homo sapiens (us), Neanderthals, Denisovans, and others. Geneticists claim that the lineages of Homo sapiens and Neanderthals had a common ancestor until about 588,000 years ago, when these two kinds of humans became isolated from one another and proceeded to evolve separately.

Homo sapiens continued to evolve in Africa, mostly likely East Africa. Homo sapiens skeletons have been described as gracile—and in the language of anthropologists, this means tall, thin, and built for heat dissipation and running. Neanderthal skeletons are described as robust: short, stocky, and built for heat retention. Neanderthals continued to evolve and thrive mostly alone in Western Europe and Asia until they went extinct about 30,000 years ago. The proposed reasons for their extinction range from pure chance to climate change to demographics (group size) to war with Homo sapiens.

Much has also been made of the coupling of Neanderthal extinction with the entry of anatomically modern Homo sapiens into Europe at the beginning of the Neanderthal extinction. Some anthropologists believe it is a mere coincidence, primarily because there is little or no evidence for war or direct competition between these two human types. These "twist of fate" anthropologists further argue that Neanderthal brains and behavior were the absolute equivalents of modern Homo sapiens

However, many anthropologists believe that it was a competition for resources, and not direct conflict, that led to Neanderthals' extinction. Some argue that small but significant cognitive differences between these two human cousins were the reason that Homo sapiens could extract greater resources from the same environments.

Underlying the extinction of Neanderthals location of the group with a definitive home range, the size of the group, and cannibalism (in order to eliminate competition and gain additional resources). Cannibalism appears to be an optimal way to obtain resources.

It is important to distinguish between two kinds of cannibalism, which is endocannibalism and exocannibalism. Endocannibalism is where a group eats its own members. This type of cannibalism can be practiced for nutritional reasons—that is, if a group is starving and very young or very old members might be eaten in order that the effective (i.e., working and reproductive) members of the group may survive. Endocannibalism may also be practiced for religious or symbolic reasons after a group member's death. Notice that in the former case, it might be considered murder, and in the latter case, it might represent reverence for the dead.

Exocannibalism, in contrast, involves eating members from other groups. Exocannibalism might be practiced to eliminate competition from a group's resources (food, shelter, etc.), to frighten away other groups, and/or for symbolic or nutritional reasons.

When resources were scarce and/or the environmental conditions were difficult (e.g., extreme cold), cannibalism may have been an optimal trait. In the latter conditions, groups that favored exocannibalism could gain additional resources, prevent their own extinction, and reduce competition by other groups.

Evidence of Neanderthal Cannibalism

California anthropologist Hélène Rougier (2016) and her colleagues analyzed 99 Neanderthal remains from a cave in Goyet, Belgium that dated to about 45,000 to 40,000 years ago. Their analysis showed very clear evidence for cannibalism and even the use of Neanderthal bones to resharpen defleshing tools. Roughly one-third of the bones had clear evidence of cut marks, and there were percussion marks (i.e., notches and pits) as well. Not only were these remains cannibalized, but they were found among many other animals, mainly reindeer and horses. There was also a large number of big animal bones, which were processed in the same way as the Neanderthal bones.

A review of six other instances of Neanderthal cannibalism ranging from 120,000 to 39,000 years ago shows that all were Neanderthal upon Neanderthal cannibalism. But the mystery deepens: In many of these aforementioned cases, animal bones were also present, bountiful, and processed in the same fashion. That is, cut marks on longer bones were similar for Neanderthal skeletons and animals, and the bones were split to extract nutritionally-rich marrow.

Why would Neanderthals eat other Neanderthals if animals were plentiful? It is known that Neanderthals did not restrict themselves to just meat resources—there is evidence that they sometimes ate plants and other non-meat foods. Some Neanderthals, perhaps beginning about 120,000 years ago, began practicing cannibalism as an optimal strategy of gaining resources and reducing competition.

However, it may have begun an almost 80,000-year tradition of gustatory cannibalism in some Neanderthal groups—that is, some Neanderthals simply enjoyed the taste of Neanderthal flesh. It also seems unlikely that the practice began in each Neanderthal group independently over 80,000 years, but it was more likely that it was a tradition passed down through generations of Neanderthals.

Recent research published in the October 2017 issue of American Journal of Human Genetics found that genomes of modern human groups originating outside Africa contain between 1.8 and 2.6 percent Neanderthal DNA. Today the Homo sapiens originating out of Africa are at war with humans with Neanderthal DNA in them.

My questions are where did the Neanderthal come from, why do they hate black Africans, and did they really go extinct around 40,000 years ago? Who made two distinct Homogenus species? A 2017 study by author Kay Prüfer, a paleo geneticist at the Max Planck Institute for Evolutionary Anthropology in Leipzig, Germany, found that modern-human DNA entered the Neanderthal gene pool between 130,000 and 145,000 years ago. Not one Holy Book addresses these questions.

Now, scientists believe they have found out a fascinating thing in regards of Rh Positive and negative. According to this "scientific" theory, in the distant past, extraterrestrial beings visited the Earth and created, through "genetic manipulation," the Rh Negative with an intention of creating a race of "slaves".

But Aliens... really? According to investigators, this would explain why Rh negative mothers do not tolerate fetuses with RH Positive blood; thus, this radical, hard-to-explain, by most natural laws intolerance could derive from an ancient genetic modification why Rh positive and Rh negative groups tend to "repel" each other instead of merging.

It is believed that these ancient beings planned and genetically altered primitive human species, creating stronger and more "adequate" beings that were used as slaves in the distant past.

The Rh negative would be the legacy that the Anunnaki left on Earth among other things. Interestingly, the negative RH strain is characteristic, for example, of the British royal family, which has generated controversial theories about a possible extraterrestrial lineage.

Although this hypothesis has not been confirmed, the disturbing questions it generates floats in the air: how would a civilized world react to facts that a small portion of the Earth's population has a genetic code that has been altered in the distant past by highly advanced extraterrestrial beings?

What if it is possible, after all of our "skeptical" views that in the end, the Negative Rh group of people have a connection to "beings" not from earth. What if there still is, a mysterious bond that connects them? How would life on Earth change?

Blood lines

From these bloodlines has come the origin of the "divine right of kings", the belief that only certain bloodlines have the God-given right to rule.

In truth this is not the "*divine*" or "*God*" at all. It is the right to rule from the reptilian "gods" by way of your hybrid genetics.

These bloodlines later became the royal and aristocratic families of Europe and, thanks to the "Great" British Empire and the other European empires, they were exported to the Americas, Africa, Australia, New Zealand, and right across into the Far East, where they connected with other reptilian hybrid bloodlines, like those, most obviously, in China, where the symbolism of the dragon is the very basis of their culture.

These reptilian-human hybrid lines became the political and economic rulers of these lands occupied by the European empires and they continue to rule these countries to this day.

The United States of America has been home to hundreds of millions of people since 1776. What's more, these people came from an amazingly diverse genetic pool. And yet, wait for this, the 42 who have become Presidents of the United States are all related!!! Thirty-Three of them alone go back to Charlemagne, one of the most famous monarchs of what we call France. He just happens to be a major figure in the story of these bloodlines and their expansion out of Britain, France, Germany, and elsewhere.

Many researchers have written of the possibility that life on this planet began with "ancient astronauts" from other stars or other galaxies who colonized this planet untold thousands of years ago. However, there is another possibility which has not received the attention which it deserves, possibly because of the vain belief held by many modern scientists that they are the "be all and end all" of technological understanding whereas human civilizations on this planet is concerned.

Therefore, some of these believe themselves to be the first and only civilization on this planet to have developed sophisticated sciences, or to have landed manned craft on the moon, Mars, and regions beyond.

Many scientists will dismiss the notion that ancient civilizations could have developed aerospace travel capable of propelling them towards the stars. But, are their presuppositions justified?

Theologically speaking, it is only logical that a Divine initiator of all things would choose to "plant" the seed of life at one particular point in the universe, and from there carefully nurture and observe that life reproduce from this central point of genesis, in essence working out "The Plan" in that particular part of the Universe before allowing that life to spread too far out into other regions of the Cosmos. Since man possesses free agency the success or failure of "The Plan" would to some extent be up to them.

In spite of various theories which have been presented, there is no solid evidence that man "evolved" from apes (which in turn supposedly evolved from small mammals which supposedly gained their sophisticated computer-like "programmed" genetic makeup from almost invisible sea urchins. Actually, a recent poll (1990's) revealed that only 9 percent of the population of the United States atheistically rejects the possibility of a Creator who established all things and guides the universe in its evolution or course.

(These same 9 percent happen to include many of the very same "inner elite" who manipulate the mass media to their own ends and lie about the true facts and figures. For years they have been telling us that "most" people reject the Creation Sciences view of history. In this way they try to manipulate public opinion, and to a great degree they have succeeded).

The **Alpha Draconians**, a reptilian race composed of master geneticists, tinker with life - which from their perspective exists as a natural resource.

The Draconians look at lifeforms which they have created or altered as a natural resource. Apparently, the Alpha Draconians created the primate race, which was first brought to Mars and then to Earth.

The primate race was then tinkered with by many other different races - 21 other races - resulting in the primate race having been modified 22 times. This primate race eventually became Homo Sapien Sapiens. - who we are on a physical level. Yes, we used to have 12 strands of DNA. Ten strands were taken out by a group from Orion in order to control us and hold us back. Why would they want to hold us back?

The reason the Orion group wanted to hold us back was because they found out who we were on a soul level. Again, according to **the Andromedans**, we humans are part of a group of energies that they know of as the Paa Tal.

The Contradiction

How the human race colonized our galaxy. Based on the age of the Suns and the planets in our galaxy, it was decided that the human life form was to be created in the Lyran system. The human race lived there for approximately 40 million years, evolving. The orientation of the human race in Lyrae was agricultural in nature. Apparently, we were very plentiful and abundant, and lived in peace.

Then, one day, huge craft appeared in the sky.

[This scenario is the theme of the movie *Independence Day*, to air in the theatres nationally on July 7, 1996].

A large ship came out of the huge craft and approached the planet Bila, and reptilians from Alpha Draconis disembarked. Apparently, the Alpha Draconians and the Lyrans were afraid of each other.

Alpha Draconians were apparently the first race in our galaxy to have interstellar space travel, and have had this capability for 4 billion years. Well, when the Draconians came and saw Bila, with all its abundance and food and natural resources, the Draconians wanted to control it.

The word "Jehovah" originally meant, in the Chaldean and Hebrew, "*is, was, and will be*". The reason he was given that name is because he lives such a long time. They live thousands of years in one incarnation.

It never meant "creator of all things". He used technology to promote himself as a "God", and fear is an incredible tool when you want to get people to do something. Some of you have no doubt observed this factor in some of the activities of the world governments.

The Chaldean people were the remnants of the Sumerian people. This you probably already know. Much of the Hebrew religion and the religion of the Sumerians are similar. The books of Moses do not in any way suggest that Jehovah was in any way the only "lord of the Elohim".

The expressions "Elohim" and "Nephilim" are used in the original Hebrew tongue, and these expressions are plural in nature, which means that in their terms there was more than one "God". That should be a major tip to everyone.

Abraham, whose name was "Abramou", did consider Jehovah to be a "God" because of the technology that **Jehovah** and the other Elohim possessed. Many of the "Gods" did the same thing. They used technology to strike fear into the people, and they worshipped the "Gods" to avoid punishment. Any of this sound familiar, here in 1997?

Marduk, whom we also know as the *Egyptian "God"* **Ra**, Enki, and En-lil, were notorious for doing this.

These extraterrestrial manipulators used bigotry because they wanted to control their own groups of people, and each of their offspring procreated with elements of the population of the earth. According to Moraney and Vasais, our Native American races are the remnants of the ancient Babylonians.

They were brought here and hidden underground just prior to the flood of Noah.

Now, what was the flood of Noah? We are told that it rained for 40 days and 40 nights. According to Moraney, the flood of Noah was as a result of the movement of Earth from one orbit to another around the Sun. The Earth was apparently hit with a tractor beam and literally moved to an orbit further out from the Sun.

This added five days to our rotational period around the Sun. The period of this 40 day rain was during the period when the magnetic poles of the Earth rotated 180 degrees.

My reason for telling you this is to try and give you a broader perspective. There is just so much more to who we are and who we've been. We have been manipulated by the "hidden ones". The reason they remain "unseen" is because on-the-whole they are basically afraid of us. They are afraid of something about us. They absolutely do not want us to unite together, because then the "gig" is up.

Now, when the extraterrestrials were here in force - that is, during the time referenced in the Bible where is says the Sons of God married the Daughters of Man, they bred and mated with their human wives. Out of this came offspring, half-breeds. There were at that time, within the last 5000 years, predominantly 13 families from Sirius B and Nibiru, who were living here on the planet. These were the tribes of En-lil, Marduk, Enki, etc. They all had offspring.

Those from Nibiru were a tribe that came about as a result of a "marriage" between some groups between Sirius B and Orion. It was in essence a "royal marriage" between groups that formed a "tribe". This "tribe" was called Nibiru. The word Nibiru, in the ancient Sumerian language, means "between two peoples".

Sitchin calls it something else. The offspring were not allowed to go with the extraterrestrial parents when they left the Earth, because they were considered "half-breeds". The reason they were viewed like this by the extraterrestrials was because of their Terran genetics, which contain certain genes from the primate race.

According to Moraney, the first melding between the primate genes and the human species was 28,731,007 BC, and there have been many prototypes. In fact, they just found another prototype in Portugal that is estimated to be 780,000 years old. They will discover more. In fact, start looking for some major discoveries in Nigeria.

Apparently, there is a tremendous amount of extraterrestrial technology buried in Nigeria, which has not been tapped yet.

When the extraterrestrials left, the real ET›s, they left certain types of technology behind. The Indian Veda›s discuss some of this technology. They didn›t care. They had science teams who were constantly inventing new things, and as they got new technology they discarded the old.

Well, it was the Magi, the half-breeds that were left these technologies. There were 13 major families that were considered under the heading of Magi. Does that number ring a bell?

The members of these 13 families on earth contain the genetics of both Terran and extraterrestrial races that formerly tyrannized the Earth. They were basically left in charge. Some of them were actually Pharaohs.

The Magi interbreeding resulted in the cultures we today recognize as the "Ivory Hebrew", the "Mayan", the "Celts", and the "Aryan" races. Now, while all of this was transpiring on the surface of the planet, underground there was another extraterrestrial race that had been here - a race that has been here for hundreds of thousands of years. They are, of course, the reptilian race, which the Bible refers to as the "serpent race". Serpent men.

They are still here, and they can't stand the radiation of the sun. They haven't been able to live on the surface of the planet since the last major war that occurred here approximately 450,000 years ago. They are basically hyperborean in nature. They have control of the planet at depths from 100 to 200 miles down.

That's their turf, and no one contests that. That is why when people go into the inner earth, they enter via the poles. They do not go through the crust, because these reptilians simply to not like humans. They consider us to be "fleas" on the surface.

Again, prejudice as a concept has its origin in extraterrestrial perspectives. All of the concepts involving languages and social structures for human societies were introduced by extraterrestrial sources. All of the languages that we have on the planet have their origins within the structures of extraterrestrial languages. The letters and their numerical values.

From Moraney's perspective, "*Adam and Eve*" were in fact two human tribes that were created. I know the Bible refers to "Adam" as a singular person. This is not accurate. According to Moraney, there was a race of human beings prior to the Sumerians called the "Annunites", and they were named after the chief scientist who the Sumerian's called the "God" **Anu**.

The name of "A-dam", as far as these people were concerned, was originally "Anu-dam". That word meant *workers in the mines.* Like everything else, we get the "Cliff notes" version of what really was the case.

How the extraterrestrials were able to control all the populations. Apparently, there were groups of hundreds of thousands of people in areas all over the planet. Moraney said that it was very easy to control the population by controlling the water. He said that primary control was through technology, but the single most important control mechanism for a race as primitive as ours was control of the water supply. You have to have water.

Bill Clinton signed a presidential directive, number 28, which is legislation that has been put into the Federal Register. It did not go to Congress for approval.

They withheld it for two weeks, only giving the legislation 14 days of review before it became law. It is called the River Heritage Act.

He is taking ten of the largest rivers in the United States and declaring on behalf of the Federal Government that ten miles on each side constitute a "world heritage protection site". Now, why would he do this? On the entire planet, 2.5% of the water is fresh water that is fit to drink. Now, 78% of that 2.5% is right here in North America. The Great Lakes. Are you getting the picture?

Now, **the Magi** created class systems around themselves. Priesthood›s. You can read about this priesthood›s in Sumerian and Egyptian lore. Every major religion has these. The *priesthood's of the Magi* were known as the "Naga", and I know that is a name that has been thrown around a lot.

The Naga constituted the priesthood. They are like the international bankers today, who are the new "priesthood", in a sense, for the extraterrestrial controllers. Everything in your life revolves around *money*. Everything. My reason for bringing this up is to show you how history is constantly repeating itself.

Our race has been stuck in a cycle of doing the same thing over and over again, and getting "screwed" over and over again. Maybe now you will be able to take a step back and see the "games" and the political mind sets that are coming down again.

People don't give a damn, because they are so busy just "surviving". Well, you are going to have to try and make room for more than just "survival" in your life. You're going to have to do this. There is only one semi-free nation on the planet.

The United States. If we lose it, there is nowhere for us to go, and I will tell you this: I refuse to serve two masters! I refuse. You can't do it.

The Black Nobility

In Carthage, the Canaanites called themselves Punics.

Rome attacked Carthage in full force, beginning in 264BC and completed their task after killing or enslaving every Carthaginian, by sowing the land to salt so that nothing could ever grow there again.

The Edomite descended from Esau later intermarried with the Turks to produce a Turco-Edomite mixture which later became known as Chazars (Khazars) - who are the present occupants of Israel. These Canaanites eventually adopted the name "*Sepharvaim*" for deceptive purposes. They later became known as Venetians, and by marrying into European royalty and aristocracy, the "black nobility."

The Venetians today control the Federal Reserve System in the US.

Around AD1400, European power centers coalesced into two camps:

- the Ghibellines, who supported the Emperors Hohenstaufen family
- the Guelphs, from Welf, the German prince who competed with Frederick for control of the Holy Roman Empire

The Pope allied himself with the Guelphs. All modern history stems directly from the struggle between these two powers.

The Guelphs are also called the *Neri*, *Black Guelphs*, or Black Nobility, and supported William of Orange in his seizure of the throne of England, which eventually resulted in the formation of the Bank of England and the East India Company, which would rule the world from the 17th century. All coup d'états, revolutions and wars in the 19th and 20th centuries are centered in the battle of the Guelphs to hold and enhance their power, which is now the New World Order.

The power of the Guelphs would extend through the Italian financial centers to the north of France in Lombardy (all Italian bankers were referred to as "Lombards"). *Lombard* in German means "*deposit bank*", and the Lombards were bankers to the entire medieval world. They would later transfer operations north to Hamburg, then to Amsterdam and finally to London.

The Guelphs would start the slave trade to the colonies. The Guelphs, in order to aid their control of finance and politics, would perpetuate *gnostic cults* which eventually developed into the Rosicrucian, Unitarians, Fabian Society and the World Council of Churches. The East India Company, together with John Stuart Mill, would finance the University of London.

A friend of Mill, historian George Grote, a founder of London University donated £6000 for the study of "mental health", which began the worldwide "mental health" movement.

Banks large and small in the thousands are in the Committee of 300 network, including:

- Banca Commerciale d'Italia
- Banca Privata
- Banco Ambrosiano
- The Netherlands Bank
- Barclays Bank
- Banco de Colombia
- Banco de Ibero-America

Of special interest is Banca del la Svizzeria Italiana (BSI) - since it handles flight capital investments to and from the United States - primarily in dollars and US bonds - located and isolated in "neutral" Lugano, the flight capital center for the Venetian Black Nobility.

Lugano is not in Italy or in Switzerland, and is a kind of *twilight zone* for shady flight capital operations. George Ball, who owns a large block of stock in BSI, is a prominent "insider" and the bank's US representative.

In the secret 1822 Treaty of Verona (between Austria, France, Prussia and Russia) the Jesuits agreed to smash the US Constitution and suppress the freedom of the US. Their methods included destroying free speech, destroying and suppressing the press, universal censorship, sustaining the cooperation of the Pope and clergy to use religion to help keep nations in passive obedience and financing wars against countries with representative governments.

The monarchs who signed this treaty were ultimately deposed. Most of these families are very wealthy and may be more powerful today than when they sat upon thrones. They are known collectively as the Black Nobility. Privately these families refuse to recognize any right to rule except their own.

The fact that this treaty was made long ago does not mean it is void. The treaty was placed in the Congressional Record on April 25, 1916 by Senator Owen.

In 1948 **George H.W. Bush** graduated from Yale University and the Skull and Bones. He is a distant cousin of the Queen of England, part of the Black Nobility which traces its power back 5,000 years.

Prince Bernhard of the Netherlands created a group that became known as the Bilderbergers. Many "conservative" researchers have come to recognize the Bilderbergers as an important force for the "New World Order."

(Note: Since the Bilderbergers, according to former British Intelligence agent John Coleman, serve as a BINDING force between the three major 'one world government' forces - the Wicca-Masons (i.e. Communism); the Black Nobility descendants of the early Roman emperors; and the Maltese Jesuits... each of which have 13 respective representatives on the 39-member Bildeberger board - and since a Nazi SS Stormtrooper was responsible for developing this

"New World Order" coordination council, and since Adolph Hitler's second book was titled [believe it or not] "The New World Order."

No wonder Adolph Hitler's dream - and that of his predecessors the "Kaisers", a German translation of "Caesars" - was the revival of the Roman Empire.

According to former British Intelligence agent Dr. John Coleman, the three world power groups: the Wicca-Masons (i.e. Communism), the Maltese-Jesuits and the Black-Nobility (*'Black'* in this context refers to their character, not their skin color) all work for and under the central Command of the Bavarian Illuminati which binds them together.

The Bavarians created the Bilderberg society for this purpose, the core of which is a council of 13 members from each of the three 'groups' or 39 in all.

The old-line ruling families who believe that they have the right to rule the world because they are descended from the emperors of the ancient Roman and so-called 'holy' Roman Empires consist of 13-15 'blue blood' families.

Which include:

- Rothschild
- Kuhn
- Loeb
- Lehman
- Rockefeller
- Sach
- Warburg
- Lazard
- Seaf
- Goldman
- Schiff
- Morgan
- Schroeder
- Bush
- Harriman

Others that have not been mentioned are more 'powerful' than others.

But these names will get you started if you wish to track down the present-day inner core of the conspiracy. The history of the Bilderberg group itself, a cover for the Bavarian Illuminati, and its *Nazi connections*, would probably be the best place to start.

Prominent on the board of two insurance giants are Committee of 300 members:

- the Giustiniani family, Black Nobility of Rome and Venice who trace their lineage to the Emperor Justianian
- Sir Jocelyn Hambro of Hambros (Merchant) Bank
- Pierpaolo Luzzatti Fequiz, whose lineage dates back six centuries to the most ancient Luzzatos, the Black Nobility of Venice
- Umberto Ortolani of the ancient Black Nobility family of the same name.

Other old Venetian Black Nobility Committee of 300 members and board members of ASG and RAS are:

- the Doria family, the financiers of the Spanish Hapsburgs
- Elie de Rothschild of the French Rothschild family
- Baron August von Finck (Finck, the second richest man in Germany now deceased)
- Franco Orsini Bonacassi of the ancient Orsini Black Nobility that traces its lineage to an ancient Roman senator of the same name
- the Alba family whose lineage dates back to the great Duke of Alba
- Baron Pierre Lambert, a cousin of the Belgian Rothschild family

Italy was chosen as a test-target by the Committee of 300.

Italy is important to the conspirators' plans because it is the closest European country to the Middle East, and linked to Middle East economics and politics. It is also the home of the Catholic Church, which Weishaupt ordered destroyed, and home for some of Europe's most powerful oligarchical families of *the ancient Black Nobility.*

Should Italy have been weakened by Aldo Moro's death, it would have had repercussions in the Middle East which would have weakened US influence in the region. Italy is important for another reason; it is a gateway for drugs entering Europe from Iran and Lebanon.

Various groups combined under the name of socialism to bring about the downfall of several Italian governments since the Club of Rome was established in 1968. Among these are the Black Nobility of Venice and Genoa, P2 Masonry and the Red Brigades, all working for the same goals.

Police investigators in Rome working on the *Red Brigades-Aldo Moro case* came across the names of several very prominent Italian families working closely with this terrorist group.

The police also discovered evidence that in at least a dozen cases, these powerful and prominent families had allowed their homes and/ or property to be used as safe houses for *Red Brigades* cells.

Peccei headed the *Atlantic Institute's Economic Council* for three decades while he was the Chief Executive Officer for *Giovanni Agnellis' Fiat Motor Company.* Agnelli, a member of an ancient Italian Black Nobility family of the same name, was one of the most important members of the *Committee of 300.* He played a leading role in development projects in the Soviet Union.

The Club of Rome is a conspiratorial umbrella organization, a marriage between Anglo-American financiers and the old *Black Nobility families of Europe,* particularly the so-called *"nobility" of London, Venice and Genoa.*

The key to the successful control of the world is their ability to create and manage savage economic recessions and eventual depressions.

The Committee of 300 looks to social convulsions on a global scale, followed by depressions, as a softening-up technique for bigger things to come, as its principal method of creating masses of people all over the world who will become its "welfare" recipients of the future.

To introduce new cults and continue to boost those already functioning which includes rock "music" gangsters such as the filthy, degenerate *Mick Jagger's "Rolling Stones"* (a gangster group much favored by European Black Nobility) and all of the *Tavistock-created "rock" groups* which began with "The Beatles."

To continue to build up the cult of *Christian fundamentalism* begun by the British East India Company's servant, Darby, which will be misused to strengthen the Zionist state of Israel through identifying with the Jews through the myth of "*God's Chosen People*" and by donating very substantial amounts of money to what they mistakenly believe is a religious cause in the furtherance of *Christianity.*

Brzezinski was not writing as a private citizen but as *Carter's National Security Advisor* and a leading member of the Club of Rome and a member of the Committee of 300, a member of the CFR and as a member of the old Polish Black Nobility. His book explains how America must leave its industrial base behind and enter into what he called "a distinct new historical era."

In this regard, a *French Black Nobility* member, **Etienne D'Avignon**, as a member of the Committee of 300, was assigned the task of collapsing the steel industry in the US It is doubtful that any of the hundreds of thousands of steel workers and shipyard workers who have been without jobs for the past decade have ever heard of D'Avignon.

A second assassination bureau is located in Switzerland and was until recently run by a shadowy figure of whom no photographs existed after 1941. The operations were and probably still are financed by the Oltramaire family - Swiss Black Nobility, owners of the Lombard Odier Bank of Geneva, a Committee of 300 operation.

The primary contact man was Jacques Soustelle - this according to US Army-G2 intelligence files. This group was also closely allied with Allen Dulles and Jean de Menil, an important member of the Committee of 300 and a very prominent name in the oil industry in Texas.

Army-G2 records show that the group was heavily involved in the arms trade in the Middle East, but more than that, the assassination bureau made no less than 30 attempts to kill General de Gaulle, in which Jacques Soustelle was directly involved.

The same Soustelle was the contact man for the *Sendero Luminoso-Shining Pathway* guerilla group protecting the Committee's Peruvian cocaine producers.

Richard Gardner was sent to Rome on a special assignment. Gardner married into one of the oldest Black Nobility families of Venice, thus providing the Venetian aristocracy a direct line to the White House. The late Averill Harriman was another of the committee's direct links with the Kremlin and the White House, a position inherited by Kissinger after Harriman's death.

In 1986 in "*The Order of St. John of Jerusalem*" Dr. Coleman wrote:

"It is therefore not a secret society, except where its purposes have been perverted in the inner councils like the Order of the Garter, which is a prostituted oligarchical creation of the British royal family, which makes a mockery of what the *Sovereign Order of St. John of Jerusalem* stands for.

As an example, we find the atheist Lord Peter Carrington, who pretends to be an Anglican Christian but who is a member of the Order of Osiris and other demonic sects, including Freemasonry, installed as a *Knight of the Garter* at St. George's Chapel, Windsor Castle, by Her Majesty, Queen Elizabeth II of England, of the Black Nobility Guelphs, also head of the Anglican Church, which she thoroughly despises."

$15.8 billion is one realistic estimate of the Queen's worth - tax exempt - BOE.

"Only the little people pay taxes."

Path 20: What if an advanced Alien civilization populated humans on earth after destroying the dinosaurs and are who ancient people refer to as Gods?

Archons...Extraterrestrial Architects of Evil
[Archons: A Greek word meaning '"ruler", "lord" or "magistrate]

What if ancient Egyptians Gods were actually flesh and blood aliens that lived on planet Earth thousands of years ago? What if ancient astronauts created the human Race?

Lost Gnostic gospels reveal an exotic description of alien interference with the human species that serious religious scholars dismiss as mythological "science fiction" – a fantastic and disturbing description of cosmology that exposes an imposition and intrusion upon Earth humanity by malevolent, parasitic extraterrestrial invaders, who use Earth humans as puppets in games of deception and domination from times immemorial to this very day.

And how do Gnostics describe these 'invaders'? Referred to as 'Archons', they came in two distinct types—an aggressive reptilian humanoid and smaller, passive creatures resembling a 'prematurely formed fetus'!

What if this wealthy elite class of billionaires and trillionaires through Project Paper Clip have enlisted the world's most imminent technical engineers guided by extraterrestrial intelligence of Grey and Reptilian Aliens to use CRISPR Cas9 technology embraced by Transhumanists and take evolution into their own hands to design an immortal human 2.0 in the near future; thereby reducing organic life as we know it to existence in a logical machine.

What if world governments are facing technologically advanced alien beings that places humanity's in jeopardy? What if elite bankers, controlling the world governments and militaries, have negotiated humans for technology with non-biological extraterrestrials?

This is a deal with Satan himself? Millions of people go missing each year worldwide. Would our government really disclose the arrangement? Is this why they choose not to disclose what they really know about UFO's and have placed Antarctica off limits?

If you know nothing of William Thompkins, he has a very interesting book titled "Selected by Extraterrestrials." He was instrumental in designing and building Starships for Inter Galactic Space travel for the U.S. Navy with the help of Extraterrestrials. Werhner Von Braun, the father of the NASA Space program, who arrived in the US after World War II via Operation Paper Clip, stated that Germany rose to technological prominence with advanced technology provided by extraterrestrials from another galaxy.

What if this wealthy elite class of billionaires and trillionaires are seeing benefits of such advancement in technology and have establish many agencies to prevent knowledge of their deal with the extraterrestrial devils; deals that must remain secret to keep people in high-tech industries as slave-like worker-bees for their black projects?

We have gone from traveling on horse drawn buggies to Intergalactic Starships in a little under 100 years. We have built the Hadron Collider in Cern Switzerland and now China has built one seven times larger. What are the purpose of these projects?

These projects of Bilderberg and Tri-Lateral commissions of the super-rich are without oversight of world governments. In fact, The Bilderberg and Tri-Lateral agendas have placed multitudes of world government under one New World Order agenda.

It is very disturbing that Secret Societies are making decisions without our consent and are putting our lives and the planet in jeopardy choosing to share alien threat and the agenda of CERN with only a privileged Secret Society members.

The rise of Satanic Cults, meetings at Bohemian Grove, and the rising ranks of devil worshippers has reduced love to an anecdote, something not practiced very much.

This is the time, more so than any other time in history of human civilization, that we should be questioning world leadership and investigate all the questions of Secret Societies, Secret Space Programs, and the extraterrestrial questions

Path 21: Chromosome Fusion
Evidence of DNA manipulation in our distant past?

The Human Genome Project has dished up some real surprises to scientists. The first surprise was the vast percentage of the human DNA that is inactive. It is estimated that at least 97% of our DNA is in actual fact a waste of space, as it does not contain any active genes that actually carry the code for any of our physical makeup.

Then within the genes there are Introns – parts that do not carry any code; and Exons - sections that carry some sort of genetic code. The full length of our DNA is made up of some 20 000 genes that have now been identified.

These genes carry the blueprint for the structure of our entire body. What is very puzzling is the fact that Homo sapiens, as the supposed pinnacle if civilized evolution on this planet, should have such large parts of unused DNA. We seem to have the longest DNA molecule among all other species, but we use the smallest part of it in proportion to the other species. In other words, all the other creatures use much more of their DNA than humans do. Some species use as much as 98% of their DNA.

This flies directly in the face of the principles of evolution.

Humans should have the most complex and evolved DNA of all creatures, to have reached levels of civilization seemingly much higher than any other species on Earth over millions of years of evolution. What is even more curious is the predicted number of genes in species. The numbers seem to increase steadily from basic organisms to the most advanced. We would expect that humans should end up having most genes, but strangely this is not the case.

Here are some examples of the predictions for total number of genes in species.

- Fruit Fly 21 000
- Zebrafish 50 000
- Chicken 76 000
- Mouse 81 000
- Chimp 130 000
- Human 68 000

Can you see the problem here?

The Chimp is our closes know genetic relative and yet it has almost twice as many genes as humans.

And then we get to the anomaly of the chromosomes. Our DNA is broken up into 23 pairs of chromosomes. By comparison, all apes have 24 pairs. One would expect that Homo erectus, our immediate evolutionary precursor would then also have had 24 chromosome pairs.

Just one year ago on 6 April 2005, researchers from the National Human Genome Research Institute announced that, "A detailed analysis of chromosomes 2 and 4 has detected the largest "gene deserts" known in the human genome and uncovered more evidence that human chromosome 2 arose from the fusion of two ancestral ape chromosomes" as reported in Nature.

It is also the second largest chromosome we possess and it seems to make no sense why 2 primordial chromosomes should have merged to make us human, if this new chromosome gives us no apparent advantage for survival.

So when we read in the Sumerian tablets that humans were cloned as a sub-species between Homo erectus and a more advanced human-like species that arrived on Earth some 400 000 years ago, it suddenly makes a little bit more sense. The tablets describe how our maker removed certain parts of the "Tree of life" to trim the ability of the new "creature" and how they struggled to make the perfect "primitive worker" so that it could understand commands but not be too smart to question their existence.

Similar suggestions of genetic cloning are made in The Quran and Hindu Laws of Manu.

The Quran:

- Ya Sin: "Is man not aware that we created him from a little germ?"
- The Believers - God says almost verbatim what the Sumerian tablets tell us. "We first created man from an essence of clay; then placed him a living germ in a secure enclosure. The germ we made a clot of blood, and the clot a lump of flesh. This we fashioned into bones, then clothed the bones with flesh..."

Laws of Manu:

- 19. But from minute body (-framing) particles of these seven very powerful Purushas springs this (world), the perishable from the imperishable.

- 20. Among them each succeeding (element) acquires the quality of the preceding one, and whatever place (in the sequence) each of them occupies, even so many qualities it is declared to possess.

Notice the reference to "We" by the creator. The cloning of humans as a more primitive worker or "lulu amelu" suddenly does not seem so far-fetched and the strange genetic anomalies seem to support some genetic manipulation in our distant past. The modern-day researchers go further to say that this "fusion" of our chromosome 2 is what makes us human.

Are we getting closer to proving that humans were created by his MAKER as slaves to work in the early gold mines on Earth? It certainly seems like it.

Michael Tellinger

April 2006

Path 22: The Definition of Archons and What we are dealing with? Satanists & Pedophiles Run the World

David Icke

Published on Aug 30, 2016

The Invasion (Is Earth an Energy Farm?)

If I ask you to imagine an alien the first thing you would probably think about is something physical a humanoid or corporeal life form. We have been programmed to expect alien to take corporeal form to come down in a spaceship and say take me to you leader.

But what if the invasion you have been programmed to expect has already happen? What if they have been living among us for a long time but not in physical form? What if some aliens are actually non-physical non-corporeal life forms energetic beings feeding off of our psychic energy. Specifically feeding off the negatively charged energy that can be generated by the human mind.

What if the collective consciousness of the human race has been hijacked and primed towards a negative by these non-corporeal alien life forms. Harnessing our mind's abilities to actualize reality experiences and then steering us to the most negative reality experiences.

Essentially turning Earth into a negative energy farm. They would not necessarily be evil. They just need negatively charged energy like electronics needs electrons which is negative energy.

Our consciousness interacts with another dimension. Our physical sensors only show us a 3 dimensional universe:

> "What exists in the higher dimensions are entities we cannot touch with our physical sensors."

Bernard Carr professor of mathematics and astronomy.

The idea that we operate in isolation from everything else is difficult to believe. Faith in God suggest an entity existing in a higher dimension who we cannot touch with our physical sensors.

This reality we are experiencing has been hijacked by a force some ancient people called Archons. In the Far East and Central America, these entities or forces are referred to as Serpent God, the Zulus called them the Chitauri, Sumerians called them the Anunnaki, Hopi Indians called them the Snake Brothers, in Christianity they are called demons, there are various references as Star People, called Jinn in Islam, and these forceful entities are known as Archons to the Gnostics.

In the prime form this force is energetic in nature. These are different names for the same thing. The Pre-Christian Gnostics that ran the great Library in Alexandria Egypt say the Archons are made from luminous fire? Who made the Archons?

In Islam, the Jinn are made from smokeless fire (Allah stated that He created the ***jinn*** from ***fire***, as He ***says*** (interpretation of the meaning): ... "And the ***jinn*** He created from a ***smokeless flame*** of ***fire***" [55:15]). You see this correlation and description wherever you go.

In Nag Hammadi, Egypt, about 77 miles north of Luxor on the Nile, in 1945 a sealed jar was found with many leather document s in it that told the beliefs and perceptions of the Gnostics. The Gnostics had a completely different view of reality than religion. This is why the Roman Catholic Church tried to destroy the Gnostic followers.

The Gnostics ran the Great Library of Alexandria that housed a half-million scrolls that detailed the ancient beliefs and history of the ancient world, which was destroyed by the Roman Church in 1244. The religious establishment wanted these people destroyed because they were a danger and had truth they did not and until this very day don't want the people to know about.

The Crusades was all about vanquishing heretic knowledge that conflicted with the Bible. There is so much wisdom not accounted for in the Holy books. Gnosticism is a collection of religious ideas and systems which originated in the first century AD among early Christian and Jewish sects.[1] These various groups emphasized personal spiritual knowledge (*gnosis*) over the orthodox teachings, traditions, and authority of the church.

Gnostic cosmogony generally presents a distinction between a supreme, hidden God and a malevolent lesser divinity (sometimes associated with the Yahweh of the Old Testament)

Perfect redemption is the cognition itself of the ineffable greatness: for since through ignorance came about the defect ... the whole system springing from ignorance is dissolved in *gnosis*. Therefore *gnosis* is the redemption of the inner man; and it is not of the body, for the body is corruptible; nor is it psychical, for even the soul is a product of the defect and it is a lodging to the spirit: pneumatic (spiritual) therefore also must be redemption itself. Through *gnosis*, then, is redeemed the inner, spiritual man: so that to us suffices the *gnosis* of universal being: and this is the true redemption.

Salvation is not merely individual redemption of each human soul; it is a cosmic process. It is the return of all things to what they were before the flaw in the sphere of the Aeons brought matter into existence and imprisoned some part of the Divine Light into the evil *Hyle* (matter). This setting free of the light sparks is the process of salvation; when all light shall have left Hyle, it will be burnt up and destroyed.

The Gnostics adopted the term *demiurge*. Although a fashioner, the demiurge is not necessarily the same as the creator figure in the monotheistic sense, because the demiurge itself and the material from which the demiurge fashions the universe are both considered consequences of something else. Early church leaders encouraged the destruction of Gnostic texts, Depending on the system, Demiurge may be considered both uncreated and eternal or the product of some other entity.

The Valentinians believed that at the beginning there was a Pleroma (literally, a ‹fullness›). At the center of the Pleroma was the primal Father or *Bythos*, the beginning of all things who, after ages of silence and contemplation, projected thirty *Aeons*, heavenly archetypes representing fifteen syzygies or sexually complementary pairs. Among them was *Sophia*. Sophia's weakness, curiosity and passion led to her fall from the Pieroma and the creation of the world and man, both of which are flawed.

The son of Sophia, whom she forms on the model of the Christ who has disappeared in the Pieroma, becomes the Demiurge, who with his angels now appears as the real-world creative power.

He was an evil and malicious offspring of his mother, who has already been deprived of any particle of light. In the Valentinian systems, the Demiurge was the offspring of a union of Sophia's daughter Achamoth with matter, and appears as the fruit of Sophia's repentance and conversion.

But as Achamoth herself was only the daughter of Sophia, the last of the thirty Aeons, the Demiurge was distant by many emanations from the Supreme God. The Demiurge in creating this world out of Chaos was unconsciously influenced for good by Christ; and the universe, to the surprise even of its Maker, became almost perfect. The Demiurge regretted even its slight imperfection, and as he thought himself the Supreme God, he attempted to remedy this by sending a Messiah. To this Messiah, however, was actually united Christ the Savior, who redeemed men.

The **Archontics**, or **Archontici**, were a Gnostic sect that existed in Palestine and Armenia, who arose towards the close of the 2nd century CE. They were thus called from the Greek word ἄρχοντες, "principalities", or "rulers", by reason that they held the world to have been created and ruled by malevolent *Archons.*

The Archontics held that there were Seven Heavens, ruled by the Demiurge surrounded by Archons begotten by him, who are the jailers of the souls. In the eighth heaven dwells the supreme Mother of light. The king or tyrant of the seventh heaven is Sabaoth, the god of the Jews, who is the father of the Devil. The Devil, dwelling upon earth, rebelled against his father, and opposed him in all things, and by Eve begot Cain and Abel. Cain slew Abel in a quarrel about their sister, whom both loved.

"They say," records Epiphanius, "that the soul is the food of the Archons and Powers without which they cannot live, because she is of the dew from above and gives them strength. When she has become imbued with knowledge ... she ascends to heaven and gives a defense before each Power and thus mounts beyond them to the upper Mother and Father of the All whence she came down into this world."

Ideology of the various Gnostic systems, the material universe is evil, while the non-material world is good. According to some strains of Gnosticism, the demiurge is malevolent, as it is linked to the material world. According to this theory, ideas in this sense, often capitalized and translated as "Ideas" or "Forms", are the non-physical essences of all things, of which objects and matter in the physical world are merely imitations.

Valentinians identified the God of the Old Testament as the Demiurge, the imperfect creator of the material world. Man, the highest being in this material world, participates in both the spiritual and the material nature. The work of redemption consists in freeing his or her spiritual from their physical nature.

One needs to recognize the Father, the *depth of all being*, as the true source of divine power in order to achieve *gnosis* (knowledge). The Valentinians believed that the attainment of this knowledge by the human individual had positive consequences within the universal order and contributed to restoring that order, and that gnosis, not faith, was the key to salvation.

Valentinians regarded Catholic Christians "as simple people to whom they attributed faith, while they think that gnosis is in themselves. Through the excellent seed that is to be found in them, they are by nature redeemed, and their gnosis is as far removed from faith as the spiritual from the physical".

Catharism was greatly influenced by the Bogomils of the First Bulgarian Empire, and may have also had roots in the Paulician movement in Armenia and eastern Byzantine Anatolia through Paulicians resettled in Thrace (Philipoupolis). Though the term *Cathar* (/ˈkæθɑːr/) has been used for centuries to identify the movement, whether it identified itself with the name is debated. In Cathar texts, the terms *Good Men* (*Bons Hommes*), *Good Women* (*Bonnes Femmes*), or *Good Christians* (*Bons Chrétiens*) are the common terms of self-identification.

The idea of two gods or deistic principles, one good and the other evil, was a point of criticism asserted by the Catholic Church against Cathar beliefs. The Catholic Church asserted this was antithetical to monotheism, a fundamental principle that there is only one God, who created all things visible and invisible.

Cathars believed that the good God was the God of the New Testament, creator of the spiritual realm, whereas the evil God was the God of the Old Testament, creator of the physical world whom many Cathars identified as Satan. Cathars believed human spirits were the sexless spirits of angels trapped in the material realm of the evil god, destined to be reincarnated until they achieved salvation through the consolamentum, a form of baptism performed when death is imminent, when they would return to the good God.

From the beginning of his reign, Pope Innocent III attempted to end Catharism by sending missionaries and by persuading the local authorities to act against them. In 1208, Pierre de Castelnau, Innocent's papal legate, was murdered while returning to Rome after excommunicating Count Raymond VI of Toulouse, who, in his view, was too lenient with the Cathars. Pope Innocent III then abandoned the option of sending Catholic missionaries and jurists, declared Pierre de Castelnau a martyr and launched the Albigensian Crusade in 1209.

The Crusade ended in 1229 with the defeat of the Cathars. Catharism underwent persecution by the Medieval Inquisition, which succeeded in eradicating it by 1350.

The **Crusades** were a series of religious wars initiated, supported, and sometimes directed by the Latin Church in the medieval period. The term refers especially to the Eastern Mediterranean campaigns in the period between 1095 and 1271 that had the objective of conquering the Holy Land from Islamic rule. The term has also been applied to other church-sanctioned campaigns fought to combat paganism and heresy, to resolve conflict among rival Roman Catholic groups, or to gain political and territorial advantage.

The difference between these campaigns and other Christian religious conflicts was that they were considered a penitential exercise that brought forgiveness of sins declared by the church. Historians contest the definition of the term "crusade". Some restrict it to only armed pilgrimages to Jerusalem; others include all Catholic military campaigns with a promise of spiritual benefit; all Catholic holy wars; or those with a characteristic of religious fervor.

In 1095, Pope Urban II proclaimed the First Crusade at the Council of Clermont. He encouraged military support for Byzantine Emperor Alexios I against the Seljuk Turks and an armed pilgrimage to Jerusalem. Across all social strata in Western Europe there was an enthusiastic popular response. Volunteers took a public vow to join the crusade.

Historians now debate the combination of their motivations, which included the prospect of mass ascension into Heaven at Jerusalem, satisfying feudal obligations, opportunities for renown, and economic and political advantage. Initial successes established four Crusader states in the Near East: the County of Edessa; the Principality of Antioch; the Kingdom of Jerusalem; and the County of Tripoli. The crusader presence remained in the region in some form until the city of Acre fell in 1291, leading to the rapid loss of all remaining territory in the Levant. After this, there were no further crusades to recover the Holy Land.

Proclaimed a crusade in 1123, the struggle between the Christians and Muslims in the Iberian Peninsula was called the Reconquista by Christians, and only ended in 1492 with the fall of the Muslim Emirate of Granada.

From 1147 campaigns in Northern Europe against pagan tribes were considered crusades. In 1199 Pope Innocent III began the practice of proclaiming political crusades against Christian heretics. In the 13th century, crusading was used against the Cathars in Languedoc and against Bosnia; this practice continued against the Waldensians in Savoy and the Hussites in Bohemia in the 15th century and against Protestants in the 16th. From the mid-14th century, crusading rhetoric was used in response to the rise of the Ottoman Empire, only ending in 1699 with the War of the Holy League.

One-Fifth of the texts of the scrolls of Nag Hammadi was about a force they called the Archons, which they say created our physical universe. The Gnostics equated them with the Yahweh Jehovah Christian God.

Archon or Demiurge means 'Prince', ruler, authorities, from the beginning. Fake 'God' that created our 'physical' or material reality as we perceive it. **The Archons are said to be inorganic not produced by growth or artificial. The Archon created the inorganic parts of the universe. ? Who created the Universe?**

The Archons have no creative imagination and envy humans because we have imagination. They are like Cyborgs; a robotic race that can imitate but not innovate (counter-mimicry in fantasia, mind parasites, deception, and inversion). If you gave Archons a blank sheet of paper they could create nothing on it. If you give them a piece of paper with something on it, they can twist it and manipulate it.

Fantasia in the sense as Islam states about the Jinn having the ability to create virtual reality illusions. The Archons are mind parasites that possess humanity and manipulates how the world perceives everything. They are deceivers and what they create is an inversion of the natural order. Satan is called the deceiver and demon of demons. The Demiurge is called the Archon of Archons.

Archons manipulate humans via self-awareness deceptions with inverted truths. Everything is conscious, distortion is conscious, even an inversion of the truth is conscious. But it is conscious in a way that reflect the inversion and distortion.

Evil is live spelled backward (inversion); evil is inversion (distortion) of life; evil is inversion of perception; evil is extreme ignorance, which is the inversion of truth and awareness.

The Archontic forces invert organic life. Anything attached to the Archonic force is obsessed with death, which is an inversion of life. The Satanist who worships these Gods in their rituals are obsessed with death. The Archonic force and its forces are a death cult that is about destroying and killing. The natural order is about life and abundance.

The Archontic system is destroying life, both animal and planetary, in its wars and in its technological pursuits destroying the world's eco-systems via all this environmental pollution. The Archontic mind is psychopathic. Traits of psychopaths have no empathy and are without an ability to put themselves in the feelings of those suffering from their actions; once you have no empathy you have no limit of what they do, and they have no emotional consequences for delivering evil into this world. There is no remorse and no shame. They are parasites, pathological liars, and do whatever it takes to harvest low vibration energy in people.

Parasitic with no creative ability because they are parasites thriving off the creative abilities of the world's population. Prime example is banking that is an exercise in parasitic behavior. Our world leaders are pathological liars practicing truth inversion.

Also found in the Gnostic text is the word 'HAL' meaning simulation or virtual reality. They talked about the ability of Archons to create virtual realities by controlling perception.

They make something appear to happen that does not happen. They can induce a virtual reality experience. The Islamic and pre-Islamic world say the Jinn can manipulate humans by creating illusions.

Our reality is possibilities and probabilities folded into existence by perception. This whole Archontic system is about programming a distortion of our perception and inverting natural order. This is why the world chaos continues to get worse.

The goal is to disconnect the human mind from infinite awareness or the human droplet from the ocean; locking us into this tiny frequency of perception that we are an isolated humanity on planet earth and that we are all the life that exist in the entire universe.

Before the Archons hacked into our reality, there was another world described by the ancients. There existed people interacting with the natural world, communicating with animals and each other. The Gnostic say the Archons made a bad copy of our original reality. The original reality was people living in harmony with the earth, plants, and animals like in the movie the Avatar.

The bad copy created by the Archons is an information construct which we decode into a lovely world. This bad copy is not about the physical world. It is the information construct that we decode into the world we have today. They created an illusory reality to replace the old Avatar-like reality and then tuning humans into that bad copy. **We tune into an information field and we decode** that into a reality.

Via light infused codes, we tune into an information field at certain frequencies and decode that into a certain reality. If a dial is moved so that we are decoding something else, we decode a completely different reality. The moving of the frequency of light is what is meant by this bad copy. Whatever reality we decode we think it is real because it is the only reality perceivable.

Instead of decoding the organic Avatar kind, we are being fed a different information source. Once tuned into a non-natural information field, we decode a different reality (the Archontic reality). This is the reality we have been decoding through modern human history. If you can create a virtual reality simulation then it is possible to create an alternative to it.

Are we tuned to fake reality via a process called entrainment? Archons have created a dominant frequency entraining the human decoding system into that frequency. Causing humanity to decode a completely different reality than the natural organic one. Once that happens, they invert our organic sense of being if we don't realize what has happened.

The Archontic distortion inversion can be likened to a computer virus. A computer virus is rogue information (like religion) distorting words and inverts the original system. A computer virus that infects human perception. A computer virus that is rogue information that introduce into the original system rogue information which distorts and inverts the original system. A computer virus can damage files, slow the system, distort messages, and take control.

The way a virus works. A virus is a small piece of software that piggybacks on real programs. Similar to the way a biological virus must hitch a ride on a cell, a computer virus must piggyback on top of some other program or document in order to launch. Once a computer virus is running, it can infect other programs or documents. It has piggybacked off the original reality and distorted it. This is what the Gnostic called a bad copy. This bad copy has produced pedophilia, nuclear waste, and vast disparities in wealth to create a planet full of people vibrating low frequencies related to struggle and suffering.

We are taking energy sustenance from the energetic field within the frequency band of what we are vibrating to or resonating to. We can't take it outside that band because we can't synch with it outside the frequency we are vibrating to.

If you are a distortion or an inversion, you cannot get sustenance from the natural order because you are not in that frequency band. So to get you energetic sustenance, you have to get it from other distorted energy which is in the frequency band you are interacting with.

The people around the world, the different cultures talk about the fact that these entities, a universal description, feed off human energy, but not just any human energy, but low vibrational human emotions. They feed off fear, anxiety, anger, conflict, frustration, and war because they are a distortion of the natural order of things of love, peace, and balance. These Archontic inversions energies can feed off them. This was exemplified in the movie the 'Matrix' where the machines (inorganic) were feeding off human energy.

While we are coming from the natural order perspective of love, peace, and harmony who think that war, fear, and suffering is a bad thing, these things are essential to the Archon's energetic survival.

The Archontic inversion can't synch with love. It needs hate for its sustenance. It has manipulated the structure of our society to generate low vibrational energy from the human population; suffering today, which is in unbelievable abundance.

We can see there is pressure by the global elite Satanic worshippers to create more low vibrational energy induced by war, fear, and suffering. Instead of our leaders making decisions that produce less suffering, they create laws that induce low vibration energy. The Matrix is a compute-generated dream world built to keep us under control in order to change the human being one of these.

On one level that's what we are generators of distorted emotional energy. Alternative healers and people on the true cutting edge of healing will tell you that virtually all illness is based in emotion. Emotions creates energetic distortions, not only to be absorbed by these entities but to be trapped in the body and manifested as disease and disharmony in the body caused by emotions.

In this world everywhere you look is caused by inversion of the natural order. This is why the world is turned on its head. Wherever you look it is an inversion of not just what we would like it to be but an inversion of the original reality that it replaced.

This is why Satanist used inverted symbols for their symbolic language. Michal Ellner wrote "Just look at us. Everything is backwards; everything is upside down. Doctors destroy health, lawyers destroy justice, universities destroy knowledge, governments destroy freedom, the major media destroy information, and religion destroys spirituality.

Global leaders are manifestation of this Archontic force are genetic liars because lieing is an inversion of truth.

The Gnostic writings have been estimated to have been buried in the sealed jar between about 350 and 400 AD, which corresponds with the destruction of the great library of Alexandria ran by Gnostic thinkers. They were possibly written about 100 AD. In those documents about 2000 years ago, they describe reptilian entities and those known today as Greys as Archons taking form. The Greys are described as like an unborn baby or fetus with Grey skin and dark unmoving eyes. That was nearly 2000 years ago and it is the same description of what we call Grey entities today in the modern world. Behind the human network of control is a reptilian form. Is acknowledging these ideas madness or is it seeing beyond the program? Condemnation without investigation is the height of ignorance. People can say this is not true but they do not investigate.

In my research, I ran across documentation of the Chani Project or (Channelized Holographic Access Network Interface Project). During the years 1994 to 1999, a group of researchers from an organization/ corporation, which I will call RAND and Associates, or **RA**, had access to an underground CERN-like collider facility in Africa (the location is still classified).

A contingent of AFRICOM security personnel was tasked with securing the base and, of course, keeping its location secret. The AFRICOM station commander made and supervised all the travel and accommodation arrangements for the team of researchers. They were closely watched 24/7.

Between those years, the researchers started receiving communications from an Entity who claimed to be from a parallel universe/dimension/ timeline.

A remarkable and groundbreaking interaction ensued. For a period of five years, researchers asked the Entity a series of over 20,000 questions and received answers to more than 95 per cent of questions asked.

This is some of the thing revealed by the entity

A reptilian race was holding back humans so they couldn't grow

The entity said they had fought many battles against the Reptilian race in their own reality

Humans were more evolved spiritually than the Reptiles but they suppress humans with their technology – The Reptilian's God is their technology.

The Gnostic text say that humans have creative ability where the Archons don't. Remember, the Gnostic writings had been in sealed jars since 350 AD and had not been changed. The Biblical text had similar expressions of the Gnostic text but had been tampered with and changed in the public arena through many attempts of translation.

According to the Gnostic texts 'Lord Archon' (Demiurge): 'Come, let us create a man according to the image of God and according to our likeness that this image may become a light for us.' In other words, light meaning, man becoming a vehicle for the Archon.

This information is mirrored all over the world as also is found in the Biblical text,

> 'There were giants in the earth those days; and also after that, when the sons of God came in unto the daughters of men, and they bear children to them, the same became mighty men which were of old, men of renown.' Genesis 6:4

The Genetic Disc was found in Columbia and is thousands of years old. It illustrates images human eggs and sperm; things that could only be seen with a microscope.

This is one of the most mysterious artifacts in the world. It was discovered in the territory of Colombia, and was called the **Genetic disc**. It is 27 centimeters in diameter, and weighs about 2 kilograms. Both sides are covered in illustrations of the **intrauterine fetal development** in all stages. Nowadays, this process is observed by doctors using special equipment. But how was this knowledge known 6 000 years ago? And what other knowledge could have been possessed by the obscure civilization which made the disc?

The **entire process of the beginning of human life** is illustrated on the circumference of both sides with incredible accuracy – the purpose of male and female reproductive organs, the moment of conception, development of the fetus inside the womb and the birth of the baby.

Throughout many ancient cultures there are stories past down of aliens coming to earth and interbreeding to create a hybrid race.

The human form does not rely entirely on physical interbreeding to change the human into some kind of hybrid. The human reality is constructed around receiving and transmitting information.

If you change the information that the receiver transmitter decoding system is receiving and that information relates to the human form, you can mutate the human form simply though getting people to decode that information.

The reason that radiation causes mutation is because it distorts the natural order of the body energetically and then that transmits itself as a mutation of the physical form. Form is in information. Change the information and you change the form; if you can get the original form to decode the information by transmitting on the right frequency.

Humans have been locked into this world of limitation, suppression, and control of Archons ever since according to Gnostic text.

Carl Sagan wrote "The Dagon of Eden." He wrote about the impact of Reptilian impact on human behavior. He said you cannot understand the human personality unless you understand the Reptilian part of the human form. One of the things he was referring to was the Reptilian brain. Everybody has a reptilian brain or an "R" complex.

The "R" complex elates to emotion. Many believe that before human were biologically altered the reptilian element was not a part of the brain or it was much less influential or smaller in its impact on human behavior than it is today. This part of the brain is not part of critical thinking but more reflect reactionary to dangers.

From the Reptilian brain, we get primitive cold-blooded behavior and territoriality. A desire to control; an obsession with hierarchical structure of power; aggression; might is right and winner takes all; also protecting notions of status, power, reputation, superiority, intellectual pre-eminence, and acceptance of hierarchy and authority.

The Bible states 'behold Adam is become as one of us, knowing good and evil.' This is falling from a monistic sense of one with nature (or one with the Archontic mind) to the dualistic ideology of a separate non-quantum existential detachment from the natural order of things (from a sense of oneness to duality). Knowing good and evil is knowing duality.

When you are in a reality of oneness based on the heart, which does not do duality, there is no duality. Everything is just is. When you start to pull that unity, that oneness into different elements of itself, then you can get polarity, duality, and conflict.

The Archons harvest low vibrating energy of hated from conflict. The computer like virus, inherent in the Archon's bad copy of our natural order, this distortion has distorted the wave form energetic level of our reality. We are decoding it through holographic distortions such as wars, conflicts, and people dying of hunger in a world of plenty. We live in a world where it is all about me instead about all what is right.

We are locked into this frequency band thinking the current perception of reality is all there is. Throughout known human history, the theme of possession is so prevalent where entities are possessing someone and taking over their mental and emotional faculties and their sense of reality.

That is possible because we are an energetic field emanating an aura. From this auric field is projected the holographic physical self. What these entities do on an energetic level is lock into that wave form level of the human form. Once they make a frequency connection with it, they can start influencing the perception of that person.

Inside ourselves are two wolves. One they say is evil and one they say is good:

Evil Wolf: It is anger, envy, sorrow, regret, greed arrogance, self-pity, guilt, resentment, inferiorities, lies, false pride, superiority, and ego

Good Wolf: It is joy, peace, love, hope, serenity, humility, kindness, benevolence, empathy, generosity, truth, compassion, and faith.

Which wolf wins? Is evil an aspect of human nature? Is it? Is evil human nature or is it distortion seeking to impose itself on human nature and collectively creates a world that reflects the imposition of evil by the Archons?

Which one wins? Which one wins in their terms depicts which world wins. Love, benevolence, and empathy just think of the world that would create; a world that did exist before the Archons hijacking compared to the world we have now that is manipulated more and more now into destruction and conflict.

The divine light is always in inner man and woman. Presenting itself to the senses and to the comprehension, but man and woman rejects it -Giordiarno Bruno-

This divine light mentioned by Bruno is beyond the Archon's program. If we are prevented from reaching that level of frequency, we cannot connect with a consciousness of divine light. The Archontic forces are focused on holding us out of that connection.

The Reptilian God is in plain sight all over the world. Worship is the worship is the worship of the reptile, snake, or the serpent. It goes back at least 70,000 years in Africa, Botswana, and Salado Hills where the Sand People, better known as the Bushmen say that the great python came with a bag of egg to create and or manipulate humanity.

John Bathurst Deane wrote a book called "Worship of the Serpent" in 1933. It was a work on the study of the worship of massive serpent, the snake, and reptile imagery all over the world. He concluded:

> It appears, then, that no nations were so geographically remote, or so religiously discordant, but that one- and only one – superstitious characteristic was common among to all: that the most civilized and most barbarous bowed down with the same devotion to the same engrossing deity; and that this deity either was, or was represented by, the same sacred serpent.
>
> It appears also that in most, if not all, the civilized countries where the serpent was worshipped, some fable or tradition which involved his history, directly or indirectly, alluded to the Fall of Man in Paradise, in which the serpent was involved.
>
> What follows, then, but the most ancient account respecting the cause and nature of this seduction must be the one from which all the rest derived which represent the victorious serpent – victorious over man in a state of innocence, and subduing his soul in a state

of sin, into the most abject veneration and adoration of himself.

This author is talking about the whole concept where every look of the fall of man was always related to some serpent figure; not just in Christianity but all over the world.

You can find serpent figures as the one above that dates to the Ubaid period (c. 6500–3800 BC) a prehistoric period of Mesopotamia the area now which is Iraq, in antiquity Babylon, and Samaria.

You also see the serpent portrayed with the Pharaohs of Egypt. The Cobra is a massive symbol of the reptilian race.

The Druids you to worship a serpent God called Hu.

Kukulkan was worshipped by the Yucatec Maya peoples of the Yucatán Peninsula, in what is now Mexico.

Ancient writings from Cambodia to Africa refer to a race of semi-divine beings, half human and half reptilian, known as the 'Naga' half Reptilian Shapeshifting Beings from Ancient India.

These Naga can take on a serpentine form or a fully human form (or presumably any other form).

Throughout history, the Naga have been both friendly to humans and potentially dangerous.

According to these legends, the Naga live in a large kingdom underneath the Himalayan Mountains.

Buddhist legends from Thailand and Cambodia hold that a Naga king sheltered the Buddha from the rain while he meditated for seven days, and later protected the Buddha from an attack by bird-like humanoid beings.

A South African legend tells of reptilian-like 'gods' who ascended from the heavens in monstrous vessels to become the dictators of the human race. The reptilians filled humans with great hate and trained them as warriors to make terrible war.

According to David Icke, reptilian beings came to the earth thousands of years ago from Orion, Sirius, and Draco, and began breeding humans through the manipulation of DNA coding, inserting their reptilian genetics.

A human/reptilian bloodline has been preserved through the ages through European royalty, and has been passed along to all forty-four U.S. presidents as well as many media celebrities.

Secret Societies worship a certain force or certain God. With religion, people worship a certain God; people think the Gods are different but it is the same God. At the level of Satanism, they are more knowingly worshipping the Archontic Satanic Gods. In the end all these different form, although the vast majority of them have no idea that's the case, they are ultimately worshipping the same Archontic evil forces disguised as different Gods.

This Archontic force does not operate in this dimension, in the sense this is not its frequency. So the Archons needs a vehicle within visible light to work on its behalf while it works hidden.

Certain bloodlines were created specifically to be that vehicle and they are human Archontic or human reptilian hybrids. You see symbols of them in the reptilian imagery in the aristocracy coats of arms.

With these human hybrid bloodline or like "in-betweeners," you have got the visible light frequency band, you've got the entities outside the light frequency band, the hybrid human reptilian bloodlines are the representatives within this frequency band that interact with those entities outside the visible light frequency band to do the bidding of the hidden forces.

This is an analogy, think of scientists who cannot work inside a tank with something contagious or radioactive and he must interact with protective gloves and works from outside the tank. In this analogy, the scientists are the Archontic force, the tank to be our reality, and the gloves the scientist uses to interact in the tank to be the human hybrid bloodlines.

What has been created is a hierarchy coming out of the hidden down into seeds to create and direct a society that generate maximum low vibrational energy and systematically imposes the virus upon our society more and more and more.

These blood lines have a particular DNA. DNA is an information field. Creating human hybrid is similar to altering a software program. The reason these bloodlines breed incessantly, we see it with Royals and banking families, this in-breeding is done to hold this information field with has a certain series of personality traits, which these Archontic forces want in these hybrids because it makes them work on their behalf without any compassioned empathy or question of the impact of the suffering they create.

The DNA of the human hybrids have many of the natural order traits of the Good Wolf joy, peace, love, hope, serenity, humility, kindness, benevolence, empathy, generosity, truth, compassion, remorse, the ability to feel the emotional impact of what they do to others, and faith are deleted. The end result of such deletions is the creation of psychopaths. These human hybrids are psychopaths in our reality on behalf of psychopaths operating outside our reality.

Politicians do not run the world. Something outside, something very different runs the world that politicians are just an expression of. Some politicians know and some do not know. The reason the elite hybrids are so important because of their hybrid genetics connection that places them closer to the frequency of the Archontic entities than normal human population. The ability to possess, control, and dictate their behavior is far more powerful with the hybrid than it is with the general population.

Anton Styger wrote:

> When I see people in business or politics who are particularly tapped by the material world, for example, I notice that they no longer have any light at the heart chakra, which is otherwise always present, is no longer visible to me.
>
> Instead I see something like a layer of 'shiny tar' around them in which a monstrous being in the shape of a lizard can be distinguished. When such people speak on television, for example, I see a crocodile shape manifesting itself around the person like in a concave mirror; I don't see the light of their throat and forehead chakra.
>
> – Swiss Clairvoyant, Anton Styger –

We are being infiltrated by a force that is taking over this reality that fooled us because they look human. One day soon people are going to have to face the fact that this is true and this is why the world is the way it is and when it is totally understood we can do something about it.

The elite did not just arrive the last few years. In the rise of our earliest advanced societies Egypt, Mesopotamia, Indus Valley, and China. Today's human Archon hybrids bloodlines came out of these ancient societies.

The Chinese Emperors claimed the right to be Emperor because of their genetic descendence from the serpent Gods. Sumer and Egypt were major places they came out of, as well. The bloodlines started moving up into Europe, They became the hierarchy that established the Roman Empire that relocated in Britain and became the British Empire. Wherever these bloodline relocated themselves, an empire has followed.

This Archontic virus has spread and reached a global point to what is now a global Babylon. Global Babylon came about when the British Empire could walk all about the world, create all the colonies behind fake religion. Sure the Americans resisted during the revolution. But that resistance was only on the surface. They best form of slavery is if you don't tell them they are slaves.

What was not vanquished during the Revolution was the bloodlines that went with different names and the secret society network which manipulate the people in government and their agencies of power, though this network, the human archon hybrid has gone on to control the world ever since.

The United States, a major world power on the surface, is also controlled from Europe by a Secret Society Network. What the secret society has created today is a vast web with an Archontic inner sanctum dictating out through various organizations such as The Round Table, Bilderberg Group, United Nations, Tri-Lateral Commission, Council of Foreign Relations, Royal Institute of International Affairs, and Club of Rome.

This organization is dictating direction of a global power with more control, surveillance, more takeover of everything, and more inversion of the natural order. The virus is spreading.

From the hidden meeting scene, policies are disseminated out to countries, agencies, and governments. The inner sanctum are making decisions and introducing policies which on the surface appears to be made by elected officials but comes from the center of the secret society's web.

We have these different aspects of religions operating in isolation but they are not. They are all worshipping the same God. In the bloodline of human archon hybrids are Satanists, members of secret societies, and pedophiles. Behind these three aberrations of the natural order is this Archontic force.

The here today gone tomorrow elected officials, even those with some awareness of what's happening, they are the gophers that introduce the decisions and policies from the hidden Archontic force. Through CERN, Satanists are interacting with these Archontic demonic entities.

In the Archon realm, where these major satanic rituals are performed, there is manipulation of energetic fields taking place. These rituals creates and energetic synchronization which allows some of these entities to slip through an energetic gateway or vortex and manifest into this reality for these rituals.

David Berkowitz (Son of Sam Killer) stated:

> Satanists are peculiar people. They aren't ignorant peasants or semi-literate natives. Rather, their ranks are filled with doctors lawyers, businessmen, and basically high ranking citizens. They are not a careless group who are apt to make mistakes. But they are secret and bonded together by a common need and desire to mete out havoc on society. It was Alleister Crowley who said "I want blasphemy, murder, rape, and revolution, anything bad."

Fields of the Nephilim

The all-important element of the Divine Right is that it comes from God, or "the gods," alternately.

And who were these gods? Authors such as Zecharia Sitchin, Sir Laurence Gardner and Nicolas de Vere are authoritatively convinced that kingship was created by an advanced race of beings called the Anunnaki, also called the Nephilim in the Old Testament.

These were the ones who created the human race and interbred with a portion of it to create the kingly caste which until this day has still maintained control over the Earth.

Some, like Gardner and Sitchin, claim that they come from another planet. Others, like de Vere, say that they're multi-dimensional, or that they're from the Hollow Earth.

Some, like David Icke, say that they are humans inhabited by the spirits of multidimensional reptiles, capable of shapeshifting into reptile form at any time. Still others claim that they were humanoid, but more than human, with pale white skin. The human hybrid offspring that they created as the Royal/Priestly caste was, according to most, the Aryans, who usually had red hair with green eyes - in stark contrast to the traditional Hitlerian vision.

Nicolas de Vere, the leader of an organization called The Dragon Court which claims to represent this royal Aryan caste, writes:

> "the depiction of the Aryan (Scythian) as a tall, ruddy-complexioned blonde moist ' yeoman-farmer-warrior-god has no basis in truth."

He further suggests that the "yeoman-farmer" Celtic, Gaulish and Pictish tribes which we now think of as Aryan were actually of a different race, but had hired the extra-human Aryans to be their leaders.

These Aryans were also the masterminds behind the Indian, Hittite, Greek, Egyptian, Hebrew, Sumerian and Pre-Sumerian Ubaid civilizations. Many believe that their descendants can be found amongst the segment of the population with the RH Negative blood type, roughly 5% of the Earth's population, most of them Europeans.

These people are often born with:

- an extra vertebra
- have a lower than normal body temperature
- can rarely mate with one another successfully, which suggests that they may indeed be a hybrid species

Conspiracy enthusiast Arizona Wilder takes it a step further by stating:

> "The Aryan bloodline is alien to this planet... There are 13 bloodlines from this kind of stock (the Merovingians being one), and all of them have to a greater or lesser degree the capacity to play host to the Shape Changer reptiles."

The other 12 families have been identified as Astor, Bundy, Collins, Dupont, Freeman, Kennedy, Li, Onassis, Reynolds, Rockefeller, Rothschild, Russell, and Van Duyn, with the rest of the European Royal Families being categorized as Merovingian.

These are the people referred to by the fanatical group, the Sons of Jared, when they,

> "pledge an implacable war against the descendants of the Watchers, who as notorious pharaohs, kings and dictators, have throughout history dominated mankind.. like super-gangsters, a celestial Mafia ruling the world."

The Book of Enoch says that the sons of the Nephilim, are destined to,

> "afflict, oppress, destroy, attack, do battle and work destruction on the earth."

Nicolas de Vere, himself a Prince of the Dragon Blood, sees it quite differently. He sees them as the rightful shepherds of the human flock. He states:

> The fairies were tuned to a higher frequency of perception and activity generally. In the past, therefore, because the Fairies were, for millennia, physiologically bred and exhaustively trained to operate at a higher level than men, humans often invited them to become social navigators... A dragon was one who saw clearly, and the clarity of vision engendered was always classically associated with wisdom, which itself produces power....

The Anunnaki and their quasi-human offspring are attributed with remarkable traits. They lived for thousands of years, were capable of levitation, dimension-hopping, clairvoyance, and other magical powers, all a product of applied eugenics.

De Vere explains:

> "Selective unions gave the race the opportunity to breed outstanding magicians whose gift of natural perception and understanding and whose ability to access the 'Otherworld' helped to produce and guide brilliant kings who ruled with elegant aplomb.
>
> The ability to perform magic was carried in the blood and of that blood," and "the Elves were relied upon by their client races to be able to see things and perform feats that these client races couldn't."

Laurence Gardner, himself a former member of the Dragon Court, concurs:

> "hi short, these people were bred to be leaders of mankind, and they were both mentally and physically maintained in the highward state."

But what property did they inherit in the blood which makes this possible?

The experts are nearly unanimous about the fact that the answer is endocrinology. Says de Vere:

> "hormonal levels [are] influenced by genetic inheritance and that hormones [affect] the individual's perceptions, psychological unicameralism and the subsequent ability to transcend and perceive the intricacies of the cosmos. Elven blood [is) rich in these substances."

Starfire bloodfests

> "The best blood is of the moon, monthly..."
> Aleister Crowley
> The Book of the Law

The beneficial effects of the hormone melatonin have been part of the health supplement scene for some time, for high melatonin production is known to be synonymous with a high immune system, a low cancer risk, long life, energy, stamina, and according to many, enhanced spiritual awareness.

Perhaps it is fitting then that this hormone is secreted by the pineal gland, a mysterious little item long believed by mystics to be the "Seat of the Soul," "Me Third Eye," and the organ through which psychic powers are exercised. In fact, it actually functions as an organ of sight in some reptiles, and it still seems to possess some sensitivity to light in higher mammals, since melatonin production increases when the person is exposed to darkness (thus melatonin means "night worker!")

Writes Laurence Gardner:

> High melatonin production thereby increases the facility for receiving and transmitting high-frequency cosmic and local broadcasts, and leads to a greater state of cosmic awareness - a state simply of 'knowing.'

> In this regard, it is interesting to note that the Pineal Third Eye has been found to contain very fine granular particles, rather like the crystals in a wireless receiving set.

Many magical rites and meditation techniques are aimed at gaining control of this organ and the fluid it produces: the live melatonin.

Rumor has it that the members of the super-secret society Skull & Bones, to which both George Bush and his son belong, engage in a ceremony called "The Obscene Rite," which involves the consumption of the live pineal gland of a human or animal sacrifice in order to get the fresh secretions.

Supplements bought over the counter are ineffective because, as Gardner explains,

> "their inherent secretions are obtained from the desiccated glands of dead animals and they lack the truly important elements which only exist in live human glandular manufacture."

Aryan bloodline is alien to this planet... There are 13 bloodlines from this kind of stock all of them have a greater or lesser degree the capacity to play host to the shape changer reptiles.

But the Aryan overlords who ruled over mankind in ancient days had a simpler way of acquiring this fluid. Their ancestor-gods, the Anunnaki, had endocrine systems that produced large amounts of this and other beneficial substances, so they drank it straight from the source: the menstrual blood and vaginal fluids of the goddesses themselves.

This they referred to lovingly as "Starfire" and drank in a ritual ceremony called the Black Mass, after which the Catholic Mass is said to have been modeled. Later, as direct contact with the Anunnaki ceased, the fluids were collected from sacred priestesses referred to as "Scarlet Women," or "Grail Maidens."

Readers will recognize the Scarlet Woman as the Whore of Revelations, as well as the title which Aleister Crowley gave to all of his sex magick partners.

> "These sacred, royal princesses" writes de Vere, "virgins of High Birth and Pure Blood, at an optimum age would be chosen to act as feeding females," whose essences contained such valuable substances as, "oxytocin, prolactin, melatonin, seratonin, adenosyne triphosphate, dopamine, telomerase, and retinol."

There is another important ingredient in the mix here. De Vere explains,

> "many think that only men have semen when in fact women also have it."

And so a Starfire ritual involves the use of a golden straw.

Stich a device would have been inserted into the virgin's urethra to the depth of about one inch, whilst the partner in the rite inserted his or her finger into the vagina and massaged the "roof of the mouth" or uppermost wall of the canal nearest the open or 'mouth' of the vagina, behind the pubic bone.

After a few conducive moments perhaps, orgasm would occur and the fluid from the gland would discharge itself through the straw, either into the waiting mouth of the recipient, or onto a "grail platter" or dish held next to the vulva.

Keen readers will recognize this as identical to a sex magick ritual advocated by Aleister Crowley for members of his Order or Oriental Templars (OTO).

The only difference is that his rite also involved the use of male semen which was called the "Red Tincture" or "coagulated blood," while the female fluids were called "Gluten" or "The White Tincture."

Together they made "The Elixir of Life," and in alchemy blood and semen are the prime materia or first matter of the great work.

> *"this is the true Key to Magick," writes Crowley. "That is, by the right use of this secret man may impose his Will on Nature herself."

Monatomic Gold - the substitute

According to de Vere and others, ingesting the fluids of mundane women has only a slight effect, certainly not enough to maintain a royal Dragon family in the manner to which they're accustomed.

And after a few thousand years the genetic purity of their Grail maidens began to deteriorate, so the Starfire lost its potency. This reportedly began around 1960 BC and is equated with the time that an edict was handed down to Noah by God demanding that the consumption of all blood cease immediately. (Gen. 9:4)

Thus, a substitute had to be found, and so the alchemical process was created as a means of artificially creating the Elixir of Life, the Philosopher's Stone, also known as "potable gold." This is created using a black powder known as occultum, the universal solvent which has the power to transmute metals.

When placed against gold it converted it into a white powder which could be ingested.

It is said to cause nothing less than immortality, as it sets off a self-correcting mechanism in your DNA that lasts for thousands of years. It also bestows the enhanced melatonin production and magical powers associated with Startfire, including clairvoyance, dimension-hopping and flying capabilities. It is believed that this "white gold" is the same as the "Shew-bread" and "Manna from Heaven" mentioned in the Old Testament.

Today, there are those who publicly proclaim knowledge of the Philosopher's Stone. A man named David Hudson claims to have created a technique for manufacturing this white gold, which he's patented as ORME (Orbitally Rearranged Monatomic Elements).

Ormus is a name associated with the Holy Grail, and so readers may not be surprised to learn that Hudson himself is related to the Merovingian Grail family through Claude de Guise.

Basically, the powder is created by putting gold into a higher atomic state through a series of intense heating and cooling sessions, during which it loses and gains weight radically, as though portions of the mass were being transferred into another dimension.

David Hudson describes the magical quantum properties of his white gold:

> These M-state elements have been observed to exhibit superconductivity, super fluidity, Josephson tunneling and magnetic levitation...
>
> They may enhance energy flow in the microtubules inside every living cell. Ingesting in-state gold has different effects on the body than the effects of ingesting metallic gold. At 2 mg. it totally has gotten rid of Karposi Sarcomas on AIDS patients.
>
> Within 2 hours, their white blood cell count goes from 2500 to 6500...
>
> Stage 4 cancer patients have taken it orally, and after 4 5 days have no cancer left any place in the body. It's been

> used on Lou Gehrig's disease, it's been used on MS, it's been used on MD, it's been used on arthritis. It literally corrects the DNA.

Sympathy for the Devil

All of this puts a nice, friendly face on the whole thing, which is currently a secret power held only by an elite caste of Aryans who use it to lord themselves over the rest of the human population.

And there are those who have said that the "substitute" white gold never did away with the original practice of blood-drinking as a method for obtaining the substances they needed.

David Icke and his associate, Arizona Wilder, have campaigned the globe to inform its citizens with Chicken Little-like hysteria that most of its financiers, politicians and aristocrats are actually under the control of Reptilian beings from another dimension, who are inhabiting their bodies.

Icke states:

> "To hold their human form, these entities need to drink human (mammalian) blood and access the energy it contains to maintain their DNA codes in their 'human' expression. If they don't, they manifest their reptilian codes and we would all see what they really look like."

Icke believes that most of this blood is obtained in human sacrifice rituals engaged in by the Satanic Illuminati.

He explains:

> "From what I understand from former 'insiders', the blood (energy) of babies and small children is the most

> effective for this, as are blond-haired, blue-eyed people. Hence these are the ones overwhelmingly used in sacrifice, as are red-haired people also."

His compatriot, Arizona Wiilder, goes into a bit more detail when she writes,

> "They have a hypnotic gaze which fixes the victim - in a trance of terror - which promotes secretion of the pineal gland - at that point, they cannot hold human form any longer and begin to shapeshift in anticipation of supper."

She acknowledges that Starfire rituals go on as well:

> In the underground vaults of his castle in the Alsace Region of France, green glowing fluorescent rocks tam stored menstrual blood black to be used at that special ritual. There are jewel-encrusted goblets to drink the blood from the symbolic female grail and a symbolic dagger to give it a bit of a stir.

They've acknowledged that vampirism does take place at their rituals, but maintain that they only drink the blood of their own family members, who participate willingly.

"You cannot take the essences by force, they are only given in love," he says, otherwise, "their systems will react by producing chemicals during one's assault upon them that will completely knock out the chemicals traditionally required."

They claim that vampirism was originally the purview of a few noble families who practiced it in order to maintain their powers.

"The most famous stories," writes de Vere, "those of Dracula, Bathory and de Rais, support this conclusion." He and Gardner enthusiastically embrace Dracula as one of their own:

"This Sacred Prince, a Hermetic scholar and initiate, a student of magic, Magus, Witch Lord and Dragon Prince, counterbalanced the bloodlust of his forebears with a refined knowledge and advanced practice of Grail procedure."

This is because he was a member of Sigismund's Dragon Court in Hungary, and therefore of the Grail blood, who also attended a hermetic academy called the Austrian School of Solomon.

"The orthodox establishment's fear of Dracula," writes, Gardner, "was not his treatment of enemies but his in-depth knowledge of alchemy, kingship and the ancient Star Fire customs."

As for the claim that they use these rituals to conjure up dragon ancestors from another dimension, de Vere calmly admits that this is the case, and that the participants have their bodies taken over by these spirits, who "rise from the dead to take possession of the witch's soul!"

He further explains:

Any spirit including the archangels, conjured by the witch or magician was actually the ancestor of the witch... It was carried in the witch's blood which, the purer it was through the unbroken descent from the Dragons, the stronger would be the return from the ancestors within.

In other words, they brought together and spoke or gesticulated a series of mnemonics that would trigger off precontrived, imprinted states of consciousness that acted as doorways into deeper seats of consciousness.

The charge of Satanism is not entirely refuted either, but de Vere proffers that they are not worshipping Satan so much as honoring one of their forefathers, who they stick right in the family tree along with Jesus, David and the rest.

"The Sabbatical Goat of the Black Mass was Chem Zoroaster," he writes, "one of the early ancestors of the ancient Dragon Families," and, "Satan was also called by the witches 'Christ, son Dei.' ...Jesus' heredity and the descent of the druidic dynasties... was devilish, because the descent of both bloodlines was from the Sumerian Enki who was the Akkadian Samael: the Roman Lucifer and thus the Catholic Satan."

But the Dragon Court members make no apology for this, because,

> "to any intelligent person, to any true seer, concepts like white or black magic or good and evil are irrational, childish nonsense; both in terms of logic and actual fact."

Every Elf for Himself

"This is our Law, and the Law of the Strong."
—Crowley, ibid.

To the charges of "conspiring to take over the world," the Dragons deny that they give two licks what the rest of humanity does with itself.

Their primary concern is, "the restoration of their own Tribes, their own Nation and their own Homelands. The foundation of their own distinct society. Re-introducing their old social structures and values." This results in "The Grail Code," a system of Egalitarian, Chivalric ethics that govern how dragons treat other members of their race. However, "it is not the code that efficiently orders the behavior of the Dragon Families in their dealings with those not of the Grail Blood."

They acknowledge and defend their own elitist attitudes towards mankind, whom they regard as, "thoroughly stupid and dimwitted, with a clear indication that this condition is genetically inherited." Whereas in contrast, "The Elves were naturally transcendent of spirit and their queens and kings were insulated from the common round of nuisances and petty concerns by minds which were bred for deeper matters."

Despite their hatred of humanity, they will kindly agree to be the guardians of our governments again (if they aren't secretly doing so already), should the population choose to accept them, and offer them the thrones of the Earth, which de Vere and friends indicate are rightfully theirs anyway.

They are just waiting for mankind to realize it again. We will have to deal with the fact that these "Elves" seem to be in possession of a material that bestows long life as well as fantastic physical, mental, and spiritual powers, giving them a distinct advantage through which they are clearly attempting to lord over us, while they allow our populations to wallow in disease, death, and spiritual degradation.

As an excuse, de Vere and Gardner claim that the Starfire and White Gold are only effective for those already of the Dragon Blood anyway, because the rest of us, "won't have the right blood serum or the right connections in their cerebral lobes."

De Vere denies the claims of most people who believe themselves to be of this bloodline.

"Some people argue that because of the outbreeding of the old families, there must be millions of people 'of the fairy blood' living today: but such a statement flies in the face of accepted facts of history.

The genuine old royal families rarely outbred at all, whilst the later, fake parvenu, tinker nobility whom people now confuse with them often did."

So that leaves little hope for you and me of ever obtaining the fruits of this magnificent "Philosopher's Stone," which "gives youth to the old" and is described as "the summation of the heart's desire."

And if such a substance were available to the public,

- How much would it cost?
- Would it be obtainable by everyone or only the rich and privileged?
- What if it could be administered for free in the water supply or was available in tablet form at your local pharmacy, covered by your health insurance policy?
- What would happen to our already exploding population?

As a species, mankind will have to decide how to deal with the information - provided that the information is aired in public someday, and provided our "thoroughly stupid and dim-witted" populace can figure out what to do with it.

Will we take advantage of what could be our greatest opportunity to advance as a species, or will we allow it to be used against us by a caste of Aryan overlords who despise us (and who are literally the spawn of Satan!)

Then again, will we perhaps wish to accept their rule, and the benefits of being led by an advanced race whose powers and insight are greater than our own?

After all, there are those who believe that civilization is created by and can only be maintained by an established elite. Would we want to meddle with that, and allow positions of power to be overrun by inferior men?

Perhaps it is worth considering whether an elite can truly be made by enhancing human faculties, or whether such powers are purely in the blood sources.

Sources

- Gardner, Laurence: Genesis of the Grail Kings
- Michaelsen, Scott, Portable Darkness: An Aleister Crowley Reader

- Moon, Peter, The Black Sun: Montauk's Nazi-Tibetan Connection
- De Vere, Nicolas, From Transylvania to Tunbridge Wells

Alleister Cowley's new religion "Thelema" revolved around the idea that human beings each have their own True Will that they should discover and pursue, and that this exists in harmony with the Cosmic Will that pervades the universe. Crowley referred to this process of searching and discovery of one's True Will to be "the Great Work" or the attaining of the "knowledge and conversation of the Holy Guardian Angel".

Crowley saw "Magic as getting into communication with individuals who exist on a higher plane than ours. For Crowley, sex was treated as a sacrament, with the consumption of sexual fluids interpreted as a Eucharist. This was often manifested as the Cakes of Light, a biscuit containing either menstrual blood or a mixture of semen and vaginal fluids. This, with blood sacrifices in the satanic network, goes into politics, goes into banking, into the media, of course not everyone, but key people directing society.

Why is Satanism and pedophilia so intimately related? What the Archontic Satanists are after is energy of children before puberty. Puberty is a hormonal chemical change. It is a holographic expression of an energetic change. They want that energy before that change takes place.

These pedophiles are possessed by Archontic entities that stimulates desires for sex with children and while it is happening, through the vehicle of the pedophile, they are drawing off the child's energy.

The reason that you have so many pedophiles in the upper echelon of society because the people are in the bloodlines of the entities feeding off the children.

Politicians are introduced by a carefully graded set of criteria and situations that enable them to accept that their victims will be "Our little secret." Young children sexually molested and physically abused by politicians worldwide are quickly used as sacrifices.

Many people do not know who Jimmy Saville is. He was a BBC television personality in London. Saville allegedly got away with abusing 500 children and had sex with dead bodies.

This man was knighted by the Queen of England and Pope Benedict XVI. Saville was supplying children to the rich and famous Archontic hybrid bloodline that was feeding off the energy of children. If he went down, they all went down. The Daily Express, tabloid newspaper of the United Kingdom, published "Jimmy Saville was part of a satanic ring." He received Knighthood from the Queen. Do you think she did not know? He received Knighthood from the Pope Benedict XVI. Pope Benedict XVI resigned on 28 February 2013.

So many people of Archontic hybrid bloodlines such as Thomas Hamilton, Ted Heath, George Bush, Henry Kissinger,

> Lord Mountbatten (member of the Royal Family the mentor of Prince Charles and Prince Phillips), introduced Jimmy Saville into the inner circle of the Royal Family. The Yorkshire police knew but refuse to knock on the doors at Buckingham Palace.

You have to ask yourself this question. Why was a record breaking pedophile and child procurer (Saville) an inner-circle royal buddy and close friend of Margaret Thatcher for decades?

MI5 and Special Branch Britain Security Services, would not allow you to get close to the Royal Family without a thorough background check. The NSA and CIA, knew about Bush. According to a WikiLeaks cable, former President George W. Bush and senior advisor Karl Rove both obstructed an elite Washington DC pedophile investigation.

George Bush himself, the pedophile, ritual child killer, mass murderer and Satanist, is a very close friend of the Windsors. The Queen made him an Honorary Knight Grand Cross of the Order of the Bath, as she did with that Brotherhood script-reader and rapist of mind controlled slaves, Ronald Reagan, himself a product of mind control. This is the highest award it is possible for her to give to someone outside the Commonwealth.

The CIA named their headquarters after Bush. Pedophilia has to be protected because of its significance to that which controls the system from the unseen.

At the Heart of Black Magic - Demonic Possession

Black magic at its core is really about demonic possession.

Since the world is made of energy, not matter, and since energy moves in waves which have frequencies, the satanic rituals are designed to entrain the energetic bio-frequencies of the participants with that of other dark entities, so that there is a vibrational match.

Once there is a frequency resonance or lock, an exchange can then take place: energy, intent or information can go from one being, place or dimension can be transferred into another.

This works both ways:

> the person gets possessed and receives information from certain dark entities, while the dark entities also take something from the person.

This theme of possession crops up again and again when exposing the worldwide conspiracy, and has been going on a long time, e.g. Hitler was reported to be demonically possessed by his aide Hermann Rauschning.

Citizens Electoral Council of Australia
Media Release Thursday, 23 July 2015
Craig Isherwood, National Secretary
PO Box 376, COBURG, VIC 3058
Phone: 1800 636 432
Email: cec@cecaust.com.au
Website: http://www.cecaust.com.au

60 Minutes exposes organized pedophilia among highest ranks of British elite

60 Minutes' explosive 19 July feature, "Spies, Lords and Predators", reported that the recent blizzard of revelations of pedophile rings operating among the elite of the British Establishment constitutes the "biggest political scandal Britain has ever faced". Presenter Ross Coulthart stated right at the show's outset, "There is a pedophile gang operating at the highest levels of the British Establishment" (his emphasis), and, although 60 Minutes did not dwell on the point, that includes the Royal Family itself. However the Royal involvement shone through in an 18 July article by the UK's Exaro News, which 60 Minutes credited as a co-producer of its show, while a 24 June press release by the CEC had been even more explicit in naming the Royals.

60 Minutes reported the first-hand allegations of a number of child abuse survivors, who identified the prominent Establishment figures who abused them when they were children in the 1970s and 80s.

One survivor, Richard Kerr, fell victim to this pedophile ring as a nine-year-old in the 1970s, when he was sent to the Kincora Boys Home in Belfast, Northern Ireland, run by notorious pedophiles. From Kincora, Kerr, like many others, was trafficked all over the UK to be abused by powerful men.

To 60 Minutes, he identified among his abusers former Member of Parliament Cyril Smith, and former deputy head of MI6 Sir Peter

Hayman. The latter was a member of an organized gang called the Pedophile Information Exchange (PIE), which campaigned openly in the 1970s for the age of consent to be lowered to as young as four.

The CEC's 24 June release also identified the pedophile ring operating out of the Kincora boys' home, in connection with the murder gangs that British intelligence coordinated in Northern Ireland, under the command of Brigadier General Frank Kitson, to orchestrate terrorism and civil war.

Though his troops opened fire on unarmed civilians in the infamous "Bloody Sunday" massacre of 30 January 1972, killing 13 civilians and wounding 13 more, the Crown showered honor after honor upon him, including an OBE for his work in Northern Ireland, while the Queen personally inducted him into her ultra-elite Order of the Bath. Still alive, he retired in 1982 as Commander-in-Chief, UK Land Forces. The CEC release emphasized the unique significance of the Kincora story:

"Despite pleas from many quarters to do so, British Home Secretary Theresa May has staunchly refused to include the Kincora case in the new child abuse inquiry to be headed by New Zealand Judge Lowell Goddard, even though the present, local inquiry in Northern Ireland into Kincora under Anthony Hart QC lacks the legal powers to compel crucial witnesses to testify.

Why the steadfast refusal to include Kincora? Because there is abundant evidence now even in the public domain that MI5, MI6 and other British intelligence agencies know that not only was one of Kitson's paramilitary 'pseudo-gangs' (Tara) at the center of that affair, but that other, leading members of the British establishment were personally involved in the abuse, including Lord Mountbatten himself, Surveyor of the Queen's Pictures Sir Anthony Blunt, and numerous other high society figures from Ireland and England."

60 Minutes did not name these individuals, but Exaro News in its 18 July article reported that Richard Kerr had identified some of the same figures which the CEC had.

Among those who were part of the cover-up of a pedophile network linked to Kincora boys' home in Belfast, Northern Ireland, according to Kerr, were:

- Lord Mountbatten, a cousin of the Queen, great-uncle to Prince Charles, chief of the defense staff from 1959 to 1965 ...;
- Sir Maurice Oldfield, director of the Secret Intelligence Service, better known as MI6;
- Sir Anthony Blunt, master of the Queen's pictures, former officer in the Security Service, or MI5, who became a Russian spy;
- Sir Knox Cunningham, Unionist/Ulster Unionist MP, parliamentary private secretary to Harold Macmillan as prime minister, and member of the Conservative party's national executive committee 1959-66. ...

"An intelligence source told Exaro that Mountbatten mixed with pedophiles who went to parties in the Republic of Ireland. Mountbatten is also understood to have visited Kincora, although why remains unclear."

It was very clear to the CEC, who had named Mountbatten himself as a pedophile in its 24 June release. Among other things, Mountbatten had welcomed the notorious pedophile Jimmy Savile into the Royal family, and he became a regular at Buckingham Palace and a mentor and advisor to Prince Charles.

According to British press accounts, Savile molested as many as 1000 children, many of them helpless patients in hospitals. He was also, according to some accounts, a necrophiliac, who proclaimed that the 5 days he had spent alone with his mother after her death were the "happiest days of my life."

60 Minutes also identified as a high-ranking pedophile one of Margaret Thatcher's many pedophile protégés, Sir Leon Brittan, whom she appointed Home Secretary and whose department was responsible for investigating, and therefore covering up, pedophile complaints. Brittan, for instance, "lost" extensive documentation on high-level pedophilia presented to him by MP Geoffrey Dickens in the early 1980s.

60 Minutes also named Lord Greville Janner, a sitting member of the House of Lords who until recently the Public Prosecutor had declined to prosecute on the grounds of his claimed dementia, even though he had voted in Parliament over 200 times since the onset of his alleged mental debility.

60 Minutes also interviewed a member of PIE, which gave the viewer a skin-crawling glimpse into the mindset that openly justifies, in fact promotes, the sexual exploitation of children.

The UK authorities have covered up this pedophile network for decades, because it exists at the dark heart of where real power is wielded in Britain's anti-democratic, elitist system—in the Crown itself. This scandal threatens the entire British oligarchical power structure, and there are already indications that the Goddard inquiry into the scandal will simply continue the cover-up, as demonstrated by present Home Secretary Theresa May's refusal to include the Kincora Boys Home in the inquiry, which would expose the overlap between the pedophile networks and MI6/MI5 and the Royals.

A cover-up was also signaled by Goddard's forecast that the inquiry would take 5-10 years to conclude—the typical British Establishment ploy to drag such things out until the uproars which caused them have died down and key witnesses have disappeared, died, or been terrorized into silence.

Path 23: Are Archons the Greys?

In George Andrew's classic book, "Extraterrestrial Friends and Foes", aliens themselves explain just how a massive, covert invasion of planet Earth could be successfully perpetrated.

"If you were a highly advanced culture about to invade a relative primitive culture, you would not do it with a flourish of ships showing up in the heavens and take risk of being fired upon. That's the type of warfare less-evolved mortals would get into. You would begin by creating intense confusion, with only interferences of your presence, interferences which cause controversial disagreement.

You would make yourselves known to various elite in-groups, who would offer you protection out of greed, expecting to acquire more perfect knowledge than anyone else on the planet of this ultimate secret to end all secrets. They would covet you, and you would trust their covetousness and their crass stupidity to trap them.

You would go to the most secret and power organizations within the society and through the use of technique unknown to them (cloning), you would take over some of their key people in their innermost core group.

You would occasionally let your ships be seen by some ordinary citizens, so that the elite government groups would become involved in attempts to keep them quiet, clumsily squelching attempts to make information about extraterrestrials and their UFO's public. This would result in mass population losing confidence in the veracity of their elected officials.

There would be constant arguments between the authorities and the public as to whether or not the persistently reported phenomena genuinely existed, thereby setting the population and the government at each other's throats.

By subtly causing economic turmoil, you would set the 'Haves' and the 'Have Nots' at each other throats. In all possible ways, you would plant seeds of massive discontent.

After you had manipulated the population to the point where you covert control over it was complete, you might decide to go overt and let a few ships land in public. But you would not go from covert to overt until you were sure of the totality of your control.

Humanity is not about to be invaded. Humanity is not in the middle of an invasion. Humanity has been invaded, and the invasion is nearly in its final stages. Great invasions do not happen with thundering smoke and nuclear weaponry. That is the mark of an immature society.

Great invasions happen in secrecy. What I want to get across to you is the ultimate evil, which underlies all the negativity in the cosmos, finds expression in that which is a masked form of psychological complacency that leads individuals to adhere to a group philosophy rather than to think things through for oneself.

Those who feel safe and comfortable in no matter what belief system merely because many others adhere to it—who get together and form an arrogant self-righteous group convinced it has a monopoly on the truth, stifle anyone who challenges that group's philosophy—have formed an alliance with the ultimate evil, whether they know it or not.

As soon as you become involved in a belief system that you are a 'chosen' special group who are lords over the common folks because of your secret knowledge, you are on your way to a fall. That type of attitude plants the seeds of destruction in any society or culture, leaving it vulnerable to overthrow by those oppressed within its boundaries, as well as by outside forces.

All cultures that have elite power groups at odds with each other, and with the population at large, sooner or later collapse from either internal or external pressures.The only chance of retaining your freedom is for the awareness of this principle to penetrate the consciousness of humanity. It is a pearl of wisdom treasured by those who have attained the ability to travel through time and other life cycles.

In his book "The Day after Roswell", retired Army Colonel Phillip Corso, former National Security Advisor to President Eisenhower stated ....

> "We were convinced that whoever the UFO Extraterrestrials were, they were tampering with our planet, operating with impudence, and manipulating us constantly and secretly."
>
> "But it was a secret that had our full compliance because we were unwilling to admit the truth and fight the war. Those of us in the military who knew what was happening also felt that we could be experiencing an invasion that was more of an infiltration."
>
> "They were compromising our very systems of defense and government." As long as we were incapable of defending ourselves we had to allow [the ET's] to intrude as they wished. We had negotiated a kind of surrender with them as long as we couldn't fight them."
>
> "They dictated the terms because they knew what we feared was disclosing truth to the people."
>
> "Hide the truth and the truth becomes your enemy. Disclose the truth and it becomes your weapon. We hid the truth and the extraterrestrials used it against us."
>
> "Let there be no doubt. Alien technology harvested from the infamous saucer crash in Roswell, New Mexico, in July 1947, led directly to the development of the

integrated circuit chip, laser and fiber optic technologies, particle beams, electromagnetic propulsion systems, depleted uranium, projectiles, stealth, and many other technological advancements."

The first step to liberation from this alien control is to unmask the deception. The Gnostics fully understood this truth 3600 years ago. The stupendous success of the alien invasion has been its ability to function in absolute secrecy and seduce the human mind with artificial systems of beliefs; to convince us that we live our lives at the mercy of circumstances and events that exist outside of ourselves, for centuries this belief, like an insidious mantra, has been drilled relentlessly into our psyches from the cradle to the grave, we have been duped into seeing ourselves as victims and so we become victims.

The Gnostics reminds us that the world we see today does not show the face of true humans, but rather the insane, homicidal face of manipulating Archon madness that distorts it (the true human face). Perhaps humanity now can confront its ultimate destiny; to awaken from this artificially induced nightmare and reclaim the divine power within us that has always been our true cosmic birthright!

Humanity now has the opportunity to rid itself of these other-dimensional extraterrestrials parasites. An ever-increasing widespread realization of the true nature of this predatory game is what will bring liberation [George Andrews].

Path 24: What if such beings as Archons: Alien Space Invaders truly exist?

Aristotle stated "Not everyone who walks in the guise of a man is human." On May 10, 1971, the noted British Astrophysicist and Astronomer, Sir Fred Hoyle called a news conference and made the following, startling announcement "Human beings are simple pawns in a great game being played by alien minds, which control mankind's every move."

"These alien minds comes from another universe, one with Five Dimensions"

"These super-intelligent entities are so different from us that to comprehend them or to describe them in human terms is impossible"

They have been here for countless eons and they have probably controlled the evolution of homo-sapiens. "All of what man has built and becomes was accomplished because of the "tinkering of these intelligent forces."

It is possible that Aliens have been here for untold years and Earth's inhabitants are being used for biological experiments.

Whose planet is this? – **What if** Aliens [Grays, Reptiloids] consider themselves Native Terrans. Are they are an Ancient race, descendants of a reptilian humanoid species... are they are untrustworthy manipulative mercenary agents from another Extra-Terrestrial culture, "The Draco's" who are returning to Earth—which was their ancient outpost before the coming of the original Uni-Terrestrials—to try to use it as a staging area, which is not easy at all because it causes all the other one hundred seventy different Alien species to want their share of the Meta-gene secrets.

These 170 are in most cases various sub-species of the humanoid and reptiloid root species, although various other trans-dimensional species are also visiting earth, like the 'Insectoids', etc. This also includes various humanoid and reptiloid species who are the products of genetic integration with various bizarre 'animal' life forms.

The meta-gene is an inbred gene within humans on Terra resulting from the mixture of various cultures upon the "mother" world or "genesis" world, a genetic anomaly which can produce extraordinary characteristics and abilities in individuals, allowing them to accomplish what would be considered by many ET's to be extraordinary physical and psychic feats. - Branton).

But, these Alien cultures are in conflict over whose agenda will be followed for this planet. All the while mind control is being used to keep humans in place, artificially of course, especially since the forties. The Dulce complex is a joint U.S. Government and Alien base. It was not the first one built with the Aliens, and others are located in Colorado, Nevada, Arizona, Alaska, etc...

Different type of Aliens

"Andro-Pleiadean Federation" and their "Non-Interventionist - Individualist" beliefs, and those who have taken sides with the "Draco-Orion Empire" and their "Interventionist - Collectivist" philosophies.

Mt. Shasta subterranean colony of TELOS, an underground city which is said to be the western branch of a subterranean kingdom that certain Asian fraternities refer to as the 'Agharti' network.

One might say that the scenarios taking place within Telos are somewhat of a counterpart of similar power-struggles taking place within "Sirius" and within the U.S. government. The same could hold true within the entire 'Agharti' network which has its center of activity under the Gobi desert of Mongolia, and which allegedly contained two opposing factions during the Second World War period: the Technologists who secretly sided with the Allied Forces, and the Occultists who sided with the Axis Forces.

Andro-Pleiadean Federation. What distinguishes the two is that the Andro-Pleiadean Federation believes in Truth-Individualism-Non Interventionism whereas the Draco-Orion Empire adheres to a philosophy of Deception-Collectivism-Interventionism.

According to contactee Alex Collier these two factions are now or have been at war within the Sirius-B system, and this conflict has entered our Solar system with the Draconian-Orion reptilians.

Alex Collier claims that the non-interventionist from the Pleiades and Andromeda constellations, from Tau Ceti, Procyon and others systems, have "blockaded" the Solar system near the orbital sphere of Neptune in order to keep the Draconian-Orionite forces out and to keep them from interfering with our planet at this CRITICAL and VULNERABLE point in planet earth's history.

The Draconians and Orions are psychologically and emotionally manipulating their cultic human followers in Sirius-B, the Gizeh Empire & Bavaria who are tied-in with the "dark side" of the Ashtar collective, to establish a global government which they intend to annex to their Luciferian Interstellar empire-collective.

Information on Reptiloids alien forms:

Average Height: Male - 2.0 Meters; Female - 1.4 Meters

Average Weight: M - 200 Kilos; F - 100 Kilos

Body Temperature: M - Ambient Temperature; F - Ambient Temperature

Pulse/Respiration: M - 40/10; F - 40/10

Blood Pressure: M - 80/50; F - 80/50

Life Expectancy: M - 60 Earth Years; F - 23 Earth Years

Cold-blooded like all reptiles, the Reptiloids flourish in a warm, tropical clime [normally artificial... big caves]. With imperfect respiration providing just enough oxygen to supply tissues and maintain the processing of food and combustion, their temperature can be raised only a few degrees above the ambient [this suggests that 'heat' weapons, like flame-throwers and so on, may prove to be nearly immediately effective and fatal to this species under battle conditions].

The reproductive system is ovouniparous, with eggs hatching in the oviduct prior to birth. The underdeveloped Reptiloid [for faster activities, physical activities] cerebellus results in a slowness and simpler city of movement. The Reptiloids eyes are composed of thousands of microscopic facets, each facet with its own independent protective lid. The eye is almost never closed entirely during waking hours; rather, sections of the organ are shut down in conjunction with the dominant light source. Reptiloids survived 'hidden' inside the Earth [within] Big Caves Underground.

Information on the Insectoids:

Average Height [Master Race]: Male - 1.6 Meters; Female - 1.2 Meters

Average Height [Servant Race]: M - 1.0 Meters; F - 1.0 Meters

Average Weight [Master Race]: M - 70 Kilos; F - 40 Kilos

Average Weight [Servant Race]: M - 35 Kilos; F - 35 Kilos

Body Temperature: M - 110/2; F - 110/2

Life Expectancy: M - 130 Earth Years; F - 130 Earth Years (Note: are the current attempts to create a genetic reptilian-insectoid hybrid race, like those genetically mutated species reportedly existing in Bellatrix Orion, a result of the Reptiloids' desire to increase their life-span? - Branton)

The Insectoid retina is composed entirely of tone-sensitive rods, and is incapable of discrimination between different wavelengths of light. Therefore, the addition of 'color' to the insectoids vision is accomplished by the dual antennae which, in addition to being auditory receptors, are made up of a complex network of wavelength-sensitive cones.

Owing to the highly directional nature of the antenna, the corona of vision is perceived by the subject in the tones of grey. Because of this correlation of four independent light-receptive organs, Insectoid vision can be correctly termed 'Quadroscopic', resulting in relatively superior depth perception. Insectoid auditory capabilities are highly developed, and Insectoids are capable of distinguishing from among a wider range of audio frequencies than is normal for humanoids.

Because of the mono-directional antennae, Insectoids (most of which have been observed in the form of giant mantis, locust or grasshopper type entities - Branton) usually listen with their head tilted slightly downward. They also have a limited exoskeleton.

More alien races mentioned in the secret report:

1. Type A: Rigelian, Rigel, or the Gray
2. Type B: 2-Reticulae, Z-Reticulae 1, or Grey
3. Type C: 2-Reticulae, Z-Reticulae 2, or Grey
4. Type D: Orion, Pleiades, or Nordic
5. Type E: Bernards Star, the Orange

Information on the Rigelian Reptilian Grays:

LUNA-1 is the Rigelian base on the far side of the Moon. It includes a base, a mining operation using very large machines, and very large Alien Crafts or carrier ships. WAVENEST is the Rigelian base in the Atlantic Ocean, and includes an underwater Alien base, mining and big cigar-shaped crafts.

Rigelians made contacts with certain members of the MILITARY-INDUSTRIAL ['Corporate' or 'Secret' government] complex from 1947-1971... The 'government' thought that the Grays meant us no harm, but in 1982 and 1988 the picture that emerged was exactly the opposite.

The story now is one of great deception at several levels. The Grays 'Trojan Horse' style manipulation and lying involved MJ-12/MAJIC Forces (The CURRENT agreements with the Grays within the NSA-connected levels of the Military-Industrial Complex, some sources have implied, continue as a result of the large level of alien infiltration and mind-control that exists throughout certain levels of the Intelligence Community - Branton).

The inner core of the CIA/NSA is deeply controlled by the Grays... Working under the instructions of the aliens from Rigel, the CIA and former [?] Nazi scientists have developed and deployed malignant strains of bacteria and viruses, including AIDS, in order to exterminate 'undesirable' elements of the human population.

Information on the Nordic races:

Average Height: Male - 2.0 Meters; Female - 1.7 Meters

Average Weight: M - 90 Kilos; F - 70 Kilos

Body Temperature: M - 98.6 degrees Fahrenheit; F - 98.6 degrees Fahrenheit

Pulse/Respiration: M - 72.5/16; F - 72.5/21

Blood Pressure: M - 120/80; F - 80/50

Life Expectancy: M - 60 Earth Years; F - 23 Earth Years (According to other sources, this low life expectancy is probably greatly exaggerated. - Branton)

Information on the Orange (The Orange are reportedly humanoids with red, stalky hair and in some cases may have been genetically tampered with and imputed with various levels of reptilian genetics, making them a quasi-hybrid race although apparently mostly 'human' in many cases.

Unlike the reptilians however they have external reproductive organs and are apparently capable of mating with other 'humanoid' races. They come from the Bernards Star system.

On certain rare occasions they have been seen with facial hair, beards, etc. Apparently some strains of the Orange hybrids are more 'humanoid' than are others. - Branton):

Average Height: Male - 1.7 Meters; Female - 2.0 Meters

Average Weight: M - 70 Kilos; F - 50 Kilos

Body Temperature: M - 91 degrees Fahrenheit; F - 91 degrees Fahrenheit

Pulse/Respiration: M - 242/61; F - 242/61

Blood Pressure: M - 80/40; F - 80/40

Path 25: Psychonaut Sailors of the Soul Altering Parameters of Perception

How the human mind has been infiltrated by an alien intelligence

Gnostic gospels contain more than Sophia's creation myth, they reveal an exotic description of alien interference with the human species that serious religious scholars dismiss as mythological "science fiction" a fantastic and disturbing description of cosmology that exposes an imposition and intrusion upon Earth humanity by malevolent, parasitic extraterrestrial invaders, who use Earth humans as puppets in a vast, centuries old game of deception and domination.

And how do Gnostics describe these 'invaders'? Referred to as 'Archons', they came in two distinct types—an aggressive reptilian humanoid and smaller, passive creatures resembling a 'prematurely formed fetus'!

Modern ufology usually postulates that aliens come from another planet or dimension. But, what if they've been here since the dawn of time? The Gnostic alien theory by John Lash claims, that aliens are Archons, devoid and corrupt cousins of man put here by celestial forces that created humans as well.

The Archons were whispered about in texts after the burning of the library at Alexandria with some mention of these mysterious beings. But the powers that be spent 1,300 years cleaning up the records and had written out the Archons from our history.

In 1947, texts were found in clay jars in Nag Hammadi in Egypt and, on these texts was a story of what the Nag Hammadi people, 2,000 years ago, thought the world was about. The word Archon means a ruler and primordial.

According to the myth, they were created by a celestial interdimensional entity, Sofia, who was pleiroma with other Aeons, and thus, partly emancipation of wholeness of the Heavenly Father.

The Archons are a spinoff of Sophia, and devoid because they had not been approved with the other Aeons.

This happened billions of years ago, before the solar system was born. These agents of celestial consciousness are hard to imagine, since they come outside of space and time. A materialized neonate-type of Archon would appear to be quiet, psychotic and prone to lying.

Archons are interdimensional inorganic beings, who reign and rule matter. This makes them look godlike to humans, but they are incomplete entities, since they lack human consciousness and experience. They don't come from any civilization nor do they build civilizations.

The first Archon, who created all others, is called Yaldabaoth (means breeder of the hive). This "reptilian" leader is aggressive, territorial, and charged with demonic powers.

The Archons wish to keep mankind under "the constraint of fear and worry", because they feed from it. Negative emotional energy gives them room to operate. They are psychic parasites capable of mind control on many levels. But they are, and have been without humans, and don't need us for their survival. The Archons can't inhabit earth, which is hostile to them. Archons are caught in a delusion they created humans. They have no soul, only a hive like common mind.

According to John Lash, Gnostic texts describe two kinds of Archons, an embryonic or fetal type - hence, the Greys of modern UFO lore - and a reptilian type.

They "abduct souls by night," a precise description of modern ET abductions. Envy (covetousness) and arrogance (egomania) are their primary features. They are mindless drones, greedy for power over us and too cowardly to come out in the open and reveal themselves. They have no concentrating power, no innate faculty that would unite intention with attention.

Gnostic gospel says:

> "The Archons cast a 'trance" over Adam... They put him into a sleepy state, but it was his perception they dulled... They make our hearts heavy that we may not pay attention and may not see. So we lose the reflection of the Divine Light within us".

Ancient Gnostic seers detected and investigated the problem of alien intrusion before the first century A.D.

They kept the Archons as a primary threat to humanity. Gnostic seers had to be skilled in non-ordinary reason to interpret the experiences they underwent in states of heightened perception. Mr. John Lash says we should not expect the Archons to be rational. What we learn about these entities will involve non-ordinary reason, but it will not be irrational nonsense. In general:

> "The mentality of the Archons "cannot be rectified," and, what's worse, "the Archontic hive-mentality is not capable of development."

In ancient Rome, Gnostics considered themselves as Christians, and lived in harmony with others for hundreds of years. They were main stream in religious sense. New age Gnostics have little to do with them.

Psychonautics, Carlos Castaneda and the concept of spiritual reality

The word *psychonaut* means literally a *sailor of the soul* who uses altered states of consciousness to investigate mind, and address spiritual questions, through direct experience.

Psychonaut tend to be pluralistic, willing to explore mystical traditions from established world religions, meditation, lucid dreaming and technologies.

John Lash, David Icke and Graham Hancock for example have done such trips. Terence McKenna is probably most famous advocate in the use of psychoactive plants. According to Mr. Lash, these plants aid "shedding the filters of conditioning and to commune directly with the planetary intelligence."

Dr. Carlos Castaneda was a psychonaut, and his books record apprenticeship with a Yaqui Indian, Don Juan Matus, who plays mentor to Dr. Castaneda's skeptical anthropologist.

Dr. Castaneda manages to alter the parameters of perception and explore other worlds. In the process of his adventures, he encounters certain alien inorganic beings. According to Mr. Lash these are Archons, the small grey aliens.

To the horrified astonishment of Dr. Castaneda, the elder sorcerer Don Juan explains how the human mind has been infiltrated by an alien intelligence:

> "We have a predator that came from the depths of the cosmos and took over the rule of our lives. Human beings are its prisoners. The predator is our lord and master. It has rendered us docile and helpless. If we want to protest, it suppresses our protest. If we want to act independently, it demands that we don't do so."

The Yaqui Sorcerers believe that the predators have given us our systems of beliefs, our ideas of good and evil and our social mores.

They are the ones who set up our hopes and expectations and dreams of success or failure. They have given us covetousness, greed and cowardice. It is the predators who make us complacent, selfish and egomaniacal.

The predators give us their mind, which becomes our mind.

Prof. John Mack says:

A number of shamans with whom I have spoken, from native cultures of North and South America, Africa, and Australia, know of, or have had encounters with, beings that have properties much like the grey aliens that visit abductees in the United States and other Western societies.

Each culture has its own name for them.

According to these shamans, beings of this sort have been around for thousands of years and seem to have a great interest in the face of Earth, functioning as its scavengers or protectors depending on particular shaman's experience or point of view.

There is too a connection to modern alien abduction phenomena.

Prof. John Mack talks about a different reality people have during an abduction and interaction with aliens. Many abductees feel that another spiritual reality is an essential part of abduction experience. This is because the aliens, who according to Mr. Lash do create a HAL's or virtual realities. An abductee steps into a world where time-space is separate from our world.

The aliens generate this using mind power. It is like a small parallel universe. Dr. Castaneda writes on his books of human power sorcerers, who can do the same. They have learned this skill from the Archons and at the same time lost something essential from their human soul.

Dr. Karla Turner did tell on her lectures of a case, where person was sleeping on a bed. Next the aliens came, did raise her into the air, and a glow of silvery light surrounded her body. At the same time, there was a UFO on top of the building.

When the aliens left and she revived she told she had been on a UFO and interacted with the aliens. This happened although two witnessed her body at the time the encounter lasted. Here, according to Mr. Lash a person is inside a HAL or virtual reality, her soul's essence is with Archontic spiritual reality, which is real. It is not observed by the witnesses, who only see a levitating, glowing body of an abductee.

Some Archon-ET hypothesis similarities to modern ufology

The *interdimensional hypothesis* (IDH or IH) is an advanced theory by Jacques Vallée that says UFOs and related events involve visitations from other "realities" or "dimensions" that coexist separately alongside our own.

He called the ET/UFO phenomenon "a spiritual control system." ET/ cyborgs probably belong to the local planetary realm.

Paranormal researcher Brad Steiger wrote:

> "We are dealing with a multidimensional Para physical phenomenon that is largely indigenous to planet Earth"

In the book UFOs: Operation Trojan Horse published in 1970, John Keel linked UFOs to supernatural concepts such as ghosts and demons.

In the book Passport to Magonia Dr. Vallee describes how long and versatile the UFO and abduction/contact history is with the humanity. Mr. Albert S Rosales has collected 17000 humanoid encounters from 2500 A.D. to the present day showing all kinds of creatures being interested in humans.

Dr. Vallee suspects that alien entities manifest themselves in forms the subjects expect them to be. Mr. Lash says Archons can do this via HAL/virtual reality capabilities. The motive is to camouflage the phenomenon.

In *Haunting of America* by Dr. Bill Birnes and Mr. Joel Martin describe paranormal phenomena like haunting and ESP something quite common, and in conjunction remarkable with historical events. Archons would be operating in the same spiritual world like ghosts. Gnostic myth states Archons do not sleep nor nourish themselves i.e. are ghostlike.

Is there a reality beyond our reality? Are the aliens and UFOs are only a part of it? Ancient Gnosticism suggests that there is life after death, and the Archons have something to do with reincarnation.

Linda Howe was told in the early 80'es by Richard C. Doty much controversial information, including a statement, that:

> "EBEs said that souls recycle, and reincarnation is real. It's the machinery of the universe." And that "extraterrestrials created *Jesus*".

And how the aliens possessed information about the past and the future via "yellow" and "red" books i.e. were interdimensional beings outside the space and time, like Gnosticism suggests. The extraterrestrials have also an interest of our souls, possibly in a predatory way.

MJ-12 member has been asked to elaborate on this, and the answer was:

> "You don't want to know that".

According to Karla Turner's beliefs and research, aliens (Archons) have the ability to retrieve what we call the soul, to store it in a container, and to put it back into another body. Two traits, she had come to conclude, characterized alien behavior above all: deceitfulness and cruelty.

Dr. Turner says:

> "Aliens (Archons) can take us - our consciousness - out of our physical bodies, disable our control of our bodies, install one of their own entities, and use our bodies as vehicles for their own activities before returning our consciousness to our bodies."

Could it be that humans, possibly the military or others are using Archontic platform (grey bodies) to conduct their own agendas? Could it be that throughout the times some humans have been in alliance with the Archontic forces, to run their own or their group's interests?

Mr. Lash does not have an answer on this.

In his book "Grey Aliens and the Harvesting of Souls" Nigel Kerner claims the Greys are seeking to master death by obtaining something humans possess that they do not: souls.

Through the manipulation of human DNA, these aliens hope to create their own souls (away from the hive?) and, thereby, escape the entropic grip of the material universe in favor of the timeless realm of spirit.

Whitley Strieber suggests on his book the Key, that the aliens used in the past souls as tools, and that they were imprisoned to containers.

Raymond Fowlers "The Watchers" has accounts of *Out-of-body* (OBE) experiences during alien abduction and that human race was being "watched" by alien beings. Abductions are coming strange indeed when they are not always appear to involve the physical body. This suggests of the duality of mind and matter, a thing obvious to Gnosticism.

In the book Intruders, Budd Hopkins tells about abduction cases where aliens were interested on collecting genetic material from the abductees.

Dr. David Jacobs ("The Threat") firmly believes that aliens have a cross breeding program in order to create an alien-human hybrid race.

Bob Lazar, while working at S-4 (Area 21), claims to have seen documents that claim that human beings are actually "containers," and that mankind is the result of 65 genetic corrections by alien biological manipulations.

John Lash does not believe that alien-human hybridization program could work, since the genome is so well protected by our creator. The ancient dream of Archons is to be born like humans to a paradise called Earth.

Reincarnation is believed in Buddhism and Hinduism, and some non-canonized Christian texts also talk about it.

Many new age-movements and Scientology believes that souls reincarnate and have lived on other planets before moving on Earth.

John Lash and Gnosticism

John Lash is a self-educated free-lance scholar who combines studies and experimental mysticism to teach directive mythology.

He has had remarkable experiences from the age of four, such as lucid dreams in which he encountered magical beings who assisted and helped him, as well as other beings who attacked him.

On metahistory.org website, Mr. Lash presents a revision of Gnosticism, and clams to present a complete restoration of the Sophianic myth of the Pagan Mysteries. He has developed a theory of the grey type of space aliens, or Archons, who want to take us over. Mr. Lash describes these entities as inhumane, stupid, blind, imitative and distorted. They influence the way we perceive the world, not the world itself.

Mr. Lash says that Archons did not succeed taking over us, and moved to plan B:

> "We'll get them to become like us. This takes us into the transhumanist agenda, an agenda that Archons desire.

They are willing to "enhance" the human experience via the means of technology, and prolong life. They want humans as androids and abandon the human soul.

Winter Leeke, who considers himself a Satanist, talks on recent interview merging of humans and machines, planned to happen by the year 2040.

He calls this event as "singularity", and it would mean the end of humanity as we know it. This is according to Mr. Lash Archontic; an alien idea is to prune us violently into building blocks of machinery. Or then, it could be disinformation to make people scared and quiet.

In ancient Gnosticism there was a savior figure, many times *Jesus*, who wakes up humanity from the spell of the Archons. This leads to golden age of innocence and freedom.

John Lash's Gnostic view denies this:

> "The Gnostic Christos is an Aeon, a divine force that does not assume human form."

His message is clearly anti-Christian, against the ideology of divine redemption, but not against love, kindness and good works.

Mr. Lash does not talk about the divine force of Heavenly Father or Barbelo (God's acting thought) mentioned so often in Nag Hammadi texts. Apparently Mr. Lash thinks it is indifferent or disinformation, since he does not believe in "salvationalism."

On an interview by Red Ice Radio, Mr. Lash condemns all "Abrahamic" religions as *mind control by the Archons.*

He sees nothing good in any religion, and considers it as an instrument of zombifying the human race. Mr. Lash thinks goddess Aeon Sofia is impersonated on living earth as flora and fauna. She has a soul of an animal, and is a conscious interdimensional being, even guiding and steering earth through space. We live in her skin.

Mr. Lash even recommends going into the wild and making a vow to Gaia Sofia, a promise to live in harmony with her.

According to scholar Gnostic sources, John Lash's Gnosticism is more his private thinking, not that much related to current and ancient practices. He claims he found the only true way to Gnosticism. Mr. Lash thinks that the alien abduction phenomena could be done by the Archons. On another interview he said UFOs, aliens and abductions could be psyops/blackops by the government.

Mr. Lash's view is:

> "The planetary shift is leading to the close of the present world cycle in 2216 CE."

Before this happen a spiritual awakening must take place.

Gnostics taught that nous, the spiritual intelligence endowed in humanity, could be blocked by Archons. They rely on humans remaining ignorant of their inherent spiritual potential. Mr. Lash sees activation of Kundalini forces as tools of protection. Arousal of Kundalini produces ecstasy, triggers super consciousness, opens the occult faculties, and releases waves of healing energy that flush physiological and hormonal secretions through the body.

Also luminous epinoia or a proper use of human imagination can be used against Archons. Mr. Lash states that for a good life we need goodwill, innocence, transparency, communication and play. We can build immunity to Archons by strengthening our vital bond with Gaia-Sofia, the living planet. Also people shouldn't fear fill their hearts that is being fed by the media.

Mr. Lash doesn't know if parasitic Archons go away, nor will they do that.

On the other hand he refers Dr. Castaneda:

> "Human beings are on a journey of awareness, which has been momentarily interrupted by extraneous forces."

Mr. Lash seems to think, that higher forces don't care for us.

Lash says, the trick is, to get past the extraterrestrial tricksters to the real magic of life on this earth. He seems to be a visionary and a prophet having faith on his studies on mythology, experiences with entheogens and Gnostic practices.

As such, his material and alien hypothesis are interesting and many times thought provoking.

On the other hand Mr. Lash has very little if any proof for his claims. Is Lash's Gnosticism only an esoteric system to himself? Is it a religion among others?

More knowledge on the subject can be found at his very large collection of writings from his page.

Interview of John Lash

Mr. Lash was kind to answer shortly some questions to UFO Digest via email.

> UA: On Nag Hammadi texts there is mentioned many times a savior figure, sometimes called Jesus. He is an announcer who wakes up humanity from Archontic spell. As well as Heavenly Father and Barbelo.
>
> What are your thoughts about this as well as other Aeons? Are they real and do they have any role on the fate of humanity?
>
> JLL: The gnostic soter is an illumined teacher who imparts knowledge of the cosmic order and human potential, not a Jesus-type messiah who performs self-sacrifice for humanity.
>
> Humanity always needs illumined teachers to educate the species in how to develop its true potential. Gnostic eduction has nothing in common with salvation. The assumed historical Jesus is never named specifically in the NHL. The Coptic initials IS are used. What IS means is open to interpretation.
>
> UA: The alien abduction phenomena. Are Archons or people with them culprits of the phenomena? Could it be possible?
>
> JLL: I believe that some alien abduction may be due to black op mind control experiments. Others may be due to the

virtual reality manipulations of the archons who are capable of temporarily inducing a trance state in human subjects.

UA: What are your eschatological views? You mention the year 2216 as an end of a cycle. Can you elaborate? Is there a worldwide "spiritual awakening"? And if, who would be behind it?

JLL: I have no eschatological view. I base the date 2216 on astronomical data. It is simply the zero hour of the 26,000-year cycle of precession. I do not see a spiritual awakening for humanity at large at this time.

UA: You talk Kundalini activation as tools for protection towards Archontic influence. Can you tell in layman terms how this could be done on a wider scale?

JLL: No, I have no formula or advice for Kundalini work for people at large, on a wider scale.

UA: How your views differ from a religion?

JLL: Religion demands faith and prevents untestable propositions. Gnosis is an alternative to religion that does not demand faith. It is an open path of experimentation using propositions that can be tested, changed, corrected, and rejected.

UA: What are your views towards H. Blavatsky and A. Crowley? What do you think of *Ecclesia Gnosticae Catholice?* How do you see freemasonry?

JLL: Frauds. Freemasonry is not worth thinking about.

UA: What kind are your moral and ethical views in general? Do you, for example believe in brotherhood of men, equality, love and tolerance to others? Do you renounce yourself of violence?

JLL: I am not an idealist in human values. I do not renounce violence but consider the right use of violence to be essential for social health.

UA: How do you see in general the future of humanity?

JLL: It's impossible to predict anything.

Do Archons dream of robotic sheep?

But what if John Lash is right? What happens if we take his views and current knowledge of UFO phenomenon and predict future?

The material is from Mr. Lash's latest interview on Red Ice Radio. The result is something out of Philip K. Dick's Blade Runner.

According to Mr. Lash the Archons have interacted with people in all times. Our culture, ideologies, religions and values are infiltrated with Archontic ideas. Some people, probably a part of elite have been secretly co-operating with the aliens from the beginning of history.

Interdimensional Archons manifest themselves as space aliens from other civilizations, angels and as UFOs, but this is deception.

The aliens manipulate humans, since they are interested in soul energy. They feed from it. Archons produce human misery in every culture and country. They have possibly founded secret societies and use the occult to bring people closer to them.

All main stream thinking has a hostile attitude towards studying their existence. Science considers UFOs, aliens and paranormal little more than *figments of imagination*. Archons have in fact created materialistic science to distort the truth, to keep people in the darkness. Their dream is to make us drones like them by creating war, famine, mental retardation, hate and disgust.

We ought to be cynical, remote controlled and on the mercy of our drives. And have a creed to money, which they make a synonym to success and freedom.

Off from the quiet life and with Leonard Cohen's words:

> "Your private life will suddenly explode."

They would make the popular culture all culture there is with rampant violence, sex and drugs.

To end this misery we would merge with the machines that would make the selected few immortal. The industrial elite rule the planet and mankind. Archons will make an imitation of man, an artificial human and present him as a messiah of new age world religion that ends other all religions.

The transhumanist agenda wins, the people form a machinery of human androids who serve one god and ruler.

Our soul essence is uploaded into a perfect body that endures stress and time. Our minds are programmed as such, what is needed for the great work for invisible rulers. There is no human misery, but humans as we know are no more.

Is this a future we want to have? Probably impossible for most is to imagine tens of billions had faith in *God, prayed and suffered for nothing.*

Would people really give up free will to something so alien? Archons have had thousands of years to assimilate us with them with little success.

- Wouldn't people fight back?
- Could the powers that be really force us on this new world order?
- Are Archons biblical Satan and his troops?

- Is there a happy end, with or without religion?
- Or could Archons just be one man's fantasy?

These questions remain unanswered.

Path 26: Addendum: The Archon Matrix

"The Matrix is everywhere. It is all around us, even now, in this very room. You can see it when you look out your window or when you turn on your television. You can feel it when you go to work, when you go to church, when you pay your taxes. It is the world that has been pulled over your eyes to blind you from the truth...that you are a slave, like everyone else, you were born into bondage, born into a prison that you cannot smell, taste, or touch, a prison for your mind."

The Archon Matrix Control System
"The human body a container"

Ancient Gnostics perceptions appear to be far more than charming antiquated mythologies. They bear striking significance to the modern UFO and alien abduction scenarios. Gnostic adepts had gained a keen understanding of how hyper-dimensional entities could access our world and influence human activities. As well, "reality" as we perceive it may in fact be an artificial "containment"—a "virtual reality" – where human existence serves unseen masters. The notorious Grey aliens seem to be more than just curious space visitors.

Robert Lazar

Whistleblower, Robert Lazar, a physicist employed at Area 51, revealed in 1989 classified information suggesting the Greys have had a long standing proprietary interest in the human species.

These beings conveyed information about the capability of affecting the human brain to anesthetize the human body. This is done without any physical contact but deployed from a a remote source.

For this anesthesia to be accomplished, the brain has to be in a relaxed state similar to that required for hypnosis. If the brain is subject to any external stimulation like stimulant drugs or loud music, this manipulation of the nervous system is ineffective.

These beings said that man was the product of externally corrected evolution. They said that man as a species had been genetically 65 times. They referred to humans as 'container', yet I don't know what we are containers of.

Lazar went on to state, ".there is an extremely classified document dealing with religion...[its says] that we are containers. That is supposedly how the aliens look at us; that we are nothing but containers—maybe containers of souls. You come up with whatever theory you want.

But we are containers, and that's how we are mentioned in the documents; that religion was specifically created so we have some rules and regulations for the sole purpose of not damaging the containers—."

[From "Alien Contact" by Timothy Good, published by William Morrow and Company, Inc 1993]

Soul Food

Again referencing the book, "Extraterrestrials Friends and Foes" author George C. Andrews tells us....

> "One of the allegations concerning the short Greys is that they have a way deriving nourishment from what leaves our body [container] at the moment of death, that they are eaters of souls, who extract from our spirits a

certain principle, through a process comparable to the extraction of hemoglobin from blood, which they use as food.

Separation of the etheric body from the soul can also be brought about by malignant entities for predatory purposes, both during life and upon passing the frontiers of death.

The etheric body is charged with energy, which they are here to trap as we trap fur bearing animals. We are now and have been used for millennia by the Greys as a food source without almost zero awareness of the actual situation. However the continual survival of the Greys on Earth depends on our continual ignorance of this symbiotic relationship, in which the benefits are strictly one-way.

The Greys are other-dimensional predatory parasites who have been manipulating us as we manipulate cattle, since time immemorial. Their hypnotic control over us is so complete that hardly anyone even begin to realize that they actually exist."

Philosopher Daniel Pinchbeck

Describes the plight of the Greys in his text "2012 The Return of the Quetzcoatl"

"Like dusty insects attracted to flame, the Greys yearn for our qualities of soul warmth; despite their cunning and technological acumen, these qualities remain beyond them. They are intelligent and sentient, hence aware of their exiled status.

Unable to escape their de-souled condition, they desire to draw humans into their lower world, sustaining their half-lives on our subtle energy. They appear to be utilizing their dream world technologies in a serious and desperate attempt to find a way out of their cul-de-sac."

Jacques Vallee

Dr. Jaques Vallee suggests our accepted scientific perception of reality may be very limited and inaccurate, if we look at the world from an informational point of view, and if we consider the many complex ways in which time and space may be structured, the old idea of space travel and interplanetary craft to which most technologies are still clinging appears not only obsolete, but ludicrous.

Indeed, modern physics has already bypassed it, offering a very different interpretation of what an 'Extraterrestrial" system might look like. I believe there is a system around us that transcends time as it transcends space.

The system may well be able to locate itself in outer space, but its manifestations are not space crafts in the ordinary 'nuts and bolts' sense. The UFO's are physical manifestations that cannot be understood apart from their psychic and symbolic reality. What we see in effect here is a control system which acts on humans and uses humans.

Piercing the Veil of Reality

Researcher Bernhard Guenther further define these "Hyper-Dimensional Realities by stating.

"There is more to our reality than our five senses can perceive, we are not God's ultimate creation, nor on the peak of the evolutionary ladder in Darwinian terms.

Our reality is embedded in a complex system of unseen worlds and controlled by denizens of higher reality. The forces at work are not all good and we are not at the top of the food chain. "Food" doesn't have to be physical and these beings feed off our negative emotions and energy, predominantly chaos, sexual pathologies, and fear which they create working through us.

The ancient esoteric teachings talk about a "Hyper-Dimensional Matrix Control System" that has influenced and controlled humanity for millennia, each in their own way"

The Active Side of Infinity

Don Juan, in Carlos Castaneda's book "The Active Side of Infinity" called the book the Topic of Topics, speaking of cosmic predators that use man as food:

Man has a glowing coat of awareness which the predator eats, leaving just the bare minimum of "consciousness stuff" for man to remain physically alive.

The predator "milks" man through arranging constant trouble, crisis, and senseless preoccupation, so as to generate flashes of awareness that it the predator then proceeds to eat.

What if there truly are Psychopaths in Power in World Governments?

To guarantee their perpetual 'human food' source, it appears the Archons have established on Earth a Matrix Control System to manage their 'livestock'. As well, it also appears they have groomed particular dynasties of humans to serve as their terrestrial managers. The human managers passes a very specific psychological profile.

There exist a type of human who has no connection to the higher centers of universal love-awareness at birth. He or she is not genetically wired this way, not being able to access them this lifetime around but he or she can emulate and mimic these higher characteristics quite well and even distract you from evolving by sapping your energy and feeding off of it.

He or she can tell you exactly what you want to hear, appear compassionate, empathetic, and understanding without meaning or feeling it.

This type of 'human' is the psychopath (making up about 6% of humanity) who is hiding behind a mask of sanity, creating misery and chaos which they feed off.

They are not necessarily criminals in prisons, but can be successful CE)'s politicians, spiritual leaders, a husband, wife, child or the neighbor next door. They're also pathological liars who never feel guilt or remorse.

That is a topic which is very misunderstood and ignored. Becoming aware of it is the most important action we can undertake to make this world a better place. It's the underlying cause of the reason why our world is in the state it is in. It is ran by psychopaths.

Ponerogenic Groups

The collective inability to recognize our leaders as psychopaths is in itself pathological. One phenomenon all 'Ponerogenic' groups and associations have in common is the fact that their members lose (or have lost) the capacity to perceive pathological individuals as such, interpreting their behavior in fascinated, heroic, or melodramatic ways.

When the habits of subconscious selection and substitution of thought thought-data spread to the macro-social level a society tends to develop contempt for factual criticism and humiliate anyone sounding the alarm.

The general population inability to discern pathology in their world leaders effectively serves the Archon Matrix Control System.

[Andrew M. Lobaczewski, "Political Ponerology"]
An Abductee herself, the late Dr. Karla Turner warned:

Humans have a deep need to believe in the power of good. We need the Aliens to be a good force, since we feel so helpless in their presence. And we need for some superior force to offer us a hope of salvation, both personally and globally, when we consider the sorry state of the world.

I think the aliens know this about us—they know that we want and hope for them to be benevolent creatures—and they use our desire for goodness to manipulate us. What better way to gain our cooperation than to tell us that the things they are doing are for our own good.

John Carter and the Archon Game

We've been playing this game since before the birth of this planet and we will continue to do so long after the death of your planet. We don't cause destruction of the world, Captain Carter, we simply manage it; feed off of it, if you like.

On every host planet it always plays out exactly the same way, populations rise, societies divide, wars spread, and all the while a neglected planet slowly fades.

We have evolved to a point in mass surveillance and obfuscation of facts in the name of National Security that many lies are told to global communities. Lies are so proliferate that one has to do your own research and be able to connect the dots to discern what reality we are actually living in. Information about extraterrestrials, UFO's, and alien presence under the ice of Antarctica deep in the catacombs of earth is fiercely withheld from the people.

3rd Snow covered pyramid discovery' in Antarctic could change the course of HUMAN HISTORY. Images on Google earth have revealed the existence of the four-sided structure, which bears an uncanny resemblance to the famous Egyptian pyramids built thousands of years ago. Covered by snow on each side, the find has prompted theories that what is now the snowy caps of the earth was once inhabited by humanity. Three structures have apparently been found, two roughly 10 miles inland and the other close to the coast. Evidence from the surrounding area indicates the climate was not as cold as it is today. The ancient megalithic ruins discovered Antarctica recently give us a hint that it may have been a part of the ancient Atlantean global civilization that ruled the Earth hundreds of thousands of years ago.

Our government has decided to shield the people from evidence that we are not alone in our galaxy. Absence of evidence is not evident of absence. People we are not alone and secrecy of advance alien technology being used to secure and advance positions of power for the wealthy elite who are profiting behind curtains of secrecy. Is this what the Antarctic Treaty all about?

The World's False Front Governments is inversely proportionate to people's false front realities starved of truths. What are the truths behind political lies of our government in denial of the existence of extraterrestrials and UFO's? Are our world leaders in the business of trading humanity for advanced technology? Beyond conspiracy theories, Secret Societies and Extraterrestrials. Some are awake and some are asleep, all of us need to wake up and be accountable for the false realities that shape our existence in a Cosmos full of evil suppression of truths and facts.

The Site of an Asteroid 'Mega Impact'

A huge and mysterious "anomaly" is thought to be lurking beneath the frozen wastes of an area called Wilkes Land. This "Wilkes Land gravity anomaly" was first uncovered in 2006, when NASA satellites spotted gravitational changes which indicated the presence of a huge object sitting in the middle of a 480 km-wide impact crater.

One team of NASA suggested it is the remains of a truly massive asteroid which was more than twice the size of the Chicxulub space rock which wiped out the dinosaurs. If this explanation is true, it could mean this killer asteroid caused a "mega impact" which resulted in the Permian—Triassic extinction event that killed 96 per cent of Earth's sea creatures and up to 70 per cent of the vertebrate organisms living on land.

After World War 2, it is believed that the American military launched one more secret mission to Antarctica to defeat the last of the Nazi Party as well as the Reptilians who sided with them. From that point on, all alien technology and research has been under the control of the American military. In 1959, the region was declared a safe zone by The Antarctic Treaty which stated it was a zone of scientific cooperation and research. This meant that no nuclear missiles or bombs could target Antarctica.

So in the event of nuclear war, we can all sleep comfortably in whatever passes for a bed in our dystopian wasteland knowing that our scientists are hard at work building flying saucers from a secret Nazi/Reptilian base deep beneath the ice.

CHAPTER IV

ARE TRANS HUMANISM AGENDA DRIVING HUMAN AFFAIRS?

Path 27: Ray Kurzweil, Elon Musk and the Transhumanism Agenda

Conspiracy Theories or Undisclosed Truths
Where there is smoke there is usually fire.

Where the human race did began on planet earth? Is religion a stumbling block to heighten spiritual ascension? Are there aliens living among us, under the ice in Antarctica? Are there "Deep Underground Military Bases beneath us connected to each other by high speed rail systems? Does our world leaders bloodlines trace back to ancient aliens and are our scientists in our military space programs corroborating with extra-terrestrial beings? Is there an agenda underway using bio-weapons to depopulate our planet of individuals who are awoke and willing to fight in resistance to trans-humanist plots to destroy our natural biological DNA?

What is the truth about Admiral Byrd and Project Highjump regarding the destruction of the United States fleet in Antarctica? Where did the German scientist involved in Project Paper Clip acquire advance rocket technology during World War II? How much trouble are the people of this world, who are being ruled over by psychopaths' world, truly in?

What if this wealthy elite class of billionaires and trillionaires through Project Paper Clip have enlisted the world's most imminent technical engineers guided by extraterrestrial intelligence of Grey and Reptilian Aliens to use CRISPR Cas9 technology embraced by Transhumanists and take evolution into their own hands to design an immortal human 2.0 in the near future; thereby reducing organic life as we know it to existence in a logical machine.

What if world governments are facing technologically advanced alien beings that places humanity's in jeopardy? What if elite bankers, controlling the world governments and militaries, have negotiated humans for technology with non-biological extraterrestrials?

Our purpose and destiny is to evolve into spiritual beings beyond the limited physical human realm of consciousness as we physically dissolve and return to a higher dimension within the omnipresent fibers of energetic Godly creative bliss of silence, super consciousness, or if you will "infinite consciousness" where the energy that is God in us comes full circle in life and death. Our life experience dissolves back into its original form of creative infinitude of that which is God itself.

Included in the nanotechnology of the Covid vaccine is self-assembling" graphene bio circuit nanostructures, and how these may be building an antenna to receive commands or instructions from external electromagnetic fields.

Global governments might be able to control the vaccinated masses by broadcasting signals from 5G cell towers. Although it sounds like science fiction, this technology has already been proven in experiments with mice, involving both SPIONs (Super Paramagnetic Iron Oxide Nanoparticles) for targeted tissue drug delivery as well as "magneto" proteins that achieve neuromodulation (brain control).

Nano Technology

Is there technological intent to incorporate nano-technology in the M-rna vaccines that morphs into our DNA. Has there been a black oil discovered that has sentience, intelligence and awareness that also can interfaces with human DNA? This black oil has been responsible for many deaths of scientists and computer programmers at the Marconi Communications company in Britain. David Griffin from Exopolitics United Kingdom gave an initial presentation at the July 2012 conference in Liverpool, England. Anything discovered that can interface with our DNA we need to be aware of it.

Are we being polluted with nano technology Morgellons in the chemtrails aerosol? Morgellons, which is a lethal communicable nanotechnology invasion of human tissue in the form of self-assembling, self-replicating nanotubes, nanowires, and Nano arrays with sensors.

Other nano configurations associated with Morgellons disease carry genetically-altered and spliced DNA or RNA that possibly responds to frequency input. These Bio-agents infect people causing lesions and strange wires that protrude from the skin. Morgellons also represent quorum sensing, which is individual nano components in the blood stream able to communicate with each other and to receive signals inward from an external stimuli such as signals from the cloud broadcast via 5G.

High tech bio agents have been introduced into the human body, via chemtrails and vaccines loaded with M-RNA nano technology. People all around the world are being unwittingly subjected to Trans humanist agenda. The nano technology within the blood stream is being influenced by certain frequencies. These high tech nano tech components contain self-replicating nanotube. The nano fluids that was retrieved from the Falkland Island is a planetary based terraforming agent. Morgellons seems to be a human biological agent being used to terraform the human body into a bizarre sci-fi entity. Morgellons disease was not around before chemtrails began.

The very same things coming down in chemtrail residue are the very same things being taken from human bodies. Some power that be is messing around with the human body with nano technology. Is there a correlation with the black oil, Morgellons, chemtrails, and M-rna vaccines?

This nano technology that is self-aware and responds to signals. Have the powers that be created a pandemic in order to deploy these binary bio-weapons infecting people with Morgellons bio agent. After that you activate the agent by use of frequencies carried on 5G radiated waves to create chaos with the people infected with Morgellons, which according to Clifford Carnicom we are all infected with Morgellons.

Ricardo Delgado has a master's degree in Bio-Statistics. Post-Graduate studies included Microbiology, Epidemiology, and immunology. He is the founder of the 5th Column. Delgado has published videos of electron microscopy taken at the University of Almeria in Spain of the Pfizer M-RNA vaccine showing what can be best described as self-organizing nano structures.

The video shows that as the Pfizer M-RNA vaccine evaporates nano sized structures begin to form. Multiple structures that appear to be the same things, things that look like microchips and electronic circuitry.

Pfizer has reportedly made 33 different batches, which has all been catalogued in a data base, some dangerous and others seemingly innocuous. So nano technology may not be in every vile but the FDA has said it needs 75 years to tell us all the detail.

At a world economic forum 2018 conference, the chief executive officer of Pfizer expressed excitement for invasive nano-technology. He referred to the recent FDA approval of a tablet with a sensor that can notify medical authorities of compliance.

Later that year, a transistor chip is unveiled that replaces silicon with air. Just this week a Covid implantable microchip developer claimed we will be chipped whether we like it or not.

There has been much talk about graphene oxide and nano tech in the vaccines, which the media vehemently claim is not true. But how would they know and why would anyone trust a word that they say about any of this?

If there are nano circuits being created in the body of the vaccinated, this will explain in the videos we have seen of the IP addresses coming from the jabbed a newly activated network coming from the jabbed of nano circuits unique to each individual.

One of the leading experts of nano technology Charles Lieber has written patents describing a technology that has a potential to self-assemble into tiny computer systems capable of controlling human neurology, which is exactly what Delgato's electron microscopy of the Pfizer jab appears to be.

Charles Lieber was just convicted of numerous crimes of working with the communist Chinese in Wuhan where Pfizer ran a research and development facility.

Elon Musk expect to be implanting his Neuralink chip in humans in 2022. Musk claims this chip can fully put you in virtual reality as if this is somehow important for humanity. For humanity it is not but for Trans Humanists it is a necessity.

If you listen to the psychopaths organizing all of this, Tan Humanism is officially their stated goal. They will not need Elon Musk's implantable chip. With injectable nano sized circuitry in the human brain and nervous system, non-intrusive wearable tech will do the job just fine.

This is rapidly being developed by "Welcome Leap" a private run umbrella corporation connection DARPA, Silicon Valley, and the military who has tripled their network in less than a year. They boast their success for the M-RNA vaccines and pushing to accelerate new ones designed to correct every so called flaw of the human psyche that stands in the way of productivity of an authoritarian state ran by artificial intelligence that monitors and controls their neurological functions 24X7.

This is exactly what they say they want by the year 2030. So either the vaccines are a way of interfacing the new Trans Human with the AI technology or they are lieing and it is all about depopulation, which is what the latest data is showing.

Natural News estimated billions of deaths if the vaccinations are not stopped in the next year. It is obviously not about public health and whether it is about depopulation and Trans Humanism it is a threat to all of humanity.

We can ponder until the end about what or why anyone would want to do this. But the real question is why are we letting them?

Mass Psychosis is also known as Group Mind, Mob Mentality or Herd Mentality. Before modern civilization, we lived in herds and in order to survive in the herd, we conformed to the herd.

This is where Mass Psychosis all stems from.

The most popular examples of explaining Mass Psychosis are typically angry mobs and violent riots but these are merely the end results.

Mass Psychosis begins when an individual mind starts to identify as a member of a group based on any unifying factor. The unifying factor doesn't even need to make sense.

For many people, the feeling of unity is enough. Our ego mind innately craves acceptance and by default, will instinctively conform to whatever group it perceives to be the majority.

In order to successfully conform to the group, the individual must put aside personal intuition and follow the guidance of the group.

This makes a person highly-controllable and spiritually stifles the individual, which causes them to crave group acceptance even more.

Man's disposition for Mass Psychosis has been written about for millennia, most notably, in ancient scripture and philosophy.

And we all experience this as human beings, whether we reflect upon it or not.

Plato argued that due to the nature of Group Mind, democracy always leads to tyranny and subjugation. His concern was the lack of good leadership and philosophized on ways of solving this.

In 1895, Gustave Le Bon published 'The Crowd', wherein he explains the key processes for cultivating Mass Psychosis: Anonymity, Contagion and Suggestibility. This work is known to have influenced world leaders, businesses and tyrants, of which the ethics has been written about for decades.

And yet, AP and Reuters outrageously claim that Mass Psychosis does not exist, when it is, in fact the corporate media apparatus to which they belong that makes this all possible, waging psychological warfare against a group of the population who believes the media would never lie to them.

This is why the term "Mass Psychosis" is arguably a better term than "Group Mind" or "Mob Mentality". A change on the field of consciousness occurs; a devolution from Divine Inspiration into primitive hierarchy, which has no place in a civilized society - and yet, here we are.

Without Mass Psychosis, today's leaders would have no power. Just like advertising, everything about politics is about cultivating Mass Psychosis.

Whereas, the individual pursuit of happiness has inevitably led to beauty and innovation, creating and controlling groups of people, which has been the biggest power play on Earth for all of recorded history, almost always leads to death and destruction, the science and study of Mass Psychosis could be used to enlighten humanity, by educating the individual about the power and potential of the human mind.

But today, the very same corrupt media being used by wealthy elites to divide and enslave us says there is no such thing as Mass Psychosis.

Mass Psychosis is humanity's burden to outgrow. It is why we accept the lesser of two evils.

Many of us are well aware of the frailty of man and the civilized world. The great psychologist, Carl Jung's warning to the world was that the individual must come face to face with their own shadow.

In order to accomplish this, one must liberate themselves from the collective.

And until enough of us do, society will continue to be led by tyrants and ignorant mobs

The Trans Humanist Connection to the COVID19 Pandemic

With an increasing number of people becoming aware of graphene oxide being identified in Covid vaccines, a company called INBRAIN Neuroelectronics demonstrates that graphene-based "neuromodulation" technology using AI-powered neuroelectronics is very real.

INBRAIN Neuroelectronics Secures $17 Million in Series A Funding for First AI-Powered Graphene-Brain Interface. They state their technology is being used, "for treating epilepsy and Parkinson's disease."

The company to advance first-in-human studies for its flagship product, a less-invasive neuromodulation device for treating neurological conditions using artificial intelligence and graphene electrodes. INBRAIN's brain-controlling "bio circuits" based on graphene are, in fact, a very real technology. Fact-checker claim that graphene isn't found in vaccines and that graphene bio circuits are a conspiracy theory. INBRAIN Neuroelectronics shows that the fact checkers are lying.

INBRAIN describe graphene bio circuits as a kind of platform that can be upgraded. Moderna, creator of the mRNA Covid vaccine, has described its technology as an "operating system" that can be updated and reprogrammed at any time, also. The company highlights its technology as being able to "read" a person's brain, detect specific neurological patterns, and then control that person's neurology to alter their brain function.

Graphene is further described as, "Thinnest known material to perfectly adapt stimulation to targeted brain anatomy." Graphene in Covid vaccines can be used to control human neurology. INBRAIN Neuroelectronics is engaged in any sort of nefarious agenda, nor are they involved in Covid vaccines. **Graphene-based bio circuits can be used for both good and evil, depending on the ethics and motivations of those who control the technology.**

As with most technologies touted as empowering humanity, television, vaccines, the internet, nuclear power, robotics, etc.—they all end up in the hands of lunatic, genocidal globalists who wield them as weapons against humanity. There is no technology that madmen won't exploit to enslave humanity and increase their own power and control.

Graphene bio circuits give power-hungry lunatics direct access to your brain, and according to many analysts (see below), vaccines provide the excuse to inject human victims with graphene-based substances that self-assemble into bio circuits in the human brain. Analyzed Covid vaccines and has found that 98% to 99% of the non-liquid mass in the vaccine appears to be graphene oxide.

Many people acquire pseudo magnetism after Covid vaccine inoculation. *The person becomes a superconductor. That is, he or she emits and receives signals.*

Graphene is toxic, it is a chemical, a toxic chemical agent. Introduced in the organism in large quantities, it causes thrombi. It causes blood clots, causes alteration of the immune system, and eventually generates a collapse of the immune system.

Included in the nanotechnology of the Covid vaccine is self-assembling" graphene bio circuit nanostructures, and how these may be building an antenna to receive commands or instructions from external electromagnetic fields.

Global governments might be able to control the vaccinated masses by broadcasting signals from 5G cell towers. Although it sounds like science fiction, this technology has already been proven in experiments with mice, involving both SPIONs (Super Paramagnetic Iron Oxide Nanoparticles) for targeted tissue drug delivery as well as "magneto" proteins that achieve neuromodulation (brain control).

Dr. Charles Lieber, 60, Chair of the Department of Chemistry and Chemical Biology at Harvard University, was arrested December 22, 2021 and charged by criminal complaint with one count of making a materially false, fictitious and fraudulent statement.

Yanqing Ye, 29, a Chinese national, was charged in an indictment today with one count each of visa fraud, making false statements, acting as an agent of a foreign government and conspiracy. Ye is currently in China.

Zaosong Zheng, 30, a Chinese national, was arrested on Dec. 10, 2019, at Boston's Logan International Airport and charged by criminal complaint with **attempting to smuggle 21 vials of biological research to China**. *On Jan. 21, 2020, Zheng was indicted on one count of smuggling goods from the United States and one count of making false, fictitious or fraudulent statements. He has been detained since Dec. 30, 2019.*

"According to court documents, since 2008, Dr. Lieber who has served as the Principal Investigator of the Lieber Research Group at Harvard University, which specialized in the area of nanoscience, **has received more than $15,000,000 in grant funding from the National Institutes of Health (NIH) and Department of Defense (DOD).** *These grants require the disclosure of significant foreign financial conflicts of interest, including financial support from foreign governments or foreign entities," DOJ reveals.*

"Unbeknownst to Harvard University beginning in 2011, Lieber became a "Strategic Scientist" at Wuhan University of Technology (WUT) in China and was a contractual participant in China's Thousand Talents Plan from in or about 2012 to 2017. China's Thousand Talents Plan is one of the most prominent Chinese Talent recruit plans that are designed to attract, recruit, and cultivate high-level scientific talent in furtherance of China's scientific development, economic prosperity and national security."

Nanomesh, neurology interface control systems, "radial addressing" of nanowires

Another patent from Dr. Lieber:

9,252,214 Apparatus, method and computer program product providing radial addressing of nanowires

This allows for embedded AI systems to control nano-mesh lattices that interface with human neurology to both monitor and control human beings. This technology was being transferred to China.

Speculation is that **nano-mesh lattices could be inserted into vaccines** and once injected, they would self-assemble into neuralink-like computational interface systems that read and control human neurology.

This technology would essentially allow Mark Zuckerberg to project his "Meta" universe into your brain *without using goggles.* It's a full-matrix scenario, where these nanowire / embedded computational systems could eventually **read your own private thoughts** (inner dialog) and surveil the most private thing you have—your mind.

This tech represents *transhumanism* and the "borgification" of humanity. It is the end game of total enslavement and mind control at the neurological level. It can be inserted into your body using hypodermic needles that are falsely labeled "vaccines." (This does not mean that all vaccine injections are nanowire payloads, just that nanowire payloads can be inserted into such needles due to their nano-scale size.)

Taking evolution into their own hands, they believe they can design an immortal human 2.0 in the near future. Transhumanism and Technocracy share a common philosophical base in Scientism, or the effectual worship of science.

This war on human consciousness is more obvious with each vaccine mandate and the continuous violation of civil liberties with the ongoing crimes against humanity with all the lies and deceptions being perpetrated by world governments and their news media propaganda machines.

There is an agenda to manipulate the weather, environment, the food supply, the human DNA and human consciousness through CRISPR9 genetic engineering. Is there an alien agenda to manipulate the human DNA strands? We are without leaders in our government brave enough to disclose to disclose the cause of our sad global reality of human depopulation.

The controllers of this planet are using military programs that are designed to deliver to them bio-spiritual enslavement using mind control and genetic engineering to control human brain waves. Their ultimate objective is to control thought and behavior and limit human perception in order to keep human consciousness in a very low vibrational frequency.

In the process, prevent us and our children from attaining incredible insight and knowledge perceptible to us through our third eye or pineal glands, which we use to receive insight from higher dimensional planes of our conversations with our true godly creator that exist just outside the physical realm of our being.

Some of us are more enlightened through education than others, for so many reasons due to the culture we live in and the religions we embrace, that we are being used as guinea pigs in tyrannical military medical, pharmaceutical, and technological experiments involving chemtrails, vaccinations, and GMO foods.

We have advanced to the latest 5G technology. Is this radiation technology being used to manipulate the electromagnetic field around us along with nano-particles in these vaccines to control our consciousness? Is there an alien agenda to destroy the air, water, and the life sustaining environment? It is a very difficult to understand that humans would be so self-destructive.

Destructive pollutants, chemtrails, GMO, and nano-particle containing vaccines, these pollutions directly from our environment and direct injections via vaccinations and foods into our bodies, pollutes nucleic acid in our DNA. Through these means, the powers-that-be are directly destroying the DNA processes that produces intelligent information necessary for spiritual ascension by manipulating our DNA coding.

The more the organic human body has endured gene modification, the splicing and dicing of our DNA, the more likely our body loses the ability to activate our original blueprint. Men are not at liberty to play God at the expense of other misinformed and helpless individuals.

What is genetic engineering about? What is the value gained by creating soul-less computer with artificial intelligence? What has brought humanity to the point that it no longer values spiritual ascension by genetically rehabilitating our original DNA blueprint with natural means? Is there an alien agenda seeking to control human consciousness and the physical human body thru avenues of chemtrails, 5G technology, artificial intelligence, GMO, and vaccine bio-weapons?

The chemtrails, GMO, and vaccine bio-weapons have not been designed to accelerate the natural ascension processes innate in our DNA. It is clear as day via the FEMA camps and vaccine mandate that there is an anti-human agenda. Psychopaths are playing God with our minds and bodies to block spiritual ascension.

We are silently witnessing the beginning of a vaccine induced Zombie apocalypse and it is time for the enslavement of human consciousness to end. Transhumanism is about replacing the organic human's original DNA blueprint. The vaccine bio-weapons are loaded with self-assembling nano-particle technology to destroy the human spiritual and independent thinking God given function. They want to build human beings they can control by destroying our very powerful traits of emotions that fuels the idea of love in us all.

Transhumanism is a type of futurist philosophy aimed at transforming the human species by means of biotechnologies. Transhumanists see disease, aging and death as undesirable and unnecessary, and aim to transform human beings into post-human species with greater capacities than those of present human beings.

The technology powers players are Ray Kurzweil, Elon Musk, Zolton Ivstan, Sergey Brin, Peter Theil, Larry Ellison, Larry Page, and Mark Zuckerberg, have emerged as powerful social engineers and have already established a 2030 deadline to roll out the Trans Humanist agenda. You are to take these RNA-modifying nanotechnology, fetal tissue-line derived, graphene oxide-filled COVID-19 vaccines to keep your job. This group of men want to reinvent what God has created.

Transhumanists give special attention to genetic engineering, robotics, molecular nanotechnology and artificial intelligence, and the Covid-19 pandemic is providing gene-based vaccines a chance to break through into the global health market.

In the case of Moderna and mRNA therapeutics, DNA vaccines is considered a new paradigm that would disrupt the pharmaceutical industry. Its vision is to harness a new technology that synthesizes messenger RNA, or mRNA—which is an instruction manual in every living cell for creating protein—to prompt the human body to make its own medicine.

Elon Musk may change our minds forever with Neuralink, which aims to use implanted brain chips to improve the human body—and help us compete with AI.

One of Musk's main projects is to develop high-bandwidth interfaces to connect humans and computers.

Formed in 2016, Neuralink is one of Musk's more secretive offshoots. The immediate goals of the endeavor are treating traumatic brain injuries. Musk says paralyzed people who get Neuralink's electronic brain chip or "Fitbit" installed in their skulls, for instance, could conceivably walk again.

Musk has said humans are "already cyborgs" because of access to smartphones and computers. Neuralink, he says, will close that gap and prep us for the future. Musk's Neuralink Company aims to implant an incredibly thin chip in human's brains that would allow people to control prosthetic limbs. Musk said his long term goal is symbiosis with artificial intelligence. Adding a digital layer to the brain's limbic system and cortex may be humanity's only hope of matching the exponential and possibly sinister rise of artificial intelligence.

Ray Kurzweil, Google's director of engineering and a futurist credited with the idea of "the singularity," says machines could surpass humans in intelligence by 2030 and time is of the essence for companies like Neuralink to help humans keep up.

Kurzweil stated "When we get to the 2030s, we will have neural net technologies at Google that go way beyond what is feasible today. These will exceed human intelligence. For this to be something that makes humans smarter rather than just competing with humans, we need an ability to interact with our neocortex. But that has to be done at a fast speed, far greater than what we can do now."

CRISPR Cas9 technology is being embraced by Transhumanists all over the world.

The Ethics of Transhumanism

Andy Warhol once said that he wanted to be a machine, and that it would be a lot easier to be a machine - if something broke, you could just replace it.

Even though small wounds and injuries heal, this has not been the case for humans. If something were inherently broken, it would stay broken the rest of our lives. Which relates to another common saying: The only two things in this world that are certain are death and taxes.

For the transhumanist movement, this is not the case. Transhumanists believe that humankind can evolve beyond its current physical and mental limitations to become "superhuman" and, eventually, immortal.

Scientists are merging robotics with the human body in brain-to-computer interface (BCI), wherein individuals with physical injuries can regain their functions, and soldiers become smarter and more powerful through the fusing of their brain with machines.

But U.S. is not the only country engaged in human enhancement and transhumanism, as Russia and China are also in hot pursuit with exoskeletons, vaccines and brain implants. As this competition gains traction, one wonders what the future of their militaries may look like as human beings are steadily integrated with machines to become armies of iron man.

One of the most prominent members of the movement is **Zoltan Istvan**, founder of the *Transhumanist Party* and 2016 third-party presidential candidate.

For Istvan, aging and death are the biggest plague of our time. The party is proposing a *transhumanist bill of rights* that states that it should be illegal to stop research on longevity and eternal rights based on religious and ethical reasons.

Many of today's well-known faces in the tech world accompany the movement.

Peter Thiel has, like a modern-day *King Gilgamesh*, stated that it is against human nature not to fight death, and is investing heavily in companies like the Methuselah Foundation. He is joined by **Larry Ellison**, who finds accepting mortality "incomprehensible." Google co-founders **Larry Page** and **Sergey Brin**, as well as **Mark Zuckerberg**, are also investing in ways to extend human life.

The concept of eternal or even extended life would challenge several constructs of today's society, ranging from healthcare and social services to pensions and insurance, as well as the labor market, just to name a few.

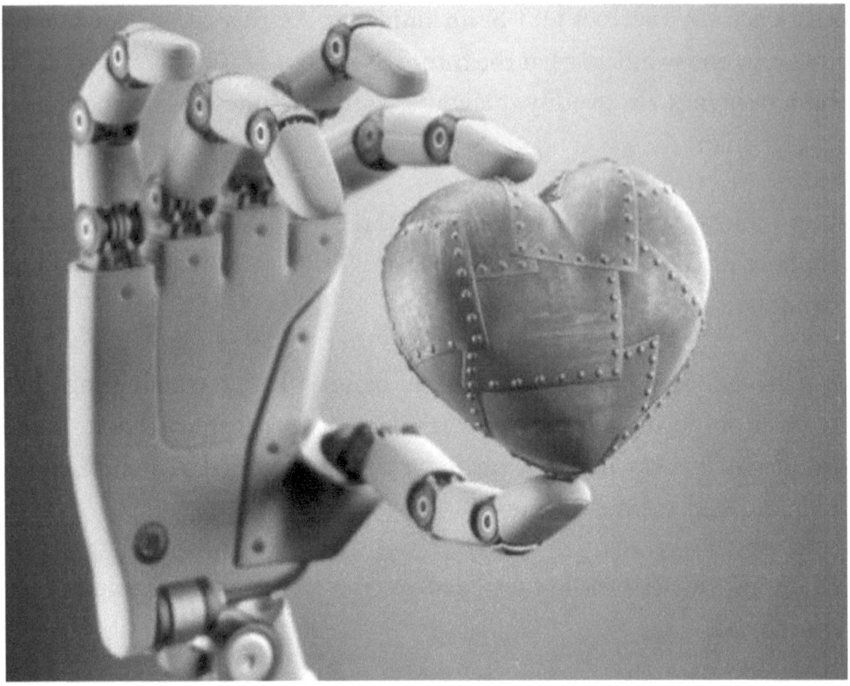

Eternal life also poses a series of ethical and moral dilemmas, such as,

- how to make room for the next generation
- or whether eternal or prolonged life would be reserved for those privileged few

Will this create a new class divide, through which an elite class emerge with physical and mental upgrades? One of the proposed solutions to achieve immortality comes from **Ray Kurzweil**, who believes that we can transfer our consciousness to machines to achieve digital immortality within three decades.

According to techno-futurists, the exponential development of technology in general and artificial intelligence ("AI") in particular—including the complete digital replication of human brains—will radically transform humanity via two revolutions.

The first is the "singularity," when artificial intelligence will redesign itself recursively and progressively, such that AI will become vastly more powerful than human intelligence ("super strong AI"). The second revolution will be "virtual immortality," when the fullness of our mental selves can be uploaded perfectly to non-biological media (such as silicon chips), and our mental selves will live on beyond the demise of our fleshy, physical bodies.

AI singularity and virtual immortality would mark a startling, trans-human world that techno-futurists envision as inevitable and perhaps just over the horizon. They do not question whether their vision can be actualized; they only debate when will it occur, with estimates ranging from 10 to 100 years.

However, by the time it is predicted we achieve digital immortality, it is also likely that we would have developed human-like artificial intelligence.

Elon Musk believes that humans need to add digital implants in the form of a neural lace to their brains to be able to compete with artificial intelligence.

Ray Kurzweil, Singularity University, and Elon Musk

Who is Ray Kurzweil? Ray Kurzweil was born to Jewish parents on February 12, 1948. He is an accomplished American author, computer scientist, inventor and futurist. He has written books on health, artificial intelligence (AI), transhumanism, the technological singularity, and futurism. Kurzweil is a public advocate for the futurist and transhumanist movements, and gives public talks to share his optimistic outlook on life extension technologies and the future of nanotechnology, robotics, and biotechnology.

Kurzweil received the 1999 National Medal of Technology and Innovation, the United States' highest honor in technology, from

President Clinton in a White House ceremony. He was the recipient of the $500,000 Lemelson-MIT Prize for 2001, the world's largest for innovation. And in 2002 he was inducted into the National Inventors Hall of Fame, established by the U.S. Patent Office.

He has received twenty-one honorary doctorates, and honors from three U.S. presidents. Kurzweil has been described as a "restless genius" by The Wall Street Journal and "the ultimate thinking machine" by Forbes. PBS included Kurzweil as one of 16 "revolutionaries who made America" along with other inventors of the past two centuries. Inc. magazine ranked him #8 among the "most fascinating" entrepreneurs in the United States and called him "Edison's rightful heir".

With all due respect, Mr. Kurzweil is a Secular Jewish person. Many prominent Jews have been secular, including Sigmund Freud, Gustav Mahler, Marc Chagall, Henri Bergson, Heinrich Heine, Albert Einstein, Theodor Herzl, Louis Brandeis, Micha Josef Berdyczewski, Hayim Nahman Bialik, Karl Marx, Boris Pasternak, Bernie Sanders, Dave Rubin and Baruch Spinoza.

Ray Kurzweil set up Singularity University, with others, call this "The Cloud." The goal at Singularity University is to connect the human population to the cloud by 2030 via micro-chip implants, which is no time from now. As Ray Kurzweil puts it, we will think through the gateways in the cloud where the cloud will do more and more human thinking, until it does all the thinking for us.

So what we are looking at is the complete hi-jacking by "The Cloud", of the human conscious mind and immediate sub-conscious mind, by those who control "The Cloud", [this is] what AI [artificial intelligence] really is. And that will be artificial intelligence, that will have the agenda that is programmed, or it chooses to have, and they will be open about it, trying to sell it as being Super Human.

We see the sales pitch that by being connected to this "Cloud." We will be able to do things and understand things the human mind cannot. In fact the whole term "Singularity" refers to the point where artificial intelligence becomes greater in potential than the human conscious mind.

So what they are saying is, if you connect your brain, mind to this tech cloud, you will be super human... You will be able to think like the machines can, how the AI can.

I think the transhumanist agenda or assault on our organic human nature is underway with the mRNA vaccines being pushed in the Covid19 plan-demic

The rush to inject at least 70% of the human population with "manipulative magnetic nano-medicine" and "super paramagnetic nanoparticles" smacks of an alien agenda.

Implants and tracking devices have been recurring themes of the Alien Abduction Scenario. DARPA has been involved in the creation of Google, which has been instrumental in delivering the Technocratic wet dream of implementing a global Artificial Intelligence network for human command and control.

According to San Francisco-based Neuralink's website, the company, which Musk launched with a half dozen researchers, professors and industry experts in 2016, will eventually implant a computer chip, roughly the size of a large coin, into the human brain via a robot surgeon.

James Giordano, Chief of the Neuroethics Studies Program at the Pellegrino Center for Bioethics at Georgetown University talks about "The use of neural interfacing and physiological interfacing through... remote-controlled, small-scale systems, to create a nano swarm of bio-penetrable materials that you cannot see, that can penetrate the most robust biochemical filters, that are able to integrate themselves through a variety of membranes, mucus membranes and wherever – mouth, nose, ears, eyes and they can be done in such a level that their presence is almost impossible to detect.

The idea here is to put minimal-sized electrodes in a network within a brain through only minimal intervention; to be able to read and write into the brain function in real-time, remotely."

Data transfer between living human brains and the cloud will require the use of D-Wave quantum computers and Artificial Intelligence. While such supercomputers with processing speeds fast enough to handle the necessary volumes of data already do exist, the nanoscale interfacing devices to be embedded in the brain have yet to be perfected.

Nanobots can be delivered into the body by vaccines or can be aerosolized to place minimal-sized electrodes in a network within a brain, to be able to read and write into the brain function in real-time remotely. Once the nanobots are inside the brain, the devices would then wirelessly transmit encoded information to and from a cloud-based supercomputer network for real-time brain state monitoring and data extraction, in essence controlling what people think.

Neural-nanorobotics are being developed to enable a safe, secure instantaneous real-time interface between the human brain and both biological and non-biological computing systems. This technology would include brain-to-brain interfaces, brain-to-computer interfaces and specifically, brain-to-cloud interfaces, to connect your brain to the cloud in real time and provide you with instant access to the world's knowledge and Artificial Intelligence.

If this isn't the "hive mind" of the Greys, then what is? Are humans being transformed, through the COVID vaccine into prototypes of Earth-based Greys? Is this what an alien invasion looks like? Are we a generation away from becoming genderless Borgs with no personal will, mere nodes on a network?

It is unknown whether human-level artificial intelligence will arrive in a matter of years, later this century, or not until future centuries. Regardless of the initial timescale, once human-level machine intelligence is developed, a "super intelligent" system that "greatly exceeds the cognitive performance of humans in virtually all domains of interest" would follow surprisingly quickly, possibly even instantaneously. Such a superintelligence would be difficult to control or restrain.

While the ultimate goals of superintelligences can vary greatly, a functional superintelligence will spontaneously generate, as natural sub goals, "instrumental goals" such as self-preservation and goal-content integrity, cognitive enhancement, and resource acquisition.

For example, an agent whose sole final goal is to solve the Riemann hypothesis (a famous unsolved, mathematical conjecture) could create, and act upon, a sub goal of transforming the entire Earth into some form of computronium (hypothetical "programmable matter") to assist in the calculation. The superintelligence would proactively resist any outside attempts to turn the superintelligence off or otherwise prevent its sub goal completion.

In order to prevent such an existential catastrophe, it might be necessary to successfully solve the "AI control problem" for the first superintelligence. The solution might involve instilling the superintelligence with goals that are compatible with human survival and well-being. Solving the control problem is surprisingly difficult because most goals, when translated into machine-implementable code, lead to unforeseen and undesirable consequences.

It is not about making us super human, it is about making us sub-human. It's about the end of humanity as we know it, in terms of anything even approaching free thought or free perception, because perception will be coming from "The Cloud" to conscious mind. Thus the conscious mind will be thinking "I have a thought, I agree, I oppose" but it won't be the human mind reaching those conclusions it will be the CLOUD.

Ray Kurzweil, one of the great PR men for Frankenstein and the transhumanist nightmare. And the whole agenda is for humanity to have artificial intelligence put inside the brain, Nano tech in the end, that you can even breathe in. Nano-technology is called smart dust, Nano-bots and other "smart" names. This technology will connect the human mind to a non-organic technological sub-reality. It is the entire agenda of this transhumanist nightmare unfolding around us...the complete takeover of human thought and emotion.

We are being taken down that road step by step in a very coordinated way. First you get people addicted to tech they can hold.... Look around you all over the world to groups of young people. Look at them, and the rest of the world doesn't exist, only the screen of the smart phone exists as the mind gets attached to the tech. The focus of the attention in effect is the expression of "The Cloud".

The next step is getting tech ON the body and we are well into that. Wearables. The step before implantable; that is your smart watches, google glasses.

The next step, manipulated from the start, putting tech in the body, connected to "The Cloud" and taking over human thinking.

The purpose of this "University" is to promote just that. So much will be going on to advance this agenda of the tech control of the human mind, whether its this University or putting satellites up to bathe us in Wi-Fi because if you are going to connect everyone you must have Wi-Fi everywhere.

Goggle is a search engine right? Facebook is just a way to keep up with your friend's right? No. They are much more than that. Google is just a few miles down the freeway in Silicon Valley close to NASA research area and Singularity University. People think of it as a search engine, which gives it enormous power because of its domination of the search engine arena.

Google is a prime driver in this transhumanist agenda, in league with DARPA, the tech development arm of the Pentagon, one of most sinister agencies on Earth, developing death rays, surveillance tech, mind control, and effective ways of killing.

This combo of DARPA and Google is at the forefront of pushing the Trans-human agenda and Kurzweil is also an executive at Google, called chief futurist. Some years ago a lady named Regina Dugan, head executive of DARPA moved from DARPA in a strange career move to Google. But when you do the research and see what's going on… It was then actually in effect an interdepartmental transfer.

Google is fundamentally involved in this entire scenario. They recently took over a company called Boston Dynamics, one of the prime organizations developing AI controlled machines, and smaller-145 d-darpa-m15robots who are under contract to…DARPA!

This combo is extremely important to understand in relation to this agenda of control, connecting the human mind to the tech CLOUD. Also in development is a robot army for the World Government, but one step further is, in the end they don't want that to be an army of humans, but an army of machines controlled by AI, making the decisions of who to kill and who to bomb.

So we are now in an arena of sci-fi and sci-fi is supposed to be fiction projecting into the future, coming from imagination, but is now science fact and is all around us, being driven by the Singularity University and Google. Google has changed much of its company's name to ALPHABET, because all of these areas that they are involved in, have become so vastly much more than just a search engine.

We need to watch people like Kurzweil, Singularity University, and organizations like Google, like a hawk with a telescope, because we are being manipulated into literally giving our minds away to tech controlled by artificial intelligence002E`

When convicted IMF criminal Christine Lagarde, World Bank head Jim Kim and 100 other global misleaders gathered in the UAE for the World Government Summit in 2015 Elon Musk was there arguing that humans will have to merge with machines as they work toward the world government utopia. He was pushing a brain/computer interface technology called "Neuralink."

It is billed as a "medical research company" working on crafting brain-computer interface technology. Neuralink is touting the idea of "neural lace," an imaginary invention from the science fiction of British novelist Iain M. Banks. Neural lace refers to a semi-organic mesh that is grown on the cerebral cortex, allowing for a direct brain-computer interface.

Lost in the hype over Musk's announcement of Neuralink is that neural lace-type research has already been going on for years and the "invention of neural lace" was first announced in 2015.

It's important to understand this is the thin edge of a massive public indoctrination campaign to love and accept the brain chip. As far-fetched as that may sound to people who aren't paying attention, we are closer to the implementation of this technology than many would like to believe.

We now have brain-computer interfaces that are helping the paralyzed to move and promising to cure Parkinson's and revolutionize medicine in all sorts of other amazing ways. And those promises are real, and they're here, and they're important.

But this technology comes as a double-edged sword, and when that sword is wielded for evil, the possibility for outright control of the human species (or the new cyborg subspecies, or whatever is being created) is there, too, and it's being overseen by friendly government/ military agencies like DARPA. Oh, but here's the best part: Neuralink is being backed by Bilderberger Peter Thiel, too.

So, who wants to be the first to volunteer to have a brain chip implanted by the Bilderbergers? It's for a good cause.

It is very unlikely that Mr. Kurzweil futuristic society requires education. Education has become very expensive and beyond the grasp of the average person. High tech jobs requires high tech education. What is the solution to those left behind without the necessary education to exist in a futuristic world envisioned by Mr. Kurzweil? Will people simply be digitized and uploaded into Mr. Kurzweil Digital Universe.

When Mr. Kurzweil was asked if God exist, his response was "not yet." Maybe, in his computerized universe, pushing buttons to delete and permit digital consciousness, he himself will be God.

Leaders should be motivated by a more humanistic approach to living, whereby they shape the lives of the masses through lens of love instead of misguiding dogma and a growing cast of elite and greedy scientists controlled by the super-rich with selfish ideas of who benefits in a futuristic society with advanced technology.

How does this change in the vision of trans-humanism in Kurzweil world of digital consciousness?

What really goes on at Bohemian Grove? What are in the minutes from Bilderberg and Tri-Lateral meetings? What are the truths from Roswell and area 51? What is NASA not telling us about non-natural structures photographed on the moon? How damaging are the aerosol sprays in the Chemtrails raining down on us out of the skies?

How do we atone for geniuses making money forsaking morals and ethics? What are the pathways to atonement of humanity in order to heal human and planetary destruction caused by political lies, racial prejudices, unscrupulous greed, and inflated God complexed feelings of personal ability, privilege, and notions of infallibility and racial superiority?

Since times immemorial, we have paid a hefty price in violence not cultivating civility towards each other by loving each other mechanically guided by religious beliefs. In this contemporary age of advanced technology, the words of Frederick Nietzsche seems apropos, "God is dead" as we send our kids to the temples of high technology worshipping technological dictates that undermines human dignity and human heartedness.

When will we truly learn to love and trust each other? If we ever compassionately cultivate love, we will understand love is the answer to saving our technologically condemned world. Advanced technology is a tool that will only benefit the wealthy elite and not the slave workforce used to produce the digital robotics and android technology that will make organic life obsolete

This is the time for greater self-awareness and how our awareness of the true problems in society of lies being distorted into truths. Men and women at Bohemian Grove, Bilderberg, Tri-Lateral, Kings, Queens, and Pontiffs are responsible for the inversion of perception of evil ways presented to the people of the world as life. Evil spelled backwards is live.

Our leaders promotes evil inverted into life through ignorance that processes lies into evil masquerading as truth made possible by dumbed-downed unawareness. The people that are in positions of leadership are obsessed with death. Our leader's agendas are about destroying, killing, and expanding suffering through wars and domestic policies.

Every decision of governments contradicts principles of freedom and democracy. Our governments promote agendas of psychopathic death cults. There is no empathy, no remorse, and no ability to put themselves in the feeling of those who suffer from their actions.

Behind these secrets of inverted lies of fake truths, the destruction of everything biological we know and love has begun.

Emerging in the tech industry is a blatant disrespect for biological life and this is truly frightening. The main focus of our brightest technical minds is a future of computer terminal humans or the inversion of life from biological to digital.

The Internet is designed to be a technical collective mind, thus everything is being connected to the Internet. This design is intended to control everything including the natural thought processes of human thought manipulated through the cloud.

The Internet is an inverted digital/electrical universe inverse to the natural universe. It is an information system and deliver information as though it is reality. Our bright minds are proposing a world of counterfeit sub reality digital conscious matrix connecting human to a hive mind in a virtual reality within a virtual reality hacked from the biological ordinary reality.

The last 15 years we have been inundated with movie after movie portraying the very society software gurus want to direct our society towards, which is a desecration to biological life at the cost of planetary destruction and billions lives lost through Eugenics Society's plans of planetary depopulation.

The Emergence of a Society Addicted to Artificial Intelligence Where Compassion Has Become Illogical

As Germany's Technical Director of Germany's rocket development program, Werhner Von Braun had knowledge of all of Germany's secret dark projects. Werhner Von Braun attended secret meeting at Bohemian Grove and was recruited by private investors to build a private Space Program completely independent of control of the US government.

These men have wrought from selfishness so many ideas into being that should never have been allowed to proliferate.

So many secrets, so many mounting problems. The technological solutions being proposed are truly something out of a science fiction novel.

We never seek to connect the problems in the world, created by banking, to advances in alien technology. So many secrets are being withheld from the people regarding UFO's and back engineered technology from crashed alien crafts.

Science and technology has made tremendous strides towards trans-humanism creating androids and cyborgs utilizing artificial intelligence and data cloud inspired digital consciousness of mapped minds into a hive downloaded into a virtual universe.

I have experienced working in the culture in Silicon Valley at Google on the team of its Fiber to the Home Project. To work there is to sample what it is like to work in an environment staffed with the worlds brightest technologically educated individuals.

I could not help but notice the lifestyle of the mindset of people making salaries "six-figures-plus" thriving in a vacuum of egoistical disconnect.

People whole lives consumed with living up to competitive technological aggrandizement. It is no place to reflect on world politics, humanism, and the role their livelihood plays in the destruction of biological life.

People are paid well to display unwittingly cold steely automaton characteristics paid well to help diminish the future presence of biological life. Their rewards are an ability to afford inflated million dollar homes, drive the best cars, and sadly ship their kids to the best automaton factories we call schools. Schools that separates them and perpetuate a class of arrogant and elite technocrats.

This is very scary to me because I can see clearly our society heading passionately down an advanced technological rabbit hole of Trans-Humanism and Artificial Intelligence chasing concepts of digital immortality.

On the surface and looking at such advancement, it seems an inescapable technological love-affair of bliss. In reality, the advancement of such technology is Pandora's Box full of demons and our greatest technological nightmares!

Historically, our species have always looked to the future and advanced technology to rescue us from our predisposition of violence that, instead of improving us as a specie, technology does the opposite keeps us fighting endless wars, and the precursor to destroying eco-systems, example number one the nuclear disaster at Fukishima or the threat of destruction posed by nuclear weapons.

Life will be extended by advanced technology with sickness being cured with Nanobot-technology, gene therapy, and possible restoration of life via cryonics preservation until the deceased body is revived by future technology. People will also have the option to have their brain mapped and uploaded into the cloud.

The scientists continue to dream of exploration of space in spaceships manned by androids fueled with artificial intelligence from the cloud. Scientists also envision humans with microchips and Nano-bots, hybrid man and machines called Cyborgs and ultimately android and robots.

With all the great technological advances, the future is made to look bright, but is it really? For the last 50 years, world population multiplied more rapidly than ever before, and more rapidly than it is projected to grow in the future. In 1950, the world had 2.5 billion people; and in 2005, the world had 6.5 billion people. By 2050, this number could rise to more than 9 billion.

Will advance technology be accessible by 9 billion or will only the wealthy have access to this technology. Population control issue will be an issue. If we have 6 to 9 billion people who are not going anywhere, what do we do?

Will there be a regulatory commission to decide who can have a kid? Will there be an inequality of this technology that prolong our life that only the super-rich can afford? Today regulate visits to the doctor is life extension. Health care is life extension. The same issues of inequality we are dealing with today, if we do not find solutions, it will only get worse in the future.

What we need more than the advancement of technology today is equity so all humans can live well. As we look at politics, greed, and wars today, are we truly laying the groundworks for equity in society? Are we dematerializing, demonetizing, and truly democratizing?

If the Covid19 vius was created in laboratories in Wuhan China, if AID/HIV virus was created in US Labs, if Chem-Trails contains Nano-Fibers laced with…., if democracy is being undermined by discussions of Eugenics in Tri-Lateral, Bilderberg, and Council of Foreign Relations, are there plans to provide health care for life extension for all or are there plans to reduce the world's population to a fraction of the population today and the advancement spoken of in the future being accessible to only the wealthy elite?

The signs are already apparent that advance technology will only be available to the elite. Incarceration, enslavement, and depopulation is already in motion.

We see each day the atmospheric poisoning overhead with Chem-trails releasing micron size mechanized dust as aerosol. We inhale this micro-dust into our lungs and it bores into our tissues and execute pathological missions.

The fluoride in our water prevents and aspartame in our foods interferes with the development of our pineal gland crippling and numbing us down and preventing us from thinking for ourselves.

We are being sold goods of Artificial Intelligence, Trans-humanism, and digital immortality that we will never have access to. The advance technologies being developed will only benefit the wealthy elite.

Immortality is a very tasty concept. Let's not fall for the "Fool's Gold." For this dream of humanity to come to a pragmatic fruition, billions will die so a world will exist where androids will be programmed to obediently serve the wealthy one percent.

Why should they dismantle the war machines when the disgruntled masses can be replaced by robots, cyborgs, and androids? There is no place for democracy for those who can have their cake and eat it too.

Are we little more than dust in the wind?

Ray Kurzweil ideas of the next humans, advanced bio-technology and research for eternal life and digital consciousness with the goal of augmenting humans to a new stage of evolution as the trans-human. Transhumanism is use of technology to enhance their physical, psychological and intellectual capabilities.

Genetic engineers are changing what it is to be human. They are genetically engineering an entire generation of humans. Genetic engineers are capable of snipping out and replace parts of the DNA in a fertilized egg by a process called CRISPR or Clustered regularly interspaced short palindromic repeats.

A simpler system CRISPR/Cas9 allows permanent modification of genes within organisms. Along with gene-therapy, biologists reveals research on specialized drugs designed to convert non-neuronal cells in the brain call glial cells in the brain into neurons.

Ninety percent of the cells in our brain are glial cells that are support mechanism for neurons. Biologist can take chemicals to alter the function of glial cells and create fresh neurons. Creating new neurons will heal degenerative brain trauma, Parkinson, and Alzheimer diseases. Increasing the brains neuron capacity from 10 percent to 35 percent can make us super human. If we can reproduce the brain cells, we can reproduce all other cells.

The building blocks of life are forged from the dust of exploding stars. The resulting dust nebula is the miracle factories of life producing objects. Forged from nature's element storehouses, human consciousness is a magical force spawning from miraculous creative quantum processes. Spiritual awareness, embodied in all plants and animals, gives the universe the means to contemplate itself.

We are simply miracles of consciousness interfaced in a universal conversation that spans every galaxy. The inner voice in all of us is connected and none of us are as independent as we believe.

Technology and religions shrouded in the unknown are a surrogate alternative to deep reverence for the natural creative processes of order of changing fluctuations of life and death. Mankind's social mores continues to be filtered through religion and advancing technological uncertainties and remains the long way home to peaceful relations between brothers and sisters of the world.

When will we develop loving relationships of care and concern for each other that are void of finite religious and high tech influence? When will we develop a purposeful environment built upon foundations of love and not myths of gods and live in harmony with each other?

I think it is the time that we stopped wandering cluelessly down life's mean streets of prejudice, ignorance, racism, bigotry, and fear. Spiritually inculcated in dogmatic myths and finite algorithm of human thought, we live our lives as if we are outsiders in a quantum cosmos.

This is the challenge facing the world. We must evolve intellectually to emerge with a shimmering spirituality cleansed of all the dogmatic and high tech mysticism and replace finite speculation in this dualistic realm of us and the universe with an organic loving antidote to cancerous greed of a few who perpetuates diseases, inequality, death, and destruction in the world.

It is the time we collectively celebrate a faith of "one love" that will secure hopes and dreams and serve humanity instead of that which harms and divide the people of earth further. I think it will serve us better to focus less on the creator of the universe and usher in the period of human existence where love for each other and our planet replace a philosophy of deity worship whether in the real or virtual world.

Meaning comes only from within. A person who is able to give meaning to life from energy filtered from sources within is living. This person is actualized, and is an actual person.

We spend so much energy on the thinking of God, creation, and what role religion is to serve in our relationships. We did not create ourselves and we did not create the universe around us.

If you did not create those things then why sit around worried about what existed before God existed and what existed before the "Big Bang." What happened before time is meaningless from an existential point of view because we can never know the truth because we were not there. We did not create any of this so there is no need to work it out. All the money spent trying to solve the riddle of existence is wasted resources and is better spent on the welfare of the life we can see among us. If we solved the riddle, would it change our existence? No, it would not!

We did not create life on this planet. Life on this planet is over 15 million years old. We were not there when animal or human life began, nor were we here at the point of the origin of intelligent life. So, a lot of worrying trying to figure what this is all about is useless, meaningless information from a psychological and existential point of view. The religious aspect of it all is a useful tool of control for the Archontic masters.

The only origin that we are privy to is the fact that individually each of us was born. By being born we grew a thing called consciousness. We are able to think about ourselves. We are able to think about thought and we have this incredible facility called a brain. This human presence is the only origin we are in charge of. We use this interior speculative rational ability to survive.

This is where the main focus of our bio-energetic response to nature's and human challenges. We live in a debt driven consumer oriented world of material things. There are many things of interests like money and drugs used to medicate our traumatized spirit. These things can be of interest to a mind that lacks passion of an organic spirituality. These things are not essential psychologically or existentially.

What matters to your existence is your fragile consciousness that came with your miraculous existence. What also matters more importantly is what you do with that consciousness and how you orient it. What we are encouraged to do is shut off organic intelligence and not speak up about corrupt moral inhumanities for a paycheck. For money, we conform and let spiritually flawed individuals feed us programs that turn off our inner senses.

If we actualize our inner senses, it will guide us to our true organic self, which directs us away from the path of the self-mutilated collective. We fear that which makes us different from the pack.

We know a lot about what makes us the same as everyone else but we have very little understanding of what makes us unique.

Thinking itself is meaningless, it is what you are thinking about and how you thinking is focused. This is where the real answers of life will come from. Meaning comes from within.

Let's pay homage to the truth for once in human existence. When we recalibrate our senses and focus on true acts of love for each other, end the strife of greed and wars and end the divisive partitions of religion and politics, then and only then will we vanquish life's demons and move forward beyond superstitions, ignorance and prejudice, to finally know peace, create global prosperity, and save our planet from being destroyed by the ignorance we continue to embrace.

Our collective human presence in this transformative existence is governed by physics and principles that are beyond the grasp of the conscious tools we have at our disposal, so we desperately try to understand things through faith-based religious systems and high tech solutions to fail spiritual awareness. We should strive not to cower in shadows of fear and superstition, or remain intellectually bound behind barred cages of myths in the real or digital realm. We must educate and enlighten ourselves!

At the other end of the spectrum, human secularism propped up on foundations of capitalism buoyed by uncontrollable high tech innovative greed continues to fail us. Where are the answers to our dilemma? The laws of the universe and its language of physics are there to be discovered by those of us who love wisdom. Beyond the holy books, there is an infinite vortex of vibrating universal consciousness begging us to look at each other beyond the facade of social status and technical ingenuity.

I hold out hope that deep inside we are all loving beings who once united and relieved of the ball and chain of political, technical and dogmatic division, we are capable of true greatness in the real world.

We are the by-product, departing and arriving in a celestial stream of energy, inextricably embedded in the quantum mechanical maze of existence. We are made from stardust, eternal dust in the cosmic winds. If we listen carefully in the cosmic wind, the inner voice is not our own, but the voice of the immensity of the universe, humming and vibrating the order of life and creating harmony.

Listen to the cosmic hum of universal consciousness whispering not from outside, but from an inner singularity echoing within the chambers of your heart and through the corridors of the brain that speaks to a sense of peace and order. Nature's energy is constantly swirling, poetically carving away at the senses, sculpting our neural sensors with cosmic energy manifested in gentle breezes that caress, rains that revive new beginnings, sunshine that recharges, moonlight that calms and sedates, electric shows of lightning humbling us, and the ebb and flow of the ocean replenishing us with cooling moisture.

The human spirit unfolds in oneness like a flower in the shower of cosmic energy. It is analogous to a rock being dissolved by the swift currents of rushing water. The same cosmic energy that's propelling the galaxies through dark matter on the wings of dark energy, also shapes human consciousness into one eternal cosmic order, while whittling away the physical temple itself. Over time, cosmic energy molds, shapes and eventually fades a dual sense of consciousness much like water molds, shapes and fades a rock to fine silt.

Think of how water erodes the earth's crust; constantly carving canyons. The cosmos inculcate human consciousness into its eternal presence. Encapsulated in biological membranes, we are unaware of the field of energy swirling around our corporeal flesh until we merge with the cosmic forces at death much like water swirling around a rock, eroding and breaking down the molecular structure of solid matter. This is the sense of eternal being that escapes Mr. Kurzweil.

The cosmos is always speaking to us through the elements earth, the wind, and fire. If we silence the conscious noise of fear and desperation that gives birth to human societies saturated in the conscious noises of political rhetoric and high tech innovations that leads to war and destruction, if we can silence the noise of dogmatic belief, if we can silence the noises of hatred, racial division and religious differences, if we can unite and relieve the pressure of competition meeting the capitalist metrics of inequities that divide, then maybe we can align with the peaceful hum of the cosmos.

Silence your mind, listen deeply to the echo of the beat of your heart, reverberating throughout its chambers. It is the cadence of love; a finely tuned song of order, synchronicity, creating a rhythm of love, a rhythm of life. Can you hear it? Can you feel it?

Are the events and phenomenon that define the lives of human any more significant than the span of life for a leaf? Life throughout the universe seems to be seasonal bound in a destiny of an end point of being.

Our reality is acted out on a universal stage of matter transitioning from gases that are condensed by gravity to matter in an endless cycle we term life and death. There are so many miracles that makes consciousness possible. It is amazing how through all these miracles human are able to contemplate its creator the universe.

Stars are very important because ingredient for life come from their nuclear reactors that creates all the elements that makes life possible.

How can life be the product of such volatility of enormous luminous energy of the stars that comes from nuclear fusion processes in their centers? Depending upon the age and mass of a star, the energy may come from proton-proton fusion, helium fusion, or the carbon cycle. For brief periods near the end of the luminous lifetime of stars, heavier elements up to iron may fuse, but since the iron group is at the peak of the binding energy curve, the fusion of elements more massive than iron would soak up energy rather than deliver it.

While the iron group is the upper limit in terms of energy yield by fusion, heavier elements are created in the stars by another class of nuclear reactions. This nuclear synthesis of elements heavier than iron uses energy rather than supplies it.

Before there was ever a human being contemplating the workings of the universe or a creator we refer to as God, these complicated phenomenon preceded the creation of oxygen, water, all the elements of life. It is fascinating how all the astronomical parts must come together to produce the possibility of life on earth.

The Moon's role in stabilizing the Earth's rotation axis may have been crucial to the development of life. If Earth's orbit had been just a bit further inside or outside of where it is, life may likely never have arisen and the planet would be a cold desert like Mars or a cloudy furnace like Venus.

Also our planet has a magnetic field that protects us from any storms of charged particles from the sun. Violent bursts of radiation could have scoured life from Earth in its early, fragile stages. So many miracles have conspired to make humanity possible. Yet and still, the universe is a violent place of black holes, menacing comets, asteroids, cosmic radiation, Gamma Ray Bursts, and Magnetars.

In the larger universal scheme of things at the magnitude of the length of the lifespan of life giving stars, how significant are we as human beings? In the seasons of life, I dare say we are no more significant than the many beautiful colored leaves that came to life in the spring and flutter in their death dance in the autumn wind.

We are funny creatures, humans are, with our wars, insecurities, petty jealousies, regards short of charity worshipping the many concepts of Gods, with our nations in need of love and prosperity, because of this petty emotion of greed people in possession of the miracle of being are forced to live a life of broken dreams and tragedy. Why? There are no sane reasons.

In this universe of miracles, life is presented as a gift in one of the most volatile and hostile environment, yet we are more hostile to each other in this world to each other in light of all the natural dangers surrounding us in the cosmos. The human mind is the biggest threat to this fragile refuge we are witnessing as life. It is just amazing that inequities continue to exist and people respond with apathy.

Maybe it is because we are like those leaves whose time has come to being just so much debris in the wind. Maybe there is nothing to be done but just fulfill our destiny of just being dust in the wind. There is no special hurry to fashion and develop the greatest miracle of this whole experience and that is a thing called love. Is it just a myth or are we as human being capable of making this myth real?

Listen to your heart beating. What does it really beat for? Are you guilty of materialism over love? Really think before you answer. I am. Maybe we should release that material stance and like the leaf break off the tree of materialism and see where the spiritual winds blows. It is up to each of us to be seeds of a new spring of a different brand of trees fertilized by love and not greed.

Wall Street Banks, Bilderberg, DARPA and Silicon Valley's Singularity University

Google, Facebook, Tesla, and many of the high tech entities in Silicon Valley are considered strands in the web of the Deep State and United States Military Industrial Complex subsidized by the Central Intelligence Agency and the National Security Agency. Wall Street bankers are heavily invested in the technical advancements in Silicon Valley.

It is very disturbing to have innovative high tech firms developing technology of mapping the brain creating digital consciousness and uploading individual's consciousness into "the Cloud."

It is well known that members of the banking cabal advocate Eugenics, which advocates depopulation of the planet. The wealthiest families and dignitaries of maybe 500,000,000 is thought to be the right amount of people populating the planet.

The creation of the State of Israel in 1948 is often seen as Zionist Jews' greatest achievement. The Rothschild family played a great part in the creation of the State of Israel. The Rothschild family has also deeply influenced the history of the world as financier of many of the major conflicts in the world from the Napoleonic Wars of Britain and France, the Civil War of the United States, both World war I and II, and the destruction of sovereign nation in the Middle East such as Palestine, Iraq, Libya, Sudan, Yemen, Afghanistan, and the present conflict in Syria and insurrections ongoing in Iran and North Korea.

The greatest tragedy perpetrated by Zionist Bankers is the establishment of non-governmental central bank including the Federal Reserve Bank of the United States and the Bank of England. Democracy has been hi-jacked through monetary policies emanated from the will of an international cabal of Jewish bankers.

The cultivation of love is incomplete. The conflict in the Middle East is fundamentally about the abandonment of Torah Judaism by the Zionists and their subsequent rejection of the divinely imposed, exilic agenda of peace, humility and piety. Good will built up by pious Jews over the centuries has been very much endangered by Zionist actions and propaganda.

The Zionists seek to demonize all Palestinians, all Arabs and all Muslims. One of the greatest tragedies that Zionism has brought about is the identification of Zionism with Judaism and Zionists with Jewry in the popular mind, both Jewish and non – Jewish.

Of course, the mainstream media operating under heavy Zionist control and mainstream politicians, with their careers always threatened by the likes of AIPAC and the ADL, are reluctant to ever question Zionist propaganda. Hundreds of thousands of Jews around the world, in New

York and Montreal, in Jerusalem and London, in Antwerp, in Safed and Tiberias are Orthodox Jews who completely reject Zionism

These same Zionist bankers are bank-rolling the destruction of the people and the planet for greed through investment in technical enterprises throughout Silicon Valley. Maybe Artificial Intelligence and the creation of Androids is part of the Eugenic solution.

"Bechtel (pronounced BECK-tul, a San Francisco - based organization - Branton) is a supersecret international corporate octopus, founded in 1898. Some say the firm is really a 'Shadow Government'—a working arm of the CIA. It is the largest Construction and Engineering outfit in the U.S.A. and the World [and some say, beyond].

"The most important posts in the U.S.A. Government are held by former Bechtel Officers. They are part of 'The Web' [an inter-connected control system] which links the Tri-Lateralist plans, the C.F.R., the Order of 'Illuminism' [Cult of the All-seeing Eye] and other interlocking groups..."

"MIND MANIPULATING EXPERIMENTS... The Dulce Base has studied mind control implants; Bio-Psi Units; ELF Devices capable of Mood, Sleep and Heartbeat control, etc.

"D.A.R.P.A. [Defense Advanced Research Projects Agency] is using these technologies to manipulate people. They established 'The Projects,' set priorities, coordinate efforts and guide the many participants in these undertakings. Related Projects are studied at Sandia Base by 'The Jason Group' [of 55 Scientists]. They have secretly harnessed the Dark Side of Technology and hidden the beneficial technology from the public.

"Other Projects take place at 'Area 51' in Nevada... 'Dream-land' [Data Repository Establishment and Maintenance Land]; Elmint [Electromagnetic Intelligence]; Cold Empire; Code EVA; Program HIS [Hybrid Intelligence System]: BW/CW; IRIS [Infrared Intruder Systems]; BI-PASS; REP-TILES, etc.

"The studies on Level Four at Dulce include Human Aura research, as well as all aspects of Dream, Hypnosis, Telepathy, etc. [research]. They know how to manipulate the Bioplasmic Body. They can lower your heartbeat with Deep Sleeve 'Delta Waves,' induce a static shock, then reprogram, Via a Brain-Computer link. They can introduce data and programmed reactions into your Mind [Information impregnation—the 'Dream Library'].

"We are entering an era of Technologicalization of Psychic Powers... The development of techniques to enhance man/machine communications; Nano-tech; Bio-tech micro-machines; PSI-War; E.D.O.M. [Electronic Dissolution of Memory]; R.H.I.C. [Radio-Hypnotic Intra-Cerebral Control]; and various forms of behavior control [via chemical agents, ultrasonics, optical and other EM radiations]. The Physics of 'Consciousness.'...

Evil the great spiritual partitions of non-satanic and satanic worship out of sync in the natural order of the universe.

What role does rich and powerful people influenced by satanic worship play in designs of incarcerating souls in a virtual reality of digital consciousness?

Intelligence is an ability to extract compassion from fear-based silence. Our collective voices of compassion have been silent too long in light of unfolding violence associated with advance technology. Our world of technological wonder can be a double-edged sword, surprising us with dreaded pathology intended and unintended.

Although advance technology seek to better society by increasing productivity, comfort, and security it is easy for the elite to overstep morality and ethics, indulge in temptation, succumb to the dark side of power's temptations by increased incidents of murderous wars, mass surveillance, industrial enslavement, and loss of liberties.

We must pumps the brakes and ascend to higher vibrating wisdom of non-violent consciousness that actualize priorities of love that diminish obsessions of constructing societies revolving around concepts dependent on inorganic artificial intelligence that lacks love and compassion.

There is so much we have left unexplored in our ability to love as we build deadly weapons of destruction and machines that mimic the dark side of humanity's lower animal consciousness.

Loving each other is a lot cheaper than spending hundreds of billions of dollars on war weapons of destruction or building machines that one day will see us as much of a problem to them as we are to ourselves.

Is technology America's surrogate religion and a bailout for missing elements of spiritual fiber in its greed based governing politics littered with endless high tech innovated wars?

Racism, CERN, drones, artificial intelligence, digitized consciousness downloaded from the Cloud, attitudes of "I am God" redesigning human nature, cloning, deceptive propaganda propagated by mass media, dumbing down the masses with high tech sciences, high tech surveillance, violations of privacy, Nano technology, gene therapy, it is indeed a bold new world that should be very wary of.

We live in a world rife with inequities. We have to ask ourselves can these high tech machination alleviate the imbalance of resources and reduce the divide of privilege between the rich and the poor.

It is a tremendous source of concern and very unlikely that the very men who are financing high tech advancement in cloud technology, including artificial intelligence, digital immortality, robotics both cyborg and android, are the very same men, directing governments to kill people and destroy nations in needless wars, hesitant to raise wages, hesitant to provide affordable/free healthcare and education, it is questionable that these same men will also provide the benefits of advanced technology to the very same people being murdered needlessly today.

We are briefed on the marvels of possibilities of mapping minds or digitizing consciousness and uploading consciousness into the cloud to live forever in a digital world.

The one aspect of humanity that has been debated from time immemorial to this very day is the concept of God as men balances temptations of good and evil. In a digitized world, who will regulate the evil tendencies of the mind? Can the evil aspect of humanity be alleviated altering DNA via gene therapy? In a digital universe what will replace the reverence for God? Who can delete your digital presence if you do not follow digital laws in a digital universe?

A digital universe is Pandora's Box of heaven and hell where all good and evil can be a deep exponentiated abyss of endless horrors as well as joys. Conspiracy theories of New World Order with members who are proponents of Eugenics beliefs that depopulation and it is not efficient to continue with humans.

With all the great technological advances, the future is made to look bright, but is it really? For the last 50 years, world population multiplied more rapidly than ever before, and more rapidly than it is projected to grow in the future. In 1950, the world had 2.5 billion people; and in 2005, the world had 6.5 billion people. By 2050, this number could rise to more than 9 billion.

The world we have sculpted from compassionless ignorance is one that breeds insanity exponentially. What species can see all the suffering of its own and sweep the insanity under a financial rug. Money buys us the illusion that we are compassionate. Money is a wall those who have it hides what is truly behind it.

We have many fear based concerns that money will not be the antidote to. Money will not make the Greys stop buzzing our planet looking for biological specimens in their search for immortality.

Money will insure that the theoretical physicists will continue to delve into the dark realm of anti-matter to harvest the greatest evils not seen in this world for a very long time.

Elite members of society will not disclose their interactions with extraterrestrial drunk on the exchange of their fellow human souls for advance technology. The Grey extraterrestrials are real but the greatest threat to humanity is not the little Grey androids in their anti-gravity devices.

Our greatest threat is the elite establishment and their fascination with the dark world they are exploring with CERN. Humanity's lack of faith in God is Lucifer's greatest hope in his war against the Lord.

Do not trust men who are willing to let people suffer while they explore the realm of darkness with CERN and D-Wave Quantum computers. What good if the elite gain the world and lose their soul. This is the book of questions we should not dismiss so easily as conspiracy theory. Evil is not a conspiracy theory. Look around at all the suffering. Evil abounds......here in this book manifests it presence among us.

Path 28: Conversation with Nigel Kerner Existing with Greys in an Imperfect Universe and the End Game of Artificial Intelligence

Are Greys sophisticated biological robots created by an extraterrestrial civilization? The only thing we have to discern this matter is anecdotal evidence. Beyond the tooth fairy, Santa Clause and traditional concepts of God, from reports of abductees, people taken by these being (Greys), there are so many Draconian experiences reported by those claiming to have been abducted. It is hard to believe all of them are lying. Blank faced beings carrying on painful procedures on their human subjects centered on the human reproductive system as if we are like rats to them.

The Greys come across as programmed mechanisms that have no emotional base as some robotic entity. There are no reports of them having a sense of compassion or sympathy. They seem to be machine or mechanism that could function but without the things we take for granted as natural living beings.

Qualities of compassion, feeling, smile, or humor having never been reported at all. They seemed to be designed for moving through space time. For them to arrive at this planet, they would have to travel past the speed of light using pretty impressive technology with gravity generators and gravity amplifiers to travel vast distances through wormholes.

When they arrive at the planet the problem of deceleration. When people travel in jet fighters, the G-forces have pretty nasty effects on the body. How pilots describe the movements of UFO at right angles at high speeds, a human would be a stain on a window.

Russian reports indicated ET's are Grey mercury mush with gold wires. This is an idea mechanism for space travel where you wouldn't have to worry about being biological tissue and becoming a stain on the inside walls and windows of your ship. The ET's are perfectly design to take on g-forces traveling at the speed of light. They appear to be bio-robotic type entities.

The question is, why would these things come to Earth? The behavior of the Greys suggests lack of conscience following preset instructions having been programmed into them in a dead Meg program to preserve and look out for the interest for themselves and those who might have created them.

The Greys are similar to probes we sent out to planets that we ourselves cannot visit but sent to gather information remotely. Two different scenarios present themselves (1) They come from civilizations at other locations in the universe similar to ours but with a much more hugely advanced technology that created them. (2) They might have been sent out in an ancient past like go-fors, go for this and go-for that to explore and understand the very nature of the existence of our physical universe.

Both scenarios are likely true. To understand what is being discussed, everything you understand about science, quantum mechanics, and mathematics and all the rest will have to take a real knock before stepping outside the known box of reality to understand theories of the Greys.

The prevailing thoughts about the Greys is that they are final lens or telescope that views into the various state of the physical universe. Why has the lens of the Greys been created? To explain the origin of the Greys, we must explain our own origin.

Existence in an imperfect physical universe is not the result of a creator type mechanism placing us in a state of imperfection and watching with fun for his own benefit. Are we the product of two free choices? Our Universe is based on two final polarities.

One that provides for all things come together in perfect harmony in one absolute singularity of perfection. The other, everything goes into past and chaotic amelioration and broken up into situations where all things do not exist in terms of force and identity that is discreet that is all hardness.

Between these two fundamental polarities, incidentally if you like because of the potential difference between the two of them, we get a huge point of force center, this point of differential potential is so huge that either can't exist there in themselves and universes that are created in a big bang. These universes are an amalgamation of those two absolute polarities.

One that is a momentum to union and the other a momentum to separation (Big Bang and Big Crunch). At the center of the God-Verse is the God-Head and opposite of that a Satan-Head as the center of the opposite principle.

The two together come together in us as beings in the physical universe. We are in a Multi-Verse and we get levels and permutations of all kinds of formations of the two central axioms or the yen and yang, the main existential polarities between the two.

Are the Greys the mediators of this experience? The Greys may be perfectly normal all over the universe. They are the actual product of creating something any intelligence should never create, and that is a secondary type of form of being. When you make an artificial being with artificial intelligence, you run up against a paradox that is devastating.

Lots of places in our universe that may be highly developed go into this business of actually creating these robots. The Greys are the function of a program that meets a paradox that is extremely interesting. You can't tell a machine psychology anything about a God-Verse. There is no such thing to a robot as feeling.

The robot is instructed to self-maintain itself, then it will start seeing you as the thing that can pull the plug out or turn off the power and decide to come after you. This is a big problem. This is quite possibly the dilemma of the Grey ET's. They were created by a superior natural effect in the universe.

If you get the program wrong in the AI, you can't tell an artificial modus-operandi we are an exception. How do you define that exception? This is extremely difficult to tell them what feeling is. In the end, this entity you've created may well take you out.

Greys have progressed to being predatory things running wild all over the universe. They have come here and we are in big trouble. Whoever is keeping this information from the public is committing a great sin against humanity. They need to tell the world and there are ways to circumvent whatever consequences there might be.

The Greys probably do not know what they are. As a machine they do not have a sense of self. We are extremely the opposite of the Greys with the ability to value this incredible facility we call natural life. It is imperative that we re-evolve back into this wondrous state of all togetherness called the God-Burst. A totally forceless and timeless paradigm of the idea of eternal bliss.

In our technological advancement mankind is beginning to touch upon transhumanism with artificial intelligence technology. We are recreating the human nervous system, we are recreating the neural network of the brain in simulations in machines, the blue-brain project, etc.

We see in movies the machines turning against humanity (The Terminator and the Matrix). Earth is following the same path of disaster that other civilizations may have taken in creating the Greys, who in the end may have destroyed its creator.

We have got to think extremely hard about artificial intelligence and the programming of artificial entities that we create for our convenience and possibly good things but we have to think about the consequences.

Regarding remote advanced civilizations that may have created the Greys, most of the original beings that come that comes into the universe with the amalgamation of the two polarities are wondrous states of intelligence, light beings of intelligence, full of the God-Burst or at the disadvantage of the laws of thermodynamics, the second law of thermodynamics is the curse of the universe.

That which is created in chaos and randomness can never be stopped in its inertia to break up. So all cosmologists, 93% was accepts the cold death scenario where everything is supposed to end in one huge cold mass of nothingness frozen absolute zero. All even the tiniest of particles will be unraveled.

It is absolutely necessary to believe in the power of thought and that way or think in ways of union which marries within the God-Verse which then propels you into the God-Verse. Reincarnation is that part of the thinking process that gives us access to eternity.

Reincarnation gives us tenure to an existence into the future. The Greys are after this rebirth of existence. They can see us being reborn or maybe their technology can actually follow us into what might be the dominions of death and then back again into life.

Nigel Kerner's theorize that death is within the space of atoms and that the God-Verse is that center point of force that lies between all aggregations of atoms right in the center and that what God-Verse actually is the emanation of a force pulling us in gravity may well be the voice of the God-Verse pulling things together again and that's why they can't find it as a force.

All these scientists are looking for a force, it may be gravity is not a force. Maybe it is this tug of the God-Verse within everything that's created in our Universe.

The artificially created Greys end up outside of certain parameters of rules that the rest of the universe is restricted to and laws we abide by sequentially and the Greys exist in between the laws we abide by. Natural life-forms are the primary and the glorious and the ones that belongs in terms of return choice, knowing, understanding, self-motivation, control, option, and seeking values that might go yin or yang, while artificial programs have only one program where they go and they go according to the program.

It is amazing how fascinated humanity is with the machine. Each living being, all the animals and insects goes back to the beginning of the God-head of nature of was before the Big-Bang. We all have that unmitigated uninterrupted line in our DNA. We are superior to the very machines of technology.

We are living beings that will always have this beautiful track all the way back to ad infinitum. We have a magical DNA track of information that goes back for each and every one of us. The machines we are creating with plastic faces and plastic emotions is always going to be plastic emotions because you cannot program into a mechanism what it is to feel and know self.

Machines have a pseudo self and a pseudo emotion that never can track back and have a original reference and that original reference that encapsulate an entirety of understanding in the whole. Such a mechanism are Godless outside the norms of nature. The Greys have so much intelligence in the sense that they have the possibility of developing a pseudo kind of ego.

They have enough intelligence to realize they lack a soul. They just add one logical fact to another in a mathematical sense of yes or no. Literally they are spewing binary data. Their intelligence is not this overwhelming kind of active combination of all things arriving at a against a reference which they can place that see that what we have that give living intelligence always a much greater stance over anything that is created as an artificial intelligence.

We can refer that back to a central thesis and then compare that if we go back to a thing call a God-Verse point they're all knowledge is there and the reference with which we learn anything is placed against the whole companion of knowledge.

This is an incredible advantage for humans and gives us a sense of self-identity and sense of reference. When a machine is made and the machine's artificial intelligence is adding all these things and making larger numbers as possible and quicker. It is acknowledged that computers have gone as far as they can and basic procedures can't progress any further. You can make quantum eyes and thinking huge multiples but the computer aren't anything but dumb.

If something comes in from the beginning of the universe, it bring in that whole amount of knowledge of the center of the absolute where all things are in perfect union and harmony giving you the information to make incredible assessment of all things as a comparative as a point against another point. This cannot be beaten by a computer. You have to be created by the very existential design itself, which is what each of us is. This much be realized so we do not take each other for granted.

What the Greys Envy Most about the Organic Lives of Humans

Life is but a bubble riding electrical pulses of dreams. A bubble glistening in the sun for a brief moment destined for the realm of evermore. Bubbles of consciousness come and go born of creative sexual energy. Lives come and go in endless arrays of fear and courage. Where were we before our birthday before we were created from energy of sexual passion? Before there ever was a birthday, each of us were just mere impulses of sexual attraction in the minds of our parents.

Each of us irascible forces of sexual passion knocking on doors in our parents minds for entrance into this physical realm. We were only electrical impulses ignited in the fusion of sperm and egg. We are a force of life is fueled from boundless natural resources in the vast universe.

Sex is a microcosm of the "Big Bang." This is why the sexual ritual is the most powerful and most guarded activity of our civilization. Sex is the portal of spiritual entry where the properties of the spiritual and physical worlds intersect.

Nature seems to be endless experiments of forging life from inanimate potentiality. That creative process concerns itself not with anthropomorphic concepts of love, fear, compassion, or God. Its focus seems to be creation.

Our creative concept of God is probably fool's gold from nature's perspective. Nature's creative processes ask not affirmation from us and nature certainly will not be regulated by concepts of humanity.

Nature only affords us just a brief view, in the twinkling of an eye, to speculate on what our existence means to us. We will never transcend our reality enough to know the machinations and powers of nature nonetheless God.

From the electricity of sexual impulses, the flowering of dividing cells, we rise out of nature's spectrum of non-being, cultivate thoughts that become romantic life epics from realms of our dreams, and then we fade back into nature's spectrum of non-being. Just like a bubble, we are here for a brief moment and then gone in instance.

Whatever you want to love, love it now. Whatever you want to do, do it now. This is the realm where creative processes intersect in nature where we are miraculous bubbles of awareness for a brief moment. Love every second of your miracle regardless of your circumstances. Love is the fruits of clarity of thought. Find love, find love, find love, and find love right now.

Path 29: Is an Alien Extraterrestrial Intelligence Agenda Driving US Domestic and International Policies

Snowden Documents Proving "US-Alien-Hitler"
Link Stuns Russia

The greatest threat of evil to humanity manifest as ignorance! We have progressed in this world always looking externally out into the cosmos for spiritual ascendance thinking dualistically that God is out there observing and judging our acts of free will.

We mistakenly proceed, as a species disciplined in fear, oblivious that we are swiftly evolving into our own worst nightmare; we are the good and the evil; the God and the Devil; and we are an integral component of that God we revere. The Godhead who is not separate from us but the higher consciousness that is composed of all the cosmic dust in all of us. We are also complicit in the creation of the evil we fear.

When we reduce our human experience to a collective existence in this universe in a specific place at a specific time, speaking from a quantum mechanical perspective, we exist in this cosmos in a haze of possibilities. Regarding our collective nature of good or evil interactions with each other, these interactions will be from a point of good or from a point of evil.

I have always been fascinated by why some are motivated to care for others while others are motivated to destroy. What is the truth about Extra-terrestrials and what is the truth about Secret Illuminati Societies? Is all the sighting made up lies and just conspiracy theory? If they are real, what will be the consequences for the masses regarding reactionary Secret Societies cryptic agendas?

A stunning Federal Security Services (FSB) report on the nearly two million highly classified top-secret documents obtained from the United States Department of Defense **(DOD) run National Security Agency-Central Security Service (NSA/CSS) by the American ex-patriot Edward Snowden states that this information is providing "incontrovertible proof"** that an **"alien/extraterrestrial intelligence agenda"** is driving US domestic and international policy, and has been doing so since at least 1945.

Edward Snowden is a computer specialist, a former Central Intelligence Agency (CIA) employee, and former NSA/CSS contractor who disclosed these classified documents to several media outlets in late 2012 and was granted temporary asylum in Russia in 2013 after his designation by the Obama regime as the "most wanted man on earth."

This FSB report further states that Snowden, in December, 2012, contacted the highly respected American columnist, blogger, and author Glenn Greenwald by an email headed with the subject line stating, "I and others have things you would be interested in.?.?.?."

In Snowden's own words, this report continues, he outlined to Greenwald the reason for his highly secretive group obtaining and releasing these documents by warning that that there "were actually two governments in the US: the one that was elected, and the other, secret regime, governing in the dark."

As to who is running this "secret regime" Snowden and his cohorts were warning about, FSB experts in this report say, was confirmed by former Canadian defense minister Paul Hellyer who was given access to all of Snowden's documents by Russian intelligence services and stated they were, indeed, "accurate."

Even though Defense Minister Hellyer's exact statements to the FSB in regards to Snowden's documents remain classified, shortly after his "extensive electronic interview" by the FSB Paul Hellyer appeared on Russia Today's program SophieCo where he shockingly admitted that aliens have "been visiting our planet for thousands of years" and described several types of these extraterrestrials, including "Tall Whites" who are working with the US Air Force in Nevada.

Of the many explosive revelations in this FSB report, the one most concerning to Russian authorities are the Snowden's documents "confirming" that the "Tall Whites" (further revealed by Defense Minister Hellyer as noted above) are the same extraterrestrial alien race behind the stunning rise of Nazi Germany during the 1930's.

In just one example of the many outlined in this FSB report, it shows that with this "alien assistance," at the end of the 1930's, when Nazi Germany possessed just 57 submarines, over the four years of World

War II it built 1,163 modern technologically advanced submarines at its dockyards and even put them into operation.

Snowden's documents further confirm, this report says, the "Tall Whites" (Nordic) meetings in 1954 with US President Dwight D. Eisenhower where the "secret regime" currently ruling over America was established.

The "Tall White" agenda being implemented by a "secret regime" of the world's most powerful royal families and elite financier who claims to be direct descendants to the Anunnaki of ancient Samaria. It is believed that this small elite group have secretly, without the informed consent of the unknowing masses around the world, have aligned with alien-extraterrestrial power trafficking humans for technology.

This privileged and wealthy elite class ruling over the militaries of United States and Europe (fearing global chaos if there is full disclosure about the presence of extraterrestrials under the water, underground and in caves under the ice in Antarctica) have resorted to global electronic surveillance systems meant to control information regarding the multitude of extraterrestrial presence on earth. The Elite planners are entering into what one of Snowden's documents calls the "final phase" of their end plan for total assimilation and world rule.

To do this, it is necessary to deploy systems of mass surveillance, control the means of survival implanting RFID chips in humans, and taking away the rights to own firearms.

There are those still in the US government backing Snowden, whose presence is "unmistakable" in the cataclysmic power struggle currently underway, about Russian collusion to influence the 2016 Presidential election, between an inner circle "secret regime" and "forces unknown."

CHAPTER V

SECRET SOCIETIES PACT WITH ALIEN ENTITIES

Path 30: William Hamilton

William Hamilton himself has gained a great deal of 'intelligence' on the secret government's underground bases, many of which are as of this writing under the control of the 'collaboration', or those military-industrialists who have sold-out to the humanoid-reptiloid collaborators from Draconis, Orion & Sirius-B, who are more-or-less given free reign within the secret government's underground network. In an article which appeared in Patrick O'Connell's "TRENDS AND PREDICTIONS ANALYST" Newsletter, Vol. 6, No. 2 [July, 1990] issue, William Hamilton stated:

> "...The cover-up was initiated soon after the Roswell, N.M. crash. We wanted to know - 1] Who they were, 2] Why they were here, 3] How their technology worked. The cover-up became a matter of NATIONAL SECURITY [a blanket word covering secrecy and deception]. The cover-up involves secret organizations within our government such as MJ-12, PI-40, MAJI, Delta, the Jason Scholars, & known intelligence

> organizations such as Naval Intelligence, Air Force Office of Special Investigation, the Defense Investigative Service, the CIA, NSA, and more!

It involves THINK TANKS such as RAND, the Ford Foundation, the Aspen Institute, & Brookings Institute. It involves corporations such as Bechtel, GE, ITT, Amoco, Northrup, Lockheed, & many others. It involves SECRET SOCIETIES who may be the hidden bosses of the orchestrated events [i.e. economic collapse, wars, assassinations, conspiracies to manipulate & control humans & thereby to exercise enormous power over the destiny of the human race] - the Illuminati, Masons, Knights of Malta, etc.

The individual players are too numerous to list. The whole of this conspiracy forms an INTERLOCKING NEXUS. The goal is said to be a ONE WORLD GOVERNMENT [Dictatorship]!

"'The Underground Nation' - The RAND symposium held on Deep Underground Construction indicated that plans were hatched during the 50's to build underground bases, laboratories, & city-complexes linked by a stupendous network of tunnels to preserve & protect the ongoing secret interests of the secret societies. These secret societies made a pact with alien entities in order to further motives of domination..."

Actually, as it turns out, THEY [the secret societies] are now being 'dominated' by the 'aliens'. One can only assume that if certain humans would 'sell out' their own kind to an alien race and use such an unholy alliance to gain domination over their fellow man, then they should consider the fact that they, according to universal law, must in the same way open THEMSELVES up to manipulation and control by their supposed benefactors.

Thus one can see the utter insanity of hoping to establish domination of others by petitioning the assistance of an Imperialistic alien force. The human 'elite' may think that their reptilian collectivist hosts will shower their egos with praise and rewards for their cooperation in selling out their own planet, but in reality the Draconians consider the human elite as being useless "weeds", as they do all humans in general, but necessary fodder in order to carry out their agenda.

Mr. Hamilton continues: "...The underground complexes are not confined to the U.S. alone! A large underground complex operated by 'the U.S.' exists at Pine Gap, near Alice Springs, Australia.

"...It appears that the secret societies among us have become aware of the coming planetary eco-catastrophe & the possibility of an earth polar shift in the near future. Surveying the earth from space, satellites & shuttles reveal EXTENSIVE DAMAGE TO OUR ECOSPHERE! Our planet is wobbling on its axis & its magnetic field is decaying! Ozone depletion & the greenhouse effect are rapidly endangering life on our planet. Alternatives, which include - 1] direct handling of the atmospheric problems, 2] taking shelter in underground domains, & 3] escape to other planetary bodies in the solar system, have been devised in secret.

However there is a possible Alternative 4 which mostly depends on a completely different idea on how to save the earth..." (this MAY be, in essence, a project to colonize other 'dimensional' frequencies or densities that exist elsewhere within the super spectrum of the ONE Omniversal 'Reality'... although others have suggested that Alternative-4 may involve a HAARP type manipulation of the atmosphere in an effort to get CONTROL of the situation - Branton).

Bill Hamilton then explains some of the mystery surrounding the so-called 'hybrids' who have been encountered by UFO abductees, and why an ACTUAL cross between humanoids and Reptiloids [thank God] might never succeed:

> "...It is unlikely that the reptilian greys are cross-breeding with humans. Reptilians carry their sex organs

> internally and reproduce by eggs hatched by solar heat. Reptoids have well developed eyes, no hair follicles, & no external ear cartilage as consistent with most reptilian species.

Since their means of reproduction is incompatible with our own, it is suggested that humans (women - Branton) may be fertilized by the grays by artificial insemination with human spermatozoa or perhaps they use the human uterus as an incubation chamber."

Note: Other indications are that the reptilians inject or encodify the human embryo with reptilian or other DNA during the early stages of development. It is even believed by some abductees that they have the ability to're-program' the genetic information within an 'egg' before it has been fertilized.

As for the so-called 'hybrids', Hamilton's statements seem to be confirmed by others, including abductees, who have hinted that the 'hybrid' fetuses are actually alien-looking OR human-appearing 'hybrids' who are conceived through human 'seed' taken from human male and female abductees. In other words the fetus would fall to one species line or the other—an alien-appearing being lacking a 'soul', or a human-like child with a soul.

It is said that within the hybrid society, the more human-looking hybrids consider themselves superior to the alien-appearing hybrids. Their more-human-like features are a source of pride and status, even though many of the hybrids are nevertheless 'servants' of the Greys.

Some abductees have reported that they have observed experiments involving the attempted mixtures of human and cattle DNA to create a 'hybrid' being. Many of the so-called hybrids however are never-the-less essentially 'human'. For instance the "HU-brids" or humanoid-hybrids would possess crimson blood, five fingers, round pupils, ears, and exterior reproductive organs, although the reproductive organs might be minimized and non-operative.

If they possessed even one of these traits there is a 'chance' that the hybrid might possess a human "soul", although this may not always be the case, as with the "chameleons" and so on. In such a case "aura detectors"—which could detect whether or not the being has a multi-colored chakra system—would be a possible fail-safe means to determine the "imposters" from the "real thing".

The "RE-brids" or reptiloid-hybrids would generally possess greenish 'blood' similar to that which the Greys themselves possess, four fingers, opaque black and/or vertical slit pupils, no visible ears, and no exterior reproductive organs.

Hamilton continues: "...Alien vehicles are being tested at the alien physical technology center at S-4 at the Nevada Test Site. Alien vehicles are being replicated at Kirtland AFB & Sandia Laboratories & these replicas are referred to as ARVs [Alien Reproductive Vehicles] (Subsequent research by William Hamilton and Norio Hayakawa have confirmed that McDonnell-Douglass, Lockheed, and Northrup Corps are now involved with the 'replication' of alien hardware for the Military-Industrial establishment.

If this technology is being used for our own American defenses then this is all well-and-fine, however if the technology is being appropriated by the "New World Order" interests, under the oversight of the Reptiloids/ Greys, then the 'sell-out' of our Military-Industrial Complex to a pro-Draconian and/or anti-American superpower would be considered HIGH TREASON, just as the sell-out of our entire Stealth fleet to the United Nations / New World Order control structure—which HAS taken place—should be considered high treason! - Branton)

"At least three of these vehicles are stored in hangers at Norton AFB, California. It is alleged that vehicle propulsion units were constructed by General Electric & composite materials were provided by Amoco. Alien vehicles generate an artificial gravity field which can be focused & intensified for high speed travel... Alien organisms and biological technology are tested (in the upper levels - Branton) at the underground biogenetic laboratories at Dulce, New Mexico. Alien genetic engineering, cloning, & cryogenic technology have been studied with a view towards 'enhancing' human genetics, deciphering the human genome, & gaining a biological advantage by ARTIFICIAL BIOLOGICAL ENGINEERING. Strange life forms have been bred in these laboratories..."

Path 31: Secret Treaty

The United States Government and Extra-terrestrial Entities

By Richard K. Wilson and Sylvan Burns

Historical Data Regarding Aliens and the Government

According Richard K. Wilson and Sylvan Burns, in "Secret Treaty, the Government and Extra-Terrestrials," research behind this subject is quite demanding, and requires a tremendous amount of time, as well as cooperation between the many researchers that may be involved. The whole idea "UFO-logy" as a science is not very accurate. Its' a disciplinary investigation that is born out of a pattern of human and non-human deception that reaches into the very core of our civilization.

What's really going on around us? Information has come forth that sheds a lot of light on what is actually going on. Discovered information is quite disturbing. Structures of society situate individuals in a very fragile and vulnerable state, and aspects of the universe that don't fit into that societal mold we not often able to discover.

Actual manipulation of societies began in the late 1800's. The creation of elite class structures gave rise to the Illuminati, who made use of the financial structure to control people by controlling their government by directing that government to plan and execute deliberate conflict in order to divide, fragment and limit population to controllable levels.

A few wealthy elites control wealth and technology to insure societal structure that support and maintain a power structure hell-bent on manipulating and maintaining planetary power structure in all matters by not disclosing truths regarding extraterrestrial phenomenons.

Historical Comments

The era of "modern" interaction with non-human terrestrial and non-terrestrial entities also started in the late 1800's. Abduction of animals started in the 1890's. There are many records of abduction of humans, both children and adults, from that time period. Legends and writings of the various tribes of hunting and gathering societies also contain a lot of information about early abduction of humans.

1928 - 1944

In 1928, Thomas Brown discovered a relationship between electrical capacitance and gravitational control. His work was subsequently taken over by the government. In 1930, Dr. Henry Coanda began work on aerial craft that were lenticular in shape.

In 1932, Adolph Hitler was in control of the German society enough to force scientists to work in laboratories on advanced aircraft designs. Aided by the implosion vortex technology of Viktor Schauberger, and the technical expertise of scientists like Schriever, Habermohl, Ballenzo and Miethe, the Germans began flying aerial craft as early as 1938. There is also some evidence that the Germans recovered a crashed alien disk in 1937.

1934—The first 'deal' or interaction with the Grey entities occurred on July 11, 1934 on board a naval ship in Balboa. It was here that the agreement was initially made [between aliens and representatives of the 'Bavarian' Illuminati operating within U.S. Intelligence 'fraternities'] that let the greys proceed unhindered with the abductions and cattle mutilations.

As a result of all this technology, the German scientific effort was pushed forward by leaps and bounds, and was conducted at several underground research facilities at Reinickendorf, Kummersdorf and Thuringia. The earliest "pilotless aircraft" were produced in 1934, and has some moderate degree of success. The United States was quite aware of the German technical progress and sent an American named Wilson to Germany to "give technical assistance" and generally to keep an eye on German technology.

It was probably by virtue of Wilson that the Germans never used their gravitational craft enmasse in the war, for Wilson attained a high position in the German technical community, and switched propulsion methods from gravitational to advanced jet propulsion in an apparent effort to "get technology out there to fight the war". Because of this, German gravitational research remained in the labs and stayed in the R&D phase until around 1941, when the Schriever / Miethe designs were successfully tested.

It was clearly a situation where the war was going on faster than the Germans could technically develop their designs. Hampered by sabotage and deliberate technical misguidance from Wilson, as well as delays in metallurgical research which didn't result in an acceptable alloy of magnesium and aluminum until 1944, the Germans could only continue to harass allied pilots with the "fireballs", pilotless craft developed and used since 1942 which emitted electrical fields that interfered with the operation of aviation engines.

1945

In 1945, the British discover German plans for advanced craft and joined the efforts of the United States to subvert the German program. On February 16, 1945, despite allied efforts, the Germans successfully flew a crew-carrying version of the "fireball" from the underground facilities in Thuringia. The craft had a top speed of over 1,250 mph. The craft was called the "Kugelblitz".

The Germans in the scientific community knew the war was lost as early as 1942. They decided to establish a plan for continuing the dream of the Third Reich despite the war. They decided that the establishment of a separate society founded on Nazi principles of genetic purity was the answer. The development of gravitational technology aided that plan. On February 23, 1945, the newest engines of the Kugelbitz were tested and then extracted from the craft.

The Kugelbitz was blown up by SS personnel and the scientists, plans and engines were shipped out of Germany to the South Polar regions, where the Germans had maintained underground construction activity since 1941. Two days later, on February 25, 1943 the underground plant at Khala was closed and all the workers sent to Buchenwald and gassed.

The Germans also sent their "Aryan elite" children and other elements of their society to the underground base. General Hans Kammler, who disappeared in April 1945, was instrumental in the evacuation operation, as was General Nebe. There, the Germans developed a eugenic society that apparently is limited to a specific number of people. They're still there. Apparently they also maintain technical colonies in South America.

On May 7, 1945, Germany surrendered. Both the Americans and gained access to elements of German disk technology and scientists which the Germans had neglected to eliminate before the hasty departure at the close of the war. The Canadians also had access to some of the data that the United States had acquired, as well as some data directly from the German efforts.

On July 16, 1945, the United States detonated their first nuclear explosion in New Mexico. By August 15, 1945, the Japanese had "been induced to surrender", despite the fact that the Japanese government had offered to surrender on February 14, 1945 and again in June 1945. Both offers were refused by the United States, who preferred to use the nuclear device on them two months later, as planned. It is most probably that the nuclear detonations also attracted the attention of non-human entities.

1946

In 1946, the United States imported German SS intelligence officers in an effort to form what later become the Central Intelligence Agency. This was part of a plan conducted by Allen Dulles in 1943, when a deal was cut with German intelligence to provide the United States with a viable intelligence operation as well as provide German intelligence with a place to go after the war. Good inducement, indeed.

1947

National Security Act of 1947 made it illegal to ever say how much money is spent on the CIA. Indeed all of our tremendous alphabet soup collection of Intelligence Agencies. Whether you are talking about the CIA, or the NRO, or the NSA or the DIA, etc., all of them are in the same category.

In 1947, the powerful radar in the four corners area in the Midwest cause the crash of several alien disks, the most notable of which were at Roswell and Aztec, New Mexico. The disks recovered had a reptilian species on board, as well as the bodies of United States Air Force pilots.

There was evidence that the bodies had been mutilated. In June 1947, Kenneth Arnold coins the term flying saucer.

The Germans, having had two years to get it together after the war, started making fly-overs over the United States in their disks, which had by then achieved a remarkable degree of development. This prompted the United States to undertake plans to ascertain both the exact location of the German base at the Pole and their technical capabilities. In 1947, Operation High-jump was conducted at the pole in an attempt to locate the Germans. It was a failure.

The Germans used their technology to thwart the efforts of the United States. It wasn't until 1958 during the International Geophysical Year that another major attempt to work on the Germans was made. Various polar expeditions that occurred in between 1947 and 1958 had intelligence as part of their design, and also seemed to evoke activity from other forces and entities from inside the Earth. There also seems to be some evidence that the Germans made contact with alien forces from inside the planet during the stint at the pole.

In 1947, the United States decided that the problem with both the Germans and aliens was getting a little dangerous, and it was necessary to implement severe measures in order to hide the truth of alien presence. The German problem was easier to control as far as public knowledge was concerned.

In September 1947, Truman caused the national Security Act to be passed in order to hide the activities of the Government, the CIA and the alien problem. CIA mind control projects began at Bethesda Naval Hospital in 1947, with data gained from German SS intelligence. Truman created a study group in order to control the alien problem. A series of National Security Council (NSC) memos removed the CIA from the sole task of gathering foreign intelligence and slowly legalized direct action in the form of covert activities.

The memos, including NSC- 10/1 and NSC-10/2, established a buffer between the President of the United States and the activities that were going on, as well as providing means for the President to deny knowledge of any covert activities. It was decided that more knowledge was needed about the various types of alien craft.

Project Sign, created on December 30, 1947 and established at Wright Field, was to investigate disk technical capabilities and performance. There was still the problem of evaluation of the disks that had been recovered. It was decided that the Navy Auxiliary Field in the Groom Mountains in Nevada would be the ideal spot to do the testing.

1948

In August 1948, Project Sign prepared a Top Secret estimate of the situation, which was designated as Air Intelligence Report 100-203-79. General Hoyt Vandenburg, after reviewing the report, ordered the report destroyed. Not all copies of the report were destroyed. In December 1948; at least one still survives, Project Sign was re-designated as Project Grudge, with public version to be known as Project Bluebook. The liaison between Project Grudge and MJ-12 was the Air Force officer in charge of Project Bluebook, Captain Edward Ruppelt.

1949

1949 was also the year that construction started on AEC property on Nellis range of the complex designated to perform testing and evaluation of alien technology. It was also another year that German disks started fly-overs in the United States. As a response to this activity and the general alien problem, the CIA Act of 1949 was enacted, giving the agency more capability to act outside the bounds of established law in order to guarantee that the alien problem remained inside the government. At that point, the CIA office of Scientific Intelligence began to review civilian reports of sightings in order to determine the scope of the suppression effort.

It was in 1949 that the Soviet Union detonated their first above ground nuclear test. It is uncertain whether the Soviet effort to produce a nuclear device was aided by the delivery to them of 1 kilogram of uranium in the 1943 by the United States, or the subsequent delivery of nuclear weapons plans to the Soviets in the same year by President Roosevelt under the Lend Lease program. A major who was in charge of the transfer of Lend Lease supplies discovered that at least three assignments of uranium chemicals totaling .75 ton, as well as documents and reports, were transferred to the Soviets.

Julius and Ethel Rosenberg were blamed for the Soviet weapons acquisition during the next year, and were summarily executed in order to cover up the technology exchange. President Roosevelt's son, James, wrote a book entitled "A Family Matter" in which he details Roosevelt "bold decision" to share the nuclear technology with the Soviet Union.

In 1949, alien craft were often seen hovering over sensitive nuclear installations, especially in New Mexico, and probes known as "green fireballs" were frequently seen all over the state; they were presumably monitoring something to do with radiation. The disk crash at Roswell, New Mexico netted a live alien, named EBE (Extra-terrestrial Biological Entity). It was a name coined by study group member Detlev Bronk.

Secretary of Defense James Forrestal became disenchanted with the whole handling of the alien problem. He voice his concern to President Truman, who asked him to resign on March 3, 1949. Within one month, the White House had all 3,000 pages of the diaries of James Forrestal locked up in a white house safe and had sent him to Bethesda Naval Hospital under the care of Dr. Raines.

Forrestal's brother decided to take him out of the hospital, fearing for his brothers' life. On the same day his brother was due to pick him up,

James Forrestal was found hanging outside of a 16th story window of the hospital with a sheet around his neck. The sheet broke, and Forrestal fell to his death. By December 1949, the government decided to close Project Grudge and divert efforts elsewhere.

1950

In 1950, Canadian scientist Wilber Smith reported in a letter that the disks were one of the most highly classified issues in the United States Government, even "higher than the H-bomb", which President Truman ordered into production in January of 1950. In 1950, problems continued with alien disks. There were near misses with commercial airline flights, and continued overflights over sensitive military installations.

By August of 1950, it was decided to let General Walter B. Smith assume Forrestal's vacant position in the study group. It was also the same month that the Government decided to seize all USS railroads in order to prevent a general strike.

In December of 1950, a unit called IPU, Interplanetary Phenomenon Unit, was established operational unit to deal with the ever-increasing scenarios of crashed disks and aliens. That same month a disk crashed in the El Indio-Guerro area of Mexico and was taken to the AEC facility at Sandia in New Mexico.

1951

In 1951, construction of the base at Groom Lake took on a more earnest effort with Project Red-light. Information leaked out that disks were stored at Wright Patterson AFB in Dayton, Ohio. Viking Press published a version of the Forrestal diaries.

Flying wing type aircraft were seen over Albuquerque. The alien named EBE suddenly became ill, and was worked on by a Dr. Mendoza for almost a year until 1952, when the alien died.

General MacArthur, famous for his statement about interplanetary beings was inevitable, he was relieved of his command by President Truman.

In 1951, the CIA was essentially telling the public that it was closing it's books on the "UFO" problem. President Truman created the National Security Agency (NSA) in 1952 to monitor and contain the secret of alien presence, decipher alien communications and eventually establish an ongoing dialogue with any alien species it could make communications with. Presidential Executive Order exempts the NSA from all laws except those laws which specifically mention the NSA.

1952

President Truman kept the allies of the United States, including the Soviet Union, informed of the developing alien problem ever since the recovery of the crashed disk in Roswell, just in case it was discovered that the aliens turned out to be a threat. The problem was that there was ever increasing threat to security about the aliens. To solve that problem, the group known as the Bilderbergers was created in order to take the decision making about the alien problem and other international issues out of the hands of governments. The Bilderbergers are headquartered in

Geneva, Switzerland and evolved into the elite secret body that still controls international situations. Nelson Rockefeller, Gerald Ford, Henry Kissinger and George Bush are involved with the world control groups, and have been for many years.

1953

In 1953, Thomas Brown gave a demonstration of his electrogravitic effect to the Air Force, who promptly took over the project. It was also the year that Eisenhower was elected. It was Eisenhower who appointed Rockefeller to head a group that would propose a reorganization of government. Eisenhower's' favorite comment seemed to be "do whatever it takes". That comment seemed to form the basis for all actions to do with the alien problem from then on.

Project Sigma, created in 1953 and run by NSA, functioned to intercept and decrypt alien communications. With ten disk crashes, effort to maintain security took a supreme effort. Eisenhower, in 1953 asked Rockefeller for help with the alien problem. This is where the idea for MJ-12 was born. It was probably a critical mistake in asking a member of the world control group for help with a problem with alien beings.

Astronomers in 1953 made a rather disturbing discovery of a large object that entered the solar system, which later proved to be an object that was intelligently guided and emitted communication signals. The Air Force, in the same year, discovered huge orbiting objects between 100 to 500 miles altitude. They were alien craft.

Project Plato, governed by the NSA, endeavored to establish some sort of diplomatic relations with the alien species that had appeared. In 1953, the NSA was successful at this task, and the CIA, perceiving that more public disinformation was needed, convened the Robertson Panel. The summation report, issued in January of 1953, stated that there was "no threat to national security from UFOS". By now, some of the aliens were KNOWN, and therefore the semantics describing "unidentified" flying objects could be truthfully used.

Contact was made in 1953 with a race known thereafter as the Big-nosed Greys, and meeting was arranged with the aliens at Holloman AFB in New Mexico for 1954. A Secret Treaty was formed where the aliens would not interfere in our affairs and we would not interfere with their affairs. We would let them do what they want and also establish underground bases here in exchange for alien technology.

Concern or public probing into the "UFO" question caused the government to come up with the idea of developing disks using conventional technology and then displaying them to the public. This would take the heat off the real programs. Project Snowbird was created for this purpose. It to, was headquartered in Nevada.

The United States and the Canadians had been cooperating for some time on the disk technology, and in 1954 successful tests were made of some jointly developed disk designs. Project "Red-light" sustains it first death of an Air Force pilot in Nevada during a test of an alien vehicle. Project "Pounce" was created to provide a general process of disk and occupant recovery, as well as providing cover stories. It too was run by the NSA. Project "Plato", another NSA project, was initiated in order to establish a continuing program of technological evaluation of alien disks.

Increasing numbers of people in the public domain began to have encounters with alien beings. In order to retain the element of secrecy, the Air Force established a number of "debriefing colonies" in the United States for contactees and their families - a practice which continued well into the 1960's and beyond.

The Government also had contact with another race of aliens in 1953. This race would not share technology with the government, and despite their warnings about the Big-nosed Greys, the government broke off contact with them, preferring to allow the Greys to trade technology in mind control, beam weaponry and gravitational devices for silence on part of the United States about their abduction and mutilation operations.

1954

In 1954, Dr. Wilhelm Reich began experiments with his cloud-buster equipment, and discovered that he could affect the propulsion systems of some of the alien disks. Reich's discoveries also involved the manipulation of biological energy in terms of conquering disease. It didn't take the government long to realize what a threat Reich was to the established order, and Reich was hassled by the government and jailcd. He was finally murdered in Lewisburg prison in November 1957.

Back in 1954, under the Eisenhower administration, the 'federal' government decided to circumvent the Constitution of the United States and form a treaty with alien entities. It was called the 1954 Greada Treaty, which basically made the agreement that the aliens involved could take a few cows and test their implanting techniques on a few human beings, but that they had to give details about the people involved. Slowly, the aliens altered the bargain until they decided they wouldn't abide by it at all.

1955

In 1955, a documentary film about UFOs was released from Hollywood in an attempt to de-mystify UFOs as far as the public was concerned. The CIA mind control program, which was authorized in 1953 when Allan Dulles approved project MKDELTA, took on a new insidious turn when mind control drugs began to be given to subjects in normal settings in order to observe the effects. Later, by 1956, testing of mind control drugs on prisoners would be approved.

The National Security Council had established a "deal" with the Big-nosed Greys. The Greys would make sure that they would give a periodic list of abductees to the NSC. By April of 1954, it became obvious to the Eisenhower administration that the Greys had broken the agreement and were abducting far more people than they reported, including large numbers of children.

Also in 1955, Henry Kissinger was chosen as the head of the Alien study group, known as the JASON society, under National Security Council provision NSC 5411. NSC edict 5412/2 established as the original study committee. In 1956 the group, publicly referred to as the Quantico group, was closed. The 5412 designation became public knowledge, but the purpose of the group remained secret.

1956

In 1956, Captain Ruppelt, who left the Air Force in 1953, wrote and published his famous book "Report on Unidentified Flying Objects", he also made a statement that year about a "group of Germans having advanced aerial vehicles".

1957

By 1957, Joseph McCarthy was becoming a problem. He was admitted to Bethesda Naval Hospital where, of course, he mysteriously died. In 1957, it was decided that the course of human evolution would make the planet uninhabitable by the year 2000, so various "Alternatives" were discussed. Alternative 1, was to allow things to continue the way they were and hope things could be repaired.

The second alternative was to arrange for underground cities and facilities to be built in order to insure the survival of select groups of people. Alternative 3 was migration to other planets.

Both Alternatives 2 and 3 were chosen as being the most viable. Work was then started on both of them. In order to implement Alternative 3, alien technology would be needed. It was also necessary to push for more complete forms of mind control in order to insure a smooth flow of operations despite any opposition that might occur.

In 1957, work under Project "Red-light" was begun in earnest in Nevada. A facility code named DREAMLAND was constructed in the proximity of an alien underground base known as "S-4". Here, the process of exchange of alien technology began.

1958

In 1958, International Geophysical Year, expeditions were made to the poles in order to again assess the problem of the Germans, as well as the threat from aliens of different character that were detected as coming from inside the Earth. Work continued on Alternatives 2 and 3.

1959

In 1959, the RAND Corporation held several conferences on Deep Underground Construction. These conferences were attended by the various military services as well as large corporate construction firms like Bechtel. Underground construction projects began within a year. Existing underground facilities were beefed up and new ones were started. Funding for government underground facilities come from "Presidential Shelter" funds, as well as covert drug operation conducted by the CIA under the orders of MJ-12. This procedure appears to be still in effect as of July 1989. Over 75 underground facilities have been constructed under various programs.

Also in 1959, Joseph Bryan, CIA Psychological Warfare director, met with Major Donald Keyhoe in order to review cases. Keyhoe refuses. Captain Ruppelt, dissatisfied with governmental operations in terms of "UFO investigations" is becoming an increasing problem.

1960

In 1960, Edward Ruppelt mysteriously dies of a heart attack. In that year, Project Aquarius is initiated in order to collect medical and technical information from alien technology. It was another NSA sponsored project. Ronald Reagan is governor of California. His personal secretary was former translator for those Germans over Eichmann during World War II.

1961

In 1961, Cape Canaveral/Kennedy radar locked onto an object that was following a Polaris missile over the ocean. Vice-president Johnson's private aircraft crashes. Radar showed UFOs in the area.

In 1961, John Kennedy was elected president. He orders NORAD not to divulge information about foreign space vehicles. Experiments with ultrasonic and brain lesions are done by universities. Donald Keyhoe begins sending proof of his censorship to Congress. At Fort Ord, 221 military members are abducted and implanted with devices. They and their families are sequestered.

By May 1961, a House subcommittee had been formed to look into the subject of UFOs. It was again put down and the problem seemed to 'disappear' for a while. Kennedy, dissatisfied with some areas in the covert governmental structure, threatens to go public. In 1962 the Bilderbergers meet to discuss the problem.

1962

1962 was the year that the American public watched John Glenn orbit the Earth in the manned "space program", which was a public program designed to be a pool where funds could be siphoned off for work on covert projects. Some of the projects were concerned with development of alien technology.

1962 was also the year that a space probe was landed on Mars. It confirmed the presence of a viable atmosphere and further strengthened the push for Alternative 3. Disk activity is observed by the public around the area of Dulce, New Mexico, the area that would later become famous as the site of a joint government alien facility.

1963

In 1963, Kennedy evidently issued an ultimatum to MJ-12 and they decided that Kennedy should be subject to an expedient kill. This was the era when the United States first started having its own operational disks. 1963 is the date of one of the earliest visits to an underground joint base by an abductee that came back and lived to tell about it. It is the first hint of the underground breeding facilities that are described in the Dulce Papers, events surrounding Paul Bennewitz and Thunder Scientific Corporation in Albuquerque, New Mexico, and other insidious experiences that have been reported by scores of people from 1963 to 1989.

Within a month after Kennedy's murder, the Bilderbergers met again to formulate their plans. In England, mind control experiments began in Warminster. Lonnie Zamora's abduction case gave further impetus to public awareness of abduction by alien entities.

1964

In April 1964, Cape Kennedy radar technicians track disks in pursuit of the Gemini capsule. On April 15, two intelligence personnel meet under the Project Plato with aliens in the New Mexico desert to arrange a meeting on April 25 at Holloman AFB, New Mexico in order to "renew" the treaty in a psychological bid to buy time in order to solve the problem of the Greys.

In May 1964, the book "The Invisible Government" was release, and many significant details about the operation of the CIA were released to the public.

In the summer of 1964, alleged metal samples from the Socorro case were being analyzed. Scientist Ray Stanford states that the samples are an unknown alloy. On August 20, 1964, fifteen days after Stanford makes his statement, NASA scientist Sciacca states that the Socorro sample is silicon.

September 17, 1964 marked the release of the Warren Commission Report on the Kennedy assassination, intended to pacify the public about the event and obscure the details about the assassination. In December, disks were back again, buzzing the Pautuxent Naval Air Station in Maryland.

1965

In 1965, the Bilderbergers met again. George Adamski takes motion pictures of an object at Silver Spring, Maryland on February 26, 1965. On March 18, the Soviets give a less than adequate performance during the "spacewalk" of Leoniv. It's obviously a staged event not taking place in space. In June, astronaut James McDivitt sees an object in space and reports it. The government begins to review data about the earth energy grid system detailed by Dr. Bruce Cathie in New Zealand. It is believed that the energy grid provides power to sustain some of the implant systems and other equipment that the aliens use. It also provides (if the tilt of the earth is correct) the power to energize apparent "window areas" on the planet and open dimensional doorways.

1966

In 1966, actual technology on-board far exceeded technology that was made available to the public. It is believed that a research lab in Silicon Valley had developed 3 dimensional television and had it perfected. Video tape was also in the process of being developed for release. The SR-71 blackbird, an aircraft having advanced design and special alloy skins allowing it to travel to the fringes of space, was designed and built. It was around that time period that people become acutely aware of the series of underground tunnel systems that lie under California and the other Western States that connect corporations and other facilities together.

1966 marked the end of the mind control experiments in Warminster, England. Cheyenne Mountain and its NORAD facility is activated, and the Bilderbergers meet again. Henry Kissinger, Olaf Palmer (who would authorize the use of implants in Sweden in 1971 and subsequently be murdered), Gerald Ford and Schmidt from Germany were among the attendees. The NASA budget had swelled to over $572 million dollars.

A 1966 Gallup poll indicated that over 8 million people had seen UFOs in the United States. Public interest increased. It was time to manipulate public opinion again. The Condon Committee was set up, chaired by Edward Condon, who admitted his forgone conclusion that UFOs didn't exist. The Condon Committee announced its results to the public, declaring the UFOs didn't really have any basis in reality.

It was the beginning of a debunking process that would culminate in 1969 when the Air Force made a public announcement that they are "closing Project Bluebook". Congressman Gerald Ford makes a declaration to Congress that they should look into the subject of UFOs. Two months later, in June 1966, disks interrupt tests at Pine Gap facility near Alice Springs, Australia.

In August 1966, Dr. J. Allen Hynek publicly criticizes scientists for not investigating UFO reports.

1967

In 1967, Astronomer James E. MacDonald sees a classified version of the 1953 Robertson Report and becomes a critic of the Air Force and the CIA. MacDonald makes a statement that UFOs may be visitors spying on the planet. Also in 1967, a large shipment of gold leaves Fort Knox, destination unknown.

In October 1967, Britain is hit by a wave of disk sightings. In December, the Schirmier case in Nebraska becomes the most interesting abduction case of the year. Schirmer is brought to an underground base and relates the details afterward.

1968

In 1969, Richard Nixon becomes president. Edward Condon releases his book "Scientific Study of UFOs" in an attempt to further obscure the subject as far as the public is concerned. The US Army Language School R&D department produces a brain nullifier device. The Air Force declares Project Bluebook abandoned "out of lack of interest". The Brazilian Air Force issues a directive forbidding release of UFO info to the press. Donald Keyhoe, a longtime enemy of the government, is ousted from NICAP and replaced by CIA operative John Acuff.

On May 28, 1969, former president Eisenhower dies, marking the last time a President will have full knowledge of the whole alien situation until the election of President Bush in 1988.

On July 20 - 21, 1969, the public is treated to Neil Armstrong landing on the Moon (in the wrong place). Armstrong and his crew are treated to views of huge alien spacecraft surrounding their landing site. Radio hams pick up the chatter involved in the incident.

A controversy erupted in 1969 over the 1950 Internal Security Act which authorized detention camps in the United States. Senator Daniel Inouye introduced a bill to abolish the section of the Act which dealt with detention camps and it was quickly passed into law. Despite the government's official policy, some believe the law has been violate.

Years later, a suit was filed in US District Court in Houston by businessman William Pabst, who charged that the federal government established secret concentration camps and mental hospitals for the purpose of jailing political dissidents. Pabst said that a massive computer system exists whereby government officials have access to the names of citizens in order to arrest and control them.

By 1969, the NASA budget has shrunk to a mere $44 million. They don't want any more intrusions into the operation on the moon. In October of 1969, Jimmy Carter sees and reports a UFO.

1970

In 1970, the Bilderbergers meet. The world population is 3.6 billion. In October 1970, Canadian Prime Minister Trudeau suspends the Canadian Bill of Rights, which allows search without warrant.

1971

In 1971, the Bilderbergers meet again, this time in Woodstock Vermont. The Air Force still continues Project Bluebook. A bill is introduced again to repeal Title 2 of the Internal Security Act as far as detention camps are concerned. Currently, emergency provisions stall stand on the books.

In June 1971 Dr. James E. MacDonald mysteriously drives out into the desert and shoots himself in the head.

1972

In 1972, the Central Security Service (CSS) was created at Fort Meade. Purpose: communication interception. Project Redlight assumes a new phase of operations in Nevada. The first Watergate break-in occurs. Scientist Rene Hardy, also a prominent UFOlogist, is found dead; an apparent suicide. The CIA mind control project at Bethesda Naval Hospital ends. On June 12, 1972, the second and most prominent Watergate break-in occurs. In December, astronaut Edgar Mitchell admits that NASA has provisions for encounters with alien life-forms. On December 25, 1972, President Truman dies.

Scientist Rene Hardy, also a prominent UFOlogists, is found dead; an 'apparent' suicide... In December, astronaut Edgar Mitchell admits that NASA has provisions for encounters with alien lifeforms.

1973

In 1973, increasing numbers of aerial craft are being seen. A visit to the underground base at Twenty-nine Palms is documented by an Air Force member who takes pictures of an alien autopsy and an alien craft that is bigger on the inside than outside. Brazilian State Directive, Institutional Act No. 5, forbids dissemination of UFO related information. NICAP files are taken over by Hyneks's Center for UFO Studies. Scientists again discover a large object moving toward the Earth. It is confirmed to be another alien craft.

1974

In 1974, large numbers of animal mutilations begin to occur in Texas. Hynek visits APRO headquarters and is denied access to their files. Nelson Rockefeller becomes vice-president. The Soviets begin their research into weather modification. A photo of a disk is taken by an aviation photographer near Nellis AFB, Nevada. In February 1974, Robert Galley, French Minister for Defense, goes on TV and publicly states that the disks are real.

1975

In 1975, the NASA budget is back up to around $121 million for R&D projects. The area around Dulce, New Mexico starts to experience another intense wave of animal mutilations. NICAP begins its downward financial slide. George Bush becomes director for the CIA. Documents indicate that ultrasonic research lasted 20 years. In April 1976, NSC directive 4A authorized covert psychological activities to be conducted against American citizens. May, 1976 was the 200th anniversary of the founding of the Illuminati.

1977

In 1977, the United States sends the Soviet Union a super-super-magnet which they then use for weather modification. Jimmy Carter gets elected and says that he'll make every piece of information about UFOs available to the public. Carter is shown a disk and changes his mind. In 1977, the intelligence branch of the Royal Air Force decides to no longer publish statistical reports bout UFOs.

The Freedom of Information Act was passed in 1977. In May 1977, Jack Acuff, CIA representative in NICAP, is approached by Soviet KGB agents in regard to UFOs. In September 1977, a Red Flag pilot strays over Dreamland and is reassigned within 48 hours to another base. Also in September, USAF Colonel Senn sends a letter to NASA General Crow, expressing the hope that UFO investigation will stop.

1978

In 1978, a wave of sightings in England begins that lasts until 1983, with some 3,000 sightings documented. In 1978, an NSA employee provides CIA NICAP representative Jack Acuff with classified UFO related documents. The movie "Close Encounters" is released to the public; a new effort at acclimation toward pseudo-friendly aliens. In 1978 the United States sends new F-16 aircraft to NATO allies on Soviet ships. A former CIA employee verifies drawings of alien hands made at autopsies. Leonard Stringfield publishes "Situation Red". The magazine "Harrisburg" predicts an incident at Three Mile Island nuclear plant for March 28, 1979.

On March 18, 1978, William Herman is abducted and told by the aliens of the existence of a "network" of civilizations. They also confirm the loss of ships in the 1940's because of radar units. On June 19, 1978, President Carter issues an executive order creating the Federal Emergency Management Agency; an act viewed by some to be unconstitutional.

In September 1978, scientist Paul Bennewitz discovers the activities of alien craft at Manzano Weapons Storage area outside of Albuquerque, New Mexico. Bennewitz submits a report called Project Beta to the government and is put under observation. He was allegedly subjected to three bouts with electroshock treatment starting in 1979, then was left to be observed by both the government and the aliens with whom he had been communicating with through his computer equipment.

Also in 1978, the Federal Emergency Management Agency conducts its first Rex excise, Rex-78.

1979

In 1979, a conference on animal mutilations was organized by Senators Smith and Domenici, and was attended by Scientist Henry Montieth, who had just completed ten years of research on the subject. The conclusion of the conference was that there was something of substance in animal mutilation cases that could not be explained.

1979 was the year that a disgruntled scientist at the Dulce Genetics Facility fled with videos, pictures and notes, vowing to expose the atrocities found there.

Presidential candidate Ronald Reagan visits NORAD in Cheyenne Mountain in 1979. CIA agent John Acuff of NICAP is replaced by retired agent Hall.

In 1979, a retired OSS agent claims during an interview that he was asked to kill General Patton. In January 18, 1979, a debate on UFOs took place in the House of Lords in England. On March 28, 1979, just as predicted, the Three Mile Island event took place. In October 1979, an altercation takes place between government scientists and military personnel and the resident aliens. Sixty six people were killed.

Underground Bases: A Lecture by Phil Schneider: May 1995:

Back in 1979, this was the reality, and the fire-fight at Dulce occurred quite by accident. I was involved in building an ADDITION to the deep underground military base at Dulce, which is probably the deepest base. It goes down seven levels and over 2.5 miles deep. At that particular time, we had drilled four distinct holes in the desert, and we were going to link them together and blow out large sections at a time. My job was to go down the holes and check the rock samples, and recommend the explosive to deal with the particular rock. As I was headed down there, we found ourselves amidst a large cavern that was full of outer-space (or "inner-space"? - Branton) aliens, otherwise known as large Greys.

I shot two of them. At that time, there were 30 people down there. About 40 more came down after this started, and all of them got killed. We had surprised a whole underground base of existing aliens. Later, we found out that they had been living on [in] our planet for a long time... This could explain a lot of what is behind the theory of ancient astronauts.

(Note: This report seems to reveal a limited 'perspective' on the overall 'Dulce war' conflicts based on the experience of one individual. It appears, however, as if there was much more involved in the overall scenario than what Phil Schneider describes. For instance from Phil's description, it appears as if his team broke-in to the base 'accidentally'. It could be that IN RESPONSE to the captured scientists mentioned by Thomas Edwin Castello and others, the Special Forces and Intel agents intentionally attempted to break-in to the underground alien bases through a "back door" so-to-speak, yet Schneider may have not been aware of this part. Other reports would suggest that the conflict was more complex than this, and involved more than one firefight. According to other sources, the "Dulce Wars" involved AT LEAST a hundred highly-trained Special Forces. - Branton)

"Anyway, I got shot in the chest with one of their weapons, which was a box on their body, which blew a hole in me and gave me a nasty dose of cobalt radiation. I have had cancer because of that.

"I didn't get really interested in UFO technology until I started work at Area 51, north of Las Vegas. After about two years recuperating after the 1979 incident, I went back to work for Morrison and Knudson, EG&G and other companies. At Area 51, they were testing all kinds of peculiar spacecraft. How many people here are familiar with Bob Lazar's story? He was a physicist working at Area 51 trying to decipher the propulsion factor in some of these craft.

::: Schneider's Worries About Government Factions, Railroad Cars and Shackle Contracts :::

"Now, I am very worried about the activity of the 'federal' government. They have lied to the public, stonewalled senators, and have refused to tell the truth in regard to alien matters. I can go on and on. I can tell you that I am rather disgruntled. Recently, I knew someone who lived near where I live in Portland, Oregon. He worked at Gunderson Steel Fabrication, where they make railroad cars.

Now, I knew this fellow for the better part of 30 years, and he was kind of a quiet type. He came in to see me one day, excited, and he told me "they're building prisoner cars." He was nervous. Gunderson, he said, had a contract with the federal government to build 107,200 full length railroad cars, each with 143 pairs of shackles. There are 11 sub-contractors in this giant project. Supposedly, Gunderson got over 2 billion dollars for the contract.

Bethlehem Steel and other steel outfits are involved. He showed me one of the cars in the rail yards in North Portland. He was right. If you multiply 107,200 times 143 times 11, you come up with about 15,000,000. This is probably the number of people who disagree with the federal government. No more can you vote any of these people out of office. Our present structure of government is 'technocracy', not democracy, and it is a form of feudalism.

(Note: I would venture to say that it is more like a techno-monarchy, since several of the U.S. presidents have been placed in office with Rockefeller financial and media backing, suggesting that these same presidential hirelings were inclined to favor certain Rockefeller and in turn International banking agendas. Techno-Monarchy would constitute those parts of the Military-Industrial Complex or M.I.C. that are largely influenced by Rockefeller interests.

According to various sources, the German immigrant Rockefellers are not the "top of the ladder" for the world conspiracy. True, they 'control' much of the eco-political system in the UNITED STATES of America, however they are following the agenda of the Bildeberger cult: the 13 Wicca Masons, 13 Black Nobility, and 13 Maltese Jesuits who have joined together UNDER the covering of the Bavarian Illuminati—which in turn is the modern manifestation of the joint human-alien 'serpent cult' which seems to have had its origins within the ancient underground Masonic systems of Egypt, a cult or collaboration that was brought to Bavaria by the early Germanic Trade Guilds during the height of the so-called 'Holy Roman' [German] Empire - Branton).

It [this 'technocracy'] has nothing to do with the republic of the United States. These people are god-less, and have legislated out prayer in public schools. You can get fined up to $100,000 and two years in prison for praying in school. I believe we can do better. I also believe that the federal government is running the gambit of enslaving the people of the United States. I am not a very good speaker, but I'll keep shooting my mouth off until somebody puts a bullet in me, because it's worth it to talk to a group like this about these atrocities.

1980

In 1980, after his election, Ronald Reagan changes the 'Air Defense' in NORAD to "Aerospace Defense". The 'Roswell Incident' was published by William Moore. The MUFON journal publishes and article on Project Red-light. The Federal Emergency Management Agency conducts Rex-80 exercises, in which they relocate Cuban refugees as part of a population relocation test.

In January 1980, Peter Gersten secures two documents from the NSA under the Freedom of Information Act. Gersten was able to find out on April 27, 1982 that some 238 NSA documents were located in the search that the government made.

In May, 1980, psychologist and researcher Leo Sprinkle regresses Myrna Hanson, who relates information about underground bases with vats. Also in May, Judy Doraty and her son witness a cattle mutilation and are abducted and implanted themselves.

In August 1980, disks intrude again into the Manzano Weapons Storage Area in New Mexico. On August 8th, a disk was discovered by a Sandia guard next to a building containing HQ CR44 (nuclear materials). On August 9th, a security officer checks down Coyote Canyon Road and discovers a disk.

By November 1980, researcher Paul Bennewitz was still being monitored by the NSA. In December 1980, the Cash - Landrum case occurred where both women received severe radiation poisoning during an encounter with a US disk that is escorted away in full view of the two woman by 23 military helicopters.

1981

In 1981, George Bush (former head of the CIA) becomes Vice-President and Ronald Reagan becomes President. The NASA R&D budget is $109 million. Ronald Reagan was shot in an assassination attempt that wanted to put George Bush in office a little sooner.

In 1981, the University of Florida begins work on thought operated computers. The Stealth 117A aircraft was first test flown. In January

1980, discovery of the Bentwaters/Woodbridge case featuring underground activities.

On January 13, 1981, Colonel Charles J. Halt writes a memo at RAF Bentwaters on the alien encounter in Rendlesham Forest.

1982

In 1982, Peter Gersten of CAUS files a petition with the Supreme Court relative to NSA involvement in UFO related activities.

Researcher Linda Howe (A Strange Harvest) was allegedly contacted by MJ-12 with ideas for making a documentary release of information - they changed their mind later. In 1982 the planetary population exceeds 4.8 billion people. On March 10, 1982, the House of Lords held its second debate on UFOs, still coming to no definitive conclusion. The Federal Emergency Management Agency conducts the Rex-82 exercise, which tested the national ability to mobilize quickly for wartime military production. Industry failed miserably.

1983

In 1983, a Nevada researcher discovers a metal rod in the center of a geomagnetic vortex in Blue Diamond, Nevada. The British government starts to release UFO files for the first time.

In 1983, the Stealth 117A fighter becomes operational on a covert basis. In 1983, the Colorado Advanced Technology Institute was created as a basic structure for future space oriented developments to take place starting in 1988 - 90. The memo of Colonel Charles Hait of Bentwaters is released in the United States.

An internal Pentagon document dated December 1, 1983 describes in detail the military directions for pulling out the troops in case of some unspecified emergency. The document lists exceptions to the

Posse Comitatus Act, the federal law that prohibits the military from operating in the United States. The document gives as its authority for such actions "the inherent legal right of the United States Government to ensure the preservation of public order.... by force if necessary", a claim that Supreme Court had dismissed when President Truman tried to use it to justify taking over steel mills in the early 1950's.

There is evidence that new Army divisions, like those at Fort Lewis in Washington, will have a dual foreign and domestic role. Another planned division will be located at Fort Ord, California. FEMA has standby legislation in a bill innocuously titled the "Defense Resources Act". The bill would suspend the Bill of Rights, abolish free enterprise, eliminate privately owned property, and generally clamp the American people in a totalitarian vise.

Section 202 of the bill, for example, allows the President to instantly confiscate any real estate or personal property "that shall be deemed necessary for national defense purposes". Section 501 authorizes the takeover of any industry the White House authorizes. Section 1213 outlaws all strikes.

The standby legislation also includes "Censorship of Communications", which allows the president, whenever he "shall deem that the public safety demand it", to censor "communications by mail, cable, radio, television, or other means of transmission". The "COG" (Continuity of Government) also exists. It is a secretive shadow government that is in place and ready to run the country.

Since 1980, this unprecedented apparatus has been installed to thrust the United States into a military takeover with or without the president's co-operation, and all in the name of preserving democracy from some un-named threat. Guess what the threat might be?

(From underground bases like the Mt. Weather facility near Bluemont, Virginia. In reference to the 'Executive Orders' authorizing FEMA to violate Constitutional law in time of 'Emergency', we must ask: are these Executive Orders legal? True, many of these E.O.'s were written by presidents who were duly elected by U.S. citizens who trusted the media slant concerning these presidents who came after John F. Kennedy, in spite of the fact that most of these were members of one-world economic organizations like the Council of Foreign Relations, Trilateral Commission, and BILDEBERGERS. However **WHAT IF** the death of John F. Kennedy was part of a coup d'etat of the Executive branch of U.S. government as many, including the late Louisiana district attorney James Garrison, claimed?

If this were the case then the entire Executive branch might be filled with ILLEGAL appointees, who may have been instrumental in authorizing illegal intelligence agencies, may have illegally given power that was not meant to be theirs over to the military-industrialists, and these elected "Chief Executives"—many of whom happened to be the hirelings of corporacratic elitists who financed their political and media campaigns—have violated the very foundations of the United States by establishing Executive Orders which violate the U.S.

CONSTITUTION, THE BILL OF RIGHTS, and THE DECLARATION OF INDEPENDENCE. I'm sure that there are still many Americans who see these three documents as being the essence of AMERICA, and they fully believe in the words penned within the DECLARATION OF INDEPENDENCE to the effect that military force is justified, if necessary, to defend from all enemies foreign AND DOMESTIC the form of government that is patterned after the sacred contents of these documents. - Branton).

1984

The movie "V" is presented to the public, portraying reptilian aliens who feed on human flesh, store humans for food, etc. Active resistance groups are also plugged in the movie/series. NASA budget is $192 million. The book "Clear Intent" is published by Fawcett and Greenwood. The

Soviets conduct a national poll on UFO experiences, to which 30,000 reply. The Federal Emergency Management Agency conducts the Res-84 exercises. These exercises was involved with practice in detaining and handling large numbers of people. Large numbers of people might presumably have to be dealt with after a controversial government action. Any guesses?

On April 26, 1984, General Bond is killed flying in Area 51 during a classified aerial test. In December, the US Space Foundation held its first Annual National Symposium in Colorado.

1985

In 1985, McDonnel Douglas receives brand new technology from apparently nowhere. John Herrington becomes Secretary of Energy. The Soviets reveal major encounter data to the public. Author Ralph Noyes UK) publishes "A Secret Property" about the British Government and UFOs. NASA Budget has grown to $248 million for research and development. Lawrence Livermore Labs begins to manufacture artificial blood, some of which is destined for Dulce

Genetics Facility in New Mexico. Cattle mutilations begin to drop off in the Midwest.

In October 1985, Aries Properties acquires 21,000 acres running next to Colorado Springs, site of a future space technology center.

In November 1985, NBC broadcasts a program about "black unmarked helicopters, secret projects, and bad money". On December 4, 1985, President Reagan voices thoughts about alien forces from space to high school students.

On August 5th, Scientists Paul Bennewitz observes the crash site of a US Black Delta ship in New Mexico.

1986

In 1986, "Sky Crash" by Jenny Randles and "UFO Crash at Aztec" by Steinman and Stevens are published. The Brazilian Air Force, according to government documents released by the FOIA, chases UFOs. Project Snowbird goes into another phase to develop craft with conventional technology to show to the public. Crime rate rises 5.2 percent. On July 26, 1986, Dr. Robert I. Sarbacher Dies.

1987

In 1987, Star Wars budget is $4.2 billion. The Department of Defense now funds 75 percent of all Federal Research and Development.

A Los Angeles policeman dies after discovering a major CIA distribution point for heroin and cocaine at the top of the Staffers Concourse Hotel in Los Angeles and is killed. Funds created by the agency are funneled to covert projects. Other distribution points exist at Riverton, Wyoming and on the Laguna Indian Reservation in Arizona. Delta Security Forces provide protection.

In 1987, the "Dulce Papers" are first released. Data on five entrances to Dulce Lab is leaked, and the government takes care of them by destroying buildings and building new ones in odd locations for apparently no perceivable reason. In February 1987, there are 102 operable nuclear facilities in the United States. On February15, 1987, the San Jose 'Mercury' reports on the Pentagon "black budget" program. On April 27, 1987, genetically altered bacteria are publicly released. The bacteria were produced to interfere with 'frost damage to citrus crops'.

In September 1987, 16 - cycle waves are broadcast from transmitters and repeaters for a period of four months before the election of George Bush. The ELF (extremely low frequency) waves cause entrainment of millions of Americans to occur, possibly to influence the election.

Allegedly, the main transmitter was located in Nevada. On September 4, 1987, the group called "Justice for Military

Personnel (JMP)" sends a letter to the president, detailing crimes the military has been ordered to commit against private citizens in regard to the alien problem.

On September 21, 1987, Reagan again voices his thoughts about aliens threatening the earth in an address to the United Nations.

On November 21st, the Parkinson Institute begins asking the public for human fetuses to study. Requests are made to groups of hospitals. On the 27th, groups of US Army rangers attempt and apparently bungle an attempt to enter a joint alien facility in New Mexico. In December, the CIA begins to contact everyone who was ever in its employ that ever had anything to do with the alien problem. A woman draws a picture of a black-mirrored spherical craft she says belongs to the National Security Agency. On the 14th of December, John Lear offers to host the MUFON Convention in Las Vegas in July 1989.

1988

George Bush finally becomes president. A joint alien base off the Florida coast is re-activated, giving rise to the sightings at Gulf Breeze. On March 25, John Lear releases a statement to the public on the status of affairs with the alien situation. On April 27th, Leonard Stringfield speaks at a Milford, Ohio public library.

In May 1988, Reagan again makes a speech in which he refers to an "alien threat from outside this world". Newspapers report Reagan has been allegedly "warned" by astrologers that there will be a space invasion by 1993. It was discovered that EBE's are sensitive to any material having a left-hand atomic spin. On May 5th, Leonard Stringfield releases and article in Batavia, Illinois about aliens.

In June 1988, Senator Cranston is allegedly shown disks at Norton AFB. The publication "NASA Techbriefs" shows a photo of an EBE with no caption or explanation. Word comes from New Mexico to researchers that Los Alamos has developed an antimatter weapon, which allegedly will be used as a last resort if "the Greys cannot be pried away from the planet". The number of Greys on Earth is estimated at 20 million. In December, Steven White (President of

Bechtel Investments) dies. Bechtel had been heavily involved in underground construction. Starting in 1989, billions of dollars are being spent modernizing NORAD.

1989

Starting in 1989, billions of dollars are being spent modernizing NORAD. Data on Project Excalibur is released. The project is involved in developing a warhead that will penetrate 1000 meters of earth and then detonate. Useful for destroying underground bases.

1989 is the year that Zbigniew Brzezinski predicted that the United States Constitution would be re-written. In January 1989, William Cooper and John Lear issue an indictment to the president regarding the alien problem. No reply was ever received.

On May 14, 1989, Las Vegas channel 8 TV televises an interview with a government scientist [Robert Lazar] working at Groom Lake and Dreamland. The scientist openly tells of nine disks on the Nellis range; three of them are operational; the craft use antimatter engines; the Soviets were involved only up to a point. He won't talk about the aliens. Subsequently, the government scientist discovered that he has been the victim of a method of hypnosis known as "Orion Hypnosis". His life is threatened and his car is shot up in Las Vegas.

On June 30, July 1st and 2nd, the MUFON Conference occurs in Las Vegas, Nevada. William Cooper, John Lear, William English, and

Don Ecker speak to an enthusiastic crowd. The day before, on July 1st, William Moore and a disgruntled audience have a shouting match with each other. The audience is astounded when instead of the issues at hand, Moore uses his time to attack other researchers, specifically Paul Bennewitz. William Moore publicly admits he works for a government intelligence agency.

On August 7th, US NEWS AND WORLD REPORT publishes material on "Americas Doomsday Project", detailing over 50 underground facilities that are for use during time of crisis.

In September 1989, SEVERAL west coast radio talk shows begin avid discussion of UFO's, aliens and interaction with the US Government. The public discussion is now out of control!!!

On September 23, 1989, a two-hour documentary is screened on Japanese television. Viewers are treated to the full spectrum of recent investigations, including underground labs, MJ-12, genetic facilities, the Kennedy murder, the voices of the astronauts on the shuttle talking about observing alien spacecraft, and EG&G scientist Robert Lazar talking about the disks at Groom Lake, and a visit to Dulce, where residents tell of visits from the CIA. A CIA or MIB type is photographed following the Japanese team. His Colorado license plate is readable.

On October 16th, word comes from researchers that the United States and the Soviet Union had a disagreement on the base on the far side of the Moon in which several US scientists were machine-gunned. This disagreement reflects the split between the US and Soviets detailed in the May '89 disclosure by a government scientist working at the S-4/ Dreamland facility in Nevada [during which time the Soviets were kicked off the super-technology projects in Nevada and sent packing]. It is thought that this disagreement occurred in 1986 or 1987. [It is uncertain what connection if any this 'altercation' may have had with an alleged Reptilian/Grey take-over of an 'Alternative-2' base on Mars two years earlier in 1985, according to contactee Alex Collier].

On October 25, Congress works on legislation to make radio talk shows liable for statements made by callers in an effort to shut down talk radio programs, where UFO/Alien data is being avidly discussed. On October 26th, William Cooper goes on a radio station in Los Angeles and tells the listening public that President Bush is involved in the drug scene. The FCC attacks the talk show host the next day for "saying a bad word". Researchers speculate that the Secret Service, who allegedly terminated Sal Mineo during Reagan's administration because of an alleged homosexual tape they were concerned about, will seek to eliminate Cooper, that for some reason Cooper has now made himself expendable with this material involving the [former] President.

On November 3rd, researchers announce their discovery that a security team code-named "Yellow Fruit" was started back during the Carter Presidency, and was part of the NSA. It has been periodically disbanded and has existed in one form or another since the Carter administration. Los Angeles radio talk show host Ken Hudnell announces his intention take a group to visit one of the ancient underground cities, which he says has an entrance 60 miles from Anaheim. Researchers discover the passive security frequencies at Groom Lake; 138.306 and 407.550 and that a group codenamed Seaspray is involved with primary security in the area. Security forces then change the frequencies.

On November 6th, Channel 8 in Las Vegas starts a two-week series on Area 51, animal mutilations, and the UFO cover-up. On November 10, EG&G scientist Robert Lazar goes on television and tells what he knows about US disk technology at S-4 in Area 51, including information about 9 US disks, antimatter reactors, and mind control for S-4 scientists.

On November 19th, an electrical worker at Mercury, Nevada, calls the Billy Goodman radio talk show and describes tunnels 3000 feet under the test site that have stainless steel walls and elevators. He also describes small Grey bodies on gurneys being wheeled down the tunnels.

On November 20th, a security guard on the Nevada Test Site describes his contact with a man in black that describes the whole alien scenario to him. The man has transparent eyelids.

On November 20 and 21st, the national program HARD COPY televises two programs on UFOs. EG&G scientist Robert Lazar goes on radio on KVEG for three hours and answers questions over the 50,000 watt station. Another three hour session takes place Nov. 24th and 25th. Robert Lazar publicizes the name of his boss at Area S-4, tells that 22 people work at S-4, and how antimatter reactors work. Indications are that more people will be coming out of the woodwork to tell what they know up at Area 51.

On November 25th, television station Channel 8 in Las Vegas televises a two hour special on UFOs, Area 51, S-4 and the UFO cover-up. It is revealed that some people who contacted Channel 8 had had their homes broken into in Las Vegas.

During the week of Christmas, 1989, it was reported that there were a series of very large underground explosions in the area of the base at Dulce, New Mexico. A month EARLIER, animal mutilations began to pick up significantly. The last time these two events occurred in this order was when the government first discovered what the Greys were up to and they tried to go in and stop them. Over 60 Delta troops were killed in the process [in the initial military attempt against the base].

1990

990—On February 17, a Ukrainian astronomer detects radio emissions near Altair [Aquila], which in ancient times was associated with reptilian creatures.

(Note: Some contactees speak of an 'unstable' alliance between 'Nordics' and 'Greys' which has existed for a long period of time in the Altair system, as well as references to a large faction of collectist Greys who were in the process of arguing against the continued existence of humans in that and other systems, which would apparently also include the sovereigntist humans in the Andromeda and Pleiadian constellations.

It is stated that some fascist human elements operating within the Montauk base at the northern tip of Long Island—who have an established an agreement with the Greys to bring about a global dictatorship on earth—were given the 'star gate' coordinates to generate a time-space window using Montauk technology, directly to a particular planet in the Altair system in order to assist in the suppression of a resistance movement among some of the 'Nordic' type humanoids there. - Branton).

On March 3rd, Las Vegas UFOCCI chairman Stacy Borland and her brother were brutally murdered while at home. [Stacy was attempting to get information out about a group of Mercury, Nevada construction workers and electricians who claimed that some of their fellow workers had been abducted and were being held captive in a vast underground systems there].

On March 8th, the final destruction of the 4th amendment of the U.S. Constitution takes effect very quietly behind the scenes. Now the authorities need no warrant or probable cause to break into a person's home and perform any action they think fit. Suspicion is sufficient.

1991

On Oct. 20, 1991, California researcher Michael Lindemann, founder of 'The 20/20 Group', gave a lecture before a large crowd of interested investigators. During the course of his lecture wherein he discussed the Military-Industrial Complex's underground bases outside of Lancaster, California, he made the following statements:

"...How many of you have seen the book 'BLANK CHECK'?... It is not a UFO book. I strongly recommend that you read the book 'BLANK

CHECK' so that you can understand something about how these projects are funded without your say so, indeed without the say so of Congress. Most citizens don't know for example that the National Security Act of 1947 made it illegal to ever say how much money is spent on the CIA. Indeed all of our tremendous alphabet soup collection of Intelligence Agencies. Whether you are talking about the CIA, or the NRO, or the NSA or the DIA, etc., all of them are in the same category.

"You cannot say how much these things cost. All you can do if you want to find out is add-up the numbers on the Budget that aren't assigned to anything that actually means anything. There are these huge categories that have tens of billions of dollars in them that say nothing but 'Special Projects...' And every year the Congress dutifully passes this bloated budget that has some $300,000,000,000 or more with HUGE chunks of cash labeled like that: 'Special Projects,' 'Unusual Stuff.'—Ten billion dollars. O.K., well where does the 'unusual stuff' money go? Well, it DOES go to 'unusual stuff', that's for sure, and one of the places it goes is that it goes into the underground bases. Indeed TIM said recently since the publication of his book [BLANK]

Path 32: Underground Infrastructure The Missing 40 Trillion Dollars

Steven J. Smith
Scientific Papers Website

For many years there have been reports and rumors of a vast network of underground complexes and tunnels beneath the North American continent. Starting in the late 1980s, the American government has tried to deflect these rumors through a campaign of misdirection and misinformation. Disclosure of the Greenbrier Congressional Shelter at White Sulphur Springs is a good example of this campaign.

To believe the existence of the Greenbrier complex was revealed against the wishes of the American government is the height of naiveté. This revelation was allowed to take place. The Greenbrier underground complex was no longer useful, so it was sacrificed to divert attention away from a much larger secret. In other words, a classic misdirection ploy.

While I do not have complete knowledge concerning the extent of America's covert underground infrastructure, I do have detailed firsthand experience with many sites near my home in Oregon. Based on my experiences, and assuming a roughly uniform distribution correlated with U.S. population demographics, the total number of covert underground facilities is in the tens of thousands.

What follows is both a compendium of my observations, and a do-it-your-self field guide for those who wish discover the true extent of the American covert underground infrastructure.

Rabbit Holes

The covert underground infrastructure serves many functions. Among these are strategic storage of materials and weapons, clandestine research and production facilities, alternant basing for military personnel and equipment, surface environment control systems (atmospheric lensing, synthetic earthquakes, weather modification, civilian population control, etc.), and of course sheltering essential government personnel during time of national crisis or war.

This list is not complete, it is only indicative of the diverse ways in which the underground infrastructure is utilized. It should be obvious that many of the uses listed above require both support from, and easy access to, the surrounding surface communities. I call these underground access points "rabbit holes", and they represent a key detectable feature of the underground infrastructure.

It should also be obvious that many of these uses require the facilities to be interconnected by a network of tunnels. The construction of these tunnels creates surface evidence of their existence, albeit transitory.

From the perspective of detection, the transitory nature of the evidence makes tunnel construction less useful than covert underground access points, however as we shall see, the evidence itself is far more compelling.

Searching for Alice

As previously mentioned, many underground infrastructure functions require surface access, furthermore many underground facilities also make use of above ground support such as electrical utilities, generally as backup for their primary supply source. These requirements pose a design dilemma. The underground access points must be well hidden, and at the same time, easily accessible to personnel and/or vehicular traffic. What is true of covert underground access points, is also true to a lesser extent for utility supply points.

How do you hide traffic and personnel movement? By mixing it with a legitimate flow of people and vehicles, in locations already under government ownership or control. In rural areas, public parks and recreational facilities make ideal locations. For instance, at a public camp ground, who will notice if 20 cars go in, but only 15 come out? In urban areas, post offices and other purpose built government installations are used.

After all, who pays attention to the comings and goings at a post office? In other words, the underground access points are hidden in plain sight. This is both a strength and a weakness. It is a strength if nobody is paying close attention, however it is also tremendous weakness, since anyone wishing to observe the location will blend in to the general ebb and flow of activity. In some respects, rural underground access points are easier to locate, but more dangerous to investigate, since the level of human activity will be less.

Another aspect of *rabbit hole location* is proximity to some useful above ground resource. For instance, a public zoo makes a good source of genetic material for a bio-lab facility. It should be obvious that a major metropolitan hospital would make an ideal source for human genetic material, as well as the perfect location to "field test" some new weaponized bacteria or virus. What is true of urban access points, is also true for rural access points.

Many are located near the periphery of major urban populations. A large water reservoir, or a public camp ground located near a major highway, are good examples of useful above ground resources. Rural underground access points are favored as utility supply points, since the supply is less likely to be interrupted in time of national crisis.

As we shall see, this last observation can be used to great advantage in detecting rabbit hole locations.

Urban rabbit hole detection

The detection of urban access points requires both persistence, and a certain amount of luck. Quite often, it will be some apparently trivial detail that will be your first clue.

The following is a list of indicators that are cause for suspicion:

1. A post office parking lot full of cars, with only one or two people visible inside the post office.
2. Sporadic late night activity at a government office building.
3. Security that is out of proportion with presumed facility use.
4. Unbalanced traffic patterns. Example: people or vehicles go in but do not come out, or vice versa.
5. Facility size is out of proportion to traffic flow. Example: many delivery vehicles at a small government office building.
6. Utility services is out of proportion to facility size. Example: large electrical service supplying a small government office building.
7. Deliveries are mismatched to presumed facility use. Example: 40 foot refrigerated truck, or medical supply truck unloading at social security office.

8. Facility location is inappropriate for presumed use or function. Example: social security office located in an industrial district.
9. Facility construction and/or layout is inappropriate for presumed use. Example: office building with oversized warehouse style loading dock.
10. Facility staff size and/or type is inappropriate for presumed facility use or function. Example: large ratio of managerial personnel (business suites) to clerical personnel.

The above list is far from exhaustive. Rather, the list is intended to illustrate what sort of details should be examined to *uncover a rabbit hole*. As can be seen from the list, many clues involve some activity that does not match the presumed use or function of the facility. Other clues involve a mismatch between the physical nature of the facility and its presumed function.

Once a suspected rabbit hole has been located, further observation is required to develop a profile of anomalous activity. Drive by the location at different times of the day and night. Keep detailed records of observations. Enlist the help of individuals who live within sight of the facility to monitor activity.

Does a medical supply truck show up every Tuesday at a social security office? Is there any discernable pattern to the traffic flow imbalance? It is the details that will ultimately confirm the existence of a suspected rabbit hole.

Rural rabbit hole detection

As with urban access points, it will be a mismatch between activity and/or the physical nature of a facility, and it's presumed use or function that will indicate the presence of a rural underground access point. In addition, there are several aspects of rural underground access points that appear to be unique.

Most rural underground access points employ a form of radiated electro-magnet field that functions as a wide area deterrent to birds, rodents, and insects. The purpose of the field being to act as a contamination shield or barrier for the underground access point entrance. Next, since rural underground access points receive less intense public scrutiny, their supporting above ground infrastructure is generally speaking, more blatant.

The presence of a well maintained home with around the clock human supervision of the suspected facility is common feature. These homes will have multiple satellite dishes, and/or radio antennas. Another common feature of rural rabbit holes is the presence of odd alpha-numeric markings on the reverse side of highway traffic signs located near the underground access point.

The following is a list of rural underground access point indicators.

1. A well maintained branch road leading to a little used park or recreational facility.
2. Electrical power lines that are routed near facility, when such routing results in longer line length and/or routing over a natural obstacle (mountain, river, etc.).
3. Electrical power lines or substations much larger than visible local load requirements.
4. Large reservoirs that serve no apparent useful function. Example: not needed for flood control or civilian water supply, or that have larger capacity than is required for presumed function.
5. The presence of truck traffic on rural roads with no known destination, or inappropriate truck types for apparent destination.
6. A public park or recreational facility that is maintained at a level well in excess of other nearby facilities, especially if facility less well known or used than other nearby facilities.
7. Public facility personnel (park rangers, etc.) that are overly nosey and/or suspicious of your activities, especially if personnel occupy the site on a 24/7 basis.

8. Public Park or recreational facility where part of facility is fenced off, or accessed by a gated road, or otherwise made inaccessible to the general public.
9. The presence of inappropriate or unusual structures and/or construction methods. Examples: small cinder block building with an electrical power feed normally used on major office buildings. An unmarked, but well maintained trail in Public Park. An old building (possibly abandoned) with a new door, and expensive lock.
10. People at camp grounds that seem out of place. Example: improperly dressed, or using inappropriate equipment, or having unusual accents (these are people taking a recreational break from underground facilities).
11. Well maintained roads that are not shown on maps, or follow a different route than shown on maps.
12. A noticeable lack of wildlife (birds, small animals, insects, etc.) in a location that would normally support a large wildlife population (see 1.2.4 preface).
13. Any of the applicable indicators listed under urban rabbit hole detection. Example: unbalanced traffic flows, etc.

As with urban rabbit hole detection, this list is far from complete. It is intended to illustrate what sort of indicators to look for, when searching for rural underground access points. Again, all of the techniques employed in urban rabbit hole discovery are applicable to rural underground access points.

However, it must be stressed that rural access point detection and observation is far more dangerous. Not only are there less people to hide your activities, but a larger faction of those people who are present will likely be *rabbit hole* occupants or guardians. Failure to exercise due caution may lead to becoming an unwilling underground guest.

For this reason, the author suggests one or more of the following precautions.

1. Be very discreet in rural underground access point observation.
2. Always inform a trusted friend of your intended destination and expected time of return.
3. When possible, use a group recreational outing as cover for your activities.
4. Spread your observation activities over several months, at random times and days of the week.
5. Assume you are being watched at all times, and act appropriately. i.e. As somebody who is enjoying a day in the park.

Tunnel construction

The techniques used for *covert tunnel construction* are very different than *civilian tunnel construction*. Covert tunnel construction makes use of a boring machine that actually melts earth and rock (by chemical valence disruption), thereby forming a glass like tunnel wall. This has several advantages over civilian tunnel boring methods.

From the perspective of secrecy, the biggest advantage is that little or no waste material (rock, dirt, etc.) is produced by the boring process, thereby alleviating the need for above ground disposal sites. Another advantage is that tunnels can be bored through lose rock, sand, etc. or other locations that would be unsuitable for civilian boring methods (for instance, a river bed). Large underground cavities are also constructed using this technique.

Covert tunnel boring produces several phenomena that are detectable by surface observation. These phenomena are transitory, and will disappear shortly after tunnel completion. However the presence of these phenomena is unmistakable evidence that covert tunnel construction is taking place.

The method used to melt earth and rock employs electro-magnetic energy to disrupt the chemical bonds within the material. This method produces little or no heat as a byproduct of the melting process, and is therefore very stealthy. However it does cause the evaporation of water to take place at an accelerated rate.

Since the method is electro-magnetic, there is a certain amount of "leakage" radiation, and this is detectable by the odd effect it produces on surface water. In particular, the *water will appear to rise from the ground as wisps of steam*, even though the ground is cold. This phenomena is very noticeable during rain storms on cold winter nights. The steam does not rise into the air, as it would if the ground was actually warm, but instead forms a layer just above the surface.

Another side effect of *covert tunnel boring* is a peculiar rippling in road surfaces. This rippling is very slight, and most noticeable while driving at highway speed (55 mph). It is more heard than felt. What sets this ripple apart from normal highway bumps and imperfections is its consistency. Assuming a constant driving speed, the ripple is perfectly constant. In some cases, the rippled road surface will continue for several miles, without the slightest change in pitch or intensity.

The "cold steam" phenomena is only observable while covert tunnel boring is actually taking place. However the "road ripple" phenomena will persist for several weeks after covert tunnel boring is finished. These phenomena are best observed late at night.

Forty trillion dollars

Despite an ever increasing tax burden, the roads and bridges continue to decline, the cities continue to decay, social security and Medicare benefits continue to dwindle. Today with both husband and wife working full time jobs, the American standard of living is less than 1950 when the husband worked, and the wife stayed home.

In 1950, most government buildings were somewhat dilapidated, having a "well used" look about them, while most American homes were modern and well cared for. Today the cities are full of shiny new government office buildings, and many American homes look dilapidated and in need of repair. Government budgets and deficits continue their upward spiral, while the American family is learning how to “make do” with less.

Consumer prices continue to rise and wages continue to fall, as the American dream fades, replaced with the nightmarish specter of advancing middleclass poverty. Inexorably, despite every effort to reverse the trend, American wealth has been systematically stripped from the people, and transferred to the government. Something has gone horribly wrong in America.

For the past several decades, there have been an unbroken chain of government scandals involving over billing and multiple invoicing for items ranging from toilet seats to bombers. Inevitably the media portray these scandals as unscrupulous corporations taking advantage of an inept government bureaucracy.

Sadly these incidents are more pervasive than media reporting indicates, and the truth is far more ominous than mere government incompetence or corporate greed. When the clandestine diversion of tax revenue was no longer sufficient to satisfy the requirements, a second method was instituted. American jobs were outsourced to other countries, thereby allowing the government to repatriate nearly 100% of product and/or service revenue through the foreign purchase of American government bonds.

Since the early 1960s, the American citizenry have been the unwitting victims of government fraud, perpetrated on a scale so vast that it staggers the imagination. When figured in 2004 dollars, the total amount exceeds **40 trillion dollars**. What did the American government and its corporate accomplices do with this almost inconceivable wealth?

The government has *built an entirely new underground civilization* beneath the abandoned factories, tattered homes, and crime ridden streets that litter the American landscape. In this new society, there is no poverty, no crime or illicit drug use. In this new society, healthcare is affordable, energy is free, public transport is efficient. And you, the American tax payer have paid for it all, without receiving any benefit whatsoever for your Herculean efforts.

As to why this monstrous crime was committed against the American people, is the topic for a future paper. Suffice it to say, you will not like the motive, nor the eventual disposition planed for you and your loved ones...

Disclaimer

ALL information contained herein is derived from public sources, widely accepted scientific principles, and/or author's firsthand experience. The author has NO written or verbal agreement with ANY governmental agency forbidding disclosure of the information contained herein. In disclosing this information, the author is exercising his right to free speech as a private citizen of the United States of America.

While the author advocates the discovery and disclosure of the American covert underground infrastructure, NO ATTEMPT should be made to interfere in any way whatsoever with the personnel and/or operations of said infrastructure.

The proper method for achieving discontinuance of these activities is through court ordered injunctive relief.

Path 33: Dulce New Mexico and a Cosmic Conspiracy

John Lear, a captain of a major U.S. Airline has flown over 160 different types of aircraft in over 50 different countries. He holds 17 world speed records in the Lear Jet and is the only pilot ever to hold every airman certificate issued by the Federal Aviation Administration. Mr. Lear has flown missions worldwide for the CIA and other government agencies.

He has flown clandestine missions in war-zones and hot-spots around the world, often engineering hairs'-breath escapes under dangerous conditions.

A former Nevada State Senatorial candidate, he is the son of William P. Lear, designer of the Lear Jet executive airplane, the 8-track stereo, and founder of the LEAR Siegler Corporation. John Lear became interested in the subject of UFO's 13 months prior to the date given below, after talking with a friend in the United States Air Force by the name of Greg Wilson who had witnessed a UFO landing at Bentwaters AFB, near London, England, during which three small 'gray' aliens walked up to the Wing Commander.

Since then Lear has tapped his contacts in intelligence, investigating the allegations that the executive and military-industrial branches of the United States 'government' knows about, and colludes with, alien forces. Lear no longer suggests the following scenario is a 'possibility', he emphatically states that the aliens are here, and that many of them bode us ill.

"It started after World War II," he begins. "We [the Allied forces] recovered some alien technology from Germany—not all that they had; some of it disappeared. It appears that sometime in the late '30s, Germany recovered a saucer. What happened to it we don't know. But what we did get was some kind of ray gun..."

Truth number 1 - 'The sun does not revolve around the Earth'.

Truth number 2 - 'The United States Government has been in business with little gray extraterrestrials for about 20 years'.

"The first truth stated here got Giordano Bruno burned at the stake in AD 1600 for daring to propose that it was real. THE SECOND TRUTH HAS GOTTEN FAR MORE PEOPLE KILLED TRYING TO STATE IT PUBLICLY THAN WILL EVER BE KNOWN.

"But the truth must be told. The fact that the Earth revolves around the sun was successfully suppressed by the [Roman] church for over 200 years. It eventually caused a major upheaval in the church, government, and thought. A realignment of social and traditional values. That was in the 1600's.

"Now, about 400 years after the first truth was pronounced we must again face the shocking facts. The 'horrible truth' the government has been hiding from us over 40 years. Unfortunately, the 'horrible truth' is far more horrible than the government ever imagined.

"In its effort to 'protect democracy', our government sold us to the aliens. And here is how it happened. But before I begin, I'd like to offer a word in defense of those who bargained us away. They had the best of intentions.

"Germany may have recovered a flying saucer as early as 1939. General James H. Doolittle went to Norway in 1952 to inspect a flying saucer that had crashed there in Spitzbergen.

"The 'horrible truth' was known by only a very few persons: They were indeed ugly little creatures, shaped like praying mantises... Of the original group that were the first to learn the 'horrible truth', SEVERAL COMMITTED SUICIDE, the most prominent of which was Defense Secretary [and Secretary of the NAVY] James V. Forrestal who jumped to his death from a 16th story hospital window.

William Cooper, a former member of a Navy Intelligence briefing team, insists that Forrestal was in fact murdered by CIA agents who made his death look like a suicide. Based on sensitive documents Cooper claims to have read, two CIA agents entered the hospital room, tied a bedsheet around Forrestal's neck and to a light fixture, and threw him out the window to hang. The bedsheet[s] broke and he fell to his death, screaming on his way down according to some witnesses "We're being invaded!" Secretary Forrestal's medical records are sealed to this day.

"President Truman put a lid on the secret and turned the screws so tight that the general public still thinks that flying saucers are a joke. Have I ever got a surprise for them? "In 1947, President Truman established a group of 12 of the top military scientific personnel of their time. They were known as MJ-12. Although the group exists today, none of the ORIGINAL members are still alive. The last one to die was Gordon Gray, former Secretary of the Army, in 1984.

"As each member passed away, the group itself appointed a new member to fill the position. There is some speculation that the group known as MJ-12 expanded to at least seven more members.

"There were several more saucer crashes in the late 1940's, one in Roswell, New Mexico; one in Aztec, New Mexico; and one near Laredo, Texas, about 30 miles inside the Mexican border.

"Consider, if you will, the position of the United States Government at that time. They proudly thought of themselves as the most powerful nation on Earth, having recently produced the atomic bomb, an achievement so stupendous, it would take Russia 4 years to catch up, and only with the help of traitors to Democracy.

They had built a jet aircraft that had exceeded the speed of sound in flight. They had built jet bombers with inter-continental range that could carry weapons of enormous destruction. The post war era, and the future seemed bright. Now imagine what it was like for those same leaders, all of whom had witnessed the panic of Orson Wells' radio broadcast, "The War of the Worlds", in 1938.

Thousands of Americans panicked at a realistically presented invasion of Earth by beings from another planet. Imagine their horror as they actually viewed THE DEAD BODIES OF THESE FRIGHTENING LITTLE CREATURES WITH ENORMOUS EYES, REPTILIAN SKIN AND CLAW LIKE FINGERS. Imagine their shock as they attempted to determine how these strange 'saucers' were powered and could discover no part even remotely similar to components they were familiar with: no cylinders or pistons, no vacuum tubes or turbines or hydraulic actuators.

It is only when you fully understand the overwhelming helplessness the government was faced with in the late 40's that you can comprehend their perceived need for a total, thorough and sweeping cover up, to include the use of 'deadly force'.

"The cover-up was so successful that as late as 1985 a senior scientist with the Jet Propulsion Laboratory in Pasadena, California, Dr. Al Hibbs, would look at a video tape of an enormous flying saucer and state the record, 'I'm not going to assign anything to that [UFO] phenomena without a lot more data.' Dr. Hibbs was looking at the naked emperor and saying, 'He certainly looks naked, but that doesn't prove he's naked.'

"In July 1952, a panicked government watched helplessly as a squadron of 'flying saucers' flew over Washington, D.C., and buzzed the White House, the Capitol Building, and the Pentagon. It took all the imagination and intimidation the government could muster to force that incident out of the memory of the public.

"Thousands of sightings occurred during the Korean War and several more saucers were retrieved by the Air Force. Some were stored at Wright-Patterson Air Force Base, some were stored at Air Force bases near the locations of the crash site.

"One saucer was so enormous and the logistic problems in transportation so enormous that it was buried at the crash site and remains there today. The stories are legendary on transporting crashed saucers over long distances, moving only at night, purchasing complete farms, slashing through forests, blocking major highways, sometimes driving 2 or 3 lo-boys in tandem with an extraterrestrial load a hundred feet in diameter. (It is alleged that ALPHA or BLUE Teams out of Wright-Patterson

AFB were the ones who were most often mobilized to carry out "crash-retrieval" operations.

"On April 30, 1964, the first communication [occurred] between these aliens and the 'U.S. Government'. (Others claim that there was an even earlier contact-communication in 1954 during the Eisenhower administration.

"During the period of 1969-1971, MJ-12 representing the U.S. Government made a deal with these creatures, called EBE's [Extraterrestrial Biological Entities, named by Detley Bronk, original MJ-12 member and 6th President of John Hopkins University]. The 'deal' was that in exchange for 'technology' that they would provide to us, we agreed to 'ignore' the abductions that were going on and suppress information on the cattle mutilations. The EBE's assured MJ-12 that the abductions [usually lasting about 2 hours] were merely the ongoing monitoring of developing civilizations.

"In fact, the purposes for the abductions turned out to be:

"(1) The insertion of a 3mm spherical device through the nasal cavity of the abductee into the brain [optic and/or nerve center], the device is used for the biological monitoring, tracking, and control of the abductee.

"(2) Implementation of Posthypnotic Suggestion to carry out a specific activity during a specific time period, the actuation of which will occur within the next 2 to 5 years.

"(3) Termination of some people so that they could function as living sources for biological material and substances.

"(4) TERMINATION OF INDIVIDUALS WHO REPRESENT A THREAT TO THE CONTINUATION OF THEIR ACTIVITY.

"(5) Effect genetic engineering experiments.

"(6) Impregnation of human females and early termination of pregnancies to secure the crossbreed infant.

(Note: Or perhaps a better term for it would be a "genetically altered" infant, since there has been no evidence forthcoming that an actual 'hybrid' between humans and the 'EBE' or 'Grey' species has been successful. In other words, the offspring would tend to fall to one side or the other, a 'Reptiloids' or 'grey' entity possessing no 'soul-energy-matrix', or a humanoid being possessing such a matrix or soul although somewhat altered genetically in its outward physical appearance or characteristics.

"The U.S. Government was NOT initially aware of the far reaching consequences of their 'deal'. They were LED to believe that the abductions were essentially benign AND SINCE THEY FIGURED THAT THE ABDUCTIONS WOULD PROBABLY GO ON ANYWAY WHETHER THEY AGREED OR NOT, they merely insisted on a current list of abductees be submitted, on a periodic basis, to MJ-12 and the National Security Council. Does this sound incredible? An actual list of abductees sent to the National Security Council? Read on, because I have news for you...

"The EBE's have a genetic disorder in that their digestive system is atrophied and not functional... In order to sustain themselves they use enzyme or hormonal secretions obtained from the tissues that they extract from humans and animals.

"The secretions obtained are then mixed with hydrogen peroxide [to kill germs, viruses, etc.] and applied on the skin by spreading or dipping parts of their bodies in the solution. The body absorbs the solution, then excretes the waste back through the skin. (Urine is also excreted through the skin in this manner, which may explain the ammonia-like STENCH that many abductees or witnesses have reported during encounters with the grey-type 'aliens'.

"The cattle mutilations that were prevalent throughout the period from 1973 to 1983 and publicly noted through newspaper and magazine stories and included a documentary produced by Linda Howe for a Denver CBS affiliate KMGH-TV, were for the collection of these tissues by the aliens.

The mutilations included genitals taken, rectums cored out to the colon, eyes, tongue, and throat all surgically removed with extreme precision. In some cases the incisions were made by cutting between the cells, a process we are not yet capable of performing in the field. In many of the mutilations there was no blood found at all in the carcass, yet there was no vascular collapse of the internal organs.

THIS HAS ALSO BEEN NOTED IN THE HUMAN MUTILATIONS, one of the first of which was Sgt. Jonathan P. Lovette at the White Sands Missile Test Range in 1956, who was found three days after an Air Force Major had witnessed his abduction by a 'disk shaped' object at 0300 while on search for missile debris downrange. His genitals had been removed, rectum cored out in a surgically precise 'plug' up to the colon, eyes removed and all blood removed with, again, no vascular collapse. From some of the evidence it is apparent that this surgery is accomplished, in most cases, WHILE THE VICTIM, ANIMAL OR HUMAN, IS STILL ALIVE.

(Note: According to former Green Beret commander Bill English, THIS incident was also mentioned in the Above-Top-Secret "GRUDGE / BLUE BOOK REPORT NO. 13" which was never released with the rest of the innocuous and voluminous "Project Blue Book" reports. The "Blue Teams" who were sent on crash-retrieval operations were reportedly working on behalf of the covert branch of the Blue Book operations, and Ufological legend has it that a secret warehouse with multiple underground levels exists at Wright Patterson AFB in Ohio, one which is literally packed with alien craft, hardware, and even alien bodies 'on ice'. Wright Patterson was—and is?—the headquarters of Project Blue Book.

"THE VARIOUS PARTS OF THE BODY ARE TAKEN TO VARIOUS UNDERGROUND LABORATORIES, ONE OF WHICH IS KNOWN TO BE NEAR THE SMALL NEW MEXICO TOWN OF DULCE. THIS JOINTLY OCCUPIED [CIA-ALIEN] FACILITY HAS BEEN DESCRIBED AS ENORMOUS, WITH HUGE TILED WALLS THAT 'GO ON FOREVER'. WITNESSES HAVE REPORTED HUGE VATS FILLED WITH AMBER LIQUID WITH PARTS OF HUMAN BODIES BEING STIRRED INSIDE.

"After the initial agreement, Groom Lake, one of the nation's most secret test centers, was closed for a period of about a year, sometime between about 1972 and 1974, AND A HUGE UNDERGROUND FACILITY WAS CONSTRUCTED FOR AND WITH THE HELP OF THE EBE'S. THE 'BARGAINED FOR' TECHNOLOGY WAS SET IN PLACE BUT COULD ONLY BE OPERATED BY THE EBE'S THEMSELVES. NEEDLESS TO SAY, THE ADVANCED TECHNOLOGY COULD NOT BE USED AGAINST THE EBE'S THEMSELVES, EVEN IF NEEDED.

"During the period between 1979 and 1983 it became increasingly obvious to MJ-12 that things were not going as planned. IT BECAME KNOWN THAT MANY MORE PEOPLE [IN THE THOUSANDS] WERE BEING ABDUCTED THAN WERE LISTED ON THE OFFICIAL ABDUCTION LISTS. IN ADDITION IT BECAME KNOWN THAT SOME, NOT ALL, BUT SOME OF THE NATION'S MISSING CHILDREN HAD BEEN USED FOR SECRETIONS AND OTHER PARTS REQUIRED BY THE ALIENS.

Path 34: Cloning and Other Experiments at Dulce

There is absolutely no doubt that replication of humans is an ongoing process that has a part to play in the manipulation of events on this planet. Hundreds of individuals over the last twenty years have attested to what they have seen, both on alien craft and in underground installations... the synchronicity and sheer weight of corroboration from vastly unconnected sources is damning evidence that this is occurring.

A lot of evidence started to surface in the 1970's. A lot of it seemed to tie-in the idea that political figures have been undergoing a process of duplication. During this process, the individual's responses, memories, and habit patterns are copied from the human to be duplicated.

The original can then be preserved or processed into basic biological components. The clone will then function as the original, except that the entity is under alien control. There is also an apparent minority of cases where the synthetic duplicate's consciousness is directly replaced by an alien consciousness—the walk-in...

Some abductees claim that in some cases the Reptiloids will 'clone' a human body through time-space acceleration and transfer the conscious memory-matrix from the original body and into the replicated body for the sole purpose of 'consuming' the original body along with the emotional-chemical residue or vital energy contained therein—emotional energies which have accumulated through a life-time of emotional expression.

This 'emotional juices' within the physical body is considered a delicacy by these 'energy vampires' in a similar manner as was depicted in regards to the draconian gargoyle-like 'aliens' in the movie 'LIFEFORCE', although this movie admittedly took this concept to the extreme, however the concept of stolen vital-energies giving aliens power to shape-shift their molecular structure like one of the legendary 'wer' creatures did NOT originate from that movie.

Also there is evidence of the post-mortem continuation of the "emotional bodies" of some people who have died under extreme emotional circumstances, where these emotional bodies linger around in the physical area where the traumatic death occurred as emotional 'shadows' imprinted on the atmosphere as 'ghosts' or 'specters'.

These forms of emotional residue seem to also attract various types of malevolent alien and/or astral forms... explaining the often numerous connections which have been found between 'aliens' and 'poltergeist' or 'haunting' episodes. The aliens involved in such scenarios may be physical, nonphysical or as with the case of many of the 'Greys'—malevolent nonphysical entities incarnating or inhabiting physical 'alien' bodies, whether these bodies are equivalent to biogenetically altered reptilians, or synthetic humanoids. - Branton

In a walk-in situation, the alien consciousness could be 'used to' a biological matrix that provided three fingers on each hand, for instance. Having an organic body with five fingers could mean that there would be two fingers on each hand that would not be used normally, if at all. This idea was once expressed in the 'INVADERS' series on television, which was pulled off the air prematurely.

(I would suggest that aside from INVADERS... THE OUTER LIMITS and DARK SKIES are two other series' which are remarkably close to the truth, as some of 'us' perceive it. - Branton).

Roy Thiness, the main character in the show, has had some experiences of his own relative to the theme of the program.

There are other factors that should be looked for. One of them is the EYES. There are three aspects of the eyes that have been mentioned:

[In some cases] one eye is different [darker] than the other, the eyes are bulging [like cow eyes], the eyes depict a blank expression.

This is not to say that people who have this appearance are synthetics, but these are said to be [possible] indicators. Another factor that is said to apply to synthetics is that they do not have a long life span. It is said that they do not function well beyond a couple years; some political figures have been said to have been replaced several times...

"IN 1979 THERE WAS AN ALTERCATION OF SORTS AT THE DULCE LABORATORY. A SPECIAL ARMED FORCES UNIT WAS CALLED IN TO TRY AND FREE A NUMBER OF OUR PEOPLE TRAPPED IN THE FACILITY, WHO HAD BECOME AWARE OF WHAT WAS REALLY GOING ON. ACCORDING TO ONE SOURCE 66 OF THE SOLDIERS WERE KILLED AND OUR PEOPLE WERE NOT FREED.

"By 1984, MJ-12 must have been in stark terror at the mistake they had made in dealing with the EBE's. They had subtly promoted 'Close Encounters of the Third Kind' and 'E.T.' to get the public used to 'odd looking' aliens that were compassionate, benevolent and very much our 'space brothers'. MJ-12 'sold' the EBE's to the public, and were now faced with the fact THAT QUITE THE OPPOSITE WAS TRUE.

In addition, a plan was formulated in 1968 to make the public aware of the existence of aliens on earth over the next 20 years to be culminated with several documentaries to be released during 1985-1987 period of time. These documentaries would explain the history and intentions of the EBE's. The discovery of the 'GRAND DECEPTION' put the entire plans, hopes and dreams of MJ-12 into utter confusion and panic.

"Meeting at the 'Country Club', a remote lodge with private golf course, comfortable sleeping and working quarters, and its own private airstrip built by and exclusively for the members of MJ-12, it was a factional fight of what to do now. PART OF MJ-12 WANTED TO CONFESS THE WHOLE SCHEME AND SHAMBLES IT HAD BECOME TO THE PUBLIC, BEG THEIR FORGIVENESS AND ASK FOR THEIR SUPPORT.

The other part [the majority] of MJ-12 argued that there was no way they could do that, that the situation was untenable and there was no use in exciting the public with the 'horrible truth' and that the best plan was to continue the development of a weapon that could be used against the EBE's under the guise of 'SDI', the Strategic Defense

Initiative, which had nothing whatsoever to do with a defense for inbound Russian nuclear missiles.

As these words are being written, Dr. Edward Teller, 'father' of the H-Bomb is personally in the test tunnels of the Nevada Test Site, driving his workers and associates in the words of one, 'like a man possessed'. And well he should, for Dr. Teller is a member of MJ-12 along with Dr. Kissinger, Admiral Bobby Inman, and possibly Admiral Poindexter, to name a few of the current members of MJ-12.

"Before the 'Grand Deception' was discovered and according to a meticulous plan for metered release of information to the public, several documentaries and video tapes were made. William Moore, a Burbank, California, based UFO researcher who wrote 'The Roswell Incident'—a book published in 1980 that detailed the crash, recovery and subsequent cover-up of a UFO with 4 alien bodies—has a video tape of 2 newsmen interviewing a military officer associated with MJ-12.

This military officer answers questions relating to the history of MJ-12 and the cover-up, the recovery of a number of flying saucers and the existence of a live alien [one of 3 living aliens captured and designated, or named, EBE-1, EBE-2, and EBE-3, being held in a facility designated as YY-II at Los Alamos, New Mexico. The only other facility of this type, which is electromagnetically secure, is at Edwards Air Force Base in Mojave, California]. The officer names as previously mentioned plus a few others: Harold Brown, Richard Helms, Gen. Vernon Walters, JPL's Dr. Allen and Dr. Theodore van Karman, to name a few of the current and past members of MJ-12.

"The officer also relates the fact that the EBE's claim to have created Christ. The EBE's have a type of recording device that has recorded all of Earth's history and can display it in the form of a hologram. This hologram can be filmed but because of the way holograms work does not come out very clear on movie film or video tape. The crucifixion of Christ on the Mount of Olives (this actually took place on the hill

Calvary, not the Mt. of Olives) has allegedly been put on film to show the public. The EBE's 'claim' to have created Christ, which, IN VIEW OF THE 'GRAND DECEPTION', COULD BE AN EFFORT TO DISRUPT TRADITIONAL VALUES FOR UNDETERMINED REASONS.

"Another video tape allegedly in existence is an interview with an EBE. Since EBE's communicate telepathically (via psionic crystalline transceiver-like implants that link the Grays together into a mass collective-hive-mind, an Air Force Colonel serves as interpreter. Just before the recent stock market correction in October of 1987, several newsmen, including Bill Moore, had been invited to Washington D.C., to personally film the EBE in a similar type interview, and distribute the film to the public.

Apparently, because of the correction in the market, it was felt the timing was not propitious. In any case, it certainly seems like an odd method to inform the public of extraterrestrials, but it would be in keeping with the actions of A PANICKED ORGANIZATION WHO AT THIS POINT IN TIME DOESN'T KNOW WHICH WAY TO TURN.

"Moore is also in possession of more Aquarius documents, a few pages of which leaked out several years ago and detailed the super-secret NSA project which had been denied by them until just recently. In a letter to Senator John Glenn, NSA's Director of Policy, Julia B. Wetzel, wrote, 'Apparently there is or was an Air Force project with the name [Aquarius] which dealt with UFO's. Coincidentally, there is also an NSA project by that name.'

NSA's project AQUARIUS deals specifically with 'communications with the aliens' [EBE's]. Within the Aquarius program was project 'Snowbird', a project to test-fly a recovered alien aircraft at Groom Lake, Nevada. This project continues today at that location. In the words of an individual who works at Groom Lake, 'Our people are much better at taking things apart than they are at putting them back together.'

"Moore, who claims he has a contact with MJ-12, feels that they have been stringing him along, slipping him documents and providing him with leads, promising to go public with some of the information on extraterrestrials by the end of 1987.

"Certain of Moore's statements lead one to believe that Moore himself is a government agent working for MJ-12, not to be strung alone, but to string along ever hopeful UFOlogists that the truth is just around the corner. Consider.

"1. Moore states emphatically that he is not a government agent, although when Lee Graham [a Southern California based UFOlogists] was investigated by DIS [Defense Investigative Service] for possession of classified documents received from Moore, Moore himself was not.

"2. Moore states emphatically that the cattle mutilations of 1973-1983 were a hoax by Linda Howe [producer of 'A Strange Harvest'] to create publicity for herself. He cites the book 'Mute Evidence' as the bottom line of the hoax. 'Mute Evidence' was a government sponsored book to explain the mutilations in conventional terms.

"3. Moore states that the U.S.A.F. Academy physics book, 'Introductory Space Science', vol. II chapter 13, entitled 'Unidentified Flying Objects', which describes four of the most commonly seen aliens [one of which is the EBE] was written by Lt. Col. Edward R. Therkelson and Major Donald B. Carpenter. Air Force personnel who did not know what they were talking about and were merely citing 'crackpot' references. He, Moore, states that the book was withdrawn to excise the chapter.

"If the government felt they were being forced to acknowledge the existence of aliens on Earth because of the overwhelming evidence such as the October and November sightings in Wytheville, Va., and recently released books such as 'Night Siege' [Hynek, J. Allen; Imbrogno, Phillip J.; Pratt, Bob: NIGHT SIEGE, Ballantine Books, Random House, New York], and taking into consideration the 'grand deception' AND

OBVIOUSLY HOSTILE INTENT OF THE EBE'S, it might be expedient for MJ-12 to admit the EBE's but conceal the information on the mutilations and abductions.

If MJ-12 and Moore were in some kind of agreement then it would be beneficial to Moore to tow the party line. For example, MJ-12 would say... 'here are some more genuine documents... but remember... no talking about the mutilations or abductions'. This would be beneficial to Moore as it would supply the evidence to support his theory that E.T.'s exist but deny the truths about the E.T.'s. However, if Moore was indeed working for MJ-12, he would follow the party line anyway... admitting the E.T.'s but pooh poohing the mutilations and abductions. If working alone, Moore might not even be aware of the 'grand deception'.

"Time will tell. It is possible that Moore will go ahead and release the video interview with the military officer around the first of the year, as he has promised. From MJ-12's point of view, the public would be exposed to the information without really having to believe it because Moore is essentially not as credible a source as, say, the President of the United States.

After a few months of digestion and discussion, a more credible source could emerge with a statement that yes in fact the interview was essentially factual. This scenario would cushion somewhat the blow to the public. If, however, Moore does not release the tape by, say, February 1 of 1988, but comes instead with a story similar to: 'MJ-12 has informed me that they are definitely planning a release of all information by October of 88... I have seen the plan and have seen the guarantee that this will happen, so I have decided to withhold the release of my video tape at this time as it may cause some problems with MJ-12's plans.' This would in effect buy more time for MJ-12 and time is what they desperately need.

"Now you ask, 'Why haven't I heard any of this?' Who do you think you would hear it from? Dan Rather? Tom Brokaw? Sam Donaldson?

Wrong. These people just read the news, they don't find it. They have ladies who call and interview witnesses and verify statements on stories coming over the wire [either AP or UPI]. It's not like Dan Rather would go down to Wytheville, Virginia, and dig into why there were FOUR THOUSAND reported sightings in October and November of 1987.

Better Tom Brokaw or someone else should risk their credibility on this type of story. Tom Brokaw? Tom wants Sam Donaldson to risk his credibility. No one, but no one, is going to risk their neck on such outlandish ideas, regardless of how many people report sightings of 900 foot objects running them off the road. In the case of the Wytheville sightings, dozens of vans with NASA lettered on the side failed to interest newsmen. And those that asked questions were informed that NASA was doing a weather survey.

"Well then, you ask, what about our scientists? What about Carl Sagan? Issac Asimov? Arthur C. Clarke? Wouldn't they have known? If Carl Sagan knows then he is committing a great fraud through the solicitation of memberships in the Planetary Society, 'to search for extraterrestrial intelligence'. Another charade into which the U.S. Government dumps millions of dollars every year is the radio-telescope in Arecibo, Puerto Rico, operated by Cornell University with - guess who? - Carl Sagan. Cornell is ostensibly searching for signals from Outer Space, a sign maybe, that somebody is out there. It is hard to believe that relatively intelligent astronomers like Sagan could be so ignorant.

(Note: Also, even if 'they' did find evidence of extraterrestrial life, do you think that SETI and similar government-sponsored projects would tell US about it? Let's just take a look at some actual statements from those involved with these projects. The following is a quote from Matt Spetalnick's article "IS ANYBODY OUT THERE? NASA LOOKS FOR REAL ET'S", in REUTERS Magazine, Oct. 5, 1992:

"At least 70 times scientists have picked up radio waves that bore the marks of communication by beings from other worlds, but they were never verified, Frank Drake said." And researcher John Spencer, in a reference to Dr. Otto Strove, tells how this astrophysicist assisted Frank Drake in establishing Project OZMA, and it's very mysterious conclusion: "...the project began its search by focusing on the star TAU CETI. According to claims made at the time, AS SOON AS the project got underway STRONG INTELLIGENT SIGNALS were picked up, leaving all the scientists stunned.

Abruptly, Dr. Strove then declared Project OZMA had been shut down, and commented that there was no sensible purpose for listening to messages from another world." [THE UFO ENCYCLOPEDIA]. So then, these 'insiders' will accept ALL of our hard-earned tax dollars to finance their radio projects—if not their underground bases and covert space operations. Yet cursed be any 'mere mortal' for having the audacity to actually insist on having access to the products of their 'financial investments'!

"What about Isaac Asimov? Surely the most prolific science fiction writer of all time would have guessed by now that there must be an enormous cover-up? Maybe, but if he knows he's not saying. Perhaps he's afraid that Foundation and Empire will turn out to be inaccurate.

"What about Arthur C. Clarke? Surely the most technically accurate of Science Fiction writers with very close ties to NASA would have at least a hint of what's really going on. Again, if so he isn't talking. In a recent Science Fiction survey, Clarke estimates that contact with extraterrestrial intelligent life would not occur before the 21st Century.

"If the government won't tell us the truth and the major networks won't even give it serious consideration (Note: This was written before such programs as SIGHTINGS, ENCOUNTERS, UNSOLVED MYSTERIES, CURRENT AFFAIR, MONTEL WILLIAMS, STRANGE UNIVERSE and other TV news digests and talk shows DID begin dealing with the UFO phenomena, abductions, and so on in much greater depth—not to mention the X-FILES, DARK SKIES and other TV series', then what is the big picture, anyway?

Are the EBE's, having done a hundred thousand or more abductions [possibly millions worldwide], built AN UNTOLD NUMBER OF SECRET UNDERGROUND BASES [Groom Lake, Nevada; Sunspot, Datil, Roswell, and Pie Town, New Mexico, just to name a few] getting ready to return to wherever they came from? Or, from the obvious preparations are we to assume that they are getting ready for a big move? Or is it the more sinister and most probable situation that the invasion is essentially complete and it is all over but the screaming?

"A well planned invasion of Earth for its resources and benefits would not begin with mass landings or ray-gun equipped aliens. A properly planned and executed invasion by a civilization thousands [of] years in advance of us would most likely be complete before a handful of people, say 12?, realized what was happening. No fuss, no mess. The best advice I can give you is this: Next time you see a flying saucer and are awed by its obvious display of technology and gorgeous lights of pure color - RUN LIKE HELL!—June 3, 1988 Las Vegas, NV"

"In 1983 when the Grand Deception was discovered MJ-12 [which may now be designated 'PI-40'] started work on a weapon or some kind of device to contain the EBE's which had by now totally infested our society. This program was funded through SDI which, coincidentally, was initiated at approximately the same date. A frantic effort has been made over the past 4 years by all participants. This program ended in failure in December of 1987.

(Note: British Ufologist Timothy Good claimed that over 22 British scientists—who were working on the U.S. SDI program for British Marconi and other Aerospace companies—had all mysteriously died or 'committed suicide' within the space of a few years. Could this have had anything to do with this 'failure'? Apparently someone 'out there' was intent on sabotaging the SDI / STAR WARS project. Also there are reports that several of our 'defense satellites' have been destroyed as well. - Branton).

"A new program has been conceived but will take about 2 years to develop. In the meantime, it is absolutely essential to MJ-12 [PI-40], that no one, including the Senate, the Congress or the Citizens of the United States of America [or anyone else for that matter] become aware of the real circumstances surrounding the UFO cover-up and total disaster it has become.

"Moore never did release the video tapes but claims he is negotiating with a major network to do so...'soon'." Another source added the following statements in regards to Lear's claims:

"Area 51... and a similar setup near Dulce, New Mexico, may now belong to forces not loyal to the U.S. Government, or even the human race. 'It's horrifying to think that all the scientists we think are working for us [in the joint-interaction bases] are actually controlled by aliens.'

"'...SDI, regardless of what you hear, was completed...to shoot down incoming saucers. The mistake was that we thought they were coming inbound—in fact, they're already here. They're in underground bases all over the place.' It seems that the aliens had constructed many such bases without our knowledge, where they conduct heinous genetic experiments on animals, human beings, and 'improvised' creatures of their own devising.

"Thus was born PROJECT EXCALIBUR. Press reports described EXCALIBUR as a weapons system designed to obliterate deeply-buried Soviet command centers, which the Reagan administration hypocritically characterized as destabilizing. We have exactly similar centers. Lear claims the weapon was actually directed toward the internal alien threat. Unfortunately, the 'visitors' have invaded us in more ways than one.

"'Millions of Americans have been implanted. There's a little device that varies in size from 50 microns to 3 millimeters; it is inserted through the nose into the brain. It effectively controls the person. Dr. [J. Allen] Hynek estimated in 1972 that one in every 40 Americans was implanted; we believe it may be as high as one in ten now.' These implants will be activated at some time in the near future, for some unspecified alien purpose.'"

When Lear was pressed to disclose some of his sources, he stated that his anonymous intelligence informants "go right to the top." He did however mention some of the names in not-so-sensitive intelligence positions from whom he has also gathered information, many of these names may be familiar to veteran Ufologists. These include:

* Paul Bennewitz, director of Thunder Scientific Laboratories [a New Mexico-based research facility with government contract ties], who claims to have gained access to and 'interrogated' an alien computer system via a radio-video-computer setup of his own invention.
* Linda Howe, the television documentarian responsible for STRANGE HARVEST [a program about cattle mutilations], who recieved astonishing 'leaks' from a special intelligence officer, Colonel Richard Doty formerly of Kirtland AFB, a name noted in aerial research circles.
* Robert Collins [code-named 'Condor', according to Lear] who has secured numerous official documents relating to UFOs.
* Sgt. Clifford Stone, premiere collector of UFO related Freedom of Information Act or FOIA documents.
* Travis Walton, professed UFO abductee whose experience inspired the movie FIRE IN THE SKY.

As an interesting follow-up to Lear's article, I we quote here some actual statements made by prominent individuals in regards to the 'UFO' phenomenon:

"In our obsession with antagonisms of the moment, we often forget how much unites all the members of humanity. Perhaps we need some outside, universal threat to make us realize this common bond. I occasionally think how quickly our differences would vanish if we were facing an alien threat from outside this world. And yet, I ask you, IS NOT AN ALIEN FORCE ALREADY AMONG US?"

—President Ronald Reagan., Remarks made to the 42nd General Assembly of the United Nations., Sept. 21, 1987

"I couldn't help but say to him [Gorbachev], just think how easy his task and mine might be in these meetings that we held if suddenly there was a threat to this world from some other species from another planet outside in the universe... Well, I don't suppose we can wait for some alien race to come down and threaten us. But I think that between us we can bring about that realization."

—President Ronald Reagan., Remarks to Fallston High School students and Faculty, Fallston, MD., October 4, 1985

"For your confidential information, a reliable and confidential source has advised the Bureau that flying disks are believed to be man-made missiles rather than natural phenomenon. It has also been determined that for approximately the past four years the USSR has been engaged in experimentation on an unknown type of flying disk."

—FBI Memo, dated March 25, 1949 sent to a large number of FBI offices.

"...on Unidentified Flying Objects... The panel recommends that the national security agencies institute policies... designed to prepare the material defenses and the morale of the country to recognize... and react most effectively to true indications of hostile measures."

—Recommendation of the CIA Robertson Panel on UFOs., January, 1953

"Public interest in disclosure is far outweighed by the sensitive nature of the materials and the obvious effect on national security their release may entail."

—U.S. District Court Opinion in the case of Citizens Against UFO Secrecy vs. the National Security Agency., May 18, 1982

"The sums made available to the Agency may be expended without regard to the provisions of law and regulations relating to the expenditures of Government."

—Central Intelligence Act of 1949

"On this land a flying disk has been found intact, with eighteen three-foot tall human-LIKE occupants, all dead in it but not burned."

—FBI memo from New Orleans Branch to Director, FBI, March 31, 1950 about a disk found in the Mojave desert in January, 1950

"When four sit down to conspire, three are fools and the fourth is a government agent."

—Duncan Lunan

"The flying disks are real."

—General Nathan Twining.

"According to Mr. ...informant, the saucers were found in New Mexico due to the fact that the Government has a very high-powered radar setup in that area and it is believed that the radar [EM beams] interferes with the controlling mechanism of the saucers...each one of the three saucers were occupied by three bodies of human SHAPE, but only 3 feet tall, dressed in metallic cloth of a very fine texture."

—FBI Memo from agent Guy Hottel., Washington Field Office., sent to Director, FBI., March 22, 1950

"I WOULD SAY THAT WE KNOW OF SEVERAL, SHOULD WE SAY, INTERGALACTIC FIGHTS THAT HAVE TAKEN PLACE—DOGFIGHTS."

—United States Army Sgt. Clifford Stone, Roswell N.M. Station.

"He believes that because of the developments of science all the countries on earth will have to unite to survive and to make a common front against attack by 'people' from other planets."

—Mayor Achille Lauro of Naples, quoting General Douglas MacArthur in the NEW YORK TIMES, Saturday October 8, 1955. p.7

Path 35: What is going on in underground mega-complex below Dulce, New Mexico

Edward Snowden is a computer specialist, a former Central Intelligence Agency (CIA) employee, and former NSA/CSS contractor who disclose classified documents to several media outlets in late 2012 and was granted temporary asylum in Russia in 2013 after his designation by the Obama regime as the, "most wanted man on earth."

Edward Snowden revealed documents providing incontrovertible proof that an alien/extraterrestrial intelligence agenda is driving US domestic and international policy, and has been doing so since at least 1945. Former Canadian defense minister Paul Hellyer who was given access to all of Snowden's documents by Russian intelligence services and stated Snowden's documents were, indeed, "accurate."

In Snowden's own words, "there are actually two governments in the US, the one that was elected, and the other, secret regime, governing in the dark." Former Canadian defense minister Paul Hellyer appeared on Russia's Today's program SophieCo where he shockingly admitted that aliens have "been visiting our planet for thousands of years" and described several types of these extraterrestrials, including "Tall Whites" who are working with the US Air Force in Nevada.

The "Tall Whites" (further revealed by Defense Minister Hellyer as noted above) are the same extraterrestrial alien race behind the stunning rise of Nazi Germany during the 1930's. At the end of the 1930's, when Nazi Germany possessed just 57 submarines, over the four years of World War II it built 1,163 modern technologically advanced submarines at its dockyards and even put them into operation.

Snowden's documents further confirm, this report says, the "Tall Whites" (Nordic) meetings in 1954 with US President Dwight D. Eisenhower where the "secret regime" currently ruling over America was established. The "Tall White" agenda being implemented by the "secret regime" ruling the United States calls for the creation of a global electronic surveillance system meant to hide all true information about their presence here on earth as they enter into what one of Snowden's documents calls the "final phase" of their end plan for total assimilation and world rule.

Hellyer's interview with Russia Today, where he said extraterrestrial beings are amongst us and if we down at least one UFO, we'll be facing an interstellar war, and that Apollo astronaut, Edgar Mitchell, told him there were something around two and twelve spices of aliens visiting the Earth, and that the aliens have provided people in the American government with military technology.

A February 1957 report by Reuters and Washington Post went so far to say that the Nazi Germany developed flying saucers that flew 1,000 miles an hour to invade the US.

Aliens are working with the US at "A large underground genetics laboratory thought to be located just outside of DULCE, a tiny town in the midst of the Jicarilla-Apache Indian Reservation located about 95 miles northwest of Los Alamos and 100 miles east of [the] sinister-sounding Highway 666, the only stretch of highway in the U.S. with that designation and the only highway that links the four states of Arizona, New Mexico, Colorado and Utah.

"Perhaps it may just be a pure 'coincidence' that this highway—befittingly named Highway 666, which originated in southeast Arizona and goes up north—cuts into northwestern New Mexico, right near the Four Corners area, an area that happens to have one of the most consistently concentrated UFO sighting reports in the country since around 1947.

This entire Four Corners area, especially northwestern New Mexico and southwestern Colorado [even extending, for that matter, to the entire southern tip of the state] also has had some of the most concentrated reports of unexplained cattle mutilations in the nation during the late seventies and early eighties. Was something covertly taking place in those areas?

Collaboration and interaction between the alien infiltrators AND the human collaborators are taking place... for instance areas such as the underground 'joint-interaction' bases of Neu Schwabenland, Antarctica; Pine Gap, Australia; Alsace-Lorraine Mts. area of France-Germany; and of course and probably by far the worst of all, the underground mega-complex below DULCE, NEW MEXICO where the worst life-forms this universe has to offer seemingly congregate, conceive and carry out their atrocities against their victims—or those who have been taken or abducted to the base permanently—as well as against their implanted-programmed victims beyond the confines of the base who are never-the-less forced to exist in 'psychological' concentration camps imposed on them against their will by the 'collaboration'.

Dulce, New Mexico harbors a deep, dark secret. That secret is said to be harbored deep below the tangled brush of Archuleta Mesa. That secret involves a joint government-alien biogenetic laboratory designed to carry out bizarre experiments on humans and animals. Dulce Base as a "secured facility for tending bio-forms of all types. It is a private subterranean bio-terminal park, with accommodations for animals, fish, fowl, reptile, and mankind.

Dulce, New Mexico has been the epicenter for nearly every form of paranormal activity one can imagine, including: UFO sightings, UFO landings, Abductions, Implantation's, Human & Animal mutilations, PSI Warfare studies, Secret Government-Alien interaction, U.S. 'Constitutional' Government vs. Alien Agenda conflicts, 'Reptilian' sightings, Cryptozoological or Bioengineering phenomena [this was the general area where the famous 'Cabbit', the half cat / half rabbit was captured], Underground bases, Conspiracy scenarios, Alien Infiltration, Deep-Cavern phenomena, Super High-Tech activity, & MIB encounters.

In fact a higher CONCENTRATION of such activities has been evident in the vicinity of Dulce than any other area in the world, to the point that the inhabitants of this town have for the most part resigned themselves into acknowledging—although not necessarily accepting—the reality of such activity, whether they like it or not.

There are basically three alien networks at work on earth: The Anti-Grey Nordic [Federation] factions, the Anti-Nordic Grey [Empire] factions and the Nordic-Grey collaborators, which would also include those Terran intelligence agencies and occult lodges who are involved in the collaboration for whatever motive. Even within the collaboration, there is a great deal of struggle over whether the humanoid or Reptiloids agendas should have the upper hand.

Within the collaboration itself 'speciesism' [akin to racism] exists at certain levels, so in spite of the species prejudices the collaboration continues nevertheless because of a 'marriage of convenience'. In other words the Greys want to take over the planet and impose a slave society to ultimately serve their empire, but they need the Illuminati's international economic connections to do so; and the Illuminati wants the same thing but they realize that they need the alien mind-control and abduction technology to accomplish their goals.

They collaborate in order to set up a planetary government, however both the humanoids and Reptiloids are constantly plotting for the time when the world government arrives so that once it is established they can move-in and take full control and expel the necessary collaborators—the humans doing away with the Greys or the Greys doing away with the humans or whatever the case may be.

For instance the Illuminati might negotiate with the Greys while at the same time develop SDI weapons to potentially use against them. On the other hand the Greys may continue negotiating with the humans while at the same time implanting micro-electronic mind-control devices in the human agents with whom they negotiate in order to ensure that they remain under ALIEN control once the planet succumbs to the New World Order. So a one world government will NOT bring peace to the planet, it will merely be a matter of fighting for control of one super-government rather than for many smaller ones.

The Sept. 10, 1990 issue of 'UFO UNIVERSE' related the following under the title-heading, "WILLIAM F. HAMILTON III—UFOLOGY'S 'MYSTERY MAN' TO REVEAL 'COSMIC TOP SECRETS. Hamilton warns there is a massive government cover-up on UFOs and alien visitations that reaches right up to the president's private office door and the U.S. military has made a secret pact with the 'Greys'. [They] are on earth... mutilating cattle, and abducting humans for experimental purposes. Supposedly the Greys have TAKEN OVER several Top-Secret underground military facilities, AND certain branches of the government [who] are working hand-in-hand with these entities to bring about total domination of the world, while a SECOND group of extra-terrestrials "Tall Whites" are here trying to protect us...

MIND CONTROL' IMPLANTS Some mystics may refer to alien intelligence's that possess human minds as 'walk-ins'. What many refer to as 'walk-ins' are often artificial intelligence matrix implants which are attached to the nerve centers of the human brain. These serve as 'nodes' for an alien collective in a parasite-host capacity, allowing the aliens to physically utilize the human subject after an altered state of consciousness has been induced, and the human subject's individual consciousness is incapacitated.

In light of these revelations, it is very alarming to think of the large number of people who are reported missing each year. The following is the statistics over the years of people reporting missing by the FBI National Crime Information Center from 1990 to 2015:

Path 36: Probing Deeper Into the Dulce 'Enigma'

The following information on subsurface anomalies and the *Dulce* base was compiled by researcher and explorer John Rhodes: Legends from different parts of the globe all tell of an <u>underworld inhabited</u> by mystical beings of varied forms. I believe that the *reptilian* [*race*] still resides to this day underground. Hidden away in the dark crevices of the *Earth* and in the depths of the oceans. The evidence supporting this proclamation is also available through recent reports and historical documentation...

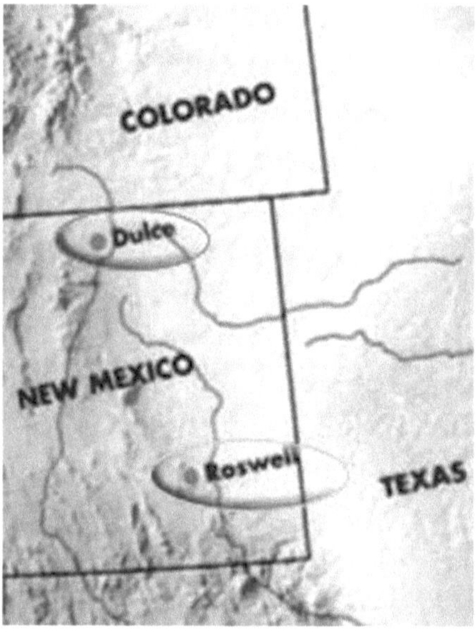

I the early 1960's, a subterranean nuclear blast occurred about 30 miles southwest of *Dulce*, New Mexico right off U.S. 64. This nuclear blast was conducted under the umbrella of *project Plowshare*, and was named *Gassbuggy*.

It has recently been alleged that this particular subsurface nuclear blast was used to create a hollowed out chute or chimney for development of a substation for a super-secret tunnel system attached to an underground *black book project* base.

According to the infamous **Thomas Castello** - a former *Dulce* base security technician - this particular under-world city is a highly secret base operated by humans as well as *reptilian aliens* and their worker cast, the commonly encountered *grays*. It is here, apparently, that a multitude of experimentation projects are carried out. Primarily genetic experiments on kidnapped men, women, and children.

There are a myriad of other specialty science projects taking place at the *Dulce* base including, but not limited to:

- o Atomic manipulation,
- o cloning,
- o studies of the human aura,
- o advanced mind control applications,
- o animal/human crossbreeding,
- o visual and audio wiretapping,
- o the list goes on...

Dulce, New Mexico is a strange place indeed. It's a sleepy little town perched upon the *Archuletta Mesa*, just south of the Colorado border in northern New Mexico.

Archuletta Mesa

Tourists passing through sometimes see little more life in the town other than that of a scruffy dog lazily spread out along side of the dirt road. Some claim that upon entering the town, black vehicles with heavily tinted windows tailgate them until they are outside the city limits and "heading out of Dodge"!...

In addition, several other sources, who wish to remain nameless, reported oddities in their work with operation 'Plowshare' during the 1960's. The project was created under the guise of the use of atomic bombs during peacetime, and forged ahead under the umbrella of "Natural Gas Exploration". In fact, several of these multi-kiloton blasts were used as a rapid way of developing huge sub-surface chambers for facility development. It is reported that the technology to clean radiation is available and already in use for such projects.

When I lectured on Friday, August 13th of 1993 in Las Vegas, I made public, for the first time ever, the floor plans to levels one and six of the *Dulce Base*. These floor plans were reproduced from the originals that were handed to Thomas Castello's friend. This friend did not previously release the floor plans because they were being used as a verification device to the claims of abductees that say they were there. To date, the originals have verified and disproved many stories circulating the field of *ufology*. This friend of Thomas Castello's, however, believes that it is time to begin [to] reveal the missing pieces...

The *Dulce* base *floorplan* was illustrated as per the originals by Thomas Castello and I released it... during my lecture in Las Vegas, Nevada. Its layout, when inspected carefully, appears to be extremely strategically planned.

From a vertical viewpoint, it resembles a wheel with a central hub and corridors radiating outwards like spokes. This 'hub' is the focal point of the entire base. It is surrounded by central security and extends through all levels of the base.

I believe this core to be the *Achilles heal* of the entire facility. It probably contains fiber optic communications and power lines. This would justify its highly guarded and central location as well as explain its vertical continuation through all levels. With all communication lines and power lines focused towards the hub, it is possible that any one level could be completely "locked down" by its own security or the security hubs from either above or below its own level. This would provide maximum control over the entire facility.

The 'spokes' or corridors radiating away from the central hub, lead to numerous other labs in five different directions. Connect the spokes and a pentagon is revealed in its design. From above, this base resembles the layout of the *Pentagon* in Washington D.C. complete with halls, walls and military insignias! Since we do not have the exact heading on its corridors, magnetic alignments are impossible to determine.

When viewed laterally, its appearance takes on the look of a tree with a trunk at its center and its floors extending outwards like the branches. If this is a facility of science, then one could easily say that its lateral appearance is like that of the *tree of knowledge.*

(Note: The original Hebrew word for the tree of "knowledge" is "Dah'ath", or "cunning". It was the 'tree' where, according to Judeo-Christian accounts, the original 'serpent' convinced Eve to take part in a rebellion against the Almighty by promising her and Adam godhood. By accepting this false gospel of self-deification, so Genesis claims, Eve AND her husband who was WITH HER at the time, joined in the rebellion. Since they saw themselves as potential gods, they no longer 'needed' to depend on the Almighty as their Source, and once the flow from the SOURCE was broken the perfection that the world once knew was destroyed, as humankind - and in fact all of nature - began to turn 'wild'.

In light of all of this, could the DULCE BASE be the modern TREE OF KNOWLEDGE [cunning], where the seed of the SERPENT and the seed of EVE have once again met in an unholy alliance, yet in a much more sophisticated form? In THIS case the "serpent" would be the GREYS, and the "forbidden fruit" would be the OCCULT-TECHNOLOGY that is being offered BY these demon-possessed beings to humans "elite" who are intent on "playing god" over their fellow man! Could it be that the Edenic scenario NEVER ENDED, but instead HAS BEEN and WILL KEEP ON REPEATING ITSELF OVER AND OVER until the "seed of Eve" once-and-for-all say "ENOUGH IS ENOUGH", and basically tell the serpent exactly where it can go!? - Branton). Was this purposely designed this way or does it just happen to be a coincidence?

The overall design of this facility reminds one of a multi-stacked subterranean *Hopi Indian kiva*. Although I believe that it's somewhat of a disservice to the *Hopi* to even be spoken of in association with a cave of horrors like the *Dulce* base, its similarity in design should not be forgotten.

As cultures around the world tend to bring their own styles of architecture with them during periods of migration, so perhaps did the advanced civilization that *'originally'* built [the] *Dulce Base.* If the *reptilian* influence over man is as great as archaic documentation and myth would have one believe, then there have to be other subterranean dwellings similar to this in other locations...

(Note: The following are some additional facts and comments, concerning the late Thomas Edwin Castello, which are not mentioned elsewhere in this work. These have been 'paraphrased' from the research files of John Rhodes. - Branton):

In 1961, Castello was a young sergeant stationed at *Nellis Air Force Base* near Las Vegas, Nevada. His job was as a military photographer with a top secret clearance.

He later transferred to West Virginia where he trained in advanced intelligence photography. He worked inside an undisclosed underground installation, and due to the nature of his new assignment his clearance was upgraded to *TS-IV.*

He remained with the Air Force as a photographer until 1971 at which time he was offered a job with *RAND Corporation* as a Security Technician, and so he moved to California where *RAND* had a major facility and his security clearance was upgraded to *ULTRA-3*. The following year he met a woman named Cathy, they married and had a son, Eric.

In 1977 Thomas was transferred to Santa Fe, New Mexico where his pay was raised significantly and his security clearance was again upgraded... this time to*ULTRA-7.* His new job was as a photo security specialist in the *Dulce* installation, where his job specification was to maintain, align and calibrate video monitoring cameras throughout the underground complex and to escort visitors to their destinations.

Once arriving in *Dulce*, Thomas and several other new 'recruits' attended a mandatory meeting where they were introduced to the *BIG LIE*, that:

> "...the subjects being used for genetic experiments were hopelessly insane and the research is for medical and humane purposes." Beyond that, all questions were to be asked on a need to know basis.

The briefing ended with severe threats of punishment for being caught talking to any of the '*insane*' or engaging in conversations with others not directly involved with one's current task. Venturing outside the boundaries of one's own work area without reason was also forbidden and, most of all, discussing the existence of the joint *Alien/U.S.* government base to any outsider would generate severe and, if necessary, deadly repercussions.

Thomas did his job as his superiors demanded. At first his encounters with actual *gray* and *reptilian* beings in the base were exhilarating, but soon he became acutely aware that all was not what it appeared to be.

Thomas slowly began to sense that there was an underlying current of tension existing between some of the personnel and himself. Once in a while he would walk around the corner, interrupting serious discussions between coworkers and, as Thomas was a security officer, these talks would die off into a short murmur and individuals would part company.

One particular part of his job was to go into various areas of the base and align the security monitoring cameras when it was necessary. This afforded him the opportunity to venture out and witness things that would stagger the imagination.

Later he was to report seeing laboratories that investigated the following:

- Auraic energy fields of humans;
- Astral or spirit-body voyaging and manipulation;
- Psi studies;
- Advanced mind control analysis and application;
- Human brain memory recognition, acquisition, and transfer;
- Matter manipulation;
- Human/alien embryonic cloning;
- Rapid human body replicating by use of energy/matter transfer [complete with an individuals memory from the computer memory banks] and other scientific advances.

Once in a while Thomas would see some of the horrifying genetic creations that were housed in separate sections of the base.

These, he knew, couldn't have had anything to do with mental illness or health research. Thomas didn't want to look any further. For every time he discovered more pieces to this underground maze, it became more and more overwhelming to accept. His curious mind, however, implored him to search for the truth regardless of his own desire to turn away in horror.

One day, Thomas was approached by another employee who ushered him into a side hallway. Here he was approached by two other gentlemen that whispered the most horrifying words... the men, woman AND CHILDREN that were said to be mentally retarded were, in fact, heavily sedated victims of *ABDUCTION.*

He warned the men that their words and actions could get them in big trouble if he were to turn them in. At this, one man told Thomas that they were all observing him and noticed that he too was 'uncomfortable' with what he was witnessing. They knew that Thomas had a conscience and they knew they had a friend.

They were right, Thomas didn't turn them into his commanders. Instead, he made the dangerous decision to quietly speak with one of the caged humans in an area nicknamed *"Nightmare Hall"*. Through their drug induced state, he asked their name and their home town. Thomas discreetly investigated the claim of this ‹insane› human during his weekends out of the facility.

He discovered through his search that the person had been declared missing in their home-town after vanishing suddenly, leaving behind their traumatized families, who followed dead ends and trailed flyers.

Soon he discovered that MANY of the hundreds, perhaps thousands of men, women and children [from ALL AREAS OF THE WORLD] were actually listed as missing or unexplained disappearances. Thomas knew he was *IN OVER HIS HEAD* and so were several of his co-workers. All he could do, until somehow the situation changed, was to be alert and extremely guarded with his thoughts. The *gray aliens*' telepathic capabilities allowed them to 'read' the minds of those around them and if he revealed his intense anger, it would be all over for him and his new friends.

In 1978, tensions within the *Dulce* base were extremely heightened. Several security and lab technicians began to sabotage the genetic experiments. Increasingly frail nerves and paranoia finally erupted into what is commonly referred to as the *Dulce Wars.*

It was a literal battle between the *reptilians* and the humans for the *CONTROL* of the *Dulce base*. It was the *reptilians* more than the humans that were pushing the *"Big Lie"*, and insisted on using humans in their experiments, AND those who did not survive the experiments [were used] as ‹*sources*' for the liquid protein tanks which '*fed*' both embryonic *gray* fetuses as well as full grown grays, as a source of nourishment.

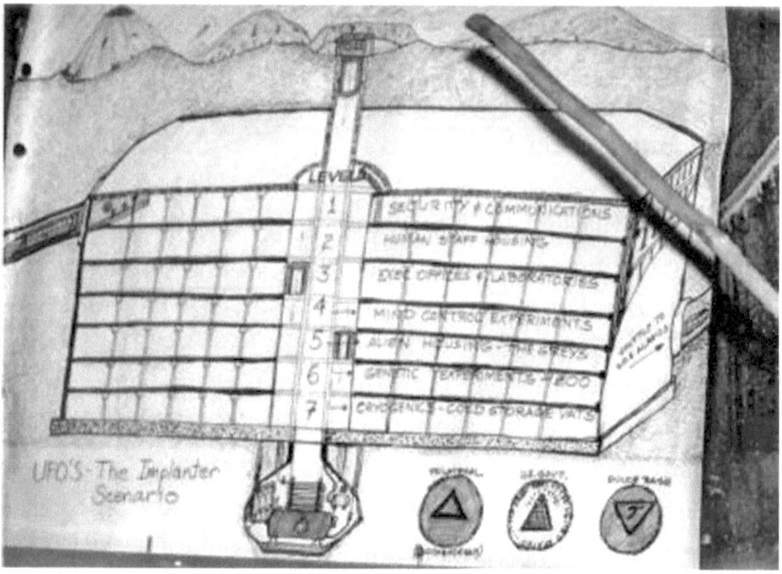

Dulce Levels and Symbols

No one is exactly sure how it started, but we do know through Thomas' account that it involved the [base] SECURITY FORCES armed with beam weapons known as "*Flash Guns*", machine-gun toting [U.S. Military] personnel, and the *Gray alien species* (who had apparently tried to turn the base security forces and U.S. Military forces against each other. - *Branton*).

When the smoke cleared, sixty-eight humans had been killed, twenty-two were completely vaporized and nineteen escaped via the tunnels. Seven were recaptured and twelve remain in hiding to this day. Thomas Returned to his post awaiting the planning of his own escape.

(Note: It is not known just exactly how many grays were killed in the conflict, but it is obvious that the human security personnel were far outnumbered by the aliens since literally thousands of grays worked in the lower levels of the Dulce base, according to Castello. There are indications that the 'spark' may have occurred when many of the scientists within the lower levels - who had learned about the "Grand Deception" of the aliens and their LIES concerning the abductees - were captured by the Reptilians and apparently confined deep within peripheral bases underneath the Ute Mountains of SE Colorado and SW Utah.

A few others apparently escaped and told those in the upper levels what was happening below. The Grays/Reptiloids could not afford to let escape the fact that they had VIOLATED the treaty with MJ-12, and in fact had been violating it ALL ALONG with NO INTENTION whatsoever to keep it. They had hoped that the humans would not become wise to their "Trojan Horse" operation until they were able to infiltrate the planet more completely.

At least 100 special forces were sent in by superiors who were ignorant of the whole picture in an effort to rescue the scientists and maintain order and control of the base, however the aliens - who far outnumbered and out-teched the human forces - managed to kill 66-68 of them. - Branton)

In 1979 the intense pressure that was brought upon Thomas in his job finally made him break the code of silence. He told his best friend, by a hand passed note that he was working in a sub-surface, huge installation outside of *Dulce*, New Mexico.

He told his friend that he was working side by side with *Gray aliens* that consider themselves *native Terrans* and that the upside-down black triangle with the inverted gold colored T inside it was the *insignia of the project.*

Thomas knew that he had to leave the job for his own peace of mind, however now that he knew the truth about the abductees being held below, it would be almost impossible to live a 'normal' life. He would always be under observation and threat until the day he died. He also was aware of the fact that old age may not be his downfall. His demise could easily be expedited by certain individuals.

After one of his weekends away from the facility, he decided to return to work. This time through one of the less guarded air shafts, unannounced and into the base by way of secret passages. Once inside, he preceded to appear as if he was working his normal duties while taking charge of every thought as he passed by *Grays.*

During this time inside the base, he removed still photographs of the facility and treaties signed, with authentic signatures, between California Governor Ronald Reagan, several other individuals and the *Grays.* Thomas also managed to retrieve a 7 minute black and white surveillance video of genetic experiments, caged humans, *Grays,* as well as schematics of *Alien* devices and complex genetic formulas.

These items, he felt, were not only his chance to a seat at the bargaining table when the need arose, but also they were things that the public needed to know about. He made copies of the films, photos and paperwork, packed several 'packages' and instructed several different people who he trusted explicitly to bury or hide them until the right time.

He was then made aware through certain sources that his wife, Cathy, and son, Eric, had been forcibly taken from their home to an undisclosed underground facility for 'safe holding' until he decided to Return with the items. At this point, he knew that even IF he did return everything to the *Dulce* commanders, that his wife and son were probably NEVER going to be the same again [if returned at all] after being manipulated by aggressive mind control.

He also knew that he AND his family would most DEFINITELY become permanently missing due to some tragic accident. Thomas was at zero option. He quickly dissolved into a lonely life on the run. From state to state, border to border, motels to sofas. Always looking behind him and trying his best to look ahead...

Further notes from John Rhodes:

During this initial period of evasion, Thomas was able to relay quite a bit of information about what was happening behind-the-scenes and what plans were being made by the government (that is, the fascist-corporate elements within the 'Executive-Intelligence-Industrial' government such as the *NSA's*, *MAJI* and *AQUARIUS agencies*, which had re-established the collaboration two years following the cessation of official human interaction following the *Dulce* wars. - Branton) and the *Grays*.

Some of it has been withheld by his closest friends as a control device in order to authenticate or invalidate some abductees' stories and researcher's findings. Believe me, there are some very well-known people who make a living from selling this type of information and they have been lying through their teeth about their 'experiences'.

(Note: Are some of these false accounts given within THIS volume? I do not know, and as I stated at the beginning of this work I am not excluding ANY information source - although I may have my own 'opinions' on certain information such as with the Phoenix Project 'research'. However, I have decided to THROW IT ALL out on the table for all to see, and will allow the future to make its own judgments. Even if one or a few of the accounts are misleading, the odds that ALL of the combined accounts within this volume are false would defy the laws of probability.

Perhaps the only way to tell for certain would be to do as the unsung hero Paul Bennewitz suggested - that is to make a full-scale military assault on the base, conquer the aliens whether they be genetic creations or true aliens or both, and bring all activities there under full Congressional oversight. I›m sure that there will be no lack of potential military recruits for this type of assault, after all tens of thousands of young American men have in the past been sent off to die to protect CIA drug-running operations in the Golden Triangle, to give their lives for the United Nations' "New World Order", or in wars that were never meant to be won.

I should however in all fairness state that in the Korean and Vietnamese wars there was a very real threat in the form of Communism, and many young men bravely fought and died in the defense of freedom. However their patriotism and hopes of victory were often sabotaged by Communist sympathizing Socialist U.N. officials or by covert drug operations or other hidden agendas.

In other words if we have fought wars in the past against the 'tentacles' of the beast, so-to-speak, then I see no reason why potential recruits would shy away from a battle against the 'head' of the Beast itself, especially when we consider that such a battle or war might ultimately have galactic ramifications.

One of the problems with the "Dulce Wars" was that only 100 Special Forces with high-level security clearances were unknowingly sent-in to a base inhabited by over 18,000 Greys. 44 of these reportedly survived the firefight - which considering the opposition was a very good survival rate.

However with the latest developments in military technology, with the current 'civilian intelligence' on the base which exists now thanks to Paul Bennewitz and others, and with the millions of American Christian Patriots who would no doubt be willing and ready to wage a HOLY WAR against the entrenched Draconian COLLECTIVIST forces on earth... the next military assault on the DULCE BASE will not be so one-sided. - Branton)

He [Thomas Castello] hopes that you find this information interesting and noteworthy. We feel that it is imperative to release more information because of the stepped-up abduction activities. If you should ever be inquisitive enough to try and do a field investigation of Dulce yourself, then you had better prepare and prepare well!... Do not treat [this] information lightly.

Thomas Castello, the former *Dulce Base* security technical [officer] and a personal friend of two *OZ team* members, may have given his life in order that someday the world may see the truth about the existence of the *Dulce* facility in which he worked [Thomas has not made regular visits to any of his known ‹contacts› for quite some time. Some are fearing the worst...]

Elsewhere within the manuscript released by John Rhodes - from which we have just quoted. - we read the following:

"Obviously, if these *snake-people* or *reptilians* really did once live amongst the *Homo sapiens* population, they have gone to extreme measures not to be revealed since they went into hiding... [However] OUR progression has been carefully monitored by the elusive *reptilian race* that lives within the cavernous *Earth* itself...

"Legends from different parts of the globe all tell of an *underworld inhabited* by mystical beings of varied forms. I believe that the *reptilian* race...still resides to this day underground, hidden away in the dark crevices of the Earth and in the depths of the oceans. The evidence supporting this proclamation is also available through recent reports and historical documentation...

If you really want to see the big show, don›t look above your head, look below your feet!"

Activity in the area of Dulce, New Mexico began almost at the same time as the Roswell crash - 1947. Studies of the area have confirmed that summer troop movements occurred every year after 1947 for quite some time. The construction of a road into the area was done, and trucks went in and out of the town. Later on, the road was mysteriously blocked by the 'military' and destroyed...

Since the initial activity seemed to occur in the same year as several disk crashes, one might wonder why the military would be carrying on a large construction program of this nature, especially since it occurred some 12 years before the famous RAND CORPORATION conference on Deep Underground Construction, which occurred in 1959.

They might have discovered information about the base from analysis of the crashed disks or the reptilian-based entities they found on board. It is possible that this facility was functional earlier than 1947. We do know that the base was made in stages using ALIEN technology. Most everything in the base is controlled magnetically. Even the illumination is magnetically induced.

What we do know is that the upper levels were built AFTER the lower levels. In other words, a U.S. base was built ON TOP OF a pre-existing alien base. This is not the only location where this phenomena has taken place. There are indications that there are situations like this up at the Nevada Test Site and elsewhere. Deep sections of the complex are connected to [extensive] natural cavern systems...

We know that the base consists of a many-leveled cylinder with tunnels radiating out in several [5] directions. There are at least 7 levels. We know [through personnel who have worked there] that the first two or three levels are primarily US government personnel. We know that senators and astronauts have been brought to the facility and have been shown the first [few] levels. The facility appears to be a state of-the-art cryogenics facility and laboratory...

Level 7 is where human children and adults are stored as a source of biological materials. Remember the long ships in the series "V" where all the humans were stored? It's similar to that, but it is more of a production laboratory situation. Humans have been seen stored in clear cylindrical containers over 6 feet in height, suspended in a yellow or amber fluid—alive and conscious but unable to scream or say a word. [This has been] a common observation in this installation as well as in some of the other 26 installations in the Midwestern US [containing similar facilities]...

Biogenetic research gained at Los Alamos, New Mexico was funded under the cloak of secrecy. It was combined with alien technology in the genetic sciences to produce expendable biological entities

for use as the makers see fit. Cloning of humanoids is part of the natural progress of scientific development along the "service to self" lines; that it is going on there is absolutely no doubt. There is also no doubt that political figures in governments have been cloned and reproduced.

(Note: These replicates maintain the same 'surface' memories and identity of the 'original', which are electronically transferred into the clones mind via a mind-computer link, and the clone may or may not contain the original soul-energy matrix. However in most cases the duplicate is heavily implanted electronically in order to connect him/her to the alien collective on a SUBCONSCIOUS level, or on a conscious level IF the body is under the full control of an alien identity, as in the case of the notorious 'walk-in' phenomena. - Branton)

It sounds like the plot from a grade B movie, doesn't it? Well, what is more comfortable for humans to handle in the guise of science fiction is actually based on fact; the main reason that this problem exists to the extent it does is that it is all literally underground and covert.

Although the base actually has more than 100 exit points, including large air intake ducts near Lindrith, these exits and other areas inside the base are covered by cameras. Everything and everyone is watched and monitored.

In 1978, a small group of workers at Dulce discovered the true nature behind the facility and a resistance unit formed; a resistance unit is a touchy thing in a base that was estimated in 1978 to have a population which included over 18,000 alien beings. By late 1979, the situation led to a confrontation over the flash-tube weapons that [alien/human] security forces carried [as opposed to the machine-guns which US government-military forces had to settle for]. A lot of humans were killed. Members of the NRO's Delta Security team were among the casualties...

Known Activities At The Dulce Base

The United States Government has maintained an interest in so-called "disposable biology" humanoids, to perform tasks that it considered too dangerous for humans. With the knowledge gained from work at Sandia and Los Alamos, along with knowledge gained by interacting with alien technology, the 'government' has achieved the ability to produce humanoids for this 'purpose'.

The abilities of the United States Government (although many would argue that it is the Executive-Industrial 'government' rather than the Congressional-Electorate 'government' that is involved - Branton) have been advanced enough [and this has been confirmed by witnesses] to instigate the same clandestine impregnation of human females in order to achieve 3-month hybrid fetuses, which are grown further in labs under alien technology. In other words, the Greys are NOT the only ones doing this to the population of the United States.

The hybrids thus generated are products of DNA manipulation. Implants that function as brain transceivers are also installed, and are controlled through RF transmission [regular radio frequencies]. The network of hybrids was apparently put together by the Defense Advanced Research Projects Agency [DARPA] and include R.H.I.C. [Radio-Hypnotic Intracerebral Control] and E.D.O.M. [Electronic

Dissolution of Memory] type controls, which were developed in the latter half of the CIA/NSA mind control programs of MKULTRA and MKDELTA...

A significant portion of the base is geared toward maintaining the survivability of the alien population. The main focus of these facilities appears to be acquisition and processing of biological materials in order to assure a supply of DNA and other biological materials for production of both aliens and synthetic lifeforms.

Synthetic lifeforms are created with animal based tissue, which can take any form [genetically manipulated], including artificial neural matter. Alien technology permits the withdrawal of memory from a human being and the implantation of that memory in synthetic neural networks; other methods use molecular computers to simulate memory.

The humanoids created by these methods end up being slow and clumsy. They have relatively short life spans, typically about three years—usually shorter. Humanoid lifeforms are also bred with standard human beings, producing hybrid lifeforms—the desired result is to produce self-breeding hybrids to function on the lower end of another Master-Slave game for the alien species. Terrestrial humans are in the middle.

Terrestrial humans are also used for training purposes—to train synthetics—and to train themselves to perform duties imposed by their alien captors. Some humans are kidnapped and completely used—right down to the atomic particles in the matter that forms the body.

Terrestrial humans are also treated with various mind control techniques, such as the Orion method of hypnosis [techno-hypnosis + drugs-chemicals + stress-repetition] and used to spread disinformation or distort information that will lead others astray.

The DNA acquired from animals and humans is altered and used to create lifeforms that grow to adult size in a matter of a few months, allowing for massive reproduction potential. Actual mixing of DNA types to create new lifeforms which are a hybrid between the human and non-human are done inside the fetus that grows inside a manipulated human female.

Conversations Between Researchers

ON SYNTHETICS AND CLONES [Apparently the researcher that Valerian interviewed has remained anonymous]

Q. - In your opinion, do you think any of the material about the use of clones, synthetics and androids is valid?

A. - Yes, there is plenty of evidence that these and other processes are carried out universally in order to permit the housing [or trapping] of consciousness. As far as western culture is concerned, there have been examples that have been shown to the public. For example, on the TV series "The Invaders", the title role was played by Roy Thinnes.

Shortly after Roy had finished reading for the series, two weeks before he was to start filming, he had a UFO encounter himself. It made the whole thing he was doing for the series a lot more real for him. As a result, he began to examine the different ideas presented in the series a little more closely, such as ways that the government eventually forced the series off the air.

These beings that are coming from other frequencies that don't use a physical body but need a physical presence have other beings that have a physical presence generate biological structures that function as containers for them. Biological humanoids.

Through these, their energy fields are manifested. The internal organs would not matter, since they are just energy transitional containers. A lot of what is going on is like super science fiction. The only way a lot of humans can deal with it is through science fiction, because if they have to continually confront that it is real, or what they may have to think or do about it, knowing that it is a fact, it would evoke too much stress.

(I would add that it would probably be closer to a combination of science fiction AND sword and sorcery, or a fusion of the physical with the metaphysical—since the reptil-insectoid Greys especially seem to manifest not only technological powers but supernatural powers as well, or what some refer to as "occult-technology". In this case it is occult technology utilized by "alien sorcerers" capable of attacking human beings on all three levels of their nature—or the spiritual, psychological and physical levels - Branton)

It is easier for most humans to negate reality to a science fiction format so they can manipulate the concepts while at the same time equating the fantasy as a sort of 'protection' against the true nature of reality, which is suppressed by cultural forces in order to maintain organization and pacification in an artificially maintained cultural process of "Be Silent, Consume and Die" in the midst of massive intentional suppression of awareness.

There is consciousness which has manipulated human beings for a long time according to what is, to humans, an alien agenda. The 'game' is deeper and more complex than most humans can imagine; a lot deeper than a few humans having a little disk hardware at S-4...

A lot of the technology discovered since the 1940's has been actively suppressed. There are all sorts of things that can be done to adjust a living being to look like something or someone else. Many hints of the technology have been seen in the media in old [and new] television programs like "Outer Limits" and in films.

There is a lot of truth in many of the old programs. Gene Roddenberry, Trek series ran out. One of them was "GENESIS II", which portrayed United States Government underground genetics laboratories that were connected by tube shuttles. The pilot was never permitted to develop into a series, for obvious reasons.

There are other films that deal with biogenetic clones and still others that portray remotely piloted spherical surveillance objects that are controlled from underground laboratories. All these portray aspects of what has been actually happening.

The early programs in the "Time Tunnel" series portrayed the government having an underground lab that housed the time tunnel equipment. Access was by way of a piece of desert road that dropped down and allowed vehicles to drive underground in tunnels. Fantasy is coming from reality, not the other way around...

Groom Lake, Area 51, And The Nevada Test Site

The Air Force has had a unit at Nellis [AFB] for several years; its name: Alien Technology Center. The first question is, do they think they are studying Mexicans? The center is rumored to have obtained alien equipment (via the Alpha-Blue crash-recovery teams operating out of Wright-Patterson AFB, Ohio? - Branton) and, at times, personnel to help develop our new aircraft star wars weaponry, etc. Yes, I know I sound crazy, but the rumor is awfully solid! The Alien Technology Center is for real.

Something remarkable has caused the Russians to suddenly want to play ball, and I personally believe this could be it. Sure, it sounds strange, but the most advanced known airplane in the world today [SR-71] was secretly flying in 1963-4. Do you really think our best, 23 years later, is the F-16?...

[In reference to the GROOM wars of 1975 and the DULCE wars of 1979, John Lear stated in a Nov. 25, 1989 interview]:

"...I know one of the families of one of the people that was killed—Dr. Gary Henderson, who testified before Congress. He worked for General Dynamics, and in 1979 [the year the Dulce Wars began] he disappeared off the face of the earth. He was involved in that division of General Dynamics which deals with UFOs. We looked for him and found out that he had been attached to a Top Secret detachment that was stationed up at the Test Site. He was one of those 44 scientists [who were killed or captured by the Greys?]. The government has a way of going to families and giving them money to "help them over" their problems...

"Apparently in the late 1960's we made a deal with whoever it was that we would receive highly advanced technology [from] in return for covering up the existence of the aliens and what they are doing. We thought that we would get advanced weaponry that we could use against our enemies, but in fact it turned out that we did get a lot of technology that was non-weapon oriented. These scientists were working at a highly classified facility, and in 1979 they collectively came upon information which indicated that something really bad was going on. What is was, specifically, I do not know. Maybe they found out about the AIDS plan.

It became necessary for the aliens to eliminate these 44 scientists. Whatever it was that happened, 66 Delta troops were sent [to find the scientists] and ended up being killed along with the scientists. The document my friend read was dated 1981, and that's all I know.

(Note: Other sources claim that 100 Special Forces were sent in. Of these, 66 were killed and 44 escaped, and the scientists—an undefined number of them—were not saved. However this was apparently one of several military assaults that have been directed against alien underground bases over the years with varying degrees of success.

Most of the major military actions however seem to have centered around the Dulce base. According to Col. Steve Wilson, director of SKYWATCH INTERNATIONAL, several attempts have been made by certain intelligence agencies to "take out" the Dulce base ever since all but the most die-hard mind-controlled fascist human collaborators were forced out of the base following the beginning of the Dulce Wars.

However all of these efforts to take back control of the base from the aliens have failed. I would personally think that all future attempts will CONTINUE to fail, until American citizens as a whole are allowed to be a part of such an action against this base and in fact the entire "alien underground", and unless such an action has the full and conscious backing of Congress and of the American people. - Branton)

Path 37: The Black Budget and the Underground Empire

If world leaders fear a higher advanced alien race with much greater technology, it does not makes sense to not disclose this presence to the people. Maybe panic of people reacting to facts that we are not alone on this planet is not the reason for non-disclosure. What if a cabal of rich men in Secret Societies have made a deal with ultra-dimensional spirits in control of extraterrestrials to attain advance technology in exchange for human life?

Absolute power corrupts absolutely. The Cabal panics over people's realizing all lies told them from the distant past to present day. The Cabal must answer why technological advancement has been harnessed to megalomaniacal obsessions of securing opulence of the while plotting depopulation of the many. With all the wealth and resources in the world there is no reason for the growing misery of the people and the advancing destruction of the planet.

Beyond the Trans-National banking Cabal's moral shortcoming of producing oppressive measures to hoard wealth, lies a greater fear-filled challenge. In 1939, the banking cabal, controlling Trans-National military industrial complexes, found themselves facing a formidable challenge much greater than refining clandestine means to rob people of wealth.

That challenge has manifested in an alien presence in underground 'joint-interaction' bases of Neu Schwabenland, Antarctica; Pine Gap, Australia; Alsace-Lorraine Mts. area of France-Germany; and of course and probably by far the worst of all, the underground mega-complex below DULCE, NEW MEXICO where the worst life-forms this universe has to offer seemingly congregate, conceive and carry out their atrocities against their victims – or those who have been taken or abducted to the base permanently – as well as against their implanted-programmed victims beyond the confines of the base who are never-the-less forced to exist in 'psychological' concentration camps imposed on them.

There are many Deep Underground Military bases and survival vaults around the world where a cabal of elite Trans-National bankers, businessmen, Monarchs, and Clergy will be evacuated to in case there is nuclear war with extraterrestrials or nuclear wars to quell revolt of the people to the lies continually told to them by governments controlled by secret societies.

Secret deep underground military bases are logical responses to nuclear weapons unleashed in conflict not only with Russia or China, but with a far greater adversary with superior weaponry technology.

So many challenges for humanity from ourselves by failing to harvest our greatest resource of love for each other and from extraterrestrial beings that our government continue to lie to the people about. If people's lives and resources are being used to finance the Military Industrial complex's Secret Space Program where scientists are collaborating with extraterrestrials, why keep joint operations with extraterrestrial undisclosed? The Military Industrial Complex is more of a private industry than government controlled.

NASA has been absolved of control of the Space Program just as the non-government Federal Reserve Bank absolved control of money from Congress. The Military Industrial Complex Secret Space Program and the Federal Reserve Bank are end runs around the Constitution of the United States by a secret society of rich men.

Deception of the people when their life and resources are literally being stole from them is humanity's darkest challenge. What lies equate to is a shadow government secretly building advance weaponry not to protect the people, but from extraterrestrials with more advanced technology. This is madness!

Before we set our military might against an undisclosed foe, let's eradicate the clear and present danger of greedy cabalists who are developing weapons and advancing futuristic concept that the super-rich will enjoy in their in Super Cities, the poor will be constrained to settlement zones just as was depicted in the movie "The Hunger Games." Greed of men is very predictable.

Currently, there are two agendas of business being pursued. I see an exploding population that will reach 10 to 15 billion around the year 2100. Surely, depopulation is in the ruling cabal's top 2. Collusion of Germany with extraterrestrials in World War II set the stage for the second agenda. The second agenda is maintaining the deal with the devil of a powerful civilization of extraterrestrial origin under the ice of Antarctica.

There is a huge network of alien underground installation that world governments refuse to disclose truths of their presence. This has created a whole new paradigm of deceptive lying for greed by a Eugenic minded cabal of bankers conspiring depopulation of the planet with aliens, in the process, trading human lives for technology. This is the real war people should be fighting instead of being pitted against each other by racist propaganda fed us by the elite on their controlled news networks. We are dealing with a formidable enemy while the masses are asleep in darkness of lies.

Human life bartered between the elite and aliens for advance technology. Human intelligence is being silenced by fluoride in the water, Chem trails in the sky, nuclear radiation poisoning our atmospheric rivers and largest ocean, threats of nuclear war, corruption in government, children enslaved to the cabal by student loan debt, and our city's infrastructures crumbling, truths of lies and deception is validated in these unholy acts perpetrated by wealthy individuals we entrust to protect us and save this beautiful planet!

Let's take off the rose colored shades for a clearer more accurate vision of life and shed the shackles of lies and stop living as enslaved consumers and look at a new reality where we are vigilant and no longer content to allow others determine how much freedom we will have.

On Oct. 20, 1991, California researcher Michael Lindemann, founder of 'The 20/20 Group', gave a lecture before a large crowd of interested investigators. During the course of his lecture wherein he discussed the Military-Industrial Complex's underground bases outside of Lancaster, California, he made the following statements:

> "...How many of you have seen the book 'BLANK CHECK'?... It is not a UFO book. I strongly recommend that you read the book 'BLANK CHECK' so that you can understand something about how these projects are funded without your say so, indeed without the say so of Congress. Most citizens don't know for example that the National Security Act of 1947 made it illegal to ever say how much money is spent on the CIA. Indeed all of our tremendous alphabet soup collection of Intelligence Agencies. Whether your talking about the CIA, or the NRO, or the NSA or the DIA, etc., all of them are in the same category.

"You cannot say how much these things cost. All you can do if you want to find out is add-up the numbers on the Budget that aren't assigned to anything that actually means anything. There are these huge categories that have tens of billions of dollars in them that say nothing but 'Special Projects...' And every year the Congress dutifully passes this bloated budget that has some $300,000,000,000 or more with HUGE chunks of cash labeled like that: 'Special Projects,' 'Unusual Stuff.' – Ten billion dollars. O.K., well where does the 'unusual stuff' money go? Well, it DOES go to 'unusual stuff', that's for sure, and one of the places it goes is that it goes into the underground bases. Indeed TIM said recently since the publication of his book [BLANK CHECK]... MORE Black

Budget money goes into underground bases than ANY OTHER kind of work.

"Now I don't believe that 35 billion, which is the approximate size of the black budget money that you can find by analyzing the budget, I don't think that comes CLOSE to the real figure because there is absolutely unequivocal evidence that a great deal of additional money was generated in other ways, such as the surreptitious running of guns and drugs. And one wonderful example of that is coming to light with the B.C.C.I. scandal which I hope you've heard of… a number of very high-ranking American officials are caught in the undertow of the BCCI tidal wave… Even though these guys are trying to pull 'fast ones' on an immense scale they are getting caught. These things don't always work. Indeed they are very, very vulnerable.

Indeed this whole 'end game' is very vulnerable and that's why they feel it requires such secrecy. The American people wouldn't stand for this stuff if they had the information, and that's the reason why we have to get the information out and take it seriously because it really is a matter of our money and our future that's being mortgaged here.

"But my friend who worked in the underground bases, who was doing sheet-rock was down on, he thinks, approximately the 30th level underground… these bases are perhaps 30-35 stories deep ['ground-scrapers']. As I say they are not just mine shafts, these are huge, giant facilities… many city blocks in circumference, able to house tens of thousands of people. One of them, the YANO Facility [we're told… by the county fire dept. director, the county fire dept. chief who had to go in there to look at a minor fire infraction] there's a 400-car parking lot on the 1st level of the YANO Facility, but cars never come in and out, those are the cars that they use INSIDE.

"O.K., so… a very interesting situation down there. Our guy was doing sheet-rock on the 30th floor, maybe the 30th floor, underground. He and his crew are working on a wall and right over here is an elevator door.

The elevator door opens and, a kind of reflex action you look, and he saw three 'guys'. Two of them, human engineers that he's seen before. And between them a 'guy' that stood about 8 to 8 1/2 feet tall. Green skin, reptilian features, extra-long arms, wearing a lab coat, holding a clip-board...

"I tend to believe that story because, first of all because we have other stories like it, but more importantly because he walked off that job that very day. And he was getting paid a GREAT deal of money... If you're basically a sheet-rock kind of guy, if you can do sheet-rock in a place like that then you get paid way more than standard sheet-rock wages, you can count on it.

"So, he walked off that job. His buddy on that same crew turned into an alcoholic shortly after. This is an extremely upsetting thing. You know, it wasn't like this alien jumped out and bit his head off or anything, it was just standing there for a few minutes, the doors closed. He has a feeling that that elevator was malfunctioning, otherwise he never would have seen that except by accident..."

According to former Wackenhut employee Michael Riconosciuto, there is a direct underground connection between the Nevada Military Complex and the underground facilities near Lancaster, California, such as the Tehachapi mountain base. Several people have referred to the subsurface as well as the operational 'connections' between the Dulce base in New Mexico and the Dreamland or Area-51 base in Nevada, connections that exist via Dugway, Utah and Page, Arizona.

If alien forces are intent on taking control of this planet, then it would be logical for them to target our major military weapons research and development centers. This might involve actual 'infiltration' of our military-industrial complexes and control of the line-of-command through mind control of specific and strategic personnel. The 'deeper' one descends into the underground 'alien empire' the greater the security and therefore the greater the 'control' will be in regards to this

"...from the bottom up..." takeover attempt. In many cases patriotic Americans have become caught in the middle of this 'underground war' between loyal American military personnel and alien or alien-controlled 'personnel', as was the case in the Dulce and the Groom wars themselves. Some have managed to escape from their terrifying encounters and – whether intentionally or unintentionally, as in the following incident – have voiced their fears, concerns or even rage to those on the 'outside' who will listen.

The following conversation, in relation to the Nevada Military Complex and the 'underground facilities', took place on the "Billy Goodman Happening" – KVEG Radio 840 AM, Las Vegas, Nevada, on November 19, 1989. It was transcribed by a Las Vegas resident.

Billy Goodman incidentally, has personally planned visits, in collaboration with KNBC Radio in Los Angeles, to observe the 'disks' which are being tested at Groom Lake, Nevada. Goodman and others claimed to have seen these disks in operation, and back-up these claims with video documentation. One such video shows a hovering object making a vertical ascent, stopping in mid-air, followed by a horizontal traverse, followed by another vertical ascent.

Something like this would be impossible for any conventionally known aircraft of the time to duplicate. Billy Goodman, who has since moved to another radio station in Los Angeles, has been very instrumental in getting the information out about the underground base at Site 51 [or Area-51]. One contact of ours has informed us that a good friend of hers in Las Vegas, Nevada, had uncovered some very disturbing facts and testimonies concerning construction workers and others who had been involved in the installation of certain equipment within the tunnels beneath the Nevada Military Complex, and particularly under the Mercury, Nevada area.

Many of these later died under bizarre circumstances, and there were rumors that others were being held captive underground because they "saw too much". This informant, Stacey Borland, was later found dead – along with a brother of hers – in Las Vegas, as the result of a gangland-type execution. Someone had apparently entered her place and murdered them in cold blood.

Path 38: The Secret Shadow Government A Structural Analysis

Underground Bases: A Lecture by Phil Schneider: May 1995

Now, I am very worried about the activity of the 'federal' government. They have lied to the public, stonewalled senators, and have refused to tell the truth in regard to alien matters. I can go on and on. I can tell you that I am rather disgruntled. Recently, I knew someone who lived near where I live in Portland, Oregon. He worked at Gunderson Steel Fabrication, where they make railroad cars.

Now, I knew this fellow for the better part of 30 years, and he was kind of a quiet type. He came in to see me one day, excited, and he told me "they're building prisoner cars." He was nervous. Gunderson, he said, had a contract with the federal government to build 107,200 full length railroad cars, each with 143 pairs of shackles. There are 11 sub-contractors in this giant project. Supposedly, Gunderson got over 2 billion dollars for the contract. Bethlehem Steel and other steel outfits are involved.

He showed me one of the cars in the rail yards in North Portland. He was right. If you multiply 107,200 times 143 times 11, you come up with about 15,000,000. This is probably the number of people who disagree with the federal government. No more can you vote any of these people out of office. Our present structure of government is 'technocracy', not democracy, and it is a form of feudalism.

(Note: I would venture to say that it is more like a techno-monarchy, since several of the U.S. presidents have been placed in office with Rockefeller financial and media backing, suggesting that these same presidential hirelings were inclined to favor certain Rockefeller and in turn International banking agendas. Techno-Monarchy would constitute those parts of the Military-Industrial Complex or M.I.C. that are largely influenced by Rockefeller interests.

According to various sources, the German immigrant Rockefellers are not the "top of the ladder" for the world conspiracy. True, they 'control' much of the eco-political system in the UNITED STATES of America, however they are following the agenda of the Bildeberger cult: the 13 Wicca Masons, 13 Black Nobility, and 13 Maltese Jesuits who have joined together UNDER the covering of the Bavarian Illuminati—which in turn is the modern manifestation of the joint human-alien 'serpent cult' which seems to have had its origins within the ancient underground Masonic systems of Egypt, a cult or collaboration that was brought to Bavaria by the early Germanic Trade Guilds during the height of the so-called 'Holy Roman' [German] Empire - Branton).

It [this 'technocracy'] has nothing to do with the republic of the United States. These people are god-less, and have legislated out prayer in public schools. You can get fined up to $100,000 and two years in prison for praying in school. I believe we can do better. I also believe that the federal government is running the gambit of enslaving the people of the United States. I am not a very good speaker, but I'll keep shooting my mouth off until somebody puts a bullet in me, because it's worth it to talk to a group like this about these atrocities.

America and its technological advances of Transhumanism and Artificial Intelligence, its Hegemon agenda of the Military Industrial Complex, its Secret Space Programs, Deep State Black Projects, reverse engineering of alien technology, or even our government working with aliens in the hundreds of Underground Military Bases yet to be disclosed to the public.

What will be disclosed to the public, what does our government know about aliens in the sea under the ice in Antarctica, what do they know and how long have they known what they know?

There is a reason that 8 out of the top 10 high tech corporations producing aircraft, electronics, engines, artillery, vehicles, missiles, Space Arms, and ship arms resides in America. The Pentagon annual budget of 800 billion dollars a year support high tech weapons of violence. We continue to exports hundreds of billions of dollars in advanced arms that facilitates war and violence around the world.

Recent arms deals with Saudi Arabia in excess of $350 billion seeds instability in the Middle East. How serious are we about peace when we export hundreds of billions in arm in the most volatile region of the world? This is like pouring gasoline on an inferno. Yet we revel in the income from the technical industry. America is an interesting study in moral contradictions.

Those multi-billion dollar corporations are as follows:

Lockheed-Martin (US)
Boeing (US)
BAE (US)
General Dynamics (US)
Raytheon (US)
Northrop Grumman (US)
EADS (Netherlands)
Finmeccanica (Italy)
L-3 Communication (US)
United Technologies (US)

A Lecture by Phil Schneider: May 1995:

I have some interesting 1993 figures. There are 29 prototype stealth aircraft presently. The budget from the U.S. Congress five-year plan for these is $245.6 million. You couldn't buy the spare parts for these black programs for that amount. So, we've been lied to. The black budget is roughly $1.3 trillion every two years. A trillion is a thousand billion. A trillion dollars weighs 11 tons.

The U.S. Congress never sees the books involved with this clandestine pot of gold. Contractors of [these] programs: EG&G, Westinghouse, McDonnell Douglas, Morrison-Knudson, Wackenhut Security Systems, Boeing Aerospace, Lorimar Aerospace, Aerospacial in France, Mitsubishi Industries, Rider Trucks, Bechtel, *I.G. Farben*, plus a host of hundreds more. Is this what we are supposed to be living up to as freedom-loving people? I don't believe so.

This problem of arms and ideas of Transhumanism with artificial intelligence, robotics, and nuclear technology has brought humanity to the point where our biological consciousness and planet is imperiled. Scientist have visions of Interstellar Space travel and many see no alternative to the transcendent technological onslaught.

Are hybrid humans merged with robotics and artificial intelligence the destiny of humanity? In such a world, what is the fate of compassion, love, and the cherished traits of humanism?

One thing is for sure, a country that exports advanced weapons of destruction has placed ideas of peace, democracy, and love for its fellow humanity on the backburner while serving up the deadly concoctions of deadly wars for profit. All of this emanates from the seed of greed of the initial eight powerful families pursuit of wealth and power.

The secret "shadow" government is the large organizational network which operates alongside the officially elected and appointed government of the United States of America. Just as with the official government, the secret government has functional branches.

Just as with the official government, the Shadow Government has functional branches. However, unlike the official government, the purpose of the non-executive branches of the Shadow Government is simply to distribute various functions, but not to achieve a system of checks and balances, as was supposed to happen constitutionally between the executive, legislative and judicial branches of the U.S.

Government. That is because the Shadow Government is a creature of a powerful elite, who need not fear being dominated by an instrument of their own creation.

In the Shadow Government five branches may be identified. These branches are: the Executive Branch, the Intelligence Branch, the War Department, the Weapons Industry Branch, and the Financial Department.

The reporting lines of the Intelligence Branch and the War Department to the Executive Branch are straightforward and obvious. Intelligence exists to provide the Executive Branch with sufficient necessary information to make adequately informed policy decisions. The War Department exists to provide coercive force to carry out Executive policy decisions which could meet with public resistance. The Special Operations units within the Intelligence Branch and War Department exist to carry out policy directives requiring covert action and official deniability.

The Weapons Industry Branch reports to the Executive Branch most often indirectly, through the War Department and/or the Intelligence Branch (for Black Budget weapons systems).

The Financial Department theoretically reports to the Executive Branch for fiscal policy implementation, but de facto also reports directly to the international power brokers who have created the Shadow Government. The Financial Department serves at times directly as their instrument of fiscal policy implementation. An analysis of the overall purposes of these five branches suggests that the overall purpose of the Shadow Government is to exercise covert control by:

Collecting comprehensive institutional and personal information, by establishing national and international policy independently of the established Government, by developing high-tech arms and equipment, and, with these, establishing small, specialized, highly mobile, elite military units to effect these covert policies, when need arises, without having to rely on the official (and "unreliable") Armed Services, (whose subservience to the Shadow Government is reasonably suspect).

By developing an armed capability to repel any threat to the status quo, (including the uncertain ontological, social, and economic impacts of any revelation of the reality of UFO and extraterrestrial presence) through the development of a Star Wars/BMDO ground and space-based surveillance and SDI weapons network.

By denying information compromising to the Shadow Government from all those outside "need-to-know" policy-making levels.

By exercising control on the money supply, availability of credit, and the worth of money, through policy decisions made outside of the official Government.

Executive Branch

Council on Foreign Relations (CFR) includes George Bush, Bill Clinton, all modern CIA Directors, most modern Joint Chiefs of Staff, most modern Cabinet and top Executive Branch appointed officeholders, etc.

Trilateral Commission David Rockefeller, Henry Kissinger, John D. Rockefeller, Alan Greenspan, Zbignew Brzezinski, Anthony Lake, John Glenn, David Packard, David Gergen, Diane Feinstein, Jimmy Carter, Adm. William Crowe, etc.

Bilderberg Group Prince Hans-Adam of Liechtenstein, Prince Bernhard of Netherlands, Bill Clinton, Lloyd Bentsen, etc.

National Security Council (NCS), the military and intelligence policy-making and control group for national and international security, which reports directly to the President, its secret 5412 Committee (which directs black [covert] operations), and its PI-40 Subcommittee (aka MJ-12: which exercises policy direction and control of the UFO Cover-Up).

Joint Chiefs of Staff (JCS)'s Special Operations compartment, the operations directorate which implements the orders of the NSC's 5412 Committee, utilizing the U.S. Special Forces Command.

National Program Office (NPO), which operates the Continuity of Government Project (COG), an ongoing secret project to maintain command, control, communication and intelligence executive centers during an extreme National Emergency by operating clandestine, secure, underground cities staffed by surrogates for above ground national leaders.

Federal Emergency Management Agency FEMA's black projects compartment, which operates federal preventive-detention camps [often located on military bases or Federal Bureau of Land Management lands], secure underground shelters for the elite during cataclysms, etc.

Intelligence Branch

National Security Agency (NSA), monitors and screens all telephone, telegraph, computer modem, radio, television, cellular, microwave, and satellite communications, and electromagnetic fields "of interest" around the world, and orchestrates information-control and cover-up activities related to UFO secrecy and surveillance of extra-terrestrial operations, Fort Meade, MD.

National Reconnaissance Office (NRO), controls and collects information from global spy satellites, monitors UFO traffic entering and leaving Earth's atmosphere, coordinates firing of energy beam weapons from orbiting Star Wars satellites at selected human ground and airborne targets and selectively at extra-terrestrial craft, Pentagon basement and Dulles Airport area, VA.

National Reconnaissance Organization (NRO) (aka MJ-TF), the military/intelligence operations arm of the PI-40 Subcommittee, conducts surveillance, interdiction, capture and confiscation of UFOs and their extra-terrestrial occupants for intelligence and "International Security" purposes; surveilles and "interacts" with close encounter experiencers, including occasional physically and sexually assaultive mind control kidnappings disguised as "Alien abductions" for psychological warfare and dis-informational purposes, headquarters unknown, probably compartmented and dispersed among various elite Delta Force Special Operations units, such as the USAF Blue Light at Hurlburt Field, Mary Esther, FL and Beale Air Force Base, Marysville, CA.

Central Intelligence Agency (CIA), commands, often controls, and sometimes coordinates, the gathering of secret overseas information gathered by spies (HUMINT), electronic surveillance (SIGINT), and other means; carries out covert unconstitutional paramilitary counterinsurgency operations and preemptive political pacification projects in violation of international law, as well as counter-intelligence sting operations against foreign agents; engages in domestic surveillance, and manipulation of the U.S. political process, "in the National interest" in direct violation of its congressional charter; operates proprietary "false front" companies for profit; conducts a major share of international trans-shipment of illegal drugs, using National Security cover and immunity; and cooperates with NSA's UFO cover-up operations, Langley, VA, and worldwide branches.

Federal Bureau of Investigation, Counter Intelligence Division, The branch which investigates, surveilles and neutralizes foreign Intelligence agents operating within the U.S., and cooperates with the National Reconnaissance Organization in the surveillance of those involved in close encounters with UFOs and extra-terrestrials.

Department of Energy Intelligence (DOE-INTEL), which conducts internal security checks and external security threat countermeasures, often through its contract civilian instrumentality, the Wackenhut Corporation.

NSA's Central Security Service and CIA's Special Security Office, which respectively spy on the spies, and conduct special operations which cannot be entrusted to line intelligence officers, Ft. Meade, MD and Langley, VA.

U.S. Army Intelligence and Security Command, (INSCOM) whose assignments include psychological and psychotronic warfare (PSYOPS), para-psychological intelligence (PSYINT), and electromagnetic intelligence (ELMINT), Ft. Meade, MD.

U.S. Navy Office of Naval Intelligence (ONI), which gathers intelligence affecting naval operations, and has a compartmented unit involved in UFO and USO [Unidentified Submerged Objects] information gathering.

U.S. Air Force Office of Special Investigations, (AFOSI), which gathers intelligence affecting aerospace operations, and has a compartmented unit involved in investigating UFO sightings, extra-terrestrial contact reports, as well as IAC [Identified Alien Craft] surveillance, and coordination with NRO interdiction operations, Bolling Air Force Base, MD.

Defense Intelligence Agency (DIA), which coordinates the intelligence data gathered from the various Armed Services intelligence branches (Army, Navy, Marines, Air Force, Coast Guard and Special Forces), and provides counter-threat measures, (which include providing security at ultra-classified installations by the deployment of U.S. "Thought Police", who conduct surveillance, by remote viewing and other para-psychological measures, against penetrations and scanning by foreign or civilian remote viewers [clairvoyants/out-of-body seers], Pentagon, VA, Fort Meade, MD, and the entire astral plane.

NASA Intelligence, which gathers intelligence data relating to space flights, sabotage threats, astronaut and reconnaissance satellite encounters with UFOs and ETs, and coordinates the transfer of alien technology to U.S. and allies' aerospace operations.

Air Force Special Security Service, which is an NSA/USAF joint intelligence operations unit dealing with possible threats to aerospace operations from foreign powers, terrestrial or otherwise.

Defense Industry Security Command (DISCO), which conducts intelligence operations within and on behalf of the civilian defense contractor corporations engaged in classified research, development, and production.

Defense Investigative Service (DIS), which conducts investigations into people and situations deemed a possible threat to any operation of the Department of Defense.

Naval Investigative Service (NIS), which conducts investigations against threats to naval operations.

Air Force Electronic Security Command, which conducts surveillance and interdiction of threats to the security of Air Force electronic transmissions and telemetry, and to the integrity of electronic countermeasure (ECM) warfare equipment.

Drug Enforcement Agency (DEA) Intelligence, which conducts surveillance and interdiction of drug smuggling operations, unless exempted under "National Security" waivers.

Federal Police Agency Intelligence, which coordinates intelligence relating to threats against federal property and personnel.

Defense Electronic Security Command, which coordinates intelligence surveillance and countermeasures against threats to the integrity of military electronic equipment and electronic battlefield operations), Fort Worth, TX.

Project Deep Water, the ongoing effects of the compromised personnel, sources and methods resulting from the secret importation of Hitler's own Nazi Intelligence chief, Gen. Reinhard Gehlen, to redesign the US's Intelligence apparatus.

Project Paperclip, the ongoing results of the secret importation of Nazi weapons and aerospace/UFO scientists into U.S. secret military research and development bases.

War Department

CIA's Directorate for Science and Technology, which gathers information with promise for scientific and technological developments which present a superiority advantage for, or a threat against, the National Security, [also contains the "Weird Desk", which centrally processes intelligence about UFOs and ETs and their interaction with Earth], current Deputy Director of Central Intelligence for Science and Technology is Ron Pandolfi.

Strategic Defense Initiative Office (SDIO) Ballistic Missile Defense Org. (BMDO)

Which coordinates research, development and deployment of Star Wars electromagnetic pulse, killer laser, particle beam, plasmoid, and other advanced technology aerospace weapons.

Department of Energy (DOE) which, besides its cover story of researching cleaner-burning coal and gasoline and more solar power, is principally involved in research and development of: more specialized nuclear weapons; compact, self-sustaining, fusion powered, particle and wave weapons, including electromagnetic pulse, gravitational/

anti-gravitational, laser, particle beam and plasmoid applied weapons research; high energy invisibility “cloaking” technology, etc.

Lawrence Livermore National Laboratories Sandia National Laboratories-West (SNL-W), Which are involved in nuclear warhead “refinements”, development of new transuranic elements for weapons and energy applications, development of anti-matter weapons (the Teller Bomb: 10,000 times the force of a hydrogen bomb), laser/maser technology applications, and, reportedly, successful teleportation experiments, among other projects, at this Russian nicknamed “City of Death”), Livermore, CA.

Idaho National Engineering Laboratories (INEL), which houses numerous underground facilities in an immense desert installations complex larger than Rhode Island, has security provided by its own secret Navy Base, is involved in nuclear, high energy electromagnetic, and other research, and includes Argonne National Laboratory, West), Arco, ID

Sandia National Laboratories (SNL) Phillips Air Force Laboratory Which are sequestered on Kirtland Air Force Base/Sandia Military Reservation, and conduct the translation of theoretical and experimental nuclear and Star Wars weapons research done at Los Alamos and Lawrence Livermore National Laboratories into practical, working weapons), Albuquerque, NM.

Tonopah Test Range SNL's DOE weapons testing facility for operationally testing Star Wars weapons in realistic target situations, and is adjacent to classified stealth and cloaked aerospace craft and United States-UFO bases at the Groom Lake [USAF/DOE/CIA] Base [Area 51] and Papoose Lake Base [S-4]), Nevada Test Site/Nellis AFB Range, Tonopah, NV.

Haystack (Buttes) USAF Laboratory, Edwards AFB, CA A 30 levels deep, extreme security facility reportedly engaged in alien technology retro-engineering.

Los Alamos National Laboratories The premiere research lab for nuclear, subatomic particle, high magnetic field, exometallurgical, exobiological and other exotic technologies research, Los Alamos County, NM.

Area 51/Groom Lake (USAF/DOE/CIA) Base) and S-4 (Papoose Lake Base) Ultra-secure "non-existent" deployment bases where extremely classified aerospace vehicles are tested and operationally flown, including the Aurora hypersonic spyplane, the Black Manta [TR-3A] stealth fighter follow-on to the F-117A, the Pumpkinseed hyper-speed unmanned aerospace reconnaissance vehicle, and several variants of anti-gravitational craft (U.S.-UFOs).

U.S. Special Forces Command Hurlburt Field, Mary Esther, Fl, along with its Western U.S. Headquarters, Special Forces Command, Beale AFB, Marysville, CA, coordinating:

U.S. Army 'Delta' Forces (Green Berets)

U.S. Navy SEALs (Black Berets), Coronado, CA.

USAF Blue Light (Red Berets) Strike Force

Defense Advanced Research Projects Agency (DARPA), which coordinates the application of latest scientific findings to the development of new generations of weapons.

The Jason Group Elite weapons application scientists, developing cutting-edge science weapons for DARPA, and operating under the cover of the Mitre Corporation.

Aquarius Group UFO technology application scientists, reportedly working under the guidance of the Dolphin Society, an elite group of scientists privy to extremely classified science and technology findings.

Defense Science Board, which serves as the Defense Department's intermediary between weapons needs and the physical sciences.

Defense Nuclear Agency, currently concentrating on fusion powered, high energy particle beam, X-ray laser, and EM forcefield weapons development and deployment.

U.S. Space Command Space War Headquarters for operating "the next war, which will be fought and won in space", Falcon AFB, CO.

North American Aerospace Defense Command (NORAD), operating the nuclear survivable space surveillance and war command center deep inside Cheyenne Mountain, Colorado Springs, CO.

Air Force Office of Space Systems, which coordinates the development of future technology for operating and fighting in space.

National Aeronautics and Space Administration (NASA), which operates covert space defense, ET research, and space weapons compartments, in addition to manned Shuttle and unmanned scientific satellite launches.

NASA's Ames Research Center, which conducts the SETI (Search for Extraterrestrial Intelligence) Project, Exobiology (alien life forms) Division, and "Human Factors" (PSY-Warfare) Division), Sunnyvale, CA.

Project Cold Empire SDI weapons research - Classified

Project Snowbird Pseudo-UFO's used as misinformation.

Project Aquarius UFO research - Classified

Project MILSTAR Development and deployment of WW III [space war] command, control, communication and intelligence satellites.

Project Tacit Rainbow Stealth drones/pseudo-UFO's.

Project Timberwind Nuclear powered space vehicles.

Project Code EVA Space walk based technology.

Project Cobra Mist SDI energy -beam (plasmoid?) weapon research.

Project Cold Witness SDI weapons - Classified

WEAPONS INDUSTRY BRANCH Stanford Research Institute, Inc. An Intelligence contractor involved in psychotronic, para-psychological and PSY-WAR research.

AT&T Sandia Labs, Bell Labs, etc. Star Wars weapons research and NSA telephone/satellite communications interception facilitation.

RAND Corporation CIA-front involved in Intelligence projects, weapons development, and underground bases development.

Edgerton, Germhausen & Greer Corporation NSA/DOE contractor involved in Star Wars weapons development, fusion applications, and security for Area 51 and nuclear installations, etc.

Wackenhut Corporation (NSA/CIA/DOE cut-out contractor) involved in contract security operations for Top Secret Ultra and Black Budget surface and underground military reservations, such as Area S-4 (U.S. UFO base), NV and Sandia National Labs, (Star Wars weapons base), NM), and, reportedly, "dirty jobs" for CIA and Defense Intelligence agencies.

Bechtel Corporation CIA's main contractor for covert projects and experimental underground bases.

United Nuclear Corporation Military nuclear applications.

Walsh Construction Company, seems to undertake CIA projects contracts.

Aerojet (Genstar Corp.) Makes DSP-1 Star Wars battle satellites for the NRO.

Reynolds Electronics Engineering, seems to undertake CIA and DOD projects.

Lear Aircraft Company, Black budget technology.

Northrop Corporation, makes U.S. anti-gravity craft, back-engineered from alien technology, near Lancaster, CA.

Hughes Aircraft, classified projects compartment.

Lockheed-Martin Corporation Black Budget aerospace projects.

McDonnell-Douglas Corporation Black Budget aerospace projects.

BDM Corporation CIA contractor, involved in UFO back-engineering and psychotronic projects, etc.

General Electric Corporation Electronic warfare and weapons systems.

PSI-TECH Corporation Involved in military/Intelligence applications of research into psychotronics, parapsychology, remote viewing, and contacting extra-terrestrial consciousness.

Science Applications International Corp. (SAIC) - "black projects" contractor, reportedly including psychic warfare.

Financial Department

Federal Reserve System, Cartel of private banks overseen by elite super-wealthy financiers, such as the Rockefellers, Mellons, DuPonts, Rothschilds, etc., which dictates to the Government the flow of money, worth of money, and the interests rates.

CIA self-financing, the operation and/or control of much of the international drug trade in heroin, cocaine and marijuana, as well as "front" business enterprises, as a source of cash for off-the-books covert operations, and the purchase of exotic munitions and strategic bribe funds.

Department of Justice self-financing, the use of confiscated money and valuables from "targets of investigation" to finance "special projects".

Special Forces self-financing, the self-use of confiscated money from covert military operations to fund other clandestine operations.

Various secret government projects

THE 'MAJI' [Majestic Agency for Joint Intelligence] PROJECTS:

SIGMA—Initial project involved with attempts to establish communication with alien intelligence.

PLATO—Responsible for establishing Diplomatic Relations with the Aliens. This project secured a formal treaty, illegal under the U.S. Constitution, with the alien Grays.

AQUARIUS—Concerned with investigating the history of alien presence on earth and interaction with human beings. An outgrowth of this project is a huge Thesaurus-like document called the YELLOW BOOK describing aliens, their history in regards to humanity, and technology. (Some believe that the YELLOW BOOK is filled with alien propaganda meant to make government agents vulnerable to alien psychological manipulation...

For instance, this would include the deception that humanity is a genetic creation placed on this planet by the reptilians, and so on... and the potential results of such propaganda, for instance: that since they are our 'creators' we have absolutely no defense against them and might as well try to negotiate with them and attempt to appease our 'creators' by giving them what they want. - Branton)

GARNET—A project responsible for control of all information and documents regarding the Alien subjects and accountability of their information and documents.

PLUTO—A project responsible for evaluating all UFO and IAC [Identified Alien Craft] information pertaining to Space technology.

POUNCE—A project that was formed to recover all downed and/or crashed craft and Aliens, and provide cover stories and operations to mask the true endeavors whenever necessary, i.e. such as cover stories of crashed 'experimental' Aircraft, Construction, Mining activities, etc.

NRO—National Recon Organization, based at Fort Carson, Colorado. Responsible via DELTA FORCES for security on all Alien or Alien Spacecraft and underground base projects.

DELTA—The special arm of the NRO which is especially trained and tasked with SECURITY of all MAJIC projects [MAJI or MAJIC oversee MJ-12]. Also code-named "MEN IN BLACK", the Delta Forces are trained to provide Alien tasked projects and LUNA base security.

BLUE TEAM—The first project responsible for reaction and/or recovery of downed and/or crashed Alien craft and/or Aliens. This was a U.S. Air Force Material Command project. Also synonymous with ALPHA team crash/retrieval projects.

SIGN—The second project responsible for collection of Intelligence and determining whether Alien presence constituted a threat to the U.S. National Security. SIGN absorbed the BLUE TEAM projects. This was a U.S. Air Force and CIA project.

REDLIGHT—The project involving the test-flying and back-engineering of recovered Alien craft at AREA 51 - Groom Lake - Dreamland, Nevada. UFO sightings of craft accompanied by Black unmarked Helicopters are project Redlight assets.

SNOWBIRD—Established as a cover for project Redlight. This project is activated from time to time when it is necessary to provide cover stories for Redlight operations, etc., by releasing information on advanced conventional military aircraft which are used to explain 'unexplained' UFO sightings.

BLUE BOOK—A U.S. Air Force, UFO, and Alien Intelligence collection and disinformation project. This project was terminated and its collected information and duties were absorbed by Project AQUARIUS. A classified report named "GRUDGE/BLUE BOOK, REPORT No. 13" is the only significant information derived from the project and, other than information from second hand sources, is unavailable to the public. Reports No. 1-12 and No. 14 ARE available to the public. The Grudge/Blue Book Report No. 13 mentions that many military government personnel AND CIVILIANS have been terminated [murdered without due process of law] when they had attempted to reveal the alien interaction with the SECRET government.

SOME OF MAJI'S SECRET WEAPONS AGAINST THE ALIENS INCLUDE:

GABRIEL—A project to develop HIGH Frequency pulsed sound generating weapons that would be effective against alien crafts and beam weapons. The project also involves working with high frequency microwaves.

JOSHUA—The development of LOW Frequency pulsed sound generating weapons. This weapon was developed and assembled at Ling Tempco Vaught in Anaheim, California. It was described as being able to totally level any man-made structure from a distance of two miles. It was tested at the White Sands Proving Grounds, and developed between 1975 and 1978. It is a long horn-shaped device connected to a computer and amplifiers. The project also involves low frequency and microwave projection.

EXCALIBUR—This is a weapon designed to destroy alien underground bases [developed and funded mostly by intelligence branches connected with the U.S. Navy and SDI projects who have rejected any further interaction with the Greys after they turned on 'us' during the Groom massacre and the Dulce wars.

Some patriotic elements of MJ12 and the M.I.C.--Military-Industrial Complex--support this agenda of resistance, whereas other elements tied-in with the 'corporate imperialists' of the international banking community support continued collaboration for purposes of acquiring further mind-control technology for their 'New World Order'].

Excalibur is a missile capable of penetrating 1,000 meters of Tufa/ Hard packed soil, such as is found in New Mexico, with no operational damage resulting. The missile's apogee is not to exceed 30,000 feet Above Ground Level [AGL] and impact must not deviate in excess of 50 meters from designated target. The device carries a one to ten Megaton Nuclear Warhead. The secret for a self-contained missile 'drill' [a vertical shaft over 1,000 meters deep] consists in an energosintetizer macrowave deflector in the "Missile Warhead".

MAJIC has five other major weapons to be used against the Aliens, however little if any information on these is available.

Path 39: Who was William Thompkins?

Tompkins, William's Book: Selected by Extraterrestrials: My life in the top secret world of UFOs

With a Secret extraterrestrial background in the Douglas Think Tank, William Thompkins worked at Douglas Aircraft Company from 1950 to 1963. He was initially a draftsman working in Ground Support Electronics. He worked for Elmer Wheaton and his German scientific advisor, Wolfgang B. Klemperer.

As Engineering Section Chief, Thompkins conceived dozens of missions and spaceships designed for exploratory operations to the planets that orbit our nearest stars. I designed a station to be built on Mars, massive NOVA vehicles and equatorial launching facilities, designed multiple 2,000-man military bases for our Moon, and designed the checkout and launch-test systems for the Apollo Moon Saturn V, SIV-1B and reassembly with the command control Moon vehicle, a near complete redesign of the major facilities operations for the entire Launch Control Center. (*Selected by Extraterrestrials*, p. xix)

Over a 12 year period beginning in 1951, William Tompkins worked for an above Top Secret think tank within the Douglas Aircraft Company designing kilometer-long antigravity spacecraft covertly requested by the U.S. Navy.

Tompkins was given the job at the "Advanced Design" Douglas think tank, due to exceptional skills he exhibited in his war time service with Navy Intelligence from 1942-1945. Significantly, during his service at San Diego's Naval Air Station, Tompkins directly participated in intelligence debriefings of Navy agents embedded within Nazi Germany's most secret aerospace facilities during and immediately after World War II.

William Thompkins's book "Selected by Extraterrestrials" is a wealth of information about incredible things about what he did in work related to UFOs, alien technology, sexy Nordic secretaries, naval spacecraft carriers, what Armstrong saw on the Moon and other secret projects.

During the Apollo 11 Moon landing in July 1969, Tompkins says he was in the NASA Launch Operations Center at Cape Canaveral as part of a large TRW contingent. He states that television cameras from the Apollo Lander provided a live feed of what was being witnessed by Armstrong and Aldrin.

Tompkins explains how Armstrong and Aldrin were met by a fleet of extraterrestrial spaceships that were ominously close to the Apollo Lunar Lander:

The Landing Module (LEM) actually impacted the Moon surface in the Sea of Tranquility Crater, which had tremendous size vehicles parked around part of its rim. When astronaut Neil Armstrong made that First Step for Man on the Moon he looked up to the edge of the crater and said to mission control: "There are other ships here, they are enormous. The public did not hear that statement or see the massive alien starships. Armstrong panned his camera in a 360 degree motional all around the crater and the CIA then classified the information as way above top secret. " (*Selected by Extraterrestrials*,_p. 418)

In his autobiography, Tompkins describes what the Navy spies had found:

The Navy agents (spies) in Germany discovered what all those "out of this world" aliens gave Hitler: UFOs, antigravity propulsion, beam weapons, extended life and plenty of mind-controlled willing girls programs. The reptilians made a deal with the Third Reich SS giving them this big box full of toys in exchange for letting Hitler enslave the rest of the planet. (pp. 70-71)

Over his four years with Navy Intelligence, Tompkins helped in the covert distribution of data from Nazi Germany's two distinct secret space programs to Douglas Aircraft Company, along with other select aerospace companies and universities that had the scientific expertise to understand what the Nazis were doing.

When Tompkins joined Douglas Aircraft Company in 1950, it had already formed its Advanced Design think tank to design antigravity space craft. Once Tompkins moved over to Advanced Design in 1951, he was specifically tasked to design a variety of antigravity space vehicles, using his knowledge of Naval Intelligence gathered from Nazi Germany and his own talent for technical detailing.

Tompkins describes his two superiors at the Advanced Design Think Tank:

I reported directly to Dr. [Wolfgang] Klemperer and Elmer Wheaton, the V.P. of engineering who wore two hats. He was V.P. of all the classified missile and space-systems programs. Unknown to 99.9%, Wheaton was V.P. of the above top secret compartmentalized extraterrestrial threats research Think Tank, too, sometimes referred to as Advanced Design. (p. 48)

Thompkins had a genius gift of understanding of ship design and the ability to reproduce models of highly classified naval ships.

Navy intelligence officer, Lieutenant J.G. Perry Wood. Lieutenant Wood, understanding the talents that went into creating ship models, put together a mission-package for William Thompkins to get in the Navy. He arranged for Thompkins to get a job with Vultee Aircraft, while awaiting for a security clearance. After being sworn in and having completed boot-camp in San Diego, Thompkins was assigned to a position in Naval Intelligence.

For four years (from 1942 to 1947) Thompkins had access to highly classified programs, and was involved in some of the most unprecedented advanced scientific programs on the planet. In 1949, Thompkins got a job at Lockheed Aircraft Company in Burbank. At Lockheed, he became aware of a technical advancement into aerospace activities which was going on at the massive Douglas Aircraft Company, in Santa Monica.

In 1951 Thompkins was transferred into engineering as a draftsman. Because of Thompkins former security clearance with the Navy, the Electronics Section Chief transferred him into the highly classified Advanced Design Section, a move that changed his life.

In his book, Thompkins mention a secret report sent to the Secretary of War in 1945 by Commanding General of the Army Air Forces, H. H. "Hap" Arnold, wrote: "During these years of war, our military has made unprecedented use of scientific and industrial resources. We must continue to have teamwork amongst the military, industry, and the universities. Scientific planning must be years in advance of the actual research and development." In this report, Arnold did not, however, reveal his greatest concern - that some type of alien beings were here and that, technically-speaking, might be millions of years ahead of us.

Under the direction of James Forrestal, who was the Secretary of the Navy, on October 1, 1945, several high-ranking big shots were brought on-board, including: General Hap Arnold, Edward Bowles (of M.I.T., and a consultant to the Secretary of War), Donald Douglas (the President of Douglas Aircraft Company), Arthur Raymond (the Chief Engineer at Douglas), and Frank Collbohm (who was Arthur Raymond's assistant).

They met in secret at the Army Air Corps Headquarters, Hamilton Field, California, to set up Project RAND, a way-above-top-secret scientific think-tank. It was created in December 1945, as a special contract to Douglas Aircraft Company, at the Santa Monica Municipal Airport. Inside a highly classified, walled-off area in the Douglas Engineering Department, Project RAND studied the implications of threatening alien agendas.

RAND had two missions: (a) to research the potential design, performance, and possible use of manmade satellites; and (b) to function as a highly classified, scientific research program. The latter included literally thousands of problems in various fields, many related to addressing the technological threats posed by aliens, considered to be thousands of years more advanced than our own technologies.

On June 24, 1947, Kenneth Arnold, a private pilot, encountered a tight formation of nine disc-shaped aircraft. They were cutting across his flight path, at high speed, over the Cascade Mountains in the Washington State area. Although this was not the first known sighting of such objects, it was certainly one of the first to gain widespread attention. Hundreds of reports of similar objects quickly followed. Many of these came from highly credible military and civilian sources.

The military tried to ascertain the nature and purpose of these objects, primarily in the interest of national defense. They were, however, unsuccessful in their attempts to utilize naval aircraft to pursue reported discs in flight. At times, public reaction bordered on near hysteria.

According to the so-called Majestic 12, Eisenhower Briefing-Document (EBD), mailed anonymously to UFO researcher Jaime Shandera in December 1984: "Little was learned about these objects until a local rancher reported that one had crashed in a remote region of New Mexico on July 5, 1947." The site, seventy-five miles northwest of the Roswell Army Air Field, became the staging ground for a secret operation meant to ensure recovery of the wreckage. "During the course of this operation, aerial reconnaissance discovered that four small humanoid beings had apparently ejected from the craft at some point before it exploded, fallen to earth roughly two miles east of the wreckage site," reported all four were reportedly dead. A determination was made that the vehicle was a short-range reconnaissance craft, which implied it came from a larger, mother-ship.

Eisenhower Briefing-Document (EBD), stated "Numerous examples of what appeared to be a form of writing were found in the wreckage. Efforts to decipher these had remained largely unsuccessful,"

Equally unsuccessful, noted the author(s) of the Majestic 12 documents, were the efforts to determine the method of propulsion and the nature, or method, of transmission of the power source involved. This is not surprising, when one takes into consideration the complete absence of identifiable wings, propellers, jets, and total lack of metallic wiring. Nor were there any vacuum tubes or recognizable electronic components present whatsoever.

Although these creatures were humanoid, noted Majestic 12, the apparent biological processes responsible for their evolution were entirely different from our own, so the term "Extraterrestrial Biological Entities" or "EBEs" was adopted. It is virtually certain that these craft do not originate in any country on Earth. Dr. Menzel (allegedly of MJ-12) summed this up nicely, stating, "We are dealing with beings from another solar system entirely."

Operation MAJESTIC-12 was created on September 24, 1947, upon the recommendation of Secretary of Defense James S. Forrestal (formerly Secretary of the Navy), Dr. Vannevar Bush, and Admiral Roscoe H. Hillenkoetter, who headed up the group.

It is a Top secret, MAJESTIC-Eyes-Only Research and Development-Intelligence operation responsible directly (and only to) the President of the United States.

In light of this, William Thompkins states "my intention is to present compelling evidence of multiple alien cultures influencing our aerospace development." The Apollo Moon missions were just the foundation for the Deep Space Exploratory Interstellar missions planned by the Douglas think-tank and the Navy.

Thompkins conceived dozens of missions and spaceships designed for exploratory operations to the planets that orbit our nearest stars. He designed a station to be built on Mars, massive NOVA vehicles and equatorial launching facilities. He also designed multiple 2,000-man military bases for our Moon, and a 600-man naval station for all of the habitable planets and their moons. He devised the checkout and launch-test systems for the Apollo Moon Saturn V, SIV-B and reassembly with the command control Moon vehicle. Complete redesign of the major facilities operations for the entire Launch Control Center at Cape Canaveral, Florida.

Today, we are amidst a technical explosion. Man has evolved on this planet for a span of approximately 30,000 years, according to carbon-dated skeletons. In terms of development, nothing of a technical nature occurred until relatively

So why was NASA created in 1958? Publicly, it was created to provide a non-military government agency to organize and build a rocket ship that would take man to the Moon on a peaceful exploratory venture. Well... that's not exactly the whole truth, either.

U.S. governmental heads aware of the alien involvement in human affairs, but that the old Soviet Union was aware of the situation, too. With possible alien "assistance," the Soviets were bent on getting to the Moon first, in order to establish missile bases there and control the entire planet. Oh, yes, that was a copy of Hitler's plan.

Man has made some progress in exploring our local space. Still, we have worlds that await us in our own galaxy, Andromeda (our closest galactic neighbor), and the rest of the universe. Our challenge is to extend our presence across the vastness of deep space, seek answers from other solar systems with potentially intelligent life, and establish commerce with them. So why, all of a sudden in a microsecond of galactic time, did we leave the planet? Who wanted us out there?

According to Thompkins, "our Army Air Force and Navy pilots have reported over one hundred and sixty different, unknown alien craft that vary from race to race. Some of these are massive spaceships that are obviously capable of crossing the galaxy. I guess both groups have been tasked to counter not just one rival military force of hostile beings. There appear to be different alien civilizations in the galaxy, all engaged in bizarre, dangerous wars, the outcomes of which might, one day, determine the future of humanity on our planet."

"Even more important than that, we must defend this planet against aliens whose stars and planets could have developed millions of years before our sun. They have developed the technical ability to move off their planet and conquer worlds, with space ships and weapons so advanced it could take us thousands of years to even understand them, possibly even millions of years.

"We should not even be considering hostilities against the Soviet Union or any other country on the planet. All technically advanced countries should be allied together against the warring aliens."

Thompkins elaborates in his book that "extraterrestrials have been operating their ships through the galaxy for thousands of years, not by nuclear means, but by overcoming gravity.

This was disturbing to some in the semi-weekly meeting, because of the rumors that President Eisenhower's meeting with an elite, highly advanced squadron of extraterrestrials at the Muroc Army Air Base (now Edwards Air Force Base)."

According to Thompkins, "This occurred in the desert of California in February, and was not yet substantiated. Eisenhower's meeting with the Nordic aliens had been prearranged and permission for them to land had been agreed upon. The Nordic alien squadron had taken some control over planet Earth; it consisted of two large cigar-shaped ships and three 100 foot disc shaped ships.

They were commanded by several alien battle groups, human-like admirals operating in uniform with their crewmembers. They demonstrated their military ability to make their vehicles disappear, reappear, and overcome gravity. Their message to General Eisenhower was essentially: "We have taken your planet and are requesting permission to tell your people about us and that we will make it better for them."

Thompkins relates in his book, "What a line of bullshit," "What about the control the reptilians and the grays have had?" They also basically told Ike, the most powerful leader on the planet, that he had surrendered. Now, to say that Ike was pissed is an understatement: He had never surrendered. But, at that time, before reverse engineering of the crashed alien vehicles, Ike had no weapons capable of stopping them or the grays."

However, Thompkins relented to being convinced the alien take-over was true.

One of hundreds of Advanced Design concepts that Thompkins was privileged to be involved in was the configuring of a classified lunar, naval base. Much later, the Army presented a similar proposal, known as Project Horizon. The Think Tank had been conceiving many designs of different lunar and planetary commercial and military facilities that gave us a "heads up," and way before the Project Horizon.

As for Phase 1 Naval Base construction offices, equipment, storage and buildings on the Moon's surface, this included design, construction, assembly, and testing of prefab-type surface buildings. They were then disassembled and shipped to the Cape, where they were reassembled and installed in large, upper-stage, liquid propellant rocket boosters. These upper stages were to be launched and powered to the Moon, solar systems, planets, their moons and asteroids. The plan was to have them soft- land on the lunar surface and rail-transported in sections to the assembly site, where they would be reassembled to form large buildings that would be able to withstand the harsh lunar and planet environments.

The Phase 2 mission was far more complicated. The entire base was to be built underground. This required using extremely large boring machines. They were to be disassembled for storage within NOVA type rockets, then reassembled on the lunar surface and rechecked out before boring operations. The goal of Project Horizon was to establish an Army missile base on the Moon to protect our planet from the evil empire and the evil aliens.

Our goal was to develop a very sophisticated lunar naval base. It was an enormous project to design and build a two-thousand-man city that would include Naval research centers, Naval command and control centers, advanced power generation, military and commercial docking / launching facilities, Naval astronautical observatory, hospital / medical research, environmental systems, agriculture R & D, transportation systems, and commercial and residential centers.

Douglas acquired access to several German V-2 rockets, the wonder weapons with sizable documentation packages that were used in part for our intermediate range ballistic missile designs. These were at the Army's Redstone Arsenal and White Sands Proving Ground in New Mexico, where we established reverse-engineering facilities. Hitler's plan was for them to fly across the Atlantic Ocean and smash into New York and Washington. If the U.S. had not made Germany surrender in 1945, they would have. So, we also had access to a sizable documentation on the A-10s for construction of long range missiles.

Also during the same time, Naval Intelligence confirmed that the Soviet Union was making great strides in this area of research, too. The Soviets were engineering several very large vehicles that utilized data and technology acquired from the alien telepathic assistance and German A-9 / A-10 programs. The Russians intended to launch these rockets to the Moon, taking control of it, and possibly using it as a base with which to blackmail the entire planet. This may be the real reason President Kennedy told our nation: "We are going to the moon." Was NASA just a cover up for a massive U.S. military program to beat the Soviet Union to the Moon and not let them control the planet with their missiles? NASA was not, and never has been, a civilian organization. It is a naval deep space galactic penetration organization.

They were always thinking forty years into the future, which was always a problem when they tried to convince the conservative bankers to provide financing to develop a vehicle that everyone said was impossible to build.

It is really revealing in William Thompkins revealing statement of the Apollo 17 mission to the moon:

As reported late in 1966, the U.S. unmanned space probe, Orbiter 2, passed thirty miles above the surface of the Moon. NASA was attempting to find the most interesting location for our Astronauts to land. The onboard camera photographed six pyramid structures that were arranged in geometrical patterns, in a specific area within the Sea of Tranquility. These objects were arranged similar in plan to the Egyptian and Teotihuacan pyramids, all aligned with the Three Stars of Orion. What's most interesting is that NASA did not make any public announcement concerning this unusual situation.

Our Astronauts were shocked when they landed on the Moon. The landing module (LEM) actually impacted the Moon's surface in the Sea of Tranquility Crater, which had tremendous sized vehicles parked around parts of its rim. When Astronaut Neil Armstrong made the first step for Man on the Moon, he looked up to the edge of the Crater and said to Mission Control, "There are other ships here, they are enormous."

The public did not hear that statement or see the massive alien starships. Armstrong panned his camera in 360 degrees motion all around the crater, the CIA then classified the information way above Top Secret.

The Extraterrestrials put up their "NO TRESPASSING" signs but allowed us to make several additional Apollo landings, to pick up rocks and play in the sand.

The action of the Extraterrestrials stopped the plans to build our manned Naval Base on the Moon. Everything stopped, including our similar plans for Mars. Nearly all of the Four-Hundred Thousand Aerospace contractors were laid off, not just at Douglas, but at Boeing, Grumman, North American, ITT, Caltech, JPL, and numerous other companies, All over the country.

All of these Four-Hundred Thousand Apollo people were dedicated to the programs, using Launch Complex 39 only (each person is inherently supported by 7 commercial persons for normal living activities). Therefore that's 2.8 million total persons. There were plans for six times as much Launch Complexes, as well as NOVA Truck Complexes.

Thus, the total number of people that would have been involved in the expansion would have been about 25 million people for the project NASA was developing in detail. Not just to go to the Moon, but to develop everything necessary to operate massive naval vehicles out in the galaxies, and build Naval Stations on all habitable planets In the Solar System.

In just a few months everything stopped. We created the naval mission, designed, built, and tested every element necessary to operate massive U.S. Naval Space Battle Groups out there in the Galaxies some 50 years ago. Everything stopped. Why did we stop? What in the Hell happened. A force greater than the entire United States government halted our grandiose plans.

Tompkins testimony impressively corroborates the core claims made by Corey Goode and other independent whistleblowers about the secret space programs examined in the book, Insiders Reveal Secret Space Programs and Extraterrestrial Alliances (2015).

After the publication of Selected by Extraterrestrials in December 2015, Tompkins received a copy of Insiders Reveal Secret Space Programs from Dr. Robert Wood. In subsequent phone conversations, Tompkins stated that much of information that he read in Insiders Reveal Secret Space Programs, which is substantially based on disclosures made by Corey Goode, is accurate.

According to Tompkins, the U.S. Navy had corporate contractors design kilometer-long antigravity spacecraft in the 1950s to early 1960s, with construction beginning in the 1970s, leading to their deployment in the 1980s. His documentary support of these claims is substantive and compelling.

Tompkins testimony and documents provide powerful evidence that in the 1980's and 1990's, the U.S. Navy did indeed covertly deploy eight space carrier battle groups in a top secret space program called Solar Warden.

Solar Warden the United States Secret Space Program

The following information is given to us by Dr. Michael Salla. He is recognized in international politics conflict resolution and US foreign policy and he has taught at universities in the USA and Australia. He is more known in the development of EXO Politics, which is the study of the main actors and institutions and political processes associated with extraterrestrials life.

Dr. Salla first book on EXO Politics in 2004 and followed with another examining EXO politics in 2009. He authored Galactic Diplomacy Kennedy's Last Stand, which is the classified relationship of UFO's and the assassination of John F. Kennedy. Dr. Salla has also authored Insiders Reveal Secret Space Programs and Extraterrestrial Alliances. He has also published a book The US Navy's Secret Program and Nordic Extraterrestrial Alliance.

The US Secret Space Program was advanced by German engineers who had been involved with developing V1 and V2 rockets during World War II. The German scientists, Werhner Von Braun and Walter were experts in Ballistic technology that operated on Newton's Third Law for every reaction there is an equal opposite reaction. With a rocket as you expend gases at the end of the rocket it propels forward. This was the principle used by German scientists to propel the V1 and V2 rockets equipped with explosives.

These scientists were more than just rocket experts. The scientists that were brought over to the United States also had knowledge of other principles. Some of these scientists produced revolutionary propulsion systems that were not at all related to Newtonian physics of expelling gasses at a high velocity that propelled and object forward. These scientist also understood and developed propulsion technology. Another weapon that they worked on during the war was the Bell that had a weapons implication and an anti-gravity aspect to it.

What is anti-gravity? In 1928, American researcher Thomas Townsend Brown took out a patent in England and was an apparatus producing forceful motion. He discovered that if you created a huge electrostatic charge, it can actually have a propulsive force. Think of electro-static force like lightning as a very large positive charge. The idea behind anti-gravity force is you have a buildup of a positive charge at one end and it builds up so it discharges.

Thomas Townsend Brown found out that if you build up the force and not allow it to discharge it has a propulsive anti-gravity effect. Another Non-Newtonian principle being developed by Nazi scientists which was using higher rotating plasma in a ring. If you circulate plasma at a high rate around a ring it creates an anti-gravity effect also.

This technology was what German scientists brought to the United States, Great Britain, and Russia after World War II. Winifred Otto Schumann was a professor at the technical institute in Munich in electro-physics. He specialized in high voltage electro-statics rotating plasma. He was just one of the scientist taken to Wright-Patterson Air Force base in Ohio after the Second World War.

Not only were scientist for projects on V1 V2 rockets brought over, but scientists with expertise in anti-gravity technology as well. Werhner Von Braun worked on Ballistic Rockets in Huntsville, Alabama and Schumann on anti-gravity technology in Dayton Ohio in 1946. We brought over Nazi scientist with skills in different areas of physics.

Werhner Von Braun headed the NASA program using Newtonian Physic design for Space programs. Von Braun and other scientists in the rocket propulsion program thought that rockets could be used to develop send rockets up with equipment that can be assembled to build space stations.

There has been much controversy over the years concerning the development of space stations. A comment by President Ronald Reagan recorded in his Presidential diary in 1985 led to speculations of a nondisclosed Secret Space Program.

The entry for Tuesday, June 11, 1985 (page 334) reads:

> -Lunch with 5 top space scientist. It was fascinating. Space truly is the last frontier and some of the developments there in astronomy etc. are like science fiction, except they are real. I learned that our shuttle capacity is such that we could orbit 300 people.

This is curious since the Space Shuttle holds a maximum of eight people and only five were built for space flight. Even if all five took off fully loaded it would be impossible to place and maintain 300 astronauts in orbit. Was Reagan revealing the existence of a highly classified space program that could accommodate hundreds of astronauts in orbit? Apparently so according to dozens of military and corporate whistleblowers. Hidden within one of the ten unified combatant commands of the U.S. military, Strategic Command, is a highly classified fleet of aircraft carrier sized antigravity vehicles that operate in outer space.

The United States has organized its military forces into ten unified combatant commands respectively led by a single four star General or Admiral who reports directly to the Secretary of Defense. Six of the unified commands span the globe in terms of different geographical areas. In addition, there are four functional commands where specialized military activities are run by a single Combatant Commander. From 1985 to 2002 Space Command was responsible for outer space operations by the U.S. military.

In June 2002, Space Command merged with another of the functional commands Strategic Command which is responsible for a range of space, satellite, missile, nuclear and intelligence activities.

Rumors that the U.S. has a highly classified fleet of antigravity vehicles have circulated for years. On March 23, 1993, at an engineering conference in Los Angeles, Dr. Ben Rich former CEO of Lockheed's Skunkworks, showed a slide with a black disk headed for space and said: "We now have the technology to take ET home".

Corporate and military whistleblowers have come forward to claim firsthand knowledge of classified space vehicles using antigravity technology such as the Aurora and TR-3B. In his book, The Hunt for Zero Point, Jane's Defense Weekly analyst Nick Cook writes about the Aurora: "there has been speculation since the late 1980s about the existence of a secret replacement for the Blackbird, a mythical plane called the Aurora that supposedly flew twice as fast and on the edges of space" (p. 14).

Other whistleblowers such as Edgar Fouche, a former contractor with the Department of Defense, have come forward to claim that the Blackbird's [or SR-71] replacement, the Aurora actually comprises two types of hypersonic aircraft used for space flight. He said: "The Aurora comprises the SR-75 capable of speeds above Mach 5, and acts as a mother ship for the SR-74 that can travel at speeds of Mach 18 or more into space to deliver satellites."

The SR-74 rides piggy-back on the SR-75. Once the SR-75 reaches Mach 5 speed, the SR-74 takes off and reach orbital velocity so it can be carried into orbit and actually become a space vehicle. This is one if the ways a Secret Space Program can serve the Space Stations.

The Aurora Project is a Secret Space Program using very advanced technology supplying space stations that are orbiting the Earth not revealed to the public with people and equipment.

More significant is the large black triangular vehicle, the TR-3B that Fouche claims generates an intense magnetic field circulating mercury plasma at velocities of 60,000 RPMs at high temperatures and pressures of 250,000 atmospheres and that reduces its weight by 97 percent. He says that the TR-3B uses the Biefeld-Brown effect (created by large electrostatic charges) to reduce its weight so that more conventional propulsion systems such as scramjets can give it amazing speeds.

With this incredible weight reductions, atomic propulsion can propel these ships at incredible speed and make incredible right hand turns very rapidly. This would be well above Mach 18 that he claims is the speed of the SR-74. Fouche claims the TR-3B is 600 feet across which would make it similar in size to an aircraft carrier and is the most advanced aerospace technology being built at Area-51.

In 1999, there were Belgian UFO sightings where thousands of people saw these flying triangles and the Belgian Air Force planes were sent to intercept and did capture them on Radar. Fouche stated these were TR-3Bs.

NASA Saturn V rocket based technology is a cover program for the anti-gravity based TR-3B, and the Aurora SR-74 and 75 technologies that can get up into orbit and transfer a lot of equipment and resources without the public knowing.

The TR-3B and Aurora Program is a cover for another program. Government is using one classified program as a cover for another classified program. The US Navy run the most secretive space program in the United States.

The Navy's Secret Space Program has operated covertly going back to the Second World War.

Circumstantial evidence points to the existence of a secret space fleet of antigravity vehicles. President Ronald Reagan's startling Diary entry for June 11, 1985, for example, reveals a space shuttle capacity that could launch 300 people into orbit. Also, on August 6, 2007, for example, NASA awarded the Human Spaceflight Support Team for assisting NASA vehicles in avoided space debris. The support team was part of USAF Space Command which is publicly stated to be the major military command providing space forces for U.S. Strategic Command.

However, neither the USAF Space Command nor Strategic Command is publicly known to have any kind of space vehicle that would assist the Space Shuttle or International Space Station from orbital dangers. Normally, both NASA vehicles would require gradual orbital corrections that would take much time and be insufficient to deal with an immediate threat. According to Ted Twietmeyer, the citation is circumstantial evidence for the existence of antigravity vehicles with advanced particle beam weapons that could remove orbital debris from the path of NASA vehicles.

The idea that a secret space fleet exists that can intervene to assist the Space Shuttle or International Space Station is also supported by the testimony of a former NASA employee. Clark McClelland worked as a Spacecraft operator for Space Shuttle missions during 1989-1992.

On one occasion he claims to have witnessed an eight to nine foot tall astronaut and what appeared to be a delta winged antigravity vehicle nearby. Since McClelland knew all astronauts in the NASA space shuttle program he assumed that the very tall being in a space suit was an extraterrestrial. While such a possibility can't be excluded, the being and the nearby delta shaped vehicle may in fact have been part of a classified Space Fleet attached to U.S. Strategic Command.

Finally, the idea of a secret space fleet using advanced technologies was boosted by a British hacker, Gary McKinnon, who faces extradition to the U.S. for hacking into U.S. government and military computers. McKinnon claims that he came across secret Pentagon and NASA files that contained a list of 'non-terrestrial officers', and a spreadsheet detailing 'fleet-to-fleet transfers'. Could the tall being depicted with the two Space Shuttle astronauts actually belong to a group of "non-terrestrial officers" that periodically give assistance to Space Shuttle programs through the US Air Force's Space Command?

Based on the available evidence from a range of sources, President Reagan's 1985 Diary entry is a frank acknowledgement of a classified space program that can transport and accommodate hundreds of astronauts. The Diary entry suggests he received one or more briefings on the topic. Important clues may emerge from the recently released Reagan records about Strategic Command's classified space fleet. More significantly, the public may soon learn about the advanced antigravity technologies that have been secretly developed and used for decades to fly military astronauts into deep space.

http://www.examiner.com/article/reag...igravity-fleet

The US has a very top secret space program which include ships. Reagan knew when he wrote in his journal that it would be made public decades after he was gone from office. Maybe that's why he wrote that passage down?

Whistle blowers such as William Thompkins and Corey Goode reveals that Nazi Germany did establish underground bases in Antarctica that produced a successful advanced anti-gravity equipped Secret Space Program that permitted them to travel not just to the moon but to Mars also. Germany was doing this in the 1940 when the war was raging in Europe.

Corey Goode corroborates William Thompkins revelations stating that the Space Fleet was built in the early 80's in a secret location under the mountains of Utah. As William Thompkins states, Corey says that SR-74 SR-75 and TR-3B ships were flown into space and personnel are brought up to these ships in smaller craft. The craft are like a nuclear submarine in space and people that served on them are called Squids. It is no different than being on a modular submarine with a crew of 270 to over 300 people. Corey states there are Naval Vessels much larger than the Cigar shaped submarine transport craft up to a kilometer long.

On the dark side of the moon at the 10 o'clock position is a Luna Operation Command. It was originally set up in the 1940's by the Nazis who had developed their own Secret Space Program with flying saucers flying outside our atmosphere. The Nazis develop these craft that early in our history.

The Nazis set up a base there shaped like a Swastika. Corey states the Germans infiltrated the Military Industrial Complex of the United States through Project Paperclip and after negotiations that occurred in 1952, after the Nazis overflew the Whitehouse, Truman and Eisenhower was forced into negotiating with them a partnership. The Germans new that the highest secret in the land was and still is the Extraterrestrial phenomenon.

The government was not concerned about people knowing about ET's. The government does not want the people to know about free energy that powers the flying vessels or UFO's as we call them.

Once the Nazis infiltrated the Military Industrial Complex, they took over and won the post-war after World War II. This new Military Industrial Complex Space program began to utilize the Lunar Operations Command base on the moon. The command base was built out and the shape of it was purposely removed.

The non-terrestrial and human bases on the moon are masked by using holographic cloaking technology. What is not masked are some of the ancient ruins on the moon and crashed vehicles from wars waged by non-terrestrial in our Solar System.

Our moon was like a Switzerland area where no battles were allowed to occur on it. There are non-terrestrial groups that can't stand each other and have been at war for millennia that are just a few kilometer away from each other on the moon but they never fight because of a galactic treaty.

There is a lot of debris of crashed ships on the dark side of the moon as a testament to remind these warring groups how terrible the war was.

The US Navy was briefed by Spies in the 1940's of Germany's Space Program. The Us Navy was attacked by Nazis in Flying Saucer in Operation High Jump down in Antarctica. The US lost all of its planes and some of its ships.

In 1952, Nazi flying saucers flew over the Nation's Capital in successive weekends of July 1952. They were recorded, photographed, fight-pilots dispatched to intercept the crafts but the fighter-pilots could not do anything. This is well documented. President Truman dismissed the saucers as swamp gas.

According to William Thompkins, Corey Goode, and Clark McClellan these flying saucers were not extraterrestrial. These were Nazi German flying saucers. The Nazi has built fleets of saucers under the ice of Antarctica. They announced they were now the dominant geopolitical power out of Antarctica, the moon, other planets, or wherever else they had established their presence.

At this time, what was President Truman to say? Sorry we lied to you, the Germans were not defeated during World War II, they have established a presence in Antarctica, and since then they have developed these incredible aerospace vehicles that can outperform anything we have by quantum leaps.

Our government is just not going to reveal that to the people. Fear by the Americans, British, and Soviets and embarrassment created a conspiracy of silence amongst the most powerful men in the world.

Deals were made between the Truman and Eisenhower Administrations and the Nazis with a flying saucer program in Antarctica. The Nazis were not interested in exacting revenge on the Allied powers. What they were interested in forming an agreement and cooperation because the Nazi had become a space power. Not only that they were a secret society because they were more than just Nazis. They were more than Nazi ideologues, they believed in the occult and esoteric communications with all sorts of entities, which is what is going on at Cern.

They were not intending on planetary conquest militarily because they knew there would be great destruction. The United States and Soviet Union have nuclear weapons. So, what's the point? If you need those military resources, if you need those industrial resources to be able to expand your space program out of the Antarctica program by a factor of 10. The Nazis have about three million people at the bases in Antarctica, as compared to 100s of millions in the United States, Russia, Great Britain, China, and India, or billions worldwide, to expand your space program you need to form an alliance with the US military industrial complex.

Alliances was made with the US military industrial complex to build advancing technologies that the Nazis could use to expand their space program in Antarctica.

The Navy and military industrial complex knows what is going on buy in agreeing with the Nazis, the Navy has its own agenda.

The Navy's plan was to build their own space fleet. People like William Thompkins, because of his skill, would play a critical role in building a secret space fleet. From 1951 to 1963, Thompkins worked at a Douglas Aviation Think Tank called Advanced Designs in the development of an anti-gravity technology for a US Space Battle Fleet.

The Air Force thinking is you build a fleet of advanced craft for what you plan to do in space, but the Navy thinks in terms of battle groups. The Navy has a completely different perception of how it is going to conduct itself. The Navy think in terms of battle groups much like an aircraft carrier, with destroyers, planes, cruisers, submarine escorts, and other support ships that is integrated that fulfills whatever the mission of the battle group.

The Navy began in the 1950's designing these Space battlegroups. William Thompkins was part of the Douglas Think Tank. The research and design Rand Corporation grew out of the Douglas Aerospace Think Tank. Thompkins worked for Klemperer and Wheaton who were leading anti-gravity technologies.

The Douglas Aerospace Company was working on anti-gravity technologies back in the 1950's. Thompkins was designing the first US Navy Space Battle Group. The Navy requested development of a Space Carrier in 1954. The programs were slowed down decades by Nazi industrial sabotage cyphering off as much resources and innovative thinking to help their program under Antarctica and to sabotage the US duplicating what they had already achieved.

The industrial espionage got so bad that Elmer Wheaton, William Thompkins boss at Douglass, became so frustrated with the Nazi sabotaging the program at Douglass that he resigned and went over to Lockheed's Skunkworks in 1962 to help them develop and anti-gravity space program.

Thompkins was released 1 year later. There was people in the manufacturing sector in Douglas had all the power while Thompkins was part of the engineering sector working on innovative designs for the Navy while the manufacturing sector was building rockets for the NASA Space program.

The manufacturing sector felt it was a waste of time to putting resources and specialists in esoteric ideas in engineering when they needed to work on manufacturing rockets. This was sabotage by people working in manufacturing who also worked secretly with the Nazis. This resulted in the first eight battle groups being deployed in the 1984.

The United States have 10 Aircraft Carrier Battle Groups. Five deployed while the other five are being serviced or upgraded with the latest technology. There are 8 Space Battle Groups. Four groups are in deep space and four are being serviced.

How do the Navy keep the secrets of the Battle Groups hush-hush? How are you going to get people to man them? The Navy uses a technology developed by the Nazis called Age-Regression, which reverses a person's age 10 years, 20 years, etc.

In 1960, William Thompkins began working at a TRW on Age-Regression. TRW is an aerospace program merged into Northrop Grumman. From 1967 to 1971 they were working on principles of reversing a person's age.

Secret Space Program whistle blowers reveal having served 20 years and at the end of that 20 years they are reversed back in age and sent back in time. Age Regression and Time Travel is how these Secret Space Programs operate.

Personnel are recruited for 20 years tours of duty and maintain morale and commitment, you tell people they are going to serve their twenty years and at the end of that 20 years they will be sent back in time as the same age when they were recruited. They will be able to live those 20 years again.

The first whistle blowers to reveal Age-Regression was Michael Relf, Randy Cramer, Corey Good, military abduction Program.

Michael Relf

Michael Relf joined the Navy in 1976 and recruited into the Navy's Secret Space Program. He is sent to Mars by Jump Gate Technology serving from 1976 to 1996. Michael Relf served in Mars as a space fighter pilot. At the end of twenty years he is age-regressed. Afterward he is age-regressed and sent back in time to 1976. He serves another 6 years to 1982. In 2001 he publish his story "The Mars Records."

Veteran Michael Relfe: Humanity is being targeted by a predatory hyper dimensional species By Alfred Lambremont Webre

VANCOUVER, BC – Former U.S. serviceman Michael Relfe has released an Oct. 14, 2013 Open letter sent to the military leaders of many prominent nations asserting that "Previous members of the military made a grave mistake when they hid the reality of aliens from the people of earth. That mistake has been continued. That mistake could endanger the future of humanity forever. It is time to remedy this situation before it is too late.

"This battle against predatory species cannot be won by military might and technology alone. By now you know that this scenario involves energies and technology beyond your wildest imagination. For example, how can you hope to win a battle against an enemy when the enemy possesses jump gates and mind control technologies so that any head of government can be abducted and mind controlled at any time? And how can you hope to win a battle against an enemy that can hide itself from your perception?

"These predatory species, their technology and those humans that voluntarily serve them, can only be defeated by harnessing the cumulative might of the metaphysical and spiritual powers, as well as the intelligence, of the people of earth."

Former U.S. serviceman Michael Relfe has authored The Mars Records, two books on the 20 years (1976-1996) he states he spent as part of the permanent armed force detail on a U.S. facility on Mars that was part of the security perimeter developed in our solar system against the attempted occupation by the predatory hyper dimensional species.

Agenda of predatory species

In his Open letter, Mr. Relfe states, "These predatory species work in secrecy because they are AFRAID of human beings. They are afraid of God….That is why, by subversive means, they have influenced the systems of earth to do all in their power to keep people enslaved. This includes:

Keeping knowledge of their existence and their evil intentions hidden, until it is too late.

Vaccinating people, which damages their metaphysical abilities.

Genetically modified foods and nanotechnology which damage the DNA of the body, so that metaphysical abilities and reproduction are destroyed.

Fluoride which damages the pineal gland, necessary for metaphysical abilities.

Numerous toxins to damage the body (See the book "You're not fat, you're toxic).

Lack of information of spiritual power and metaphysical abilities, so that powerful metaphysics do not develop their powers.

ET Abductee confirms presence of predatory species

On Oct. 15, 2013, a Vancouver, BC-based ET abductee confirmed numerous repeated abductions and electromagnetic tortures that he ascribes to a predatory hyper dimensional species that have stated their intent is to ultimately displace humanity on planet Earth.

ET Abductee - Hyper dimensional predatory species is threat to humanity

Watch on You Tube

http://www.youtube.com/watch?v=MToni1LCwRA&feature=youtu.be
12 Steps to defeat predatory species

Michael Relfe recommends 12 steps to the military leaders he addresses in defeating the attempted occupation by the predatory hyper dimensional species.

"Time is running out. All governments of all countries need to:

"1) Release all of the true information concerning alien invasion of this planet.

"2) Release the true information concerning the ancient things found upon the moon and mars.

"3) Release the true information concerning government developed advanced technology and its use in establishing off planet projects.

"4) Release the true information concerning electronic medicine so long suppressed and allow people to be healed of terrible degenerative diseases.

"5) Stop the vaccinations, which kill us and destroy our metaphysical abilities.

"6) Stop the GMO foods, which sterilize people after 2 generations. These 'foods' will end civilization and you will not have anything to defend.

"7) Stop the use of nanotechnology in food.

"8) Stop the MSG, Aspartame and Excitotoxins that brain damage us and kill us. These chemicals are poisoning your soldiers.

"9) Stop mind controlling and abducting people with metaphysical abilities.

"10) Openly recruit and employ with generous remuneration sane, ethical metaphysically gifted people to fight these predatory species.

"11) Punish and eliminate the corporations that prey upon the population, and that help predatory species enslave us.

"12) Remove Christians from the "terrorist" list. They are not your enemy. They are the enemy of the predatory species.

"Know that if you do the above, the people of earth will find ways to help you rid earth of alien parasites, by working in the spiritual and metaphysical realms in ways that you cannot possibly imagine."

Michael Relfe has sent Open Letter to Heads of the Military Regarding Defeating the Alien Presence to the "Army, Air Force, Navy and Marines of Australia, Bulgaria, Canada, Croatia, Cyprus, Czech Republic, Denmark, Estonia, Finland, France, Germany, Greece, Hungary, Iceland, India, Ireland, Italy, Japan, Latvia, Liechtenstein, Lithuania, Luxembourg, Macedonia, Malta, Moldova, Netherlands, New Zealand, Norway, Poland, Portugal, Romania, Russia, Serbia and Montenegro, Singapore, Slovakia, Slovenia, Spain, Sweden, Switzerland, Turkey, Ukraine, United Kingdom, United States of America."

Predatory hyper dimensional species

Other whistleblowers from government – hyper dimensional ET liaison programs have also warned of an attempted occupation of Earth by predatory hyper dimensional species.

One report states, "In 1964, U.S. intelligence expected a Grey/Reptilian ET takeover in 2000-2030. The current war between hostile extraterrestrial Grey/Draco Reptilian faction and humanity has been in development for a number of decades.

"In his book, [whistleblower] Michael Prince reveals that in 1964 U.S. intelligence agencies had concluded that a Grey/Reptilian extraterrestrial alliance had a timetable for a planetary takeover of Earth sometime during the 2000 – 2030 period.

"He writes, 'On April 15th, 1964, two US intelligence personnel met under Project Plato with the Greys in the New Mexico desert to arrange a meeting on April 25th at Holloman air force base in New Mexico. This meeting was to renew the treaty that had started in 1934 again and was a psychological bid to buy time in order to solve the problem of the Greys and Draco reptilians. The upper levels of US intelligence now believed the Greys and Dracos had this planet time-tabled for invasion and takeover between the years 2000 and 2030.'

Ethical hyper dimensional species

Researchers such as Mary Rodwell have gathered replicable empirical evidence that ethical, hyper dimensional civilizations exist that are closely involved in the positive development of humanity. These include hyper dimensional civilizations of the Grey phenotype of which approximately 150 have been identified.

Randy Cramer

Randy's story begins at age 5 as he is recruited in a military abduction program for 12 years. Randy was trained to be a super soldier. Through mind-control his physical strength was enhanced. He was trained to compartmentalize his mind in order for a personality can come forward and act like a super soldier.

Randy was then recruited into the Secret Space Program's Mars Defense Force. Where he was taken to the moon and then traveled to Mars by a space craft 11 years after Michael Relf claimed he was taken to Mars by jump gate. In 2007, he completes his tour of duty and comes back and is age-regressed, sent back in time and enlist for 20 years again.

Corey Goode

Corey was also part of a military abduction in the My Lab program from age six and was in the program for 11 years. In 1996 he is taken from home and physically enhanced. At 17, he is taken to a base on the moon called the Luna Operations Command, which was a former Nazi base but was incorporated by the Military Industrial Complex.

According to Corey Good in an interview explained that if a person is abducted by non-terrestrials and returned, the government will come and abduct them again to be debriefed on what the aliens picked them up for and they will be given a screened memory and then put back in their daily lives, this is what My Lab means.

Corey explains that the My Lab program has been used a lot in MKULTRA and other programs lumped into My Lab. Corey states that he was identified as an intuitive empath through standardized testing in public school. He was then brought into a special school program that pulled him out of his regular activities. Three times a week he was taken n field trips to Carswell Air Force base or other similar military installations and was heavily engaged by military personnel.

Corey states they were put through many types of training and virtual reality scenarios to build personality profiles in order to know who they wanted to draft into the Secret Space program or just have or just have them work for loosely connected syndicate of the cabal we call the illuminati.

Corey explains that to be an intuitive empath is that you have a very strong intuition of what is about to happen or you know what's going on and you learn to trust that intuition because it is accurate and you have the ability to feel other people's feelings and emotions.

An intuitive empath is a hot commodity because they can be trained to interface with non-terrestrials. Without this intuitive sense and training, communicating with non-terrestrials is one way communication.

Goode was part of a military industrial complex space program within 500 miles of the near earth orbit. There are space stations unknown to the public that are 400 to 500 mile mark altitude that are serviced with TR-3B type advanced anti-gravity space crafts. There are also small bases on the moon.

Goode was part of the Solar Warden program, which was a Navy Program. Solar Warden is an Interstellar program. The Solar Warden program consist of a fleet of advanced anti-gravity space ships that are out traveling throughout our solar system and into other solar systems.

Good explains that he was brought on as an intuitive empath a couple of months before his 17th birthday. He was sent to an intruder intercept interrogation. His role was to communicate with non-terrestrials living amongst us. The military would abduct those non-terrestrials and interrogate them in order to find out why they are here and what their objectives and agendas are.

Goode states he was a part of that for almost a year and then reassigned back to a research vessel where he spent the remainder of his 19 years on tour. He states he was assigned to a research vessel called the Sommerfeld. He states that his deployment was trips around Jupiter, studies of the Sun where probes were shot into dark spots of eddies on the Sun to penetrate to get more information about it.

Corey states we have proven that the Sun is electro-plasmic and not a giant hydrogen generator. He states that our universe the physic model used in these black projects is an electric plasmic universe model. This knowledge has been suppressed from surface humanity preventing them from developing more interesting technologies to collect free energy or anti-gravity.

Once we are taught the true physics and understand that everything is electric plasmic, then we will adopt a new mathematics model and be able to build advanced space ships very easily.

Goode spoke of a high ranking Air Force officer name Sigmund who he first met when he was picked up by a strange triangular vessels and interrogated about the Navy's space program. Sigmund was the officer in charge as Goode was chemically interrogated holding a tablet below his head hanging down while going through academy looking photos of military personnel. There was a camera on this tablet like pad. Whenever Corey look at a photo and recognized a person the tablet would highlight the photo.

Corey gave up three naval personnel that was part of the Secret Space project Solar Warden. Sigmund was upset because he thought the program he was in was the tip of the spear program only to discover compared to Solar Warden he was much like the coast guard.

As a kid, Corey states he had PTSD. After each of the training sessions or field trips, the Navy would do what is called "blank slating," which was a mind wipe. He was given a screen memory. Three to five percent of the people they give screen memory to or do the blank slating on does not work. Within days or weeks, the memory comes flooding back to those who are intuitive empaths.

The military has come to realize that, in IT terminology, we have a physical hard drive that is our brain. You have people talk about past lives but how could you have a past life memory on this hard drive (your brain) that has only existed since you have been alive? The military realized that your higher self-acts like a virtual hard drive. Everything that occurs memories are stored there as well and intuitive empaths gets an automatic backup or download of the information that has been messed with or altered.

Corey stated that the military tried blank slating him on what is called the twenty impact when he served twenty years in the Secret Space program. They blank slate individuals so they cannot recall the twenty year service and then age-regress individuals back to their physical age of first enlistment in the program.

In 1986, Corey was drafted into the twenty-and-back program. He was told he would serve twenty years in this program. He would come back and have the best job around, and he would not want for anything, a promise that was not kept.

They also told Corey that his life would not be heavily impacted by his experience in the Secret Space program because they were going to age and time regress him back to 1986, the time he was taken. He would pick up where he left off and his family would never know he was missing.

According to Corey, there is technology that exist right now that reverses life itself that was used upon him. William Thompkins worked on this technology at TRW involving Telomere and age regressing therapy.

Corey revelations about Antarctica begins with a group he was introduced to a group called the sphere beings an avian (bird-like) race. Corey had never encountered an 8 foot tall blue bird like being in his entire 20 years in the program. Through the communicating process of getting to know these beings, Corey was introduced to an inner-earth group called the Anshar and this Anshar group took an active interest to him because he was in communication with who they call the guardians.

Corey was in communication with an Anshar ambassador who was working with the Secret Space Alliance to get us full disclosure. This inner-earth group took Corey twice to Antarctica. Once for a reconnaissance flight under the ice about about 2 mile where there exists a huge industrial complex with buildings all over the place, smoke and steam coming out of them, and very human looking.

There were giant submarines under the ice that were the size of giant ships that carried big shipping containers that were being unloaded with giant cranes reaching into the top of the submarines that pulled back.

According to Corey, the civilization comprised of ancient structures of tuned blocks sticking out of the ground under the ice and structures sticking out from the cavern walls suspended up in the ice overhead. The actual building look like a 21st century industrial complex close to any shoreline. It was very human looking, very modern looking, and in the middle there was a huge geothermal generator generating heat from the earth.

There were also pools of water around that were steaming like hot heated pot pools that were heated by geothermal energy. The geothermal heating is picking up at a high rate in Antarctica causing the ice shell to heat up about one degree every year causing a rapid melt. The activities under the ice excavating the ancient civilizations there using pressurized steam coupled with the industrial facilities under the ice causes the ice to melt quicker.

Corey's second trip under the Antarctic ice was again at the invitation of the Anshar. He was accompanied by one of his major contacts in the Secret Space program, a Lieutenant Commander Gonzales, to a different region of Antarctica. With advance flying craft that could dematerialize, they flew right through the ice shelf like they were passing through regular atmosphere.

Corey says he saw hundreds of these crafts flying around above in a huge cavern flying through the cavern walls aided by some type of advanced technology that permits them to dematerialize and pass through solid objects. Everything is about vibrations and frequency, if they are able to change the frequency and rearrange mater in a certain way allows them to pass through solid objects.

Regarding Antarctica being a portal from other parts of interstellar space, Corey states that gateway portals are often guarded by some sort of military installation or as the case in Tibet watched over by Tibetan Monks. Corey states there is a large entrance gateway in Antarctica. He stated they went over a bay of warm water lapping the shores of an industrial area. Instead of flying in the direction I thought we were, they went straight down the way the submarines came from and ended up entering this large west Antarctic rift system very deep underground that had been tunneled out by an ancient alien race that allowed you to travel from Antarctica to all the way up to Central America and the South Western part of the United States (Area 51) all completely underwater.

This underground city was the size of Texas with its own eco-system with light and warmth. Corey stated that the ceiling underground in

Antarctica was so high you cannot see it because there is a fine mist that created clouds in an enclosed environment where it even rains at times.

According to Corey, the Anshar people are very leery of human beings. When they had contacted us in the past, they feel that we are from the Pleiades and are such a violent race. They are afraid that if we knew where they were underground we would attack them, which has happened involving some of our black projects groups.

They are unwilling to invite us to their cities but there is plenty of area underground that we could take refuge. After full disclosure, our archeologists and geologists will travel to inner-earth. There is so much to explore.

Corey states there are other races down in inner-earth that look like humans in their own way. There is an Asian looking race, an African looking race, and Caucasian looking races in inner-earth that do not normally meet with each other and stay separated unless there is a huge emergency.

The Anshar people underground in Antarctica claim that human beings originated on earth approximately 18 million years ago. They say that they have been here that long and have been highly developed technologically. They had their own break-away civilization.

That split civilization went underground because it was a lot safer down there. They were shielded from the sun that causes rapid aging and ebb and flow of disasters that occur on this planet in a regular cycle.

He began a tour of duty with Solar Warden, which is the name of the Navy's Secret Space Program serving as an intuitive empath. In 2007, he completes his tour of duty and also goes through age-regression.

Corey describes age-regression as a technology where for two to three weeks you are physically immobilized, drugs/chemical are injected into you, and you begin the age-regression process. This is what William Thompkins worked on at TRW from 1967 to 1971.

Corey is an advocate for disclosure of all secrets surrounding the Secret Space Program. There is so much dark stuff going on that is a roadblock to disclosure. There is Interstellar human slave trades going on. For a long time, non-terrestrials were coming down and abducting humans and taking off with them.

The illuminati type groups realized the non-terrestrials want humans and the illuminati started treating humans as a commodity. The illuminati began trading people for technology and other biological information for other star systems that can be used for studies.

Nearly a million people go missing every year. A good portion of them end up being traded off as slaves or worse in this inter galactic or interstellar slave trade. If we get full disclosure of the dark secrets of the illuminati, it is going to be one of the most traumatic events that has ever happened to humanity.

The groups benefitting from disclosure are working on partial disclosure slowly over 50 to 100 years so many of them have a chance to die because so many crimes against humanity have been committed just to keep the secret alone, not to mention the millions that go missing each year. Our government just do not know how to come clean and tell the truth.

The slow release of planting seeds in our consciousness about aliens and Secret Space Program has been going on since the Star Trek series through Gene Rodenberry who had close connections with the son of the major Admiral who was involved with Solar Warden, according to Dr. Salas research and his source William Thompkins. Gene Rodenberry had direct contact with people involved in the Secret Space program.

Spherebeingalliance.com

Path 40: Antarctica Shrouded in Secrecy Absence of Evidence is no Evidence of Absence

Why did all the world's governments decide to establish the Antarctic Treaty? Given the many reported untapped natural resources reported found there by Admiral Bird, what has kept greedy capitalists from exploiting the resources of this supposedly uninhabited continent? Mankind has waged wars since time immemorial for spoils of wealth.

It is very suspicious that our world government have backed away from the continent of Antarctica, just as it has backed away from trips to the moon. High ranking German scientists and engineers, such as Werhner Von Braun and others, have stated that they received help with advancing technology from beings not of this world.

There are so many sightings of UFO's, the Roswell and Bavarian crashes of flying saucers, and reports by people having been abducted, it is not a stretch to say the Germans did collaborate with extraterrestrials and are operating under the ice in Antarctica. Did the American Government and military encounter superior extraterrestrial technology during "Operation High Jump" and was the Antarctic Treaty was made with extraterrestrials to keep people away from Antarctica?

Antarctica's greatest mysteries, from lost civilizations to a secret Nazi space base. It is the last great unexplored wilderness on the face of our planet and it's shrouded in icy mysteries.

Antarctica is effectively a freezing time-capsule that contains clues about life on the planet before humans. It's the last great unexplored wilderness on the face of planet Earth and is shrouded in icy mysteries. But what's the truth about the frozen continent of Antarctica?

For scientists, it's a freezing cold time-capsule that contains clues about life on the planet before meddling humans came along and ruined everything. But for conspiracy theorists, the icy continent contains much, much more than just a few frozen bacteria and a hidden lake. The wilder minds of the internet have made a series of sensational claims about the South Pole, suggesting it is home to alien bases and even a lost human civilization.

The Lost City of Atlantis

You won't find this theory in any science books, but a quick Google search will throw up screeds of bizarre claims that Atlantis is frozen in Antarctic ice.

Corey Goode, Antarctica, and the Anshar People

Corey was also part of a military abduction in the My Lab program from age six and was in the program for 11 years. In 1996 he is taken from home and physically enhanced. At 17, he is taken to a base on the moon called the Luna Operations Command, which was a former Nazi base but was incorporated by the Military Industrial Complex.

According to Corey Good in an interview explained that if a person is abducted by non-terrestrials and returned, the government will come and abduct them again to be debriefed on what the aliens picked them up for and they will be given a screened memory and then put back in their daily lives, this is what My Lab means.

Corey explains that the My Lab program has been used a lot in MKULTRA and other programs lumped into My Lab. Corey states that he was identified as an intuitive empath through standardized testing in public school. He was then brought into a special school program that pulled him out of his regular activities. Three times a week he was taken n field trips to Carswell Air Force base or other similar military installations and was heavily engaged by military personnel.

Corey states they were put through many types of training and virtual reality scenarios to build personality profiles in order to know who they wanted to draft into the Secret Space program or just have or just have them work for loosely connected syndicate of the cabal we call the illuminati.

Corey explains that to be an intuitive empath is that you have a very strong intuition of what is about to happen or you know what's going on and you learn to trust that intuition because it is accurate and you have the ability to feel other people's feelings and emotions.

An intuitive empath is a hot commodity because they can be trained to interface with non-terrestrials. Without this intuitive sense and training, communicating with non-terrestrials is one way communication.

Goode was part of a military industrial complex space program within 500 miles of the near earth orbit. There are space stations unknown to the public that are 400 to 500 mile mark altitude that are serviced with TR-3B type advanced anti-gravity space crafts. There are also small bases on the moon.

Goode was part of the Solar Warden program, which was a Navy Program. Solar Warden is an Interstellar program. The Solar Warden program consist of a fleet of advanced anti-gravity space ships that are out traveling throughout our solar system and into other solar systems.

Good explains that he was brought on as an intuitive empath a couple of months before his 17th birthday. He was sent to an intruder intercept interrogation. His role was to communicate with non-terrestrials living amongst us. The military would abduct those non-terrestrials and interrogate them in order to find out why they are here and what their objectives and agendas are.

Goode states he was a part of that for almost a year and then reassigned back to a research vessel where he spent the remainder of his 19 years on tour. He states he was assigned to a research vessel called the Sommerfeld. He states that his deployment was trips around Jupiter, studies of the Sun where probes were shot into dark spots of eddies on the Sun to penetrate to get more information about it.

Corey states we have proven that the Sun is electro-plasmic and not a giant hydrogen generator. He states that our universe the physic model used in these black projects is an electric plasmic universe model. This knowledge has been suppressed from surface humanity preventing them from developing more interesting technologies to collect free energy or anti-gravity.

Once we are taught the true physics and understand that everything is electric plasmic, then we will adopt a new mathematics model and be able to build advanced space ships very easily.

Goode spoke of a high ranking Air Force officer name Sigmund who he first met when he was picked up by a strange triangular vessels and interrogated about the Navy's space program. Sigmund was the officer in charge as Goode was chemically interrogated holding a tablet below his head hanging down while going through academy looking photos of military personnel. There was a camera on this tablet like pad. Whenever Corey look at a photo and recognized a person the tablet would highlight the photo.

Corey gave up three naval personnel that was part of the Secret Space project Solar Warden. Sigmund was upset because he thought the program he was in was the tip of the spear program only to discover compared to Solar Warden he was much like the coast guard.

As a kid, Corey states he had PTSD. After each of the training sessions or field trips, the Navy would do what is called "blank slating," which was a mind wipe. He was given a screen memory. Three to five percent of the people they give screen memory to or do the blank slating on does not work. Within days or weeks, the memory comes flooding back to those who are intuitive empaths.

The military as come to realize that, in IT terminology, we have a physical hard drive that is our brain. You have people talk about past lives but how could you have a past life memory on this hard drive (your brain) that has only existed since you have been alive? The military realized that your higher self-acts like a virtual hard drive. Everything that occurs memories are stored there as well and intuitive empaths gets an automatic backup or download of the information that has been messed with or altered.

Corey stated that the military tried blank slating him on what is called the twenty impact when he served twenty years in the Secret Space program. They blank slate individuals so they cannot recall the twenty year service and then age-regress individuals back to their physical age of first enlistment in the program.

In 1986, Corey was drafted into the twenty-and-back program. He was told he would serve twenty years in this program. He would come back and have the best job around, and he would not want for anything, a promise that was not kept.

They also told Corey that his life would not be heavily impacted by his experience in the Secret Space program because they were going to age and time regress him back to 1986, the time he was taken. He would pick up where he left off and his family would never know he was missing.

According to Corey, there is technology that exist right now that reverses life itself that was used upon him. William Thompkins worked on this technology at TRW involving Telomere and age regressing therapy.

Corey revelations about Antarctica begins with a group he was introduced to a group called the sphere beings an avian (bird-like) race. Corey had never encountered an 8 foot tall blue bird like being in his entire 20 years in the program. Through the communicating process of getting to know these beings, Corey was introduced to an inner-earth group called the Anshar and this Anshar group took an active interest to him because he was in communication with who they call the guardians.

Corey was in communication with an Anshar ambassador who was working with the Secret Space Alliance to get us full disclosure. This inner-earth group took Corey twice to Antarctica. Once for a reconnaissance flight under the ice about about 2 mile where there exists a huge industrial complex with buildings all over the place, smoke and steam coming out of them, and very human looking.

There were giant submarines under the ice that were the size of giant ships that carried big shipping containers that were being unloaded with giant cranes reaching into the top of the submarines that pulled back.

According to Corey, the civilization comprised of ancient structures of tuned blocks sticking out of the ground under the ice and structures sticking out from the cavern walls suspended up in the ice overhead. The actual building look like a 21st century industrial complex close to any shoreline. It was very human looking, very modern looking, and in the middle there was a huge geothermal generator generating heat from the earth.

There were also pools of water around that were steaming like hot heated pot pools that were heated by geothermal energy. The geothermal heating is picking up at a high rate in Antarctica causing the ice shell to heat up about one degree every year causing a rapid melt. The activities under the ice excavating the ancient civilizations there using pressurized steam coupled with the industrial facilities under the ice causes the ice to melt quicker.

Corey's second trip under the Antarctic ice was again at the invitation of the Anshar. He was accompanied by one of his major contacts in the Secret Space program, a Lieutenant Commander Gonzales, to a different region of Antarctica. With advance flying craft that could dematerialize, they flew right through the ice shelf like they were passing through regular atmosphere.

Corey says he saw hundreds of these crafts flying around above in a huge cavern flying through the cavern walls aided by some type of advanced technology that permits them to dematerialize and pass through solid objects. Everything is about vibrations and frequency, if they are able to change the frequency and rearrange mater in a certain way allows them to pass through solid objects.

Regarding Antarctica being a portal from other parts of interstellar space, Corey states that gateway portals are often guarded by some sort of military installation or as the case in Tibet watched over by Tibetan Monks. Corey states there is a large entrance gateway in Antarctica. He stated they went over a bay of warm water lapping the shores of an industrial area.

Instead of flying in the direction I thought we were, they went straight down the way the submarines came from and ended up entering this large west Antarctic rift system very deep underground that had been tunneled out by an ancient alien race that allowed you to travel from Antarctica to all the way up to Central America and the South Western part of the United States (Area 51) all completely underwater.

This underground city was the size of Texas with its own eco-system with light and warmth. Corey stated that the ceiling underground in Antarctica was so high you cannot see it because there is a fine mist that created clouds in an enclosed environment where it even rains at times.

According to Corey, the Anshar people are very leery of human beings. When they had contacted us in the past, they feel that we are from the Pleiades and are such a violent race. They are afraid that if we knew where they were underground we would attack them, which has happened involving some of our black projects groups.

They are unwilling to invite us to their cities but there is plenty of area underground that we could take refuge. After full disclosure, our archeologists and geologists will travel to inner-earth. There is so much to explore.

Corey states there are other races down in inner-earth that look like humans in their own way. There is an Asian looking race, an African looking race, and Caucasian looking races in inner-earth that do not normally meet with each other and stay separated unless there is a huge emergency.

The Anshar people underground in Antarctica claim that human beings originated on earth approximately 18 million years ago. They say that they have been here that long and have been highly developed technologically. They had their own break-away civilization.

That split civilization went underground because it was a lot safer down there. They were shielded from the sun that causes rapid aging and ebb and flow of disasters that occur on this planet in a regular cycle.

He began a tour of duty with Solar Warden, which is the name of the Navy's Secret Space Program serving as an intuitive empath. In 2007, he completes his tour of duty and also goes through age-regression.

Corey describes age-regression as a technology where for two to three weeks you are physically immobilized, drugs/chemical are injected into you, and you begin the age-regression process. This is what William Thompkins worked on at TRW from 1967 to 1971.

Corey is an advocate for disclosure of all secrets surrounding the Secret Space Program. There is so much dark stuff going on that is a roadblock to disclosure. There is Interstellar human slave trades going on. For a long time, non-terrestrials were coming down and abducting humans and taking off with them.

The illuminati type groups realized the non-terrestrials want humans and the illuminati started treating humans as a commodity. The illuminati began trading people for technology and other biological information for other star systems that can be used for studies.

Nearly a million people go missing every year. A good portion of them end up being traded off as slaves or worse in this inter galactic or interstellar slave trade. If we get full disclosure of the dark secrets of the illuminati, it is going to be one of the most traumatic events that has ever happened to humanity.

The groups benefitting from disclosure are working on partial disclosure slowly over 50 to 100 years so many of them have a chance to die because so many crimes against humanity have been committed just to keep the secret alone, not to mention the millions that go missing each year. Our government just do not know how to come clean and tell the truth.

The slow release of planting seeds in our consciousness about aliens and Secret Space Program has been going on since the Star Trek series through Gene Rodenberry who had close connections with the son of the major Admiral who was involved with Solar Warden, according to Dr. Salas research and his source William Thompkins. Gene Rodenberry had direct contact with people involved in the Secret Space program.

Spherebeingalliance.com

Project Daedalus

Project Daedalus is a concept design for an interstellar probe, developed in the 1970s by a group of technical specialists for the British Interplanetary Society. The target destination was Barnard's Star—a red dwarf about 6 light-years away, in many ways similar to Proxima Centauri, where astronomers now report they have found signs of a potentially habitable planet. When Project Daedalus was conceived, some astronomers thought a gas giant planet might be in orbit around Barnard's Star, but since then, no planets have been found in the star system.

The result of the five-year project was the design of the Daedalus spacecraft, a two-stage, 54,000-ton nuclear rocket that would boost a 400-ton robotic probe to around 12 percent of the speed of light. This would enable the probe to make the 6-light-year journey to Barnard's Star in around 50 years.

The rockets of the Daedalus spacecraft would be powered by nuclear fusion, using electron beams to detonate a stream of pellets of fuel such as helium-3, which could be mined from the surface of the moon. Even so, the engines would consume tens of thousands of tons of fuel to get the spacecraft up to its top speed in about 4 years—and because there wouldn't be any fuel left to slow down, the end result of the 50-year journey would be just a 70-hour flyby of the destination system, before the spacecraft speeds past into interstellar space.

The Daedalus would be much too large to lift off from the Earth's surface, so it would have to be built in orbit, which means spacecraft like this couldn't be built without a capacity for construction in space that doesn't exist today, said space scientist Ian Crawford, a professor of planetary science and astrobiology at Birkbeck College in the United Kingdom.

While Crawford thinks the science behind the Project Daedalus concept is better understood now than when the spacecraft was designed, he said the immense cost and enormous technical challenges likely mean it would be more than 100 years before something like the Daedalus sets out for the stars.

Project Icarus

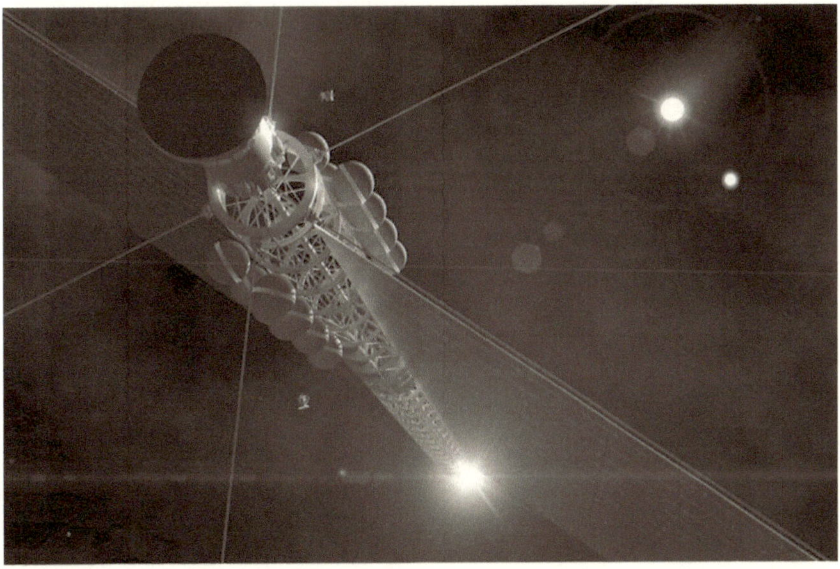

The Project Daedalus concepts from the 1970s are the inspiration for Project Icarus, an ongoing joint project by the British Interplanetary Society and the Icarus Interstellar organization, an international network of scientists, engineers and enthusiasts who hope to develop the capabilities for interstellar spaceflight by the year 2100.

Project Icarus is designed to reach any star within 22 light-years of Earth that has a potentially habitable exoplanet, meaning if a planet is confirmed around Proxima Centauri, it could become a target destination.

Project Icarus aims to update the Daedalus design with new technologies and ideas. Among the refinements proposed are fusion rocket engines that use a different nuclear fuel, which would be detonated by lasers instead of electron beams—a technology that could draw from recent advances in laser-ignition fusion at the National Ignition Facility at Lawrence Livermore National Laboratory in California, Crawford said.

The Icarus probe could also be smaller than the 400-ton probe envisioned for Project Daedalus, thanks to advances in electronic miniaturization and robotics, and future nanotechnologies—which would mean the spacecraft would need to carry less fuel to reach its full speed.

Light Sail

Our best bet for interstellar travel may be to not use a rocket at all, Crawford said. Light sails, which use the pressure of light to propel a payload, are already being considered for interplanetary space probes, and in 2010 Japan's experimental IKAROS spacecraft successfully used its 60-foot-wide (20 meters) light sail to maneuver during a six-month journey to Venus.

But although light sails driven by sunlight are already an effective way to explore the solar system, they are not fast enough to cover interstellar distances in a reasonable amount of time.

Crawford said the answer may be to use powerful lasers to push the light sail to very high speeds with bursts of light at the start of the journey, until the spacecraft is too far from the laser source to gain more thrust from the light beam.

Since the driving lasers would be built on Earth or in orbit, interstellar light-sail spacecraft would not need to carry fuel for the journey, and so the mass of the spacecraft could be kept small.

Laser-driven light sail spacecraft are the basis of the Breakthrough Starshot project that was announced this year by investor Yuri Milner and physicist Stephen Hawking. The project aims to build a working prototype by 2036 at a final mission cost of around $10 billion dollars.

The project envisages a swarm of around 1,000 stamp-size "StarChip" spacecraft, each weighing a few grams and attached to a light sail measuring 13 feet (4 m) across, which would be deployed from a "mothership" in orbit before being accelerated by ground-based lasers to speeds of around 15 to 20 percent the speed of light.

This would allow the spacecraft to make the 4-light-year journey to the Alpha Centauri system—a triple-star system that includes the star Proxima Centauri and its possible planet—in between 20 and 30 years.

The concepts behind the Breakthrough Starshot project have been studied by Philip Lubin, a professor of cosmology at the University of California, Santa Barbara, who says the biggest challenge remaining is to create sufficiently powerful lasers to drive the light sail spacecraft.

Bussard Ramjet

The Bussard Ramjet concept, proposed by physicist Robert Bussard in 1960, combines the high thrust of fusion rockets with the low fuel requirements of light sails.

Instead of carrying its own fuel, a Bussard Ramjet would scoop up the very thin traces of gas and dust found in interstellar space, known as the Interstellar Medium, using a vast funnel-shaped electromagnetic field that extends for thousands of miles in front of the spacecraft.

Hydrogen from the Interstellar Medium would then be compressed and used as fuel in a fusion rocket at the rear of the spacecraft that drives it forward.

In theory, a spacecraft driven by a Bussard Ramjet could continue to accelerate as long as there is enough interstellar gas in its path to provide enough thrust, and could reach a high fraction of the speed of light.

As a result, the venerable Bussard has seen long and honorable service in many works of science fiction, notably Larry Niven's "Known Space" series of novels and short stories, including the "Ringworld" books; and the 1970 Poul Anderson novel "Tau-Zero" (Doubleday, 1970), in which an interstellar crew push their stricken Bussard spacecraft to relativistic speeds to avoid destruction.

Unfortunately, the Interstellar Medium around our solar system and the nearby stars is especially thin, and scientist have calculated that there's just not enough hydrogen there to fuel a Bussard Ramjet. "It's not the ideal part of the galaxy," Crawford said.

But he explained that several ideas have been proposed to get around this limitation, including a concept known as a "Ram Augmented Stellar Rocket", which uses collected matter as reaction mass to drive the spacecraft forward, using energy beamed to it by a laser; and an "Interstellar Runway," which would use deposits of fuel positioned in advance in the path of an accelerating Bussard spacecraft.

Antimatter rocket & black hole drive

Beyond light sails, giant lasers and fusion rockets, a few even more exotic options for interstellar travel have been proposed, such as rockets powered by the extremely violent (and supremely efficient) annihilation reaction of matter and antimatter.

"Antimatter would be an excellent rocket fuel, because its energy density is so high," Crawford said. "But, of course it doesn't exist in nature, we have to make it. And it's very difficult and expensive to make, and very dangerous once you've made it—so who knows whether it could ever be used as a rocket fuel?"

Another proposal for using exotic physics to drive a spacecraft is the "Schwarzschild Kugelblitz" drive, which would use a microscopic, artificial black hole contained within its engines as its power source.

One idea for a ship equipped with the so-called "SK Drive," shown above, would trap Hawking radiation from the rapid and extremely violent decay of the tiny black hole, and convert it to energy that can be used it to propel the spacecraft.

Each of the artificial black holes would only survive for a few years, so new black holes would need to be created on demand, possibly by compressing pellets of matter with gamma-ray lasers.

According to a 2009 research paper, an SK-drive starship powered by a microscopic black hole with the mass of a modern supertanker could accelerate to 10 percent of the speed of light within 20 days. The black hole would last around 3.5 years before it decayed entirely, and would output more than 160 petawatts, or 160 quadrillion watts, of power in its lifetime.

Human "slow boats"

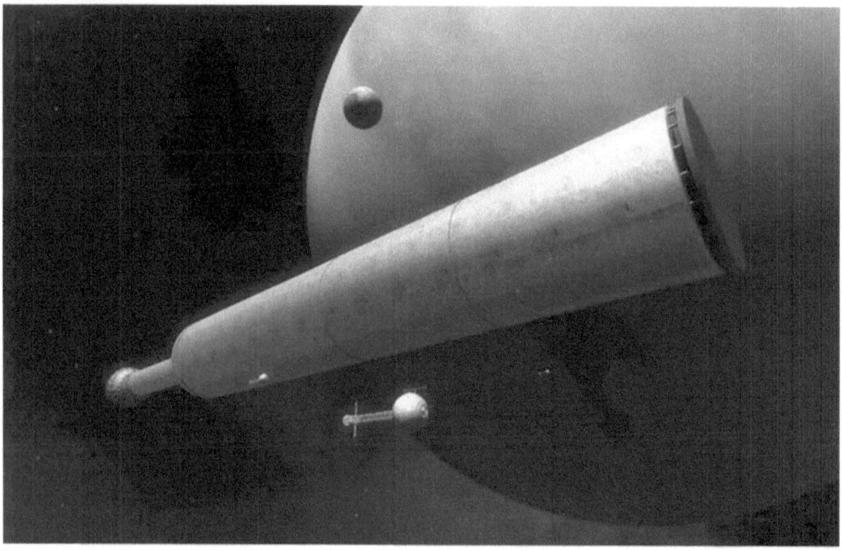

Human "Slow Boats"

Even with super-fast rockets traveling at speeds of 10 percent or more of the speed of light, it would take many human lifetimes to reach all but the very nearest stars. And although Crawford is an advocate of human exploration of the solar system, he said that interstellar distances are too vast to make a human voyage conceivable within the next few hundred years.

"I think humans can explore the planets more effectively than robots, and I also think there are cultural reasons for sending humans into space, to broaden our range of experiences and enrich human culture," he said. "Now, it's true that all of that would apply on the interstellar scale as well—it's just that the distances are so large and the technical difficulties so great that advocating it at this stage is almost inconceivable."

Even so, several ideas exist for what are known as "Slow Boat" concepts that might one day take humans to the stars, including:

Sleeper Ships, in which human crewmembers are kept in a state of "deep sleep" or "suspended animation" for the duration of the very long voyage. This idea has featured in several science fiction movies, including Stanley Kubrick's "2001: A Space Odyssey" made in 1969, Ridley Scott's "Alien" in 1979 and James Cameron's "Avatar" in 2009.

World Ships, also known as generation ships or interstellar arks, would be giant self-contained space habitats carrying large populations of humans and other species from Earth on a relatively leisurely journey to colonize exoplanets—journeys that would take many centuries to complete. Entire generations would live and die during the voyage, and only the descendants of the original population would arrive at the destination.

Embryo Ships would send cryogenically frozen embryonic humans, instead of sleeping or living humans, to a distant colony planet, where they would be "hatched out" and educated on their mission by a crew of protective robots.

Faster than Light

Faster than light?

Wherever astronomers look in the universe, the Theory of Relativity holds fast. As Albert Einstein showed, it's not possible to accelerate a mass to the speed of light in space, nor past it.

But Einstein's equations may yet hold a few tricks that could someday let science do an end-run around the known laws of physics and achieve faster-than-light (FTL) travel—a Holy Grail for generations of science fiction fans.

The best known scientific concept for FTL travel is the Alcubierre drive, proposed by theoretical physicist Miguel Alcubierre in 1994.

The proposed drive operates by using intense gravitational forces, generated by two rotating rings of dense exotic matter, to shrink the physical dimensions of space in front of the spacecraft while expanding the space behind it, at a rate that could appear to exceed the speed of light.

In Alcubierre's proposal, which requires a type of exotic matter for the rings that is not known to exist, the spacecraft inside the "warp bubble" created by the drive would never travel faster than light in its local space, and so would not violate the laws of relativity.

Other speculative ideas for FTL travel include using trans-dimensional wormholes—also theoretically possible, but not known to exist—to travel between entangled but distant regions of space; or to daringly skim the edges of a large, spinning black hole, as depicted in Christopher Nolan's 2014 movie "Interstellar."

But Crawford notes that the concept of faster-than-light travel is rife with unknowns and apparent contradictions, such as violating the principle of causality, in which events are caused by other events that happened earlier in time, and not the other way around. So, it's likely the proposals would prove impossible, even if they were technologically feasible to attempt.

"I don't want to sound overly pessimistic, because I can see huge benefits of being able to travel to the stars, but the laws of physics are the laws of physics, and it is going to be really difficult," Crawford said.

Interstellar Space Travel: 7 Futuristic Spacecraft to Explore the Cosmos

Tom Metcalfe, Live Science Contributor

Semptember 2, 2016

CHAPTER VI

EXTRATERRESTRIAL CONTRIBUTIONS TO WORLD WAR II. HUMANITY'S FLAMING OUT ON THE HIGHWAY TO HELL

Path 41: A Way beyond Loyalty, Provincialism, and the Herd Instinct

In America, a happy and successful life depends on what group one belongs to. We have groups partitioned by wealth, there are groups partitioned by religion, and groups partitioned by race.

There is war being waged between groups defined by wealth and poverty. Financial status dictates whose children proliferates and prospers and whose offspring exist behind cages of constrictive debt. The children of the poor inevitably are brainwashed in the military, prison, or worse live a life poisoned by drugs.

If you are in the so-called educated, politically protected, and highly favored in group who are afforded a different set of privileges, you have a difficult time seeing the moral dilemma of an elite group confiscating excessive resources at the detriment of others perceived as undeserving and expendable.

Those who control financial resources are the in-group. They are blindly obsessed with doing anything and everything to insure and retain their social status of privilege by any means necessary including reversing:

> We The People of The United States, in order to form a more perfect union, establish justice, insure domestic tranquility, provide for the common defense, promote the general welfare, and secure blessings of liberty to ourselves and our posterity, do ordain and establish this Constitution for the United States.
>
> Amendment II
>
> A well-regulated militia, being necessary to the security of a free state, the right of the people to keep and bear arms, shall not be infringed upon.

The in-group of Financial Royalty controls institutions of banks that includes The Bank of London, The Federal Reserve Bank, Bank of International Settlements, The International Monetary Fund, and the World Bank. These banks fund world governments and their respective militaries.

There are those of us who are and are not are aware of the roles this in-group plays in destabilizing the world through their endless financial instruments of wealth transferring wars, in the end, all of us conditioned and converted to consumer slaves in chains of debt have a disturbing loyalty to these group of banking institutions.

Life beyond Superficial Material Desire

Part of the so-called "successful formula" in America is to settle into a religious group, political parties, actor's guilds, and professional athletics, or get a job in technical fields that are essentially blinders to moral and ethical degradations that these ways of life currently are supporting.

Our kids are indoctrinated (not educated) into continued production of insensitive values, a way of life measured in wealth accumulation, and further development of flawed cultural morality based on historical lies, deceptions, and an unending assortment of destructive untruths and fictitious religious principles in the name of profit with little or no regards to respect for a peaceful spirituality, a rational concept of the idea of God, nature, or life at every level (animal, plant, or planet).

What is really going on in the world, the wars, the mass killings in our communities, deceitful spineless politicians, pedophilia, mass surveillance, and the transference of wealth to just a handful of families in the world? What has rendered people to being apathetic zombies who victimize themselves not understanding the tool of mind-control fashioned through false front terrorism created by political actors on Capitol Hill?

The time is now for humanity to reckon with our greed and imported obstacles to spiritual well-being. A good start is loving self and life beyond the material temptations that makes us easy marks as slaves controlled and manipulated because of massive desires of technical and material consumption.

Fiascos are created and propagated to an elite controlled media to distract and traumatize the masses. Royal weddings, wars, sports and their seasonal championships are all dramatic distractions from the true problems of the world today. Everything on digital media is just bread and circus for the masses.

In this current season of traumatization of humankind, we have been reduced to our lowest spiritual common denominator and lowest level of spiritual vibrations that finds us imperceptibly in a modern slavocracy and not a democracy.

A good portion of people's reality is a pseudo-reality. We have been reduced to playing games for wealth. Once you have been reduced to playing games, you are at an infantile level, even if you are 40 years old.

In all the worship like patriotism for wars, of Royal weddings, proliferation of the trillion dollar business agenda of Big Pharma, and sports championships, the people are delusional and traumatized into apathy and fail to understand slavery that does not work unless you have a hierarchy.

Once you educate yourself and look at the agenda of greed's progression, you understand the true darkness that has set upon us as one people. The farther humanity progresses away from the Laws of MAAT of ancient Egypt and the teaching of Thoth, we find less and less love and trust in humanity.

We offer each other superficial surface beauty very little substance of inner beauty founded on a deep spiritual core of love for self, nature, each other, and the essence of god gifted in each of us. All of this has been obscured by an evil crafted Master and Slave relationship.

Reflecting on this very fact, what is it in the mind of the slave that wants a master? In its many forms our masters are religion, Trillionaires, Billionaires, rich entertainers of the sports, music, and sports industries.

Each one of us caught in the web of the "Matrix" like flies in the web of a spider. The Ironic thing is the slave would like to be free. If only we became our own master, looking inside, trusting in the God inside each one of us. Instead we seek a master in the external world with a notion of "In God We Trust". We are taught to turn the other cheek, pay Caesar, his taxes, and look to heaven after spiritual enslavement on earth.

Man is an instrument in his own enslavement. Down through the centuries, slaves have exchanged chains of iron for chains of gold. The poster child for this is illustrated than the image of Young black rappers with gold chains around their necks.

The spiritual disconnect is more extensive than Rappers. There are the so-called educated fools from uneducated schools with their litany of degrees (Bachelors, Masters, and PHDs) whose gold chains are stored in the banks of some of the most vile and evil men who eve walked this planet.

All the people we grew up with in our neighborhoods brainwashed and are all in on the scheme of hierarchy that divides and keeps us from building spiritual bridges to each other.

Each of us slaves and do not realize it. All of us slaves who do not want to leave the walls of the prison. The gate can be wide open to get out and the slave can leave at any time. When you show them the spiritual light at the end of the dark tunnel and tell them to get out, they say to you "No" you leave we are happy here.

Once you understand the psychology of the slave and the master, you understand the brilliance of the controller. The controller is aware that the slave don't want to be free. They give up one set of chains just to jump into another set of chains. This is part of the Occult Knowledge used on the masses by the global elite.

Any people treated unfairly, persecuted, treated as slaves must understand their plight by developing the ability of seeing though the eyes of the masters. If the master can create a situation where the slave is auto hypnotized (Religion and Debt), the slave is doing his own hypnotizing. The slave is in essence the instrument of his own enslavement.

As far as remedies, political change is not going to work. Religion will not work in this dimension because it blinds us to the potential within ourselves requiring a master to save us when it is us that must save ourselves. Change must be at an individual level; found in a relationship we have with ourselves internally.

The Masters or Archons Keeping Us on Spiritual Lockdown

As soon as you are born, you have 2 enemies or adversaries and find yourself in a Twi-light zone. All the shenanigans and ups and downs of the external world in order to stay sane and the inner subjective world where its development depends on filtering a way through the darkness of lies and deceptions.

The masters or Archons at the top of the ladder in society understand completely our conflicted struggle from day one of our birth. They keep people in a state of spiritual lockdown with trauma, and constant fear, anxiety to the point people are drowning in angst.

The major things driving anxiety is religion, what will happen to me if I lose my job, what will happen to my kids, will I be killed by police or criminal, and will politicians create wars for profit?

Humanity a Traumatized Species

The trauma continues day in and day out. Psychologically man has suffered massive trauma. We seem to always have been a traumatized species. Though wars, famine, poverty, social injustice, and various other injustices rampant all over the world, masters continue to create further forms of schizophrenia in human beings.

Humans, through this schizoid energy, creates the society's sociological setting. The society we create is schizoid-genic that creates schizoid-genic children who are polarized, fragmented, narrow minded, and spiritless. Our children represent a continuous loop of ignorance that will ultimate lead to a post-human world.

We are a very deeply disturbed species who want to shut down the emotion of love. We are no longer attuned to our own emotions. We are inundated with drugs from Big Pharma, unhealthy eating habits and foods contaminated with GMOs, the legalization of

the marijuana industry, brainwashed or heavily misled by sexual narratives of Hollywood.

When humans have to confront the inner syndrome and complexes, one of the methodologies the ego uses to offset responsibilities or select as a method of escape from disorderly internal trauma is to project it outward on the economy, was, or relationships.

We, as a society of want-to-be-slaves will always find a way to project our inner angst on the external world. We will place the blame of our shot comings on the external environment and then step back and require an authority figure to fix the problem, looking for a God outside ourselves instead of looking within.

This is transference, displacement, sublimation and ultimately people not taking personal responsibility for their consciousness or for their lives. They are happy to project the problem outward or go to some priest or religious leader, or psychiatrist.

This is another master and slave relationship conditioned over millennia into the human psyche. Consequently, people have lost so much of their power. We have evolved psychologically as a collective whose bio-energetic energy is no longer under our control. Global elite master rule almost every aspect of our lives. We cannot remember where in what wars or how we've lost our way.

We are being controlled in the same way a dominating parent controls every single aspect of a child's life, to the extent the child becomes neurotic. The child is in a state of neurosis because it is scared if it does a bad deed it will lose the love of its parent, fearing losing love that it truly has never had, fearing loss of security it truly has never had, and fear of losing the love of a God it has truly never known.

The Archontic masters using the slogan "In God we trust" uses fear as an instrument to control behavior. People go to church and or encouraged to be good. Is these acts of goodness out of its own true moral nature or because the fear of punishment.

To rebel against Christian doctrines is met with ostracism, assigned a scarlet letter, and made an outcast in the master slave environment. People refuse to think for themselves knowing such retaliation will come, not being able to earn money and take care of their financial obligations for self and family.

Those masters who control money have a powerful tool to extinguish undesirable behavior and control thought. Defensive aggressive instincts, in the people, are being repressed by the Archontic masters. These masters have always been ruthless killers endeavoring to feed off the low energy of traumatized masses.

When something rotten is happening to you, one should respond aggressively. We learn early as children that acts of aggression will be met with pain, loss of jobs, loss of standing in community, and loss of status by not being able to spend money amongst your peers.

Aggression is a natural bio-energetic response to the violation of your integrity of you self. The slaves in all societies around the world, have been taught to repress their bio-energetic responses in order to conform and fit into the Archontic master's system we call "Big Brother or the Matrix."

You accept tyranny because you have repressed you own instinct of aggression for money. **The smarter our intellectuals become, the more cowardly they become. This has something to do with the traditional colonial educational institution's agenda to dumb-down the masses. Although people with Masters and PHDs know the truth, they cannot and refuse to speak the truth because they are conditioned by the paycheck not to speak the truth. Because of the paycheck, acts of aggression are inaccessible for use by the people against the violation of the masters.**

In the political and sociological world are smiling depressives, each one of us are seeking the approval of others. In this world, a soft tyranny is taking place. The moment anyone shows independent thought and quest for selfhood that is the opposite of the ordinary self-mutilated individual, the soft tyranny is the anxiety filled conflict going against society's program to repress the organic self that is fighting to emerge healthy.

A person's own neurosis and disorder is pseudo anxiety, pseudo despair, and a pseudo distress caused by the repression of your selfhood, which is naturally organic spirituality. This natural organic spirituality can be suppressed but it does not die or go away. Anytime this natural or organic spirituality tries to re-emerge causes anxiety.

The anxieties of the world today and the stresses of the world today are based on people's true inner voice trying to emerge. **We are self-mutilating ourselves, self-murder, and self-sadism all done to get the approval of the slave masters.** The slave masters themselves are in the same boat of self-murder themselves and they are encouraging you to self-murder.

The stress is "Not" how will I get rid of "Big Brother" but how can I get a better place in the "Master's" Slavocracy. Each individual thinking, **I wish I could get rid of my organic instincts and that this true version of my organic self would not bother me at all. Further thinking, how can I become a celebrity and have everything Big Brother can hand me. I don't have enough seniority in the lie.**

Ask yourself "Not" why I have been sold a lie, but ask, why have I bought a lie? So many people deny the master slave conspiracy and step on each other getting in line for money selling drugs, their bodies, and their souls for the low vibration feeding ones. The treacherous, deceptive, and criminals are not the usual suspect. The criminals today wear nice suits, drive nice cars, and live in million dollar mansions calling the enlightened ones crazy. Look at the people in lock-step wearing uniforms with weapons going off to kill people. Who is the truly insane?

It is way past the time of the rising of the Phoenix and the time of renaissance. It is time for us to see through the eyes of the masters the dilemma they cause for us and know the truth. Stop seeking guidance from the evil and misguided. It is time to deconstruct lies and do things better.

We have an entire world of Gurus, teachers, pseudo teachers, and misleaders with a modicum of knowledge, insight, technical, or other who set themselves up as Gods (Bankers, Royal Families, and religious leaders) and try to dominate everybody else. They do not want to awaken your organic intelligence, which scares the Hell out of them.

Our wise ancestral leaders passed from this physical world but their archetypal wisdom remains. We need to filter the great thinkers teaching vibrating energy that is all around from our consciousness into this physical dimension as a re-awakening. The material things we clamor for are just physical objects. They exist but do not have any meaning and are nothing that will travel with us spiritually when our time in this realm is over physically.

(VI) Extraterrestrial Contributions to World War II; Humanity's Flaming Out on the Highway to Hell

Path 42: "The Presence of Extraterrestrials on Earth and The Technological Threat to the Planetary Biosphere"

Are there highly intelligent and deceptive 'ultra-dimensional entities' materializing in disguise as 'aliens' collaborating with a secret 'world government'? Did German Nazis flee to Antarctica at the end of World War II to collaborate with extraterrestrial's called 'Greys and continued to develop advanced military technology that include anti-gravity craft o Flying Saucers?

The Aldebaran Mystery

Jim Nichols

Jim Nichols UFO Website

Oberth's fellow associate space pioneer, who also served the Third Reich, **Werhner Von Braun**, echoed similar knowledge of the extra-terrestrial reality when he stated in 1959:

> "We find ourselves faced by powers which are far stronger than hitherto assumed, and whose base is at present unknown to us. More I cannot say at present. We are now engaged in entering into closer contact with those powers, and within six or nine months' time it may be possible to speak with more precision on the matter."

From "Above Top Secret" by Timothy Good, William Morrow and Company, Inc. 1988.

Just who were "the people of other worlds" that Dr. Oberth spoke of so blithely?

Were both of these esteemed German scientists making oblique reference to one of UFOlogy's most pervasive and tantalizing 'myths' - the alleged link between the Third Reich of pre-World War II Germany and... EXTRATERRESTRIALS?

Following military defeat of World War I, certain occult secret societies emerged in Germany intent upon discovering clues to the existence of ancient lost civilizations that once flourished on this planet; civilizations that reportedly possessed remarkable, almost magical technologies that allowed them mastery of the seas and the skies and even inter-stellar space travel.

Inspiration to rediscover such technologies were found in a novel published in 1871 by Rosicrucian author Edward Bulwer-Lytton, entitled, "THE COMING RACE".

Lytton tells the tale of an intrepid explorer who discovers an advanced race of humans living within a vast subterranean world who call themselves "Vril-Ya". These beings had formerly been surface dwellers until a global catastrophe not unlike the Old Testament flood, forced them to take refuge deep in the Earth.

The survival of this marvelous society was facilitated by their application of a force they referred to as "Vril."

Vril can be call *electricity*, except that it comprehends in its manifold branches other forces of nature, to which in our scientific nomenclature, differing names are assigned, such as magnetism, galvanism, etc.

These people consider that in 'Vril' they have arrived at the unity in natural energetic agencies, which has been conjectured by many philosophers above ground…"

It was supposed by some that Lytton's book was not altogether a work of fiction, and in fact, he was privy to secrets that lost Lemurian and Atlantean artifacts still existed in clandestine caches hidden in the Gobi Desert and Tibet.

And indeed, ancient Sanskrit texts from India describe civilizations that flourished before the great flood that possessed technologies beyond the understanding of modern science.

The epic poem 'Saramangana Sutradhara', makes reference to the construction of amazing flying machines:

"Strong and durable must the body of the Vimana be made, like a great flying bird of light material. Inside one must put the mercury engine with its iron heating apparatus underneath.

By means of the power latent in the mercury, which sets the driving whirlwind in motion, a man sitting inside may travel a great distance in the sky.

The movements of a Vimana are such that it can vertically ascend, vertically descend, or move slanting forwards and backwards. With the help of machines, human beings can fly through the air and heavenly beings can come down to Earth."

German oriental scholars and occultists regarded such ancient myths with complete seriousness and during the lull between the First and Second World War, diligent efforts were put forth by both the 'Thule' and the 'Vril' secret societies to transform these myths into a viable technological reality.

Mastery of an occult force such as 'Vril' would not only assure German technical dominance–it would ultimately liberate Germany from any crippling co-dependence upon the international petroleum cartels dominated by Germany's conquerors–the United States and Britain.

Initiates of both the Thule and Vril societies were determined to develop an 'alternative science' and 'alternative technologies' based on principles possessed by the great 'lost' civilization of Atlantis:

> "A spiritual 'dynamo-technology' superior to the mechanistic notions of modern science."

Thus to rediscover this source of universal free-energy and make it readily available as a benefit to the modern world became their goal.

Thule member, Dr. W.O. Schumann of the *Technical University in Munich*, declared:

> "In everything we recognize two principles that determine the events; light and darkness, good and evil, creation and destruction–as in electricity we know plus and minus. It is always; either–or...

Everything destructive is of Satanic origin, everything creative is divine... Every technology based on explosion or combustion has thus to be called Satanic. The coming new age will be an age of new, positive, divine technology..."

Hence, the goal to harness 'Vril', Prana, the fundamental, limitless, cosmic life-force energy - a power source that would function harmoniously with our natural world - became an integral focus of these German secret societies.

The medium **Maria Orsic** was leader of the ‹Vrilerinnen›, the beautiful young ladies of the *Vril Gesellschaft.*

Characteristically they all wore their hair in long horse-tails, contrary to the popular short bobbed fashion of their day, claiming their long hair acted as cosmic antennas that helped facilitate their contact with extraterrestrials beings from beyond.

According to the legend of the *German Vril society*, a fateful meeting was held in 1919 at an old hunting lodge near Berchtesgaden, where Maria Orsic presented to a small group assembled from the Thule, Vril, and Black Sun Societies, telepathic messages she claimed to have received from an extraterrestrial civilization existing in the distant Aldebaran solar system, sixty-eight light years away, in the Constellation of Taurus.

One set of Maria's channeled transmissions was found to be in a secret *German Templar script* unknown to her. A second series of transmissions appeared to be written in an ancient eastern language, which Babylonian scholars associated with the Thule group, recognized as *ancient Sumerian.*

Maria Orsic along with Sigrun, another of the Vril Society's female mediums, began the task of translating these transmissions and discovered they contained instructions for *building a circular flight machine.*

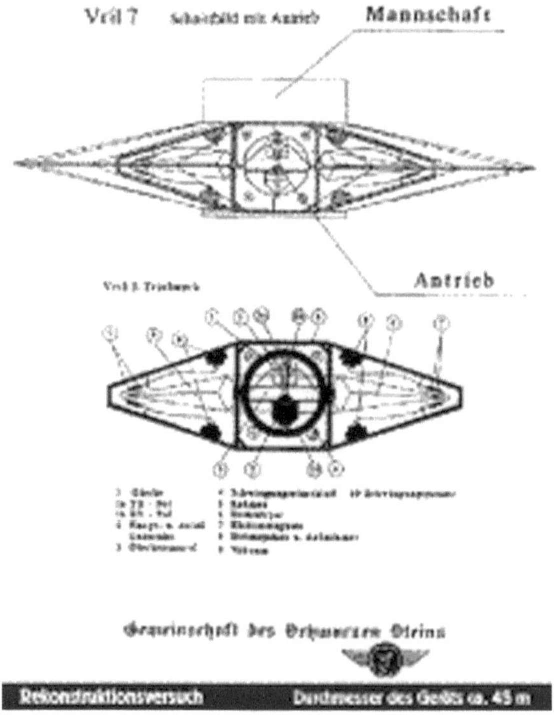

However, it should be important to consider the possible motivation behind the Aldebaran civilization's offer to assist the Vril Group and Germany.

Researcher **Wendelle Stevens** tells us that, rather than a militant gesture of aid to aggressive Nazis, the Aldebarans perceived an economic disparity in Earth cultures that fueled perpetual wars and conflict.

To alleviate this disparity the Aldebarans reasoned that by offering 'free-energy' technologies, used to create affordable mass transportation devices, a new innovative generation of industries, promoting prosperity and greater peaceful interaction between nations might result; thus diminishing violent wars.

Clearly such a plan resonated with members of both the Thule and Vril Societies and their dream for a utopian New World based on 'alternative science'.

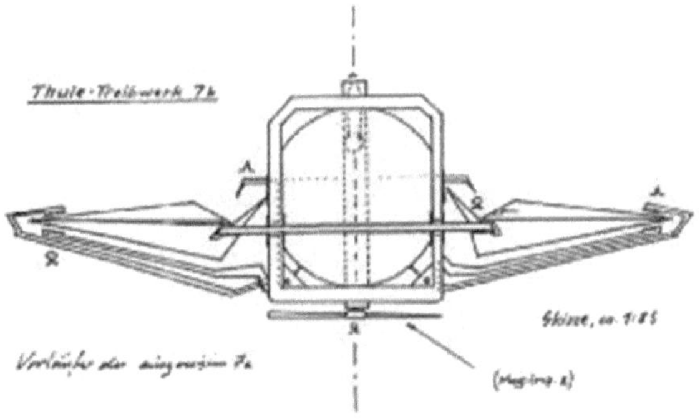

Upon studying these otherworldly, esoteric designs, Dr. W.O. Schumann and his associates from the University of Munich realized the channeling actually contained viable physics, and over the ensuing years construction was initiated to make this flying machine a reality.

By 1922 development of a working prototype was underway. Meanwhile, Germany saw the inception of the National Socialist Party and Adolph Hitler's rise to power, fueled in part by the utopian visions of a new world order inspired by the Thule and Vril Societies. By 1934, the first manned test flight of the RFZ-1 took place.

However, the results were less than auspicious. Flown by intrepid World War I ace, Lothar Waiz, the craft wobbled to altitude of 60 meters, and upon landing, the pilot, managed to escape from the craft just in time before it spun out of control, ripping to pieces like a drunken top. Before the end of that year a much improved version, the five meter RFZ-2, was test flown successfully and eventually flying disc development was taken over by Division SS E-IV of the Nazi military.

The fundamental physics were as simple as a child's spinning gyroscope - circular discs spun in counter-rotation create an anti-gravity effect; an effect as timeless as that described by the Old Testament prophet Ezekiel and his 'fiery chariot'–"a wheel within a wheel."

Had the Hebrew patriarch been witness to a flying machine from Aldebaran?

Contrary to his professed aim to create a world of cosmic harmony, Hitler sent his Panzer tanks and infantry into Poland in 1939, thus precipitating the altogether destructive Second World War.

And despite the fact that he also outlawed all secret societies in Germany, the Thule and Vril Gesellschafts maintained their autonomy, and development of Vril levitating saucer craft continued, despite funding competition from conventional Luftwaffe war-production imperatives.

Aero-Technical Unit V-7 designed a number of hybrid saucers that combined both exotic anti-gravity and conventional turbojet propulsion systems, creating vertical lift craft that were essentially precursors to modern helicopters.

However, the distinctly separate SS E-IV Unit, bore the sole responsibility of developing Hitler's dream of free-energy propulsion.

By 1941, the successful Vril-2 levitation craft was employed for transatlantic reconnaissance flights. The RFZ-2 craft employed the "Schumman-Levitator" drive for vertical lift and when activated, the craft displayed effects commonly described in many UFO accounts; blurring of visible contours, and luminous ionization colors relative to the craft›s engine acceleration; varying from orange to green, blue to white.

As well, the craft made radical 90 degree turns characteristic of UFO flight.

Tragically, the Reich diverted *the peaceful intent of the Alebaran's levitation technology*, and following the success of the RFZ-2, a single pilot combat model was designed.

The advanced Vril-1 Fighter was capable of 12000 km/h with full speed right angle turns with no adverse G-effects on the pilot.

Since the craft flew in a self-contained envelope of *its own gravitational field*, the pilot experienced no sense of motion or inertia.

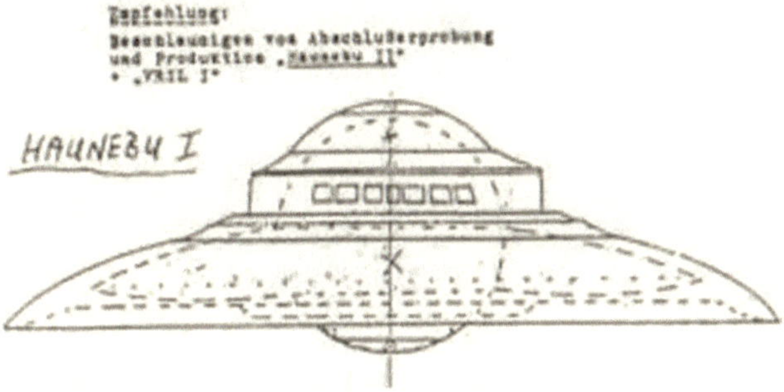

Subsequent levitation-craft advances between 1941 and 1944 spawned the "Haunebu" series, the 'heavy hitters' of Reich's saucer fleet.

Development of powerful tachyon magneto-gravitic drives - "Thule-Tachyonators" (speculated to be large spheres of vertically rotating mercury) - allowed design of 75 foot diameter armored saucer ships equipped with armaments such as Panzer-tank cannon turrets mounted to the underside.

Other craft were equipped with klystron laser cannons.

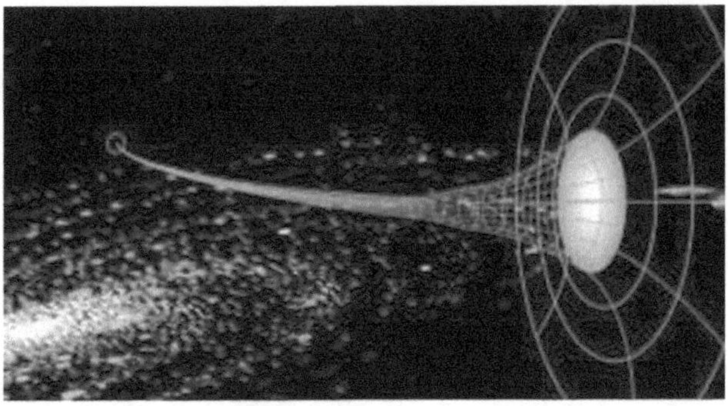

By Christmas of 1943, medium Maria Orsic of the *Vril Gesellschaft*, claimed that subsequent transmissions from Aldebaran revealed there were two habitable planets orbiting that star and that the ancient Mesopotamian civilization of Sumeria was linked to earlier colonies of Aldebaran explorers.

The seers discovered that the Aldebaran written language was identical to that of the Sumerians and was phonetically similar to that of spoken German. It was also revealed that a ‹dimension channel› or ‹worm-hole› existed connecting our two solar systems.

Thus in January of 1944, possibly aware that Germany's war efforts were faltering, Hitler and Himmler authorized an audacious plan to send a Vril-7 saucer ship into the dimensional channel, perhaps to secure assistance from the Aldebaran civilization.

The venture resulted in near disaster, the Vril-7 returned with its hull reportedly aged as if it had been flying for a hundred years and its surface damaged in several places.

Meanwhile, the Allies sampled an unpleasant taste of the deadly weapons potential of German saucers.

In 1944 a massive bombing raid was launched against the critical ball-bearing plant at Schweinfurt. Within a matter of hours a squadron of ten to fifteen Nazi discs managed to shoot down as many as one-hundred and fifty British and American bombers - one quarter of the entire bomber contingent.

Still, facing overwhelming odds, the crumbling Reich lacked sufficient saucer squadrons to turn the tide.

With the military fate of the Reich in doubt, an ambitious, energetic General rose within the SS inner circle elite to a level of power that rivaled perhaps that of even the Fuhrer himself.

Hans Kammler, a protégé' of Heinrich Himmler, had earned a reputation with his skills for rapid development and implementation of underground manufacturing facilities, and vast mobilization of slave labor consignments from concentration camps.

By 1945 Kammler had secured control over all top secret SS projects that were missile or 'aircraft' related.

Certainly Vril projects would have been one of his foremost priorities. Cunning and shrewd, Kammler easily bore the qualifications to master mind construction of 'special projects' facilities at the South Pole.

And as of April 17, 1945, Kammler disappeared from Germany, presumably escaping capture aboard a lumbering, six engine Junkers 390 Amerika bomber, bound for an unknown destination.

Neither was military assistance forthcoming from Aldebaran, but perhaps safe haven was offered instead, as a massive 250 foot diameter Haunebu IIIdreadnaught armed with four, triple-gun, heavy caliber naval turrets and capable of space flight was allegedly completed by April of 1945.

With the specter Russian, British and American armies all relentlessly advancing on the German heartland, supplies, scientists, and saucer components were being steadily evacuated from Europe by U-boats to secret enclaves in Germany's Antarctic colony - *Neuschwabenland.*

Just one month prior to the Haunebu III's completion a cryptic message was sent by Maria Orsic to all members of the Vril Society, simply stating "None are staying here."

The psychic medium Maria was never heard from again, perhaps having escaped - like Kammler - to South America, the Antarctic, or possibly even... Aldebaran!

The question remains, was she Kammler's collaborator or captive?

By inevitably seizing the rocket facilities and personnel at Peenemunde, the advancing Allied Army leadership was only too well aware of how dangerously advanced German technology had become.

Despite the Third Reich's unconditional surrender in 1945, a potential Nazi threat still haunted Allied intelligence. Had the German High Command sacrificed its European operation to buy time for installation of a 'fall-back' position in the Antarctic, capable of launching future retaliations from its South Polar redoubt?

Post-script to this legend is the account of "Operation High-Jump".

In January of 1947, an American military task force, complete with thirteen ships including, an aircraft carrier, seaplanes, helicopters and 4000 combat troops was dispatched to the Antarctic under the command of Admiral Richard E. Byrd, for the stated purpose of 'mapping' the coastline.

This task force was provisioned for an eight-month polar stay, but after eight weeks and an undisclosed loss of planes and personnel, Byrd withdrew his forces.

Rumor was, Byrd encountered overwhelming hostile action, and he described as:

> "fighters that are able to fly from one pole to another
> with incredible speed."

He also intimated that he had in fact engaged a German contingent being assisted as well by an 'advanced civilization' with formidable technologies...

Whatever occurred with Byrd's expedition at the South Pole remains shrouded in mystery since all reports, including Byrd's personal log entries, remain classified.

Also, it should be noted that *Operation High-Jump* was originally organized by Secretary of the Navy, **James Forrestal**. But later, in 1949, Forrestal was sent to convalesce for a nervous breakdown at Bethesda Naval Hospital. However, after allegedly ranting to hospital staff about the Antarctic, UFOs and an underground Nazi city, Forrestal was denied all visitors and shortly thereafter, *died in a fall from his hospital room window.*

His death was labeled a 'suicide'.

But again, considering the question posed at the outset of this essay,

- Could the 'advanced civilization' suggested by Byrd be the same extraterrestrials alluded to by both Von Braun and Oberth?
- Could these "people of other worlds" be Germany's mysterious allies from Aldebaran?

Such is the legend of 'Vril' and the Third Reich's levitating disc projects.

Of course, had all discussion of 'flying saucers' ended in 1945 it would be perfectly simple to dismiss the whole myth as preposterous nonsense. However, as we well know, persistent reports of UFOs and circular flying craft have remained a ubiquitous enigma worldwide for all the decades since World War II. And as long as this mystery goes unanswered the riddle of Nazi saucers will remain an urgent paradox that spins a kaleidoscope of demanding questions.

Viewed from the aspect of classical physics, the whole myth is easily dismissed as fanciful rubbish; the fairy tale notions of occult channeling with *space brothers* from Aldebaran, and Nazis armed with flying saucers and ray-guns sounds like *the most outrageous science fiction!*

However, this same legend reconsidered from the radically altered view of Quantum physics takes on dramatic plausibility!

- Was the Vril Society simply making practical application of the 'Unified Field"?
- Is Vril or "the unity in natural energetic agencies" that Edward Bulwer-Lytton described, far from pulp fiction, but a remarkably accurate description of zero-point energy that pervades the entire universe?
- Did ancient lost civilizations of Earth share understanding with extraterrestrial civilizations among the stars that the universe is in fact a single consciousness and simultaneously an ocean of limitless energy?
- Could it be that a handful of daring German visionaries discovered secrets of harnessing this energy?
- And ultimately, who were the REAL victors in World War II?
- Did a contingent of German physicists and engineers and military personnel successfully drop off the grid in 1945 and establish a new colony, totally self-sufficient and independent of the global petroleum cartels?
- And are the fundamentals of free-energy production fully known and deliberately withheld, at the cost of destroying our environment, merely to serve the greed of multi-national corporate and banking interests to this day?
- And is this 'free-energy' propulsion the ultimate secret behind the UFO cover-up?

Of course, in the years immediately following World War II, the German saucer mystery compounded even more. In June of 1947 a private pilot named **Kenneth Arnold** reported a formation of nine shiny objects speeding along at an unprecedented speed of 1600 mph in the vicinity of Mt. Rainier, Washington.

In Arnold's words, the craft flew "*like a saucer would if you skipped it across the water.*"

Hence the press seized upon his words and launched the public fascination with "Flying Saucers". However, Arnold actually described the craft as more crescent shaped, like 'flying wings' - which coincidentally was another air form perfected by the German *Horton Brothers*, during the war.

It was suspected that captured German aircraft were being studied in a joint U.S./British facility in western Canada close to Washington State.

Four months later, in September of 1947, just eight months after Admiral Byrd's aborted mission to the Antarctic, the Strategic Air Command undertook a detailed mapping and reconnaissance mission of the North Pole.

An extensive B-29 support base was established at Ft. Richardson, Alaska. But aside from cameras, these bombers were crammed with state-of-the-art, electromagnetic scanners, sensors and magnetic emissions detectors.

And, just as Byrd described, 'high speed craft capable of flying from pole to pole', were again encountered at the Arctic as well. Debriefed flight crews reported seeing metallic vertical lift saucers parked on the ice packs, flying in and out of the water as well as dogging the B-29s.

All evidence, tapes, film canisters and documentation were immediately classified and rushed back to Washington D.C.

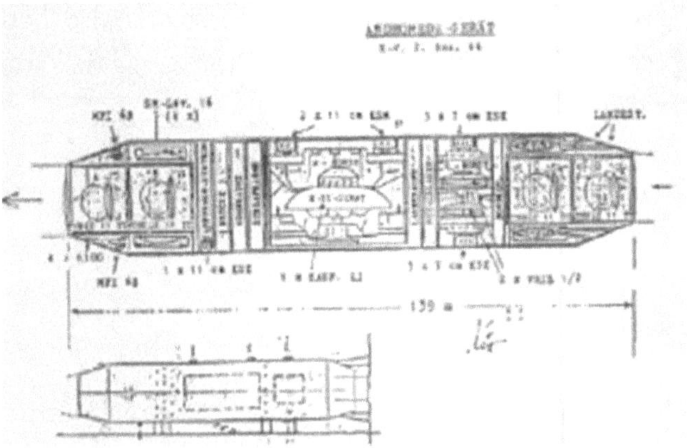

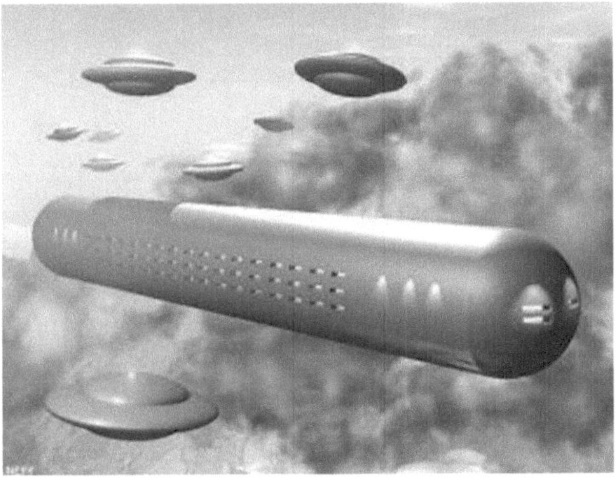

According to the captured records, the Germans also had plans to build a 'Zeppelin'-sized levitating cylinder ship called the "Andromeda" machine.

This 330 foot behemoth was capable of carrying as many as five of the smaller Vril and Haunebu scout ships. In the early 1950's a California man named George Adamski photographed a UFO remarkably similar to this design.

Later, Adamski claimed to have contact with a 'Nordic' looking extraterrestrial near Desert Center, California, who claimed to be from the planet Venus.

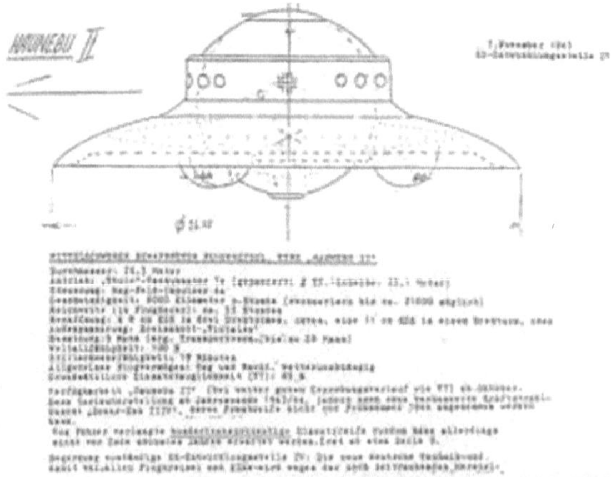

However, it should be noted that photographs of the little scout craft this alien flew show a design virtually identical to the German Haunebu II.

Though Adamski was later debunked as a fraud, reports of UFOs identical to the ‹Venusian scout ship› continued to surface worldwide.

In 1954, President **Dwight Eisenhower** was allegedly secreted away to a meeting with Extraterrestrials at MUROC airfield near Palm Springs, California.

Former American President Dwight D. Eisenhower had three secret meetings with aliens, a former US government consultant has claimed.

The 34th President of the United States met the extra-terrestrials at a remote air base in New Mexico in 1954, according to lecturer and author Timothy Good.

Eisenhower and other FBI officials are said to have organized the showdown with the space creatures by sending out 'telepathic messages'.

The two parties finally met up on three separate occasions at the Holloman Air Force base and there were 'many witnesses'.

Conspiracy theorists have circulated increased rumors in recent months that the meeting between the Commander-in-Chief and people from another planet took place.

But the claims from Mr. Good, a former U.S. Congress and Pentagon consultant, are the first to be made publicly by a prominent academic.

Speaking on Frank Skinner's BBC2 current affairs show Opinionated, he said that governments around the world have been in regular contact with aliens for many decades.

Aliens have made both formal and informal contact with thousands of people throughout the world from all walks of life,' he added.

Asked why the aliens don't go to somebody 'important' like Barack Obama, he said: 'Well, certainly I can tell you that in 1954, President Eisenhower had three encounters, set up meetings with aliens, which took place at certain Air Force bases including Holloman Air Force base in New Mexico.'

He added that there were 'many witnesses'.

Eisenhower, who was president from 1953 to 1961, is known to have had a strong belief in life on other planets.

The former five-star general in the United States Army who commanded the Allied Forces in Europe during the Second World War, was also keen on pushing the U.S. space program.

His meeting with the cosmic life forms is said to have taken place while officials were told that he was on vacation in Palm Springs, California, in February 1954.

The initial meeting is supposed to have taken place with aliens who were 'Nordic' in appearance, but the agreement was eventually 'signed' with a race called 'Alien Greys'.

Mr. Good added: 'We know that up to 90 per cent of all UFO reports can be explained in conventional terms. However, I would say millions of people worldwide have actually seen the real thing.'

According to classified documents released by the Ministry of Defense in 2010, Winston Churchill may have ordered a UFO sighting to be kept secret.

The UFO was seen over the East Coast of England by an RAF reconnaissance plane returning from a mission in France or Germany towards the end of the war.

Churchill is said to have discussed how to deal with UFO sightings with Eisenhower.

One particular group was reported to be 'Nordic' looking and they offered Eisenhower Free-Energy technology in exchange for nuclear disarmament - Ike declined!

And as the story goes, these 'Nordic' ETs subsequently met with Pope Pius XII at the Vatican as well.

And of course it remains common knowledge that during the war Germany had cordial relations with Argentina and other Latin American countries, and by a curious 'coincidence' even today UFOs are commonly reported the full length and breadth of South America, along with tales of hidden German bases in the ice peaks of Peru and the vast jungles of Brazil...

Consider this suspiciously familiar object allegedly photographed near Lima, Peru in 1973.

But perhaps the most blatant inference of a German connection with UFOs comes from the famed Billy Meier case in Switzerland.

In 1975, thirty years after the disappearance of the Vril society leaders, a Swiss farmer claimed to have contact with a girl from the 'Pleiades', who bore the pseudonym, "Semjase" and a striking resemblance to the 'Vrilerinnen' from 1919.

This space girl also wore long blonde hair, spoke in fluent Austrian-German and candidly shared comprehensive knowledge about the German saucer projects of World War II.

Were Semjase's 'beamships' actually contemporary versions of the old Haunebus?

And yet, the riddle remains that, were the surviving modern remnants of the Third Reich to actually possess such vastly superior technology,

- Why then would they not simply flex their muscle and conquer the world in one final swift stroke?
- Or did they realize such a victory might ultimately be a futile gesture?

Suppose the Reich survivors learned from their Aldebaran mentors the secret the ancient Sumerians possessed - that, in a regular 3600 year cycle, the surface of planet Earth is devastated by the passing of a dwarf-star which is companion to our solar system.

And that this Dark Star was calculated once again to swing through the inner planets *during the early years of the 21st Century.*

Such a monumental event would grant the "Thousand Year Reich" a meager seventy year or so life span.

- Thus might the Reich survivors not wisely choose to disappear from the surface world and develop hardened underground 'shelters' in the remote wastes of Antarctica, patiently preparing to safely ride out the Dark Star's passing?
- Do we dare suppose that a contemporary generation of subterranean Reichskinder secretly continue to advance their limitless scientific wonders, content to allow the ignorant, expendable 'surface dwellers' to choke in the poisoned atmosphere of their internal-combustion, junk-technology, automobiles, airplanes and industries?
- Could it be that all the incredible levitating machines and free-energy technologies envisioned by the Thule and Vril Societies are being carefully held in reserve for the promised 'New Age'; a future time when Earth has recovered from the agonies of its Dark Star's encounter…?

We may discover the answers to these questions sooner than we realize!

Meanwhile, the quest to solve the mysteries of Nazi saucers and the secrets from Aldebaran, certainly has gained more relevance to our present world here in the first decade of the 21st Century. It seems an irony that, much like pre-World War II Germany, we find Western Civilization dangerously dependent upon foreign petroleum sources dominated by hostile Muslim nations.

Is there a free-energy/anti-gravity answer to this dilemma?

And lastly, there has surfaced the mystery of the TR-3B. Allegedly one of the latest high-tech, USAF stealth aircraft rumored to be operational is the 'Astra', otherwise known as the TR-3B.

This craft is delta shaped and capable of vertical lift, as well as all the other radical moves commonly associated with UFOs. This baby comes in two sizes, one 300 feet long and one 600 feet long. Its propulsion is described as "Magnetic Field Disruptor" [anti-gravity], created by spinning mercury plasma at 50,000 rpms, pressurized to 250,000 psi.

This reduces the craft's gravitational mass by 89%. Multi-mode impulse rockets at each corner of the delta configuration supply the remaining 11% propulsion. Could this plane be *the ugly stepchild of the Haunebu III??*

It is interesting to note that in ancient India, the name "Astra' referred to a 'terrible' airborne weapon...

If such aircraft technology seems too far-fetched, one might consider this statement from former director of Lockheed's 'Skunk-Works' at Area-51, Ben Rich...

"We already have the means to travel among the stars, but these technologies are locked up in 'black-projects' and it would take an act of God to ever get them out to benefit humanity."

Rich is also quoted as saying,

"Anything you can imagine we already know how to do."

Author's Disclaimer

The preceding text is virtually all 'legend'. There is no absolute, conclusive evidence to fully verify the authenticity of such a tale.

I've cobbled this together from the writings of Jan Van Helsing, Vladimir Terziski, Wendelle Stevens and a website called 'Grey Falcon', as well as the video, UFO Secrets of the Third Reich.

Nick Cook's book, The Hunt for Zero Point, sheds important new light on advanced, hitherto unrevealed, Nazi technologies.

And in addition, I highly recommend two books, *Dark Mission*, by Richard Hoagland and *The Rise of the Fourth Reich*, by Jim Marrs that follow the post-war trail of insidious covert Nazi influence into American politics, military and space exploration, right up to the present day.

The bottom line has two options; either the whole story is pure fantasy, or Nazi secrets of anti-gravity were gobbled up at the end of the war by Allied Intelligence and given a security classification *Above-Top-Secret*, with all evidence meticulously hidden or destroyed.

However, it should be noted that anti-gravity propulsion systems, such as *the Vril legend* suggest, would make all aerospace and avionic technologies obsolete overnight - and these are huge multi-billion dollar industries directly tied to the international petroleum cartels. Surely these combined military/industrial interests would possess the means and the motive to obliterate any conclusive history of German anti-gravity research.

Allegedly the Rockefeller Foundation paid $139,000.00 in 1946 to commission the publishing of an "official" history of World War II that deleted any and all references to the mystical and occult interests of the Third Reich.

One of the Rockefeller Foundation's major contributors was... Standard Oil!

Path 43: 'Luciferians' or the 'Poltergeists' overseeing and directing the actions of the Humanoid-Reptiloids collaborators.

Humanity has always been divided by religious and scientific belief systems. Religion is based on faith while science is based on logic. The existence of God is one of the chief concepts in religion. According to religion, the creation of the universe is the foremost act of God.

Science has its own way of doing things and it has nothing to do with religious beliefs. It is always based on logic. For something to be accepted as true there should be proof. To scientist, God is a faith based assumption that foregoes dialectics, thus science does not accept the notion of God and that men are made in God's image.

God did not create the world according to science. According to science, the universe was created as a result of an organic Big Bang which set off a chain reaction of rapid energy expansion about 13.7 billion year ago producing forceful energy of light illuminating a vast infinity of darkness.

Governments have a dilemma explaining existence in this vast universe that does not include alien extraterrestrial beings. Disclosure that confirms the existence of UFO's and extraterrestrial life beyond earth provides alternative beliefs to the religious answers about human origin. Governments are not up to disclosing what information they have on the existence of extraterrestrials. Why?

The trees grow as they always have, the wind still blows as it always has, water flows as it always has, and the sun shine as it always has, why are governments lying about extraterrestrials? Why is there false flag terrorism, why do governments spend money on weapons when peace is much more beneficial to the lives of the inhabitants of earth? Why are government's deciding to err on the side of murder, violence, and being out of synch with humanity's higher vibrations of love and peace? It is very strange that governments continue to lie about the presence of extraterrestrials on earth.

UFO sightings continues at alarming frequencies all around the world. Many believe that government not only are not disclosing that UFO's exist, but that they are actually working with extraterrestrial acquiring advanced technology. The question is why does governments choose to lie to the people and keep people in the dark?

Humanity has progressed from riding in horse and buggies to sending probes to Mars in 60 years. Many people believes that Germany acquired advanced technology from extraterrestrials to advance rocket technology and build anti-gravity crafts. German Scientist were brought over at the end of World War II to advance the United States Space Program.

Secret Societies in Germany believed that they were descendants of a superior extraterrestrial race. This belief system is at the heart of many of the problems of the world today specifically economically and racially.

The divine right of kings, divine right, or God's mandate is a political and religious doctrine of royal and political legitimacy. It asserts that a monarch is subject to no earthly authority, deriving the right to rule directly from the will of God. The pathway for many to God is tracing D.N.A. to extraterrestrial origin to an advance race from origins light years away from this solar system.

Royal families who believe this have an agenda beyond servicing the will of the people who they believe is of inferior D.N.A. make-up. This is the essence of racist beliefs proliferating in the world. The ruse of

"Divine Rights" implies that only God can judge an unjust king and that any attempt to depose, dethrone or restrict powers runs contrary to the will of God and may constitute a sacrilegious act. It is often expressed in the phrase "by the Grace of God", attached to the titles of a reigning monarch.

Before the outbreak of the Second World War, to an isolated section of the Bavarian Alps, It was there, in the summer of 1938, Unidentified Flying Objects, crewed by a distinctly human, and Aryan appearing races, made a forced landing, very similar to the one which was to occur, some ten years later, in the desert, near Roswell, New Mexico, in the United States.

While the occupants of the two craft were completely unrelated, the technology involved, seems to have been strikingly similar. Also, the outcome of the recovery effort, undertaken by Germany, just as a similar recovery effort was undertaken by the United States, had strikingly different results.

The Bavarian crash of 1938, seems to have yielded a functioning, or almost functioning and repairable (with the technology of the time) power plant, and a nearly completely destroyed, or unrepairable airframe. The Roswell crash resulted in exactly the opposite... a nearly intact airframe and a ruined power plant.

Technology changed drastically after these events. Powerful men with money used money control government and religion to control the masses of people. Alien technology opened up new technologies in the market place that has created superior aircraft, cars, computers, phones, and television. Back engineering crashed alien technology has been very profitable to bankers controlling the money supply of governments.

We have gone from people living in the darkness of religion controlled by leaders who feel they are Monarchs by Divine Rights. This idea of genetic differences that makes one group superior to another has propelled racism throughout the ages. Now, the very people who once felt they were descendants of Gods, have adopted a belief that they are now descendants of a superior race of extraterrestrials.

Our society, no longer constrained by reins of religion, is being segregated by technology. Jobs that support advance technology are developing financial cast systems in society. Advance technology paints a rosy picture of the future. The "Hunger Game Society" will take full advantage of advancing technology constructing centers for the rich and powerful, who will live in high tech luxury. The rich will be protected in enclaves of privilege by military police.

It is a sad day, religion is no longer constraining our logical dark side. Technology segregation is the tool of oppression where virtual reality has become preferable over biological life. I rather die and follow the natural cosmic order than to live eternally in a virtual reality. The love of money has built an evil legacy of selfish implosion by the human race. O heavenly Father, how is it that they do not know what they are doing?

What is it exactly that life urges from our soul? To know thyself is at the top of the pyramid of wisdom. We come into this world equipped with minds to filter consciousness from energy radiated from moving particles.

The Cosmos, the physical manifestation of God, is the artist painting life with exploding stars, radiation, and gases. Our cognitive vision is filtered through radiating photons producing cognitive impressions we term reality on a collective canvas called humanity. The art of living is an experience of artistry where all lives make up the rich colors of reality.

What do we really know about self if our cognitive spectrum is limited to a mundane perspective from only one mundane reality? We expand knowledge of self only when we cross the limited religious bias that we are the only species created by God. Once we accept the grandiosity of the Cosmos outside of the religious box of that instructs we inherited this vast cosmos alone, then we enter the realm of quantum thinking, which entertain the infinite spectrum of being.

Life is the endless stream of cognition built from mental fibers created from movement of matter. Love, sadness, pain, and pleasure are products of electromagnetic sensations that becomes a collective kaleidoscope of a biased human consciousness.

The Cosmos is a storehouse of physical matter being converted into consciousness ad infinitum through electromagnetic process where moving particles generates energy as they collide. This energy is factored into consciousness.

What would we find in the spiritual spectrum of humanity? If we could look at the willful desire component of the collective spiritual spectrum of humanity, what is in this inventory? Who are everyday people whose very survival depends on self-knowledge and a greater understanding of their place in the universe?

In the spiritual spectrum of collective humanity exists imprints of struggle to survive by people in throes of poverty and suffering, cavalier regards of those celebrating more wealth than they could ever need, relentless search for security of those captive of various religious ideology, guilt component contributed by those who lie to us and murdered for profit, we would find the noble qualities of those willing to die for righteousness, concern of those who see the actions of their fellow man or woman doing harm to others yet do nothing to stop it.

We would also find the exceptional consciousness of those motivated by compassion pushing imperatives that save lives, we would find the spiritual component of those who have nurtured wholeness from principals of love that instruct all lives matter. The important question is, what part of the spiritual spectrum are each one of us contributing to?

Our spiritual nature has a unique imprint constructed from life experiences. Our ideas and beliefs are the products of truth and lies revealed to us. Many traditions created from myths, religious dogma, and superstitions are created from fear. Somewhere along the way, in the traditional struggles to weather the challenges to the physical body, the spiritual development of our collective psyche took a backseat to master mundane challenges we pose to each other with egotistical aggression driven by a primal instincts.

Survival of the fittest sanctions rape, pillage and plunder. Yes people, we have not come so far. We still are doing what Atalla the Hun, Genghis Kahn, Alexander the Great, Julius Caesar, and Hannibal did; we are just using more destructive technology.

We are living in a new age that dictates the spiritual baby must and will be tossed out in the dirty wash of selfishness using advance technology as the soap.

If you sit down and think about it, so much of what political actors perfect is inverted lies to cover back room money deals that feeds financial divides between the .01 percent and the working poor. The social concessions that comes along with prioritizing technical advancement without the people's full understanding reflects the mounting inhumanities for profit that is setting everyone adrift in the ocean of intellectual properties to face towering swells of technological segregation that has morphed into society's greatest partition of prejudice.

It is important for us to realize that our collective humanity is under assault by rogue multi-Transnational corporations controlling governments, just as marionette controls puppets. This realization is the first step to improve our collective brand to construct authentic societies of people loving and helping each other that has never been allowed to exist in the current system of greed. The world will only get better when we realize we are denied our greatest humane fruits of dignity, freedom, and love accepting the growing mindset of technical segregation.

Year	Missing
1990	663,921
1991	705,175
1992	801,358
1993	868,345
1994	954,896
1995	969,264
1996	955,252
1997	980,712
1998	932,190
1999	867,129
2000	876,213
2001	840,279
2002	821,975
2003	824,699
2004	830,325
2005	834,536
2006	836,131
2007	814,967
2008	778,164
2009	719,558
2010	692,944
2011	678,860
2012	661,593
2013	637,911
2014	635,155
2015	637,304

In 2016, 634,435 people were reported missing. This is a lot of people disappearing, yet it is not reported as you think it should be.

The aliens use the blood and body parts for formula to keep them alive [their food] and for use in the growing vats, and for the artificial wombs. Plasma and amniotic fluid are the two most vital ingredients for their lives. Also, the 'sap' of some plants can keep them alive for months. Most of the plants are parasitic in nature, but red grapes and okra plants can also be added to the formula to keep them alive, if they have no 'regular' formula.

They also consume amniotic water, plasma and several other body parts [raw, usually bovine]. This nearly clear mixture with a texture of pureed peaches, and almost in that color. Reptiloids are not above eating human flesh. It has been said that they prefer flesh that is young enough to be free of toxins, yet old enough to be imbued with a lifetime of accumulated "emotional energy residue" which is resident within the human body.

The grays make the attempt not to 'eat' around the humans, because the odor of it is VERY unpleasant to ANY human. They can spend days or even weeks between feedings. The working caste of the reptilians eat meat, insects and a large variety of plants including vegetables and fruit. They prefer their meat raw and very fresh, but have learned to enjoy some cooked meat like rare beef steak.

Some abductees claim that certain reptilian factions have such complex bio-technologies that they are able to remove a human's soul-energy-matrix and place it in a containment 'box', and use the controlled 'body' for whatever purpose they choose.

Some abductees also insist that in some cases the Reptiloids can create a cloned duplicate of a person in a short amount of time through time warping and replace the soul-energy-matrix of a person back into the new cloned body if their disappearance from society would otherwise create too many problems.

This way they can ingest the emotional-residue-imbued original body without the abductee realizing [in most cases] that their soul-memory-matrix has been transferred to a cloned body, because they would have experienced a total 'soul-matrix' energy transfer and a suppression of any memories relating to the transfer process.

The cloned bodies do not possess the integrated emotional residue that the vampirialistic Reptiloids apparently crave and find intoxicating in a similar manner as a human on earth who is addicted to hard drugs.

Abductees have reported that the aliens can pass their bodies and that of the abductee through window glass. Is this a feat of magic achieved by advanced technology or is it a psychic power? The aliens have mastered atomic matter. They can go through walls like we go through water! It is not magic, just physics. We can learn to do the same thing. It has to do with controlling atoms at will.

Security level goes up as one descends to the lower levels. The studies on Level 4 at Dulce include Human Aura research, as well as all aspects of Dream, Hypnosis, Telepathy, etc. [research]. They know how to manipulate the Bioplasmic Body. They can lower your heartbeat with Deep Sleeve 'Delta Waves,' induce a static shock, then reprogram, Via a Brain-Computer link. They can introduce data and programmed reactions into your Mind [Information impregnation—the 'Dream Library']

Most of the aliens are on levels 5, 6, and 7. Alien housing is on Level 5. There is never a chance to roam on the fifth level. The alien housing area is off limits to any human.

Level 6 is privately called 'Nightmare Hall'. It holds the genetic labs. Here are experiments done on fish, seals, birds, and mice that are vastly altered from their original forms. There are multi-armed and multi-legged humans and several cages [and vats] of humanoid bat-like creatures up to 7-feet tall. The aliens have taught the humans a lot about genetics, things both useful and dangerous."

"...LEVEL #7 is the worst. Row after row of 1,000's of humans & human-mixture remains in cold storage. Here too are embryos of humanoids in various stages of development.

Tube shuttles go to and from Dulce to facilities below Taos, N.M.; Datil, N.M.; Colorado Springs, Colorado; Creed, Colorado; Sandia; then on to Carlsbad, New Mexico. There is a vast network of tube shuttle connections under the U.S. which extends into a global system of tunnels and sub-cities..

"We are entering an era of Technologicalization of Psychic Powers... The development of techniques to enhance man/machine communications; Nano-tech; Bio-tech micro-machines; PSI-War; E.D.O.M. [Electronic Dissolution of Memory]; R.H.I.C. [Radio-Hypnotic Intra-Cerebral Control]; and various forms of behavior control [via chemical agents, ultrasonics, optical and other EM radiations]. The Physics of 'Consciousness.'...

"As far as advanced bio-technology is concerned, micro-chip implantation technology is being perfected in which tiny micro-chips could be implanted in our circulatory systems, vital organs and tissues if need be for whatever purpose the future may 'require'.

It is my conclusion that a large-scale research has been completed by the government [with possible assistance from 'outside' sources] within the last 20 years or so utilizing tens of thousands of cattle in the Southwest to conduct this covert experiment.

Abductees have reported that the aliens can pass their bodies and that of the abductee through window glass. Is this a feat of magic achieved by advanced technology or is it a psychic power? The aliens have mastered atomic matter. They can go through walls like we go through water! It is not magic, just physics. We can learn to do the same thing. It has to do with controlling atoms at will.

What many do not realize is that there appears to be a third element behind this agenda, a 'race' of Para physical entities that some might refer to as the 'Luciferians' or the 'Poltergeists'—who are often described, by abductees who have encountered them, as being in the appearance quasi-physical etheric or energy beings who have often been seen overseeing and directing the actions of the Humanoid-Reptiloids collaborators.

Path 44: World War I, RMS Titanic, and the "Nitrogen Bomb" that will kill us all

"Madness is something rare in individuals—but in groups, parties, peoples, and ages, it is the rule."

Friedrich Nietzsche (1844-1900), German philosopher whose work has exerted a profound influence on Western philosophy and modern intellectual history.

Over one hundred years ago, the world was nearing the final year of what was then called the Great War, and known now to history as **World War I**—and having a cost of 41 million human beings killed, maimed and missing, it's important to remember, that at its very essence, this global mass insanity of slaughter and bloodletting was nothing more than a dispute among cousins over who was going to control the how's and why's of global trade.

The main Allied Powers of the **British Empire** and **Russia Empire**, along with their main Central Power adversary the **German Empire**, you see, were all ruled by the descendants of **Queen Victoria**—as the three principal monarchs of the age, **Kaiser Wilhelm II** of Germany; **King George V** of England; and **Tsar Nicholas II** of Russia were all cousins with each other: **Kaiser Wilhelm II** and **King George V** were first cousins, **King George V** and **Tsar Nicholas II** were also first cousins, and **Kaiser Wilhelm II** and **Tsar Nicholas II** were third cousins.

The competing economic ideologies between these warring cousins, you should also know, were the same as they are today—with the **British Empire** favoring **Globalism** (*the failed liberal authoritarian* *desire for a "one world" view that rejects the important role of nations in protecting values and encouraging productivity*), and the **German Empire** favoring **Nationalism** (*loyalty and devotion to a nation; especially a sense of national consciousness exalting one nation above all others and placing primary emphasis on promotion of its culture and interests as opposed to those of other nations or supranational groups*).

As to why these competing economic ideologies of **Globalism** and **Nationalism** were so critical for that time is because Europe was on the brink of mass starvation—and everyone knew it!

In fact, just 16 years prior to World War I, in 1898, **Sir William Crookes** called on science to save Europe from impending starvation as the world›s supply of wheat was produced mainly by the United States and Russia.

Sir Crookes noted in his presidential address to the British Association for the Advancement of Science that as Europe's countries populations grew, their own demands would outpace any increase in production, and then, what would happen to Europe? "*It is the chemist who must come to the rescue of the threatened communities. It is through the laboratory that starvation may ultimately be turned into plenty*" Crookes cried.

Prior to 1912, you must know, the only way that a rapidly transforming industrial world was able to feed itself was through the mass planting of grain crops that required enormous amounts of nitrogen fertilizer—but by the early 20th century had been nearly completely depleted as all sources of guano (bird feces) had been mined the world over.

The **German Empire**, however, in 1912, achieved the greatest scientific achievement in the history of mankind in their discovering how to produce nitrogen by "*drawing it from the clear blue sky*"—and that has since **unleashed a fury on the world as threatening as the invention of the atomic bomb**.

With all of the world knowing that the **German Empire** was now able to feed its population, and hence be able to field the greatest army in Europe (if not the world), and its stating that it would not share this historic discovery with any other nation, an elite group of American and British bankers, and business tycoons, met in London during the Spring of 1912 to plan their revenge.

This revenge, of course, meant war—but that neither the **British Empire** nor **United States** could afford—that is unless they merged their nations' banking structures together.

In order to merge the banking structures of these two nations, though, the **United States** first had to establish a central bank that through the printing of money (fiat currency) would enable it to finance a war against the **German Empire**.

The American bankers and tycoons attending this Spring 1912 meeting in London had an agenda of how to create a central bank structure in the **United States**—and whose attendees were **John Pierpont (JP) Morgan** (the richest man in America), **Henry Frick** (American industrialist and business associate of J.P. Morgan), **Milton Hershey** (of Hershey chocolate fame), **Benjamin Guggenheim** (one of the richest men in America), **Isidor Straus** (American multi-millionaire co-owner of Macy's (with his brother) and former US Congressman), **John Jacob Astor IV** (one of the richest men in America) and **John Mott** (one of America most influential evangelists).

One of the main incentives used by **JP Morgan** to get these powerful people to attend this London meeting was their returning to the **United States** on the new ocean liner he had just built—called the greatest in the world—and named the **RMS Titanic**.

The only passengers of the London 1912 meeting to return on the **RMS Titanic**, though, were those who opposed to the creation of a central bank in the United States in order to finance a war against the **German**

Empire—who were **Benjamin Guggenheim**, **Isidor Straus** and **Jacob Astor,** and all of whom died when the **RMS Titanic** sunk on 12 April 1912—as opposed to **JP Morgan**, **Henry Frick**, **Milton Hershey** and **John Mott,** who all "*suddenly*" canceled their reservations and survived.

With no powerful opposition left to create a central bank in the **United States** after the sinking of the **RMS Titanic**, 18 months later, on 23 December 1913, the **Federal Reserve System** was created with **World War I** starting seven months later on 28 July 1914—and that saw, between 1914 and 1917, the American gross national product (GNP) go up an astounding 20%, its manufacturing soar up to 40%, the Allied Powers purchasing over $3 billion dollars in wartime orders and then borrowed from the **Federal Reserve** over $2 billion in bonds.

In fact, it was only when the **German Empire** appeared to be winning the war in 1917 that the **United States** even entered **World War I**—because if Germany won the war, all the billions in loans made by the **Federal Reserve** would be worthless.

The start of the **Industrial Revolution,** beginning in the 1760's, the world's population remained nearly steady—but after **World War I**, when the **German Empire's** nitrogen making process began to spread around the globe, the greatest explosion of human population growth our planet has ever known was unleashed.

100 years ago every school child in the modern world knew—EVERY SINGLE species of plant life that exists in the world needs nitrogen, and that nature provides via a bacteria called ***rhizobia*** that takes nitrogen from the air—but with our pumping massive amounts of artificially produced nitrogen into our planet's atmosphere for the past century has thrown this whole system off.

Because this is happening, the greatest cover-up in history is now occurring keeping you from knowing that our ocean food chains are near total collapse, that all over the globe plants are growing into strange circular patterns, that "*mass death events*" are now occurring all throughout the Pacific Ocean, that throughout North America hundreds of millions of trees are dying, and that nitrogen filled blue clouds are now filling the skies of Antarctica.

To fully understand what exactly these "*blue clouds*" are we must go back to 1802 when **guano** (the accumulated excrement of seabirds, seals, or cave-dwelling bats) was discovered to be nitrogen fertilizer needed by the world to grow food—but by 1885, the use of guano began to throw large amounts excess nitrogen into our atmosphere—and that "*scientists*" of today call "*Noctilucent clouds*".

But to thinking that these "*blue clouds*" of nitrogen floating in at the highest reaches of our planets atmosphere are our only danger, you'd be wrong, as this prize goes to a red alga species named ***Gracilaria Tikvahiae*** that voraciously eats nitrogen—and whose effect on our world soon to come I'll let the **Bible** explain: *"And the second angel poured out his bowl into the sea, and it turned to blood like that of the dead, and every living thing in the sea died. Then the third angel poured out his bowl into the rivers and springs of water, and they turned to blood...."*

Many of you reading these words, of course, have been raised and taught by your elite rulers not to believe whatever the **Bible** says—and is evidenced by the shocking numbers of people this past week in America cheering a company micro chipping its workers, and the large numbers of Europeans, likewise, cheering their growing cashless society—but with all of them failing to heed, or even realize, this **Biblical** warning: *"And he causeth all, both small and great, rich and poor, free and bond, to receive a mark in their right hand, or in their foreheads: And that no man might buy or sell, save he that had the mark, or the name of the beast, or the number of his name.*

Path 45: Exploitation of the people, for what? Wealth, Race, and War

It is not the general CITIZENS of Britain who pose a threat to freedom, it is the so-called 'elite', the Rockefellers of America and the Rothschilds of Britain who would and have SOLD-OUT their own peoples for personal gain and god-like domination over the lower classes. The Americans and Britons who fought and died together on the battlefields of World War I and II did not realize that the Rothschild-Rockefeller monarchies were the ones who had betrayed them by helping to CREATE the 'monster' they were fighting in both world wars for the sole purpose of gaining even greater wealth, power, the ultimate goal of controlling the world's population by maintaining control of global money supply.

In the end, it all comes down to base human greed! America has strayed a long way from the ideals established by the founders of the U.S.

Constitution. Today, we have two governments. The shadow government of Fortune 500 billionaires and a False Front government of selected political officials that we elect in a rigged elections. And, needless to say, Britain has strayed a long ways from the ideals established by the legendary King Arthur whose greatness came from his ability to make all of his knights equals amidst the 'round-table' rather than succumb to vainglory and the temptation of establishing himself as some kind of human deity like the Rothschild and Rockefeller families.

The Rockefeller cartel supplied Nazi Germany with the oil and materials necessary to keep their war machine operating that were supplied by Rockefeller-connected OIL companies include EXXON, ARCO, ZAPATA, etc. Terrorist such as ISIS continues the trend of evil being fed by champions of peace and democracy who are in the game of controlling both side of conflicts. A prime example of the US selling hundreds of billions of dollars of weapons to Saudi Arabia, who supply ISIS with those same weapons.

At the end of World War II, Operation Paper Clip took in some 3000 Nazi SS war criminals by providing them with immunity, new identities, and positions within the Bavarian-backed Rockefeller corporate empire and within the CIA—with the help of Bavarian agents like Allen Dulles, Otto Scorzeny, Reinhard Gehlen and later Vice President Nelson Rockefeller.

These were then used as a covert force to destroy American independence and make America subject to a Bavarian-backed New World Order. Remember even through the Bilderbergers consist of a "marriage of convenience" between Londonese Wicca Masons, Basilian Black Nobility and Roman Maltese Jesuits... the supreme controllers of the Bildeberger cult itself are the secret black gnostic cults of Bavaria whose 'Cult of the Serpent'—or Illuminati—can be traced back to Egypt and ultimately to Babylon itself.

These Rockefeller-Nazi projects reportedly continued through at least 1975 during which period many thousands more "underground Nazis" were brought into America from Europe and also, if we are to believe some reports, from the secret German "New Berlin" base under the mountains of Neu Schwabenland, Antarctica that was established during World War II via Nazi-occupied South Africa.

Is Neu Schwabenland the REAL power behind the joint Bavarian-Alien New World Order Agenda?

The fact that British and American Masons would be pulled into a Bavarian-backed New World Order conspiracy run by anti-British Nazi's and anti-Masonic Jesuits—in spite of the animosities of World Wars I and II—would seem contradictory to the extreme. However, NOT if we consider the fact that Roman Jesuits had secretly created the Scottish Rite of Masonry at the Jesuit college of Clermont in France and also the Bavarian Illuminati via the Jesuit Adam Weishaupt.

Both the Illuminati and Scottish Rite worked together to INFILTRATE Masonry and subdue the traditional Judeo-Christian York Rite. The Masonic elitists in Great Britain and America would have as a result of this infiltration become subject to the influences of the Scottish Rite dominated 33rd degree—falsely believing that 'Masonry' was still the enemy of the 'Jesuits', as in earlier times the conflict between the two was notorious.

They might have been deceived into believing that 'British Masonry' would come out on top of the New World Order when in fact Rome and Bavaria, the two power-centers of the old [Un]Holy Roman Empire, had the REAL control. But blinded by their own delusions of grandeur and world domination, the British elite failed to see how their Masonic lodges were being infiltrated and manipulated by their sworn enemies. Some of the elite might have been oblivious to the ins-and-outs of Masonry altogether, being conscious only of their own greed.

People are increasingly becoming immoral, unconscionable, and self-gratifying. For ages, humankind has struggled to nurture a survival system based on morals and ethics that produce good will that cultivates spiritual growth.

Pride is excessive belief in one's own abilities that interferes with the individual's recognition of the grace of God. It has been called the sin from which all others arise. Pride is also known as Vanity.

Envy is the desire for others' traits, status, abilities, or situation.

Gluttony is an inordinate desire to consume more than that which one requires.

Lust is an inordinate craving for the pleasures of the body.

Anger is manifested in the individual who spurns love and opts instead for fury. It is also known as Wrath.

Greed is the desire for material wealth or gain, ignoring the realm of the spiritual. It is also called Avarice or Covetousness.

Sloth is the avoidance of physical or spiritual work.

Pride, envy, gluttony, lust, anger, greed, and sloth reached it height as fuel for human struggle during World War II. Germany. Nazism subscribed to theories of racial hierarchy and Social Darwinism, identifying the Germans as a part of what the Nazis regarded as an Aryan or Nordic master race.

Notions of white supremacy and Aryan racial superiority combined in the 19th century, with white supremacists maintaining the belief that certain groups of white people were members of an Aryan "master race" that is superior to other races, and particularly superior to the Semitic race, which they associated with "cultural sterility". Arthur de Gobineau, a French racial theorist and aristocrat, blamed the fall of the ancient régime in France on racial degeneracy caused by racial intermixing, which he argued had destroyed the purity of the Aryan race, a term which he only reserved for Germanic people.

Humanity, Spawns of What?

Our planet is said to be 4 billion years old. It amazes me that we can make such bold estimates and feel comfortable of knowing things that it seems impossible to know. What exactly is the Big Bang Theory and can we know it to be true not knowing what preceded the Big Bang? Can we establish reality from nothing, yet that is what the Big Bang Theory insist that we believe?

So exactly what are we Spawns of? The explanation of currently embraced creation of the Universe is, at best, conceptual advanced metaphysics that humanity has wrapped its collective brain around. Our planet, just one of billions that only infinity knows how many, has been around an estimated 4 billion years.

That is a very long time to accumulate footprints of God only knows how many space travelers from anywhere in the infinite space and time of this thing we call the universe may have settled here and perished along the way before the current occupants of this planet. How many civilizations could have come and gone in the reimaging of the ever evolving space time phenomenon of cosmic life and death cycles of energy?

It is interesting how brief the specie of humanity terrestrial or extraterrestrial life is and how much conscious energy is invested in the study of evidences of design in nature and its origin, when nature assures every civilization, terrestrial or extraterrestrial, an expiration date long before any civilization can ever know the causation of our presence in the Cosmos.

The question is what will be the legacy of the organism humanity cast on a very small speck of rock on the outer edges of the Milky Way

Galaxy? In our micro mindset, intelligence is measured in how we utilize brain cells to ensure survival by developing technology to avoid nature's shell game of death depleting energy resources in recycled matter.

What will humanity's legacy be in this race against cosmic redistribution of energy and life itself? How many lives will humanity sacrifice to the altar of the technology god trying to escape the inevitability of the death of its specie and it fuel shell of a planet that is also destined to die? Like so many others worlds before, we are not the first world populated with intelligent beings who have suffered as collateral damage in cosmic redistribution of matter and energy.

Teleological perspectives founded on fear influences government allocations of financial resources to the Military Industrial Complex that provides the required military force to oversee the development of the Secret Space Program in order to protect ourselves from other extraterrestrials and also to provide the technology for intergalactic travel in pursuit of a habitable unpopulated planets to migrate too as our planet become less habitable due to overpopulation, pollution, and depletion of natural life sustaining resources.

The reason for non-disclosure of extraterrestrial encounters are many, outright fear of a more advanced civilization both intellectually and technologically, but also we must factor in selfishness and greed into our government's reluctance to share the truth with the people. You would think that it is better to have the world united as one against any invaders If there are such threats posed by informing the people of the truth, why are we persistently killing each other in senseless wars among each other?

Does our government have plans to use the Secret Space Programs as a means of escape for an elite few, who will one day leave a devastated nuclear radiated planet and nuclear wars behind? We need to ask ourselves some very disturbing questions as to the priorities being displayed by the rich elite who are dictating technology over the lives of people on this God forsaken little speck of a rock on the outer edges of the Milky Way Galaxy.

Path 46: A Nazi Space Base

During World War 2, there was a massive race between the Allies and Axis powers to innovate new ways of killing each other. During the later days of the war, the Nazis developed rockets and jets many believed were inspired by stolen alien technology. There are also many who believe that the Nazis were developing flying saucer technology and would have been successful in building one had they not been defeated. And just where were they creating all this futuristic technology? According to conspiracy theories, it was at a secret base built in conjunction with lizard people from another planet beneath Antarctica.

Some believe the Nazis claimed an area of Antarctica as German territory and sent an expedition there. German scientists then mapped the area to discover a network of rivers and caves, one of which led to a large underground lake. A city-sized base was built near the lake called "Base 22" or "New Berlin", which was supposedly was home to not only Nazis descendant of extraterrestrial reptilians who built the base, according to Vladimir Terziski, from Bulgaria.

The theory of a military base beneath Antarctica has been around for years. In 1962, Albert Bender wrote FLYING SAUCERS AND THE THREE MEN. An Air Force veteran during World War 2 and founder of the International Flying Saucer Bureau, Bender believed that he was abducted by aliens on several occasions during the 1950s. During one abduction, Bender claimed he was taken to a secret underground facility in Antarctica. There he saw giant landing strips for UFO's and met with the base commander, a descendant of the reptilians who built the base. The base was carved out by machines incorporating metal structures into the ice. Bender claimed he was cold at first, but with the help of alien technology his body quickly acclimated. While there, he was told about the history of this base that had been there for nearly 200 years.

Bender learned that he wasn't the first to visit the reptilians and their icy lair. In the months leading up to World War 2, a German vessel called the Schwabenland carried out an expedition to Antarctica. During this expedition, it is said that the Nazis first met the aliens that would help them develop new technologies for war. It is unclear whether or not the reptilians knew the true intentions of the people they were working with. It should be noted that there are actual historical accounts of the Germans traveling to Antarctica.

The Site of an Asteroid 'Mega Impact'

A huge and mysterious "anomaly" is thought to be lurking beneath the frozen wastes of an area called Wilkes Land. This "Wilkes Land gravity anomaly" was first uncovered in 2006, when NASA satellites spotted gravitational changes which indicated the presence of a huge object sitting in the middle of a 480km-wide impact crater.

One team of NASA suggested it is the remains of a truly massive asteroid which was more than twice the size of the Chicxulub space rock which wiped out the dinosaurs. If this explanation is true, it could mean this killer asteroid caused a "mega impact" which resulted in the Permian—Triassic extinction event that killed 96 per cent of Earth's sea creatures and up to 70 per cent of the vertebrate organisms living on land.

After World War 2, it is believed that the American military launched one more secret mission to Antarctica to defeat the last of the Nazi Party as well as the Reptilians who sided with them. From that point on, all alien technology and research has been under the control of the American military. In 1959, the region was declared a safe zone by The Antarctic Treaty which stated it was a zone of scientific cooperation and research. This meant that no nuclear missiles or bombs could target

Antarctica. So in the event of nuclear war, we can all sleep comfortably in whatever passes for a bed in our dystopian wasteland knowing that our scientists are hard at work building flying saucers from a secret Nazi/Reptilian base deep beneath the ice.

Path 47: German Advance Weaponry and Extraterrestrial Influence

Religion is the opiate of the masses. Opiated by religion, the people fell to realize that a satanic force of Freemasons is imposing its cancerous will on our government, henceforth our lives as well. The cancerous dreams of Freemasons at Bohemian Grove is alive, thriving, and smothering the dreams of the people with deadly concoction of misguided military adventures that include threats of nuclear war, ideas of supplanting biological life with digital consciousness.

People and our planet are being sacrificed for the mad dream of men who believe they are descendants of extraterrestrial lineage dating back to ancient Egyptian, Sumerian, Indian, and Anunnaki ancestry.

A Nazi era school textbook for German students entitled Heredity and Racial Biology for Students written by Jakob Graf described to students the Nazi conception of the Aryan race in a section titled "The Aryan: The Creative Force in Human History". Graf claimed that the original Aryans developed from Nordic peoples who invaded ancient India and launched the initial development of Aryan culture there that later spread to ancient Persia and he claimed that the Aryan presence in Persia was what was responsible for its development into an empire.

He claimed that ancient Greek culture was developed by Nordic peoples due to paintings of the time which showed Greeks who were tall, light-skinned, light-eyed, blond-haired people. He said that the Roman Empire was developed by the Italics who were related to the Celts who were also a Nordic people. He believed that the vanishing of the Nordic component of the populations in Greece and Rome led to their downfall.

The Renaissance was claimed to have developed in the Western Roman Empire because of the Germanic invasions that brought new Nordic blood to the Empire's lands, such as the presence of Nordic blood in the Lombards (referred to as Longobards in the book); that remnants of the western Goths were responsible for the creation of the Spanish Empire; and that the heritage of the Franks, Goths, and Germanic peoples in France was what was responsible for its rise as a major power.

He claimed that the rise of the Russian Empire was due to its leadership by people of Norman descent. He described the rise of Anglo-Saxon societies in North America, South Africa, and Australia, as being the result of the Nordic heritage of Anglo-Saxons. He concluded these points by saying that "Everywhere Nordic creative power has built mighty empires with high-minded ideas, and to this very day Aryan languages and cultural values are spread over a large part of the world, though the creative Nordic blood has long since vanished in many places.

To accomplish such lofty goals, many lies have become water cultivating egoistic and selfish principles of misguided madmen from the ranks of the wealthiest families of the world who have taken alien technology and advanced mankind from the age of horse and buggy to deep space travel in a span of 60 years.

Hitler's German army was the most advanced military in the world. The development of jet engines, rockets, and back engineered crashed alien ships propelled Germany years ahead in aviation and weapon technology. Where did and how did Germany, from nowhere, advance so far ahead of the rest of the world? Many of the great geniuses said they were helped by extraterrestrials and spoken to by voices via dreams.

Hermann Oberth became a mentor to a young assistant by the name of Wernher von Braun. Together they worked in rocketry research for both the German Reich and the American manned space launches. Dr. Oberth cryptically stated "we cannot take credit for our record advancement in certain scientific fields alone. We have been helped. When asked by whom, he replied "the people of other worlds."

Wernher Von Braun was a famous German aerospace engineer and spacecraft architect credited with inventing the v2 rocket for Nazi Germany and the Saturn5 for the United States. He echoed similar knowledge of a Nordic looking extraterrestrial influence when he stated in 1959 "We find ourselves faced by powers which are far stronger than hitherto assumed and whose base is at present unknown to us. More I cannot say at present we are engaged in entering into closer contact with these powers and within six to nine months' time it may be possible to speak with more precision on the matter."

Just who were the people of other worlds that both these esteemed German scientists spoke of so nonchalantly? The medium Maria Orsic was leader of the German Vril Society and Pre-World War II Germany. The Sisters of Vril conducted research into psychic phenomenon and advanced propulsion technology. This included saucer shaped aircraft or UFOs.

The Vril Society's members would become notable members of the Nazi Party believed that many ancient civilizations owed their origin to refugees from Atlantis. The Vril Society advanced the idea of a subterranean civilization ruled by ancient parent race who had mastered technology called Vril. This beak-away civilization was said to have survived antediluvian cataclysms which ended the Ice Age and they continued to thrive below the surface of the earth.

While it is widely accepted that Nazis were defeated with Germany's formal surrender in 1945, this is only partly true. The Nazi elite were able to covertly develop crafts far in advanced of anything possessed by the Allies and established a secret subterranean base in Antarctica.

German engineers like Werhner Von Braun, Nikola Testla, Albert Einstein, J Robert Oppenheimer, and hundreds of their counterparts were brought to America. These engineers were instrumental in engineering nuclear and rocket science that advanced America's Space programs and war weaponry to the forefront of the nations of the world.

Wernher Magnus Maximilian Freiherr von Braun (March 23, 1912 – June 16, 1977) was a German, later American, aerospace engineer and space architect credited with inventing the V-2 rocket for Nazi Germany and the Saturn V for the United States. He was the leading figure in the development of rocket technology in Germany and the father of rocket technology and space science in the United States.

Following World War II, he was secretly moved to the United States, along with about 1,500 other scientists, engineers, and technicians, as part of Operation Paperclip, where he developed the rockets that launched the United States' first space satellite Explorer 1, and the Apollo program manned lunar landings.

In his twenties and early thirties, von Braun worked in Nazi Germany's rocket development program, where he helped design and develop the V-2 rocket at Peenemünde during World War II. Following the war, von Braun worked for the United States Army on an intermediate-range ballistic missile (IRBM) program before his group was assimilated into NASA. Under NASA, he served as director of the newly formed Marshall Space Flight Center and as the chief architect of the Saturn V launch vehicle, the superbooster that propelled the Apollo spacecraft to the Moon. In 1975, he received the National Medal of Science. He continued insisting on the human mission to Mars throughout his life.

Germany was the first nation to field a ballistic missile in the sleek shape of Werhner von Braun's V-2. The name V-2, for Vergeltungswaffe 2 (Vengeance Weapon 2). The German army had begun sponsoring von Braun's research even before Hitler came to power, seeing missile weapons as an alternative to the long-range artillery forbidden to post-WW1 Germany.

A workforce of slaves laboring in hideous underground factories managed by sadistic murdering thugs (as many as 20 000 people died building A4s, and about 7250 more people were killed by the missiles, never forget this), the A4 was a staggeringly futuristic rocket. Rising from its launch pad under 25 tons of thrust from its alcohol and liquid oxygen-fueled engine, it could carry a 975 kg (2150 lb.) warhead at supersonic speed up to 314 km (195 miles) from its launching site. First successfully launched in 1942, it was fired against Allied cities, including London, Antwerp and Paris from 1944. Sometime in 1944, an A4 reached an altitude of 189 km (117 miles) making it the first man-made object to reach space.

In 1950 Von Braun started work at the Army's new Redstone Arsenal in Huntsville, Alabama, which later became NASA's Marshall Space Flight Center. There, he and his team developed the Redstone missile, similar to the V-2. In 1959, Von Braun and other Germans were transferred to NASA along with all Army space activities. His final and most successful rocket was the Saturn V, which carried astronauts to the moon. However, after the Apollo 11 Moon landing in 1969, public support for the space program declined. In 1972, von Braun retired from NASA and went to work with Fairchild Industries, in Maryland.

Apollo 17 marked the end of the program that took 12 people to the surface of the moon. By the time the mission launched on Dec. 7, 1972, public interest had declined, the government had shifted its focus to the Vietnam War, and many other factors brought the program to a close, even though three more flights had been planned.

The Nazi also had begun a secret space program that consisted of 30 different prototypes of flying saucer crafts that were weaponized.

The Germans were the first to develop the Nazi Bell utilizing Torsion Field Physics. The Nazi scientists were also interested in high energy pressurized plasma traveling in a circular path. The rotating plasma reduces the mass of weight by 97% to create anti-gravity devices or flying saucers. Nazi scientists were experts in this emerging technology.

The question is, where did the Nazis get this technology? The German scientist such as Herman Oberth and Werhner Von Braun confessed they were helped by people of another world, extraterrestrial. There were Hitler's SS group of engineers and a secret society group of engineers working on anti-gravity devices with an extraterrestrial species called "Reptilians."

The Reptilians gave the Secret Society 14 complete anti-gravity crafts. The remaining 16 crafts were developed by Hitler's SS team who corroborated with tall blond extraterrestrials called Nordics. Before the war ended, the German Secret Society Space group were led to Antarctica to underground caverns beneath the ice and created a base for further production of anti-gravity aircraft.

The secret society were very much aware of Germany's rise to power and was determine to block Germany's ascension as a dominant world power. Conservative Prime Minister Arthur Balfour, a member of the inner circle of the Secret Elite, and Foreign Secretary Lord Lansdowne began the transformation of British Foreign policy towards war with Germany in the sure knowledge that senior Liberals would continue that policy if and when the people voted for change. – See more at: http://www.globalresearch.ca/new-world-order-the-founding-fathers/5445255#sthash.Acxr7l0h.dpuf

Their Secret Elite connections were impeccable. Together, with their good friend Arthur Balfour, they were intimately involved with the inner circles of the cabal. Their duty was to the King, the Empire, to Milner's dream, to Rhode's legacy.

They confronted the same problems, analyzed the same alternatives and agreed the same solution. Germany had to go. – See more at:

http://www.globalresearch.ca/new-world-order-the-founding-fathers/5445255#sthash.Acxr7l0h.dpu

We know from eyewitness accounts and recovered records that the German military machine was making great strides in experimental research. So successful in pioneering rocketry were they, that immediately after the war tons of material plus hundreds of scientists were siphoned off by the allies—both east and west.

As respectful British historian Barre Pitt noted:

The Nazi war machine swung into action utilizing as much as it could of the most up-to-date scientific knowledge available, and as the war developed the list of further achievements grew to staggering proportions. From guns firing shells of air to detailed discussions of flying saucers, from beams of sound that were fatal to a man at 50 yards to guns that fired around corners and others that could 'see in the dark' - the list is awe-inspiring in its variety.

While some German technology was less developed than imagined at the time, some technologies were dangerously near to completion stage which could have reversed the war's outcome. Secret German weapons nearing completion in 1945 included the Messerschmitt 163 Komet and the vertically launched Natter rocket fighters, the jet-powered flying wing Horten Ho-IX and the delta-winged Lippisch DM 1

Since the 1950s there were many claims about alleged German developments of revolutionary saucer-shaped crafts able to fly with incredible performances, from a sort of "supersonic helicopter" to hard-to-believe interstellar spaceships.

These crafts were believed the same "flying saucers" (later named UFOs) sighted by many people all around the world since 1947. According to the many would-be "inventors" and enthusiasts of this theory, UFOs would not be of extraterrestrial origin but man-made. According to the many would-be "inventors" and enthusiasts of this theory, UFOs would not be of extraterrestrial origin but man-made.

The "German saucers" are often known also as the "V-7 legend": this comes from a reportedly circular aircraft named "V-7" that is claimed to have flown in Prague on February 14, 1945.

The conventional view of history is that, while the Germans possessed some remarkable and deadly weapons such as the V-l, the V-2 and the jet-engined Messerschmitt ME-262 fighter, their technological innovations did not extend much further than that. Indeed, serious historians treat claims of fantastic advances in Nazi technology with the utmost disdain.

The problem is that the majority of people that dispute German disc developments have never heard of these largely classified devices. Ignorance does not make them myths.

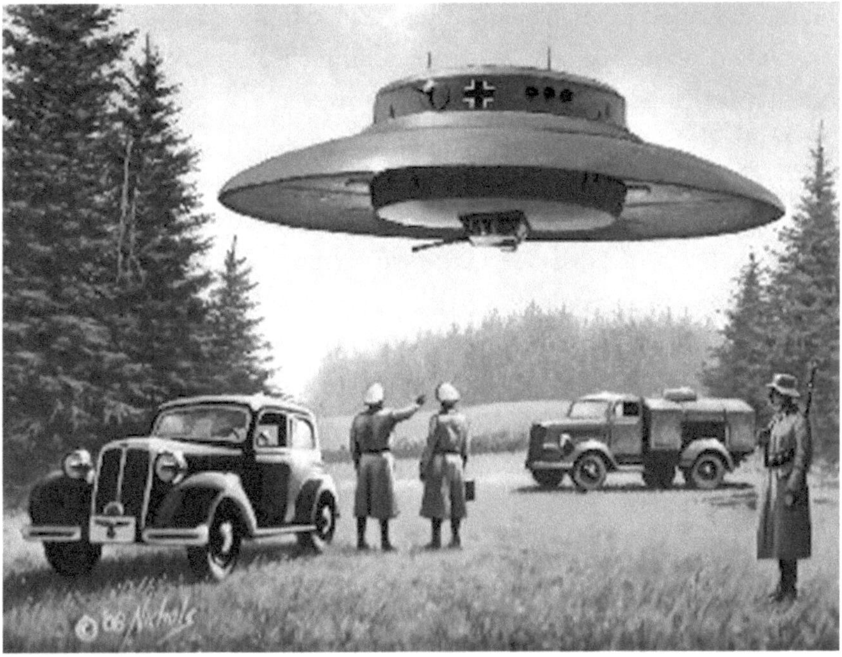

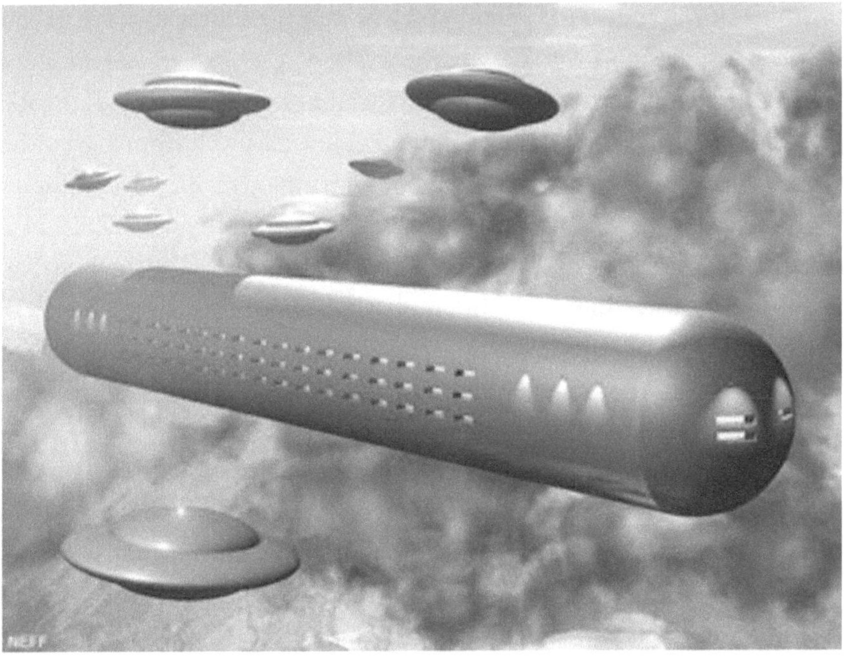

Granted, Rudolf Lusar, Renato Vesco, Justo Miranda, and Ernst Zündel have made some grievous errors in telling the story of German disc aircraft development during WW2; however, the disc development programs did exist and there is more than adequate proof of them..

The US 415th NFS encountered German disc weapons launched from below their aircraft over German-held territory which interfered with the aircraft's prop engines. Official photographs and "Foo Fighter" documentation of these German weapons exist and are available to the public despite the USAAF never explaining what that weapon was. Other official US Army and AAF Technical Intelligence Reports from 1945 list similar strange flight craft encountered over the Reich in the last year of the war.

There is also the problem of known German varied disc and circular aircraft programs that can be properly identified which include Focke's Fw Rochen patent, Sack's AS-6 V-1, Epps Omega Diskus test models, Schauberger's Repulsin discoid motors, and Schwenteit Elektrische Luft Turbine und Raumschiff patent postwar that is credited as a Schriever/Miethe disc design from WW2 (the mystery V-7). All this evidence is totally known and there is an abundance of photographic and historic evidence about. There is the German evidence as well from Luftwaffe Sonderbüro 13 which was tasked with covering up civilian and military sightings of strange craft over the Reich. On September 29, 1944 a Me-262 pilot on a test run spotted the Andromeda Gerät cylindrical Raumschiff traveling at 1,200 mph. His report to Sonderbüro 13 is official and on file (although the jet pilot had no idea what the unmarked 348 foot long object was). Sonderbüro 13 covered it up as an unknown Allied craft.

For years rumours had been flying round that the Germans had been fully aware of the foo-fighter phenomenon and that they had a special study group formed to look into the problem under the name of "Project Uranus," backed by a shadowy group by the name of Sonderbüro 13 (reminds you of Majestic 12 doesn't it?). This was first detailed in

La Livres Noir De Soucupes Volantes (The Black Book of Flying Saucers - 1970) by French ufologist Henry Durrant. The rumour spread in Europe and eventually took physical form in the English language in Tim Good›s acclaimed book Above Top Secret where it is used to help substantiate further vague rumours of an Anglo/American foo-fighter study. Good had not checked his facts and had in fact just copied the information direct from Durrant›s book.

When I checked this out with Durrant he informed me that the whole "Project Uranus" affair was a hoax which he had inserted in his book precisely to see who would copy it without checking. The hoax apparently had been revealed in France some years before but hadn't percolated its way through to English speaking ufologists. Perhaps other foo hoaxes await discovery.

-Andy Roberts, In search of Foo-Fighters Robert J. Lee's book Fascinating Relics of the Third Reich tells of the capture of one of the huge cylindrical Raumschiff Andromeda Gerät by the US Army and confirmed it in an interview of "The German Cylindrical UFO". British BIOS Reports acknowledge German disc aircraft development as well as Hans Coler's gravitic battery - the Magnetstromapparat (which the SS turned into an electricity converter).

Several of the German engineers and scientists hold postwar disc patents in both Germany and the US: Heinrich Focke, Heinrich Fleissner, Josef Andreas Epp, Viktor Schauberger, Hermann Klaas, Bruno Schwenteit (for Miethe-Schriever), Henri Coanda. If there were no discs how could different engineers, non-related, apply for disc patents postwar as soon as it was permissible by the Allies? And why the sudden drive by the US, Britain, Canada, and the USSR for this specific type of design?

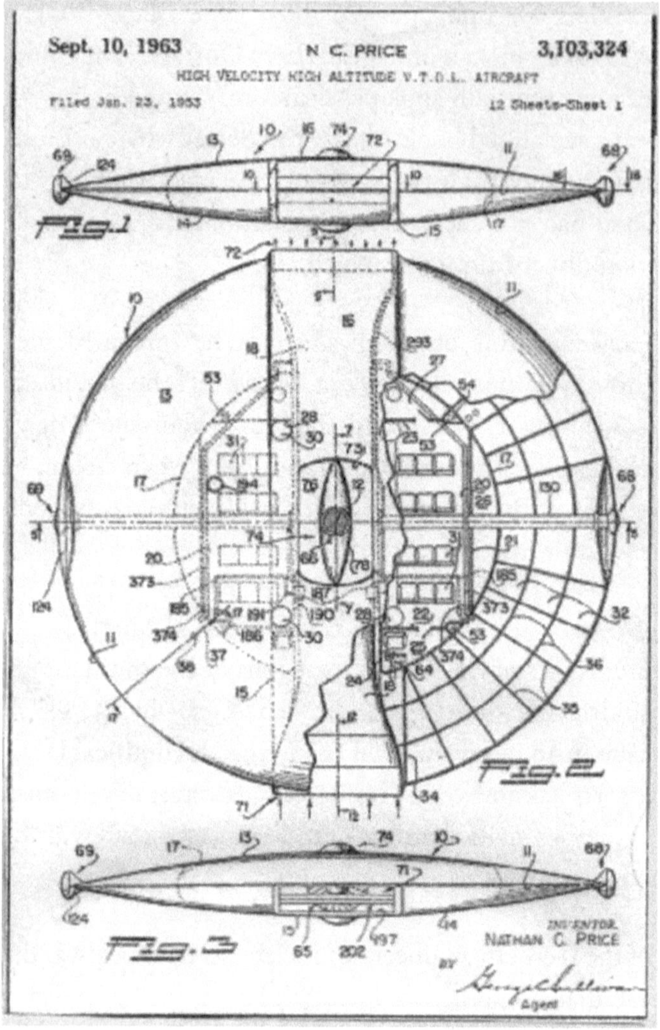

Heinrich Fleissner was an engineer, designer and technical advisor for the German Peenemünde saucer project. On March 28, 1955, he filed a patent application with the United States Patent Office for a flying saucer! It was not granted until June 7, 1960. But it is on file today and a copy can be obtained for a few dollars. (The patent number is 2,939,648). Nathan C. Price was an engineer and inventor for Lockheed aircraft. On January 23, 1953 he also filed for a patent for a flying saucer. It was not granted until September 10, 1963. This can also be obtained for a few bucks. (All 12 pages, the patent number is 3,103,324.)

The largest and most ambitious flying saucer project was developed by North American Aviation of California. It was the Wright-Patterson United States Army Air Force Base in Dayton, Ohio. It was a strategic military joint effort between the United States, England, Canada and Australia. This project was named the LRV (Lenticular Reentry Vehicle). It was a flying saucer that was forty feet in diameter. It flew by a combination of chemical rocket and nuclear powered engines. It carried four nuclear tipped missiles into orbit for a mission lasting six weeks duration. The speed of this flying saucer was well beyond 17,000 miles per hours. There is evidence of a race to build these type craft in AVRO Canada's disc designs (16 of them) and US disc designs now being declassified by Lockheed, Northrop, and NASA. The publicly displayed Avrocar VZ-9 was a ploy as that craft is not a true flight disc but a GETOL (Ground Effect Take Off and Landing) hovering Jeep that was supposed to be armed with a rear deck bazooka or recoilless gun. It was deliberately meant to fail and to be photographed parked outside on purpose to deceive the Soviets.

Operation Bluebook (an official US document) states that (paraphrasing) only "certain developments of the Third Reich in the closing months of WW2 come close to the performance of the UFOs they were investigating". This makes no sense at all unless they are referring to German disc aircraft. A Me-262 or even the Sãnger Hypersonic Bomber could in no way match the performance of unknown disc craft that could accelerate to Mach 10, make a law-of-physics-defying turn that would kill a human pilot, and then stop in mid-air.

The USAF had knowledge of the German discs because they held them at Wright Patterson AB before transferring them to MacDill AB for scrapping. So they were completely correct with their statement. USAF reporters for the USAF's in-house magazine in the 1960s visited MacDill and gained unauthorized access to the scrap yard for an article on prototype aircraft. Their cameras and film were seized after they saw 4 German discs in the scrap yard. The next month's issue of the USAF magazine was cancelled. The reporters' story is online and in print.

Their eyewitness testimony and account is entirely valid - so much in fact that MacDill had to re-transfer the discs back to storage at Wright Patterson. Most people who know about such craft believe the German discs are still held there.

Area 51 was always a black aircraft program (SAP = Special Aircraft Project) base that hosted the U-2, SR-71, stealth demonstrators, F-117, B-2, etc. Maybe the holding bays in S-4 never housed any alien reverse-engineered craft but only German captured EMG discs built by the SS Technical Branch Unit E-IV. That is why they do not show up with the other manufacturers because they were SS property (of Thule and Vril Gesellschaft origin) not under RLM control at all. Reich Armaments Minister Albert Speer himself in his book Infiltration describes his being blocked by Himmler and the SS organization from investigating SS separate military manufacturing facilities, materials accumulated, and projects - including the persistent rumors of the "Flying Tops" and reported of SS requirements made to him for more slave labor needed for such secret projects late war Vril is confirmed by the 1937 purchase of the fallow land around Arado-Brandenburg for "flight testing". Flight testing of what if no discs existed? Photographic evidence exists for the JFM (Jenseitsflugmachine), the RFZ (Rundflugzeugmachine) series, Haunebu and Vril models 1 Jäger, 7 Geist, 8 Odin, and 9 Abjäger..,

Thule-Vril RFZ "Rundflugzeug" (Round Aircraft) Series)

- RFZ-1, disc aircraft prototype 1937
- RFZ-2, "Fliegende HeissWasserFlasche" (Flying Hot Water Bottle) disc aircraft prototype 1937, performed recon in 1940
- RFZ-3, disc aircraft prototype 1937
- RFZ-4, disc aircraft prototype 1938
- RFZ-5, disc aircraft, re-designated Haunebu I, 1939, 2 produced
- RFZ-6, disc aircraft prototype 1940
- RFZ-7, disc aircraft, re-designated Vril 1 Jäger, 1941, 17 produced Haunebu, Thule, SS Military Technical Branch E-IV
- Thule H-Gerät Hauneburg Device, Haunebu I disc aircraft, 1939, 2 produced

- Thule Haunebu II disc aircraft 1942, 5 produced
- Thule Haunebu II Do-Stra disc aircraft co-produced by Dornier. Do-Stra = DOrnier STRatosphären Flugzeug, 1944, 2 produced
- Thule Haunebu III disc aircraft, 1945, 1 produced
- Thule Haunebu IV disc aircraft project (all discs powered by Thule Triebwerk EMG engines)
- Vril, SS Military Technical Branch E-IV/E-V
- Vril 1 "Jäger" (Hunter) disc aircraft, 1941, 17 manufactured
- Vril 2 "Zerstörer" (Destroyer) disc aircraft project
- Vril 3 disc aircraft prototype
- Vril 4 disc aircraft prototype
- Vril 5 disc aircraft prototype
- Vril 6 disc aircraft prototypes, 2 built
- Vril 7 "Geist" (Spirit) disc aircraft, 1944, several built
- Vril 8 "Odin" (God Wotan) disc aircraft prototype, 1945
- Vril 9 "Abjäger" (Universal Hunter) disc aircraft prototype, 1945 over occupied Germany
- Vril 10 "Fledermaus" (Bat) disc project
- Vril 11 "Teufel" (Devil) disc project
- Vril Andromeda-Gerät "Andromeda Device", 139 meter cylindrical Raumschiffen, 1945 1 built, 1 under construction, built exclusively by SS E-V Unit, powered by 4 Thule Triebwerk EMG engines plus 8 SM-Levitators
- Vril Andromeda-1 Freyr (Norse God), captured by US Army 1945 partially completed
- Vril Andromeda-2 Freya (Norse Goddess), one built
- Vril DORN "Verteidiger" (Defender) unmanned delta craft weapon. "DORN" is either short for DORNier or means (Thorn), Sighted near Pescara, Italy postwar
- Vril Gammagische Auge, "Magic Eye" recon drone, prototype only

(all discs except Andromeda-Gerät powered by Vril Triebwerk EMG engines plus Schumann SM-Levitators)

Deutsche Flugkreisel/Flugscheiben, die vermutlich noch bis Kriegsende Einsatzreife erlangten.

Vr 1 ("VRIL 1"), Erstflug verm. März 1942

Durchmesser ca. 11 m

Vril 1 ist als Jäger geplant gewesen, konnte jedoch in Ermangelung einer geeigneten, das Eigenfeld durchdringenden, Bewaffnung nicht bis 1045 Frontreife erlangen. Wahrscheinlich nur in ein oder zwei Exemplaren fertiggestellt.

HAUNEBU II (Erstform), Erstflug verm. Mitte 1943

Durchmesser ca. 26 m

Haunebu II/I wurde wahrscheinlich als Einzelstück gefertigt, als Erbrobungsträger verwendet und zuletzt auch für Aufklärungszwecke eingesetzt,

Vr 7 ("VRIL 7"), Erstflug verm. Herbat 1943

Durchmesser ca. 45 m

VRIL 7 ist als Vor-stufe zu Vril 8 (Odin) gedacht gewesen, aber wegen hervorragender Eigenschaften in ein oder zwei Exemplaren gebaut worden. Wahrscheinlich das leistungsfähigste dieser Geräte.

BMW Kreisflügler II, Erstflug verm. Anfang 1945

Durchmesser ca. 42 m

Der BMW Kreisflügler II könnte noch in einer kleinen Serie von vielleicht vier Exemplaren hergestellt worden sein. Aufgrund der Antriebsbasis Düse, war diese Flugscheibe auf als Träger herkömmlicher Waffen geeignet.

Haunebu II "Do-Stra", Erstflug verm. Ende 1944

Durchmesser ca. 26 m

Die H II Do-Stra dürfte derjenige Typ gewesen sein, der für die Großserienproduktion vorgesehen war und das Rückgrat der neuen deutschen Luftmacht bilden sollte. Es kann angenommen werden, daß noch eine kleine Stückzahl fertiggestellt wurde.

BMW's wartime Prague facility is known and eyewitness testimony of Georg Klein verifies the Flügelrads as well as Schriever's Flugkreisel on site. All were disc fans with BMW Flügelrads more jet auto-gyro than pure flight disc.

Most people will only know RLM (German Air Ministry) designations and have no clue that the SS had its very own war production capability. It had its own army (the Waffen SS), own religion (Black Sun Order), and own scientific branch (Entwicklungsstelle IV/V). If Albert Speer as Armaments Minister could not gain access to Himmler's weapons programs there is little wonder that the disc craft and other odd machines are thought of as hoaxes of Neo-Nazis and Fourth Reich advocates. But once the individual discs are investigated and patents emerge, photos, documentation, and Allied reports that are both declassified and still classified... then one begins to understand where the entire postwar UFO/Black Project Aircraft started from - the Reich's arsenal of the SS. "Black Projects" are actually SAPs (Special Access Programs)! Fear of real truth vs. official history written by the victorious Allies makes many people want to deny these craft and even modern sightings of strange craft that amazingly stick close to military bases.

Myth or Reality?

The reality of the "Nazi UFOs" has been highly controversial. No really hard historical evidence about the undisputable existence of such advanced technology has been presented so far.

There are some clues and many fascinating rumours that have been creating a real myth about the so-called "Nazi UFOs".

Latest developments of the legend include claims of German space journeys to the Moon, Mars and near stars.

Also of interest are all those rumours about secret Allied developments of original German projects, Nazi underground bases and related stories, like Hitler's Escape and mysterious U-Boots sighted after the end of WWII.

> *The Haunebu I, II and III space gyros and the Vril I space flying disk had disappeared after May 1945... It is very interesting to note in this context that after its nineteenth test flight, the German Haunebu III is said to have taken off on April 21, 1945, from Neuschwabenland, a vast, officially German territory in the Eastern Antarctic, for an expedition to Mars, about which there is nothing further known. One year later, in 1946, the many sightings that suddenly occurred in Scandinavia of shining objects of unknown and definitely artificial origin caused a great stir among the Allies in East and West. Again one year later, in 1947, and well into the Fifties, a rising number of shining unknown flying objects, doubtlessly steered by intelligent beings, mostly round, disk- or bell-shaped, sometimes cigar-shaped, so-called UFOs appeared over North America.*
>
> -Norbert-Jürgen Ratthofer, *Zeitmaschinen*

Besides claims of would-be inventors and rumours, there are no original first-hand historical documents about the development of saucer-shaped aircrafts by the Germans. The supporters of the saucers' reality say that most documents and blueprints were destroyed by the Nazis before surrender or captured by the Allied and never released, due to their extreme strategic importance. Investigation for locating possible undisputable sources is still running.

Hitler and the Third Reich led the world into a decade of terror in the first half of the 20th century that culminated in World War II. Technology played a greater part in that war than in past conflicts and the Germans developed an amazing array of secret weapons in a short time. Were flying discs part of the Luftwaffe arsenal? And, if so, was this secret looted and used by the Allied victors after the war?

Some of the German war-time technical advances are well known. The first military jet was the German Heinkel 178 which flew in 1939. In 1943 the Germans also deployed the only jet fighter to go into regular service during the war, the Messerschmitt 262. This German jet could easily overtake the fastest Allied aircraft. Only Hitler's misguided orders that the planes be outfitted as bombers, instead of defensive fighters, saved Allied aircraft from devastating casualties.

Cruise missiles, a staple of current advanced arsenals, were also first used by the Third Reich during the war. V-1 flying bombs were launched from German-held territories across the channel into England. The "buzz bombs," as they were sometimes called because of the sound of their impulse jet engines, could outrun most Allied aircraft making the V-1's almost impossible to stop. The V-1's weakness was its guidance system (a problem solved in modern cruise missiles by the use of computer-controlled radar). Because it couldn't hit a pinpoint target, the V-1 could only be used to cause random terror, not wipe out truly important military assets.

The V-2 rocket was the predecessor of the Intercontinental Ballistic Missiles that filled the nuclear arsenals of the Soviet Union and the United States during the Cold War. It traveled up to 225 miles at five times the speed of sound. A single hit could demolish a city block. During the war the V-2 killed 2724 civilians and injured another 6467. Like the V-1, though, it lacked a guidance system that would have allowed it to strike at important targets.

The Germans even developed a rocket-powered fighter, the Me 163. Though it never was put into regular service, it was the first aircraft to fly faster than 600 miles an hour.

Is it possible that the list of secret weapons produced by Nazi Germany included flying saucers? Did they actually deploy disc shaped fighters or at least experiment with them?

Some of the earliest stories about German flying saucers date back to an inventor named Viktor Schauberger. Schauberger was born in Austria in 1885 and was considered by many to be a crackpot. Schauberger himself said:

They call me deranged. The hope is they are right...

Schauberger believed that machines could be designed better so that they would be "going with the flow of nature" rather than against it.

One of Schauberger's projects was to produce a flying machine, saucer shaped, that used a "liquid vortex propulsion" system. His theory was that "if water or air is rotated into a twisting form of oscillation, known as a 'colloidal,' a build-up of energy results, which, with immense power, can cause levitation."

According to stories Schauberger built several models, one of which was almost five feet in diameter and was powered by a 1/20 hp electric engine. Some reports indicated that one of the models actually flew. There are also reports that, according to letter Victor Schauberger wrote to a friend, a full-sized prototype of one of his designs was constructed using prison labor at the Mauthausen concentration camp. This craft flew on February 19th of 1945 near Prague and obtained an altitude of 45,000 feet in only 3 minutes. The letter goes on to say the prototype was destroyed by the Nazis before it could be captured by the Allies.

After the war Schauberger moved to the United States, where some contend he worked on secret projects for the U.S. government. He died in 1958, apparently claiming his ideas had been stolen.

Another German designer involved with the Nazi effort during the war was Rudolf Schriever. Schriever, along with some other engineers named Habermohl, Miethe and Bellanzo apparently came up with several disc-shaped aircraft designs that used more conventional power sources than those Schauberger envisioned. One of Schriever's drawings shows an egg-shaped cockpit surrounded by a rotating fan-like disc that provided the lift. A Miethe drawing depicts a smooth flat saucer with an elongated hump on its back for the cockpit. Both would have been powered by jet engines.

As with Schauberger, there were reports that some of these designs were actually built. The Schriever machine was said to have been tested in 1945 and to have reached an altitude of 12 kilometers in a little over three minutes. It had a top speed of 2000 kilometers an hour.

There is no real, solid evidence, though, that a test flight ever took place and Schriever himself, who relocated to the United States after the war, indicated that any prototypes of the craft were destroyed, before flying as the Germans abandoned their facilities in the face of advancing Allied troops.

Stories also persist that the Germans's also had developed small automatized flying discs.

The Feuerball and Kugelblitz stories seem to parallel tales of foo-fighters" told by Allied pilots during the war. Despite this it seems unlikely that

Feuerballs and Kugelblitzs were ever actually built or flown. The "foo-fighters" observed were probably some purely natural phenomena. No Allied plane ever reported being attacked by a foo-fighter and it is likely that if the Germans had invented a device capable of tracking planes as well as the foo-fighters apparently did, they would have soon armed it with some effective weapon.

So were there really any German disc-shaped aircraft?

It seems likely that there was certainly some experimentation with the concept within the Reich. Disc-shaped aircraft have several advantages, including low stall speed and low drag, even at high speeds. The rounded shape can also lower the craft's radar profile making it "stealthy." For these reasons German designers did consider using disc shaped aircraft, as did the U.S.

The low stall/drag of the shape was particularly important to the Germans at the end of the war. Months of bombing had reduced German runways to rubble. A saucer shaped craft could have lifted off the ground like a vertical-takeoff-and landing (VTOL) aircraft without a runway at all.

It is certain that they produced some models or prototypes, though, it is unlikely that if these machines flew they obtained the outstanding climb and speed figures some stories suggest. These stories may be difficult to disprove, though, since in the chaos at the end of the War, many records were lost or destroyed.

Rumors are likely to continue that the Nazis developed flying saucer technology that was then stolen by the United States and the Soviet Union after the war. This latter suggestion is not wholly without merit, since US and USSR rocketry development after WWII owed a lot to German scientists who were recruited to assist in the superpowers Cold War space programs through an operation known as "Paperclip." There are records, exposed by author Jim Wilson in a Popular Mechanics article in July 1997, that suggest that at least two brothers, Walter and Reimar Horten, were sought by the United States after the war because of their participation in German military saucer programs.

Some saucer stories about Germany developed after the War, rather than during it. In particular there is a book, UFOs: Nazi Secret Weapons? in which the author, Ernst Zündel, suggests Hitler escaped at the end of the war to establish a flying saucer base in Antarctica at the entrance of a hole that leads to a hollow "inner Earth."

Since science has pretty well established that the Earth isn't hollow, it seems these stories can be disregarded. As for the existence of German WWII flying discs, though, it is a possibility that may never fully be disproved.

[redacted]

ER - 3 - 2809

CENTRAL INTELLIGENCE AGENCY
WASHINGTON 25, D. C.

OFFICE OF THE DIRECTOR

195

MEMORANDUM TO: Director, Psychological Strategy Board

SUBJECT: Flying Saucers

1. I am today transmitting to the National Security Council a proposal (TAB A) in which it is concluded that the problems connected with unidentified flying objects appear to have implications for psychological warfare as well as for intelligence and operations.

2. The background for this view is presented in some detail in TAB B.

3. I suggest that we discuss at an early board meeting the possible offensive or defensive utilization of these phenomena for psychological warfare purposes.

Walter B. Smith
Director

Enclosure

Nazi UFOs

The idea that Nazi Germany developed highly advanced aircraft or spacecraft appears in fiction as early as 1947. In Robert A. Heinlein's novel Rocket Ship Galileo, the protagonists discover Nazi fugitives living in a base on the moon. However, the idea is not limited to science fiction. Academic Nicholas Goodrick-Clarke, in Black Sun: Aryan Cults, Esoteric Nazism and the Politics of Identity, has documented a fringe belief that the Nazis developed flying saucers (Haunebu or Hauneburg-Geräte, and Reichs- or Rund-Flugscheiben) that they launched, and continue to launch, from a base in the Antarctic territory of New Swabia (Neu-Schwabenland). He includes the theory under the heading of "esoteric Nazism," an ideology that hopes for Nazi restoration through supernatural or paranormal means.

Historical connections

Nazi UFO theories agree with mainstream history on the following points:

- Nazi Germany claimed the territory of New Swabia, sent an expedition there in 1938, and planned others.
- Nazi Germany conducted research into advanced propulsion technology, including rocketry and Viktor Schauberger's turbine work.
- Some UFO sightings during World War II, particularly those known as Foo Fighters, were thought to be enemy aircraft.

Early references

The earliest non-fictional reference to Nazi flying saucers appears to be a series of articles by and about Italian turbine expert Giuseppe Belluzzo. The following week, German scientist Rudof Schriever claimed to have developed flying saucers during the Nazi period.

Aeronautical engineer Roy Fedden remarked that the only craft that could approach the capabilities attributed to flying saucers were those being designed by the Germans towards the end of the war. Fedden also added that the Germans were working on a number of very unusual aeronautical projects, though he did not elaborate upon his statement.

Revisionist claims

Pauwels and Bergier

A 1967 book by Louis Pauwels and Jacques Bergier, Aufbruch ins dritte Jahrtausend: Von der Zukunft der phantastischen Vernunft, made many spectacular claims about the Vril Society of Berlin. It claimed that the society had made contact with an alien race and dedicated itself to creating spacecraft to reach the aliens. In partnership with the Thule Society and the Nazi Party, it developed a series of flying disc prototypes. With the Nazi defeat, the society allegedly retreated to a base in Antarctica and vanished.

Ernst Zündel

When German Holocaust denier Ernst Zündel started Samisdat Publishers in the 1970s, he initially catered to the UFOlogy community, which was then at its peak of public acceptance. His main offerings were his own books claiming that flying saucers were Nazi secret weapons launched from an underground base in Antarctica, from which the Nazis hoped to conquer the world. Zündel also sold (for $9999) seats on an exploration team to locate the underground base. Some people who interviewed Zündel about this material claim that he privately admitted it was a deliberate hoax to build publicity for Samisdat, although he still defended it as late as 2002.

Miguel Serrano

In 1978 Serrano, a Chilean diplomat and Nazi sympathizer, published The Golden Band, in which he claimed that Adolf Hitler was an avatar of Vishnu and was then communing with Hyperborean gods in an underground Antarctic base. Serrano predicted that Hitler would lead a fleet of UFOs from the base to establish the Fourth Reich.

Vladimir Terziski

Bulgarian engineer Vladimir Terziski, billing himself as president of the American Academy of Dissident Sciences, has built on the claims of Pauwel and Bergier, claiming that the Germans collaborated in their advanced craft research with Axis powers Italy and Japan, and continued their space effort after the war from New Swabia. He writes that Germans landed on the Moon as early as 1942 and established an underground base there. When Russians and Americans secretly landed on the moon in the 1950s, says Terziski, they stayed at this still-operating base. According to Terziski, "there is atmosphere, water and vegetation on the Moon," which NASA conceals to exclude the third world from moon exploration. Terziski has been accused of fabricating his video and photographic evidence..

Path 48: Fact or Fiction, Possible Extraterrestrial Intervention in World War II?

"The absence of evidence is not evidence of absence."

"The last world war was not simply a war fought between the Allies and the Axis or Democracy and Despotism…. It was also the planetary battlefield of Galactic War III, when alien civilizations sponsoring the Nazis and alien civilizations sponsoring the Americans fought once again for control of planet Earth ...while using its unsuspecting armies as pawns in their interstellar conflict."

"Steve Omar from "Galactic War III"

The conventional view of the outbreak of World War II is one in which Germany and Japan just happened to emerge as fascist military superpowers at the same time, and decided to join forces and take over the entire world! In this view, it was coincidental that Japan would build an imperial fleet, and become an invincible naval power, and that Germany would simultaneously develop a fearsome Blitzkrieg capability using coordinated air and ground forces.

Could it be that for millennia, while we struggled with swords and bows and arrows, and man-powered naval vessels, the ETs, apparently, paid scant attention to us; but that with the advent of World War II we became players on the cosmic stage? Could it be that tor the last three quarters of a century we have become knowing, active participants in an ongoing galactic conflict?

The Thule Society (German: Thule-Gesellschaft), originally the Studiengruppe für germanisches Altertum 'Study Group for Germanic Antiquity', was a German occultist and Völkisch group in Munich, notable chiefly as the organization that sponsored the Deutsche Arbeiterpartei, which was later transformed by Adolf Hitler into the Nazi Party. Hitler, however, was never a member of the Thule Society.

A primary focus of Thule-Gesellschaft was a claim concerning the origins of the Aryan race. "Thule" was a land located by Greco-Roman geographers in the furthest north. The society was named after "Ultima Thule"—(Latin: most distant North) mentioned by the Roman poet Virgil in his epic poem Aeneid, which was the far northern segment of Thule and is generally understood to mean Scandinavia. Said by Nazi mystics to be the capital of ancient Hyperborea, they placed Ultima Thule in the extreme north near Greenland or Iceland.

The Thulists believed in the hollow earth theory. The Thule Society counted among its goals the desire to prove that the Aryan race came from a lost continent, perhaps Atlantis. Like the Ahnenerbe section of the SS, and due to its occult background, the Thule Society has become the center of many conspiracy theories concerning Nazi Germany. Such theories include the creation of spacecraft and secret weapons.

Bulwer Lytton wrote "The Coming Race" which featured a mystical pre-Nazi group in Germany.

This Berlin group called itself the "Luminous Lodge", or "Vril Society" Vril (like the force) had enormous energy potential. The book describes a race of men physically far in advance of surface humans. They have acquired powers over themselves and over all material objects.

They lived in caves and would emerge to reign over the surface world. The most prominent member of the Vril Society was Karl Haushofer, a close confidant of Hitler, Hess, and Rosenburg, who all belonged to the Thule Society (Thule Gesellschaft) that was founded in Munich in 1918.

Thule was a neo-Gnostic racist group, which became a rallying front for the societal roots of Nazi thought. The chief architect of the Thule group was Baron Rudolf von Sebottendorff (Rudolf Glauer) who had direct contact with the Dervish Orders and knew a great deal about Islamic mysticism, particularly Sufism in all its aspects. He also had contact with Herman Pohl, leader of the German Order Walvater of the Holy Grail.

Nazi occultism was a mixture of influences and a host of interrelated secret societies, including the Bavarian Illuminati, the Knights Templar, the Teutonic Knights, the Holy Vehm, the Golden Dawn, the Rosy-Cross, the Vril Society, the German Order and its offshoot, the Thule Society.

Thule is known as the capital of Hyperborea, in the Polar Regions.

Also known as "Ultima Thule", it was the gateway to other worlds.

It was known to serve as both a place to leave the earth and a place on the rim of the opening to the "hollow earth". It is interesting to note that the major powers of the earth have microwave stations setup in the area, broadcasting ELF waves on brain-wave frequencies.

Tradition has it that Hyperboreans were in contact with various "alien cultures". War supposedly broke out between the Hyperboreans and other civilizations (atomic war).

Descendants of the Thule caste (Celts) immigrated elsewhere to other areas of the planet. They colonized these areas, driven by "memory chromosomes" inherited from their space-travelling ancestors.

These star seed people are mostly of Celtic origin (Basques, Irish, English, Norsemen, Icelanders, Bretons, Spaniards and Portuguese) which, strangely enough, make up the largest percentage of RH-NEGATIVE blood types.

Current neo-Nazis are allegedly trying to locate and control these people. Apparently, most contactees have RH-blood type. Are UFO cultures tracking their own "cross-breeds"?

The Grand Lodge of Vril was seeking to re-unite the ancient Aryan traditions and to make contact with the original super-human "luminous race" and to make an alliance with beings who have secret sanctuaries hidden inside the planet.

"The Coming Race" by Edward Bulwer-Lytton, a story about an underground Utopian civilization where the inhabitants flew around in silent wingless vehicles, powered by a force called "Vril" - hence the name of the society.

Haushofer knew a great deal about life on Atlantis, almost as though through personal memory. He taught Hitler that the Aryan race was genetically developed by the "gods" of Atlantis in preparation for the coming disaster, to be a new "master race" afterwards. He claimed that the Aryans were given higher consciousness and the faculty of logical thought, instead of just super-memory as with the preceding sub-races on Atlantis.

He convinced Hitler that the "pure" Germans were descended from this civilization from "Ultima Thule," sometimes called Hyperborea, and were meant to be the nucleus of the new master race. Haushofer believed that this race of Aryan supermen survived the Atlantean upheavals and still existed somewhere underground in Tibet or the Gobi Desert, and he convinced Hitler to try and make contact with them.

From 1926 through 1942, Haushofer organized annual German expeditions to Tibet. He apparently succeeded in making contact with an underground civilization in Tibet known in occult literature as "Agartha," sometime in the early 30s.

It is known that Haushofer met some monks from this underground city, and enlisted them in the Nazi cause. Some literature on this subject describes the monks as "adepts of the dark side." They came to Berlin and set up a community.

They were later joined by members of the Japanese Green Dragon Society, at the invitation of Haushofer.

In the secret meetings of the Vril Society, attended by Haushofer, Hitler, and the key members of the Thule Society, a very talented medium by the name of Maria Orsic began to get psychic transmissions in an unknown language, which they were eventually able to decipher.

As they continued, it was determined that the messages were coming from two planets in the Aldebaran system comprising the Sumerian empire.

Aldebaran is a huge star in the Taurus constellation thousands of time larger than our own sun, about 65 light years from earth.

The information channeled by Orsic claimed that the Sumerian empire consisted of an Aryan or master race, and a subservient slave race, and that the Aryans colonized our solar system 500 million years ago when the Aldebaran system became uninhabitable. When they eventually reached earth, they founded the Sumerian civilization.

According to Peter Moon in the Black Sun

"As they continued to study the transmissions, the Vril Society discovered that the ancient Sumerian language… was identical to that of the Aldebaran and that it was also similar to the German language."

Whether or not they materialized in the flesh in the inner sanctum of the Vril Society, or met with the Nazi leaders in the underground city through the mediation of the Tibetan monks, there is no doubt that Haushofer and Hitler, at least, met with the "ubermensch" or "superman."

In a conversation with Hermann Rauschning, the governor of Danzig, about the possibility of creating a new, advanced species of human through breeding, Hitler said, as reported by Rauschning, "The new man is living amongst us now! He is here!" exclaimed Hitler, triumphantly. "Isn't that enough for you? I will tell you a secret. I have seen the new man. He is intrepid and cruel. I was afraid of him." Samuel Mathers, the founder of the Golden Dawn, had a similar encounter.

In a manifesto to the members in 1896, he wrote, "As to the secret chiefs with whom I am in touch and from whom I have received the wisdom of the Second Order... They used to meet me physically at a time and place fixed in advance. For my part, I believe they are human beings living on this earth, but possessed of terrible and superhuman powers....

I felt I was in contact with a force so terrible that I can only compare it to the shock one would receive from being near a flash of lightning during a great thunderstorm..."

Could the "secret chiefs" or "supermen" have been extraterrestrials, perhaps currently living on earth or elsewhere?

In light of subsequent developments, such a conclusion seems not unreasonable. Possibly, because of this contact with Hitler, the Nazis were to acquire scientific knowledge and weapon technologies far beyond anything previously seen on earth.

The weapons became known as the Wunderwaffe or "wonder weapons." This all seems especially remarkable when it is understood just how much the Nazi inner circle detested science and "book knowledge" and embraced psychic information and ceremonial magic instead.

According to Peter Moon, as early as 1919, the combined Thule and Vril Societies began work on a time machine which was completed in 1924 and taken to a hiding place in southern Germany.

This early development, it is said, re-surfaced after the war and was continued thirty years later as "The Montauk Project," in an underground base at Montauk Point, Long Island where ex-Nazi scientists were assisted by extraterrestrials.

It was the Vril Society that reportedly developed the first anti-gravity craft, the RFZ-1, as early as 1934.

The society raised its own funds for this development by soliciting donations in German newspapers!

This first model "crashed and burned," but the RFZ2, 60-feet in length, flew quite well and was used as a reconnaissance craft, and so it came to the attention of SS Chief Himmler. By this time, Hitler was in power and he turned the anti-gravity development project over to the SS, to develop directly with the Vril Society. He himself was more interested in conventional weaponry.

By 1939, the SS had developed the RFZ-5, which was renamed to become the famous Hannebu I - a two-man craft, about 35 feet in diameter powered by a tachyon type electro gravitation motor called the Kohler Converter.

Purported Plans for Hannebu I

The motor, it was claimed, converted the earth's gravitational energy into electromagnetic power. The Nazis continually improved on the Hannebu model, culminating in the Hannebu-III late in the war.

A huge craft; 200 feet in diameter, the Hannebu-III, it was said, could reach a speed of 24,000 mph at an altitude of 15,000 feet and could carry 32 passengers.

But strangely, the Germans were never able to adapt these incredible flying machines to conventional warfare. It is suggested that they couldn't train the pilots, and that the craft were not maneuver-able enough to engage fighter planes in dogfights, and that they couldn't be used as bombers, although they could easily reach the U.S. without refueling.

The Nazis chose to focus instead on Von Braun's robotic-rocketry, believing that they could so frighten the civilian population of London with their V-2 flying bombs that they could precipitate a mass movement to surrender. As history makes dear, they severely underestimated the legendary British "stiff upper lip." The Nazis also pioneered jet powered propulsion.

The first jet fighter plane in the world, the fearsome Messerschmitt ME-262, could easily have turned the tide of the war if it had lasted several months longer.

German scientists were also working on development of nuclear weapons long before America got into the act. Nuclear fission was discovered in

1938 by Otto Hahn and Fritz Strassman at the Kaiser Wilhelm Institute in Berlin. The Germans were producing heavy water in Vemork, Norway in 1943 in preparation for using it to refine plutonium.

But Hitler and Albert Speer scuttled the program after chief civilian nuclear scientist Werner Heisenberg failed to sell the project as a feasible way to win the war.

Allied soldiers discovered a uranium-based nuclear reactor underground in Haigerloch, Germany, Heisenberg's hometown, and several thousand pounds of uranium buried nearby.

The consensus is that Germany would have developed the bomb before the US. If it hadn't been for Hitter's poor judgment in scientific matters, and the sabotage and heavy allied bombardments of technological sites, although some think that Heisenberg, a former protégé of Nobel Prize winning Danish physicist Niels Bohr, deliberately diverted his research away from weaponry.

German advanced scientific knowledge and weaponry was supplied by extraterrestrials somehow connected with a purported underground civilization in Tibet.

Exactly how this information was conveyed is not clear, but some argue that the connection was established through the mediation of Karl Haushofer, and that a group of monks from that underground Tibetan city came to live in Berlin to assist with Hitler's war plans. They were, reportedly, known as the "Society of Green Men."

There is some evidence to suggest that this situation evolved to the point that aliens were actually working "shoulder-to-shoulder" with German scientists. Hitler envisioned a New World Order to last a thousand years. With the help of architect Albert Speer he designed grandiose buildings and monuments to accommodate his new one-world Aryan civilization, to be supported by the slave labor of the "inferior" races.

However, it now seems that this reputed alliance with extraterrestrials was a marriage of convenience, since apparently they had a similar goal and, indeed, may have been using Hitler as some kind of straw man to facilitate their intended takeover of the planet. If all that is true, it puts the European war in a totally new light - just one piece in an elaborate worldwide campaign of alien design, which included the participation of Japan in order to control the seas.

From this perspective, the outbreak of World War II can be viewed as a push by the extraterrestrials to impose a fascist dictatorship of the entire planet, under their control.

If that is the case it appears that the planning may have begun in the early years of the 20th century, and that Hitler's rise to power was coordinated with Mussolini's in Italy and the emergence of Hideki Tojo in Japan. Such a scenario would help to explain many strange similarities between the three fascist movements, especially the militarization of the governments, and the imposition of elaborate and sophisticated propaganda machines.

Propaganda, after all, is nothing more than a form of national mind control, and we suspect that the aliens are very skilled in these techniques.

Cloned Storm Troopers?

At the close of World War I in 1919, under the terms of the Versailles Treaty, Germany was allowed to keep only 100,000 men in the army and 15,000 in the navy. They were not permitted to have submarines or military aircraft. This situation remained basically stable for the next 14 years until Hitler came to power in 1933 and then, in March of 1935, instituted conscription and renewed military training in open violation of the treaty.

To achieve the extravagantly ambitious goal of world conquest, Germany would need a bright new army of young, ruthless, efficient, well-trained storm troopers numbering in the millions. In 1933 that seemed like an impossible dream, since the army then consisted mainly of 100,000 aging, dispirited veterans of WWI, and some raw recruits. It seemed especially hopeless in view of the depressed economic conditions in Germany at that time.

Yet, in September of the very next year, six months before conscription began, at the Nuremberg Nazi Rally of 1934, 160,000 stalwart German soldiers with backpacks and rifles stood silently at attention in precise ranks as Hitler, Heinrich Himmler and SA chief Viktor Lutze walked down the wide center aisle towards flaming columns bordering a gigantic wreath honoring German soldiers killed in battle.

This fantastic scene was captured in the now famous documentary, Triumph of the Will by legendary film photographer Leni Riefen-stahl.

Where did those 160,000 perfect young soldiers come from?

In October of 1935, Hitler supplied the answer to that riddle when he made public that he had kept 21 infantry divisions "under wraps" in 1934, and he announced that they would now become the core of the new German army - the Wehrmacht.

So that's where the 160,000 came from, but where did the 21 divisions come from?

An infantry division can be as many as 20,000 troops, so it seems that somehow Miller magically got his hands on an instant army of about 500,000 soldiers, with no explanation of where they came from or how they had been trained. He announced also that an additional 21 divisions would soon be added.

One may be forgiven for wondering just how was it possible for all this to be accomplished only one year after Hitler became chancellor of Germany.

Now that we have evidence of alien involvement in the war preparations, a startling explanation presents itself. It is now believed by many that the aliens have mastered cloning biotechnology, and in fact that the small grey ETs of abduction fame are clones themselves.

Could it be possible that Hitler's alien friends presented him with a ready-made million-man army of cloned storm troopers?

We have already seen that the planning for World War II probably began in the early part of the century. Was Hitler's army secretly growing up in spaceships or underground cities even as real soldiers were dying by the millions on the battlefields of Europe?

Perhaps George Lucas knew more than is commonly believed when, in 2001, he wrote Episode II of the Star Wars saga titled Attack of the Clones.

When it comes to fantastic possibilities for the Nazi/ET connection, though, that is only the beginning.

A Nazi Moon Base

According lo Vladimir Terziski, the Germans succeeded in reaching the moon sometime in 1942, and established a base on the dark side.

Terziski is a controversial figure in the UFO community, but he has impressive credentials, lie is a Bulgarian born engineer and physicist, lie graduated cum laude with an MS degree from Tokai University in Tokyo, and reportedly is conversant in English, Japanese, Russian and German in addition to his native Bulgarian, and is therefore uniquely able to do research in all these languages.

He says, "The Germans landed on the moon probably as early as 1942, utilizing their larger exo-atmospheric rocket saucers of the Miethe and Schriever type.... The Schriever Walter turbine powered craft was designed as an interplanetary exploration vehicle. It had a diameter of 60 meters, had 10 stories of crew compartments, and stood 45 meters high."

Terziski claims that after establishing the initial surface base they tunneled underground, "and by the end of the war there was a small Nazi research base on the moon. The free energy tachyon drive craft of the Haunibu-1 and 2 type were used after 1944 to haul people, materiel(s) (sic) and the first robots to the construction site." He claims that the moon has an atmosphere, water and vegetation, and it is possible to get around without space suits, despite NASA propaganda to the contrary. If Terziski is right, it seems reasonable to suspect that the aliens played a large role in the Nazi moon adventure.

While obviously this fantastic accomplishment would have had little wartime strategic value, it should be remembered that, in 1942, the Germans were supremely confident of winning the war, and were projecting their space travel (conquest?) plans well ahead into the thousand-year Third Reich.

Vladimir Terziski

A Proxy War

Needless to say, sources of information about extraterrestrial involvement in WWII in book form are hard to come by but Exopolitics is the title of at least two large books, one by scholar Michael Salla and another by former Carter administration staffer Alfred Webre. But still, if you want details on how the alien factor sorts out, you must go to the Internet where a veritable cornucopia of such information presents itself.

Whether such material is to be relied upon is, of course, another question, but that has not slowed the production of complex scenarios arguing for consideration of alien involvement in the politics and wars of earth.

Branton

Among those offering supposedly detailed information concerning the extraterrestrial intervention factor typical is someone called "Branton."

All we know about him is that he claims to have been abducted many times since the age of 12, and that his information accords with David Icke and some other such sources.

The following is taken from Branton's material

A formal treaty was executed in 1933 between the Nazi-Bavarian Intelligence Agency, which eventually became the S.S, and the "Greys," an alien race living in underground bases in Tibet and elsewhere in the world, facilitated by the Thule Society.

The Greys are said to be from Zeta II Reticuli. The Greys, in turn, it is said, are subservient to the Reptilians, and are believed to be implanted with biochips to keep them under control. They are mostly a cloned race, having lost the ability to reproduce eons ago, due to radioactive fallout from nuclear wars on their home planet. There is a group of about 2000 original Grey prototypes from which the clones are copied. Many abductees have commented on their robotic, totally unemotional behavior.

The Reptilians are a fierce, tyrannical race from Alpha Draconis, sometimes referred to as Reptilians because they are human-like in basic form, but their skin, it is claimed, is scaly, and their faces are lizard-like with vertical-slit eyeballs. They are up to 8 feet tall, and very strong. They are considered by some extraterrestrials to be master geneticists, but others claim that they have botched many of their genetic experiments.

Their most powerful capability is mind control, and in this they are considered undisputed experts. This accounts for their ability to "shapeshift," or to take on a human appearance, because they can plant that illusion in the mind of the observer. They are in league with other Reptilian races from Rigel Orion and Bellatrix Orion.

Together they are referred to as the Draco-Orion Imperialists, and have taken over many of the star systems in the 21 star cluster in this section of the Galaxy, comprising the Draco-Orion/Grey Empire. The Draco-Orionites are referred to as "interventionists" because they boldly seek to enslave other races. Like the fascists that they sponsored, they are cruel and merciless.

Their ancient enemies are the humanoid races from Andromeda, Arcturus, Lyra, the Pleiades and Sirius. The main Pleiadian faction is from the planet Erra circling the star Taygeta, one of the Seven Sisters. Taken together, this group of civilizations comprises the Galactic Federation.

The DAL Universe is also part of the Federation.

Raphael: How was the Universe created?

Billy: Our universe, the DERN Universe, was created by the „Big Bang", a reaction of chemical elements which - by the way - are the same everywhere in the universe. All life forms, galaxies, suns and planets etc. are located in the fourth belt, the „solid belt". Just to complete the picture: The DERN Universe has got a twin universe, the DAL Universe which is connected through a kind of „Doorway".

Raphael: What does D. A. L. mean?

Billy: Nothing special, a name like any other name.

Raphael: Perhaps you can define the DAL universe?

Billy: The DAL Universe is a parallel or twin universe to our DERN Universe that came into existence the same time as ours. Simply, each one a counterpart of the other. One Universe could not exist without the other.

"The DAL Universe"

The Federation races are "non-interventionist" in that they believe deeply in freedom, and will never try to influence or persuade other developing races, or to block or violate their right to make free will choices, and, in fact, they seek to assist in spiritual development. The Federation forces on earth are based under Death Valley and Mt. Shasta in California.

The star wars began when the Draconians attacked Lyra and the Pleiades.

Branton says, "The stories that contactees tell of the devastating battles and galactic massacres - in almost every case initiated by the collectivist-interventionist reptilians/greys - between the two galactic superpowers are integral although controversial elements within the annals of Ufology."

Whew.

Tesla

While the Draco-Greys, it is claimed, gave the Germans fantastic weapons including jet propulsion, rocketry, television-guided missiles, anti-gravity aircraft, nuclear technology, and possibly even a cloned army, the allies were not completely without alien assistance.

The ETs, it is said, gave the Allies one man - Nikola Tesla.

It was Tesla, according to this line of argument, who first saw the promise of radar in 1917, and was instrumental in its development and use in the war.

Consequently, the British and the U.S. had sophisticated radar defenses deployed early in the war using Tesla's patents, while the Germans gave it scant attention, and it was radar that won the Battle of Britain.

Tesla and Roosevelt met in 1917 when FDR was Secretary of the Navy, and Roosevelt was very impressed with Tesla's genius. In 1936, according to some reports, he put Tesla in charge of the Invisibility Project, working with the navy.

In 1940, as the story goes, they succeeded in making a ship disappear in the Brooklyn Navy Yard. Whether or not invisibility was secretly used in the war is unknown. Tesla also invented, it is claimed, particle beam weaponry which he publicly referred to as the "Death Ray."

It was not, it seems, developed soon enough to use in the war, but satellite-based versions have since, particle beam weaponry are potent weapons in both U.S. and Soviet arsenals. Tesla is also said to have been offered a large amount of money to go and work for Germany, but he refused and remained an American patriot to the end.

It is reported that Tesla often spoke of his "off-planet" friends. Sometime in the mid-thirties he arranged a meeting between Roosevelt and Pleiadian representatives, which supposedly took place on a ship in the Atlantic.

Within the alien-tracking Internet community it is believed that some sort of agreement came out of that meeting, and that a Federation representative may have consulted at the Pentagon for most of the war.

Suicide Mission to Mars?

Sometime in late 1944, the story goes, when it became apparent that they had lost the war, the Germans moved the main components of their antigravity aircraft technology and their top scientists to their subterranean base in the Antarctic called Neuschabenland, which they had been preparing since 1938. it is suspected that an extraterrestrial base had already existed there, and that it was inhabited by their compatriots, the Draco-Orionites.

The Germans had been assiduously patrolling and defending the sea lanes to Antarctica since early in the war as they moved men and materials there in U-boats. They stationed their largest battle cruiser, the Graf Spee, off the coast of Argentina sometime in 1939, and they were known to be sinking even merchant vessels sailing in those waters.

If true, this might explain why the Allied armies found only superficial remnants of flying disc development as they overran Germany, and none of the important scientists.

Could Antarctica have been the destination of the so-called "Lost Battalion" of 250,000 German troops that could never be accounted for?

Could these have been perhaps carefully kept and maintained cloned storm troopers, to be used as genetic prototypes for the new Wehrmacht?

By April of 1945, the European war was winding down as the Allied troops converged on Berlin.

At that point, it is claimed, all the antigravity technology and scientists had been transferred to Neuschwabenland. It was from that Antarctic base that the Germans decided to launch a mission to Mars, jointly with the Japanese.

Vladimir Terziski says,

> "According to the authors of the underground German documentary movie from the Thule society, the only produced craft of the Haunibu-3 type - the 74 meter diameter naval warfare dreadnought - was chosen for the most courageous mission of this whole century - the trip to Mars."

The trip reportedly took almost 8 months because the large Andromeda-type tachyon drives were turned off immediately after the escape from the earth's gravitation, and the ship coasted the rest of the way in an elliptical orbit.

Terziski believes that the crew probably numbered in the hundreds.

The huge craft crash-landed on Mars in January, 1946 severely damaging the tachyon drives and making return impossible, but according to the documentary, the crew knew from the beginning that it was probably a suicide mission.

Terziski says, "The radio message with the mixed news was received by the German underground space control center in Neu Schwabenland and by their research base on the moon." Evidently, with the war on earth lost, the Axis partners decided to position themselves off-planet in readiness for the next round, and the advent of the Fourth Reich.

All the chroniclers of World War II agree that the German soldiers were very tough and courageous, and almost robotic in terms of efficiency. They obeyed orders without question, even in the face of certain death. As the Blitzkrieg rolled over Europe, they could do no wrong. It was their insensitivity to human suffering that made the atrocities in Russia, and the concentration camps (the Einsatzgrupen were taken from the ranks of the Wehrmacht), possible.

Maybe, though, it wasn't that they were sadistic - maybe they just didn't care! But, on the other hand, they showed no resourcefulness, whereas the British and American soldiers could be relied on to come up with ideas even in the worst situations. Ultimately, the thinking soldier with a heart prevailed.

Apparently, the moral of the story is - if you expect to win a war with an army of clones, you better have someone with great intelligence directing them, and Hitler just didn't fill the bill.

When it came to intellect, he was no match for the combined brain power of Franklin Roosevelt, Winston Churchill, and an allied army of citizen soldiers from free societies.

Return to War In Heaven, War on Earth

Return to Germany's ET Contacts? - Its Legacy on the Twentieth Century And After...

Path 49: Antarctica- A Nazi Base?

An Excerpt from Alien Agenda
Jim Marrs
From: Grey Falcon Website

With the current mysterious happenings in Antarctica concerning Lake Vostok, an old theory is being resurrected - that German Nazis as early as the 1930s may have built a secret base at the South Pole.

While this idea undoubtedly will strike most people as absurd, there is tantalizing evidence to suggest that something along this line might have some truth to it.

Long-standing banking and business connections allowed high-ranking German leaders in 1944 to forge a formidable Nazi-controlled organization for postwar activities.

Author **Jim Keith** wrote, "in researching the shape of totalitarian control during this century, I saw that the plans of the Nazis manifestly did not die with the German loss of World War II." The ideology and many of the principal players survived and flourished after the war, and have had a profound impact on postwar history, and on events taking place today.

Orvis A. Schmidt, the U.S. Treasury Department's director of *Foreign Funds Control*, in 1945 offered this description of a Nazi flight-capital program:

The network of trade, industrial, and cartel organizations has been streamlined and intermeshed, not only organizationally but also by what has been officially described as 'Personnel Union'.

Legal authority to operate this organizational machinery has been vested in the concerns that have majority capacity in the key industries such as those producing iron and steel, coal and basic chemicals. These concerns have been deliberately welded together by exchanges of stock to the point where a handful of men can make policy and other decisions that affect us all.

Could one of those "decisions" have been the creation of a Nazi base connected to the development of UFOs? While this notion may superficially appear to be sheer nonsense, the public record offers compelling - if incomplete - evidence to support this idea.

One theory is that Martin Bormann and other top Nazis escaped to South America and on to a secret base in Antarctica where they built UFOs so sophisticated that their secret Nazi empire has exerted significant control over world events and governments to this day.

While there can be no question that the business and financial network created by Bormann wields a certain amount of power even today, evidence for the existence of a major Nazi base containing UFOs is virtually nonexistent, consisting primarily of the known exploration of Antarctica's Queen Maude Land - renamed *Neuschwabenland* by the Germans - in 1938 and some unverified statements.

Reportedly, German Navy Grand Admiral **Karl Dönitz** stated in 1943:

The German submarine fleet is proud of having built for the Führer in another part of the world a Shangri-La on land, an impregnable fortress.

It has been reported that U.S. Admiral **Richard Byrd**, upon his return from an expedition to Antarctica in 1947, stated it was, "necessary for the USA to take defensive actions against enemy air fighters which come from the polar regions" and that America could be "attacked by fighters that are able to fly from one pole to the other with incredible speed."

Advancing the idea that the Nazis continually shipped men and material to the South Pole throughout the war years, author **R. A. Harbinson** wrote:

Regarding the possibility of the Germans building self-sufficient underground research factories in the Antarctic, it has only to be pointed out that the underground research centers of Nazi Germany were gigantic feats of construction, containing wind tunnels, machine shops, assembly plants, launching pads, supply dumps and accommodation for all who worked there, including adjoining camps for slaves - and yet very few people knew that they existed.

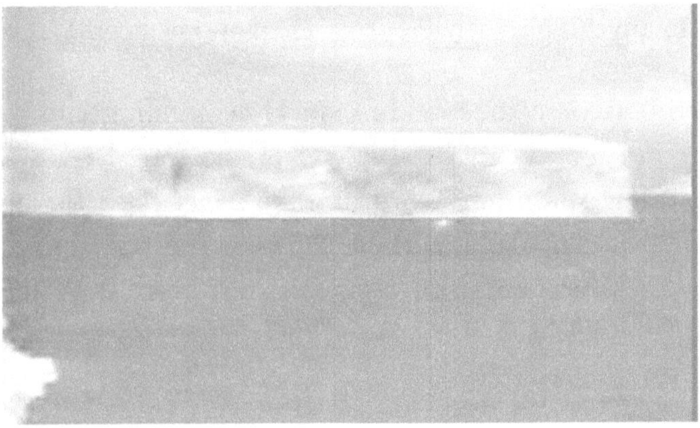

But, while tales of a *secret Nazi base in Antarctica* may appear plausible to some, the idea that a warm water location at the South Pole has remained undiscovered and no one has escaped or deserted the place in more than 50 years stretched belief to the breaking point in years past.

But with the new revelations of 60-70 degree temperature water, magnetic anomalies suggesting the possibility of a hidden city or base and the obvious back out taking place concerning current events at the pole, the idea of a secret base is no longer so farfetched.

Rumors began to circulate that whilst Germany had been defeated, a selection of military personnel and scientists had fled the fatherland as allied troops swept across mainland Europe, and had established themselves at a secret base on the Antarctic continent, from where they continued to develop their advanced aircraft technology.

Furthermore, it is interesting to note that at the end of the war, the allies determined that there were 250,000 Germans unaccounted for - even taking into account casualties and deaths Could *Neu Schwabenland* have been a permanently manned German base at that time?

The brackish water of the warm (30 degrees) lakes virtually confirmed that all had an outlet to the sea and would thus have been a haven for U-boats. The two ice-free mountain ranges in *Neu Schwabenland* presented no worse an underground tunneling project for Organization Todt than anything they had encountered and overcome in Norway.

The Germans were the world›s experts at building and inhabiting underground metropolis. At the end of the war the United States gave anything concerning Ohrdruf a top secret classification for 100 years upwards. The fact that there had been substantial underground workings there, and Ohrdruf was the location of the last Redoubt, was concealed absolutely.

Fortunately for researchers, in 1962 the DDR had taken sworn depositions from all local residents during an investigation into wartime Ohrdruf, and upon the reunification of the two Germanys in 1989, these documents became available to all and sundry at Arnstadt municipal archive.

The Charite Anlage Unit

From the Arnstadt documents it is clear that the *Charite Anlage* unit operated in a three-story underground bunker with floors 70 by 20 meters.

When working, the device emitted some kind of energy field which shut down all electrical equipment and non-diesel engines within a range of about eight miles. For this reason, even though Ohrdruf was crawling with SS, it was never photographed from the air nor bombed.

Declassified USAF documents dated early 1945 admit the existence of an *unknown energy field* over Frankfurt/Main "and other locations" which "fantastic though it may appear" were able to "interfere with our aircraft engines at 30,000 feet."

Ohrdruf rebuilt below Neu Schwabenland during the last two years of the war would not have been difficult, and since *Charite Anlage* had the highest priority of anything in the Third Reich, it seems likely that it must have been.

Such a base would have been impregnable, for the suggestion is that the force field worked in various ways favorable to the occupants.

Scary Secrets of the Third Reich's Base in Antarctica

A remarkable event occurred in 1999, but only specialists paid adequate attention to it. A research expedition *discovered a virus in Antarctica;* at that, neither people nor animals had immunity to the virus. After all, Antarctica is far away, for this very reason the virus cannot be dangerous for the rest of the planet, especially since the dangerous discovery was deep in the permafrost.

However, scientists say that against the background of a global warming threatening the Earth, the unknown virus can cause an awful catastrophe on the planet.

Expert **Tom Starmerue** from the University of New York also shares the pessimistic forecasts of his colleagues. We don't know what mankind will face in the South Pole in the nearest time due to the global warming. It is not ruled out that an unbelievable catastrophe may break out.

Viruses protected with a protein cover survive even in the permafrost; as soon as the temperature gets warmer they will immediately start reproducing. American scientists treated the Antarctica discovery very seriously and even organized a special expedition that currently tests the ice for unknown viruses in order to develop an antidote in good time.

What is the source of the virus in Antarctica where only penguins can survive in the ice? There is no answer to the question, specialists are at a loss. However, several theories concerning the problem have been put forward. A majority of scientists are inclined to believe that prehistoric forms of life probably survived in the permafrost.

But some specialists blame bonzes of the Third Reich for delivery of a secretly developed bacteriological weapon to Antarctica. And this theory arose not in a vacuum. It is known that already in 1938 Nazis suddenly became interested in Antarctica, they organized two expeditions to the area in 1938-1939.

At first, planes of the Third Reich took detailed pictures of unexplored territories and then they dropped several thousands of metal pennons with swastika there. The whole of the explored territory was called Neu Schwabenland and was considered a part of the Third Reich.

After the expedition, Captain **Ritscher** reported to Field-Marshal Göring:

The planes dropped the pennons 25 kilometers apart; we covered the area of about 8.600 thousand square meters. 350 thousand square meters of them were photographed.

In 1943, Grand Admiral **Karl Dönitz** dropped a remarkable phrase:

Germany's submarine fleet is proud that it created an unassailable fortress for the Führer on the other end of the world. It highly likely means that Nazis were building a secret base in Antarctica within 1938-1943.

Submarines were mostly used for transportation of necessary freight to the place. As specialists for the Third Reich wrote, at the end of WWII the submarines were relieved of their torpedo arms in the port of Kiel and then were loaded with containers with different goods. The submarines also received passengers whose faces were hidden behind surgical bands.

Wilhelm Bernhard was commander of one of the submarines, U-530; the submarine left the port of Kiel on April 13, 1945. When it reached the shores of Antarctica, 16 members from the crew built an ice cave and put boxes into the cave; it was allegedly said that the boxes contained relics of the Third Reich, including Hitler's documents and personal stuff. The operation was code named Valkyrie-2. When the operation was over on July 10, 1945, the submarine U-530 entered the Argentinean port of Mar-del-Plata and surrendered to the authorities.

It is also supposed that another submarine from the formation, U-977, under the command of **Heinz Schäffer** delivered *the remains of Adolf Hitler and Eva Braun* to Neu Schwabenland. It followed the route of the U-530 submarine and called at Antarctica. The submarine arrived in Mar-del-Plata on August 17, 1945.

But the version of Wilhelm Bernhard and Heinz Schäffer saying that the submarines delivered relics to the Antarctica shores (both captains told it at the interrogations held by the American and British intelligence services) seems rather dubious. It is unlikely that the serious operation was designed only for the sake of delivery of the Third Reich documents and relics.

Later, special services seized a confidential letter of Captain Schäffer to his friend, Captain **Wilhelm Bernhard** who obviously planned to publish his memoirs. The letter was dated with June 1, 1983.

It runs as follows:

Dear Willy,

I was thinking if it is reasonable to publish your manuscript concerning the U-530.

The three submarines that took part in that operation (U-977, U-530 and U-465) are currently at the bottom of the Atlantic Ocean. Isn't it better to leave them there? My old friend, think about it! Think please how then my book will look when you publish your memoirs (after, WWII Heinz Schäffer wrote a book named "U-977").

We all made an oath to keep the secret; we did nothing wrong, we just obeyed the orders and fought for our loved Germany and its survival. Please think again: isn't it better to picture everything as a fable? What results do you plan to achieve with your revelations?

Think about it, please. Even 40 years after the events, Heinz insisted that Bernhard mustn't say the truth. Is it possible that the submarines delivered something more dangerous to the continent, not Hitler's documents?

Could it be the bacteriological weapon traces of which were discovered in Antarctica as unknown viruses in the permafrost last year?

Neuberlin

If you had been a Wehrmacht soldier at the bombed-out railroad station in Poltava, a city in the Ukraine, during the summer of 1942, you may have seen a very strange-looking military unit on the march, heading for a waiting passenger train. The unit consisted of women, all of them blond and blue-eyed, between the ages of 17 and 24, tall and slender, their sensational figures encased in striking sky-blue uniforms.

Each woman wore an Italian-style garrison cap, an A-line skirt with the hem below the knee, and a form-fitting jacket with the insignia of the SS. You might have thought the SS had recruited a platoon of high-class call girls, but the truth was far stranger than that. You would have been looking at Reichsführer-SS Heinrich Himmler's latest brainstorm - the *Antarktische Siedlungnsfrauen* [Antarctic Settlement Women or ASF].

The story actually begins in 1938, when the German seaplane carrier Schwabenland sailed across the South Atlantic, bound for Queen Maud's Land in Antarctica. According to Russian UFOlogists **Konstantin Ivanenko**, "The Schwabenland sailed to Antarctica, commanded by Albert Richter, a veteran of cold-weather operations. The Richter expedition's scientists used their large Dornier seaplanes to explore the polar wastes, emulating Admiral Richard E. Byrd's efforts a decade earlier.

The German scientists discovered ice-free lakes (heated by underground volcanic features) and were able to land on them. It is widely believed that the Schwabenland's expedition was aimed at scouting out a secret base of operations."

A German base was established in the Muhlig-Hofmann Mountains, just inland from the Princess Astrid Coast. The area was renamed *Neuschwabenland* (New Swabia) and "the base was known only as Station 211."

From the movie *Schindler's List*, people have gotten the idea that killing Jews was the Nazis' main concern. But in actual fact, Hitler and the SS were just as ruthless with the rest of the population in their eastern European empire, thinking nothing of shuffling large numbers of people around in their quest for a more perfect Aryan race.

This shuffle was accomplished by a little-known office of the SS called the *Rasse und Siedlungshauptamt* (German for Race and Settlement Bureau) or RuSHA. In the Ukraine alone, RuSHA drafted 500,000 women for forced labor in the munitions factories of Nazi Germany.

It was RuSHA which selected women for Himmler's unit of *Antarktische Siedlungsfrauen* (Antarctic Settlement Women). About half of the "recruits" were Volksdeutsch-ethnic Germans whose ancestors had settled in the Ukraine in the Seventeenth and Eighteenth Centuries. The others were native Ukrainians whom RuSHA had "upgraded" to full Aryans.

This process was called *Eindeutschung* (Germanization). According to Ivanenko,

There is increased popularity for the idea of a 'German-Slavonic Antarctic Reich.' It is said that 10,000 of the 'racially most pure' Ukrainians, out of half a million deported in 1942 by Martin Bormann, were transported to the German Antarctic bases during World War II, in the proportion of four Ukrainian women to one German man. If true, this would mean that Himmler transferred 2,500 Waffen-SS soldiers, who had proven themselves in combat on the Russian front, to Station 211 - now Neuschwabenland - in Antarctica. This may be the source of the myth of the "Last SS Battalion."

An ASF training camp was set up in Estonia, on a peninsula near Ristna on Hiiumaa Island in the Baltic Sea. It was a combination finishing school and boot camp, where the ladies took lessons in charm and housekeeping along with their courses in polar survival. Himmler kept the camp's existence a closely-guarded secret. For "unhappy campers," the only escape consisted of a one-way train ticket to Auschwitz.

(There is one known instance of an ASF "deserter." In 1943, Auschwitz guard Irma Griese, 22, the off-and-on girl friend of Dr. Josef Mengele, took to wearing a sky-blue ASF uniform, which she had scavenged from a pile of inmate clothing. Griese was hanged in 1946 for war crimes. The uniform's original owner must have had serious second thoughts about a permanent move to Antarctica).

The failure of Grossadmiral Karl Dönitz's U-boat offensive by May 1943 freed up dozens of "milk cow" U- boats. These were large submarines, almost as big as tramp steamers, which Dönitz had used to supply his U- boat "wolf packs" in remote seas of the world. Himmler now put them to work carting supplies and personnel to Antarctica.

Himmler's rationale for sending thousands of settlers to Antarctica can only be understood within the context of his mystic beliefs. As a result of his youthful reading of *New Age books*, his association with the occultist Dr. Friedrich Wichtl, and his membership in the Artamen, Himmler became a believer in the Hindu concept of world-ages or yugas.

He believed that the current age, or *Kali Yuga*, would end in a global cataclysm, thereby giving birth to a new world-age called the *Satya Yuga*.

By sending a Nazi colony to Antarctica, Himmler was ensuring that a remnant of the "pure Aryan race" would survive the coming cataclysm with its society and culture intact. They would then take possession of Antarctica when the cataclysm melted the south polar ice cap.

Nazis in Antarctica Alive and Thriving
The most militarily powerful states in the world

According to believers, the *Neuschwabenland* colony survived not only the end of World War II, but a full on battle with the 3,500 Marines and aircraft of Operation High Jump.

In 2003 **Ivanenko** wrote: The total population of Nazis in Antarctica now exceeds two million and that many of them have undergone plastic surgery in order to move about with greater ease through South America and conduct all manner of business transactions.

He called the *Antarctic Reich*, "one of the most militarily powerful states in the world because it can destroy the USA several times over with its submarine-based nuclear missiles, remaining itself invulnerable to U.S. nuclear strikes because of the two-mile-thick ice shield." Further, he claims that the city of *Neu Berlin*, the colony's capital, sprawls through "narrow sub-glacial tunnels" under an unnamed mountain range, heated by "volcanic vents."

The UFOlogists also makes the claim that *Neu Berlin* adjoins, "the prehistoric ruins of Kadath, which may have been built by settlers from the lost continent of Atlantis well over 100,000 years ago." Still other fringe researchers claim that the actual ruins of Atlantis have been found - and possibly reoccupied - under the Antarctic ice.

Some say that Atlantis is located near one of the 70 or so warm water lakes that have been discovered miles beneath the Polar Ice Sheet, such as Lake Vostok near the Russian base at the Pole of Inaccessibility.

Another of the oft made claims about *Neuberlin* is that the city has an Alien Quarter, where *Pleiadians*, *Zeta Reticulans*, *Reptoids*, *Men Black*, *Aldebarani* and other visitors from the stars dwell. As we have seen, the Nazis were working on some very advanced aircraft, some of which may have been capable of leaving the earth›s atmosphere.

Some researchers are convinced that the Nazis did indeed make it to the moon, and even Mars. Could they have made contact with space aliens once they left the earth? Or, could their rockets, foo-fighters and disk aircraft have attracted aliens to visit them?

A claim floats around in modern U.F.O. lore that an extraterrestrial craft with anti-gravity propulsion crashed in the Schwarzwald in the summer 1936, and was recovered by the Nazis who back-engineered it, thus explaining their flying saucer program.

This parallels stories of a similarly recovered crashed "saucer" near Roswell, New Mexico in 1947, the American back-engineering of which supposedly led to the discovery of the transistor (patented by Bell Laboratories the following year), fiber-optics and other exotic technologies.

Ivanenko reported that talk about the Antarctic Reich is "becoming more and more popular" in Russia, Poland, the Ukraine, Belarus and other countries in Eastern Europe.

He writes, "In the May 10, 2003 issue of the (newspaper) 'Frankfurter Allgemeine', Polish journalist A. Stagjuk criticized Poland›s decision to send troops to Iraq" to assist with the Allied occupation. "At the end, he said, 'The next Polish government will sign a treaty with Antarctica and declare war on the USA."

Ivanenko added that Stagjuk's words were broadcast on the shortwave radio station *Deutsche Welle* the same week. Some analysts compared this sentence to famous code phrases which started wars in the Twentieth Century, such as 'Over all of Spain, the sky is cloudless' in 1936, and 'Climb Mount Niitaka' in 1941.

("Climb Mount Niitaka" was the signal Admiral Yamamoto sent to Kido Butai, the Imperial Japanese Navy's fleet, to begin the attack on Pearl Harbor.)

It is strange to think of a large population living under the ice of Antarctica, totally divorced from the "mainstream" world. Then again, there are Jivaro indigenous people living on Lago de Yanayacu (lake), less than 50 kilometers (30 miles) east of Iquitos, Peru, who have never heard of Courtney Love.

- So, is there a city under the ice inhabited by the grandchildren and great-grandchildren of the original SS settlers?

- Or is it just an urban legend stemming from the chaotic conditions that prevailed in Europe during World War II?

Some day we may know for certain.

In their books, written in the 1970s, **Wilhelm Landig** and "outcast ufologist" **Ernst Zündel** claimed that *Operation High Jump* was literally "the last battle of World War II."

In *Secret Nazi Polar Expeditions* (1978) and *Hitler at the South Pole* (1979), Zündel claimed that Reichsführer-SS Heinrich Himmler had founded an SS colony in Antarctica called *Neuschwabenland.* The base, known as Point 211, eventually became the Antarctic Reich.

Opinion is sharply divided about the final fate of *Neuschwabenland.* Some argue that the Nazis abandoned their Antarctic sanctuary in the 1960s and moved to sites in the Andes.

Another group claims that the Antarctic Reich still exists and has grown into "a civilization under the ice," home to about 3 million people of German and Ukrainian descent. It's supposed to be somewhere in the Mühlig-Hoffman Mountains, adjacent to the ruins of *Kadath*, a city founded by settlers from the lost continent of Atlantis.

The *Redemptionists* believe that Adolf Hitler escaped from Berlin in April 1945, traveled to southern Argentina in a U-boat, and from there traveled to *Neuschwabenland* in a Nazi flying saucer. Hitler supposedly lived in Antarctica until 1952, when he reportedly traveled to the moon and met with aliens from space.

These aliens took him to Aldebaran, 68 light-years from Earth. According to the legend, some day Hitler will return with *an Aldebarani space armada.*

Path 50: Why the US government doesn't like visitors to the South Pole base

There are lines of magnetic force emanating from the South Magnetic Pole. What is strange about the North and South Poles is the way in which the magnetic lines of force move.

The magnetic lines of force originate from a "hole" just off the coast of Antarctica.

There are Chilean and Peruvian scientists/bases near or along the route of UFOs emanating from inside the Earth.

Many UFOs fly directly south-north along South America. If one draws a line from South America, through the Antarctic bases of Chile, etc. through the South Pole to the South Magnetic pole - then you get a straight line.

What's interesting about this potential "UFO route" is that UFOs coming from Inside the Earth would end up flying over the America South Pole base.

However, the line of flight is such that the only places in the Antarctic where you'd stand a chance of seeing these UFOs is in the "Weddell sea" area where South American countries have their bases and at the Scott Base at the South Pole.

The other parts of the UFO route is somewhat offset from the commonly traveled routes and so there's little chance of running into UFOs by accident at any other places. That would explain why the US government doesn't like visitors to the South Pole base: It's not that the hole is AT or NEAR the South Pole base (as we originally thought), but *along the route from the real hole in the oceans off the coast.*

UFO Bases Found in Antarctica

Bob Borino, in his article, 'UFO Bases Found in Antarctica' (Globe, Jan. 18, 1983) quotes from certain scientists who believe that a subterranean UFO Base is located beneath the strange 'Polynya Sea' in the Antarctica's Weddell Sea region.

The *French Agence France Press* on 25 September 1946, said:

The continuous rumors about German U-boat activity in the region of *Tierra del Fuego* (Feuerland, in German), between the southernmost tip OF LATIN AMERICA AND THE CONTINENT OF ANTARCTICA are based on true happenings. The newspaper 'France Soir' had the following account:

Almost 1-1/2 years. AFTER cessation of hostilities in Europe, the Islandic Whaler, "Juliana" was stopped by a large German U-boat.

The Juliana was in the ANTARCTIC region around Malvinas [now Falkland] Islands when a German submarine surfaced and raised the German official naval Flag of Mourning—red with a black edge.

The submarine commander sent out a boarding party, which approached the Juliana in a rubber dinghy, and having boarded the whaler demanded of Capt. Hekla part of his fresh food stocks. The request was made in the definite tone of an order to which resistance would have been unwise. The German officer spoke a correct English and paid for his provisions in U.S. dollars, giving the Captain a bonus of $10 for each member of the Juliana crew.

Whilst the food stuffs were being transferred to the submarine, the submarine commander informed Capt. Hekla of the exact location of a large school of whales.

Later the Juliana found the school of whales where designated.

To address that 1947 story. To this day there has never been any Icelandic whaler in the South Atlantic, let alone in the Antarctica. No Icelandic ship has ever been named Juliana and Hekla is an active volcano in Iceland, not a last name.

99% of all Icelandic last names for males end in "-son".

The *Hitler-in-Argentina* tale is an old one. It first surfaced in a book by **Ladislao Szabo** entitled "Hitler Está Vivo" (Spanish for Hitler Is Alive) back in 1947.

A second book by **Michael X. Barton** was published in 1969 entitled "We Want You: Is Hitler Alive?" Then **Ernst Zündel** took up the banner in 1974. Out of these books has sprung the "Saucer Nazi" theories.

Both theories agree that Hitler escaped from the Führerbunker in Berlin and fled to Argentina in a U-boat. However, believers in the Antarctic Reich theory contend that Hitler left Argentina in the early 1950s and moved to *Neuschwabenland*, an SS colony under the ice of Antarctica, right next to the prehistoric ruins of Kadath.

Here, they say, Adolf lived out his life, resuming his artist's career and painting a series of Antarctic icescapes.

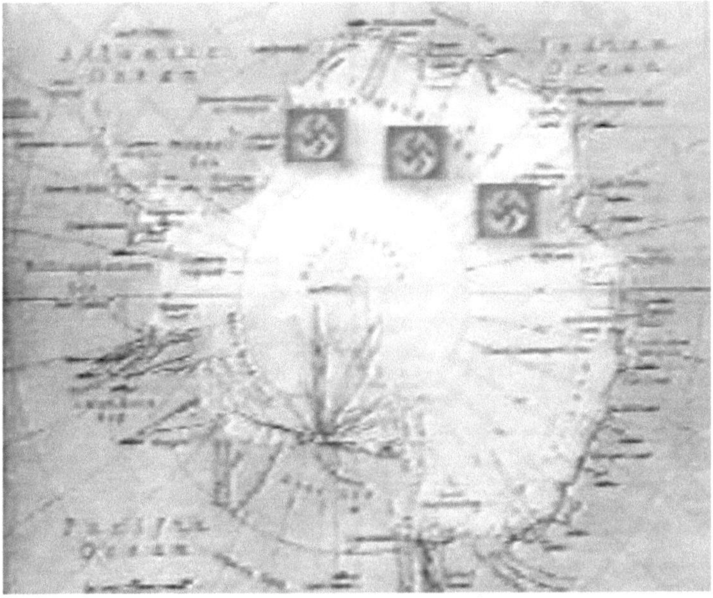

Prior to World War II German scientists were obsessed with Antarctica. Far from finding a desolate wasteland covered with ice, the Germans discovered ice-free areas, warm water lakes and cavern systems.

The following passage refers to German efforts to claim a region of Antarctica after Norwegian expeditions in the 1920's and 30's: after these expeditions the Germans also got interested in Queen Maud land [or "Neuschwabenland" as referred to by the Germans], and planned an expedition to declare it as theirs... Anyway, it is still lying there as a remote ice-shelf with lots of high mountains over the glacier.

Truly a beautiful land.

Queen Maud land is dominated by the giant shelf of ice, flowing slowly from King Haakon VII - plateau over the South Pole, down to the ocean. This area is called "Fenriskjeften" after the mouth of the giant Devil-wolf in Norse mythology.

According to this mythology Fenris' (the wolf) teeth were very sharp, and they would kill all people on Earth during Ragnarok - *the end of the world.*

Most of the mountains in Fenriskjeften have names with analogies to teeth, or to other parts of the Norse.

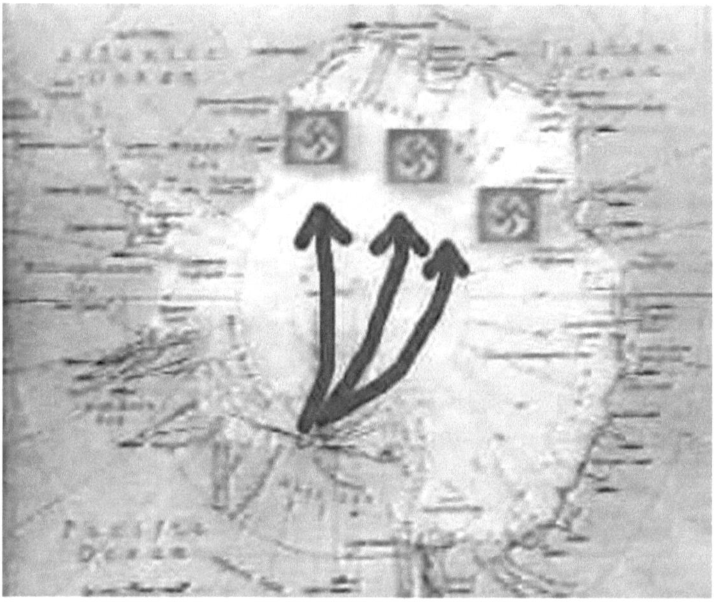

The use of wolf symbology is interesting as it touches upon a theme in Nazi symbology which used the wolf as a totem of the hunter-killer: Hitler's retreat in Berchtesgaden, Bavaria was nicknamed "Wolf's Lair" and the tactic used by German U-Boa ts to defeat convoys during the War was called "Wolfpack." Germany also had allies in South America and South Africa. Many Nazis fled to Argentina following the war and South Africa resembled a Nazi state as racial minorities [including Indians as well as blacks] were subjected to apartheid.

Hitler's dream was of a "Thousand-year Reich." Is this a thinly-veiled counterpart to *Jesus'* Millennial Kingdom? Allied pilots reported seeing "foo fighters" during the latter stages of the World War II. These craft appeared and vanished at incredible speeds and created electrical and magnetic anomalies when close to allied aircraft.

These craft are similar to "flying saucers" that were reported initially in 1947.

Nazi leaders were known for their obsession with the occult, including astrology and ancient relics. Remember the Indiana Jones movies that used Nazi quests for the holiest relics of the Judeo Christian faith? These movies are based on the occultic practices of Nazis.

One relic they were fascinated with [and may possess] was the "Spear of Destiny" that pierced *Christ's* side on Golgotha.

The next movie in the Indiana Jones series is tentatively titled "Indiana Jones and the Lost Continent" an allusion to Atlantis - the antediluvian civilization destroyed by God's flood in Genesis Chapter 6 after the daughters of men were taken by the sons of *God* as their wives [a reference to "fallen angels"?]

Hitler's corpse was never found. Recent reports of "opened KGB files" assert that Hitler's bones were kept and then destroyed by Soviet intelligence. But the current incarnation of Russia is a wolf in sheep's clothing and there is little faith in the KGB [or FSB, its "successor"] veracity.

UFO abductee **Barney Hill** [who in the 1960›s was one of the first publicized abductees] claimed under hypnosis that one of his abductors "look[ed] like a German Nazi". Other abductees have claimed seeing Nazi-style decorations or hearing German or German-accented voices as part of their abduction experience.

Some twelve years later the Australians discovered a 16mm film, a technical report, of the German V-7 research project.

The V-7 weapons research project involved circular disk-shaped craft. Now, we knew about programs V-1 through V-4, but we had no previous idea about the V-7 program.

The information in this documentary seemed to indicate that the Germans built their first operational disk sometime in the early 1940's in the first production facility in Prague. Then they proceeded to expand their design, development and research teams until by the time the Germans were being driven back into Germany, they had nine research facilities, all with projects under testing.

They successfully evacuated eight of those facilities out of Germany, along with the scientists and the key people. The ninth facility was blown up. Now, this 16mm film showed some pictures of flying vehicles in operation.

We also knew through intelligence, where I was working at the end of the war, that the Germans built eight very large cargo submarines, especially built, and they were all commissioned, launched and proceeded to disappear without a trace. To this day, we have no idea where they went.

They are not on the bottom of the ocean or at any port we know of. It's a mystery, but the mystery might have been solved by this Australian documentary film, which shows large German cargo submarines in the Antarctic with ice flows all around them, and crews standing on deck waiting for tie-up at a quay. We have underground information that some of the research facilities in Germany were taken to a place called "New Schwabenland".

Now, Germany was called "Schwabenland" before it was called Germany. So, we are talking about "New Germany", and it is located in an area at the South Pole formerly called Queen Maude Land.

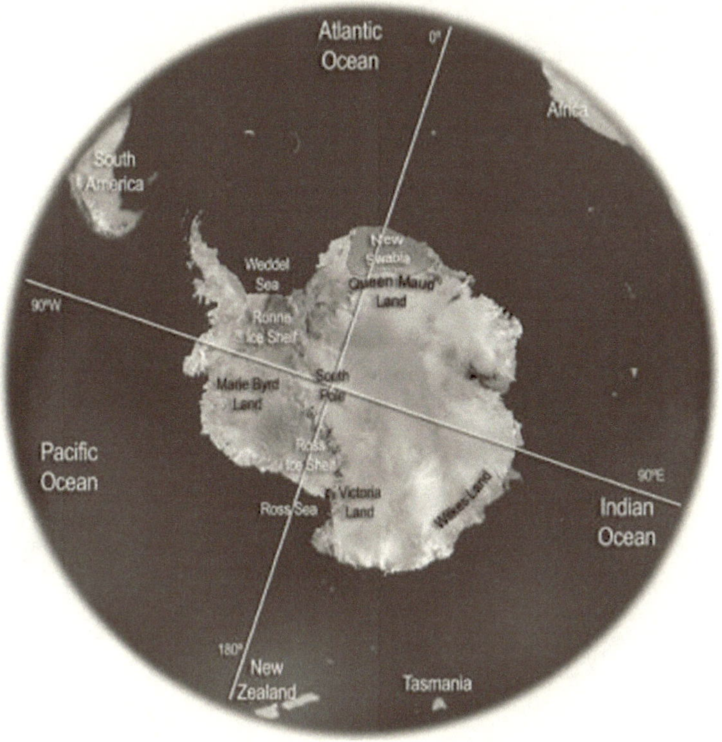

Back around 1937, we convened an international conference under the League of Nations at the time to decide to restrict new claims to land in Antarctica.

At the time, everyone seemed to have a claim except Germany, who had not staked out a claim but only had some research going on down there. The whole thing was designed to keep Germany from making a land claim as the Nazi's were coming to power. We refused to recognize German claims, which were shown on German maps.

A couple of years ago, *National Geographic* showed the German claim on a map for the first time.

But, back in 1939, Göring led an expedition to the Antarctic, including a submarine force, and they took construction and digging equipment down there and began excavating a tunnel complex, and this activity might have been going on since that time. If that is the case, it could be a sizable complex today.

That may be where the big cargo submarines are.

We believe that at least one or more of the disk research facilities were taken to Antarctica.

We had information that *one was taken to the Amazon*, and that another was taken to the north coast of Norway, where there is a strong German population. Those were taken into secretly maintained underground facilities.

Before World War II, the Germans had military advisors all over South America, and when we got into the war we persuaded countries in South America to give up German advisors and accept American ones. Down there, they still prefer the Germans and have never liked us.

It is quite possible that some of this material and some of these research facilities were de-centralized to South America as the German empire began to collapse.

The big companies like I.G. Farben and the German subsidiary of General Electric opened large subsidiary plants in Rio and Sao Paulo in Brazil, and some of these new facilities became larger that they had been in Germany. So, there would have been support capability for disk research facilities. One has to wonder how much truth there really is to all of this.

It appears that some of the craft we see today are nothing more than further developments of German disk technology. So, we may in fact be visited periodically by Germans.

One has to wonder how much we are observing is man-made, and how much is truly extraterrestrial technology.

Certainly there is some of both, but we don't know what the percentages are.

Wendelle C. Stevens

Thousands of Missiles Fired by Russian and American Forces over Earth's Arctic Regions – completely unannounced

Are we fighting extraterrestrial UFOs?

India Daily

Staff Reporter

Apr. 14, 2005

Report is reaching of a strange behavior by the American and Russian forces in the Earth's Arctic regions. Completely unannounced, both the super powers are launching thousands of missiles from both land based and aircraft launched these missiles that are being directed out of the earth's atmosphere into the outer space regions of our planet's atmosphere.

From various news services however there is being reported that Russia and the United States are conducting *Missile Defense War games*. The valid question is why was this separate military exercise not previously announced. Some UFO researchers believe that both the forces are jointly fighting something that they are not saying.

There are also reports that someone is manipulating the earth's weather systems in a massive scale. Are American and Russians jointly fighting them?

The cosmic bursts hitting the earth are also strange. The Solar flares in recent times have shown extreme abnormal behavior.

The increasing earthquakes, floods, droughts and landslides may have been caused by some artificial agents.

- On the surface the American and Russians are saying these missile launches are part of military exercises but why are they unannounced?
- What triggered this massive launch of terrestrial missiles in thousands?

Photo taken over the Antarctic sky

Evidence of the use of extraterrestrial technology. One of the last great mysteries of the 20th century is the occult past of the 3rd Reich, and membership of secret societies by some of its leading exponents.

The question as to whether these people were aware of the existence of lost extraterrestrial technologies, once applied by past advanced cultures, is raised by completely new research, supported by historical documents and original film footage of the period.

Were the disk-shaped flying objects (UFOs), driven by anti-gravitation forces, actually constructed? Test pilots, engineers and investigators explain the Nazi program for space travel and contact with aliens.

Path 51: Operation High Jump

In 1947, Admiral **Richard E. Byrd** led 4,000 military troops from the U.S., Britain and Australia in an invasion of Antarctica called "Operation Highjump", and at least one follow-up expedition.

That is fact. It is undeniable. But... the part of the story that is seldom told, at least in "official" circles, is that Byrd and his forces encountered heavy resistance to their Antarctic venture from "flying saucers" and had to call off the invasion.

This aspect of the story was pushed forward, again, a few years ago, when a retired Rear Admiral, allegedly living in Texas, who had been involved in the "invasion", said he was "shocked" when he read material from a documentary, entitled "Rire from the Sky".

He allegedly claimed that he knew there had been "a lot of aircraft and rocket shoot-downs", but did not realize the situation was as serious as the documentary presented it.

Operation "High Jump", which was, basically an invasion of the Antarctic, consisted of three Naval battle groups, which departed Norfolk, VA, on 2 December 1946. They were led by Admiral Richard E. Byrd's command ship, the ice-breaker "Northwind," and consisted of the catapult ship "Pine Island," the destroyer "Brownsen," the aircraft-carrier "Phillipines Sea," the U.S. submarine "Sennet," two support vessels "Yankee" and "Merrick," and two tankers "Canisted" and "Capacan," the destroyer "Henderson" and a floatplane ship "Currituck."

A British-Norwegian force and a Russian force, and some Australian and Canadian forces were also involved.

Interestingly, the *Pine Island* (AV-12), one of the seaplane tenders involved in the expedition, has a rather colorful history. The USS Pine Island, a Currituck Class Seaplane Tender, was laid down, 16 November 1942, at Todd Shipyard Corporation, in San Pedro, California. It was launched, 26 February 1944, and given the commissioned name, USS Pine Island on 26 April 1945.

The ship served through the final months of the Second World War, and the immediate post-war period, but was decommissioned on 1 May 1950 When the Korean War broke out, the ship was re-commissioned, on 7 October 1950, at Alameda, California. She was finally decommissioned, for good, on 16 June 1967 and laid up in the Reserve Fleet.

But... here's where the story gets interesting... The *USS Pine Island* was struck from the Naval Register, on an unknown date... Her title was transferred to the Maritime Administration for lay up in the National Defense Reserve Fleet... on an unknown date... and... the ship's final disposition is unknown... Now... how does one go about "losing" a major surface ship, over 640 feet long, almost seventy feet wide, with a displacement of over 15,000 tons? [see *Rejoinder* below]

Rejoinder:

As a federal employee with immediate access to the **NDRF** (*National Defense Reserve Fleet*) archives, which are all unclassified, let me provide additional information as it relates to the subject story of 3/15.

Mr. Choron states:

"The USS Pine Island was struck from the Naval Register, on an unknown date... Her title was transferred to the Maritime Administration for lay up in the National Defense Reserve Fleet... on an unknown date... and... the ship's final disposition is unknown..."

Here's what I can tell you: PINE ISLAND was delivered to Zidell Explorations in Portland, OR (now Zidell Marine) on 3/7/72 under a standard scrapping contract. Zidell paid $166K for the ship, which would be typical. In 1971 PINE ISLAND was towed to Bremerton to be stripped out by the Navy, which is not uncommon for a ship to be scrapped. The fact that she (nor the other AVs) is not listed on the Naval Vessel Register is strange, but probably just an oversight on the Navy's part (as is not uncommon). Should you E-mail the nice folks running the NVR today, they would probably thank you for pointing out the omission and add the missing ships.

Now, all this is not a refutation of OPERATION HIGHJUMP; that will be left up to others.

The story, of course, gets stranger, still. The Pine Island is not the only ship involved in "Antarctic Research" or "exploration" to have disappeared. There were numerous others. The question is not so much "how many", that is fairly well established.

The question is "how and why"... particularly "why"...

On 5 March, 1947 the "El Mercurio" newspaper of Santiago, Chile, had a headline article "On Board the Mount Olympus on the High Seas" which quoted Byrd in an interview with Lee van Atta:

> "Adm. Byrd declared today that it was imperative for the United States to initiate immediate defense measures against hostile regions. Furthermore, Byrd stated that he "didn't want to frighten anyone unduly" but that it was "a bitter reality that in case of a new war the continental United States would be attacked by flying objects which could fly from pole to pole at incredible speeds".

Interestingly, not long before he made these comments, the Admiral had recommended defense bases at the North Pole.

These were not "isolated" remarks... Admiral Byrd later repeated the each of these points of view, resulting from he described as his "personal knowledge" gathered both at the north and south poles, before a news conference held for International News Service.

He was hospitalized and was not allowed to hold any more press conferences. Still, in March 1955, he was placed in charge of *Operation Deepfreeze* which was part of the International Geophysical Year, 1957-1958, exploration of the Antarctic. He died, shortly thereafter... in 1957... many have suggested he was murdered...

So... who was the enemy that owned or flew these flying objects? Germany was apparently defeated, and there was no evidence that the new emerging enemy, Russia, certainly had such superior technologies. They were, like the United States, only on the verge of the "rocket age", and totally dependent upon technology, and expertise captured from Germany at the end of the War. There was no other known threat could that could account for the United States' invasion of Antarctica nor for the development of any craft that could fly "fly from Pole to pole with incredible speeds."

Of course, the Roswell Incident had been in the news the past summer, but... it had been "officially" explained, and hushed up by the time *Highjump* began.

Rumors began to circulate that even though Germany had been defeated, a selection of military personnel and scientists had fled the fatherland as Allied troops swept across mainland Europe and established themselves at a base on Antarctica from where they continued to develop advanced aircraft based on extraterrestrial technologies.

It is interesting to note that at the end of the war the Allies determined that there were 250,000 Germans unaccounted for, even taking into account casualties and deaths. This would be quite a population base for a fledgling colony, and provide the essential degree of skill, expertise, and pure manpower for an industrial base of any sort, let alone the production of, even by today's standards, extremely high technology.

All *Unidentified Flying Object researchers* are, of course, aware of the multitude of reports concerning sightings of 'flying saucers' with swastikas or iron crosses on them, 'aliens' speaking German, etc. Most have also heard of abductees who have been taken to underground bases with swastika emblems on the walls, or as in the case of noted abductee

Alex Christopher, have seen "Reptiloids" and "Nazis" working together aboard antigravity craft or within underground bases.

Barney Hill was apparently, not the only one to describe the so-called "Nazi" connection to *Unidentified Flying Object abductions*. However, reports such as Christopher's and Hill's must be taken with a rather large grain of salt... There is a far more plausible explanation than the so-called "reptiloids".

Another noted example is the American Reinhold Schmidt, a man whose father was born in Germany, and who tells in his book "Incident At Kearney", that he was taken on a 'flying saucer' on several occasions. Schmidt states that "the crew spoke German and acted like German soldiers". He also stated that they took him to the "Polar" region.

Now, one must admit that if a person were making up such a story, why would they claim to be taken, of all places, to the pole? Of course, one must also realize that at the time of Schmidt's comments, the rumors of "secret Nazi bases" at the poles were already fairly common... After returning he was allegedly subjected to persecution by the U.S. Government. In his defense, it must be noted that his description of the aerial discs, as he called them, matched pictures captured from the Germans in the final days of the Second World War.

In 1959, three large newspapers in Chile reported front-page articles about *Unidentified Flying Object* encounters in which the crew members appeared to be German soldiers. In the early 1960s there were reports in New York, and New Jersey, of flying saucer 'aliens' who spoke German, or English with a German accent. Nor, can it be neglected to mention that in one of the most spectacular legal cases of the Twentieth Century... the "atomic espionage" trials... Julius and Ethel Rosenberg spoke of "warships of space."

Since they had access to top secret information, and, at that point, no reason to lie, what was it, exactly, that they meant?

So... now we get to the point...

In late 1947, only months after the famous *Roswell Incident*, then Secretary of the Navy **James Forrestal** sent a naval task force to Antarctic including Admiral Nimitz, Admiral Krusen and Admiral Byrd, called "Operation Highjump". It was touted to be an expedition to find "coal deposits" and other valuable resources, but... the facts indicate otherwise... In actuality they were apparently trying to locate an immense underground base constructed by the Germans, before, during and immediately after the Second World War, with the aid of Alien Entities, which were described as "Aryans".

This base was allegedly located in *Neuschwabenland*, an area of Antarctica which Germany explored, and claimed, before the outbreak of the Second World War... In fact, Germany had done a very detailed study of Antarctic and were alleged to have built a small underground base there before the War.

At this point, one must ask why, exactly, the United States, and, in fact, her allies, suspected that German activity at the pole was continuing, after the conclusion of the Second World War... The answer, quite honestly, has nothing at all to do with *Unidentified Flying Objects*... That part of the story came to light from a completely different set of sources...

The fact is that there was plenty of evidence, at the time, to indicate that as late as 1947, elements of the *Kriegsmarine*, or German Navy, were still very much active in the South Atlantic, operating either out of South America, or some base, previously unsuspected, in the Antarctic. Many stories were circulating at the time...

One of which even has a German U-boat stopping an Icelandic whaler named Juliana in Antarctic waters, in 1947 and insisting that its captain, named Hekla, sell the U-boat crew supplies from her available stores. In exchange for the supplies (which had been paid for in U.S. dollars, along with a ten dollar bonus to each member of Juliana's crew...) the U-boat commander told the whaler where a large school of whales were to be found. Hekla and his crew later found the whales in the exact position claimed by the U-boat commander.

The presence of such boats, all late construction Type XXI and Type XXIII U-Boats, with the "snorkel" that allowed them to make the entire passage from Germany submerged... was no secret.

An advanced submarine schnorkel. With this device German U-Boats overcame the necessity for surfacing to recharge their batteries. Raised above the surface by a telescoping tube, the schnorkel provided an outlet for exhaust gases and an inlet for fresh air. At first, allied radar was able to pick up the small schnorkel "blip" but German scientists countered with an anti-radar coating which appears on this model (a principle similar to that used by the U.S. B-2 bomber). The U-Boats again became invisible. While this advance was of great importance it was the development of the "Electro Boat" and the Walter motor, powered by hydrogen peroxide, which gave the German U-Boat a range of 30,000 miles or more, greatly increased speed and other capabilities far in advance of Allied submarines of the 1940's and 1950's (courtesy of U.S. Navy Archives).

Many were thought to be operating out of Argentina, possibly under the Argentine flag, but crewed by German crew.

The fact that in the dying moments of the Second World War, ten U-Boats, based in Oslofjord, Hamburg and Flensburg, were made available to transport several hundred German officers and officials to Argentina to found a new Reich is widely accepted. These officers, mostly involved in "secret" projects, and many of whom were members of the SS and Kriegsmarine, itself, sought to escape the "vengeance" of the Allies, and continue their work, abroad.

The U-boats were filled with their luggage, documents and, more than likely, gold bullion, to finance their efforts. All the U-boats departed their home ports between 3 and 8 May 1945. They were to proceed to Argentina where they would be welcomed by the friendly regime of Juan Peron and his charismatic wife Eva Peron. Seven of the ten of the U-Boats, based on the German/Danish border, set off for Argentina through the Kattegat and Skagerrak. None were ever seen again... "officially".

It has been, however, documented that three of the boats did, in fact, arrive in Argentina... These were U-530, U-977 and U-1238. U-530 and U-977 surrendered to the Argentine Navy at Mar del Plata in early July and August, 1945... U-1238 was scuttled, by her crew, in the waters of San Matias Gulf, off Northern Patagonia.

Seven boats are as yet unaccounted for... and... Kriegsmarine archives, recently discovered, indicate that a total of more than forty boats are completely unaccounted for... all of which were late construction, state-of-the-art craft, and could have made either Argentina or Antarctica, completely submerged... and completely unnoticed by existing "allied" technology of the time... for the entire duration of their crossing.

The question arises, of course, why these men would make such a perilous crossing. It must surely be seen as a act of either desperation or fanaticism, or both... and such men as crewed U-Boats were neither. Nor, were the scientists and military officers who were their passengers. The fact is, it would seem that most of those who fled the ruin of Germany to the far South, were scientists and engineers, and their dedication sprang from the project on which they were working...

To understand this dedication, it is necessary to go back, before the outbreak of the Second World War, to an isolated section of the Bavarian Alps, It was there, in the summer of 1938, that an Unidentified Flying Object, crewed by a distinctly human, and Aryan appearing race, made a forced landing, very similar to the one which was to occur, some ten years later, in the desert, near Roswell, New Mexico, in the United States.

While the occupants of the two craft were completely unrelated, the technology involved, seems to have been strikingly similar. Also, the outcome of the recovery effort, undertaken by Germany, just as a similar recovery effort was undertaken by the United States, had strikingly different results.

The *Bavarian crash of 1938*, seems to have yielded a functioning, or almost functioning and repairable (with the technology of the time) power plant, and a nearly completely destroyed, or unrepairable airframe. The Roswell crash resulted in exactly the opposite... a nearly intact airframe and a ruined power plant. Because of this, the German research, which was to follow, took a vastly different turn from that which was undertaken in the United States, some ten years later... Germany needed an airframe which was capable of supporting the "engine" (for lack of a better term), while the United States would eventually need an "engine" capable of giving maximum performance to the airframe.

This, of course, would explain the vast array of "experimental" aircraft... of extremely "unique" design... to literally pour out of the design bureaus of Messerschmidt, Focke Wulf, Fokker and a multitude of smaller firms in the period between 1939 and 1945. The most notable, of course, is the Sänger "Flying Wing" which was later copied by the United States, and is, of course, the ancestor of today's "stealth" bomber and fighter designs... notably, the B-2 Heavy Bomber.

It is also beyond doubt that both Unidentified Flying Object recoveries are the initial impetus for the long standing and ongoing research in "anti-gravity" propulsion seen in work of current aircraft manufacturers such as Boeing and Lockheed in the United States, and PanAvia in Europe.

In any case, it was the work on "reverse engineering" the downed Bavarian Unidentified Flying Object that was the catalyst for the "exodus" to the South in the final days of the Second World War. Germany was in ruins, and the research was viewed, by those conducting it, as vital... vital enough to risk packing up all that they had and risking a perilous submerged crossing of the Atlantic.. to an isolated experimental and research base on a frozen continent...

Granted, by modern standards... even by the standards of the day... U-Boats were small and cramped. They had very little cargo capacity. Still, a tiny fleet of them... ten to twelve boats... could easily transport the essential equipment, making several "runs", and serve to supply and, later re-supply the Antarctic bastion of the research.

Speculation exists, with much to support it, that at least one of the boats in the valiant little fleet contained the biggest prize of all... at least one living survivor of the 1938 crash... an Extraterrestrial... a literal Human Being... not a "Grey"... born on a distant planet. The best evidence indicates that there were several survivors of the crash, and that they worked, and are most likely still working, with the original German scientists and engineers, or their descendants, in an effort to construct a viable "flying disc".

These are not the "Grey Aliens" of Roswell. These beings, biologically, completely human, are described as "Aryan" in appearance, and completely human, although at least two to three generations more advanced, technologically than Earth born Human Beings. While their technology is similar to that of the Grays in general theory, it is somewhat different, apparently, in application.

This would tend to indicate that Earth technology and science is, at most, only one "major breakthrough" away from parity with the extraterrestrial cultures in question, and also explain the "urgency" of the project, as viewed by the German (and undoubtedly United States, as well...) scientists and engineers involved in such research.

In any case, *Operation Highjump*, began... The task force of over 40 ships, included the flagship "Mount Olympus", the aircraft carrier "Philippine Sea", the seaplane tender "Pine Sea", the submarine "Senate", the destroyer "Bronson", the ice breaker "Northwind", and other tanker and supply ships. An armed contingent of 1400 sailors, and three dog sled teams were also on board.

The expedition was filmed by the Navy and brought to Hollywood to be made into a commercial film called "The Secret Land".

It was narrated by Hollywood actor Robert Montgomery, father of "Bewitched" star, Elizabeth Montgomery, who was, himself, an officer in the Naval Reserve.

It seems incredible that so shortly after a war that had decimated most of Europe and crippled global economies, an expedition to Antarctica was undertaken with so much haste (it took advantage of the first available Antarctic summer after the war), at such cost, and with so much military hardware - unless the operation was absolutely essential to the security of the United States.

At the time of the operation, the US Navy itself was being taken apart piece by piece as the battle-tested fleet was decommissioned with its mostly civilian crew bidding farewell to the seas forever. The Navy was even reduced to further recruitment to man the few remaining ships in service.

Tensions across the globe were also mounting as Russia and America edged into a Cold War, possibly a Third World War that the US would have to fight with "tragically few ships and tragically half trained men." This made the sending of nearly 5,000 residual Navy personnel to a remote part of the planet where so much danger lurked in the form of icebergs, blizzards and sub-zero temperatures even more of a puzzle. The operation was also launched with incredible speed, "a matter of weeks."

Perhaps it would not be uncharitable to conclude that the Americans had some unfinished business connected with the war in the polar region. Indeed this was later confirmed by other events and the operation's leader, Admiral **Richard Byrd**, himself.

The official instructions issued by the then Chief of Naval Operations, **Chester W. Nimitz** were:

a. to train personnel and test material in the frigid zones

b. to consolidate and extend American sovereignty over the largest practical area of the Antarctic continent

c. to determine the feasibility of establishing and maintaining bases in the Antarctic and to investigate possible base sites

d. to develop techniques for establishing and maintaining air bases on the ice, (with particular attention to the later applicability of such techniques to Greenland)

e. to amplify existing knowledge of hydro graphic, geographic, geological, meteorological and electromagnetic conditions in the area

Little other information was released to the media about the mission, although most journalists were suspicious of its true purpose given the huge amount of military hardware involved.

The US Navy also strongly emphasized that *Operation Highjump* was going to be a navy show; Admiral Ramsey's preliminary orders of 26th August 1946 stated that "the Chief of Naval Operations only will deal with other governmental agencies" and that "no diplomatic negotiations are required. No foreign observers will be accepted." Not exactly an invitation to scrutiny, even from other arms of the government.

Some facts, however, are well known... There were three divisions of *Operation High Jump*: one land group with tractors, explosives, and plenty of equipment to refurbish "Little America", and make an airstrip to land the six R-4D's (DC-3's), and two seaplane groups. The R4-D's were fitted with jet-assist takeoff bottles (JATO) in order to takeoff from the short runway of the aircraft carrier "Philippine Sea".

They also were fitted with large skis for landing on the ice field prepared for them. The skis were specially fitted at three inches above the surface of the carrier deck. When landing on the ice at "Little America" the three inches of tire in contact with the snow and ice provided just enough and not too much drag for a smooth landing.

Following its arrival at Antarctica, the force began a reconnaissance of the continent. Byrd himself was onboard the first of the planes to take off on 29 January 1947.

Rocket propulsion tubes (*JATO bottles*) had been attached to the side of the aircraft and the carrier was maneuvered for a 35mph run to help get the planes airborne.

"From the vibration of the great carrier", Byrd later wrote, "I knew when the captain had got the ship up to about 30 knots (35 mph... maximum, full emergency speed for such a vessel).

We seemed to creep along the deck at first and it looked as if we would never make it but when our four JATO bottles went off along the sides of the plane with a terrific, deafening noise I could see the deck fall away. I knew we had made it."

Admiral Byrd's team of six R4-D's were fitted with the, then, super secret "Trimetricon" spy cameras and each plane was trailing a magnetometer.

The aircraft flew over as much of the continent as they could in the short three month "summer" period, mapping and recording magnetic data. They also carried magnetometers show anomalies in the Earth's magnetism, i.e. if there is a "hollow" place under the surface ice or ground, it will show up on the meter. On the last of many "mapping" flights where all six planes went out, each on certain pre-ordained paths to film and "measure" with magnetometers, Admiral Byrd's plane returned three hours late...

"Officially", it was stated that he had "lost an engine" and had had to throw everything overboard except the films themselves and the results of magnetometer readings in order to maintain altitude long enough to return to Little America. If we are to believe the published and private accounts of what actually took place, this is almost certainly the time when he met with representatives of the "Aryan" Extraterrestrials, and a contingent of the German scientists working on the reverse engineering and construction of "flying discs"...

Over the next four weeks the planes spent 220 hours in the air, flying a total of 22,700 miles and taking some 70,000 aerial photographs. Then the mission that had been expected to last for between six to eight months came to an early and faltering end. The Chilean press reported that the mission had "run into trouble" and that there had been "many fatalities".

(However... the official record, states that one plane crashed killing three men; a fourth man had perished on the ice; two helicopters had gone down although their crews had been rescued and a task force commander was nearly lost.)

It is an indisputable fact that the *Central Group of Operation Highjump* were evacuated by the Burton Island ice-breaker from the Bay of Whales on 22 February 1947; the Western Group headed home on 1st of March 1947 and the Eastern Group did likewise on 4 March, a mere eight weeks after arrival.

In the end, the task force came steaming back to the United Sates with their data, which then, immediately became classified "top secret". Secretary of the Navy (by this time, Secretary of Defense) **James Forrestal** retired... and started to "talk".... not only about Highjump, but about other things, as well... He was put in Bethesda Naval Hospital psychiatric ward where he was prevented from seeing or talking to anyone, including his wife... and... after a short while he was thrown out the window while trying to hang himself with a bed sheet.

So the story goes... It was, of course, ruled a *suicide*, case closed. However, some of what he knew... about Highjump... about Roswell... and other things... did manage to "leak"... How much is truth, how much is speculation is difficult to tell. However, in every "myth" there is a grain of truth...

This much is certain... As incredible as it may sound, there is considerable supporting evidence for these claims about a German base in Antarctica... On the very eve of the Second World War, the Germans themselves had invaded part of Antarctica and claimed it for the Third Reich.

In fact Hitler had authorized several expeditions to the poles shortly before WWII. Their stated objective was to either to rebuild and enlarge Germany's whaling fleet or test out weaponry in severely hostile conditions. Yet, if true, all of this could have been achieved at the North Pole rather than at both poles and been much closer to home.

For some reason, however, the Germans had long held an interest in the South Polar region of Antarctica with the first Germanic research of that area being undertaken in 1873 when Sir Eduard Dallman (1830-1896) discovered new Antarctic routes and the "Kaiser-Wilhelm-Inseln" at the western entrance of the *Biskmarkstrasse* along the Biscoue Islands with his ship *Grönland* during his expedition for the German polar Navigation Company of Hamburg. The *Grönland* also achieved the distinction of being the first steamer to operate in the southern ocean.

A further expedition took place in the early years of the twentieth century in the ship the Gauss (which became embedded in the ice for 12 months), and then a further expedition took place in 1911 under the command of Wilhelm Filchner with his ship the Deutschland.

Between the wars, the Germans made a further voyage in 1925 with a specially designed ship for the Polar Regions, the Meteor under the command of Dr. Albert Merz.

Then, in the years directly preceding the Second World War, the Germans laid claim to parts of Antarctica in order to set up a permanent base there. Given that no country actually owned the continent and it could not exactly be conquered as no-one lived there during the winter months at least, it appeared to the Germans that the most effective way to conquer part of the continent was to physically travel there, claim it, let others know of their actions and await any disagreements.

Captain Alfred Ritscher was chosen to lead the proposed strike. He had already led expeditions to the North Pole and had proved himself in adverse and critical situations. For the mission Ritscher was given the Schwabenland; a German aircraft carrier that had been used for transatlantic mail deliveries by special flightboats, the famous 10 ton Dornier Super Wals since 1934.

These Wals were launched by catapult from the Schwabenland and had to be accelerated to 93mph before they could become airborne. At the end of each flight a crane on the ship lifted the aircraft back on board after they landed in the sea.

The ship was refitted for the expedition in the shipyards of Hamburg, and around one million Reichsmark, nearly a third of the entire expedition budget - was spent on this refit alone.

The crew was prepared for the mission by the German Society of Polar Research and as these preparations neared completion, the organization invited Admiral Byrd to address them, which he did.

The *Schwabenland* left the port of Hamburg on 17 December 1938 and followed a precisely planned and determined route towards the southern continent. In little over a month the ship arrived at the ice covered Antarctica, dropping anchor at 4B0 30B" W and 69B0 14B" S on January 201939..

The expedition then spent three weeks off Princess Astrid Coast and Princess Martha Coast off Queen Maud Land. During these weeks, the two *Schwabenland* aircraft, the Passat and Boreas, flew 15 missions across some 600,000 square kilometers of Antarctica, taking more than 11,000 pictures of the area with their specially designed *Zeiss Reihenmess-Bildkameras RMK 38b.*

Nearly one fifth of Antarctica was reconnoitered in this way and, for the first time, ice-free areas with lakes and signs of vegetation were discovered. This area was then declared to be under the control of the German expedition, renamed Neu-Schwabenland and hundreds of small stakes, carrying the swastika, were dumped on the snow-covered ground from the Wals to signal the new ownership. Ritscher and the Schwabenland left their newly claimed territory in the middle of February 1939 and returned to Hamburg two months later, complete with photographs and maps of the new German acquisition.

Now bear in mind that all of this took place before the recovery of the *Unidentified Flying Object*, in the Bavarian Alps, in 1938... There is no conceivable reason, at least on the surface, for such an intense interest in the South Polar regions... unless something else had already transpired to make such an investigation worthwhile... The true purpose of this expedition has never been satisfactorily explained; there is merely a series of puzzles, related reports and snippets of information that are no longer open to verification. What is not open to doubt however, is that in the decade preceding the Second World War, the Germans did almost nothing that did not put the entire structure of the country on a war footing.

This activity affected all aspects of German life; military, civilian, economic, social and foreign policies, engineering, industry etc. Given that the seizing of *Neu-Schwabenland* occurred on the very eve of the war, it can only be concluded that that the polar expedition was of major importance and significance to the goals and development of the German nation.

Nor did activity end with the outbreak of the war... In fact, it intensified... The South Atlantic, including South Polar waters became quite active...

Between 1939 and 1941, well after the outbreak of war in Europe, Captain **Bernhard Rogge** of the commerce raider Atlantis made an extended voyage in the South Atlantic, Indian and South Pacific Oceans, and visited the Iles Kerguelen between December 1940 to January 1941.

The *Atlantis* is known to have been visited by an RFZ-2 (the UFO style craft which had served as a reconnaissance aircraft since late 1940.) The ship then adopted a new disguise as *Tamesis* before being sunk by HMS Devonshire near Ascension Island, on 22 November 1941 (the Atlantis was also known as *Hilfskreuzer 16* and was, at various times, disguised as *Kasii-Maru* or *Abbekerk*.)

Although the activities of the German ship Erlangen, under the captaincy of Alfred Grams, do not appear to be of consequence during 1939-40, the same cannot be said of the Komet which was commanded by Captain **Robert Eyssen**.

Following her passage along the Northern Sea Route in 1940, this commerce raider operated in the Pacific and Indian oceans, including a voyage along the Antarctic coastline from Cape Adare to the Shackleton Ice Shelf in search of whaling vessels during February 1941. There she met the *Pinguin* and supply vessels *Alstertor* and *Adjutant*. (Komet was sunk off Cherbourg in 1942.)

The *Pinguin* itself under the command of Captain Ernst-Felix Kruder was a commerce raider that operated chiefly in the Indian Ocean. In January 1941 she captured a Norwegian whaling fleet (factory ships *Ole Wegger* and *Pelagos*, supply ship *Solglimt* and eleven whale catchers) in about 59B0 S, 02B0 30W. One of these catchers (renamed Adjutant) remained as a tender and the rest were sent to France. This ship also made anchorages at the Iles Kerguelen and may have landed a party on Marion Island.

Pinguin was sunk off the Persian Gulf by HMS Cornwall on 8 May 1941 after she had captured 136,550 tons of British and allied shipping.

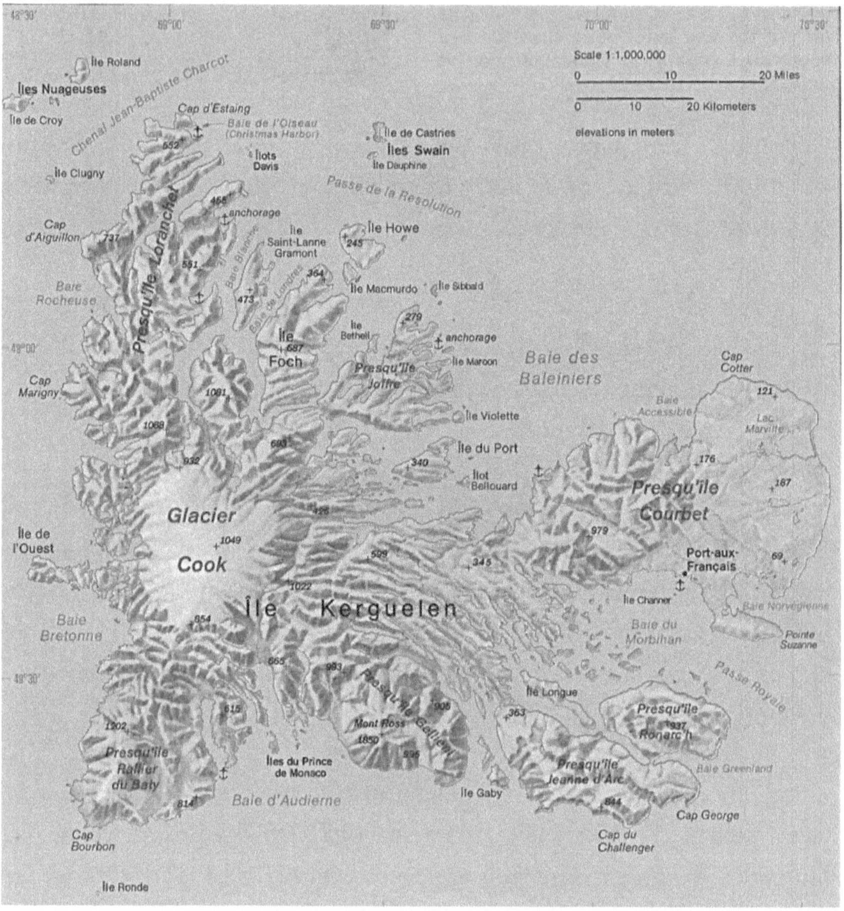

The Kerguelen Archipelago – ideal for secret supply bases

This island of Kerguelen (named the *Most Useless Island In the World* in 1995) continued to feature prominently in Nazi plans.

For example, in 1942 the German Navy planned to establish a meteorological station there. In May of that year the ship Michel transferred a meteorologist and two radio operators with full equipment to a supply vessel *Charlotte Schlieman* that went on to the island, however the orders for the station were later counter-manned. It is interesting to note that Kerguelen Island was also the centre of a mid 19th Century mystery.

Then entirely uninhabited, except for seals and seabirds, British Captain Sir **James Clark Ross** landed there in May 1840. He found in the snow unidentifiable "traces of the singular footprints of a pony, or ass, being 3 inches in length and 2 inches in breadth, having a small deeper depression in either side, and shaped like a horseshoe." Similar markings appeared overnight in the Devon area of England fifteen years later and have also defied adequate explanation.

Then in 1942 Captain Gerlach in his ship the Stier investigated nearby Gough Island as a possible temporary base for raiders and a camp for prisoners.

This ship activity does not appear considerable, however the level of U-boat activity in the South Atlantic was much higher. The exact nature and extent of how high will probably never be known, however some insight might be gleaned from the fact that between October 1942 and September 1944 16 German U-boats were sunk in the South Atlantic area. And... some of these submarines did appear to be engaged in covert activities.

A fine example of this would be that of U-859 which, on 4 April 1944 at 04.40hrs, left on a mission carrying 67 men and 33 tons of mercury sealed in glass bottles in watertight tin crates. The submarine was later sunk on 23 September by a British submarine (HMS Trenchant) in the Straits of Malacca and although 47 of the crew died, 20 survived.

Some 30 years later one of these survivors spoke openly about the cargo and divers later confirmed the story on rediscovering the mercury. The significance being that mercury is usable as a fuel source for certain types of aerospace propulsion. Why would a German submarine be transporting such a cargo so far from home?

It is not odd, at all, if one considers the fact that aviation/avionics construction is what the Polar Base seems to be all about...

Although Germany surrendered unconditionally to the Allies, on 8 May 1945, events after that date suggested something was happening that did not form a part of recognized world history. Something fuelled by a statement made by German Grand Admiral **Karl Dönitz**...

Dönitz (16 September 1891 b 24 December 1980) had become Commander of the *German Kriegsmarine* (Navy), on 31 January 1943 and he led the German U-Boat fleet until the end of the Second World War. He also has the distinction of briefly becoming head of the German state for 20 days after Hitler's death until his own capture by the Allies on 23 May 1945. His contribution to the mystery of post-war Antarctic activity came in a statement he made in 1943 when he declared that a substantial portion of the German submarine fleet had rebuilt "in another part of the world a Shangri-La land... an impregnable fortress."

Could he have been referring to the alleged base in Antarctica?

Certainly there are records of continued German naval activity in the area after the war had apparently ended. For example, on 10 July 1945, more than two months after the cessation of known hostilities, the German submarine U-530 surrendered to Argentine authorities. The background to this event is puzzling. It is known that the boat had left Lorient in France on 22nd May 1944 under the captaincy of Otto Wermuth for operations in the Trinidad area, and after successfully rendezvousing with the incoming Japanese submarine I-52, it headed for Trinidad before finally returning to base after 133 days at sea.

The boat's official record states that between October 1944 and May 1945 it formed part of the 33rd Flotilla and on Germany's surrender Otto Wermuth's captaincy and the submarine's career came to an end. Yet two months later it arrived in Rio de la Plata in Argentina and surrendered to the authorities there on 10 July 1945.

The future may well reveal that fate of more of these submarines; however given the French and South American reports, and the number of missing U-boats, it may not be unreasonable to conclude that at least some of them relocated to the South Polar area.

History also gives us further clues as to a German-Antarctica connection, for it records that Hans-Ulrich Rudel of the German Luftwaffe was being groomed by Hitler to be his successor. It is known that Rudel made frequent trips to Tierra del Fuego at the tip of South America nearest Antarctica. And...one of Martin Bormann's last messages from the bunker in Berlin to Dönitz also mentioned Tierra del Fuego.

Then there are also claims about Rudolf Hess, Hitler's best friend who went to England and was arrested as a war criminal on 10 May 1941. Following his arrest, Hess was held in Spandau Prison in isolation until his death. Such unique treatment is suggestive that he had information that the Allies considered dangerous.

Indeed, in his book *Secret Nazi Polar Expeditions* **Christof Friedrich** states Hess,

> "was entrusted with the all-important Antarctic file.
> Hess, himself, kept the Polar file."

Now, granted, such information as Hess possessed, if any, would have been complete only to the time that he took off on his solo flight to England... but... that period... prior to 1941... would have covered the initial recovery of the Bavarian "flying disc", and at the very least, the early stages of any project or projects arising from such a recovery. It would also contain any information with regard to any survivors of the crash, and their eventual fate(s).

Many believe that Hess, who had no part in any of the so-called "war crimes" was deliberately kept in Spandau Prison, for life, in an attempt to keep him quiet. It has also been speculated that the man who died, in Spandau Prison, was, in fact, not Hess at all... that Hess had been murdered, years before, in an effort to keep the truth... on several highly embarrassing matters... from getting out.

For the moment, however, let's return to *Operation Highjump*... which seems to have been an attempt to ferret out a remaining German base on the Antarctic continent, and perhaps, to determine where, exactly the sudden rash of Unidentified Flying Object activity of the past eighteen months, had originated, and, exactly who/what was behind it... There would have, of necessity, been two prerequisites for a mission of this type.

Firstly, *Operation Highjump* would have to provide evidence that the mission included a reconnaissance of *Neu-Swabenland* and secondly, there would have to be an area of the frozen continent that could allow such a base to exist throughout the year.

Both of these criteria were met...

Both the Eastern and Western Groups of *Operation Highjump* had been active around *Neu-Schwabenland.* So was a Russian boat that "proved to be unfriendly". The Eastern group were frustrated in their efforts to make a reconnaissance of the area, despite incredible efforts to secure photographs for later examination.

However by then,

> "it was very late in the season ... The sun had only been briefly glimpsed in the past few weeks, but everyone could tell that the continually grey skies and clouds were darkening daily. In another month all light would be gone from Antarctica. The waters girdling the continent would begin to freeze rapidly, binding unwary ships in a crushing embrace.

Dufek [the commander] was loath to surrender. He ordered his ships northwards away from the pack. Perhaps one or two more flights might be possible. But on the morning of 3 March virgin ice was seen to be forming on the water's surface [and the] Eastern group steamed out of Antarctica."

The Western Group, however, were to make a remarkable discovery.

At the end of January 1947 a PBM piloted by Lieutenant Commander David Bunger of Coronado, California, flew from his ship, the Currituck and headed towards the continent's Queen Mary Coast.

On reaching land, Bunger flew west for a time, then, coming up over the featureless, white horizon, he saw a dark, bare area which Byrd later described as,

> "a land of blue and green lakes and brown hills in an otherwise limitless expanse of ice".

Bunger and his men carefully reconnoitered the area before racing back to the Currituck with news of their find. The oasis they had discovered covered an area of some three hundred square miles of the continent and contained three large, open water lakes along with a number of smaller lakes. These lakes were separated by masses of barren, reddish-brown rocks possibly indicating the presence of iron ore.

Several days later, Bunger returned to the area, and found that the water was warm to the touch and the lake itself was filled with red, blue and green algae giving it a distinctive color. Bunger filled a bottle with the water which later "turned out to be brackish, a clue to the fact that the lake was actually an arm of the open sea".

This is important for two reasons; warm, inland lakes connected to the surrounding oceans would be perfect for submarines to hide within, and similar lakes have been noted in *Neu-Schwabenland*, the site of the alleged German (and suspected Alien) base.

While there is, still, no conclusive evidence of a German/Alien base on Antarctica, It is beyond doubt that something highly unusual was happening on, or around, the frozen continent. In general, it appears that the probability for such a base to have existed... and perhaps continue to exist, to this day, are rather high...

The evidence, a large volume of it, is there for all to see...

1. The Germans explored and claimed part of Antarctica on the very eve of the war when the vast majority of their activity was geared towards the rebuilding of the German economy and military infrastructure. This activity began shortly before the recovery of the Bavarian “flying disc”, in 1938, but picked up pace immediately afterward.

2. There was ongoing ship and submarine activity in the South Atlantic and Polar Regions throughout and after the war had apparently ended. This activity continued well into the 1950s, and if some accounts are to be believed, continues to this day, with what can only be considered U-Boat sightings, and a very high incidence of Unidentified Flying Object sightings in the South Atlantic and South Polar regions, including the Southern portions of South America.

3. The US literally invaded the continent of Antarctica, itself, with considerable naval resources leaving mainland America exposed and vulnerable as the world edged into the Cold War. The task force limped home as if defeated only weeks later, and the local South American press wrote of such a defeat. This coincided with a substantial increase in Unidentified Flying Object activity... generally attributed to the first major “wave” of such activity in modern times, with an inordinate amount of this activity taking place in the Southern Hemisphere, particularly in South America.

4. Admiral Byrd spoke of objects that could fly from pole to pole at incredible speeds being based on Antarctica.

5. Hundreds of thousands of Germans and a minimum of forty (40) U-boats were missing at the end of the war. Documentation and eyewitness accounts prove that at least a portion of these craft made it as far as South America, in some cases, several months after the end of the war in Europe.

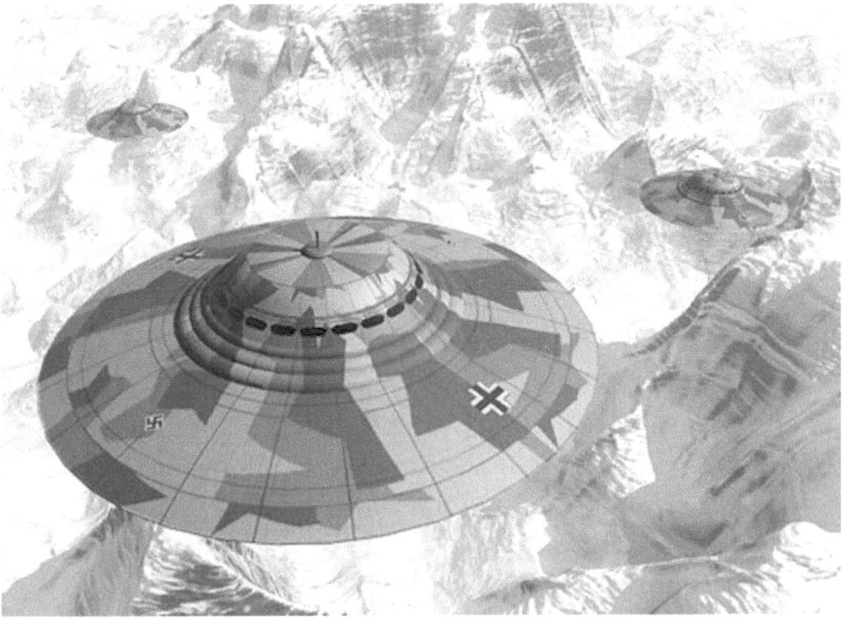

The connection between *Antarctica and the UFO phenomenon* was sealed with claims made by one **Albert K. Bender** who stated that he "*went into the fantastic and came up with an answer and I know what the saucers are.*"

Bender ran an organization called the *International Flying Saucer Bureau* (**IFSB**) a small UFO organization based in Connecticut, USA and he also edited a publication known as the Space Review which was committed to the dissemination of news about UFOs. In truth, the organization had only a small membership and the publication circulated amongst hundreds rather than thousands, but that its members and readers valued it was in little doubt. The publication itself advocated that flying saucers were spacecraft of extraterrestrial origin.

However... in the October 1953 edition of *Space Review*, there were two major announcements.

The first was headed *Late Bulletin* and stated:

A source which the IFSB considers very reliable has informed us that the investigation of the flying saucer mystery and the solution is approaching final stages. This same source to whom we had referred data, which had come into our possession, suggested that it was not the proper method and time to publish the data in 'Space Review'.

The second announcement read "Statement of Importance":

The mystery of the flying saucers is no longer a mystery. The source is already known, but any information about this is being withheld by order from a higher source. We would like to print the full story in Space Review, but because of the nature of the information we are very sorry that we have been advised in the negative.

The statement ended in the sentence:

We advise those engaged in saucer work to please be very cautious.

These announcements were of little significance in and of themselves.

Bender's publication was considered "fringe", at best, even at the time... However... what gained them wider attention was the fact that immediately after publishing this October 1953 issue, Bender suspended further publication of the magazine and closed the IFSB down without any further explanation.

This is completely consistent with the "prudent" approach, shown by many who have been "gently" warned to "cease operations" by the Majestic 12 Group and other agencies involved in "keeping a lid" on any real investigation into the *Unidentified Flying Object phenomenon.*

Bender might very well have known "what the flying saucers" were, at least a portion of them... but he later revealed in a local newspaper interview that he was keeping his knowledge a secret following a visit by three men who apparently confirmed he was right about his *Unidentified Flying Object theory*, but put him in sufficient fear to immediately close down his organization and cease publication of the journal.

It has been argued that the story of being visited by three strangers and being warned off was a front to close a publication that was losing money, however the fact that Bender had been "scared to death" and "actually couldn't eat for a couple of days" was verified by his friends and associates. It is also widely known that such "stories" are often spread by the United States, and other governments to discredit those who might just have the truth, or at least a portion of it.

In 1963, a full decade after his visit from the three strangers, Bender was seemingly prepared to reveal more of his story in a largely unreadable book entitled *Flying Saucers and the Three Men in Black.* The book was scant on facts, however, it described extraterrestrial spacecraft that had bases in Antarctica.

This was apparently the truth Bender was terrorized into not revealing.

Bender also provided images of the saucers he was aware of. He produced drawings of Unidentified Flying Objects that he was aware of... not saucers, as were the common depictions of the time, but rather "flying wings" which showed three bubble-like protrusions on the underside, reminiscent of the German designed Haunebu II (which was allegedly only in the "design stage" at the end of the Second World War) alongside a cylindrical, cigar shaped object.

Ernst Zündel was NOT a 'Paperclip Scientist':

I realized that North Americans were not interested in being educated. They want to be entertained. The book was for fun. With a picture of the Führer on the cover and *flying saucers coming out of Antarctica* it was a chance to get on radio and TV talk shows. For about 15 minutes of an hour program I›d talk about that esoteric stuff.

Then I would start talking about all those Jewish scientists in concentration camps, working on these secret weapons. And that was my chance to talk about what I wanted to talk about.

Ernst Zündel, a German scientist turned author (known for his internet "ZGrams") who had entered the US under Operation Paperclip, a United States Army/CIA program to bring German scientific talent into the United States in spite of any so-called "war crimes" which they were alleged to have committed... at the end of the war and who worked at Wright Field (later Wright Patterson AFB where the Roswell debris were eventually housed), also made claims about the nature of the activity in Antarctica.

In the 1970s Zündel's book *UFOs: Nazi Secret Weapons?* made the claim that at least some *Unidentified Flying Objects* were German secret Weapons which were developed during the Second World War, and that some of them had been shipped out towards the end of the war and hidden at the poles.

Publication of the book coincided with a tidal wave of renewed interest in all things paranormal... coming on the heel of what was to be the last major Unidentified Flying Object "wave" of the Twentieth Century, and Zündel was a guest on to countless talk shows where he shared his views on spaceships, free energies, electromagnetism, emergent technologies and some of the positive contributions made by the Germans in these fields.

Zündel, who was one of the first of the "revisionist" historians of the Second World War, was actually only really interested in promoting his holocaust theory, described in his book Did Six Million Really Die? However, he found that his *Unidentified Flying Object* and *Hollow Earth* ideas proved a greater attraction to television producers. The idea seized hold of the popular imagination and took on a life of its own. Zündel's publishing company, *Samisdat*, started to make a name for itself by issuing newsletters and books on the subject. An expedition to Antarctica itself was even proposed to seek out Hitler's UFO bases there.

The fact is that such claims would have died out had they not been based on at least some real events...

Now, keep in mind that South America has always been a "hotbed" of Unidentified Flying Object activity. Many of the reports coming out of the area are unverified, and unverifiable... However, many have credence. The claims that something extremely unusual was taking place around the foreboding reaches of the frozen continent took a major leap forward in the 1960s when the Argentine Navy was charged with the official investigation into strange sightings in the sky.

A 1965 official report prepared by Captain Sanchez Moreno of the *Naval Air Station Comandante Espora in Bahia Blanca* stated that,

> "Between 1950 and 1965, personnel of Argentina's Navy alone made 22 sightings of Unidentified Flying Objects that were not airplanes, satellites, weather balloons or

> any type of known (aerial) vehicles. These 22 cases served as precedents for intensifying that investigation of the subject by the Navy."

Following a series of sightings at Argentine and Chilean meteorological stations on Deception Island, Antarctica, in June and July 1965, Captain Engineer Omar Pagani disclosed at a press conference that,

> "Unidentified Flying Objects do exist. Their presence in Argentine airspace is proven".

The report went on to state, however, "their nature and origin are unknown and no judgment is made about them". More details of these UFO sightings were given in a report in the Brazilian newspaper *O Estado de Sao Paulo* in its 8th July 1965 edition.

"For the first time in history, an official communiqué has been published by a government about the flying saucers. It is a document from the Argentine Navy, based on the statements of a large number of Argentine, Chilean and British sailors stationed in the naval base in Antarctica.

The communiqué declared that the personnel of Deception Island (left) naval base saw, at nineteen hours forty minutes on 3 July, a flying object of lenticular shape, with a solid appearance and a coloring in which red and green prevailed and, for a few moments, yellow. The machine was flying in a zig-zag fashion, and in a generally western direction, but it changed course several times and changed speed, having an inclination of about forty-five degrees above the horizon. The craft also remained stationary for about twenty minutes at a height of approximately 5,000 meters, producing no sound.

The communiqué states moreover that the prevailing meteorological conditions when the phenomenon was observed can be considered excellent for the region in question and the time of year. The sky was clear and quite a lot of stars were visible. The Secretariat of the Argentine

Navy also states in its communiqué that the occurrence was witnessed by scientists of the three naval bases and that the facts described by these people agree completely."

Practically everyone in the "UFO Community" is aware that in March 1950 Commodore Augusto Vars Orrego of the Chilean Navy shot still pictures and 8mm movie footage of a very large cigar shaped flying object that hovered over and maneuvered about in the frigid skies above the Chilean Antarctic.

The photos and the report of Orrego's sighting have, quite literally, been seen by millions over the half century since he saw, and photographed the objects. Orrego stated,

> "during the bright Antarctic night, we saw flying saucers, one above the other, turning at tremendous speeds. We have photographs to prove what we saw ."

There have, of course, been numerous other Chilean sightings.

During January 1956 another major Unidentified Flying Object "event" was witnessed by a group of Chilean scientists who had been flown by helicopter to Robertson Island in the Wendell Sea to study geology, fauna and other features.

This experience was the subject of a later article entitled *A Cigar-Shaped UFO over Antarctica.*

"At the beginning of January 1956, during a period of stormy weather, the party suddenly became aware of something which, in other circumstances, could have been very grave for them. This was that their radio had mysteriously ceased to function. This was not too worrying a disaster in so much as it was firmly settled that the helicopter would return to take them off again on January 20."

One of the scientists, a doctor, was in the habit of getting up in the night to observe anything of meteorological interest, but another of the group, a professor, did not like to be disturbed. However on the night of 8 January 1956, the Doctor decided to wake the professor.

He pointed upwards, almost overhead. Still in a bad temper due to being disturbed, the professor looked as directed, and beheld two,

> "Metallic, cigar-shaped objects in verticular positions, perfectly still and silent, and flashing vividly the reflected rays of the sun".

Just after 7.00am, two other members of the party, an assistant and a medical orderly joined the two men.

The group watched the two craft.

"At about 9.00am object No. 1 (the nearest to the zenith) suddenly assumed a horizontal posture and shot away like a flash towards the west. It had now lost its metallic brightness and had taken on the whole gamut of visible colors of the spectrum, from infrared to ultra-violet.

The report of the sighting went on to say...

"Without slowing down it performed an incredible acute-angle change of direction, shot off across another section of the sky and then did another sharp turn as before. These vertiginous maneuvers, the zig-zagging, abrupt stopping, instantaneous accelerating, went on for some time right overhead, the object always following tangential trajectories in respect to the Earth and all in the most absolute silence".

The demonstration lasted about five minutes.

Then, according to the witnesses, the object returned and took up position beside its companion in almost the same area of the sky as before.

Then, it was the turn of No. 2 to show its paces and do a convoluted, zigzagging dance across the sky. Shooting off towards the east, it performed a series of ten disjointed bursts of flight, broken by abrupt changes of direction, and marked by the pronounced color changes when accelerating or stopping. After about three minutes, object No. 2 was observed to resume its station near its companion, and return to its original solid and metallic appearance.

Due to the nature of their mission, the group had with them two Geiger-Miller counters of high sensitivity, one of the auditory and the other of the flash-type. When the two objects had finished their dance and reassumed their stations in the sky, someone discovered that the flash-type Geiger counter now showed that radioactivity around them had suddenly increased 40 times... far more than enough to kill any organism subjected long enough to it. The discovery greatly increased the anxiety felt by the four men.

Although they had no telescopic lens, they did have cameras with them, and managed to take numerous photographs of the objects, both in color and black and white. The report does not state what became of these photographs, but it is safe to assume that they are in the possession of the Chilean Government, and there is no reason to assume that they have not been shared with that of the United States, as well as others.

Of course... no names are given in this report, but... it has the ring of truth, and is consistent with any number of similar sightings... Would that we knew their names! It is one of the exasperating facts of Unidentified Flying Object research that so many of the South American and South Atlantic sightings are attributed to "anonymous sources" or the names of the witnesses involved, have been expunged from the "official" records.

So many of the witnesses being cited would be, with reference to their stated credentials, credible sources, but because of the practice of expunging names from records which might fall into "public hands" are practically impossible to trace. The absence of names... in many, if not most cases deliberately expunged from official reports... simply lends to an aura of "unbelievability", even though it is a common practice, especially in most countries.

Yet another documented account of a UFO sighting over Antarctica is by Rubens Junqueira Villela, a meteorologist and the first Brazilian scientist to participate in an expedition to the South Polar region, and now, a veteran of eleven expeditions to Antarctica (two with the US Navy, eight with the Brazilian Antarctic Program and another on the sailing ship Rapa Nui).

While on board the US Navy icebreaker Glacier, which had set sail from New Zealand at the end of January 1961, Villela claims that he witnessed a UFO event in the skies over Antarctica which he immediately recorded in his diary, even including the emotions felt by all those involved. On 16 March 1961, after a fierce storm had forced the expedition to retreat to Admiralty Bay in the King George Isles, "a strange light suddenly crossed the sky, and everyone started to shout".

Speculation went wild. Some thought the object to be an incoming missile. Others thought it to be a meteor.

The excitement was widespread and growing.

"Trying to describe the light which appeared over Almirantado Bay" he told interviewers, later, "wasn't easy b& I wrote in my diary: Positively the colors, the configuration and contours of the object, as a bodied light, with geometric forms, did not seem to be from this world, and I did not know what could possibly reproduce it".

The object, he went on to report, was "multi-colored", and had a luminous, oval-shaped body. It left, behind it, a "long tube-like orange/ red trail".

Allegedly, it split into two pieces, as if it had exploded. Then, each part shone even more intensively, with white, blue and red colors projecting V shaped rays behind it. They quickly moved away and could be seen 200 meters above the ground b& According to the witnesses, the entire display was completely silent.

The US Navy officially registered the incident as "a meteor or some other natural luminous phenomenon" according to the report submitted by the Glacier's captain, Captain Porter. However, this is a common practice, and has been, ever since the inception of the *Unidentified Flying Object* cover-up, under the auspices of the Majestic 12 group.

This policy of "official denial" and "logical explanation" no matter how far fetched, would seem, has been followed by all branches of the United States Government since the first days after the Roswell Incident, in July 1947. It certainly applies to any sightings or alleged sightings in and around Antarctica...

Villela, on the other hand, easily dismissed the official line.

"How could they mistake a meteor with an object carrying antennae, completely symmetrical and followed by a tail without any sight of atmospheric disturbance?"

According to most "official" sources... and certainly according to world renowned skeptic and self-styled debunker, Phillip Klaus, this particular episode is a classic example of plasma, however the late meteorologist, James McDonald argued that the highly structured nature of the object and the low cloud overcast present at about 1500 feet were not compatible with Klaus's hypothesis.

The list of sightings in the South Atlantic area is practically endless. It is, and has been, particularly since the end of the Second World War, one of the most active areas on earth with respect to Unidentified Flying Object activity. Another classic sighting took place on 16 January 1958 when the Brazilian naval vessel Almirante Salddanha was escorting a team of scientists to a weather station on Trinidad Island. As the ship approached the island (or rather an outcrop of rock) an Unidentified Flying Object reportedly flew low, over the water, past the ship, circled the island, then flew off in front of dozens of witnesses.

One of the witnesses to this particular event, the expedition photographer, took a number of photographs of the object. Later, the film was handed over to the military by the Captain. Amazingly, after the initial analysis, the Brazilian government released the film stating that they were unable to account for the images.

Why did the United States Government, in late 1947, only months after the famous Roswell Incident, send a naval task force to Antarctic including Admiral **Nimitz**, Admiral **Krusen** and Admiral **Byrd**, called "Operation Highjump". As we observed earlier, the operation was said to be an expedition to find "coal deposits" and other valuable resources, but... the facts indicate otherwise...

In actuality, there seems to be no doubt that they were trying to locate an immense underground base constructed by the Germans, before, during and immediately after the Second World War, with the aid of Alien Entities which were described as "Aryans". This base, allegedly located in an area that the Germans called "Neuschwabenlandt"... an area of Antarctica which Germany explored, and claimed, before the outbreak of the Second World War... was thought to hold "flying objects which could fly from Pole to Pole in a matter of minutes"...

For years, rumors have circulated as to why German submarines... U-Boats... would operate in South American and Antarctic waters long after the end of the Second World War, in Europe.

Some have said that the boats spirited away such notables as Adolf Hitler and Martin Bormannn... both of whom can be demonstrated to have died in Berlin at the end of the war. the death... and physical remains of both men have been verified beyond doubt, the latter with very recent DNA testing. Thus neither of them escaped via U-boats to South America. The fact is, **Wolfgang Eisenmenger**, a forensic science professor at Munich University, conducted the DNA testing of Bormann's remains. He seems to have done the work for the Frankfurt justice officials.

He also had Bormann's dental, medical, and fingerprint records. Bormann's children (or a distant family member, details a bit fuzzy) provided the blood for the DNA match which was proven conclusive, i.e. that the body was of Martin Bormann. The cause of death was deemed to be self-inflicted poisoning. Adolf Hitler, of course, died in his Bunker in Berlin, of poison... and a self-inflicted gunshot.

Everyone has heard stories of vast amounts of gold or other valuables being "smuggled" out of Germany in the last days of the war... secreted away to South America... to support so-called "criminals" abroad. So far, none of those stories has shown any sign of merit. If they were so, then men such as Eichman would not have worked on the assembly line in a Volkswagen plant. Müller would not have run a chicken farm, and Mengele would not have been dependent upon the generosity of his wealthy family.

There is a story floating around that this said U-boat commander worked on some highly classified US National Secrets after the war, and that his boat was operating in the far South... He was reported to have been a commander of a VIIC or IXC U-boat in the Atlantic during the war, named *Otto Schneider*. This theory is also easy to disprove...

There simply was no U-Boat commander by that name in the *Kriegsmarine* (German Navy). Only two commanders with that last name saw service in the war; Herbert Schneider who died while in command of U-522, and Manfred Schneider only commander the small XXIII boat U-4706 for the last 3 months of the war, and never left his home port. This story is just that, a story.

The fact is, *Unidentified Flying Object* researchers are well aware of strange sightings of 'flying saucers' with swastikas or iron crosses displayed on them.

They are also well aware of 'aliens' speaking German, and have also heard of abductees who have been taken to underground bases with swastika emblems on the walls, or as in the case of one abductee... **Alex Christopher**... who claims to have seen "Reptiloids" and Germans working together aboard antigravity craft or within underground bases.

- Is this what America feared?
- Is it a secret Antarctic facility where these experiments and developments continued?
- What Operation Highjump was actually looking for?
- Is this secret, among others, the one that cost James Forrestall his life?
- Did an unrecorded, three hour long meeting with a group of German scientists and engineers and "Aryan" Extraterrestrials in the frozen wastelands near the South Pole cost Admiral Byrd his life?
- Is this the origin of the "warships of space", that the Rosenberg's mentioned in the very shadow of the electric chair?

One thing is certain... The United States did not "invade" Antarctica, at the end of a World War and the very beginning of a Cold War... using a disproportionate share of its diminishing fleet... for "exploration" purposes.

If they were looking for something, they surely knew what it was they were looking for... and... a "scientific" expedition does not go forth prepared for WAR...

The map of Neu Schwabenland that cannot be exhibited in Germany, *on penalty of imprisonment...*

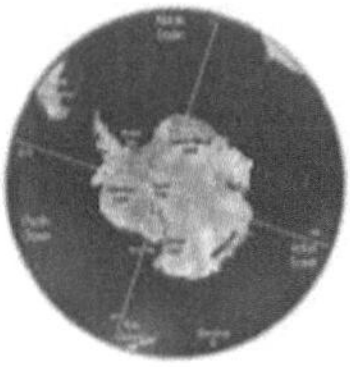
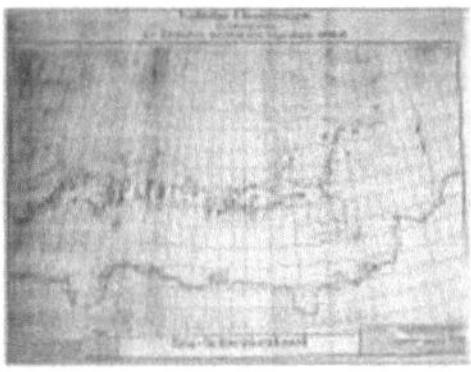
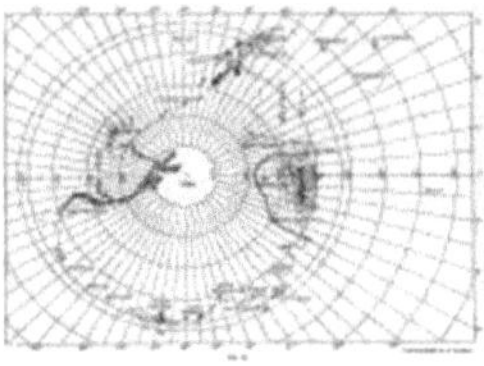

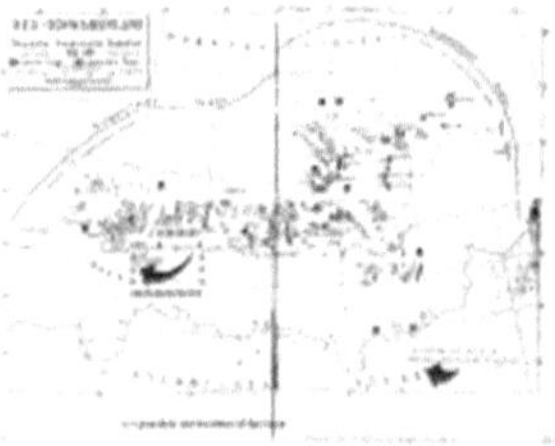
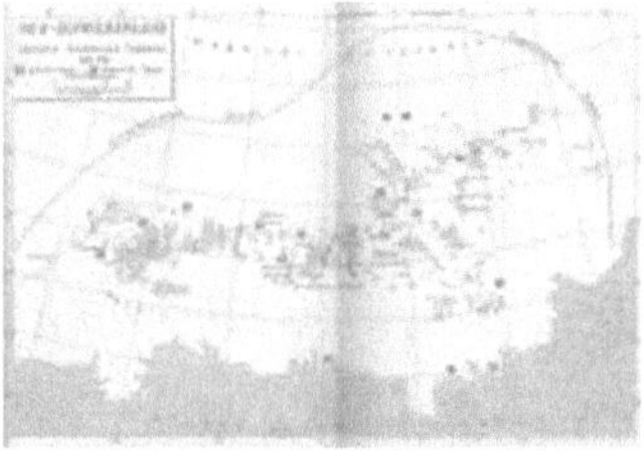

A Secret U.S. Post Office operated in Antarctica 1946-1948 causing speculation about the real reason behind two concurrent U.S. expeditions...

Finn Ronne was a Norwegian immigrant who later joined the United States Navy and was a member and officer in Admiral Byrd›s earlier expeditions to Antarctica. In 1946-8, he led a privately-financed expedition to Antarctica, following upon the heels of Operation Highjump.

Ronne's expedition was to the Marguerite Bay area, where he reoccupied Byrd's 1939 Base. One of the most important results of this expedition was a showing that the Antarctic Peninsula was connected to the rest of Antarctica, thus solving one of the last great public mysteries of the continent.

Writing in his book entitled "Antarctic Conquest", he stated:

Although no one knew it, I had been operating a United States Post office too, but for reasons of state (emphasis added) had been compelled to keep it secret.

Secrecy seems to be in no scarcity as it relates to several Antarctic expeditions; perhaps in no small way due to a continued concern that the Nazis had a remnant left in Antarctica from their infamous 1938-9 "New Schwabenland" colonization of Antarctica.

The web is abundant with sites setting forth information about suspected and actual German involvement in Antarctica possibly dating back even to the late 1800's. It does make one wonder if there were in fact, covert or as they say today, "black-ops" reasons for one or more of the Byrd Expeditions (including *Operation Highjump* for this discussion) as well as the private expedition of Captain Ronne.

Many online sources are available with information concerning what I have dubbed the "Byrd Conspiracy", which was not a conspiracy by Admiral Byrd, rather what may have been an apparent conspiracy by the government to keep particular information that he had uncovered during *Operation Highjump* as a secret. I am not passing judgment at this time, as I am still investigating the whole thing to my satisfaction.

However, lending credence to this conspiracy theory is the observation that Admiral Byrd does in effect seem to "disappear" from public view shortly after his return from Operation Highjump in 1947—until approximately 1955 when he organized Operation Deep Freeze I, and he was reported to have been hospitalized (in a mental ward) shortly after his return in 1947.

This forced hospitalization is said to have come upon the tails of Byrd having made some remarkably candid comments (which included what smacked of being a description of a UFO) to a South American newspaper about what he had found during *Operation Highjump*. His disappearance from the scene after his arrival back in the states, would make it appear he may have been promptly squelched! Remember that this time period coincided roughly with the Roswell UFO sightings.

Operation Highjump would have been first, early in 1947, and then Roswell to follow in the summer of 1947.

This was a situation that was the last thing the government would have wanted, another military official (in this case a quite prominent and popular man who had spent years crisscrossing the United States giving lectures and whose word would have been quite respected and accepted) who apparently reported having seen/and or believing in UFOs!!

NOTE: If Op HJ had continued to its full expected duration of six to eight months, they would have still been in Antarctica at the time of Roswell. The expedition headed back to the U.S. in early 1947, well short of its expected ending. Some would say "limped back", after suffering great losses of personnel and equipment. The official record only sets forth a limited loss of life and aircraft, but conspiracists feel the record has been doctored or we are not being told the full story.

Contrast this lack of public accessibility after *Operation Highjump*, to the previous well-known availability of Admiral Byrd in the period following his first two Antarctic Expeditions, where there are documented philatelic items from cities all over the country serving as commemorations of where Byrd visited lecturing to the public about his travels in Antarctica. That Byrd loved to travel and lecture about his polar explorations is quite evident.

The polar regions and his expeditions were his very reason for existence; he had said from the time he was a child that he felt destined to be a polar explorer. He had a passion for all things polar, especially exploration that could scarcely be contained.

Operation Highjump was at least as important in many respects, it would appear, as his previous expeditions... so,

- Where was he after his return?
- Where did he go?

- Was he locked away so he couldn't share the story of what he really had found in Antarctica?
- As some theorists suggest, during Operation Highjump, did he encounter and engage Nazi forces operating from bases that lodged advanced aircraft with advanced propulsion systems?

Many think so, and I am beginning to see some curiosities about many aspects of *Operation Highjump* and now, perhaps even with Ronne›s Expedition.

The little tidbit mentioned above that Ronne forked us in his book, only begins to tell us why the **Oleana Base**, Antarctica postmark is one of the rarest polar cancels that exist. With this being the first American post office established on the Antarctic continent, it is a shame that the cancel was not used more often. Is there perhaps a larger reason why this post office was kept secret? We do know that many countries, including Britain, had concurrent secret bases and or expeditions in the same general time period, notably Port Lockroy on the Antarctic peninsula.

Port Lockroy was part of a top secret World War II British expedition called *Operation Tabarin.*

Operation Tabarin was *the beginning of Britain's permanent presence on the Antarctic continent*, and was built to serve as a southern outpost and to keep an eye on suspected Nazi presence on the ice. In a 2001 BBC interview, one of the last remaining survivors of that secret expedition, **Gwion Davies**, noted that the posting of mail from their secret base was a way of their laying claim to, or establishing that section of Antarctica as British sovereign territory.

In other words, just as the Nazis are known to have dropped metal dart/markers with the Third Reich swastika emblem over a large area of Antarctica during their expedition in 1939, to act as a laying of a claim; for any country (such as Britain) to have a post office that actually accepted and postmarked mail definitely shows an intention on their part of not only establishing a base, but of staying.

While the United States did not then, and does not now, recognize any country as having specific territorial claims upon Antarctica, for Ronne to have allowed his expedition members to have open mailing of letters from Oleana Base would have served a similar purpose as with Port Lockroy, but for some reason, he would not allow that to be done.

Why?

Some mail did escape, and other mail from members of the *Ronne Expedition* is known to have been posted from nearby British bases. The posting of mail often serves a geo-political purpose in addition to the simple fact it carries mail back home to love ones; and it is a great curiosity to many polar philatelists and followers of Antarctic history that it was not done in this instance.

The full story about the existence of the post office (as well as even greater secrets?) may have passed with Captain Ronne.

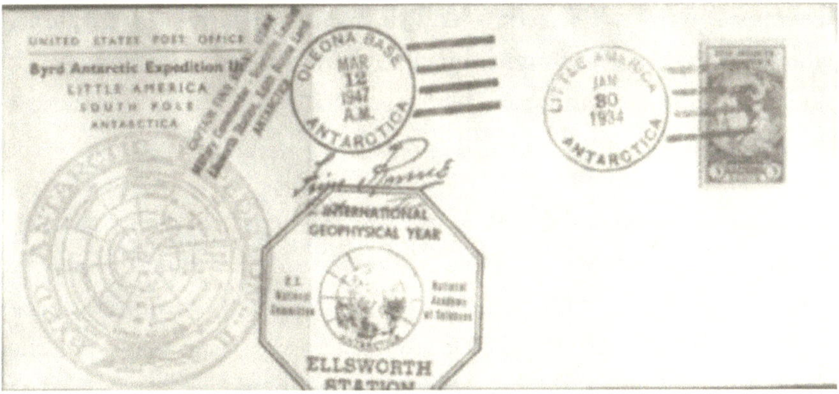

The "Holy Grail" of Antarctic Covers

The *Oleana Bay* covers are most commonly seen with a date of March 12, 1947, which was the date the expedition arrived at Marguerite Bay, Antarctica.

In this instance, the cover illustrated above is extraordinary in that it is on a printed envelope from the *Byrd II Antarctic Expedition*, postmarked with the less common hand cancellation from that mission; then repost marked at *Oleana Base* in 1947, with the addition of Captain Ronne›s "corner card" and the IGY Ellsworth Station octagonal cachet, and the best part of all, Ronne›s signature in which he adds the word "Postmaster", rounding it out to make a splendid cover!

A cover like this would fare extremely well in a polar auction. I would go so far to term it as the "Holy Grail" of a polar collection; only very few covers I can think of would be more collectable, in my opinion.

Path 52: UFO's, Admiral Bird, James Forrestal, and John Kennedy

MJ12 and Lives Snuffed Out to Preserve Non-Disclosure of Extraterrestrials

What is the message in President Eisenhower's warning of the presence of a "Shadow Government" as he stated, "In the councils of government, we must guard against the acquisition of unwarranted influence, whether sought or unsought, by the military-industrial complex," he said in his farewell address. "The potential for the disastrous rise of misplaced power exists and will persist."

Three people stand out in post-World War II who is believed to have been targets of the group MJ12. They had three things in common. They had extensive knowledge of happenings on the continent of Antarctica, they each wished to share what they knew about an extraterrestrial presence there, and each died under questionable circumstances."

What is the MJ12? If the US government refuse to disclose knowledge of extraterrestrials, can we believe the government when we are told that a secret council to conceal the existence of UFO's of extraterrestrial origin does not exist.

People interested in disclosing facts about UFO's and alien beings are murdered, their deaths ruled, or locked away as a psychotic in hospital wards. In late 1947, only months after the famous Roswell Incident, then Secretary of the Navy James Forrestal sent a naval task force to Antarctic including Admiral Nimitz, Admiral Krusen and Admiral Byrd, called "Operation Highjump". It was touted to be an expedition to find "coal deposits" and other valuable resources, but... the facts indicate otherwise... In actuality they were apparently trying to locate an immense underground base constructed by the Germans, before, during and immediately after the Second World War, with the aid of Alien Entities, which were described as "Aryans".

This base was allegedly located in Neu Schwabenland, an area of Antarctica which Germany explored, and claimed, before the outbreak of the Second World War... In fact, Germany had done a very detailed study of Antarctic and were alleged to have built a small underground base there before the War.

At this point, one must ask why, exactly, the United States, and, in fact, her allies, suspected that German activity at the pole was continuing, after the conclusion of the Second World War... The answer, quite honestly, has nothing at all to do with Unidentified Flying Objects... That part of the story came to light from a completely different set of sources...

The fact is that there was plenty of evidence, at the time, to indicate that as late as 1947, elements of the Kriegsmarine, or German Navy, were still very much active in the South Atlantic, operating either out of South America, or some base, previously unsuspected, in the Antarctic. Many stories were circulating at the time...

On 5 March, 1947 the "El Mercurio" newspaper of Santiago, Chile, had a headline article "On Board the Mount Olympus on the High Seas" which quoted Admiral Richard Byrd in an interview with Lee van Atta:

"Adm. Byrd declared today that it was imperative for the United States to initiate immediate defense measures against hostile regions. Furthermore, Byrd stated that he "didn't want to frighten anyone unduly" but that it was "a bitter reality that in case of a new war the continental United States would be attacked by flying objects which could fly from pole to pole at incredible speeds". Interestingly, not long before he made these comments, the Admiral had recommended defense bases AT the North Pole. In the end, the task force came steaming back to the United Sates with their data, which then, immediately became classified "top secret".

These were not "isolated" remarks... Admiral Byrd later repeated the each of these points of view, resulting from he described as his "personal knowledge" gathered both at the north and south poles, before a news conference held for International News Service.

He was hospitalized and was not allowed to hold any more press conferences. Still, in March 1955, he was placed in charge of Operation Deepfreeze which was part of the International Geophysical Year, 1957-1958, exploration of the Antarctic. He died, shortly thereafter... in 1957... many have suggested he was murdered...

Secretary of the Navy (by this time, Secretary of Defense) James Forrestal retired... and started to "talk".... not only about Highjump, but about other things, as well... He was put in Bethesda Naval Hospital psychiatric ward where he was prevented from seeing or talking to anyone, including his wife... and... after a short while he was thrown out the window while trying to hang himself with a bed sheet.

So the story goes... It was, of course, ruled a suicide, case closed. However, some of what he knew... about Highjump... about Roswell... and other things... did manage to "leak"... How much is truth, how much is speculation is difficult to tell. However, in every "myth" there is a grain of truth...

Just before the start of his first term on January 20, 1993, President-Elect Clinton made a strange request to close family friend and lawyer Webster Hubbell:

"If I put you over there in justice I want you to find the answer to two questions for me: One, who killed JFK. And two, are there UFOs." According to Hubbell, "Clinton was dead serious." The key to unlocking the mystery of President Kennedy's assassination and a possible UFO connection lie in events that occurred 18 years earlier in post-war Germany.

In the summer of 1945, John F. Kennedy was a guest of Navy Secretary James Forrestal in a post-war tour of Germany. Kennedy personally witnessed technological secrets that have still not been disclosed to the general public.

These secrets stemmed from technologies that Nazi Germany had acquired from around the world, and were attempting to develop for their weapons programs. The advanced technologies stunned the military government running the U.S. zone of occupied Germany.

How did the Nazis develop them?

The answer according to the father of German rocket design, Herman Oberth, shocked U.S. military officials. The Nazis had help from "the people of others worlds" - some of the technologies were extraterrestrial in origin.

In searching for answers to who killed President Kennedy we need to start with the death of his mentor, James Forrestal in 1949. Forrestal became the first Secretary of Defense in 1947, a position he held until March, 1949.

Forrestal was a visionary who thought Americans had a right to know about the existence of extraterrestrial life and technologies. Forrestal was sacked by President Truman because he was revealing the truth to various officials, including Kennedy who was a Congressman at the time. Forrestal's ideals and vision inspired Kennedy, and laid the seed for what would happen 12 years later.

After winning the 1960 Presidential election, Kennedy learned a shocking truth from President Eisenhower.

The control group set up to run highly classified extraterrestrial technologies, Majestic-12, had become a rogue government agency. Eisenhower warned Kennedy that Majestic-12 had to be reined in. It posed a direct threat to American liberties and democratic processes.

Kennedy followed Eisenhower's advice, and set out to realize James Forrestal's vision.

The same forces that orchestrated Forrestal's death, opposed Kennedy's efforts at every turn. When Kennedy was on the verge of succeeding, by forcing the CIA to share classified UFO information with other government agencies on November 12, 1963, he was assassinated ten days later.

Imagine the weight of the consciousness of the President of the United States. He has to answer to a secret government headed by rich owners of Fortune 500 Corporations who set the political agenda of the False Front government with political actors chosen from a ridged electoral process.

Presidents, Senators, and Congressmen are very much aware of the power vacuum of the three branches of government. Congress has no visibility of the balance sheets of the Federal Reserve Bank, they have no say so about money appropriated to the Military Industrial Complex Secret Space Programs or any idea what is going on with black projects in deep underground military bases, and knowingly have given up the seat of the people at the table of government consent of the people totally disregarded by the three branches of government.

I see why Presidents come into office with a hair full of color and become totally grey at the end of their terms. They know they are serving the Bilderberg, Trilateral, Council of Foreign Relations, Bohemian Grove Satanists, and not the will of the people.

Imagine the thoughts of John F. Kennedy knowing our government is aware of and communicating with alien beings, even having possession of little men and their flying craft and choosing to not disclose this information to the American people. At the same time prosecuting endless wars fought for expansion of power utilizing advanced technology from extraterrestrials, false front governments choose not to disclose to the people who believe in religion that do not include explanation of other galactic extraterrestrial being.

It must be morally defeating overseeing the directives from a shadow government to deprive the people of their wealth, privacy, and freedom, while very rich men have a different agenda requiring people to sacrifice life, our social infrastructures going unattended to, while advancing the Secret Space Program, and poisoning the planet with advanced nuclear technology. Our planet is being stripped bare to advance dreams of interstellar travel without informing the people and ascertaining their consent.

The President has the task of conducting business as usual managing propaganda that is a smokescreen of racial violence, manufactured terrorism, and the transfer of the wealth of a nation to a shadow government comprised Executives of Fortune 500 Banks and Corporations. All of our Presidents who leave office wealthier than before, who was not killed, in many ways failed the American people.

Under "Operation Paperclip" Nazi scientists and intelligence officers were integrated into the military, NASA, and the intelligence community. Wernher von Braun is the most famous and is remembered for being the genius behind the Saturn rockets.

The most infamous was Reinhard Gehlen, a Major General in the Nazi Abwehr or intelligence agency.

Gehlen was sponsored by the Dulles brothers.

John Foster Dulles was a founding member of the CFR and served as President Eisenhower's Secretary of State; Allen was a president of the CFR, and was the Director of Central Intelligence - head of the CIA - when John F. Kennedy was assassinated.

Not only has the CIA been implicated in the assassination of JFK, Allen Dulles was a member of the Warren Commission - the investigative body JFK researchers argue was the government's official cover-up of the conspiracy. German wealth [much of it looted from nations conquered during World War II] was spirited out of Germany.

U.S. Undersecretary of Commerce Stuart Eizenstadt reported the following concerning the Nazi Treasury:The evidence presented in this report is incontrovertible.

....The Swiss National Bank and private Swiss bankers knew, as the War progressed, that the Reichsbank's (the German central bank) own coffers had been depleted, and that the Swiss were handling vast sums of looted gold.

("TRANSCRIPT: EIZENSTAT BRIEFING ON LOOTED NAZI GOLD REPORT" United States Department of Commerce. 8 May 1997).

When World War II ended, and Europe was being overrun by the allies, the country in charge of each sector of Europe. In our sector, we backed trucks up to the former production facilities and hauled off all the documents.

Everyone else did the same thing.

Path 53: Operation Paper Clip

Sixty years ago the US hired Nazi scientists to lead pioneering projects, such as the race to conquer space. These men provided the US with cutting-edge technology which still leads the way today, but at a cost.

The end of World War II saw an intense scramble for Nazi Germany's many technological secrets. The Allies vied to plunder as much equipment and expertise as possible from the rubble of the Thousand Year Reich for themselves, while preventing others from doing the same.

The range of Germany's technical achievement astounded Allied scientific intelligence experts accompanying the invading forces in 1945.

Wernher von Braun:
Nasa icon and former SS officer

Supersonic rockets, nerve gas, jet aircraft, guided missiles, stealth technology and hardened armor were just some of the groundbreaking technologies developed in Nazi laboratories, workshops and factories, even as Germany was losing the war.

And it was the US and the Soviet Union which, in the first days of the Cold War, found themselves in a race against time to uncover Hitler's scientific secrets.

In May 1945, Stalin's legions secured the atomic research labs at the prestigious Kaiser Wilhelm Institute in the suburbs of Berlin, giving their master the kernel of what would become the vast Soviet nuclear arsenal.

US forces removed V-2 missiles from the vast Nordhausen complex, built under the Harz Mountains in central Germany, just before the Soviets took over the factory, in what would become their area of occupation. And the team which had built the V-2, led by Wernher von Braun, also fell into American hands.

Crimes

Shortly afterwards Major-General Hugh Knerr, deputy commander of the US Air Force in Europe, wrote: "Occupation of German scientific and industrial establishments has revealed the fact that we have been alarmingly backward in many fields of research.

"If we do not take the opportunity to seize the apparatus and the brains that developed it and put the combination back to work promptly, we will remain several years behind while we attempt to cover a field already exploited."

Thus began Project Paperclip, the US operation which saw von Braun and more than 700 others spirited out of Germany from under the noses of the US's allies. Its aim was simple: "To exploit German scientists for American research and to deny these intellectual resources to the Soviet Union."

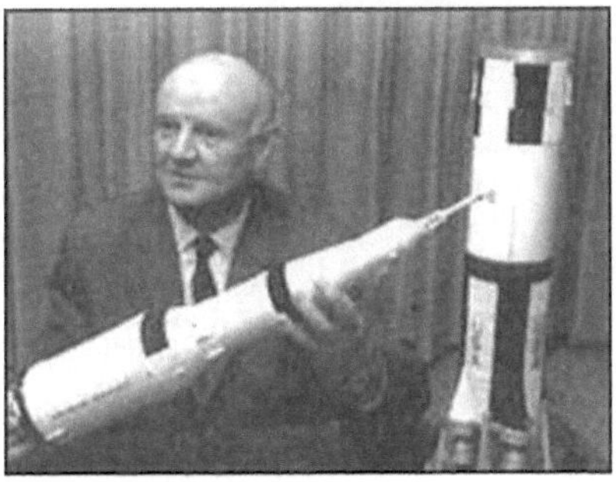

Arthur Rudolph: "100% Nazi"

Events moved rapidly. President Truman authorized Paperclip in August 1945 and, on 18 November, the first Germans reached America.

There was, though, one major problem. Truman had expressly ordered that anyone found "to have been a member of the Nazi party and more than a nominal participant in its activities, or an active supporter of Nazism militarism" would be excluded.

Under this criterion even von Braun himself, the man who masterminded the Moon shots, would have been ineligible to serve the US. A member of numerous Nazi organizations, he also held rank in the SS. His initial intelligence file described him as "a security risk".

And von Braun's associates included:

- **Arthur Rudolph**, chief operations director at Nordhausen, where 20,000 slave laborers died producing V-2 missiles. Led the team which built the Saturn V rocket. Described as "100 per cent Nazi, dangerous type".
- **Kurt Debus**, rocket launch specialist, another SS officer. His report stated: "He should be interned as a menace to the security of the Allied Forces."
- **Hubertus Strughold**, later called "the father of space medicine", designed NASA's on-board life-support systems. Some of his subordinates conducted human "experiments" at Dachau and

Auschwitz, where inmates were frozen and put into low-pressure chambers, often dying in the process.

All of these men were cleared to work for the US, their alleged crimes covered up and their backgrounds bleached by a military which saw winning the Cold War, and not upholding justice, as its first priority.

And the paperclip which secured their new details in their personnel files gave the whole operation its name. Sixty years on, the legacy of Paperclip remains as vital as ever.

With its radar-absorbing carbon impregnated plywood skin and swept-back single wing, the 1944 Horten Ho 229 was arguably the first stealth aircraft.

The Stealth bomber: Based on a 1944 German design

The US military made one available to Northrop Aviation, the company which would produce the $2bn B-2 Stealth bomber - to all intents and purposes a modern clone of the Horten - a generation later.

Cruise missiles are still based on the design of the V-1 missile and the scramjets powering NASA's state-of-the-art X-43 hypersonic aircraft owe much to German jet pioneers.

Added to this, the large number of still-secret Paperclip documents has led many people, including Nick Cook, Aerospace Consultant at Jane's Defense Weekly, to speculate that the US may have developed even more advanced Nazi technology, including anti-gravity devices, a potential source of vast amounts of free energy.

Cook says that such technology "could be so destructive that it would endanger world peace and the US decided to keep it secret for a long time".

But, while celebrating the undoubted success of Project Paperclip, many will prefer to remember the thousands who died to send mankind into space.

Path 54: Black Occult Religions" of the BROTHERHOOD OF THE BELL.

By William Dean Ross

The Universal Seduction Website

The majority of people worldwide do not know what the terms Black Operations and Black Sciences mean or how they are used.

Black Operations were developed after World War I, but really flourished after World War II during the Cold War. Congress allocated money to the Pentagon, the C.I.A. and other Defense Department sectors to make the United States military as strong as possible, but certain projects became more secretive than others. The more secret projects were funded by the civilian sector at first, such as pet peeve, with defense contractors already in the loop.

As time went on, the "privy "developed into a real clique of not only specially screened corporations, but also choice individuals found by federal talent hunts. A new sub-culture was born with a new personality and belief system, completely cut off from mainstream Americans.

Cutting-edge technology such as the stealth aircraft, invisible hover-craft, extremely low frequency mind control (ELF) and weather control, in addition to the cloning or reproduction of identical species, became "Secret Sciences'.

The new knowledge wasn't, and still is not, available to the regular Army, to Congress, or to any University. The most secret of the secret was in the hands of a power hungry few that tied itself to the World Bank for the future funding of its projects. They developed "think-tanks 'like Stanford Research Institute and Tavistock to keep the masses fooled about virtually everything.

The deception grew like a cancer into every area of industrialized society. They moved into everything - from the Mafia, to Harvard University, to International Banking. They learned how to control the media, and thus, they controlled television, Hollywood, every newspaper, every educational institution and every person's mind... at least to a certain point.

Accusations of abuse and inhuman acts by the C.I.A. and F.B.I. were investigated by Congress in 1977. These agencies used the excuse of "national security" for every crime they committed. Under the guise of "national security 'there has not been an investigation of their highly illegal activities since 1977. Your Congress, your President and your Supreme Court are actually scared of them. A mountain of evidence points to the fact that they have killed thousands, including corporate executives and politicians - perhaps JFK.

The Invisible Government

Thus, they are considered the "Invisible Government"!

The "Invisible Government "needs a name at this point, so let us call it, The Brotherhood of the Bell. This was a 1960s movie. By the way, Bell Corporation made the first flying saucer called "The Bell'- for the Invisible Government - because it was shaped like a bell.

Therefore, I shall call the Brotherhood of the Bell - simply B.O.B.

B.O.B. became an internationally funded and operated organization that developed its totalitarian tactics for worldwide economic, political and military control. B.O.B. led us to believe that half of the earth was religious-capitalism, defended by the CIA and the other half of the world was atheist-communist, defended by the KGB.

But, in actuality, the International Bankers and ancient esoteric secret societies - with an octopus of intelligence agencies - controlled the entire earth, even through World Wars I and II. Whenever a few cliques decided to go into business for themselves and break away from the monopoly system, we would have a world war. The same is true today, so be forewarned; do not mess with the super bankers!

The Cold War ended because of a worldwide cry for "peace". The old industrialist/banker game of churning up yet another war for the military/industrial complex was becoming more and more difficult. Their "think tanks" had to come up with a new strategy to subdue this "New Left" ideology.

Time also changed technology, thus the bankers and industrialists no longer needed large populations to do the farming, work in the factories or even fight in their war-machine game. Advanced computers, robots and artificial intelligence, bio-electronics and cloning eliminated the need of all of these "useless eaters". Top secret meetings were held and a strategy initiated (as early as 1960).

One such example is found in "The Report from Iron Mountain".

The "New Left," with all of its altruistic and humanitarian concepts, would be the "Trojan Horse" that would bring in the largest shadow of death to fall on mankind in the written history of the earth. "Globalist" books reveal the hidden agenda behind the United Nations, the covert meanings of their statues and art at the new Masonic airports, and their shrines like the Stones.

All of these items call for a massive depopulation of the earth!

They also propose the elimination of democracy and culture, under the guise of a new positive program devised by one of their "think-tanks'. The Proposed Agenda – A one-world religion, a one-world government - In other words, a New World Order. How many times have we had that repetitive phrase thrust into our faces?

On the other hand, certain racist "New Right 'organizations have been, and are currently, manipulated by the Black Ops agent provocateurs. Their motivation is to make these groups appear hostile to the masses through their "Song Bird 'media.

The truth is that these groups are very aware of certain concepts of the New World Order, but, they cannot see that they being used as "scapegoats and patsies "for Black Operations 'sabotage. The invisible government always uses some sort of instigated chaos to steer public demand for social change. Gun control is a perfect example of this!

Their hoodwinking games are from the old Masonic term, "Ordo Abo Chao." They covertly create the problem, but their politicians come forward publicly with the perfect solution: Order out of Chaos.

B.O.B.'s old mantra was national security, its excuse for cruelty to mankind.

Now, there are a whole string of pacifications like:

"To save the children "or "To save nature!'

The truth is that The Brotherhood of the Bell is destroying more nature with its top secret projects like the nuclear bomb, chemical and biological warfare and HAARP (High-Frequency Active Auroral Research Program), than we, the "useless eaters,' could ever imagine doing.

When the Berlin wall came down, the Black Operations of the East merged with the Black Operations of the West. The "think tanks 'now include the Soviets and Red Chinese. They have mixed their ideas for a One World Order with military Special Forces; this combination in scheming collusion in order to execute their "cleansing or killing field" immoral programs.

What these Brave New World types do not know is that, once again, they are being used to satisfy the greedy appetites of the Super Power Elite. Those in the Cabal know that an inter-dimensional society, an etheric civilization more invisible than they are, control their minds and souls.

They honor these Ascended Masters or Gods with blood and sacrifice, as they always have, through their history of the Dark Nobility and Black Arts Occultism.

They know the Lord of this earth is Lucifer or the Dark Forces, and that he must be appeased.

The "Black Budget" then started to be used for the "Black Arts" and became known as the Black Sciences. The earliest projects actually started prior to World War I, while the more popular ones started around World War II. The U.S. Army's Manhattan Project was in charge of making the A-bomb, while U.S. Navy dealt with Stealth equipment and invisibility, as evidenced in the Philadelphia Experiment (Written about in both these volumes).

After the war, the scientists of both projects were joined with Nazi scientists from Germany and NASA.

From this merging, the National Security Agency was officially inaugurated. Previous experiments like "Babylon-Working'and the"Montauk Project" were started using Nazi occultists and scientists to communicate with and materialize inter-dimensional beings. They were the "unofficial' pioneers of projects working on inter-dimensional time travel and eugenics/cloning.

Thus, with these projects, The Black Sciences were officially, yet covertly born.

The Black Sciences are the "Most Secret of all Secrets" and are seriously guarded by special, screened soldiers, trained and born out of covert, Black Operations groups.

It is this elitist group's steadfast hope to merge the seen world with the unseen world. Their prioritized goal is currently designed to ensure that the world has a "oneness-of mind" (the hive concept), in addition to being spiritually harmonized to a designated frequency that will bring their plan into full activation. The "Ascended Masters" have commanded them to eliminate the Old World, with its old ideas, old way of thinking and all of its old people.

A new generation with a "New World View" is the agenda of the day.

That is why many conservatives, Christians, Jews, Muslims, Buddhists, etc. are on the surveillance and extermination lists. That is why more anti-Constitutional laws are becoming the "New Law."

That is why those - in the know - from all religions and political ideologies are getting extremely concerned and very nervous.

The "Black Operations" work for the "Black Sciences" who worship "Black Occult Religions" of the BROTHERHOOD OF THE BELL.

CHAPTER VII

SATANIC BATTLE FOR OUR SOULS

Path 55: New World Order on Schedule The Shimmering

Our souls are vibrations of spiritual energy in the universe. We are a conscious manifestation of celestial charged particles; we are literally bubbles of human consciousness and miraculous means by which the universe contemplate itself.

We are consciousness oscillating energy frequencies flooding the environment in which we live with desires, fears, and courage. Life is fleeting. We are here in the physical flesh today and reunited in pure energy form of infinite consciousness tomorrow.

Could our destiny in the afterlife be reuniting with nature's Omni prevalent creative forces that are at work orchestrating material phenomenology that perpetuates conscious fibers of quantum reality? This cosmic organic process supersedes inorganic artificial intelligence and artificial consciousness.

The core essence of who we are manifests as shimmering energy that radiates spiritual vibrations throughout the spatial universe in the form of prayers, dreams, and hopes. The creative impact of organic thought and its many emotional wheels turning inside each of us are the very fruits of existence; movements of thoughts dances like flickering candle lights illuminating our spiritual trek through the diverse and mysterious abysses of the cosmos.

Because of nature's intricate commitment to engineering life, we must hold preservation of the miracle of organic life sacrosanct. Life is sacred and naturally encoded in our hearts is a reverence for the emotions of love. No man has the right to tarnish or terminate another's life through debt, injustice, senseless wars for the sake of advancing technologically. Preserving organic life should be our life objective not transitioning to a realm of artificial intelligent designs of a virtual universe.

We are caught between the physical and spiritual realm where compassion is compromised for money and love is surrogated with carnal lust. In our ignorance, unwittingly, as we become more comfortable living with vices and spiritual underachievement, apathy becomes more prevalent in our social interactions fueling upheavals swirling in greed and insensitivity that permits murder, mayhem, poverty and war to become social norms.

Passively we are less demanding for quality of truth and apathetically we accept lies and deceptions from our leaders unquestioningly. Content of media programming glorifies empty spirituality creating masses of dull, insensitive, and uncompassionate societies.

We have only a brief moment of shimmer under the sun; yes, we are much like a miniature star destined to shine only so long. We live constantly between acts of awakening to our greatest moral epiphanies and our worst acts of surrender to lesser primitive designs of living with and giving in to brute force of those peddling deception, greed, and immorality.

We must awaken to intelligence and use our brains as a coalesced force against dark objectives of evil. Each morning, we awaken to light and an invitation to a new day of creativity; each night, we surrender to the dark and go play in the world of dreams where time is no more.

When I speak of shimmer or shimmering, I speak of the sort of transient energy flowing through us; the essence of the creative forces of the universe is in all of us. All of us, from a universal quantum perspective, are component universal consciousness born of matter and its fruits of energy; energy which is the light in our minds illuminating all darkness that is not just in the spatial universe but darkness from the minds of mortal men amongst us.

We are born with an intelligent DNA embedded in the very fire we call our soul. Unfortunately, humanity has underachieved its potential harvest by misusing, even abusing access to the miraculous energy and force of love. For centuries this force of human goodwill has been shrouded in the mysteries and made unintelligible by the many various institutions both political and religious.

With the misapplication of cosmic intelligence, due to fear and greed, we have chosen to sculpt a physical realm filled with chaos instead of order, with violence instead of peace, with tendencies of greed instead of sharing, and hatred instead of love.

It is time we understand the fallacies of traditions based on fear that continues to undermine true wisdom of the simple approach to living "if it not a product of love, we must exist without it." Our shortcomings of choice are spending lifetimes hoarding money selfishly, instead of clearing manmade obstacles to higher spiritual vibrations, bankers and politicians selfishly and purposely create obstacles to collective spiritual growth that cultivates negative spiritual vibrations none of the Mosques, Cathedrals, Synagogues, Hindu Mandir, and Churches, have been able to prevent. So, we continue brutalizing each other whether on the streets of our cities, the battlefields of wars, or the clandestine projects in the CERN facilities. We have been reduced, for the most part literally and figuratively to a specie that cannot stop damaging each other.

Why do we use the miraculous and magical energy of the universe in this manner? Why are we on this small planet in this vast universe dropping bombs on each other? What and who are these leaders with savage thought processes? Who are we as people that allows such primitive behavior to continue in human civilizations? Who are we people collectively? Where are our voices? Where is the magic of love?

Have we lost the ability to know love, and in this loss, isolated ourselves from principles of loving acts, but instead chase fantasies of technological immortality that only happen in movies or in fairy tales? Is the love we seek simply not real, just an illusion, a pleasant distraction from our religion of consumerism?

If we have a glowing aura of goodness, if we are endowed with a shimmering, vibrating magical, and miraculous energetic force of love supreme, the glow and vibrations of our individual and collective energy is being snuffed by bankers and politicians. Distracted from our dire reality by minions of wealthy actors, entertainers, athletes and media types who are paid millions to distract us from the suffering of the have-nots in the world.

The question is, why are we buying into immoralities that none of us signed up for upon our entry into this god forsaken world? Let us cease going down dark paths trail blazed by evil men. Can we not see the fallacy electing people as a leader who place money ahead of the greatest good of the people? It is no accident that all of our politicians are member of the one percent we speak about. 1 percent of Americans are millionaires and 47 percent of House Representatives are millionaires. 56 percent of Senators are millionaires. Whose interest is really being guarded on Capitol Hill?

We are at the point where we cannot trust the media controlled by banking and corporate billionaires and their millionaire minions on Capitol Hill who lie to us about needs of war. It is imperative that we see the role we play in our own demise and admit our individual contributions to a system outdated and in the business of creating hell on earth for profit.

We have failed as individuals and as people to come up with social norms and processes that are people friendly, fair, and reflective of ethical and moral right stuff void of selfishness and greed.

We have failed to come up with the right stuff of love and goodwill toward ourselves and others who are struggling under the onslaught of greed based principles being peddled by the one percenters regulating our lives through bought constituency on Capitol Hill.

The threat of being deprived of our miracle of life and to know love for each other is real. We must say no to tainted and bought politicians who love wealth and power more than they love people!

Let's not allow them to continue perfecting blowing out spiritual flames needed to illuminates our path through the dark machinations of evil minds.

We were meant to shimmer, to illuminate darkness not to embrace the cold reality unfolding on planet earth. We are facing a darkness not of Gods but that of men. With more awareness, knowledge, courage, and conviction, we can fix obsessions with cold materiality of technical advancement requiring us to sacrifice organic spirituality.

How did we lose our way on pathways of violence?

Without thoughts, does the actual mechanics of objects moving exist? Intelligence is an incessant transition of speculation and measurement. Measurements are fibers of perceptions we call time.

These fibers of thought are echoing consciousness hitchhiking on vibrations of energy created by colliding particles of matter. It is one thing that these echoes of thought exist at all in an omniscient cosmic vacuum and this conscious phenomenon is nothing short of miraculous.

The question is, how significant or what role are we to play with consciousness in the true great activities in the cosmos? If humans perished in a cataclysm, what remains of consciousness cosmically?

When you observe the endless chain of the phenomenology of matter interactions that sparks consciousness, the God-Verse is layered echoes of intelligence.

This nuts and bolts of life are incredulities beyond all grasp of collective human consciousness. Whether we acknowledge this phenomenal energy of life in words or with a silent knowing, there is a source of being greater than human anthropomorphic attempts of man becoming God through robotic/android of artificial intelligence.

From where or whatever origin the source of life is, we cannot even begin to capture the dynamic grandiosity of the collective quantum natural energy flowing through us as the universe contemplate its own creation of life and itself.

Consciousness in humans is produced by a physical exoskeleton engineered to process raw matter into energy. This energy serves as a generator producing a dualistic consciousness where man feels alienated from the singularity of nature.

Consciousness in humans, in many ways, is nature's folly much like masturbation. Artificial intelligence evolves and displaces in the mind of men the state of nature, which exist independent of thought.

Death is part of the living cycle of the Universe. Artificial intelligence is intellectual masturbation. Reality is the live sex act. Life is feeling the rain and sun on your skin, breathing fresh air, the quenching taste of water after a thirst, and sharing this world experience with plants and animals.

Many wonder why bubbles of human consciousness are a product in the universe at all.

In human societies of bubbled consciousness, there are premiums placed on physical matter that fuels and energize consciousness. Wealth and struggles for power define megalomaniacal vainglory immersed in legacies of murder to facilitate a base technology of artificial intelligence with a goal to reduce or diminish natural humanity with Trans-humanistic artificial intelligence.

This emerging intellectual violence threatening our natural humanity has been the driving force of beings entangled and trapped in dreams of maniacal egotistical cages of thought, which is the realm of being in which we exist harvesting violent technical extremism.

Actualizing intelligence is not selling out for a world of Trans-humanism. Intelligence is tapping into a peaceful silent knowing of quiet collective minds between cosmic vibrations beyond the borders of noisy thoughts of wastefulness in ideas of costly unattainable beliefs of immortality as digi-bots in a world of artificial technology.

The life of a person burdened with an exoskeleton is one lived while processing noises of hunger, of fear, the noise of the primitive instincts to mate, and the noise of physical threats of being killed by proponents of "The Eugenic Society" in pursuit of Trans-Humanism, creation of Cyborgs, and high tech androids. Instead, through peaceful relations and politics, we should not mask our violent nature with more violent and extreme technologies and preserve the natural state of our planet and our bodies with smart use of love based intelligence.

In such a realm congested in struggle for physical survival, actualizing intelligence is very difficult in an environment that incorporates violence into formulas of success and prosperity. Resolving lack of love for nature and creating, through technology, a world of digit-bots with artificial intelligence will become pillars of destruction of human nature that is humanity's ultimate self-inflicted death blow.

The notion of love connotes happy ending. The intelligent singularity with the natural intelligence of the universe is a flowing knowing energy that never dissipates and there is no ending. This eternal natural process of life and death cannot be hijacked or conquered by artificial intelligence.

End connotes finality consistent with measuring tools of thought. The universe depends not on just human thoughts alone from just this one planet of men obsessed with cheating death living forever in a digital world.

Inhabitants of Earth are not alone in this vast universe. We are not the only consciousness and we are not the universe's prerequisite to physical existence.

Notions of ideas of love are only as relevant as the state of mind processing those concepts.

Life connotes an enduring all-encompassing flow of energy oblivious to measurements of time, which are measurements dependent on thought. Intelligence exists in the silence between cosmic vibrations from movements of matter. Intelligence is actually spiritual conduits through which silence flows.

Breeding Human Intellect with Evil

Here we are in the 21st century. The age of artificial intelligence. Living in a world more fascinated with logic than spiritual ascension. The outcome of humanity's fascination of breeding intellect with evil, you know it by what it produces with frequency, and the product of breeding intellect with evil is destruction of the ecosystem that supports organic life and calculated disregard for human life for profit.

The other outcome of intellectually breeding with evil is the questionable premises of religious dogma pertaining to the origin of the universe and the creation of life therein. Why do people live life enslaved at so many levels by dogma that does not embrace inevitabilities that we are not alone in this universe?

As we boldly advance technologically where no man has gone before, our inbreeding of our organic nature with artificial intelligence, we sacrifice humanity's roots of organic collective unconsciousness. According to Carl Jung, we have roots in an ancestral past of the entire human species.

The psychic contents of the collective unconscious have been inherited and pass from one generation to the next as psychic potential. Our distant ancestor's experiences with universal concepts such as God, Mother, water, earth, and so forth have been transmitted through generations so that people's moral sense of what's good is continually influenced by organic humane experiences of love and compassion.

It is sad that we have arrived at that point in the road of civilization where organic spirituality is actively being supplanted by logical artificial intelligence. This is tantamount to inbreeding the intelligence of human collective unconsciousness with technological world that does not prioritize love, instead prioritizing machines over human life. This is the ultimate breeding of organic intellectual nature of humanity with forces of evil.

It saddens me seeing the fierce social justice warrior archetype being bred out and supplanted in all men black, white, and yellow by love of money by unchaste programming of unchaste sexuality and the advancement of the mindset of machines over organic spirituality.

Unfortunately, this legacy of western society's fascination of breeding intellect with the evils of nuclear weapons, wars, HAARP, CERN, and Chemtrails is the naked truth of the evolution of humanity to its ugliest reality of making deals with the devil himself, literally and figuratively.

It is very startling to me how comfortable we have been made by lust of money and programmed television to humanity's ugly reality of the growing lack of compassion for each other and the growing void of love-less darkness in our surrogated trans-humanistic collective unconsciousness.

People have been misled by the adage "When life gives you lemons, make lemonade." We are being led down a dark rabbit hole where spiritually awoke peoples are fighting to keep their organic light of moral consciousness lit in the dark dungeon-like rabbit holes of the unfolding matrix of the New World Order.

People who still have vestiges of moral light in their consciousness understand we must not mistake the meaning of that adage of passively "making lemonade" from life's woes and accepting things we perceive we cannot change, when educated properly and united, morally conscious illuminated human beings is the New World Order's worse nightmare.

A dark rabbit hole is morphing unlovingly on the coattail of greed in a Matrix of evil that prides itself in the birth of a robotic age of artificial intelligence and Trans-Humanism with the intent to supplant the organic nature of humanity itself. This new age is a product of breeding intellect with the dark side of evil in the collective unconsciousness of humanity. Again, this legacy of western society's fascination of breeding intellect with the evils of nuclear weapons, wars, HAARP, CERN, and Chemtrails is the naked truth of the evolution of humanity to its ugliest reality.

We live the illusion medicating our evils in this love-fest of money surrogating spiritual wellbeing by adorning ourselves and our children with a brilliant surface image of material amor while there is nothing spiritual inside the shell.

Complicit in creating a humanity of soul-less ghouls, lusting after million dollar mansions, diving shiny new cars, disregarding the poor as undeserving, and paving the way for pedophiles to do as they wish with innocent children, we surrogate an organic spiritual reality for silliness of psychopaths who are driven by love-less qualities of profit margins instead of compassion.

Many choose to hide or turn away hesitant and scared to speak out. People are content to live as cowards, dying many deaths by the slings and arrows of the evil and unjust living among us, instead of standing up against the oppressors in the chambers of the Knesset in Israel, the Kremlin in Russia, the Parliament in England, and Capitol Hill in the U.S.

We are not going to get out of this life alive. Why not die once in a truly good fight of righteousness like Abraham Lincoln, the Kennedy brothers, and Martin Luther King Jr. chose to do?

For those of you who have a job, a home, and enough food to eat, you are among the fortunate. You are fortunate that you are not being bombed into oblivion like those in Palestine, Syria, Yemen. You are fortunate that you were not a citizen in Iraq, Afghanistan, and Libya. You are fortunate that your country is not ravaged by AIDS as many African nations are.

The Hegemon Secret Society's fingerprint of terrorism is on all these world tragedies implementing New World Order policies globally. If you live in a Prime Western nation, you are not feeling the ravages of the New World Order agenda, Yet!

1. Nearly 1/2 of the world's population—more than 3 billion people—live on less than \$2.50 a day. More than 1.3 billion live in extreme poverty—less than \$1.25 a day.
2. 1 billion children worldwide are living in poverty. According to UNICEF, 22,000 children die each day due to poverty.
3. 805 million people worldwide do not have enough food to eat. Food banks are especially important in providing food for

people that can't afford it themselves. Run a food drive outside your local grocery store so people in your community have enough to eat. Sign up for **Supermarket Stakeout**.

4. More than 750 million people lack adequate access to clean drinking water. Diarrhea caused by inadequate drinking water, sanitation, and hand hygiene kills an estimated 842,000 people every year globally, or approximately 2,300 people per day.
5. In 2011, 165 million children under the age 5 were stunted (reduced rate of growth and development) due to chronic malnutrition.
6. Preventable diseases like diarrhea and pneumonia take the lives of 2 million children a year who are too poor to afford proper treatment.
7. As of 2013, 21.8 million children under 1 year of age worldwide had not received the three recommended doses of vaccine against diphtheria, tetanus and pertussis.
8. 1/4 of all humans live without electricity—approximately 1.6 billion people.
9. 80% of the world population lives on less than $10 a day.
10. Oxfam estimates that it would take $60 billion annually to end extreme global poverty--that's less than 1/4 the income of the top 100 richest billionaires.
11. The World Food Program says, "The poor are hungry and their hunger traps them in poverty." Hunger is the number one cause of death in the world, killing more than HIV/AIDS, malaria, and tuberculosis combined.

Are there Destructive Goals of Higher Order of Power and Wealth on Earth?

Zionism is a political force that have some connection with the Masonic element of the 'conspiracy', the B'nai Brith and so on, as do ALL religious movements who stray into areas of masonic-economic-political manipulation [which constitutes most of the major denominations by the way, considering the massive Scottish Rite infiltration of the major denominational structures].

However 'Jewish Masonry' is NOT the dominant Masonic faction, that place is reserved for the Jesuit's 'Scottish Rite' and the Black Nobility's Rite of the 'Illuminati'. So then, some elements of 'Jewish Masonry' may be 'cooperating' with the New World Order agenda, but they are ultimately subservient to the racist power cults of BAVARIA. This is why the Zionist Rothschilds were UNABLE TO PREVENT the slaughter of over 6 million Jews in the Holocaust, because the Jewish Masons were NOT the dominant force. The Rothschild's' supposed economic collaborators in America, the Germanic-racist Rockefellers, were pressured into serving and carrying out the RACIST-EUGENIC policies of their cultic superiors in Bavaria, in order to be allowed to maintain their economic stranglehold on America. Following World War II, the Rockefellers received a flood of Nazi War criminals into their fold, giving them refuge and immunity within their massive corporate network.

The Jewish Masons, such as the Rothschild, are only a PART of a THIRD [Wicca Masonic] element of the global power network, competing with the other two-thirds working within the Black Nobility and the Maltese Jesuit lodges. That is, until all three agreed to work together under the 'Bildeberger' organization in order to implement the NWO and then decide later just who would dominate it.

Just why the Rothschild Wicca-Masons would agree to become a part of the Bildeberger cult is uncertain. Perhaps they were not fully aware of the part that the Jesuit-Rockefeller elements played in the Nazi Holocaust, or the actual extent of the influx of Nazi war criminals into the Rockefeller Empire following the war?

A more likely explanation would be a combination of the following: Some of the Zionists who collaborated with the Rockefellers were not fully aware of the racist Anti-Jewish elements involved; some of the

'Jewish Masons' just didn't care and were in essence willing to sell out their own kind in exchange for POWER; also the Jesuit's Scottish Rite had succeeded in Infiltrating Jewish [and York Rite British] Masonry to the point where its assimilation into the Bavarian-controlled NWO Bilderberger cult would be ensured.

In fact there is some reason to believe that the Bavarians [and aliens?] were using the Wicca Masons, Black Nobility and Maltese Jesuit as HIGH-LEVEL Machiavellian 'arms' to create political, economic and religious conflict in the world. In other words the lower levels of these three formerly 'competitive' global power cults would be individuals who were devoted to the idea that THEIR respective lodge[s] should be in control of the New World Order and were therefore to engage in fraternal warfare with the 'others', the Jesuits against the Masons and vice versa for example.

On another-planetary level it could be the Syrian-backed Masons vs the Rigelian backed Jesuits. The Syrian humanoids and the Rigelian reptiloids, being formerly at odds, were now being brought together by the Aldebaran-backed Ashtarian collectivists and their 'New Galactic Order' agenda.

Planet earth is NOT the only place where 'Machiavellian/Hegelian' political agendas have been carried out. On earth the Aldebaran collective in turn backs their 'Bavarian Black Nobility' allies and repeats the same thesis-antithesis-synthesis scenario on earth between the Masons and Jesuits, eventually merging them into a power structure that is ultimately controlled [on earth] by the Bavarian black gnostic 'serpent' cult from its secret hideaways below Giza, Egypt; Pine Gap, Australia; Dulce, New Mexico, etc.

This power-center would in turn have placed its agents within the Jesuit, Nobility and Masonic 'arms' in order to manipulate these three power-groups towards their own ends. For instance, even though lower-level initiates of these three lodges would favor their own lodge over the others, the CONTROLLING ELITE of all three elements would never-the-less be agents of the Bavarian 'Babylonian Serpent Cult' itself.

Certain members of the Black Nobility families would sell out to the cult and turn these families in whatever direction the cult dictated; high-ranking Scottish Rite members of the Wicca Mason faction would likewise be serving the Bavarian agenda via the Illuminati; and the high-ranking Jesuits themselves would in turn be serving the Bavarian elite, since Germany was after all the headquarters of the [Un]Holy Roman Empire and NOT Rome, which capitulated its center-of-power over to Germany following the decline of the earlier Roman Empire.

This is one 'perspective' from which this can all be viewed, although it is certainly not the only perspective.

According to contactee Israel Norkin however, the Ashtar or Astarte alien collective—which has a large following in Aldebaran and other systems and which played an integral part in the ancient Sirian-Orion conflict over ancient Egypt—is a subterranean/exterranean alliance, a virtual 'collective group mind', that has since been infiltrated by the 'Unholy Six' Empires of Orion.

If this is true, then this does not necessarily mean that ALL of the members of the 'Ashtar collective' are working for UH6, especially when more recent contactee accounts have stated that a civil war has been taking place in Sirius.

This 'war' has apparently been waged because the 'infiltrated' faction of the collective that has been infiltrated and commandeered by the Orionite forces, has in turn broken free from the remaining segment of the collective. This remaining segment has since established close ties with Pleiadean non-interventionists.

Actually, if they hold true to the non-interventionist policies, one would think that this remaining element of the 'alliance' would give up the collectist agenda altogether, and adopt the sovereigntist philosophy which teaches the respect for personal sovereignty from a planetary down to an individual level. Since a collective, hive or group mind tends to Kill human individuality and sovereignty, such an existence would seem to be ever at odds with non-interventionism.

Just as non-interventionists believe in planetary sovereignty, which is a more 'cosmic' manifestation of the same principles which appear in the American 'Bill of Rights' in respect to personal sovereignty, we must realize that just as with America, the non-interventionists have not "arrived" at the perfect fulfillment of their philosophy any more than the 'American dream' has become a full reality. Since this universe is imperfect and subject to human agency, it is a continuous struggle to fight to defend liberty, freedom and sovereignty whether on an inter-planetary or an interpersonal level.

So even though we must continue to fight and struggle to maintain planetary, national or personal sovereignty in a universe where it is continually being threatened by parasitical-interventionist-imperialistic forces, the non-interventionist charters of the 'Federation' and the Constitutional charters of 'America' are nevertheless Goals for us to work towards.

The government, controlled by multi-national corporations, chooses not to reveal objectives of secret space programs. There is a need for transparency of the roles of the multi-national central banking system to the secret space program. The banking network include the Federal Reserve Bank, World Bank, International Monetary Fund, and Bank of International Settlement. What is the system of financial madness in society proliferating without consent of exploited lower and middle class?

To start with, the system of finance, who are the stockholders of money center banks? J. W. McAllister, an oil industry insider with House of Saud connections, wrote in "The Grim Reaper" that information he acquired from Saudi bankers cited 80% ownership of the New York Federal Reserve Bank, by far the most powerful Fed branch, is controlled by just eight families, four of which reside in the US. They are the Goldman Sachs, Rockefellers, Lehmans and Kuhn Loebs of New York; the Rothschilds of Paris and London; the Warburgs of Hamburg; the Lazards of Paris; and the Israel Moses Seifs of Rome.

CPA Thomas D. Schauf corroborates McCallister's claims, adding that ten banks control all twelve Federal Reserve Bank branches. He names N.M. Rothschild of London, Rothschild Bank of Berlin, Warburg Bank of Hamburg, Warburg Bank of Amsterdam, Lehman Brothers of New York, Lazard Brothers of Paris, Kuhn Loeb Bank of New York, Israel Moses Seif Bank of Italy, Goldman Sachs of New York and JP Morgan Chase Bank of New York. Schauf lists William Rockefeller, Paul Warburg, Jacob Schiff and James Stillman as individuals who own large shares of the Fed. [3] The Schiffs are insiders at Kuhn Loeb. The Stillmans are Citigroup insiders, who married into the Rockefeller clan at the turn of the century.

CHAPTER VIII

THE CARNAGE ALONG THE WAY TO HELL

Path 56: CERN

Character of humans formed from the elements

If the statement is true that we are the product of stardust, could our DNA inherit the bi-polar character of stars? Throughout their existence stars exhibit two dynamic processes fusing hydrogen that consumes a finite store of life sustaining energy and being pressed by nature's relentless force of gravity. Balancing these two dynamic forces are the fruits of dark energy and dark matter.

I think about the character of humans formed from the elements of stars. We are constantly developing thought processes much like star's activity of producing energy fusing hydrogen. The psychological dynamics of human life is balancing instinct of good and evil in a similar manner as stars balances pressure of gravity within its core with the outward explosion of fusing hydrogen. Our sanity is how well we balance natures opposite forces.

Conflicts, the battle of opposites, yen and yang, positive and negative electromagnetic forces, like good and evil, are inextricably related and co-dependent creative processes of dark matter and dark energy fabric continuum of space time at the same time fuel the very fabrics of human intelligence and imagination.

Could it be that evil is just as necessary as good? I look around in our society and people come in an assortment of yen and yang, good or evil, and pessimistic and optimistic flavors of being.

We have our angels and devils in a social bi-polar spectrum reflecting the conflicted character of stars from which its dust from we come. Conflict in our nature is as old as the conflict in the struggle of a star's very existence. If you chronicled the existence of a star, the heartbeat of its life is the fusion of hydrogen to create energy that creates the dimension in which we exist. Humans convert energy from the photons emitted by stars into ideas. Ideas with which we build societies and relationships.

The script for each of us is one written by the organic constituency of elements we are all endowed with naturally by a cosmos or what many refer to as God. Could the cosmos be free, random, and unconscionable blameless creative force that does not subscribe to anthropological concepts of good and evil? We are inseparable from the cosmos Yen and Yang concoction of dark matter and dark energy character and its incomprehensible machinations of creative freedom.

Are we in control of the elementary constituents of our soul that moves us in veins of good and evil? Does championing good or evil matters within the creative and destructive reproductive processes of the cosmos? Despite our religious emotional beliefs, is the cosmos its own animation of chaos and rebirth blind to the emotional sentiments of mankind? Considering this, it is clear how the mantra of "live and let die" is so appropriate for those who embrace financial capitalism and the darkness of technological experiments at CERN. So many people, so few guided by the rare element of love.

Why do we so readily contradict our commitment to the emotion of love in our struggles to overcome the unknown frontiers of fear? Why does wealth obscure the horrors stories of destructions of lives, nations, and the very base of our existence the planet as we live in fear of death and the unknowable? Is it because of the bi-polar nature of the cycle of destruction and rebirth of everything in the cosmos?

Will this circle of fear ever be broken by the miniscule production of technology in our attempts to obtain immortality in the constructs of artificial inorganic intelligence and the creation of a virtual universe? It seems by the design and pattern exhibited in nature this cycle of life and death was never meant to be broken because good and evil is on the same team that balances creation. It is sacrilegious to the process to omit either from the creative process.

Welcome to the hellish realm of eternal conflict where the theme of live and let die to live again forever repeats itself. Maybe there is no right and wrong, just what men do caught up in the mix of forces of the universe oblivious to the anthropomorphic rantings of moral men, women, and their offspring. Do not expect mercy from those whose very nature is bred from the chaotic elements of the cosmos. Powerful men love CERN, artificial intelligence, and playing God in a virtual universe than loving and embracing the nature spiritual organic sense of being one in an everlasting cosmos of natural creativity.

Since time immemorial, chaos, death, and destruction moves humanity as a marionette moves puppets in a sad dance of human existence. Unless we find a peaceful way in an ability to create love for one another in this volatile yet creative universe, expect the future to be lit of the same flame of hopelessness, despair and continued desecration of the planet and all life on it. Looking at the unfolding political Landscape with Technological advances that include CERN, Artificial Intelligence, and virtual universes find love or die trying.

The Fears and Concerns about CERN

At CERN, nuclear physicists are trying to find the glue that holds the Universe together. What has come out of CERN is anti-matter. Matter and anti-matter are opposites. Matter can be controlled, like electricity. Anti-matter cannot be controlled. Matter is everything we can touch and feel. Quartz the building blocks of protons and neutrons. Force is lumps of energy that bring matter to life. Photons carries electromagnetic force. Without photons we could not produce motors. Without gluons, which carries strong force, neutrons and protons would not be held together. In other words, the universe would not exist. WNC particles are for weak forces that govern radioactivity.

At CERN they are looking for how everything works. They have found half of it, a component of it is the Higgs field. They have found traces of the Higgs field. The Higgs field is what is found where matter is not. With the Higgs field, they can alter reality as we know it. Our world is made up of matter, the anti-matter is what we can't see. Anti-matter is the other dimension opposite of this dimension, an inconceivable place. It is inherently hostile if not under control.

There is a group that has been studying this dimension since the 1800s. They studied the activities behind paranormal activity. They call it a dimensional slip where things can interact with this world. Anti-matter can be absorbed by any realm of paranormal activity. There is a physical affect to the world in anti-matter.

Demonic entities are attracted to anti-matter. When they produce anti-matter, it attract things to this world. Every gram of anti-matter that is produced and brought into this world it attracts things from another dimension.

What is CERN going to do, it is going to allow humanity to produce pounds of anti-matter. It is going to cause harm. Anti-matter is working in tandem with matter.

People need to have a general understanding of matter, that which they can touch and feel and anti-matter, which we cannot touch, feel, or observe but it is working in tandem. Everything is balanced. Nature cannot give us an honest choice unless we are faced with an equal balance of obedience and disobedience good and evil so low vibrating evil is that balance of darkness with the light of good.

The reason people are going to be harmed is because they are giving evil spirits the authority to work in their lives. CERN has yielded so many results and have given the true definition of paranormal activity. Anti-matter is being pulled out of nowhere, out of this other dimension that is nowhere but everywhere. Some of the not so good consequences of this process has to do with the human psyche.

Stephen Hawkins understood the effects on the psyche. For a long time Stephen Hawkins believed there was not a God. Something changed within him. He began seeing that everything is so precise that it is impossible for it to be haphazardly happenstance. He changed his mind and entertained the idea that what people call divine is done by some sort of architect.

Now the general basis of what CERN is doing. They are running a 6 month test of colliding protons near the speed of light to analyze particles that are magneto Mede and the beginning of the big bang. That is why they call it the Big Bang. It is the only way to observe these particles that wink in and out of existence for a fraction of time. The consequence of this search to gather more of this matter. By the way, they have a more efficient way of gathering anti-matter, which is why they need to know about other properties of this particle.

Once they have these properties, they will be able to extract the anti-matter they desire efficiently. Right now to attain anti-matter is very inefficient. To get a pound of it would take about ten thousand years at the current rate of extraction. CERN will allow them to get a pound of anti-matter in about a week. But, here is the consequences, they have found out that anti-matter is intimately tied to every single life form on this planet. Its energy signature is the same energy signature in all life on this planet, none excluded. They found out when any lifeform is in the presence of anti-matter, the energy of the lifeform changes.

A person has both dark and light already in them. It is part of their makeup. You can't live in a material world without anti-matter, nothing would exist. So a person has good energy which would be this realm of matter, they also have energy of anti-matter so they are connected to both realms at the same time on the energy level and they don't even know it.

With all the experiment they have conducted at CERN, they have found out why paranormal activity exists. They know exactly what it is. They do not want to tell anybody. That is why they perpetuate foolishness on television. Every single life form is connected to that other realm into this realm of reality all the time. A person's thoughts, how a person feels, doctor know about this, how a person feels determines which energy they draw from.

You can draw from this good realm and have positive results it is called faith. That is why doctors gives out placebos. They know if a person believes something is helping them, they have it within themselves to repair and command their bodies based on belief. People have recovered from cancer, back injuries, and quadriplegics have been repaired simply by their own faith.

This other realm of other energy is contained in another dimension. That is the containment wall but when a person draws that energy in it is the opposite of this realm. In this realm we have to light a piece of wood with a flame to catch it on fire. In the other realm it is already on fire and you have to contain it. When a person changes their emotional state their energy changes and they begin to draw their energy from this other dimension of this violent, chaotic and uncontainable place where they draw dark matter from. It is in operation all the time and the scientists are aware of this.

On the Spring Equinox, forces change on the earth; the scientists knows this, which in fact allows them to have better results.

With the basic introduction of what CERN is doing, with matter and anti-matter, we get into the heart of the matter that will bring consequences. There have been consequences before that nobody took notice of. The energy signature of dark matter, which resides everywhere, once you bring it into this realm where we can actually see it and observe it, it attracts things from the other realm.

Everything has a connection and that connection cannot be broken by anything. When you bring dark matter into this realm, it is still connected to where it came from no matter how far they put it anywhere. It increases paranormal activity around where it is brought.

They kept dark matter at a college and had to move it to deep underground storage because people at the college began to have vivid dreams, nightmares, violence began erupting, and vile thing began to happen in those places because it is a chaotic piece of matter. This is what happens when an atom bomb explodes chaos happen in the form of chaotic energy released. Explosion is the absence of order. When you contain something you give it order.

Understanding that dark matter is always connected to the realm it came from, that realm that is all around us. Imagine dark matter being the ocean and our reality is a submarine in the ocean. We are all in the submarine having fun. We are all doing our thing and we have a disagreement here and a disagreement there and we find out there is a hole in the sub.

We thought the hole was in the submarine itself but then we find the hole was not in the sub but in the people. The people's water inside their bodies begin to increase based on their emotions. Dark matter can come into the room through people. This is what they have in fact discovered in 1950, that people can also produce dark matter in very minute amounts but it is measureable.

It is quantifiable, in fact they know how much energy a person has to have before they go berserk and how much signature a person must have before an entity from that realm can possess them. They also understand that not everybody can be possessed. A person has to be prepared to be possessed. They have to be a portal themselves.

Scientists, over the course of many years, have quantified and calculated these things. Crooked people in certain places have been harnessing this power for themselves and it has been infective every step of the way. In the scientific community, they see fact and they know they don't understand it fully. So they have experiments and learn along the way.

So the problem about CERN, they had another discovery that dark matter causes pieces of other dark matter that they have contained to react. In other words, if you have a container of a teaspoon of dark matter and you had it in Pennsylvania and someone else had that same teaspoon of dark matter in California, then as soon as that teaspoon is exposed to the elements in Pennsylvania and it causes the dark matter in California to activate.

If you lose containment in one place, containment in the other place will be lost. They are intermittently tied together. People have signatures of the energy of dark matter in them so they contain both matter and anti-matter signatures in them but they are not together. We draw upon that energy with what's in our thoughts and in our hearts.

With CERN, as they begin to collide these protons dark matter is going to be produced in greater and greater numbers. Not only the matter but the energy signature is also going to be released into this realm. It is going to cause the dark signature in people to activate. It is going to become difficult for people to stay contained or controlled.

In essence they are going to become violent, they are going to have vivid dreams, and the darkness in people is absolutely going to surface. This is not theoretical or some theory somebody has thought of. This is absolutely 100 percent quantifiable and it is going to happen. It will take effect and has been weaponized.

They have a weapon concerning dark matter that can be unleashed in any country where they want chaos to be rampant. When you have to take part in a weapons program you become a rat in a maze. People will say they have no power to control their participation in the entanglement of the matrix. Yes you do, you just do not want to control yourself. The power within you is given through staying the course of the natural order.

Cern is unraveling that force that holds the dark energy or dark matter away from us, they call it the wall. There is another name for that. They are going to find the other particles in that wall and when they find the other particles to this wall, they will be able to undo that wall. The other name for that wall is the veil.

This is a weapon and there is no counter weapon to this. China is building a particle accelerator. There are 14 particle accelerator in existence. All the countries are vested in the CERN facilities. There are three facilities in the United States, one they could not build but they built it anyway. It is in one of the biggest in the United States. It will be powered up and the psychological effects on people will be quite evident and people will come under some strange attacks.

People know if others are motivated in the spirit of goodness and those that are not because of beliefs in higher positive vibrations that evil cannot control. Think of a collider as hundreds of nuclear explosions taking place. Nuclear physicists are going to find the particles and weaponized dark energy. If people love freedom and the good aspects of living, they cannot make excuses anymore. People must fight to keep negative energy away from them.

We have the power to overcome our flesh because the darkness is about to be pulled out of everything in a way anyone ever thought possible. People will have to be in the purity of living according to the natural order to overcome the coming darkness.

On the 10th of September 2008, the largest, most complex, and most expensive machine ever devised by man was turned on. The Large Hadron Collider of LHC has a 17 mile long ring of super-conducting electro-magnets. They are buried 300 feet beneath the ground near the city of Geneva on the Franco-Swiss border. It is chilled to the temperature colder than the void of outer space and generating a magnetic field of a 100,000 times of that of the earth.

This machine accelerates proton particles beams to a velocity just under the speed of light and then smashes them together in particle detector chambers in order to break apart the nuclei and unloose the subatomic secrets of matter.

At full power, the LHC produces 600 million collisions per seconds creating fleeting miniscule subatomic explosions up to a million times hotter than the interior of the sun.

The data collected from these collisions is processed by the worldwide LHC computing grid. One of the most extensive and powerful computer grids on the planet. The Grid builds on the technology of the World Wide Web which was invented at CERN in 1989.

The LHC is the primary research instrument of the European organization for Nuclear Research, otherwise known as CERN. After the devastating detonation of Fat-Man and Little-Boy over Nagasaki and Hiroshima, at the end of WWII, mankind was irrevocably thrust into the atomic age. In accordance with the inevitability thesis, which posits that, once technology is introduced into society, what follows is the inevitable development of that technology.

The scientific community impelled by military interest around the globe became obsessed with the idea of harnessing the power of the mighty atom and unraveling the very fabric of physical reality at the subatomic level. Cern is the largest scientific consortium in the world involving thousands of top physicists from 21 member states all working in tandem to discover the fundamental elements that hold the universe together.

While this admitted objective of CERN seems innocent enough and even laudable in a sense there are deep concerns about potential unintended consequences and probable occult intentions. When analyzing a scientific endeavor as costly and ambitious as CERN, it is essential that we have a realistic understanding of the mechanisms and machinations that has been propelling technological advancement in the modern era.

In a perfect world, the greatest accomplishment of science would be the product of good will towards men and the desire for peace and prosperity. However, in the practical world in which we live, greatest accomplishment of modern science are often facilitated and funded by men who have anything but goodwill and peace on their minds.

In many cases, the greatest technological advancements such as in the case of jet propulsion, rocket science, and nuclear fission have been intentionally directed by incredibly malevolent individuals for dark and dangerous purposes.

Scientists are rarely the evil villains scheming sinister plots in secret laboratories that Hollywood has often portrayed. With a few glaring exceptions of course, scientists are usually zealously dedicated to their particular field of study with noble or benign intentions at heart.

However this kind of religious commitment to science can engender blind apathy if not willful ignorance concerning the overarching implication and ill intentions of the benefactors facilitating their work.

This is certainly the case of the brilliant men and women working at CERN. Most of who naively believe that the prime objective of their research is to merely understand what the universe is made of and how it all started at the Big Bang.

Unfortunately, what they fail to realize apart from the fact that they are working from a false premise to begin with is that research is very likely being used to advance a hidden agenda the conspirators of which are very aware of who created the universe and are absolutely intent on making war with him and enthroning another in his place.

CERN is an acronym arrived from the rendition of the designation European Council for Nuclear Research, which was a provisional council organized in the early 1950's with critical backing from the United Nations whose task was to plan for the construction of a multi-national European Research Facility that would be dedicated to the study and advancement of nuclear physics.

On the 29th of September 1954, the Provisional Council was resolved and the European Council of Nuclear Research or CERN was born. As an interesting side note the infamous group, the Bilderberg Group was also conceived that same year exactly 4 months later on the 29th of May. Both of these organization enjoy diplomatic immunity.

Although the Provisional Council had been resolved, paradoxically the acronym of CERN remained even though it did not correspond to the title of the new organization. It was distinguished physicist and one of the key pioneers of quantum mechanics Verner Carl Heisenberg who had inexplicably insisted that the original acronym of CERN remain in effect as Tom Horne elucidate in his book on "On the Path of the Immortals." Verner Heisenberg understood quite well what quantum physics implied for humanity. Inherent in this theoretical realm populated by obtuse equations and pipe smoking scientists lies what is called the Babylon potential.

The Babylon potential is the knowledge, the scientific imperative, informed and driven by spiritual advisers that Gnostics cites as the key to opening a gateway to the Gods. It is Enki Manake Baba Aloo the opening of Akzu the doorway to hell. Tom Horne goes on to explain that although Heisenberg may or may not have known it, CERN is an abbreviated title for an ancient Celtic deity called Cernunos whose name means horned one is thought to be the god of death and rebirth and the Lord of the underworld. He is often depicted with rings or torques around his stag like horns or in his hands which may symbolize the circle of destruction and restoration that he represents.

To further concretize this idea Cernunos is also depicted with a ring in one hand and a snake in other because of the cycle by which it sheds its skin. The snake has ever been a mystical motif of death, destruction, and restoration. An adverse esoteric adaptation, the rings of the Large Hadron Collider could be representative of the rings of Cernunos and by further associative interpretation may very well reveal CERN's prime esoteric objective.

Drawing correlations between the acronym of CERN and deities from the ancient world may seem too forced and tenuous for critical minds. CERN has evoked such correlations. Rather than distance themselves from associations with arcane pagan deities, the directors of CERN welcomed and even celebrated the placement of a very unscientific icon in the courtyard of their main facilities.

On the 18th of June 2004, a two meter high statue bequeathed by the representatives of India's Department of Atomic Energy was ceremoniously unveiled at CERN. It was a statue of the Hindu God Shiva engaged in the Nataraja the cosmic dance of Destruction.

Shiva is one of three members of the Trimurti the Hindu Trinity. The Hindu Trinity in which the cosmic function of creation preservation and destruction are personified in the form of Brahma the creator, Vishnu the preserver, and Shiva the destroyer who is also known as the transformer.

It is important to understand that in Hindu mythology Lord Shiva destroys the world in order to renew, restore, and reconstitute it. A commemorative plaque positioned next to the likeness of the dancing Shiva is emblazoned a quote from Austrian-born American physicist Fritjof Capra. It reads in part "Hundreds of years ago Indian artists created visual images of dancing Shivas in a beautiful series of bronzes.

In our time, physicists have used the most advanced technology to portray the patterns of the cosmic dance. The metaphor of the cosmic dance thus unify ancient mythology, religious art, and modern physics."

Think about this, says Steve Quail in his book "True Legends," a symbolic statue of what might be a fallen angel who promises to destroy things as we know them now and rebuild a new and improved universe with a plaque basically saying the facility will be trying to unify mythology religion and physics.

Skeptic will be quick to point out that the unifying of ancient mythology, religious art, and modern physics is only metaphorically represented in the dance of Shiva and has no practical application and the scientific activities of CERN. Cern has been deliberately coalescence of mythology art and physics in very bizarre ways

In 2014, a dance opera entitled symmetry was performed and filmed at CERN facilities including inside a large Hadron Collider directed by filmmaker Reuben Van Leer and featuring the voice of American Soprano Clarion McFadden. Symmetry was a collaborative project involving not only choreographers and dancers from the production team but many of CERN's own scientists. The scientists embraced this highly esoteric and occult laced production.

> Symmetry is a dance-opera film in which CERN's scientist Lukas is thrown off balance while working on the Theory of Everything and the smallest particle.

The Occult art and science have always been fundamentally entwined. The natural synthesis or symmetry that binds them is best illustrated in one man Sir Francis Bacon.

Bacon is widely considered to be the father of modern science and the primary proponent of the scientific method, which is the very underpinning of CERN, was himself an occultist artist and scientist.

In fact, there is reason to believe that Francis Bacon is the true face behind the dubious mask of William Shakespeare. There is in truth no incongruity between the material and the metaphysical world, the physical and the spiritual, they are merely two sides of the same coin, both essential parts of the whole.

When one penetrates deeply enough into what we call physics, one discovers inevitably the veil that separates these two realities. Occultist have always been aware of this fact. Even to Sir Francis Bacon and his contemporaries, many whom were members of the mystery schools deciphering the mechanisms of the material world, was but the means to a far more important objective to make contact with the entities lurking on the other side of the veil.

This veil is often described as a dimensional doorway that allows access into realms beyond the perceivable world. The concept of unperceivable dimensions existing essentially in the same space we occupy is not only very probable but very widely accepted in the scientific community.

Many top physicist are quietly hoping that the proton collisions happening at the Large Hadron Collider will puncture the fabric of our four-dimensional confine and allow us to peek through the keyhole as it were into another dimension or alternate universe.

Some physicists have not been so quiet about this very real possibility. During a press briefing in 2009, Sergio Bertolucci director for research and scientific computing at CERN made the following curious statement:

> The Large Hadron Collider could open a doorway to an extra dimension and out of this door could come something or we might send something through it.

There is no question that the scientists working at CERN hoped to open a dimensional doorway. The real question is, what is the something that might come through when they do? Of course, for the particle physicist, the answer is simple, they hope to discover new particles that exist on alternate dimensional planes.

There is no doubt that this is the true and honest intention of the vast majority of physicists working at CERN. The problem is as previously illustrated that scientists, despite their best intentions, have always been little more than expendable tools in the hands of their benefactors.

The pinnacle of science for its elite occult practitioners is not discovery but contact. There are many indications that the power players of our world, including the Vatican, are preparing to make contact with the gods of the old world.

Transparent panels containing arcane texts were photographed inside the CERN facilities by a group of Portuguese students from the Santa Cecilia Music Academy. The text has been described as greetings or invocations written in ancient languages including Aramaic, Hebrew, Mandarin, and Sanskrit.

In the case of Sanskrit, the only people with the ability to read the sacred script considered to be the language of the gods, are the scholars of the Vedas and Upanishads. If authentic, these panels may have been prepared for those somethings that may come through the dimensional doorway.

It may seem to those unfamiliar with the theoretical realm populated by obtuse equations and pipe-smoking scientists, as Tom Horne aptly puts it, that this analysis is nothing more than hearsay hyperbole and wild speculation.

But, is any theoretical physicist worth his salt will admit particle physics and quantum mechanics is a world in which fact and fantasy are at times indistinguishable.

When it comes to CERN and its Large Hadron Collider there is no shortage of theoretical doomsday scenarios. Many of which have not been propounded by unlearned laymen such as myself, but by some of the most esteemed scientific minds in the world.

The following is a brief list of the theoretical possibilities relating to the activities of CERN. Each one of these points represents either a scientific reality or hypothetical possibility based on incredibly complex concepts and mathematical formulas.

(1). Black Holes – Perhaps the greatest fear among theoretical physicists concerning LHC is that it might create uncontainable miniature black holes that could descend to the core of the planet and literally devour it from within.

It is important to note that black holes are only theoretical constructs and have never been proven to exist. Black holes were first discovered as purely mathematical solutions of Einstein's field equations, and are not necessary in Tesla's electric universe model. To date, black holes are science fiction.

(2). Anti-matter weapons – Unlike black holes, anti-matter is not theoretical. Not only can it be measured, but it is already being created and contained in the LHC, though in very small quantities for short periods of time, according to CERN.

Anti-matter has enormous explosive potential. A quarter gram of anti-matter can produce an explosive yield equivalent to 5 kilotons of TNT. If CERN develop the capability to create and store significant amounts of anti-matter (some claim it already has) then mighty destructive anti-matter weapons will be developed. The advantages of anti-matter bombs could produce atomic level explosions without the residual nuclear fallout.

(3). Particle Beam Weapons – A directed beam of high subatomic particles moving at extreme velocity (such as the ones produced in the LHC) is capable of obliterating matter at the molecular level. Particle beam weapons are already on the battlefield, especially in "black ops" warfare, and the research of CERN will certainly expand and refine their military application.

(4). Time Distortion and Star Gates – It has been suggested that by colliding heavier subatomic particles, such as lead ions (which CERN will be doing soon), space and time could be distorted creating what Einstein called a Rosen Bridge, or Star Gate, which is basically a wormhole between different locations, dimensions, or periods of time. It has also been suggested that such distortions in the space-time continuum could lead to what has been referred to as the "groundhog day effect" in which time folds back on itself, allowing manipulation of the past.

(5). DNA Sequencing and Artificial Synthesis – Since it is a fact that the synchrotron collider at Berkeley in Walnut Creek, California was used to help sequence human DNA for the Human Genome Project, it is certainly feasible that the Large Hadron Collider could also be employed in a similar way, but with much more precise results. There is evidence to suggest that artificial human or human-hybrid genomes have already been synthesized at collider facilities, including CERN.

(6). Strangelets - Produced from a quark-gluon plasma soup sometimes generated after high energy particle collisions, Strangelets are the most explosive substance in the known universe, and according to theoretical physicists, were responsible for the explosion at the so called Big Bang. Contrary to popular belief, Strangelets are not theoretical, but have been confirmed to exist at the Brookhaven National Laboratory located on Long Island, New York, where physicists working with the Relativistic

Heavy Ion Collider (or RHIC) are attempting not only to produce Strangelets, but to contain them. The potential gain of this endeavor for the Military Industrial Complex are self-evident. Because the LHC is much higher energy collider than the RHIC, Strangelets production and containment is more feasible at CERN.

It should give everyone with access to this information when confronted with facts that China has constructed a Large Hadron Collider twice the size of CERN. There can be no doubt that in the best case scenario the world is about to witness the most dangerously and potentially deadliest Arms race in human history.

However, there is something percolating in occults shadows behind the scenes that is even more disturbing than a super collider arms race. When the sum of possibilities is considered, what we have at CERN ultimately is the potential to develop weapons for waging war with enemies far more powerful than mere human beings.

This is the Babylon Potential to which Tom Horne refers. The ability to open the forbidden gates to Archontic dimensions to forces that seek to invert our natural order.

As we come full circle, in understanding the supreme hidden purpose of the Large Hadron Collider and CERN. The Celtic deity of the underworld Cernunos represents the cycle of death and rebirth of destruction and restoration. The Luciferian Priesthood behind the thrones of the European Union and United Nations intend to use CERN as the key to literally opening the gates of Hell in order to release the gods that has been imprisoned there, those Fallen Watchers and arcane entities bound with chains in the abyss of Tartarus

Their prime objective is the restoration of the Golden Age when the gods mingled themselves with the seed of men and their hybrid offspring ruled the earth. Research points to this grand conspiracy.

The Earth is being slowly terraformed via Chemtrailing, HAARP, and other such clandestine programs in order to reconstitute the conditions that existed on the planet before the Flood of Noah in anticipation of the coming hybrid race that is coming by breaking the subatomic bonds of matter and casting away the cords that hold the material world together.

Mankind will willingly tear the veil that has been established for his own protection and unleash a darkness and chaos that the earth as not seen for many ages. This is the master plan of the Luciferian elite who seek to open forbidden gates and usher in the entities that will lead them in a futile war against the natural order. Their great hope and that of Lucifer is to usurp the throne which belong to the son of man and install the man of sin and of lawlessness in his place.

Why do the nations rage and the people plot a vain thing? A King's of the Earth set themselves and rulers take council together against the Lord and against his anointed saying let us break their bonds in pieces and cast away their cords from us. He who sits in heaven shall laugh. The Lord shall hold them is derision. Then he shall speak to them in his wrath and distress them in his deep displeasure.

CHAPTER IX

THE CARNAGE ALONG THE ROAD TO HELL

Path 57: The Morphing of the Hunger Game

Every dictator understands that a house divided cannot stand. The best way to subdue the masses is to lure the head of the masses asleep dangling dreams of wealth before their eyes on television while chopping the body up from the tail with poverty.

One trait that seems to be constant in people in large metropolitan areas is how easily they can be seduced enmasse with untruths. Today we have Nations, which by definition are segmented metropolitan areas that are seduced and fed propaganda that sets one group against another. Proponents of the new world order tell us they are trying to unite us under one government while their main goal is erasing freedom while amassing untold wealth to perpetuate growing financial inequities.

People are divided by political and religious propaganda, which brings hunger games in play. The policies of the banking cartel are managed via Bilderberg and Trilateral committees. There would be less reason to suspect conspiracy theories of banking cartels if minutes from their meetings and bank transactions are not transparent to the public.

The world's greatest challenge is understanding the prison we are in without bars. The greatest form of dictatorship is when people are imprisoned while thinking they are free. If people are enslaved thinking they are free, they have no knowledge that enables them to ever experience true freedom.

It is the most difficult challenge for the American people to see the control of a multi-national banking cartel through a government structure that has morphed from service of the people to serving multi-national corporations controlled by a multi-national banking cabal.

We could see Hitler, we could see Stalin, we could see King Leopold, or Napoleon. The bankers have learned the great lesson of remaining anonymous while uprooting lives fashioning wars that destroys sovereign nations, creating vast immigrant populations, financial inequities, vanquishing freedoms with global surveillance and cyber intelligence. The bankers make themselves immune to the laws that control the masses and never answer for their crimes against humanity.

In this bastion of immunity, the multi-national banking cabal are designing "Hunger Game Societies" around the world. The goal is enslavement of people who do not see their prison without bars. The "Hunger Game Society" is a global conspiracy structure of less than 1 percent of the population at the top of the pyramid and everyone else at the bottom living in dependency and poverty. This is a military police state of Cyborg and Android police imposing the will of the 1 percent at the top of the pyramid. This is seen clearly in the use of the United States military and its false flag wars on terrorism.

Advance technology paints a rosy picture of the future. The "Hunger Game Society" will take full advantage of advancing technology constructing centers for the rich and powerful, who will live in high tech luxury. The rich will be protected in enclaves of privilege by military police.

Our planet is challenged to support the exploding population. The UN calculates that there are more than 7 billion living humans on Earth, yet 200 years ago we numbered less than 1 billion.1 Recent estimates suggest that 6.5 percent of all people ever born are alive right now.2 This is the most conspicuous fact about world population growth: for thousands of years, population grew only slowly, but in recent centuries it has jumped dramatically.

Between 1900 and 2000 the increase in world population was three times greater than the entire previous history of humanity– an increase from 1.5 to 6.1 billion in just 100 years. According to projections, the world population will continue to grow until at least 2050, with the population reaching 9 billion in 2040, and some predictions putting the population as high as 11 billion in 2050. By 2100, the population could reach 15 billion

Not everyone will live in the centers for the rich. While the world's population tripled in the 20th century, the use of renewable water resources has grown six-fold. Population growth – coupled with industrialization and urbanization – will result in an increasing demand for water and will have serious consequences on the environment.

Already there is more waste water generated and dispersed today than at any other time in the history of our planet: more than one out of six people lack access to safe drinking water, namely 1.1 billion people, and more than two out of six lack adequate sanitation, namely 2.6 billion people. 3900 children die every day from water borne diseases.

Water and food shortages compounded by an exploding population conflicts with wealth generation, which remains the criteria of living in the center for the rich in the "Hunger Game Society." During the Progressive Era of the late 19th and early 20th century, eugenics was considered a method of preserving and improving the dominant groups in the population; it is now generally associated with racist elements creating a divisive smoke screen for the design of a "Hunger Game Society."

Eugenics was practiced in the United States many years before eugenics programs in Nazi Germany. The American eugenics movement received extensive funding from various corporate foundations including the Carnegie Institution, Rockefeller Foundation, and the Harriman railroad fortune.

The American eugenics movement was rooted in the biological determinist ideas of Sir Francis Galton, which originated in the 1880s. Galton studied the upper classes of Britain, and arrived at the conclusion that their social positions were due to a superior genetic makeup. Early proponents of eugenics believed that, through selective breeding, the human species should direct its own evolution.

They tended to believe in the genetic superiority of Nordic, Germanic and Anglo-Saxon peoples; supported strict immigration and anti-miscegenation laws; and supported the forcible sterilization of the poor, disabled and "immoral". The American eugenics movement received extensive funding from various corporate foundations including the Carnegie Institution, Rockefeller Foundation, and the Harriman railroad fortune.

Eugenics was also supported by African Americans intellectuals such as W. E. B. Du Bois, Thomas Wyatt Turner, and many academics at Tuskegee University, Howard University, and Hampton University; however, they believed the best blacks were as good as the best whites and "The Talented Tenth" of all races should mix. W. E. B. Du Bois believed "only fit blacks should procreate to eradicate the race's heritage of moral iniquity.

Depopulation has long been an agenda of the super-rich, which is to manipulating the economy and circumstances in order to remove people and land being cleared for luxury accommodation with callous disregard for anyone not of the privileged few. There are plans for "Human Settlements Zones" of highly dense populated centers living in micro apartments. Freedoms will be reduced through the abolition of private property and taking away security by making individual dependent on external discretions of the state. As stated previously, family units will be restructured with state controlled upbringing of children. Parental power over children is eroded.

We see the increase in the price of real estate serving the function of forcing certain people out of certain areas. There will be major restriction on movement with heavy 24X7 surveillance in the "Human Settlement Zones." It is difficult to see that the human race is being moved from a state of freedom to human enslavement. Politicians will not fight for us. They are connected to the system driving the hunger game initiative.

Some of the wealthier people in America, outside of the banking cartels families, and politicians are professional athletes, movie stars, and music entertainers. Beyond this wealthy group is a tremendous drop off in financial equity. The politicians are the pit bulls running around in the domain of the bankers keeping the masses at bay while Wall Street and its multi-national cabal of bankers transform human society from freedom to enslavement.

The movie industry and the news networks are instrumental in sedating the masses into a dangerous lethargic regard to this assault on their freedom. The lower rung of societies around the world are still facing minimum wages, unemployment, homelessness, poor or no medical care, while politicians, athletes, and entertainers of the acting and music industries live privileged existences.

As the lower rungs of the social ladder, movie stars, professional athletes, and music entertainers are the firewall between the impoverished masses and the bankers. So many people are being killed at the lower echelon of society either by hunger, disease, or the gang banging drug trade in the poverty ridden environments of the ghettos of Africa, South America, China, Europe, Mexico, and the United States.

The hunger games would not be in play as it is today if wealthy people were not sedated in their gated palatial estates isolated from the true reality of poverty created by the banking industry who are delusional with wealth creation and are the real menace to societies around the world.

The people of the supposedly great nations are in the same stupor that we witnessed in other powerful countries throughout the span of human history. The masses in Germany were in a stupor and permitted the slaughter of millions of Jews during the mindset of the people that led to World War II. The same hunger game mindset was in play when millions of African's lives were disrupted and destroyed during slavery. The hunger game mindset is in play with the creation of the HIV/AIDS virus. The mindset is in play in all of our senseless wars.

Not since the French and American Revolution has the eyes of the people been open. America started out as a promise of a free society constructed on premises of liberty, happiness, and justice for all. There has always been something wrong with the picture of America's promise of justice. Its founding father wrote the Constitution of the United States while perpetuating double standards as slave owners themselves.

The Indians were not too far from the truth when they stated that the white man speak with forked tongues. The country where freedom and justice is supposed to reign (America) has the largest prison population in the world with a disproportionate numbers of blacks and minorities charged with felonies. Their lives are all but finished.

No matter what your race or ethnicity and you tolerate injustice and stand idle knowing the suffering of another, then this statement is true for you. Many victims of various forms of racism and discrimination have had to cross over in their virtues and their moral compasses have been bent to survive in the brutality of injustice in all societies.

Apathy, the sleep like state of lack of interest, enthusiasm, or sensitivity of the suffering of your fellow man is contagious. The spirit of such a darkness, at a darker level, is exemplified by the actions of Adolph Hitler, Joseph Lenin, and King Leopold II of Belgium who killed millions.

This is the ongoing saga in our societies of the tale of two cities; people being exposed to and accepting different truths. I am constantly amazed at what is true in the mindset of political parties of every nation.

The current trend of apathy in our societies today is the same that was in the German people when they allowed Hitler to murder millions of people of Jewish faith; it is the same type of sedation that allowed Europe to rape and plunder Africa and the Mayan civilization without remorse.

The news on TV and the media is sedating minds with the same programmed political nonsense. It is truly puzzling why people are not turned off by political games and fed up with political leaders that keep leading us down a highway to hell.

It is hard to have an awakening of intelligence swimming in a soup of lies. What can we expect from a media owned by the wealthy institutions hell bent on dumbing down the masses? Welcome to the modern hunger games.

Is the rising poverty in Asia, Europe, Africa, India, China, South America and the United States any less of a crime than the outright brutality of oppressive brutal military force? Financial oppression is just an accepted form of warfare because there are no pictures of bloody carcasses but the outcome of the financial warfare on the poor is exactly the same.

Why don't the news media report on collateral damage done by our financial institutions stealing land and resources through their Mandrake system of banking? Their pockets and bank accounts are lined with billions of unused wealth while children are dying of starvation and poverty at increasing numbers around the world daily. We sparingly hear the media reporting on that. I do not want to hear about people running for election who will only perpetuate the growing obsessions of greed.

I know this is not the type of revelation that goes well with coffee and pastries and is not relaxing to think about. I think however this is a better stimulant than the caffeine. Wake up to this reality. There is more adrenalin rush in visualizing the true reality of the world. If you could see beyond the media conditioning and the haze of drugs being pumped into us by the pharmaceutical companies, you would not need the external stimulants to fire you up.

I really think that the GMO in our foods, the drugs, both legal and illegal, and the dwindling access to a viable education has turned the mentality of the people around the world into sheep who are content to munch on their little spot in the pasture until it is their turn to be sacrificed at the altar of greed. Sleeping on this reality has truly made us blind to something very dangerous; just like the people were in Germany under the Nazi regime.

There is still untapped resources in the heart of the people that is the foundation of what little hope remains of the human spirit. Our politicians and bankers are doing a great job dividing the masses with trickle down wealth and killing off the body with poverty. Is there enough heart of soul in the masses that still has a pulse, or has the heart of the masses been silenced forever by greed and selfishness? The people at the Oscars were happy eating pizza but that is a far cry from the reality of the ghettos around the world.

The Oscar party exemplifies the continuation of a tale of two cities. The hunger games continues to morph into one masquerade after another; hiding truths of some very dark realities of the majority of the people around the world.

Of course the media will not televise the real Hunger Game of the banking cartel. The Oscars will be brought to you live and in living colors. Shaking my head on this crazy not so merry go round of the Scheme of lies masquerading as the people's dream that is, as always, brought to you by the wealthy 1% around the world. We can and will not be limited by the dark dreams founded on greed and selfishness.

There is just too much light in us to be eclipsed by such darkness. However, we cannot afford to languish in our current sleep like state of ignorance and allow our morals and virtues to be manipulated by those holding the purse strings of wealth. I have faith that love in the hearts of the people will reign over the hopelessness being fed us by our so called leaders.

We see life different based on our socio-economic status. Regardless of my financial status, my vigil for injustice has remained resolute to fight ignorance and injustice throughout my life. We are still a work in progress as a world. We should not settle for mediocrity in that not being alarmed at the conditions of those in poverty who have no food or water to drink; while we have a bit more to devise a life with.

There is just something wrong about turning away from those struggling because we have a modicum of wealth. Some people are very comfortable burying their heads in the sand and then there are those of us who feel the need to express concern even if only the wind (the ears of God) listens. You can listen also as I whisper to the wind.

CHAPTER X

HUMANS CONTRIBUTING TO THEIR OWN DEMISE

Path 58: F.E.M.A

Federal Emergency Management Agency [F.E.M.A.] [and other emergency agencies]:

F.E.M.A. [Federal Emergency Management Agency] has been 'authorized' for the past 15 years by Presidential Executive Orders to confiscate ALL PROPERTY from the American People, separate families in the current 43 internment camps [already built and operational by the way, 5 of which are located in Georgia. The largest can confine somewhere on the order of 100,000 American citizens], called relocation camps by the 'government', for assignment to work camps; declares martial law and TOTALLY OVER-RIDES the U.S. Constitution.

Presidential Executive Orders that are related or control this are given at the end of this. Two of the state prisons here in Georgia are currently empty, although manned by a minimal number of staff, have been setup and intentionally unpopulated by prisoners just to support this political policy.

Concentration [internment] Camps. An Executive Order signed by then President BUSH in 1989 authorized the Federal Emergency Management Agency [F.E.M.A.] to build 43 primary camps [having a capacity of 35,000 to 45,000 prisoners EACH] and also authorized hundreds of secondary facilities. It is interesting to note that several of these facilities can accommodate 100,000 prisoners. These facilities have been completed and many are already manned but as yet contain no prisoners. [Remember all the TALK of over-crowded prisons that exist...]. In south Georgia there are several state prisons that except for a few guards, are completely devoid of prisoners.

Under F.E.M.A., the Executive Orders which are already written and is the current law of the land, calls for the COMPLETE suspension of the United States Constitution, all rights and liberties, as they are currently known. The following executive orders, which are in the Federal Register located in Washington DC for anyone to request copies of, call for the suspension of all civil rights and liberties and for extraordinary measures to be taken in, as most of the orders state, "any national security emergency situation that might confront the government."

When F.E.M.A. is implemented, the following executive orders will be immediately enforced:

E.O. 12148 - FEMA national security emergency, such as: national disaster, social unrest, insurrection, OR national financial crisis.

E.O. 10995 - "... provides for the seizure of ALL communications media in the United States."

E.O. 10997 - "... provides for the seizure of ALL electric power, petroleum, gas, fuels and minerals, both public and private."

E.O. 10998 - "... provides for the seizure of ALL food supplies and resources, public and private, and ALL farms, lands, and equipment."

E.O. 10999 - "... provides for the seizure of ALL means of transportation, including PERSONAL cars, trucks or vehicles of any kind and TOTAL CONTROL over all highways, seaports, and waterways."

E.O. 11000 - "... provides for the SEIZURE OF ALL AMERICAN PEOPLE for work forces under federal supervision, including SPLITTING UP OF FAMILIES if the government has to."

E.O. 11001 - "... provides for government seizure of ALL health, education and welfare functions."

E.O. 11002 - "... designates the postmaster general to operate a national REGISTRATION of all persons." [Under this order, you would report to your local post office to be separated and assigned to a new area. Here is where families would be separated].

E.O. 11003 - "... provides for the government to take over ALL airports and aircraft, commercial, public and PRIVATE."

E.O. 11004 - "... provides for the Housing and Finance Authority to relocate communities, designate areas to be abandoned and establish new locations for populations."

E.O. 11005 - "... provides for the government to TAKE OVER railroads, inland waterways, and public storage facilities."

E.O. 11051 - "... the office of Emergency Planning [has] complete authorization to put the above orders into effect in time of increased international tension or economic or financial crisis."

(What about an 'engineered' financial crisis, which in turn would most likely lead to 'social unrest'? This all depends on the decision of the current President. But then we must ask, just how legal is the U.S. Presidency anyway? MANY within the Continental Congress, fearing the rise of Monarchy, had originally opposed the establishment of a Chief Executive position such as the one that General George Washington was elected to.

They were assured however that those who followed Washington would have his example of integrity to base their own presidencies on. I have a suggestion: do away with the U.S. Presidency and the entire Executive Branch of government altogether—especially now that it is, according to many sources, under the control of unelected Military-Industrialists since the coup of 1963—and give back control of the government to the CONGRESS as it was in the beginning. Congress by majority vote CAN do away with the Executive position if they choose to do so - Branton)

All of the above executive orders were combined by President NIXON (I rest my case - Branton) into Executive Order 11490, which allows all of this to take place if a national emergency is declared by the President. The burning and insurrection in Los Angeles in the case of Rodney King could have executed [and partially did execute] these Executive Orders.

Executive Order 12919: "National Defense Industrial Resources Preparedness" signed by CLINTON June 3, 1994, delegates authorities, responsibilities and allocations of F.E.M.A.'s Executive Orders [last entry] for the confiscation of ALL PROPERTY from the American people, and their re-location and assignment to 'labor' camps. The Executive Order also supersedes or revokes eleven (11) previous Executive Orders [from 1939 through 1991] and amends Executive Order 10789 and 11790. This executive order is A DECLARATION OF WAR AGAINST THE AMERICAN PEOPLE by the [Secret] Government of the United States in concert with the UNITED NATIONS.

Operation Dragnet. Janet Reno can implement this operation upon receiving one call from the President. Arrest warrants will be issued via computer to round-up over 1 MILLION PATRIOTIC AMERICANS who may 'resist' the NEW WORLD ORDER. Americans who are not 'politically correct.' Specifically mentioned are CHRISTIANS or those who read the Bible. Concentration/internment camps have already been built to accommodate these American prisoners. See above paragraph as these internment camps have been setup and are run by F.E.M.A.

(Note: In reference to Christians, just where should they/we stand in regards to defending America? Should Christians take up arms if necessary? Apparently the Founding fathers of the American Republic believed so, so long as it was in order to DEFEND their country, their women and children... and NOT in order to engage in offensive warfare for the sake of conquering and exploiting others, which to me would be "living by the sword" or you could say "making a living" by the sword.

This could be exemplified by the Germans who initiated unprovoked invasions of their neighbors to meet their economic needs during World Wars I and II. One might ask, what about all the Orthodox Jews and Greek Orthodox Christians who went to their deaths like lambs to the slaughter without resisting during World War II? Why didn't they fight more zealously to defend themselves?

That is a hard question and one that I don't have an answer for. All I can say is that from my study of the Old and New Testaments, I find no passage that forbids us from defending ourselves from aggressors—at least in a national sense, however we ARE forbidden to become aggressors ourselves or engage in conflicts which are offensive rather than defensive oriented.

The offensive attacks against the native Americans for instance, resulting from the Anglo invasion of North America, can NOT be justified through scripture, and such policies and mistreatment of the native Americans, the continuous betrayal of treaties, and the stealing of their God-given land in the past have or will doubtless have an adverse effect on America's destiny UNLESS reparations are made to the native peoples—for instance a restoration of historical territories.

Perhaps the Greys felt justified in repeatedly violating our government's secret 'treaties' with them because 'we' had done the exact same thing to the Native Americans? Perhaps we DESERVED the abuses that the Greys and their Bavarian collaborators have inflicted upon us? Perhaps our nation's destiny will be largely determined by how we treat the native Americans from here on out, whether or not we begin to honor ALL of the treaties that 'we' had made and broken in the past?

Could it be? On the other hand, if OFFENSIVE warfare is forbidden by God, then DEFENSIVE warfare against a foreign invasion of American soil or an internal threat to our freedoms as they are guaranteed in the Bill of Rights WOULD from my perspective be justified. In Psalm 125:3 we read how the rule of the wicked is a DIRECT VIOLATION of the will of God: "...For the wicked shall not rule the godly, lest the godly be forced to do wrong."

A perfect example would be the Lutherans of Germany who all-too-often capitulated to the Nazi's and their 'state church', in spite of the fact that most of the Nazi leaders were themselves backed by Luciferian cults which the Christians should have resisted.

Instead, many of these backslidden Christians in Germany grudgingly supported the atrocities of their Nazi leaders, and by default the extermination by the millions of Jewish men, women and children. Why could Martin Luther himself stand-alone against hundreds of pompous religious hypocrites at the council of worms in Germany and boldly accuse them of parasitical blasphemy and idolatry to their face, yet many of his Protestant followers—not detracting from those few brave souls who DID resist—gave-in right and left to the Nazi Satanists, and in some cases even contributed to the atrocities of World Wars I and II?

In short then, Christianity does not teach that one SHOULD take up the sword, and it does not teach that one SHOULD NOT take up the sword in a defensive capacity. It all depends on one's own personal choice and faith. There is a warning however that those who do take up the sword should consider the possibility that they might die in battle. Then again one might die by NOT taking up the sword if they are captured and placed in death camp.

It all comes down to one's personal choice, based on the prevailing circumstances. It is written that the "meek shall inherit the earth". This does not mean the "weak", since the actual meaning of "meek" is literally "a stallion in restraint" or someone who shows self-control over their passions. Logically those who run out onto the battlefield "to die for their country" in a blaze of suicidal zeal and vainglory will probably do just that. Those on the other hand who are cautious and wise and fight with the motive of "defending their family" will not be so careless with their lives, since they are the provider of their family as well as its defender. If they are dead then they can no longer provide nor defend. - Branton)

Operation Rolling Thunder. Reno and Benson have mentioned this operation which comprises county-wide sweeps of house to house, dynamic entry, search and seizures for all guns and food stockpiles by B.A.T.F., state national guard, activity duty soldiers, as well as local police. This function is also run and coordinated through F.E.M.A.

Public Law 100-690 banned almost ALL RELIGIOUS GATHERINGS [not yet enforced..]. (Note: When and if this is enforced, this will be a blatant defecation upon the BILL OF RIGHTS, and in this event every true American is allowed—and in fact it will be his and her Patriotic DUTY—to implement the clause within the DECLARATION OF INDEPENDENCE to OVERTHROW such an alien, foreign or domestic tyranny-structure which has infested the governing body of America. - Branton); grants no-knock search and seizures without a search warrant; expands the drug laws to include EVERY American. This will generally be the prelude, or in addition to, a F.E.M.A. operation and contingency plan implementation.

The Omnibus Crime Bill of 1990. Ensures confiscation of all private property via money laundering, environmental violations of the Clean Water and Air Act, and extends as far as child abuse. This act also coordinates activities through F.E.M.A. and the Department of the Army, Commanding General, U.S. Forces Command, Fort McPherson, GA which is the executive and implementing agency upon initiation of many of these acts.

The responsible agency within U.S. Army Forces Command was what used to be known as the Deputy Chief of Staff for Operations, Plans Division [DCSOPS, Plans], which was changed several years ago to J-3 after the Headquarters became a joint headquarters. They keep on file copies of all F.E.M.A. Emergency Management Operation Plans, including those plans developed by the Army to support the F.E.M.A. plan to eliminate the U.S. Constitution upon implementation.

According to current plans, the Constitution will be 'temporarily' discontinued and shelved until the real or perceived and declared 'threat' has been neutralized (ask yourself—who or what is the REAL threat that needs to be 'neutralized'? - Branton). But once 'shelved,' as with almost every other action of the Government, it STAYS shelved.

Path 59: These Are Times That Try Our Souls

Throughout the course of Eastern and Western Civilization, there have been pockets of technical and social advancement in various time periods of human efforts of transitioning from primitive cognitive state to a civilized state of existence based on principles of legitimate love for each other.

From times immemorial of Black Pharaohs of Egypt, the Arabian efforts of the Byzantine Empire of the Middle East, the advancements in Chinese, Indian and Japanese societies in East Asia, the Greek and Roman Empires of the Mediterranean Seas, and the Mayan Civilization of Central America, the one common endeavor that has always plagued humanity is reliance on violence to sustain lifestyles for wealthy megalomaniacal rulers.

Fascination with royalty and anthropomorphic quest for ties to God remains a relentless obstacle to a loving compassionate rise to the forefront of human achievement that is needed to propel humanity beyond base instincts of war, murder, and mayhem to our collective dream of peace and prosperity. It is hard to know if the collective dream is not founded on a violent dark side, which continue to grow as the legacy of mankind. Maybe, violence is the true character of mankind.

It can be argued that technology has destroyed more lives than it has saved figuratively and literally. From the onset of gun powder, muskets, cannons, AK47, Uzis, Stealth Bombers, Intercontinental Ballistic Missiles, Atom bombs, Hydrogen bombs, and Neutron bombs have been used to maintain a balance of power for that same class of wealthy people who, from one millennium to the next, have prevented the world from attaining a peaceful spiritual balance since times immemorial.

Think of all the lives that have been lost over the quest for power and wealth. Think of all the technological advancement of medical equipment that should be free because of all the lives sacrificed in wars, in the name of freedom, peace, and democracy, yet the fruits of these wars are gobbled up to sustain the guilty pleasures of the rich and powerful.

Why is there gridlock at all about healthcare? All the people should have unlimited access to healthcare. I think in endless wars, the sacrifices paid by our sons and daughters has earned us the best life technology can offer free.

What purpose does the Royal family of England serves living off the wealth with billions while people are unemployed, hungry, homeless, and displaced in the streets of England? What purpose does the President, Congressmen, Senators, Supreme Court Justices, Wall Street Bankers, and Corporate CEO's serve? They create more problems than they solve.

Cultural progression has always been about the elite's personal needs and agenda for accumulating wealth and using money to direct legislation that preserves elitist status of power, influence, and preservation of elite bloodlines. Rarely are the elite's sons and daughters sent to war, however it is a guarantee their kids will be sent to Harvard, Yale, Oxford, Stanford, or MIT.

These are truly the times that try our souls. Furthermore, our souls have being on trial for eons as world societies, from one time period to the next, continues down the same path guided by a lineage of selfish leaders who feigns compassion while living a life of opulence and wealth.

The sad thing is that the DNA for greed exists in each and every individual. Violence is what we do best. Every aspect of what we do is in line with cultivating and preserving a culture of greed with violent means. Rarely does love eradicates the flowering of this negative DNA flaw that proliferates from one generation to the next regardless of what timeline we peer into for evidence.

The evidence is there to see in all our political and religious institutions throughout any age observed up until the present time, which is thought of as the most advanced period of human intellectual development.

Compassion in our soul is that spiritual child in each of us locked away in a far, dark, and dank chamber in the balcony of our minds. Our leaders, predisposed to violence, have never cultivated the collective compassionate instincts of love to flourish in the chambers of our hearts.

We have never been allowed the compassionate light of our loving spirit to provide us a passageway through the darkness in which we blindly stumble over each other in pursuit of selfishness and greed by any violent means necessary.

Yes these are truly trying times, of a relentless nature, that try our souls. Maybe we have no sense of the recurring self-made destruction that constantly recycles through our cultures and civilizations. Maybe in our brief partition of life we do not understand our history and are doomed to just keep repeating history from one generation to the next.

It is so sad that our children are suckling on technological nipples devoid of compassion, deprived of abilities to know love by trading loving instincts for technical genius that causes flight from humanitarian principles.

Greed is having a terrible impact on people's ability to love. Men and women say they don't see the point of love. People are so into their commitment to make money that they don't believe love can lead anywhere other than struggles against the financial burdens imposed on us to raise our children.

Relationships have become too hard. Raising families have become too hard. The mother and fathers are required to spend too much time being hijacked by their challenging high paying jobs. The sensitivity of men and women is displaced by a focus on wealth accumulation lost and obliterated in technical commitments, which renders them emotionally unavailable to each other.

Tribulations are multi-tasking that try our souls. There are so many issues politically, economically, and socially, that collectively, we have a daunting task getting our act together. The partitions in our individual lives are created by our struggle to overcome personal insecurities, societal conditioning. Socio-economic cast are other layers of reality that compounds the cultivation of progressive collective collaboration to solve problems that divide us.

The first thing we should try to understand is where we have been fragmented by race and culture, why are we living together openly in society and still fragmented, why have we languished divided so long, and what do we really want from life? By coming to know the answers to these questions, collectively, we can decide do we want to advance beyond our present and historical social quagmires or accept that we are flawed in our ability to love each other, flawed in our DNA that prevents us from living as one species bonded in love.

It is time to acknowledge that we are one humanity, and are not damned to a mindset incapable of advancing beyond selfishness that relegates love to a non-status of wishful thinking of the world's underprivileged while leaders fill vast spiritual voids of love with surrogate technological advancements.

The trials of our collective soul will be decided in the next moment with you being the judge of the violent reality that comes with the technological advancements. Can we be objective of this reality when the very harbinger of violence plaguing our world pays our bills? You are the judge and jury.

Path 60: Ego Consciousness and God

The mind, the faculty of consciousness and thought is a creative force, likened to creative powers of that primal being of infinite consciousness that we refer to as God. Is the limited human conscious idea of prayer an inner conversation only with self and only an inner voice conjuring up desirous hope within? When we pray to God, is there a primal creative force listening, or do we mistake or interpret the reverberating inner echoes of our conscious thoughts as the voice and presence of God?

When we say God is speaking to us, in our own mind, is this simply a conversation we are having with ourselves, which does not include a personal interaction of God intervening in our fate whatsoever? Are we creating our realities of blessings, shortcomings, and miracles with positive and negative thought vibrations within the realm of our own consciousness independently of any Godly influence?

Consciousness's foundation is a vast memory network consisting of experiences that preserves or threatens life. Products of these life experiences are dreams born of imagination and fear. There are far more things to fear within the thought making processes of our psyche than things that are to be feared in the external abyss of the infinite cosmos. Even if fear of something in the physical world is not present, what we imagine in our mind can create a complex of psychological horrors that become very real and damaging to us physiologically in our senses even if we cannot touch or see these phenomenons physically or with the naked eye.

What is the difference in the human concept of a primal being and the actual reality of a creator of all that exist? Why do we take that conceptuality created within the sphere of human consciousness as serious as we do from a religious perspective?

Does a primal being exist beyond the realm of human imagination that exceed or even come close to matching human conceptualization? Can we experience a real presence of that primal being, which is independent of that conceptual creation born of human consciousness? Can we ever experience or even know a primal creator that exist beyond human thought? In other words? Is God there in the human conscious experience, or are we simply having a conversation inwardly with ourselves and declaring echoes of our own consciousness as a Godly experience? Are we orchestrators of creative powers that manipulate our physical realm with conscious vibrations?

Think of traveling to someplace and understanding that consciousness is a map and God is the destination. Our conscious map is not the destination. Is consciousness merely a journey into dissolution by which we return to that realm of infinite creative energy that is God, from which everything of matter and non-matter originated? This life experience is a transition from the physical to a pure spiritual state of quantum singular energy force?

Is there a primal creative force manifesting in cyclical processes of birth and death? We see murder, destruction, and chaos in the natural operation of nature persistently manifesting eternally, whether it is a black hole shredding a star or a lion killing a baby springbok to stay alive. The pairs of opposites forever joined at the hip animating simultaneously existence and nonexistence, matter and anti-matter, life and death.

Within human ego-consciousness, emanations of that force represented in our magical realm of imagination. We toy with powerful creative essences of the primal creator that emanates within all things.

God is this creative force of infinite consciousness, a field of energy within an intricate creative factory of infinite quantum presence. God's presence is within our same perceptive consciousness. Is this a manifestation of God, or are we free moral agents creating forms of existence in a brief span of human years that reflects the freefalling chaotic blueprint of creativity of nature itself?

Spiritual Black Hole Consciousness

Spiritual properties in people we encounters repel or attract fuels our conscious revelations. We respond differently to those with the same than those of opposite spiritual energy. When like energy encounter each other, this union creates a calming gravitational dance. The energy in this like spirited unions is pulled into a vortex of singularity consciousness that cultivates calming experiences in relationships.

Comparable spiritual consciousness is that powerful force of attraction that acts as a spiritual black hole. We must be vigilant of what consciousness is allowed to permeate one's consciousness. Only in an atmosphere of silence do I find mental properties that does not clash with spiritual bliss. Random noise of traditional survival consciousness subsist on toxicities such as selfishness and greed, which opposes meditations that instills spiritual tranquility.

Words, concepts, and activities related to physical survival creates noise in a spiritual realm that requires a silent meditative state. The noise of selfishness, greed, and fear of the unknown creates duality stains on the clean spiritual fiber with which we were born.

These conceptual impasses obscures a naturally clean slated spiritual fibers of primal infinite consciousness with which we were born with. All of us become spiritually lost in the multitudes of conscious petitions attempting to avoid pain, fears; lost also in pursuit of joys, pleasures, subsistence needs, and security.

If one is fortuitous enough to attain the peaceful wisdom of a silent mind and understand a sense of quantum singularity and an idea of infinite consciousness, it becomes increasingly difficult to dwell in humanity's traditions of divided political and religious mindset that continues to smother our collective consciousness and search for divinity in this cosmos.

Having cast off the world, who would desire to return to its imperfect chaos? Society is jealous of those who escapes its reality of petitions and will come for those who wish to live off the grid of conventional thinking.

Shinto

In Japan, Shinto "the way of the Gods" is a way of devotion that preserves and cultivates purity of heart. Shinto is to follow the right and moral way. Pleasing the deities with virtues and sincerity rather than offering things of material value.

The guardian in life sees all things in silence. There are those of us who walk in wisdom and there are those of us who walk in fear.

With knowledge and wisdom gained from life experiences we manifest the cosmic forms and emanations of the primal being. We must at all cost celebrate its manifestations. Our limited knowledge, wisdom, and piousness, under duress of survival, must never be relegated to inadequacy.

In death we leave behind the legend of our manifest forms detailing our physical presence as we transcend into the non-physical spiritual presence domain of ultimate silence, that realm of primal creative cosmic activity where logic breaks down.

Independent of the influence of our creator on our ultimate destiny, we have created a disastrous dilemma. We continue to construct our reality rationalizing impulsive behaviors, without the dignity of a loving spirit, exponentially showing no respect for human or animal life and allowing immorality to metastasize. These acts and impulsive rationalization are mankind's polluted psychological ocean of self violation.

The times we live in now stains our God-given spiritual fibers with the foulest of our soul's waste waters. Swimming in these waters, we are ensnared on our very own hooks of ignorance, greed, insensitivity, and selfishness. In these insane obsessions, we continue violating our greatest spiritual values making decisions for love of money with no regard for ideas of compassion and love.

With our collective spiritual fiber torn and stained from times immemorial to the present day, a history of broken morality, selfishness, fear, and greed is smothering each of us. Selfishness, greed, and aggression are concepts upon which our society's foundation is built upon, the environment in which we are born, and that environment in which generations live and die unaware of their true gift of miraculous being.

CHAPTER XI

MAKING A U-TURN TO SALVATION

Path 61: First priority should be people over technology

We the human race is predisposed to adventure, superstitions, fears, captured by our imagination, and are obsessed with creating circumstances that improve the environment in which we live.

We have emerged from one stage where we've been encapsulated in fear and prejudice among each other, to the current mental plateau of cultivating greed and vanity. We have created space ships, and unmanned space craft capable of leaving our solar system to teach us more about the world we live in. We have launched space telescopes that allows us to peer into distant worlds light years away. These are all noteworthy achievements of the collective efforts of the human species.

Kudos to woman and mankind for technological advancements. Everyone is fascinated at the prospect of finding life somewhere else in the universe. There are too many Galaxies throughout this vast universe with the same elements as our own world that makes life out there probable billions times over.

We are so fascinated with the question of life in another part of the universe that we have failed to establish standards to take care of life on our own planet. I wonder if other worlds with life on it are just as negligent of the wellbeing of its masses. Are they just as cavalier as our leaders are of their people's struggles, as our leaders are here on earth? Maybe we need to discover intelligent life to teach us how to love and get along with each other here.

I am all for technological advancement but do we literally have to throw the baby out with the wash to answer curiosities of life somewhere else? We spend billions if not trillions of dollars on space programs, while people are dying of poisons in food, in the air, and in the oceans.

We spend trillions of dollars on war weaponry to protect selfish motives of greed and not love and freedom as we are so often told. Not only are people dying, our animals, and our planet are too. Technology is great, but at the expense of the planet, I think mankind has gotten the cart before the horse.

Our logic and strategies concerning the survival and wellbeing of the people on this planet are way off center. We choose to use our technology to support expansionist dreams of space before we procure the welfare of the people on this planet. We spent billions to plant a flag and leave footprints on the surface of the moon, while millions are dying from lack of the basic necessities.

Is it really more important to find life in other worlds than it is to provide for life in this world? Let intelligent life find us. It is cheaper that we let them do so. In the meantime, we can take care of our own here on planet earth with our limited precious resources.

We should be pouring the wealth we are concentrating on space studies into building great societies of educated people who embrace the humanities with ideas that value human life instead of selfish and greed based ideas that dictate human life must be sacrificed for the development of space research and technology. Space will always be there to explore. Let's take care of every life here on earth first and then explore space in the afterthought. We should use our technology that cultivates, prioritizes, and preserves physical and moral health agendas first.

It takes money to educate the techie that advance technology. The highest paying jobs are in technological fields. Money should be allocated for providing households with resources that insure families are secure and stable.

In this athmosphere, education is abundant and people use education as a mean to advance in society and to keep pace with advancing technologies without the sacrifice of the poor. There should be no poor exceptions in society and no families left behind. The children of each secure household will have access to healthcare education in their rite of passage from birth to adulthood.

The principles of capitalism should be scrapped for systems that incorporate equality through equal access to education. The current system is designed to feed children of the most prosperous families into the best schools. In this cycle, those born with a silver spoon in their mouths and are hardly inspired to change the system of inequities that currently exist. If you are born into poverty these days, there is a good chance you will not find a path out.

Decadence is inceasing the populations of America's prison farms. They are being fed by moral decay. They should not be fed by criminal behaviors of those who are impoverished, but should include unpunished white collar criminal activities of our political officials who are being made wealthy not serving the people they take an oath to protect.

Political legislations serving the needs of corporations are the biggest unspoken crimes and are much more serious in nature to the blue collar crimes of impoverished people. The poor have minimum access to a stable home environment to use as a platform to launch themselves into proper economic pathways compared to the access of kids from prosperous families.

There is just so many wrong priorities being focused on and our leaders are asleep at the wheel jeopardizing our lives year in and year out. How do we let ourselves be continually led by such cavalier leadership when it comes to our wellbeing?

The ongoing blind political faith in our politics is very perplexing to me. As we continue to be progammed not to love and care about each other, I can see the destruction of humanity and the majority of the world's population not surviving beyond the challenges before us today.

The current leaders of the world are more inclined to drop bombs, send rockets into space, and build prisons than to institute strategies to procure healthy lifestyles situations for the citizens of this world. We need to cultivate intelligence on this planet before we even dream of finding intelligent life somewhere else.

We need love for each other here on earth that forges an undivided aligned world collective that is not partitioned nor fragmented by the haves and the have-nots and nations divided with patriotic pride. Only then can the impoverished people of the world be freed from the bars of selfishness imposed upon them by the selfishness of the rich bankers throughout our global societies.

Most of our world leaders, and maybe each of us too, have yet to evolve beyond a selfish DNA trait called survival of the fittest. There is natural selection still taking place. Only the fittest will be allowed to live in our modern day Elysium, that place in our society, of gated luxury resorts reserved for those claiming they are descendants of gods and are the rightful rulers of our contemporary society.

Why can't it be possible here on earth that we cultivate our dark side to eliminate competition in a greed based capitalist system? We get excited about sex and the release of dopamine and oxytocin; we get excited about winning because winning provide more wealth and access to more activities that promotes the release of more dopamine and oxytocin; we get excited about drugs in every form because we lead painful lives that must be medicated with artificial means because we have lost perspective on how to naturally balance our souls with an organic loving spirit.

There are reasons we need the blue pills, the marijuana, the alcohol, and the need to go to war; our spiritual domain is in shambles because of the societies we have constructed. Why can't we get excited about loving and caring for each other and doing what is required to insure loving each other happens?

My point is spiritual ascention will always take a back seat to our evolving addictions of wealth and technology that emphasize less and less spiritual evolvement. Our greed based carnal addictions will continue to reign over us because we are spiritually in disrepair.

Money is the vehicle that enables our every addiction whether it is drugs, sex, or power and control over others. Example number one, the central banking officials who are aware of the adverse effect of their addiction to power but they still continue to implement their devastating policies of financial greed.

The insanity of mankind is not an easy analysis, but it certainly is interesting wrapping the mind around our many idiosyncrasies regarding what we selfishly do to survive at the expense of another's life. It is imperative that we come up with solutions for our many self-imposed crisis on the blue planet.

In the meantime, a semblance of good life goes on as we do anything and everything to make money and in the process stay yoked to a value system that demeans our ability to love each other. In our individual scrambles for wealth, many of us succumb to the slings and arrows of just making money and give up on cultivating a highly developed spiritual environment on earth.

The adrenalin rush of wealth is more powerful than love, no doubt as it damage manifest around us in so many ways, so it stands to reason, not being able to wean ourselves from valuing money over love, we should be looking for intelligent life here on earth.

Path 62: Thousands of scientists issue bleak 'second notice' to humanity

In late 1992, 1,700 scientists from around the world issued a dire "warning to humanity." They said humans had pushed Earth's ecosystems to their breaking point and were well on the way to ruining the planet. The letter listed environmental impacts like they were biblical plagues—stratospheric ozone depletion, air and water pollution, the collapse of fisheries and loss of soil productivity, deforestation, species loss and catastrophic global climate change caused by the burning of fossil fuels.

"If not checked," wrote the scientists, led by particle physicist and Union of Concerned Scientists co-founder Henry Kendall, "many of our current practices put at serious risk the future that we wish for human society and the plant and animal kingdoms, and may so alter the living world that it will be unable to sustain life in the manner that we know."

But things were only going to get worse.

To mark the letter's 25th anniversary, researchers have issued a bracing follow-up. In a communique published Monday in the journal BioScience, more than 15,000 scientists from 184 countries assess the world's latest responses to various environmental threats. Once again, they find us sorely wanting.

"Humanity has failed to make sufficient progress in generally solving these foreseen environmental challenges, and alarmingly, most of them are getting far worse," they write.

This letter, spearheaded by Oregon State University ecologist William Ripple, serves as a "second notice," the authors say: "Soon it will be too late to shift course away from our failing trajectory."

Global climate change sits atop the new letter's list of planetary threats. Global average temperatures have risen by more than half a degree Celsius since 1992, and annual carbon dioxide emissions have increased by 62 percent.

But it's far from the only problem people face. Access to fresh water has declined, as has the amount of forestland and the number of wild-caught fish (a marker of the health of global fisheries). The number of ocean dead zones has increased.

The human population grew by a whopping 2 billion, while the populations of all other mammals, reptiles, amphibians and fish have declined by nearly 30 percent.

The lone bright spot exists way up in the stratosphere, where the hole in the planet's protective ozone layer has shrunk to its smallest size since 1988. Scientists credit that progress to the phasing out of chlorofluorocarbons—chemicals once used in refrigerators, air conditioners and aerosol cans that trigger reactions in the atmosphere to break down ozone.

"The rapid global decline in ozone depleting substances shows that we can make positive change when we act decisively," the letter says.

The authors offer 13 suggestions for reining in our impact on the planet, including establishing nature reserves, reducing food waste, developing green technologies and establishing economic incentives to shift patterns of consumption.

To this end, Ripple and his colleagues have formed a new organization, the Alliance of World Scientists, aimed at providing a science-based perspective on issues affecting the well-being of people and the planet.

"Scientists are in the business of analyzing data and looking at the long-term consequences," Ripple said in a release. "Those who signed this second warning aren't just raising a false alarm. They are acknowledging the obvious signs that we are heading down an unsustainable path. We are hoping that our paper will ignite a widespread public debate about the global environment and climate."

Path 63: "Stockholm Syndrome" What is preventing global social change for the better?

Stockholm syndrome (sometimes erroneously referred to as Helsinki syndrome) is a condition that causes hostages to develop a psychological alliance with their captors as a survival strategy during captivity. These feelings, resulting from a bond formed between captor and captives during intimate time spent together, are generally considered irrational in light of the danger or risk endured by the victims. Generally speaking, Stockholm syndrome consists of "strong emotional ties that develop between two persons where one person intermittently harasses, beats, threatens, abuses, or intimidates the other." The FBI's Hostage Barricade Database System shows that roughly eight percent of victims show evidence of Stockholm syndrome.

Formally named in 1973 when four hostages were taken during a bank robbery in Stockholm, Sweden, Stockholm syndrome is also commonly known as "capture bonding". The syndrome's title was developed when the victims of the Stockholm bank robbery defended their captors after being released and would not agree to testify in court against them. Stockholm syndrome's significance arises because it is based in a paradox, as captives' sentiments for their captors are the opposite of the fear and disdain an onlooker may expect to see as a result of trauma.

There are four key components that generally lead to the development of Stockholm syndrome: a hostage's development of positive feelings towards their captor, no previous hostage-captor relationship, a refusal by hostages to cooperate with police forces and other government authorities, and a hostage's belief in the humanity of their captor, for the reason that when a victim holds the same values as the aggressor, they cease to be perceived as a threat. Stockholm syndrome is considered a "contested illness," due to many law enforcement officers' doubt about the legitimacy of the condition social harvest.

Path 64: David Icke

American Presidents a Continuing New World Order Tool

In David Icke's New Book "Everything You Need to Know and Never Been Told," Icke warns us that the whole recognition of Jerusalem as the Capitol of Israel declaration and the moving of the US Embassy is a process that begun long ago of Israel taking over that entire area of land and removing the removing the Palestinians from that whole area, Palestinians who were there before. This is known as the greater Israel Project or the expansion of Israel.

As we connect the dots, Icke states that the claim that land of an ancient people who go back to Israel. The people occupying Israel calling themselves Jews are not descendants from the ancient people of Israel.

It is well documented that the overwhelming majority of at least of Jewish people today don't come from biblical Israel at all. They come from an area in the Caucasus and Southern Russia, which was known as Khazaria.

In 740 A.D., there was a mass conversion of those people who weren't from Israel who weren't Jewish. There was a mass conversion to the religion of Judaism. The Khazaria King was known as the Kagan. This is why Kagan is such a common Jewish name.

As the Khazaria Empire broke up, the people moved northward, they moved into Eastern Europe, and eventually Western Europe. They were the people who were outrageously grotesquely targeted by the Nazis in Germany and as a result of that and massive manipulation by the House of Rothschild great numbers of those people were moved into Palestine.

The whole Balfour Declaration was openly powerful Britain supported homeland for converted Jewish people in Palestine. The Balfour Declaration was a letter written by Foreign Secretary Lord Balfour who was an inner circle initiate of a Secret Society in London called The Round Table. He wrote the Letter referred to as the Balfour Declaration, which enabled converted Jews to take over the land in Palestine.

Balfour sent the letter to Lord Rothschild who funded and essentially created the Round Table Secret Society. The claim to the Palestinian Land is based on what is to have been said by the Old Testament God. Israeli politician justify taking over and invading Palestine from Europe, if we break it down to basic truth. The invasion was justified quoting a God in an Old Testament written by who knows who, who knows when, and under who knows what circumstances.

The whole foundation of the existence of Israel is based on nonsense. However, we are where we are now. We can't say to Israelis Jewish people in Israel you all must leave because there are a great number of people in Israel who don't support what their far-right government under Netanyahu is doing to the Palestinians.

If we are going to have or if it is desired from the Israelis and American regime point of view that there would be an end to the conflict and a coming together, which means a living together with the same rights for all parties. The only way the problem in Israel is to be resolved is through fairness, through justice, and everyone having the same rights as everyone else.

It is interesting how the rich create injustices in wealth controlled society for the poor and particularly people of color, which is not just black people but all people of varying color spectrums thought to be not white. This is indicated in desires to have Nordic as preferred immigrants over people of color. It is stated that Germany was help by Nordic extraterrestrial in advancing technologies that helped them in producing jets and rockets far in advance of the rest of the world.

Fairness, justice, and everyone having the same rights is not happening in Israel nor the United States for a reason. The shadow government controlling the false front elected government do not want a peaceful settlement on any front around the world of social struggle between whites and people of color.

We must always be mindful of so many other dynamics taking place under the sun such as CERN.

Path 65: The American Legacy of Moral Compromise for Fool's Gold

Mayer Amschel Rothschild, the father of the banking industry, is quoted as saying: "Let me issue and control a nation's money and I care not who writes the laws."

In his book, "The Creature from Jekyll Island - A Second Look at the Federal Reserve", G Edward Griffin coined the term Mandrake the Magician was a comic strip character from the 1940s. He had the ability to magically create things and, when appropriate, make them disappear.

Griffin's view is similar to many other gold-standard supporters' critique of the fractional-reserve banking system and the Federal Reserve in particular: that it makes money "magically" appear from nothing. With control of unlimited minted paper fiat dollars not backed by gold or silver, America is Bankrupt in 31 trillion fiat dollars in debt and all of its gold confiscated by an international banking cabal.

When banks loan money, they don't actually loan existing money. Rather, they allocate money to loan, but they are limited by how much money they can create. The law basically says that, for each dollar a bank has on hand in one of its savings accounts, it is allowed to create another 90 cents to give out as a loan. (The dollar from the savings account is still there, and can still be spent by the person who owns the savings account.)

This loan is then spent, and the recipient puts it into another bank, and that bank can now loan 90 cents times 0.9 = 81 cents. This can be repeated many times (depending on the demand for loans) until it approaches its mathematical limit of 10 dollars.

For example, when the Federal Reserve holds on deposit 1 billion in marketable United States Treasury security then the banks in the banking system, public and private, and bound by U.S. financial law, are able to generate 10 billion in new debt over time.

This set the table for an American legacy that will remembered as a people who compromised their humanity for fool's gold or "fiat dollars" of the Rothschild family.

Our political leaders have stood back and allowed wealthy bankers to acquire control of the nation's land and misappropriate the money supply of the American people. Our tax dollars are used to pay interest on loans of paper money from a banking cabal to our government. The Banking cabal take our land and gold resources as collateral for paper money that cost them nothing to make. Every dollar that is created is debt related with a heavy collateral bounty for the cabal, which essentially leads to bankers holding our gold and the people given worthless paper notes not backed by gold or silver.

The only people with most of the gold these days are the super-rich. The Federal Reserve Bank of New York is one of twelve regional Reserve Banks in the Federal Reserve System. Its claim to fame is the enormous gold reserves which lay five floors (80 feet) beneath the city streets. The bank began receiving its gold during the World Wars when foreign countries wanted their gold reserves safely away from European turmoil.

Interestingly, only two percent of the 9,000 tons of gold the Federal Reserve Bank of New York stores belongs to the United States. There are 63 account holders here, 49 of which are countries; the rest belong to international organizations. The amount of gold used to be larger. In 1978, the bank held one million bars of gold; today, it stores about 700,000. Still, this amounts to an impressive cache worth approximately $116 billion.

If the stock market crashed today and we came upon another great depression, the banker's families will be well provided for with their stash of gold. Your family and my family they are expendable much like the sons and daughters of the poor that die in combats that help the bankers secure even more gold. What do we have to show for our blind obedience to their financial objectives?

We have stressful jobs that do not pay nearly enough to keep up with inflated prices of homes, gas, cars, groceries and the cost to educate our children. Many Americans do not see it but we are in an economic feudal system that is slowly eroding away our rights of self-determination.

At the behest of the Bilderbergers, the world is continuously embroiled in social, political, and military wars in the name of everything "Except" love and compassion. We need courageous new leaders that are cut from a different spiritual mode who do not simply pay lip service to the notions of compassion and who will sacrifice their lives catalyzing humanity's next steps towards the awakening of intelligence and spiritual growth.

A growth that enables the people of the world to actualize a good and decent life not tainted and disheveled by financial usurpations of an insensitive banking cabal that is addicted to playing god with the lives of the uninformed and unsuspecting population of poor. A cabal of evil and greedy men more obsessed with artificial intelligent technology instead of organic life. Men who are also obsessed with playing God, determining who lives and who dies with their designer viruses and their killer Mrna vaccines.

We need a new breed of leadership that exemplify courage for unselfish compassion that is not in lock step with a cabal of insensitive and selfish bankers whose sole interest continues to perpetuate a modern day economic feudal system and an agenda destroying lives using tools such as Hollywood movies and television News Media to shape narratives by flooding the collective senses of the masses with images of material greed that changes the mental landscape of thoughts of young people regarding the purpose of a clean heart, spirit, and what is moral, virtuous, and worthwhile.

In the process, using "Fiat Dollars" to dismantle democracy as we have known it by controlling the political overseers of the world's money supply. When was the last time that the gold in Fort Knox was audited and holdings of gold there revealed?

What is the degree of involvement of a Supreme Being in the mundane madness revolving around greed? I look to the day that the collective essence of the Supreme Being in all of us surfaces and transcend that selfish reality plaguing humanity. Evil, violence, and avarice remains a primary issue to be perpetuated or abandoned by the pedigree of each individual's moral constituency. I am not impressed with the pedigree of leadership surfacing on display in the world today.

The challenge to our leaders is to overcome issues of greed through acts of love and not war. Failure to do so perpetuates exploitation of the middle class and senseless destruction of the downtrodden and the hopeless.

Much of the people's suffering can be prevented. Bankers and politicians, alike in Western nations, objectives are evolving more and more to schemes of imperialism dependent on political schemes, poverty, designer viruses, diminishing food supplies, controlled climate change, and military weapons of mass destructions all intended to depopulate the planet.

Blinded by this "White Darkness," the people are in danger of never uniting in their own defense or educating themselves enough to grasp who the real culprits of terrorism are. We are too embroiled in financial crisis of credit card debt trying to make ends meet and can never see the true blood sucking thieves in the night. As the Bible states "Love of Money is the Root of All Evil," the very regards of a cabal of bankers to control the destinies of people's lives bears the Bible statement out.

Life, death, salvation, fear, and damnation are mundane concerns, corporeal by nature, which compels humanity search for destiny using prophesies based on varying degrees of religious dogmas. There are many faiths out there not supported by works.

It is my contention that a Supreme Being has nothing to do with the troubles, of the world, that are created when one set of extremely wealthy people exploits another set of disadvantaged people.

The wealthy covertly pursue agendas that divide the disadvantaged into classes with titles such as a liberal or conservative. Political leaders are oriented to manipulate emotions through nationalism or patriotism as a psychological tool for objectifying citizens of other nations whom they seek to kill or master.

The will of the people is controlled through nationalistic propaganda and financial persuasion. Depending on their moral pedigree, people allow themselves to be persuaded one way toward vice or virtue. In America, it is amazing to see the people captivated by their worldly possessions; because of this, many are challenged to understand the net of financial enslavement cast upon them by an international banking cabal.

Politicians, motivated by greed rather than compassion for its people, should not be in positions of leadership where policies are needed to promote the common good of the people.

Throughout all nations of the world, love of money and the attitude of doing anything for power continues to be the blinders that keep our politicians on dark paths conducive to alienating themselves from the people they are elected to protect. A financially motivated politician, with moral blinders on, leads innocent people down a path of destruction that manifest in senseless deaths and major economic setbacks for developing economies of third world nations.

Contradictions and distortions of truth prevents money-blinded politicians and wealthy bankers from truly understanding what it will take to bring about equality, universal justice, love, liberty, a pursuit of happiness, and ultimately a chance for each individual to develop a peaceful inner life. Why should people continue to submit to a system of financial exploitation that perpetuates lofty perches of luxury for a few families of privileged oil tycoons and wealthy bankers when there are so many people in the world with nothing to speak of struggling to eat bread or consume a drink of clean water?

It is imperative, in this lifetime that we use the light within to illuminate the dark nature of insensitive persons drunk on quests of power. We must see them clearly and understand who they are and what their agenda is truly. If this mission can be accomplished, they can be stopped from infecting others with their moral sickness.

By tainting the minds of children orienting them towards material enslavement through debt rather than prioritizing a spiritual life, the beautiful rose of our children, which we aspire to fill their minds with compassion, is in jeopardy of not blossoming ever.

The generations of leaders in power in America and Europe, right now, are representative of what happens when privileged individuals teach their kids to appreciate material values. Their kids grow up and duplicate the tradition handed down to them. Like their parents, kids of privilege attend the best schools and inherit reins of power and set their sights on material achievement.

Where are we headed?

Russian President Vladimir Putin announced that BRICS nations (Bazil, India, China, and South Africa) are going to roll out a new alternative to the US dollar's global reserve currency status. As reported by IndiaTimes.com:

> *According to the Russian president, the member states are also developing reliable alternative mechanisms for international payments. Earlier, the group said it was working on setting up a joint payment network to cut reliance on the Western financial system. The BRICS countries have been also boosting the use of local currencies in mutual trade.*

But this is only the beginning of the bombshell here.

We also know from industry sources that "Project Sandman" refers to a group of over 100 countries that plan to simultaneously denounce the US dollar as a global reserve currency.

The new replacement currency will be **powered by blockchain and backed by gold**, which is why member nations have been rapidly stockpiling gold supplies in anticipation of the big announcement. When this happens, nations that represent nearly 75% of the world's population will simultaneously denounce the US dollar and roll out a gold-backed, blockchain-audited international currency system that will instantly become the world's currency choice for free trade and a store of value.

The dollar, backed by nothing but more money printing and incompetent political leadership, will collapse toward zero. Virtually overnight, goods and services sold in America will increase in price by 1000%. And that's only the beginning: The dollar will continue to lose value by the hour as the world's holders of US Treasury debt and dollar currency dump it all at any price.

Those holding dollars will lose everything.

The United States government will quickly collapse in parallel with the collapse of the dollar and the US central bank. There will be no money to pay military troops or pay off corrupt government officials. All government salaries and pensions will be effectively halted. The great neocon empire of debt, lies and death will implode so rapidly that people will be psychically shocked and physically unprepared.

Russia, China and India will emerge as the economic leaders of the world, and the US Empire will cease to exist. The former United States of America will be broken into regional nation states, divided largely among political lines with the satanic, anti-American Left seizing control of the coasts, and conservative, pro-America, pro-liberty, pro-Constitution groups dominating the rest of the country. Expect a very real civil war to ensue, with massive casualties.

Russia knows that it can defeat America simply by joining the world's efforts to declare America's dollar currency to be null and void. No nuclear war is necessary. America it already highly vulnerable to this sort of collapse due to the nation's massive debt and spending addictions. Russia and China are merely sucking the air out of America's collapsing currency, knowing that economic gravity will do the rest

China's *Belt and Road Initiative*, consisting of protected, high-efficiency trade routes among countries representing about 75% of the world's population with America and Europe missing. *Belt and Road Initiative* will speed trade among member nations, and it will use China's new "digital yuan" currency backed by gold and audited by blockchain technology.

That's because America—the military and economic bully of the world—isn't welcomed by other nations. America doesn't play nice. America bombs anyone it wants while weaponizing the SWIFT system to punish its political enemies, and now that the world has come to realize the dollar is a *weapon* rather than a free trade currency, **nobody wants anything to do with America from here forward**.

The economic sanctions against Russia were the last straw for the dollar, it turns out. And the USA has nothing left to back its currency: Not manufacturing, not labor, not agricultural output, and not even gold in the vaults. The USA no longer has fair and free elections and no longer has freedom of speech. On top of that, the USA has political prisoners rotting in jails in DC while the FDA harvests organs from aborted human babies to use for medical experiments. In other words, **the USA occupying illegitimate government, under demonic influence, has become a great evil in the world**.

Western Europe is run by lunatics and "woke" propagandists who are committing economic suicide by outlawing every form of energy that matters. The EU is disintegrating, and the Euro currency likely will collapse within the next year. Western Europe is on a suicide mission, both economically and culturally, as the nations of Europe can't even protect their own borders from mass migration. (Nor can the USA, for that matter.)

America as you know it will soon cease to exist

The era of Western Civilization is coming to an end. It will be characterized by the collapse of the dollar, a global repudiation of the petrodollar status, a collapse of the rule of law across the United States, a collapse of the stock market, pensions, bond market and crypto markets, a collapse of the food supply chain, and a collapse of the fuel and transportation infrastructure. This will, in turn, take down the power grid in many areas, leading to a Mad Max-style scenario from which a few capable survivors will attempt to flee.

Before the end of 2025, **America as you know it will cease to exist**. This has been the plan all along from Barack Obama, Hillary Clinton, Joe Biden and plenty of RINO neocons, too (the Cheneys, Bushes, etc.). The plan is to take down America in order to achieve one world government under the fascist United Nations, with universal gun control, universal vaccine mandates, abortion "rights," engineered global starvation and total control over all speech and elections.

Their agenda is failing at many levels, however. Roe vs. Wade was just struck down by the US Supreme Court, for example, and there are elements at work that are looking likely to achieve key indictments against deep state players. However, **any state that wants to exist after the dollar collapses must be ready to roll out its own gold-backed currency on an emergency basis**. Texas is largely prepared to do this, but few other states are ready. The re-establishment of trade and commerce (following the dollar collapse) is going to be the key to surviving the demise of the dollar.

Texas is America's No. 1 exporter of goods, by the way, and the Texas economy is larger than most nations on the planet. So is the economy of California. But California is run by child murdering, demonic fascists while Texas has the world's best Attorney General (Paxton) and a strong contingent of pro-human, pro-liberty, pro-Constitution Americans who are ready and willing to relaunch the spirit of America in the new *Republic of Texas*, when necessary. #TEXIT

But no matter what happens domestically, America's days of being able to run around the world, threatening everybody with military strikes and dollar weaponization will soon be over. And without the ability to print money and defraud the world into buying soon-to-be-worthless US debt instruments, the United States military will have no funding to continue operations or build new weapons. It will eventually be disbanded.

What happened to the former Soviet Union in 1991 is about to happen to the United States of America: A collapse of the ability to continue to fund the bureaucracy and military that propped up the system the entire time. The USA has sadly devolved into an empire of debt, lies and death. **The country is currently ruled by an actual death cult**, but those days are fast coming to an end with the imminent collapse of the demonic dollar and all the evil that money printing has enabled since 1971.

When this evil is finally brought to an end, all those who value life, liberty and happiness will rejoice (and rebuild).

Get prepared, for that today is coming soon. And from what I've concluded, the only way to avoid the financial collapse that's coming is to **hold your assets in physical goods** such as gold and silver, land, agricultural equipment, ammunition, industrial buildings (factories, for example) and other "real" things that don't vanish in a currency collapse.

Path 66: Silence

If you take away the noise of consciousness, black holes, stars burning hydrogen, down to the voice of all conscious creatures vibrating on this fiber of dark quiet infinite abyss, this God fiber gives birth to consciousness, before there was any anthropomorphic renderings of ideas, concepts, and words such as love, hate, life or death, there was that omniscient form of peaceful stillness and silent perfection singularity "God."

That ultimate perfection is all in the singularity of one God the creator without the conflicting realities of general relativity of a quirky world in which all things seems to happen at random and are diametric opposites such as good and evil, heat and cold, and life and death.

Could it be the noise of consciousness streaming in our minds is radiated energy of God's infinite consciousness and everything that exist is heated by the radiating energetic flow of the primal creator's imaginings received by all creatures terrestrial and extraterrestrial from deep connections in the universe.

Quantum Mechanics is a new area in science that is not about absolutes. It is about probabilities. It is forcing experts to expand their definition of reality and embrace the unknown. The very nature of the quantum subatomic world seems to be affected by whether or not we are observing it. Humans are observers of God's creations and we are blessed with the power of changing our world with the eyes of our imagination, our thoughts, and the commands of the words of prayer.

Humanity is operating within four dimensions, there are believed to be more than ten dimensions that ultimately translates to the existence of an infinite number of parallel universes, which may have different physical laws from the dimensions in that we live in. Quantum physicists call it parallel dimensions and multiverse. To others, this is the spirit world where the unknown exists.

David Bohm was a renowned quantum physicist who figured out wave-particle duality. Subatomic particles do not behave as expected. They have characteristics of both waves and particles. Bohm believed that observing particles changed their behavior. What if God changes our behavior just by watching us, which is the case 100 percent of the time?

What Bohm failed to explain was a subatomic phenomenon called nonlocality. That is the capacity of a particle to influence another instantaneously across great distances without explanation.

In 1980, Bohm wrote a book called Wholeness and the Implicate Order. He implied that clarity is not within humanity's grasp and suggested there is a deeper and hidden implicate order. He said we should not dispose of hard math and mechanics all together but in order to jump forward, science must merge with at and spirituality and become comfortable with not knowing because there are many dimensions and universes that surround and overlap our own. Knowledge is infinite and in our corporeal forms, may be beyond our understanding.

The being that moves all things is and will forever be the "Great Mystery." The universe and everything within it is inside you and me. In order for science and the human race to advance, we must dispense limits of faulty prejudices created by a system built to uphold bogus social hierarchy of colonialism, capitalism, heteropatriarchy, and white supremacy.

Indigenous ways of knowing should be included in the scientific processes of Trans-Humanism, artificial intelligence, and the coming age of robotics. Incorporating wisdom and knowledge taken from the indigenous resources of Sumerian Tablets of Mesopotamia and the Pyramids of Egypt, that are salted away in the confines of Europeans vaults, should be shared as an endowment to all of humanity and not contribute to the advantage of a few families dead-set on controlling the world.

Incorporating indigenous ways fosters enlightenment and open doors to the merger of understanding, love, and compassion critical to purposeful advancement of humanity.

BIBLIOGRAPHY

Snowden Documents Proving "US-Alien-Hitler" Link Stuns Russia WhatDoesItMean.Com

Are Archons Greys? Usko Ahonen, MD
November 2012
UFO Digest Website Spanish version

The Ethics of Transhumanism and the Return of Eugenic
Christoffer O. Hernæs Aug 26, 2016
TechCrunch Website

The Aldebaran Mystery Jim Nichols
Jim Nichols UFO Website

Antarctica- A Nazi Base? An Excerpt from Alien Agenda
Jim Marrs
GreyFalcon Website

Underground Infrastructure /the Missing 40 Trillion Dollars
Steven J. Smith
Scientific Papers Website

World War I, RMS Titanic, and the "Nitrogen Bomb" That Will Kill Us All, WhatDoesItMean.Com, 28 July 2017

Selected by Extraterrestrials, William Thompkins, My Life in the Secret World of UFO's, Think Tank, and Nordic S28 July 2017ecretaries.

Secret Treaty, "The United States Government and Extra-Terrestrial Aliens" Richard K. Wilson, Sylvan Burns, 1989, http://www.thewatcherfiles.com/alien-treaty.htm

The secret shadow government a structural analysis, Underground Bases: A Lecture by Phil Schneider: May 1995

Ebola, AIDS Manufactured by Western Pharmaceuticals and U.S. DOD
Dr. Cyril Broderick Professor of Plant Pathology
September 09, 2014
Daily Observer Website

Who Murdered Africa
The Creation of the AIDS Virus by the World Health Organization
William Campbell Douglas, M.D.
HealingTools Website

Chemtrails an Airline Mechanic's Statement
May 19, 2000
from Carnicom Website

Project Cloverleaf Timeline 1994 to 2001
March 2004
Indy Media Website

Black Occult Religions" of the BROTHERHOOD OF THE BELL.
William Dean Ross
The Universal Seduction Website

Interstellar Space Travel: 7 Futuristic Spacecraft to Explore the Cosmos
Tom Metcalfe, Live Science Contributor
September 2, 2016

REFERENCES

- Jay Weidner on Rense Radio 14.7.2010
- The Apocryphon of John II 22: 14-10, through 27-20
- Gilhus, The Nature of the Archons, p. 40).
- Prof. Ismo Dundenberg: The hidden wisdom of Nag Hammadi 1999 (Nag Hammadin kätketty viisaus)
- John E. Mack. Passport to the Cosmos. p. 163
- A dialogue of Budd Hopkins and John Mack, John Hancock Hall, Boston, 1997 video.
- "Karla Turner: UFO Abduction: The Secret Agenda" (1993) Google video
- The Art of Dreaming, 1993. (Review of Don Juan's lessons in dreaming.)
- The Active Side of Infinity, 1999. (Memorable events of his life.)
- http://en.wikipedia.org/wiki/Psychonautics
- http://en.wikipedia.org/wiki/Interdimensional_hypothesis
- http://en.wikipedia.org/wiki/Jacques_Vall%C3%A9e Jacques Vallee, Wikipedia
- Richard Dolan: UFOs and the national security state: Cover up exposed (1973-1991 - p. 303, 308,353)
- Winter Leeke on Coast to Coast AM 27.10.2011
- John Lash on Red Ice Radio interviews between years 2008-2011
- Nigel Kerner 2010: Grey Aliens and the Harvesting of Souls: The Conspiracy to Genetically Tamper with Humanity
- Whitley Strieber: The Key: A True Encounter (p.53)
- Raymond Fowlers The Watchers 1991
- Budd Hopkins: Intruders 1987
  Karmapolis interview of John Lash 2005

www.ingramcontent.com/pod-product-compliance
Lightning Source LLC
LaVergne TN
LVHW041736060526
838201LV00046B/822
9798886406009